To dear
John Rose O'
&
Peggy O'

Happy Play Acting !

Love
Gráinne

GREAT
IRISH PLAYS

GREAT IRISH PLAYS

The Beaux' Stratagem

She Stoops to Conquer

The School for Scandal

The Colleen Bawn

The Importance of Being Earnest

Pygmalion

Spreading the News

The Rising of the Moon

The Land of Heart's Desire

On Baile's Strand

Riders to the Sea

The Playboy of the Western World

GRAMERCY BOOKS
New York • Avenel

This 1995 edition is published by Gramercy Books,
distributed by Random House Value Publishing, Inc.,
40 Engelhard Avenue,
Avenel, New Jersey 07001.

Random House
New York • Toronto • London • Sydney • Auckland

Printed and bound in the United States

Library of Congress Cataloging-in-Publication Data
Great Irish plays
p.   cm.
ISBN 0-517-12429-7
1. English drama—Irish authors.   2. Ireland—Drama.
PR8865.G74   1995   95-19796
822.008′09415—dc20   CIP

10   9   8   7   6   5   4   3   2   1

Contents

FOREWORD

After the great flowering of English drama during the Elizabethan period, one finds that the majority of the great dramatists of the English language are, curiously, Irish. Playwrights like George Farquhar, Oliver Goldsmith, and Richard Brinsley Sheridan were Irishmen, although the English often claim them as their own. While it is true that many Irish playwrights are of English ancestry, as George Bernard Shaw pointed out: "There is no Irish race any more than there is an English race or a Yankee race. There *is* an Irish climate, which will stamp an immigrant more deeply and durably in two years, apparently, than the English climate will in two hundred."

There is a distinctive quality that sets an Irish writer apart. Ireland for much of its history has been a conquered land under English domination. It was subjected to both military and cultural control by the English. The ethnic Gaelic language was almost wiped out, and its ancient civilization was treated with condescension by the "superior" English conquerors. As a result, a contentious, outsider point of view often informs the writing of the best Irish playwrights. Before the advent of a national Irish theater early in the twentieth century, Irish playwrights from Sheridan to Shaw made a good living on the London stage with hilarious and accurate dissections of British hypocrisy, pretension, and illusions. As Shaw wrote: "The Englishman is wholly at the mercy of his imagination, having no sense of reality to check it," while "the Irishman, with a far subtler and more fastidious imagination, has one eye always on things as they are."

Another quality that stands out among Irish writers is their unique transformation of the English language. The Irish novelist James Joyce, one of the great masters of English prose in the twentieth century, wrote in *A Portrait of the Artist as a Young Man*: "The language in which we are speaking is his before it is mine. . . . I cannot speak or write these words without unrest of spirit. His language, so familiar and so foreign, will always be for me an acquired speech." He was speaking for the Irish nation, a subjugated people who had a foreign language forced upon them. But the inherent discontent with the British did not stop Irish writers from mastering the language. There is an obvious pride in the virtuosity with which they use the language in comparison with its originators. To quote Shaw again: "My native language is the English of Swift and not the unspeakable jargon of the mid-XIX century London newspapers." The English spoken by the Irish uniquely retains many of the language's colorful archaisms that have long since fallen from use among the British. It is also infused and colored with the singular musicality, syntax, and poetic dash of Gaelic, which adds to Irish-English a revitalizing freshness and energy.

The plays collected in this volume trace the vital contribution Ireland has made to drama from the Restoration to the twentieth century. From the eighteenth century are three great comedies: George Farquhar's *The Beaux' Stratagem*, Oliver Goldsmith's *She Stoops to Conquer*, and Richard Brinsley Sheridan's *The School for Scandal*. Although little remembered today, Dion Boucicault was one of the most popular playwrights of the nineteenth century. His *The Colleen Bawn*, with its depiction of Irish peasant life, was a major influence on such later Irish playwrights as John Millington Synge. Oscar Wilde and George Bernard Shaw, two of the theater's greatest writers of comedy, are represented by their most famous plays. Wilde's *The Importance of Being Earnest*, with its infectious wit and inspired and memorable dialogue is his finest work. Shaw's *Pygmalion*, the story of a Cockney flowergirl's transformation, was later turned into the Lerner and Loewe musical *My Fair Lady*, which was enormously popular on the stage and on the screen.

At the turn of the twentieth century, the Irish struggle for political independence from England spurred what would later be called the Irish Literary Renaissance. It was a movement to create a vital and unified cultural Ireland. Initiated by the poet William Butler Yeats and Lady Augusta Gregory, what was later to become the Abbey Theatre was established to "build up [an] . . . Irish school of dramatic literature." As Yeats wrote: "our movement is a return to the people" and—referring to the derogatory and stereotyped image of the stage Irishman—would "show that Ireland is not the home of buffoonery and easy sentiment, as it has been represented, but the home of an ancient idealism." The plays written for the new Irish theater reflected the rich cultural heritage of Ireland's myths and folklore and presented a realistic portrayal of its rustic life. Included here are the finest plays the movement produced: two of Yeats's poetic dramas, *The Land of Heart's Desire* and *On Baile's Strand*; Lady Gregory's most famous one-act plays, *Spreading the News* and *The Rising of the Moon*; and John Millington Synge's *Riders to the Sea* and *The Playboy of the Western World*.

GEORGE FARQUHAR

Although George Farquhar was one of the most popular playwrights of Restoration England, very little is known about his life. He was born in Londonderry, Ireland, around 1678 and at the age of seventeen he entered Trinity College, Dublin, to study for the Church. In 1696, he left without a degree and became an actor in Dublin's sole playhouse, the Smock Alley Theatre. His acting career was cut short when he forgot to use a blunted foil and wounded a fellow actor in a duel scene. In 1697, he went to London to become a playwright.

In December 1698, his first play, *Love and a Bottle*, was produced at the Theatre Royal on Drury Lane. Running for nine nights, it was a successful debut. His next play, *The Constant Couple*, opened a year later and successfully ran for five months. His next three plays, however, were commercial failures. Adding to his financial strain was his marriage, in 1703, to Margaret Pemell, a widow with two daughters. Knowing Farquhar needed money, she pretended to be an heiress and tricked him into marrying her.

In 1704, Farquhar acquired a commission as a lieutenant in the Earl of Orrery's Regiment of Foot and was sent to Ireland. The post guaranteed him a small yearly income of fifty pounds. While recruiting for the army in Shrewsbury in 1705, he wrote *The Recruiting Officer*. Produced a year later in London, it was an overwhelming success. Despite this he was forced to sell his officer's commission to help pay his ever-mounting debts, and he soon became ill. He wrote his last and finest play, *The Beaux' Stratagem*, in six weeks under the strain of increasing ill health. It turned out to be another success when it opened on March 8, 1707, at the Queen's Theatre in Haymarket. However, Farquhar died soon afterward, most likely of tuberculosis. He was buried at St. Martins in the Fields on May 23, 1707.

Farquhar's plays, especially *The Recruiting Officer* and *The Beaux' Stratagem*, have remained popular with actors who have kept these works in the repertory. He stands apart from other Restoration playwrights in that he broadened the scope of comedy by moving his characters out of the superficial atmosphere of the blue-blooded drawing room and into the world of innkeepers, the military, and highwaymen, and by thematically exploring such social issues as human equality. The typical Restoration comedy of manners highlighted, with wit and licentious wordplay, the cynical and amoral behavior of the aristocracy. Farquhar's approach was a blast of fresh air for English comedy in that he brought a new and substantial degree of realism. His plays are considered transitional, positioned between the traditional Restoration comedy of wit and the later Sentimental Comedy, and were a direct influence on later Irish playwrights Oliver Goldsmith and Richard Brinsley Sheridan.

The expansion of the social environment of the plays reflects the emerging importance of the bourgeoisie, who were more religious and moralistic and who made up a growing part of the theater audience. While *The Beaux' Stratagem* exhibits the Restoration comedy's typically casual attitude toward sex, virtue prevails by the play's end. The plot focuses on Aimwell, a man initially inspired by monetary gain, and his efforts to court Dorinda, a rich heiress. While there is much talk of sex, no adultery actually takes place, and in the end the bride is won not by wit or trickery, but by true love.

THE BEAUX' STRATAGEM

BY GEORGE FARQUHAR

Advertisement

The reader may find some faults in this play, which my illness prevented the amending of; but there is great amends made in the representation, which cannot be matched, no more than the friendly and indefatigable care of Mr. Wilks, to whom I chiefly owe the success of the play.

GEORGE FARQUHAR

Dramatis Personae

(As play was originally acted at the Queen's Theatre in the Haymarket, March 8, 1707)

Men

AIMWELL	two gentlemen of broken	*Mr. Mills*
ARCHER	fortunes, the first as master, and the second as servant	*Mr. Wilks*
COUNT BELLAIR,	a French officer, prisoner at Lichfield	*Mr. Bowman*
SULLEN,	a country blockhead, brutal to his wife	*Mr. Verbruggen*
FREEMAN,	a gentleman from London	*Mr. Keen*
FOIGARD,	a priest, chaplain to the French officers	*Mr. Bowen*
GIBBET,	a highway man	*Mr. Cibber*
HOUNSLOW	his companions	
BAGSHOT		
BONIFACE,	landlord of the inn	*Mr. Bullock*
SCRUB,	servant to Mr. Sullen	*Mr. Norris*

Women

LADY BOUNTIFUL,	an old civil country gentlewoman, that cures all her neighbors of all distempers, and foolishly fond of her son Sullen	*Mrs. Powell*
DORINDA,	Lady Bountiful's daughter	*Mrs. Bradshaw*
MRS. SULLEN	her daughter-in-law	*Mrs. Oldfield*
GIPSY,	maid to the ladies	*Mrs. Mills*
CHERRY,	the landlord's daughter in the inn	*Mrs. Bicknell*

Scene: *Lichfield*

Prologue

Spoken by Mr. Wilks

When strife disturbs or sloth corrupts an age,
Keen satire is the business of the stage.
When the Plain-Dealer writ, he lashed those crimes
Which then infested most—the modish times.
But now, when faction sleeps and sloth is fled,
And all our youth in active fields are bred;
When through Great Britain's fair extensive round,
The trumps of fame the notes of Union sound;
When Anna's scepter points the laws their course,
And her example gives her precepts force,
There scarce is room for satire; all our lays
Must be or songs of triumph or of praise.
But as in grounds best cultivated, tares
And poppies rise among the golden ears,
Our products so, fit for the field or school,
Must mix with nature's favorite plant—a fool.
A weed that has to twenty summers ran,
Shoots up in stalk and vegetates to man.
Simpling our author goes from field to field
And culls such fools as may diversion yield;
And, thanks to nature, there's no want of those,
For rain, or shine, the thriving coxcomb grows.
Follies, tonight we show, ne'er lashed before,
Yet, such as Nature shows you every hour;
Nor can the pictures give a just offense,
For fools are made for jests to men of sense.

Act I

Scene: an inn.
Enter Boniface *running*.

BONIFACE:
> Chamberlain, maid, Cherry, daughter Cherry! All asleep, all dead?

Enter Cherry *running*.

CHERRY:
> Here, here, why d'ye bawl so, father? D'ye think we have no ears?

BONIFACE:
> You deserve to have none, you young minx. The company of the Warrington coach has stood in the hall this hour, and nobody to show them to their chambers.

CHERRY:
> And let 'em wait farther; there's neither redcoat in the coach nor footman behind it.

BONIFACE:
> But they threaten to go to another inn tonight.

CHERRY:
> That they dare not for fear the coachman should overturn them tomorrow.—Coming, coming.—Here's the London coach arrived.

Enter several people with trunks, bandboxes, and other luggage, and cross the stage.

BONIFACE:
> Welcome, ladies.

CHERRY:
> Very welcome, gentlemen.—Chamberlain, show the Lion and the Rose. *Exit with the company.*

Enter Aimwell *in riding habit,* Archer *as footman carrying a portmantle.*

BONIFACE:

This way, this way, gentlemen.

AIMWELL:

Set down the things, go to the stable, and see my horses well rubbed.

ARCHER:

I shall, sir.   *Exit.*

AIMWELL:

You're my landlord, I suppose?

BONIFACE:

Yes, sir, I'm old Will Boniface, pretty well known upon this road, as the saying is.

AIMWELL:

O, Mr. Boniface, your servant.

BONIFACE:

O, sir, what will your honor please to drink, as the saying is?

AIMWELL:

I have heard your town of Lichfield much famed for ale. I think I'll taste that.

BONIFACE:

Sir, I have now in my cellar ten tun of the best ale in Stafford-shire; 'tis smooth as oil, sweet as milk, clear as amber, and strong as brandy, and will be just fourteen year old the fifth day of next March old style.

AIMWELL:

You're very exact, I find, in the age of your ale.

BONIFACE:

As punctual, sir, as I am in the age of my children. I'll show you such ale—Here, tapster, broach Number 1706, as the saying is.—Sir, you shall taste my Anno Domini. I have lived in Lich-field man and boy above eight and fifty years and, I believe, have not consumed eight and fifty ounces of meat.

AIMWELL:

At a meal, you mean, if one may guess your sense by your bulk.

BONIFACE:

Not in my life, sir. I have fed purely upon ale. I have eat my ale, drank my ale, and I always sleep upon ale.

Enter Tapster *with a bottle and glass.*

Now, sir, you shall see. (*Filling it out.*) Your worship's health. Ha, delicious, delicious! Fancy it Burgundy, only fancy it, and 'tis worth ten shillings a quart.

AIMWELL (*drinks*):

'Tis confounded strong.

BONIFACE:

Strong! It must be so, or how should we be strong that drink it?

AIMWELL:

And have you lived so long upon this ale, landlord?

BONIFACE:

Eight and fifty years, upon my credit, sir, but it killed my wife, poor woman, as the saying is.

AIMWELL:

How came that to pass?

BONIFACE:

I don't know how, sir. She would not let the ale take its natural course, sir; she was for qualifying it every now and then with a dram, as the saying is. And an honest gentleman that came this way from Ireland made her a present of a dozen bottles of usquebaugh, but the poor woman was never well after. But howe'er, I was obliged to the gentleman, you know.

AIMWELL:

Why, was it the usquebaugh that killed her?

BONIFACE:

My Lady Bountiful said so. She, good lady, did what could be done: she cured her of three tympanies, but the fourth carried her off. But she's happy, and I'm contented, as the saying is.

AIMWELL:

Who's that Lady Bountiful you mentioned?

BONIFACE:

'Ods my life, sir, we'll drink her health. (*Drinks.*) My Lady Bountiful is one of the best of women. Her last husband, Sir Charles Bountiful, left her worth a thousand pound a year, and I believe she lays out one half on't in charitable uses for the good of her neighbors. She cures rheumatisms, ruptures, and broken shins in men; green sickness, obstructions, and fits of the mother in women; the king's evil, chin-cough, and chilblains in children. In short, she has cured more people in and about Lichfield within ten years than the doctors have killed in twenty, and that's a bold word.

AIMWELL:

Has the lady been any other way useful in her generation?

BONIFACE:

> Yes, sir, she has a daughter by Sir Charles, the finest woman in all our country, and the greatest fortune. She has a son too by her first husband, Squire Sullen, who married a fine lady from London t'other day. If you please, sir, we'll drink his health?

AIMWELL:

> What sort of a man is he?

BONIFACE:

> Why, sir, the man's well enough, says little, thinks less, and does—nothing at all, faith. But he's a man of a great estate and values nobody.

AIMWELL:

> A sportsman, I suppose?

BONIFACE:

> Yes, sir, he's a man of pleasure: he plays at whisk and smokes his pipe eight and forty hours together sometimes.

AIMWELL:

> And married, you say?

BONIFACE:

> Ay, and to a curious woman, sir. But he's a—he wants it here, sir.   *Pointing to his forehead.*

AIMWELL:

> He has it there, you mean.

BONIFACE:

> That's none of my business; he's my landlord, and so a man, you know, would not—but—Icod, he's no better than—sir, my humble service to you. (*Drinks.*) Though I value not a farthing what he can do to me. I pay him his rent at quarter day, I have a good running trade, I have but one daughter, and I can give her—but no matter for that.

AIMWELL:

> You're very happy, Mr. Boniface. Pray, what other company have you in town?

BONIFACE:

> A power of fine ladies, and then we have the French officers.

AIMWELL:

> O, that's right; you have a good many of those gentlemen. Pray, how do you like their company?

BONIFACE:

> So well, as the saying is, that I could wish we had as many more of 'em. They're full of money and pay double for everything they have. They know, sir, that we paid good round taxes

for the taking of 'em, and so they are willing to reimburse us a little. One of 'em lodges in my house.

Enter Archer.

ARCHER:

Landlord, there are some French gentlemen below that ask for you.

BONIFACE:

I'll wait on 'em.—([*Aside*] *to* Archer.) Does your master stay long in town, as the saying is?

ARCHER:

I can't tell, as the saying is.

BONIFACE:

Come from London?

ARCHER:

No.

BONIFACE:

Going to London, mayhap?

ARCHER:

No.

BONIFACE:

An odd fellow this.—(*To* Aimwell.) I beg your worship's pardon. I'll wait on you in half a minute.   *Exit.*

AIMWELL:

The coast's clear, I see. Now, my dear Archer, welcome to Lichfield.

ARCHER:

I thank thee, my dear brother in iniquity.

AIMWELL:

Iniquity! Prithee leave canting. You need not change your style with your dress.

ARCHER:

Don't mistake me, Aimwell, for 'tis still my maxim that there is no scandal like rags nor any crime so shameful as poverty.

AIMWELL:

The world confesses it every day in its practice though men won't own it for their opinion. Who did that worthy lord, my brother, single out of the side-box to sup with him t'other night?

ARCHER:

Jack Handycraft, a handsome, well dressed, mannerly, sharping rogue, who keeps the best company in town.

AIMWELL:

Right; and pray who married my Lady Manslaughter t'other day, the great fortune?

ARCHER:

Why, Nick Marrabone, a professed pickpocket and a good bowler, but he makes a handsome figure and rides in his coach that he formerly used to ride behind.

AIMWELL:

But did you observe poor Jack Generous in the park last week?

ARCHER:

Yes, with his autumnal periwig shading his melancholy face, his coat older than anything but its fashion, with one hand idle in his pocket and with the other picking his useless teeth; and though the Mall was crowded with company, yet was poor Jack as single and solitary as a lion in a desert.

AIMWELL:

And as much avoided for no crime upon earth but the want of money.

ARCHER:

And that's enough. Men must not be poor; idleness is the root of all evil; the world's wide enough, let 'em bustle. Fortune has taken the weak under her protection, but men of sense are left to their industry.

AIMWELL:

Upon which topic we proceed, and I think luckily hitherto. Would not any man swear now that I am a man of quality and you my servant, when if our intrinsic value were known—

ARCHER:

Come, come, we are the men of intrinsic value who can strike our fortunes out of ourselves, whose worth is independent of accidents in life or revolutions in government. We have heads to get money and hearts to spend it.

AIMWELL:

As to our hearts, I grant ye, they are as willing tits as any within twenty degrees, but I can have no great opinion of our heads from the service they have done us hitherto, unless it be that they have brought us from London hither to Lichfield, made me a lord and you my servant.

ARCHER:

That's more than you could expect already. But what money have we left?

AIMWELL:

But two hundred pound.

ARCHER:

> And our horses, clothes, rings, etc. Why we have very good fortunes now for moderate people; and let me tell you, besides, that this two hundred pound, with the experience that we are now masters of, is a better estate than the ten thousand we have spent. Our friends indeed began to suspect that our pockets were low, but we came off with flying colors, showed no signs of want either in word or deed.

AIMWELL:

> Ay, and our going to Brussels was a good pretense enough for our sudden disappearing; and I warrant you our friends imagine that we are gone a-volunteering.

ARCHER:

> Why, faith, if this prospect fails, it must e'en come to that. I am for venturing one of the hundreds, if you will, upon this knight-errantry, but in case it should fail, we'll reserve the other to carry us to some counterscarp where we may die as we lived, in a blaze.

AIMWELL:

> With all my heart. And we have lived justly, Archer; we can't say that we have spent our fortunes, but that we have enjoyed 'em.

ARCHER:

> Right; so much pleasure for so much money. We have had our pennyworths, and had I millions, I would go to the same market again. O, London, London! Well, we have had our share, and let us be thankful. Past pleasures, for aught I know, are best, such as we are sure of; those to come may disappoint us.

AIMWELL:

> It has often grieved the heart of me to see how some inhumane wretches murther their kind fortunes, those that by sacrificing all to one appetite shall starve all the rest. You shall have some that live only in their palates, and in their sense of tasting shall drown the other four. Others are only epicures in appearances, such who shall starve their nights to make a figure a-days and famish their own to feed the eyes of others. A contrary sort confine their pleasures to the dark and contract their spacious acres to the circuit of a muff-string.

ARCHER:

> Right, but they find the Indies in that spot where they consume 'em, and I think your kind keepers have much the best on't, for they indulge the most senses by one expense; there's the seeing, hearing, and feeling amply gratified, and some philosophers will tell you that from such a commerce there

arises a sixth sense that gives infinitely more pleasure than the other five put together.

AIMWELL:

And to pass to the other extremity, of all keepers I think those the worst that keep their money.

ARCHER:

Those are the most miserable wights in being; they destroy the rights of nature and disappoint the blessings of providence. Give me a man that keeps his five senses keen and bright as his sword, that has 'em always drawn out in their just order and strength, with his reason as commander at the head of 'em, that detaches 'em by turns upon whatever party of pleasure agreeably offers, and commands 'em to retreat upon the least appearance of disadvantage or danger. For my part, I can stick to my bottle, while my wine, my company, and my reason holds good; I can be charmed with Sappho's singing without falling in love with her face; I love hunting, but would not, like Actaeon, be eaten up by my own dogs; I love a fine house, but let another keep it; and just so I love a fine woman.

AIMWELL:

In that last particular you have the better of me.

ARCHER:

Ay, you're such an amorous puppy that I'm afraid you'll spoil our sport. You can't counterfeit the passion without feeling it.

AIMWELL:

Though the whining part be out of doors in town, 'tis still in force with the country ladies. And let me tell you, Frank, the fool in that passion shall outdo the knave at any time.

ARCHER:

Well, I won't dispute it now. You command for the day, and so I submit. At Nottingham, you know, I am to be master.

AIMWELL:

And at Lincoln, I again.

ARCHER:

Then at Norwich I mount, which, I think, shall be our last stage, for if we fail there we'll embark for Holland, bid adieu to Venus, and welcome Mars.

AIMWELL:

A match!

Enter Boniface.

Mum.

BONIFACE:

What will your worship please to have for supper?

AIMWELL:

What have you got?

BONIFACE:

Sir, we have a delicate piece of beef in the pot and a pig at the fire.

AIMWELL:

Good supper meat, I must confess. I can't eat beef, landlord.

ARCHER:

And I hate pig.

AIMWELL:

Hold your prating, sirrah, do you know who you are?

BONIFACE:

Please to bespeak something else. I have everything in the house.

AIMWELL:

Have you any veal?

BONIFACE:

Veal! Sir, we had a delicate loin of veal on Wednesday last.

AIMWELL:

Have you got any fish or wildfowl?

BONIFACE:

As for fish, truly, sir, we are an inland town and indifferently provided with fish, that's the truth on't. And then for wild-fowl—we have a delicate couple of rabbits.

AIMWELL:

Get me the rabbits fricasseed.

BONIFACE:

Fricasseed! Lard, sir, they'll eat much better smothered with onions.

ARCHER:

Pshaw, damn your onions!

AIMWELL:

Again, sirrah!—Well, landlord, what you please. But hold, I have a small charge of money, and your house is so full of strangers that I believe it may be safer in your custody than mine, for when this fellow of mine gets drunk, he minds nothing.—Here, sirrah, reach me the strongbox.

ARCHER:

Yes, sir.—(*Aside.*) This will give us a reputation.

Brings the box.

AIMWELL:

Here, landlord, the locks are sealed down both for your security and mine; it holds somewhat above two hundred pound.

If you doubt it, I'll count it to you after supper. But be sure you lay it where I may have it at a minute's warning, for my affairs are a little dubious at present. Perhaps I may be gone in half an hour; perhaps I may be your guest till the best part of that be spent. And pray order your ostler to keep my horses always saddled. But one thing above the rest I must beg, that you would let this fellow have none of your Anno Domini, as you call it, for he's the most insufferable sot.—Here, sirrah, light me to my chamber.

Exit lighted by Archer.

BONIFACE:

Cherry, daughter Cherry?

Enter Cherry.

CHERRY:

D'ye call, father?

BONIFACE:

Ay, child, you must lay by this box for the gentleman; 'tis full of money.

CHERRY:

Money, all that money! Why, sure, father, the gentleman comes to be chosen Parliament-man. Who is he?

BONIFACE:

I don't know what to make of him. He talks of keeping his horses ready saddled and of going perhaps at a minute's warning, or of staying perhaps till the best part of this be spent.

CHERRY:

Ay, ten to one, father, he's a highwayman.

BONIFACE:

A highwayman! Upon my life, girl, you have hit it, and this box is some new-purchased booty. Now could we find him out, the money were ours.

CHERRY:

He don't belong to our gang.

BONIFACE:

What horses have they?

CHERRY:

The master rides upon a black.

BONIFACE:

A black! Ten to one the man upon the black mare, and since he don't belong to our fraternity, we may betray him with a safe conscience. I don't think it lawful to harbor any rogues but my own. Look ye, child, as the saying is, we must go cunningly to work. Proofs we must have. The gentleman's servant loves drink: I'll ply him that way; and ten to one loves a wench: you must work him t'other way.

CHERRY:

Father, would you have me give my secret for his?

BONIFACE:

Consider, child, there's two hundred pound to boot.—(*Ringing without.*) Coming, coming.—Child, mind your business.

CHERRY:

What a rogue is my father! My father! I deny it. My mother was a good, generous, free-hearted woman, and I can't tell how far her good nature might have extended for the good of her children. This landlord of mine, for I think I can call him no more, would betray his guest and debauch his daughter into the bargain—by a footman, too!

Enter Archer.

ARCHER:

What footman, pray, mistress, is so happy as to be the subject of your contemplation?

CHERRY:

Whoever he is, friend, he'll be but little the better for't.

ARCHER:

I hope so, for I'm sure you did not think of me.

CHERRY:

Suppose I had?

ARCHER:

Why then you're but even with me, for the minute I came in I was a-considering in what manner I should make love to you.

CHERRY:

Love to me, friend!

ARCHER:

Yes, child.

CHERRY:

Child! Manners. If you kept a little more distance, friend, it would become you much better.

ARCHER:

Distance! Good night, saucebox.   *Going.*

CHERRY:

A pretty fellow! I like his pride.—Sir, pray, sir, you see, sir (Archer *returns*), I have the credit to be intrusted with your master's fortune here, which sets me a degree above his footman. I hope, sir, you an't affronted.

ARCHER:

Let me look you full in the face, and I'll tell you whether you can affront me or no. S'death, child, you have a pair of delicate eyes, and you don't know what to do with 'em.

CHERRY:

Why, sir, don't I see everybody?

ARCHER:

Ay, but if some women had 'em they would kill everybody. Prithee, instruct me; I would fain make love to you, but I don't know what to say.

CHERRY:

Why, did you never make love to anybody before?

ARCHER:

Never to a person of your figure. I can assure you, madam, my addresses have been always confined to people within my own sphere. I never aspired so high before.

A Song.

But you look so bright,
And are dressed so tight
That a man would swear you're right
As arm was e'er laid over.

Such an air
You freely wear
To ensnare
As makes each guest a lover.

Since then, my dear, I'm your guest,
Prithee give me of the best
Of what is ready dressed.
Since then, my dear, etc.

CHERRY (*aside*):

What can I think of this man?—Will you give me that song, sir?

ARCHER:

Ay, my dear, take it while 'tis warm. (*Kisses her.*) Death and fire, her lips are honeycombs!

CHERRY:

And I wish there had been bees, too, to have stung you for your impudence.

ARCHER:

> There's a swarm of Cupids, my little Venus, that has done the business much better.

CHERRY (*aside*):

> This fellow is misbegotten as well as I.—What's your name, sir?

ARCHER (*aside*):

> Name! I gad, I have forgot it.—Oh! Martin.

CHERRY:

> Where were you born?

ARCHER:

> In St. Martin's parish.

CHERRY:

> What was your father?

ARCHER:

> St. Martin's Parish.

CHERRY:

> Then, friend, good night.

ARCHER:

> I hope not.

CHERRY:

> You may depend upon't.

ARCHER:

> Upon what?

CHERRY:

> That you're very impudent.

ARCHER:

> That you're very handsome.

CHERRY:

> That you're a footman.

ARCHER:

> That you're an angel.

CHERRY:

> I shall be rude.

ARCHER:

> So shall I.

CHERRY:

> Let go my hand.

ARCHER:

> Give me a kiss. *Kisses her.*
> *Call without,* Cherry, Cherry.

CHERRY:

> I'mm—my father calls. You plaguy devil, how durst you stop my breath so? Offer to follow me one step, if you dare.
>
> (*Exit* Cherry.)

ARCHER:

A fair challenge, by this light. This is a pretty fair opening of an adventure, but we are knight-errants, and so fortune be our guide. *Exit.*

Act II, Scene i

Scene: A gallery in Lady Bountiful's house.
(*Enter*) Mrs. Sullen *and* Dorinda *meeting.*

DORINDA:

Morrow, my dear sister, are you for church this morning?

MRS. SULLEN:

Anywhere to pray, for heaven alone can help me. But I think, Dorinda, there's no form of prayer in the liturgy against bad husbands.

DORINDA:

But there's a form of law in Doctors' Commons, and I swear, Sister Sullen, rather than see you thus continually discontented I would advise you to apply to that. For besides the part that I bear in your vexatious broils, as being sister to the husband and friend to the wife, your example gives me such an impression of matrimony that I shall be apt to condemn my person to a long vacation all its life. But supposing, madam, that you brought it to a case of separation, what can you urge against your husband? My brother is, first, the most constant man alive.

MRS. SULLEN:

The most constant husband, I grant ye.

DORINDA:

He never sleeps from you.

MRS. SULLEN:

No, he always sleeps with me.

DORINDA:

He allows you a maintenance suitable to your quality.

MRS. SULLEN:

A maintenance! Do you take me, madam, for an hospital child, that I must sit down and bless my benefactors for meat, drink, and clothes? As I take it, madam, I brought your brother ten thousand pounds, out of which I might expect some pretty things called pleasures.

DORINDA:

You share in all the pleasures that the country affords.

MRS. SULLEN:

Country pleasures! Racks and torments! Dost think, child, that my limbs were made for leaping of ditches and clambering over stiles; or that my parents, wisely foreseeing my future happiness in country pleasures, had early instructed me in the rural accomplishments of drinking fat ale, playing at whisk, and smoking tobacco with my husband; or of spreading of plasters, brewing of diet drinks, and stilling rosemary water with the good old gentlewoman, my mother-in-law?

DORINDA:

I'm sorry, madam, that it is not more in our power to divert you. I could wish indeed that our entertainments were a little more polite or your taste a little less refined. But pray, madam, how came the poets and philosophers that labored so much in hunting after pleasure to place it at last in a country life?

MRS. SULLEN:

Because they wanted money, child, to find out the pleasures of the town. Did you ever see a poet or philosopher worth ten thousand pound? If you can show me such a man, I'll lay you fifty pound you'll find him somewhere within the weekly bills. Not that I disapprove rural pleasures as the poets have painted them; in their landscape every Phyllis has her Corydon, every murmuring stream and every flowery mead gives fresh alarms to love. Besides, you'll find that their couples were never married. But yonder I see my Corydon, and a sweet swain it is, heaven knows. Come, Dorinda, don't be angry. He's my husband and your brother, and between both is he not a sad brute?

DORINDA:

I have nothing to say to your part of him; you're the best judge.

MRS. SULLEN:

O, sister, sister, if ever you marry, beware of a sullen, silent sot, one that's always musing but never thinks. There's some diversion in a talking blockhead, and since a woman must wear chains, I would have the pleasure of hearing 'em rattle a little. Now you shall see, but take this by the way. He came home this morning at his usual hour of four, wakened me out of a sweet dream of something else by tumbling over the tea table, which he broke all to pieces. After his man and he had rolled about the room like sick passengers in a storm, he comes flounce into bed, dead as a salmon into a fishmonger's basket, his feet cold as ice, his breath hot as a furnace, and his hands and his face as greasy as his flannel nightcap. Oh matrimony! He tosses up the clothes with a barbarous swing over his shoulders, disorders the whole economy of my bed, leaves me half naked, and my whole night's comfort is the tuneable serenade of that wakeful nightingale, his nose. O, the pleasure of counting the melancholy clock by a snoring husband! But now, sister, you shall see how handsomely, being a well-bred man, he will beg my pardon.

Enter Sullen.

SULLEN:
   My head aches consumedly.
MRS. SULLEN:
   Will you be pleased, my dear, to drink tea with us this morn-ing? It may do your head good.
SULLEN:
   No.
DORINDA:
   Coffee, brother?
SULLEN:
   Pshaw.
MRS. SULLEN:
   Will you please to dress and go to church with me? The air may help you.
SULLEN:
   Scrub.

Enter Scrub.

SCRUB:
   Sir?
SULLEN:
   What day o'th' week is this?
SCRUB:
   Sunday, an't please your worship.
SULLEN:
   Sunday! Bring me a dram, and, d'ye hear, set out the venison-pasty and a tankard of strong beer upon the hall table. I'll go to breakfast.   *Going.*
DORINDA:
   Stay, stay, brother, you shan't get off so. You were very naught last night and must make your wife reparation. Come, come, brother, won't you ask pardon?

SULLEN:

For what?

DORINDA:

For being drunk last night.

SULLEN:

I can afford it, can't I?

MRS. SULLEN:

But I can't, sir.

SULLEN:

Then you may let it alone.

MRS. SULLEN:

But I must tell you, sir, that this is not to be borne.

SULLEN:

I'm glad on't.

MRS. SULLEN:

What is the reason, sir, that you use me thus inhumanely?

SULLEN:

Scrub.

SCRUB:

Sir?

SULLEN:

Get things ready to shave my head.   *Exit.*

MRS. SULLEN:

Have a care of coming near his temples, Scrub, for fear you
meet something there that may turn the edge of your razor.

Exit Scrub.

Inveterate stupidity! Did you ever know so hard, so obstinate
a spleen as his? O, sister, sister, I shall never ha' good of the
beast till I get him to town. London, dear London, is the place
for managing and breaking a husband.

DORINDA:

And has not a husband the same opportunities there for hum-
bling a wife?

MRS. SULLEN:

No, no, child, 'tis a standing maxim in conjugal discipline that
when a man would enslave his wife he hurries her into the
country, and when a lady would be arbitrary with her husband
she wheedles her booby up to town. A man dare not play the
tyrant in London because there are so many examples to
encourage the subject to rebel. O, Dorinda, Dorinda, a fine
woman may do anything in London. O' my conscience, she
may raise an army of forty thousand men.

DORINDA:

> I fancy, sister, you have a mind to be trying your power that way here in Lichfield; you have drawn the French count to your colors already.

MRS. SULLEN:

> The French are a people that can't live without their gallantries.

DORINDA:

> And some English that I know, sister, are not averse to such amusements.

MRS. SULLEN:

> Well, sister, since the truth must out, it may do as well now as hereafter. I think one way to rouse my lethargic sottish husband is to give him a rival. Security begets negligence in all people, and men must be alarmed to make 'em alert in their duty. Women are like pictures of no value in the hands of a fool till he hears men of sense bid high for the purchase.

DORINDA:

> This might do, sister, if my brother's understanding were to be convinced into a passion for you, but I fancy there's a natural aversion of his side. And I fancy, sister, that you don't come much behind him, if you dealt fairly.

MRS. SULLEN:

> I own it. We are united contradictions, fire and water. But I could be contented, with a great many other wives, to humor the censorious mob and give the world an appearance of living well with my husband, could I bring him but to dissemble a little kindness to keep me in countenance.

DORINDA:

> But how do you know, sister, but that instead of rousing your husband by this artifice to a counterfeit kindness, he should awake in a real fury?

MRS. SULLEN:

> Let him. If I can't entice him to the one, I would provoke him to the other.

DORINDA:

> But how must I behave myself between ye?

MRS. SULLEN:

> You must assist me.

DORINDA:

> What, against my own brother?

MRS. SULLEN:

> He's but half a brother, and I'm your entire friend. If I go a step beyond the bounds of honor, leave me; till then I expect you should go along with me in everything. While I trust my honor

in your hands, you may trust your brother's in mine. The count is to dine here today.

DORINDA:

'Tis a strange thing, sister, that I can't like that man.

MRS. SULLEN:

You like nothing; your time is not come. Love and death have their fatalities and strike home one time or other. You'll pay for all one day, I warrant ye. But, come, my lady's tea is ready, and 'tis almost church time.

Exeunt.

Act II, Scene ii

Scene: the inn.
Enter Aimwell, *dressed, and* Archer.

AIMWELL:

And was she the daughter of the house?

ARCHER:

The landlord is so blind as to think so, but I dare swear she has better blood in her veins.

AIMWELL:

Why dost think so?

ARCHER:

Because the baggage has a pert *je ne sais quoi.* She reads plays, keeps a monkey, and is troubled with vapors.

AIMWELL:

By which discoveries I guess that you know more of her.

ARCHER:

Not yet, faith. The lady gives herself airs, forsooth; nothing under a gentleman.

AIMWELL:

Let me take her in hand.

ARCHER:

Say one word more o' that, and I'll declare myself, spoil your sport there, and everywhere else. Look ye, Aimwell, every man in his own sphere.

AIMWELL:

Right, and therefore you must pimp for your master.

ARCHER:

In the usual forms, good sir, after I have served myself. But to our business. You are so well dressed, Tom, and make so handsome a figure that I fancy you may do execution in a country church. The exterior part strikes first, and you're in the right to make that impression favorable.

AIMWELL:

There's something in that which may turn to advantage. The appearance of a stranger in a country church draws as many gazers as a blazing star. No sooner he comes into the cathedral but a train of whispers runs buzzing round the congregation in a moment: "Who is he? Whence comes he? Do you know him?" Then I, sir, tips me the verger with half a crown. He pockets the simony and inducts me into the best pew in the church. I pull out my snuffbox, turn myself round, bow to the bishop—or the dean, if he be the commanding officer—single out a beauty, rivet both my eyes to hers, set my nose a-bleeding by the strength of imagination, and show the whole church my concern by my endeavoring to hide it. After the sermon the whole town gives me to her for a lover, and by persuading the lady that I am a-dying for her, the tables are turned, and she in good earnest falls in love with me.

ARCHER:

There's nothing in this, Tom, without a precedent. But instead of riveting your eyes to a beauty, try to fix 'em upon a fortune; that's our business at present.

AIMWELL:

Pshaw, no woman can be a beauty without a fortune. Let me alone, for I am a marksman.

ARCHER:

Tom.

AIMWELL:

Ay.

ARCHER:

When were you at church before, pray?

AIMWELL:

Um—I was there at the coronation.

ARCHER:

And how can you expect a blessing by going to church now?

AIMWELL:

Blessing! Nay, Frank, I ask but for a wife.

ARCHER:

Truly the man is not very unreasonable in his demands.

Exit at the opposite door.

Enter Boniface *and* Cherry.

BONIFACE:

Well, daughter, as the saying is, have you brought Martin to confess?

CHERRY:

Pray, father, don't put me upon getting anything out of a man. I'm but young, you know, father, and I don't understand wheedling.

BONIFACE:

Young! Why you jade, as the saying is, can any woman wheedle that is not young? Your mother was useless at five and twenty. Not wheedle! Would you make your mother a whore and me a cuckold, as the saying is? I tell you his silence confesses it, and his master spends his money so freely and is so much a gentleman every manner of way that he must be a highwayman.

Enter Gibbet *in a cloak.*

GIBBET:

Landlord, landlord, is the coast clear?

BONIFACE:

O, Mr. Gibbet, what's the news?

GIBBET:

No matter, ask no questions, all fair and honorable. Here, my dear Cherry (*gives her a bag*), two hundred sterling pounds as good as any that ever hanged or saved a rogue; lay 'em by with the rest. And here—three wedding or mourning rings, 'tis much the same, you know. Here, two silver-hilted swords; I took those from fellows that never show any part of their swords but the hilts. Here is a diamond necklace which the lady hid in the privatest place in the coach, but I found it out. This gold watch I took from a pawnbroker's wife. It was left in her hands by a person of quality; there's the arms upon the case.

CHERRY:

But who had you the money from?

GIBBET:

Ah, poor woman! I pitied her. From a poor lady just eloped from her husband. She had made up her cargo and was bound for Ireland as hard as she could drive. She told me of her husband's barbarous usage, and so I left her half a crown. But I had almost forgot, my dear Cherry, I have a present for you.

CHERRY:

What is't?

GIBBET:

A pot of cereuse, my child, that I took out of a lady's under-pocket.

CHERRY:

What, Mr. Gibbet, do you think that I paint?

GIBBET:

Why, you jade, your betters do. I'm sure the lady that I took it from had a coronet upon her handkerchief. Here, take my cloak, and go secure the premises.

CHERRY:

I will secure 'em.   *Exit.*

BONIFACE:

But, hark ye, where's Hounslow and Bagshot?

GIBBET:

They'll be here tonight.

BONIFACE:

D'ye know of any other gentlemen o' the pad on this road?

GIBBET:

No.

BONIFACE:

I fancy that I have two that lodge in the house just now.

GIBBET:

The devil! How d'ye smoke 'em?

BONIFACE:

Why, the one is gone to church.

GIBBET:

That's suspicious, I must confess.

BONIFACE:

And the other is now in his master's chamber; he pretends to be servant to the other. We'll call him out and pump him a little.

GIBBET:

With all my heart.

BONIFACE:

Mr. Martin, Mr. Martin.

Enter Martin (Archer) *combing a periwig, and singing.*

GIBBET:

The roads are consumed deep; I'm as dirty as old Brentford at Christmas. A good pretty fellow that.—Whose servant are you, friend?

ARCHER:

My master's.

GIBBET:

Really?

ARCHER:

Really.

GIBBET:

That's much. The fellow has been at the bar, by his evasions.—But, pray, sir, what is your master's name?

ARCHER:

Tall, all dall. (*Sings and combs the periwig.*) This is the most obstinate curl.

GIBBET:

I ask you his name.

ARCHER:

Name, sir,—tall, all dall—I never asked him his name in my life. Tall, all dall.

BONIFACE:

What think you now?

GIBBET:

Plain, plain, he talks now as if he were before a judge.—But, pray, friend, which way does your master travel?

ARCHER:

A-horseback.

GIBBET:

Very well again, an old offender, right.—But I mean does he go upwards or downwards?

ARCHER:

Downwards, I fear, sir. Tall, all.

GIBBET:

I'm afraid my fate will be a contrary way.

BONIFACE:

Ha, ha, ha! Mr. Martin, you're very arch. This gentleman is only traveling towards Chester and would be glad of your company, that's all.—Come, captain, you'll stay tonight, I suppose. I'll show you a chamber. Come, captain.

GIBBET:

Farewell, friend.   *Exit* (*with* Boniface).

ARCHER:

Captain, your servant.—Captain! a pretty fellow. S'death, I wonder that the officers of the army don't conspire to beat all scoundrels in red but their own.

Enter Cherry.

CHERRY (*aside*):

> Gone, and Martin here! I hope he did not listen. I would have the merit of the discovery all my own because I would oblige him to love me.—Mr. Martin, who was that man with my father?

ARCHER:

> Some recruiting sergeant or whipped-out trooper, I suppose.

CHERRY:

> All's safe, I find.

ARCHER:

> Come, my dear, have you conned over the catechize I taught you last night?

CHERRY:

> Come, question me.

ARCHER:

> What is love?

CHERRY:

> Love is I know not what, it comes I know not how, and goes I know not when.

ARCHER:

> Very well; an apt scholar. *Chucks her under the chin.* Where does love enter?

CHERRY:

> Into the eyes.

ARCHER:

> And where go out?

CHERRY:

> I won't tell ye.

ARCHER:

> What are the objects of that passion?

CHERRY:

> Youth, beauty, and clean linen.

ARCHER:

> The reason?

CHERRY:

> The two first are fashionable in nature and the third at court.

ARCHER:

> That's my dear. What are the signs and tokens of that passion?

CHERRY:

> A stealing look, a stammering tongue, words improbable, designs impossible, and actions impracticable.

ARCHER:

> That's my good child. Kiss me. What must a lover do to obtain his mistress?

CHERRY:

He must adore the person that disdains him. He must bribe the chambermaid that betrays him and court the footman that laughs at him. He must, he must—

ARCHER:

Nay, child, I must whip you if you don't mind your lesson. He must treat his—

CHERRY:

O, ay, he must treat his enemies with respect, his friends with indifference, and all the world with contempt. He must suffer much and fear more. He must desire much and hope little. In short, he must embrace his ruin and throw himself away.

ARCHER:

Had ever man so hopeful a pupil as mine? Come, my dear, why is love called a riddle?

CHERRY:

Because, being blind, he leads those that see, and though a child he governs a man.

ARCHER:

Mighty well. And why is love pictured blind?

CHERRY:

Because the painters out of the weakness or privilege of their art chose to hide those eyes that they could not draw.

ARCHER:

That's my dear little scholar. Kiss me again. And why should love, that's a child, govern a man?

CHERRY:

Because that a child is the end of love.

ARCHER:

And so ends love's catechism. And now, my dear, we'll go in and make my master's bed.

CHERRY:

Hold, hold, Mr. Martin. You have taken a great deal of pains to instruct me, and what d'ye think I have learnt by it?

ARCHER:

What?

CHERRY:

That your discourse and your habit are contradictions, and it would be nonsense in me to believe you a footman any longer.

ARCHER:

'Oons, what a witch it is!

CHERRY:

Depend upon this, sir, nothing in this garb shall ever tempt me, for though I was born to servitude, I hate it. Own your condition, swear you love me, and then—

ARCHER:

And then we shall go make the bed.

CHERRY:

Yes.

ARCHER:

You must know then that I am born a gentleman. My education was liberal, but I went to London a younger brother, fell into the hands of sharpers who stripped me of my money. My friends disowned me, and now my necessity brings me to what you see.

CHERRY:

Then take my hands, promise to marry me before you sleep, and I'll make you master of two thousand pound.

ARCHER:

How!

CHERRY:

Two thousand pound that I have this minute in my own custody; so throw off your livery this instant, and I'll go find a parson.

ARCHER:

What said you? A parson!

CHERRY:

What, do you scruple?

ARCHER:

Scruple, no, no, but—two thousand pound you say?

CHERRY:

And better.

ARCHER:

S'death, what shall I do? But hark'ee, child, what need you make me master of yourself and money when you may have the same pleasure out of me and still keep your fortune in your hands?

CHERRY:

Then you won't marry me?

ARCHER:

I would marry you, but—

CHERRY:

O, sweet sir, I'm your humble servant. You're fairly caught. Would you persuade me that any gentleman who could bear the scandal of wearing a livery would refuse two thousand pound, let the condition be what it would? No, no, sir. But I hope you'll pardon the freedom I have taken, since it was only to inform myself of the respect that I ought to pay you. *Going*.

ARCHER:

Fairly bit, by Jupiter.—Hold, hold, and have you actually two thousand pound?

CHERRY:

Sir, I have my secrets as well as you. When you please to be more open I shall be more free, and be assured that I have discoveries that will match yours, be what they will. In the meanwhile be satisfied that no discovery I make shall ever hurt you, but beware of my father.

(*Exit* Cherry.)

ARCHER:

So, we're like to have as many adventures in our inn as Don Quixote had in his. Let me see—two thousand pound! If the wench would promise to die when the money were spent, Igad, one would marry her, but the fortune may go off in a year or two, and the wife may live—Lord knows how long? Then an innkeeper's daughter—ay, that's the devil. There my pride brings me off.

For whatsoe'er the sages charge on pride,
The angels' fall, and twenty faults beside;
On earth I'm sure, 'mong us of mortal calling,
Pride saves man oft, and woman too, from falling.

Exit.

Act III, Scene i

Scene: Lady Bountiful's house.
Enter Mrs. Sullen, Dorinda.

MRS. SULLEN:

Ha, ha, ha, my dear sister, let me embrace thee. Now we are friends indeed, for I shall have a secret of yours as a pledge for mine. Now you'll be good for something: I shall have you conversable in the subjects of the sex.

DORINDA:

But do you think that I am so weak as to fall in love with a fellow at first sight?

MRS. SULLEN:

Pshaw, now you spoil all. Why should not we be as free in our friendships as the men? I warrant you the gentleman has got to his confidant already, has avowed his passion, toasted your health, called you ten thousand angels, has run over your lips, eyes, neck, shape, air, and everything, in a description that warms their mirth to a second enjoyment.

DORINDA:

Your hand, sister. I an't well.

MRS. SULLEN (*aside*):

So, she's breeding already.—Come, child, up with it—hem a little—so—now tell me, don't you like the gentleman that we saw at church just now?

DORINDA:

The man's well enough.

MRS. SULLEN:

Well enough! Is he not a demigod, a Narcissus, a star, the man i'the moon?

DORINDA:

O, sister, I'm extremely ill.

MRS. SULLEN:

Shall I send to your mother, child, for a little of her cephalic plaster to put to the soles of your feet, or shall I send to the gentleman for something for you? Come, unlace your stays; unbosom yourself. The man is perfectly a pretty fellow. I saw him when he first came into church.

DORINDA:

I saw him too, sister, and with an air that shone, methought, like rays about his person.

MRS. SULLEN:

Well said; up with it.

DORINDA:

No forward coquette behavior, no airs to set him off, no studied looks nor artful posture, but nature did it all.

MRS. SULLEN:

Better and better. One touch more, come.

DORINDA:

But then his looks—did you observe his eyes?

MRS. SULLEN:

Yes, yes, I did. His eyes, well, what of his eyes?

DORINDA:

Sprightly, but not wandering; they seemed to view but never gazed on anything but me. And then his looks so humble were, and yet so noble, that they aimed to tell me that he could with pride die at my feet though he scorned slavery anywhere else.

MRS. SULLEN:

The physic works purely! How d'ye find yourself now, my dear?

DORINDA:

Hem, much better, my dear. O, here comes our Mercury.

Enter Scrub.

Well, Scrub, what news of the gentleman?

SCRUB:

Madam, I have brought you a packet of news.

DORINDA:

Open it quickly, come.

SCRUB:

In the first place I enquired who the gentleman was; they told me he was a stranger. Secondly, I asked what the gentleman was; they answered and said that they never saw him before. Thirdly, I enquired what countryman he was; they replied 'twas more than they knew. Fourthly, I demanded whence he came; their answer was, they could not tell. And fifthly, I asked whither he went, and they replied they knew nothing of the matter. And this is all I could learn.

MRS. SULLEN:

But what do the people say? Can't they guess?

SCRUB:

Why, some think he's a spy, some guess he's a mountebank, some say one thing, some another; but for my own part I believe he's a Jesuit.

DORINDA:

A Jesuit! Why a Jesuit?

SCRUB:

Because he keeps his horses always ready saddled, and his footman talks French.

MRS. SULLEN:

His footman!

SCRUB:

Ay, he and the count's footman were gabbering French like two intriguing ducks in a millpond, and I believe they talked of me, for they laughed consumedly.

DORINDA:

What sort of livery has the footman?

SCRUB:

Livery! Lord, madam, I took him for a captain, he's so bedizened with lace. And then he has tops to his shoes up to his mid-leg, a silver-headed cane dangling at his knuckles. He carries his hands in his pockets just so (*walks in the French air*) and has a fine long periwig tied up in a bag. Lord, Madam, he's clear another sort of man than I.

MRS. SULLEN:

That may easily be.—But what shall we do now, sister?

DORINDA:

I have it. This fellow has a world of simplicity and some cunning; the first hides the latter by abundance.—Scrub.

SCRUB:

Madam.

DORINDA:

We have a great mind to know who this gentleman is, only for our satisfaction.

SCRUB:

Yes, madam, it would be a satisfaction, no doubt.

DORINDA:

You must go and get acquainted with his footman and invite him hither to drink a bottle of your ale because you're butler today.

SCRUB:

Yes, madam, I am butler every Sunday.

MRS. SULLEN:

O brave, sister! O' my conscience, you understand the mathematics already. 'Tis the best plot in the world. Your mother, you know, will be gone to church, my spouse will be got to the alehouse with his scoundrels, and the house will be our own; so we drop in by accident and ask the fellow some questions ourselves. In the country, you know, any stranger is company, and we're glad to take up with the butler in a country dance and happy if he'll do us the favor.

SCRUB:

O, madam, you wrong me. I never refused your ladyship the favor in my life.

Enter Gipsy.

GIPSY:

Ladies, dinner's upon table.

DORINDA:

Scrub, we'll excuse your waiting. Go where we ordered you.

SCRUB:

I shall.   *Exeunt.*

Act III, Scene ii

Scene changes to the inn.
Enter Aimwell *and* Archer.

ARCHER:
Well, Tom, I find you're a marksman.

AIMWELL:
A marksman! Who so blind could be as not discern a swan among the ravens?

ARCHER:
Well, but heark'ee, Aimwell.

AIMWELL:
Aimwell! Call me Oroondates, Cesario, Amadis, all that romance can in a lover paint, and then I'll answer. O, Archer, I read her thousands in her looks. She looked like Ceres in her harvest: corn, wine and oil, milk and honey, gardens, groves, and purling streams played on her plenteous face.

ARCHER:
Her face! Her pocket, you mean; the corn, wine and oil lies there. In short, she has ten thousand pound; that's the English on't.

AIMWELL:
Her eyes—

ARCHER:
Are demicannons, to be sure, so I won't stand their battery.
Going.

AIMWELL:
Pray excuse me; my passion must have vent.

ARCHER:
Passion! What a plague! D'ye think these romantic airs will do our business? Were my temper as extravagant as yours my adventures have something more romantic by half.

AIMWELL:
Your adventures!

ARCHER:
Yes,
    The nymph that with her twice ten hundred pounds
    With brazen engine hot, and coif clear starched
    Can fire the guest in warming of the bed—
There's a touch of sublime Milton for you, and the subject but an innkeeper's daughter. I can play with a girl as an angler does with his fish: he keeps it at the end of his line, runs it up the stream and down the stream, till at last he brings it to hand, tickles the trout, and so whips it into his basket.

Enter Boniface.

BONIFACE:

Mr. Martin, as the saying is, yonder's an honest fellow below, my Lady Bountiful's butler, who begs the honor that you would go home with him and see his cellar.

ARCHER:

Do my *baisemains* to the gentleman, and tell him I will do myself the honor to wait on him immediately.

Exit Boniface.

AIMWELL:

What do I hear—soft Orpheus play and fair Toftida sing?

ARCHER:

Pshaw, damn your raptures! I tell you here's a pump going to be put into the vessel, and the ship will get into harbor, my life on't. You say there's another lady very handsome there?

AIMWELL:

Yes, faith.

ARCHER:

I'm in love with her already.

AIMWELL:

Can't you give me a bill upon Cherry in the meantime?

ARCHER:

No, no, friend, all her corn, wine, and oil is engrossed to my market. And once more I warn you to keep your anchorage clear of mine, for if you fall foul of me, by this light you shall go to the bottom. What, make prize of my little frigate while I am upon the cruise for you?

Exit.

Enter Boniface.

AIMWELL:

Well, well, I won't.—Landlord, have you any tolerable company in the house? I don't care for dining alone.

BONIFACE:

Yes, sir, there's a captain below, as the saying is, that arrived about an hour ago.

AIMWELL:

Gentlemen of his coat are welcome everywhere. Will you make him a compliment from me and tell him I should be glad of his company.

BONIFACE:

Who shall I tell him, sir, would—

AIMWELL:

Ha, that stroke was well thrown in.—I'm only a traveler like himself and would be glad of his company, that's all.

BONIFACE:

I obey your commands, as the saying is. *Exit.*

Enter Archer.

ARCHER:

S'death, I had forgot! What title will you give yourself?

AIMWELL:

My brother's, to be sure. He would never give me anything else, so I'll make bold with his honor this bout. You know the rest of your cue.

ARCHER:

Ay, ay. *Exit.*

Enter Gibbet.

GIBBET:

Sir, I'm yours.

AIMWELL:

'Tis more than I deserve, sir, for I don't know you.

GIBBET:

I don't wonder at that, sir, for you never saw me before, *(aside)* I hope.

AIMWELL:

And pray, sir, how came I by the honor of seeing you now?

GIBBET:

Sir, I scorn to intrude upon any gentleman, but my landlord—

AIMWELL:

O, sir, I ask your pardon. You're the captain he told me of.

GIBBET:

At your service, sir.

AIMWELL:

What regiment, may I be so bold?

GIBBET:

A marching regiment, sir, an old corps.

AIMWELL *(aside)*:

Very old, if your coat be regimental.—You have served abroad, sir?

GIBBET:

Yes, sir, in the plantations; 'twas my lot to be sent into the worst service. I would have quitted it indeed, but a man of honor, you know—besides 'twas for the good of my country that I should be abroad. Anything for the good of one's country. I'm a Roman for that.

AIMWELL (*aside*):

One of the first, I'll lay my life.—You found the West Indies very hot, sir?

GIBBET:

Ay, sir, too hot for me.

AIMWELL:

Pray, sir, han't I seen your face at Will's Coffeehouse?

GIBBET:

Yes, sir, and at White's too.

AIMWELL:

And where is your company now, captain?

GIBBET:

They an't come yet.

AIMWELL:

Why, d'ye expect 'em here?

GIBBET:

They'll be here tonight, sir.

AIMWELL:

Which way do they march?

GIBBET:

Across the country.—(*Aside.*) The devil's in't, if I han't said enough to encourage him to declare, but I'm afraid he's not right. I must tack about.

AIMWELL:

Is your company to quarter in Lichfield?

GIBBET:

In this house, sir.

AIMWELL:

What, all?

GIBBET:

My company's but thin, ha, ha, ha; we are but three, ha, ha, ha.

AIMWELL:

You're merry, sir.

GIBBET:

Ay, sir, you must excuse me, sir. I understand the world, especially the art of traveling. I don't care, sir, for answering questions directly upon the road, for I generally ride with a charge about me.

AIMWELL (*aside*):

Three or four, I believe.

GIBBET:

I am credibly informed that there are highwaymen upon this quarter; not, sir, that I could suspect a gentleman of your figure. But truly, sir, I have got such a way of evasion upon the road that I don't care for speaking truth to any man.

AIMWELL:

Your caution may be necessary. Then I presume you're no captain?

GIBBET:

Not I, sir. Captain is a good traveling name, and so I take it. It stops a great many foolish inquiries that are generally made about gentlemen that travel. It gives a man an air of something and makes the drawers obedient. And thus far I am a captain and no farther.

AIMWELL:

And pray, sir, what is your true profession?

GIBBET:

O, sir, you must excuse me. Upon my word, sir, I don't think it safe to tell you.

AIMWELL:

Ha, ha, ha, upon my word I commend you.

Enter Boniface.

Well, Mr. Boniface, what's the news?

BONIFACE:

There's another gentleman below, as the saying is, that hearing you were but two would be glad to make the third man if you would give him leave.

AIMWELL:

What is he?

BONIFACE:

A clergyman, as the saying is.

AIMWELL:

A clergyman! Is he really a clergyman, or is it only his traveling name, as my friend the captain has it?

BONIFACE:

O, sir, he's a priest and chaplain to the French officers in town.

AIMWELL:

Is he a Frenchman?

BONIFACE:

Yes, sir, born at Brussels.

GIBBET:

A Frenchman, and a priest! I won't be seen in his company, sir. I have a value for my reputation, sir.

AIMWELL:

Nay, but captain, since we are by ourselves—Can he speak English, landlord?

BONIFACE:

Very well, sir. You may know him, as the saying is, to be a foreigner by his accent, and that's all.

AIMWELL:

Then he has been in England before?

BONIFACE:

Never, sir, but he's a master of languages, as the saying is. He talks Latin. It does me good to hear him talk Latin.

AIMWELL:

Then you understand Latin, Mr. Boniface?

BONIFACE:

Not I, sir, as the saying is, but he talks it so very fast that I'm sure it must be good.

AIMWELL:

Pray desire him to walk up.

BONIFACE:

Here he is, as the saying is.

Enter Foigard.

FOIGARD:

Save you, gentlemens, both.

AIMWELL (*aside*):

A Frenchman!—Sir, your most humble servant.

FOIGARD:

Och, dear joy, I am your most faithful shervant, and yours alsho.

GIBBET:

Doctor, you talk very good English, but you have a mighty twang of the foreigner.

FOIGARD:

My English is very vel for the vords, but we foregners, you know, cannot bring our tongues about the pronunciation so soon.

AIMWELL (*aside*):

A foreigner! A downright Teague by this light.—Were you born in France, doctor?

FOIGARD:

I was educated in France, but I was borned at Brussels. I am a subject of the King of Spain, joy.

GIBBET:

    What King of Spain, sir? Speak.

FOIGARD:

    Upon my shoul, joy, I cannot tell you as yet.

AIMWELL:

    Nay, captain, that was too hard upon the doctor. He's a stranger.

FOIGARD:

    O, let him alone, dear joy. I am of a nation that is not easily put out of countenance.

AIMWELL:

    Come, gentlemen, I'll end the dispute.—Here, landlord, is dinner ready?

BONIFACE:

    Upon the table, as the saying is.

AIMWELL:

    Gentlemen—pray—that door—

FOIGARD:

    No, no, fait, the captain must lead.

AIMWELL:

    No, doctor, the church is our guide.

GIBBET:

    Ay, ay, so it is.   *Exit foremost; they follow.*

Act III, Scene iii

Scene changes to a gallery in Lady Bountiful's house. Enter Archer *and* Scrub *singing, and hugging one another,* Scrub *with a tankard in his hand,* Gipsy *listening at a distance.*

SCRUB:

    Tall, all dall. Come, my dear boy, let's have that song once more.

ARCHER:

    No, no, we shall disturb the family. But will you be sure to keep the secret?

SCRUB:

    Pho, upon my honor, as I'm a gentleman.

ARCHER:

    'Tis enough. You must know then that my master is the Lord Viscount Aimwell. He fought a duel t'other day in London, wounded his man so dangerously that he thinks fit to withdraw till he hears whether the gentleman's wounds be mortal or not. He never was in this part of England before, so he chose to retire to this place; that's all.

GIPSY:

And that's enough for me.   *Exit.*

SCRUB:

And where were you when your master fought?

ARCHER:

We never know of our masters' quarrels.

SCRUB:

No, if our masters in the country here receive a challenge, the first thing they do is to tell their wives, the wife tells the servants, the servants alarm the tenants, and in half an hour you shall have the whole county in arms.

ARCHER:

To hinder two men from doing what they have no mind for. But if you should chance to talk now of my business?

SCRUB:

Talk! Ay, sir, had I not learnt the knack of holding my tongue, I had never lived so long in a great family.

ARCHER:

Ay, ay, to be sure, there are secrets in all families.

SCRUB:

Secrets, ay, but I'll say no more. Come, sit down. We'll make an end of our tankard. Here—

ARCHER:

With all my heart. Who knows but you and I may come to be better acquainted, eh? Here's your ladies' healths. You have three, I think, and to be sure there must be secrets among 'em.

SCRUB:

Secrets! Ay, friend. I wish I had a friend.

ARCHER:

Am not I your friend? Come, you and I will be sworn brothers.

SCRUB:

Shall we?

ARCHER:

From this minute. Give me a kiss. And now, Brother Scrub—

SCRUB:

And now, Brother Martin, I will tell you a secret that will make your hair stand on end. You must know that I am consumedly in love.

ARCHER:

That's a terrible secret, that's the truth on't.

SCRUB:

That jade, Gipsy, that was with us just now in the cellar, is the arrantest whore that ever wore a petticoat, and I'm dying for love of her.

ARCHER:

Ha, ha, ha. Are you in love with her person or her virtue, Brother Scrub?

SCRUB:

I should like virtue best because it is more durable than beauty; for virtue holds good with some women long, and many a day after they have lost it.

ARCHER:

In the country, I grant ye, where no woman's virtue is lost till a bastard be found.

SCRUB:

Ay, could I bring her to a bastard I should have her all to myself, but I dare not put it upon that lay for fear of being sent for a soldier. Pray, brother, how do you gentlemen in London like that same Pressing Act?

ARCHER:

Very ill, Brother Scrub. 'Tis the worst that ever was made for us. Formerly I remember the good days when we could dun our masters for our wages, and if they refused to pay us we could have a warrant to carry 'em before a justice. But now if we talk of eating they have a warrant for us and carry us before three justices.

SCRUB:

And to be sure we go if we talk of eating, for the justices won't give their own servants a bad example. Now this is my misfortune: I dare not speak in the house while that jade Gipsy dings about like a fury. Once I had the better end of the staff.

ARCHER:

And how comes the change now?

SCRUB:

Why, the mother of all this mischief is a priest.

ARCHER:

A priest!

SCRUB:

Ay, a damned son of a Whore of Babylon, that came over hither to say grace to the French officers and eat up our provisions. There's not a day goes over his head without dinner or supper in this house.

ARCHER:

How came he so familiar in the family?

SCRUB:

Because he speaks English as if he had lived here all his life and tells lies as if he had been a traveler from his cradle.

ARCHER:

And this priest, I'm afraid, has converted the affections of your Gipsy.

SCRUB:

Converted, ay, and perverted, my dear friend, for I'm afraid he has made her a whore and a papist. But this is not all. There's the French count and Mrs. Sullen; they're in the confederacy, and for some private ends of their own, to be sure.

ARCHER:

A very hopeful family yours, Brother Scrub. I suppose the maiden lady has her lover too.

SCRUB:

Not that I know. She's the best on 'em, that's the truth on't. But they take care to prevent my curiosity by giving me so much business that I'm a perfect slave. What d'ye think is my place in this family?

ARCHER:

Butler, I suppose.

SCRUB:

Ah, Lord help you. I'll tell you. Of a Monday, I drive the coach. Of a Tuesday, I drive the plough. On Wednesday, I follow the hounds. A-Thursday, I dun the tenants. On Friday, I go to market. On Saturday, I draw warrants. And a-Sunday, I draw beer.

ARCHER:

Ha, ha, ha! If variety be a pleasure in life you have enough on't, my dear brother. But what ladies are those?

SCRUB:

Ours, ours. That upon the right hand is Mrs. Sullen, and the other is Mrs. Dorinda. Don't mind 'em. Sit still, man.

Enter Mrs. Sullen, *and* Dorinda.

MRS. SULLEN:

I have heard my brother talk of my Lord Aimwell, but they say that his brother is the finer gentleman.

DORINDA:

That's impossible, sister.

MRS. SULLEN:

He's vastly rich, but very close, they say.

DORINDA:

No matter for that. If I can creep into his heart I'll open his breast, I warrant him. I have heard say that people may be guessed at by the behavior of their servants. I could wish we might talk to that fellow.

MRS. SULLEN:

> So do I, for I think he's a very pretty fellow. Come this way. I'll throw out a lure for him presently.

They walk a turn towards the opposite side of the stage.

ARCHER (*aside*):

> Corn, wine, and oil, indeed! But, I think, the wife has the greatest plenty of flesh and blood; she should be my choice.
> > Mrs. Sullen *drops her glove.*
>
> Aha, say you so—

Archer runs, takes it up, and gives it to her.

> Madam, your ladyship's glove.

MRS. SULLEN:

> O, sir, I thank you.—(*To* Dorinda.) What a handsome bow that fellow has!

DORINDA:

> Bow! Why I have known several footmen come down from London set up here for dancing-masters and carry off the best fortunes in the country.

ARCHER (*aside*):

> That project, for ought I know, had been better than ours.— Brother Scrub, why don't you introduce me?

SCRUB:

> Ladies, this is the strange gentleman's servant that you see at church today. I understood he came from London, and so I invited him to the cellar that he might show me the newest flourish in whetting my knives.

DORINDA:

> And I hope you have made much of him?

ARCHER:

> O, yes, madam, but the strength of your ladyship's liquor is a little too potent for the constitution of your humble servant.

MRS. SULLEN:

> What, then you don't usually drink ale?

ARCHER:

> No, madam, my constant drink is tea or a little wine and water. 'Tis prescribed me by the physician for a remedy against the spleen.

SCRUB:

> O la, O la! A footman have the spleen!

MRS. SULLEN:

I thought that distemper had been only proper to people of quality.

ARCHER:

Madam, like all other fashions it wears out and so descends to their servants, though in a great many of us, I believe, it proceeds from some melancholy particles in the blood occasioned by the stagnation of wages.

DORINDA (*aside*):

How affectedly the fellow talks.—How long, pray, have you served your present master?

ARCHER:

Not long. My life has been mostly spent in the service of the ladies.

MRS. SULLEN:

And pray, which service do you like best?

ARCHER:

Madam, the ladies pay best. The honor of serving them is sufficient wages; there is a charm in their looks that delivers a pleasure with their commands and gives our duty the wings of inclination.

MRS. SULLEN (*to* Dorinda):

That flight was above the pitch of a livery.—(*To* Archer.) And, sir, would not you be satisfied to serve a lady again?

ARCHER:

As a groom of the chamber, madam, but not as a footman.

MRS. SULLEN:

I suppose you served as footman before.

ARCHER:

For that reason I would not serve in that post again, for my memory is too weak for the load of messages that the ladies lay upon their servants in London. My Lady Howd'ye, the last mistress I served, called me up one morning and told me, "Martin, go to my Lady Allnight with my humble service. Tell her I was to wait on her ladyship yesterday and left word with Mrs. Rebecca that the preliminaries of the affair she knows of are stopped till we know the concurrence of the person that I know of, for which there are circumstances wanting which we shall accommodate at the old place; but that in the meantime there is a person about her ladyship, that from several hints and surmises, was accessary at a certain time to the disappointments that naturally attend things that to her knowledge are of more importance."

MRS. SULLEN *and* DORINDA:

Ha, ha, ha! Where are you going, sir?

ARCHER:

Why, I han't half done. The whole howd'ye was about half an hour long, so I happened to misplace two syllables and was turned off and rendered incapable.

DORINDA:

The pleasantest fellow, sister, I ever saw.—But, friend, if your master be married, I presume you still serve a lady.

ARCHER:

No, madam, I take care never to come into a married family; the commands of the master and mistress are always so contrary that 'tis impossible to please both.

DORINDA (*aside*):

There's a main point gained. My lord is not married, I find.

MRS. SULLEN:

But, I wonder, friend, that in so many good services you had not a better provision made for you.

ARCHER:

I don't know how, madam. I had a lieutenancy offered me three or four times, but that is not bread, madam. I live much better as I do.

SCRUB:

Madam he sings rarely. I was thought to do pretty well here in the country till he came, but alack-a-day, I'm nothing to my brother Martin.

DORINDA:

Does he? Pray, sir, will you oblige us with a song?

ARCHER:

Are you for passion or humor?

SCRUB:

O la, he has the purest ballad about a trifle.

MRS. SULLEN:

A trifle! Pray, sir, let's have it.

ARCHER:

I'm ashamed to offer you a trifle, madam, but since you command me—

Sings to the tune of "Sir Simon the King."

A trifling song you shall hear,
Begun with a trifle and ended.
All trifling people draw near,
And I shall be nobly attended.

Were it not for trifles, a few
That lately have come into play,
The men would want something to do,
And the women want something to say.

What makes men trifle in dressing?
Because the ladies (they know)
Admire, by often possessing,
That eminent trifle, a beau.

When the lover his moments has trifled
The trifle of trifles to gain,
No sooner the virgin is rifled,
But a trifle shall part 'em again.

What mortal man would be able
At White's half an hour to sit?
Or who could bear a tea table
Without talking of trifles for wit?

The court is from trifles secure;
Gold keys are no trifles, we see;
White rods are no trifles, I'm sure,
Whatever their bearers may be.

But if you will go to the place
Where trifles abundantly breed,
The levee will show you his grace
Makes promises trifles indeed.

A coach with six footmen behind
I count neither trifle nor sin,
But, ye gods, how oft do we find
A scandalous trifle within?

A flask of champagne, people think it
A trifle, or something as bad;
But if you'll contrive how to drink it
You'll find it no trifle, egad.

A parson's a trifle at sea,
A widow's a trifle in sorrow,

A peace is a trifle today,
Who knows what may happen tomorrow?

A black coat a trifle may cloak,
Or to hide it the red may endeavor;
But if once the army is broke,
We shall have more trifles than ever.

The stage is a trifle, they say;
The reason pray carry along,
Because at every new play
The house they with trifles so throng.

But with people's malice to trifle
And to set us all on a foot
The author of this is a trifle,
And his song is a trifle to boot.

MRS. SULLEN:

Very well, sir, we're obliged to you. Something for a pair of gloves. *Offering him money.*

ARCHER:

I humbly beg leave to be excused. My master, madam, pays me, nor dare I take money from any other hand without injuring his honor and disobeying his commands.

DORINDA:

This is surprising. Did you ever see so pretty a well-bred fellow?

MRS. SULLEN:

The devil take him for wearing that livery.

DORINDA:

I fancy, sister, he may be some gentleman, a friend of my lord's, that his lordship has pitched upon for his courage, fidelity, and discretion to bear him company in this dress, and who, ten to one, was his second too.

MRS. SULLEN:

It is so, it must be so, and it shall be so. For I like him.

DORINDA:

What, better than the count?

MRS. SULLEN:

The count happened to be the most agreeable man upon the place, and so I chose him to serve me in my design upon my husband. But I should like this fellow better in a design upon myself.

DORINDA:

But now, sister, for an interview with this lord and this gentleman; how shall we bring that about?

MRS. SULLEN:

Patience! You country ladies give no quarter if once you be entered. Would you prevent their desires and give the fellows no wishing time? Look ye, Dorinda, if my Lord Aimwell loves you or deserves you he'll find a way to see you, and there we must leave it. My business comes now upon the tapis. Have you prepared your brother?

DORINDA:

Yes, yes.

MRS. SULLEN:

And how did he relish it?

DORINDA:

He said little, mumbled something to himself, promised to be guided by me. But here he comes.

Enter Sullen.

SULLEN:

What singing was that I heard just now?

MRS. SULLEN:

The singing in your head, my dear. You complained of it all day.

SULLEN:

You're impertinent.

MRS. SULLEN:

I was ever so since I became one flesh with you.

SULLEN:

One flesh! Rather two carcasses joined unnaturally together.

MRS. SULLEN:

Or rather a living soul coupled to a dead body.

DORINDA:

So, this is fine encouragement for me.

SULLEN:

Yes, my wife shows you what you must do.

MRS. SULLEN:

And my husband shows you what you must suffer.

SULLEN:

S'death, why can't you be silent?

MRS. SULLEN:

S'death, why can't you talk?

SULLEN:

Do you talk to any purpose?

MRS. SULLEN:

Do you think to any purpose?

SULLEN:

Sister, hark ye. (*Whispers.*)—I shan't be home till it be late.

Exit.

MRS. SULLEN:

What did he whisper to ye?

DORINDA:

That he would go round the back way, come into the closet, and listen as I directed him. But let me beg you once more, dear sister, to drop this project, for, as I told you before, instead of awaking him to kindness you may provoke him to a rage. And then who knows how far his brutality may carry him?

MRS. SULLEN:

I'm provided to receive him, I warrant you. But here comes the count. Vanish. *Exit* Dorinda.

Enter Count Bellair.

Don't you wonder, Monsieur le Count, that I was not at church this afternoon?

COUNT:

I more wonder, madam, that you go dere at all or how you dare to lift those eyes to heaven that are guilty of so much killing.

MRS. SULLEN:

If heaven, sir, has given to my eyes, with the power of killing, the virtue of making a cure, I hope the one may atone for the other.

COUNT:

O largely, madam. Would your ladyship be as ready to apply the remedy as to give the wound? Consider, madam, I am doubly a prisoner: first to the arms of your general, then to your more conquering eyes. My first chains are easy—there a ransom may redeem me—but from your fetters I never shall get free.

MRS. SULLEN:

Alas, sir, why should you complain to me of your captivity, who am in chains myself? You know, sir, that I am bound, nay, must be tied up in that particular that might give you ease: I am like you a prisoner of war—of war indeed. I have given my parole of honor. Would you break yours to gain your liberty?

COUNT:

Most certainly I would were I a prisoner among the Turks. Dis is your case; you're a slave, madam, slave to the worst of Turks, a husband.

MRS. SULLEN:

There lies my foible, I confess. No fortifications, no courage, conduct, nor vigilancy can pretend to defend a place where the cruelty of the governor forces the garrison to mutiny.

COUNT:

And where de besieger is resolved to die before de place. Here will I fix; (*kneels*) with tears, vows, and prayers assault your heart, and never rise till you surrender; or if I must storm— love and St. Michael. And so I begin the attack.

MRS. SULLEN:

Stand off!—(*Aside.*) Sure he hears me not, and I could almost wish he—did not. The fellow makes love very prettily.—But, sir, why should you put such a value upon my person when you see it despised by one that knows it so much better?

COUNT:

He knows it not though he possesses it. If he but knew the value of the jewel he is master of he would always wear it next his heart and sleep with it in his arms.

MRS. SULLEN:

But since he throws me unregarded from him—

COUNT:

And one that knows your value well comes by and takes you up, is it not justice? *Goes to lay hold on her.*

Enter Sullen *with his sword drawn.*

SULLEN:

Hold, villain, hold.

MRS. SULLEN (*presenting a pistol*):

Do you hold.

SULLEN:

What, murther your husband to defend your bully?

MRS. SULLEN:

Bully! For shame, Mr. Sullen. Bullies wear long swords. The gentleman has none; he's a prisoner, you know. I was aware of your outrage and prepared this to receive your violence, and, if occasion were, to preserve myself against the force of this other gentleman.

COUNT:

O, madam, your eyes be bettre firearms than your pistol; they nevre miss.

SULLEN:

What, court my wife to my face!

MRS. SULLEN:

Pray, Mr. Sullen, put up; suspend your fury for a minute.

SULLEN:

To give you time to invent an excuse.

MRS. SULLEN:

I need none.

SULLEN:

No, for I heard every syllable of your discourse.

COUNT:

Ay, and begar, I tink de dialogue was vera pretty.

MRS. SULLEN:

Then I suppose, sir, you heard something of your own barbarity.

SULLEN:

Barbarity! Oons, what does the woman call barbarity? Do I ever meddle with you?

MRS. SULLEN:

No.

SULLEN:

As for you, sir, I shall take another time.

COUNT:

Ah, begar, and so must I.

SULLEN:

Look'ee, madam, don't think that my anger proceeds from any concern I have for your honor, but for my own, and if you can contrive any way of being a whore without making me a cuckold, do it and welcome.

MRS. SULLEN:

Sir, I thank you kindly. You would allow me the sin but rob me of the pleasure. No, no, I'm resolved never to venture upon the crime without the satisfaction of seeing you punished for't.

SULLEN:

Then will you grant me this, my dear? Let anybody else do you the favor but that Frenchman, for I mortally hate his whole generation. *Exit.*

COUNT:

Ah, sir, that be ungrateful, for begar, I love some of yours, madam. *Approaching her.*

MRS. SULLEN:

No, sir.

COUNT:

No, sir! Garzoon, madam, I am not your husband.

MRS. SULLEN:

'Tis time to undeceive you, sir. I believed your addresses to me were no more than an amusement, and I hope you will think

the same of my complaisance. And to convince you that you
ought, you must know that I brought you hither only to make
you instrumental in setting me right with my husband, for he
was planted to listen by my appointment.

COUNT:

By your appointment?

MRS. SULLEN:

Certainly.

COUNT:

And so, madam, while I was telling twenty stories to part you
from your husband, begar, I was bringing you together all the
while.

MRS. SULLEN:

I ask your pardon, sir, but I hope this will give you a taste of
the virtue of the English ladies.

COUNT:

Begar, madam, your virtue be vera great, but garzoon, your
honeste be vera little.

Enter Dorinda.

MRS. SULLEN:

Nay, now you're angry, sir.

COUNT:

Angry! Fair Dorinda.

Sings Dorinda *the opera tune and addresses to* Dorinda.

Madam, when your ladyship want a fool, send for me. "Fair
Dorinda, Revenge, etc."   *Exit.*

MRS. SULLEN:

There goes the true humor of his nation: resentment with
good manners and the height of anger in a song. Well sister,
you must be judge, for you have heard the trial.

DORINDA:

And I bring in my brother guilty.

MRS. SULLEN:

But I must bear the punishment. 'Tis hard, sister.

DORINDA:

I own it, but you must have patience.

MRS. SULLEN:

Patience, the cant of custom! Providence sends no evil without
a remedy. Should I lie groaning under a yoke I can shake off I

were accessary to my ruin, and my patience were no better than self-murder.

DORINDA:

But how can you shake off the yoke? Your divisions don't come within the reach of the law for a divorce.

MRS. SULLEN:

Law! What law can search into the remote abyss of nature? What evidence can prove the unaccountable disaffections of wedlock? Can a jury sum up the endless aversions that are rooted in our souls, or can a bench give judgment upon antipathies?

DORINDA:

They never pretend it, sister. They never meddle but in case of uncleanness.

MRS. SULLEN:

Uncleanness! O, sister, casual violation is a transient injury and may possibly be repaired, but can radical hatreds be ever reconciled? No, no, sister, nature is the first lawgiver, and when she has set tempers opposite, not all the golden links of wedlock nor iron manacles of law can keep 'um fast.

Wedlock we own ordained by heaven's decree,
But such as heaven ordained it first to be:
Concurring tempers in the man and wife
As mutual helps to draw the load of life.
View all the works of Providence above;
The stars with harmony and concord move.
View all the works of Providence below;
The fire, the water, earth, and air we know
All in one plant agree to make it grow.
Must man, the chiefest work of art divine,
Be doomed in endless discord to repine?
No, we should injure heaven by that surmise;
Omnipotence is just, were man but wise.

Act IV, Scene i

Scene continues.
Enter Mrs. Sullen.

MRS. SULLEN:

Were I born an humble Turk, where women have no soul nor property, there I must sit contented. But in England, a country whose women are its glory, must women be abused? Where women rule, must women be enslaved, nay, cheated into slavery, mocked by a promise of comfortable society into a wilderness of solitude? I dare not keep the thought about me. O, here comes something to divert me.

Enter a Countrywoman.

WOMAN:

I come, an't please your ladyship. You're my Lady Bountiful, an't ye?

MRS. SULLEN:

Well, good woman, go on.

WOMAN:

I come seventeen long mail to have a cure for my husband's sore leg.

MRS. SULLEN:

Your husband! What, woman, cure your husband?

WOMAN:

Ay, poor man, for his sore leg won't let him stir from home.

MRS. SULLEN:

There, I confess, you have given me a reason. Well, good woman, I'll tell you what you must do. You must lay your husband's leg upon a table, and with a chopping knife you must lay it open as broad as you can. Then you must take out the bone and beat the flesh soundly with a rolling pin. Then take salt, pepper, cloves, mace and ginger, some sweet herbs, and season it very well. Then roll it up like brawn and put it into the oven for two hours.

WOMAN:

Heavens reward your ladyship. I have two little babies too that are piteous bad with the graips, an't please ye.

MRS. SULLEN:

Put a little pepper and salt in their bellies, good woman.

Enter Lady Bountiful.

I beg your ladyship's pardon for taking your business out of your hands. I have been a-tampering here a little with one of your patients.

LADY BOUNTIFUL:

Come, good woman, don't mind this mad creature. I am the person that you want, I suppose. What would you have, woman?

MRS. SULLEN:

She wants something for her husband's sore leg.

LADY BOUNTIFUL:

What's the matter with his leg, Goody?

WOMAN:

It come first, as one might say, with a sort of dizziness in his foot, then he had a kind of a laziness in his joints, and then his leg broke out, and then it swelled, and then it closed again, and then it broke out again, and then it festered, and then it grew better, and then it grew worse again.

MRS. SULLEN:

Ha, ha, ha.

LADY BOUNTIFUL:

How can you be merry with the misfortunes of other people?

MRS. SULLEN:

Because my own make me sad, madam.

LADY BOUNTIFUL:

The worst reason in the world, daughter. Your own misfortunes should teach you to pity others.

MRS. SULLEN:

But the woman's misfortunes and mine are nothing alike. Her husband is sick, and mine, alas, is in health.

LADY BOUNTIFUL:

What, would you wish your husband sick?

MRS. SULLEN:

Not of a sore leg, of all things.

LADY BOUNTIFUL:

Well, good woman, go to the pantry; get your bellyful of victuals; then I'll give you a receipt of diet drink for your husband. But d'ye hear, Goody, you must not let your husband move too much.

WOMAN:

No, no, madam, the poor man's inclinable enough to lie still.

Exit.

LADY BOUNTIFUL:

Well, Daughter Sullen, though you laugh, I have done miracles about the country here with my receipts.

MRS. SULLEN:

Miracles indeed if they have cured anybody, but I believe, madam, the patient's faith goes farther toward the miracle than your prescription.

LADY BOUNTIFUL:

Fancy helps in some cases, but there's your husband, who has as little fancy as anybody. I brought him from death's door.

MRS. SULLEN:

    I suppose, madam, you made him drink plentifully of ass's milk.

Enter Dorinda, *(who) runs to* Mrs. Sullen.

DORINDA:

    News, dear sister, news, news.

Enter Archer *running*.

ARCHER:

    Where, where is my Lady Bountiful? Pray, which is the old lady of you three?

LADY BOUNTIFUL:

    I am.

ARCHER:

    O, madam, the fame of your ladyship's charity, goodness, benevolence, skill, and ability have drawn me hither to implore your ladyship's help in behalf of my unfortunate master, who is this moment breathing his last.

LADY BOUNTIFUL:

    Your master! Where is he?

ARCHER:

    At your gate, madam. Drawn by the appearance of your handsome house to view it nearer and walking up the avenue within five paces of the courtyard, he was taken ill of a sudden with a sort of I know not what, but down he fell, and there he lies.

LADY BOUNTIFUL:

    Here, Scrub, Gipsy, all run. Get my easy chair downstairs, put the gentleman in it, and bring him in quickly, quickly.

ARCHER:

    Heaven will reward your ladyship for this charitable act.

LADY BOUNTIFUL:

    Is your master used to these fits?

ARCHER:

    O, yes, madam, frequently. I have known him have five or six of a night.

LADY BOUNTIFUL:

    What's his name?

ARCHER:

    Lord, madam, he's a-dying. A minute's care or neglect may save or destroy his life.

LADY BOUNTIFUL:

Ah, poor gentleman! Come, friend, show me the way. I'll see him brought in myself.

Exit with Archer.

DORINDA:

O, sister, my heart flutters about strangely. I can hardly forbear running to his assistance.

MRS. SULLEN:

And I'll lay my life he deserves your assistance more then he wants it. Did not I tell you that my lord would find a way to come at you? Love's his distemper, and you must be the physician. Put on all your charms, summon all your fire into your eyes, plant the whole artillery of your looks against his breast, and down with him.

DORINDA:

O, sister, I'm but a young gunner. I shall be afraid to shoot for fear the piece should recoil and hurt myself.

MRS. SULLEN:

Never fear; you shall see me shoot before you, if you will.

DORINDA:

No, no, dear sister, you have missed your mark so unfortunately that I shan't care for being instructed by you.

Enter Aimwell *in a chair, carried by* Archer *and* Scrub; Lady Bountiful, Gipsy. Aimwell *counterfeiting a swoon.*

LADY BOUNTIFUL:

Here, here, let's see the hartshorn drops.—Gipsy, a glass of fair water. His fit's very strong.—Bless me, how his hands are clinched.

ARCHER:

For shame, ladies, what d'ye do? Why don't you help us?—(*To* Dorinda.) Pray, madam, take his hand and open it if you can whilst I hold his head.   Dorinda *takes his hand.*

DORINDA:

Poor gentleman. Oh! He has got my hand within his and squeezes it unmercifully.

LADY BOUNTIFUL:

'Tis the violence of his convulsion, child.

ARCHER:

O, madam, he's perfectly possessed in these cases; he'll bite if you don't have a care.

DORINDA:

Oh, my hand, my hand!

LADY BOUNTIFUL:

What's the matter with the foolish girl? I have got this hand open, you see, with a great deal of ease.

ARCHER:

Ay, but, madam, your daughter's hand is somewhat warmer than your ladyship's, and the heat of it draws the force of the spirits that way.

MRS. SULLEN:

I find, friend, you're very learned in these sorts of fits.

ARCHER:

'Tis no wonder, madam, for I'm often troubled with them myself. I find myself extremely ill at this minute.

Looking hard at Mrs. Sullen.

MRS. SULLEN (*aside*):

I fancy I could find a way to cure you.

LADY BOUNTIFUL:

His fit holds him very long.

ARCHER:

Longer than usual, madam.—Pray, young lady, open his breast and give him air.

LADY BOUNTIFUL:

Where did his illness take him first, pray?

ARCHER:

Today at church, madam.

LADY BOUNTIFUL:

In what manner was he taken?

ARCHER:

Very strangely, my lady. He was of a sudden touched with something in his eyes, which at the first he only felt but could not tell whether 'twas pain or pleasure.

LADY BOUNTIFUL:

Wind, nothing but wind.

ARCHER:

By soft degrees it grew and mounted to his brain; there his fancy caught it, there formed it so beautiful and dressed it up in such gay pleasing colors that his transported appetite seized the fair idea and straight conveyed it to his heart. That hospitable seat of life sent all its sanguine spirits forth to meet and opened all its sluicy gates to take the stranger in.

LADY BOUNTIFUL:

Your master should never go without a bottle to smell to.— Oh, he recovers,—The lavender water—some feathers to burn under his nose—Hungary water to rub his temples.—O, he comes to himself.—Hem a little, sir, hem.—Gipsy, bring the cordial water.

> Aimwell *seems to awake in amaze.*

DORINDA:

How d'ye, sir?

AIMWELL (*rising*):

Where am I?
> Sure I have passed the gulf of silent death,
> And now I land on the Elysian shore.
> Behold the goddess of those happy plains,
> Fair Proserpine. Let me adore thy bright divinity.
> > *Kneels to* Dorinda *and kisses her hand.*

MRS. SULLEN:

So, so, so, I knew where the fit would end.

AIMWELL:

Eurydice perhaps—
> How could thy Orpheus keep his word
> And not look back upon thee?
> No treasure but thyself could sure have bribed him
> To look one minute off thee.

LADY BOUNTIFUL:

Delirious, poor gentleman.

ARCHER:

Very delirious, madam, very delirious.

AIMWELL:

Martin's voice, I think.

ARCHER:

Yes, my lord. How does your lordship?

LADY BOUNTIFUL:

Lord! Did you mind that, girls?

AIMWELL:

Where am I?

ARCHER:

In very good hands, sir. You were taken just now with one of your old fits under the trees just by this good lady's house. Her ladyship had you taken in and has miraculously brought you to yourself, as you see.

AIMWELL:

I am so confounded with shame, madam, that I can now only beg pardon and refer my acknowledgments for your ladyship's care till an opportunity offers of making some amends. I dare be no longer troublesome.—Martin, give two guineas to the servants.

> *Going.*

DORINDA:

Sir, you may catch cold by going so soon into the air. You don't look, sir, as if you were perfectly recovered.

Here Archer *talks to* Lady Bountiful *in dumb show.*

AIMWELL:

That I shall never be, madam. My present illness is so rooted that I must expect to carry it to my grave.

MRS. SULLEN:

Don't despair, sir; I have known several in your distemper shake it off with a fortnight's physic.

LADY BOUNTIFUL:

Come, sir, your servant has been telling me that you're apt to relapse if you go into the air. Your good manners shan't get the better of ours. You shall sit down again, sir; come, sir, we don't mind ceremonies in the country. Here, sir, my service t'ye. You shall taste my water; 'tis a cordial, I can assure you, and of my own making. Drink if off, sir. (Aimwell *drinks.*) And how d'ye find yourself now, sir?

AIMWELL:

Somewhat better, though very faint still.

LADY BOUNTIFUL:

Ay, ay, people are always faint after these fits.—Come, girls, you shall show the gentleman the house.—'Tis but an old family building, sir, but you had better walk about and cool by degrees than venture immediately into the air. You'll find some tolerable pictures.—Dorinda, show the gentleman the way. I must go to the poor woman below. *Exit.*

DORINDA:

This way, sir.

AIMWELL:

Ladies, shall I beg leave for my servant to wait on you, for he understands pictures very well?

MRS. SULLEN:

Sir, we understand originals as well as he does pictures, so he may come along.

Exeunt Dorinda, Mrs. Sullen, Aimwell, Archer, (Gipsy). Aimwell *leads* Dorinda.

Enter Foigard *and* Scrub, *meeting.*

FOIGARD:

Save you, Master Scrub.

SCRUB:

Sir, I won't be saved your way. I hate a priest, I abhor the French, and I defy the devil. Sir, I'm a bold Briton and will spill the last drop of my blood to keep out popery and slavery.

FOIGARD:

Master Scrub, you would put me down in politics, and so I would be speaking with Mrs. Shipsy.

SCRUB:

Good Mr. Priest, you can't speak with her. She's sick, sir. She's gone abroad, sir. She's—dead two months ago, sir.

Enter Gipsy.

GIPSY:

How now, impudence; how dare you talk so saucily to the doctor? Pray, sir, don't take it ill, for the common people of England are not so civil to strangers as—

SCRUB:

You lie, you lie. 'Tis the common people that are civillest to strangers.

GIPSY:

Sirrah, I have a good mind to—get you out, I say.

SCRUB:

I won't.

GIPSY:

You won't, sauce-box?—Pray, doctor, what is the captain's name that came to your inn last night?

SCRUB:

The captain! Ah, the devil, there she hampers me again. The captain has me on one side, and the priest on t'other. So between the gown and the sword I have a fine time on't. But, *cedunt arma togae.*   *Going.*

GIPSY:

What, sirrah, won't you march?

SCRUB:

No, my dear, I won't march, but I'll walk.—(*Aside.*) And I'll make bold to listen a little too.

                              Goes behind the side-scene, and listens.

GIPSY:

Indeed, doctor, the count has been barbarously treated, that's the truth on't.

FOIGARD:

Ah, Mrs. Gipsy, upon my shoul, now, gra, his complainings would mollify the marrow in your bones and move the bowels of your commiseration. He veeps, and he dances, and he fistles, and he swears, and he laughs, and he stamps, and he sings. In conclusion, joy, he's afflicted *à la Francaise,* and a stranger would not know whider to cry or to laugh with him.

GIPSY:

What would you have me do, doctor?

FOIGARD:

Noting, joy, but only hide the count in Mrs. Sullen's closhet when it is dark.

GIPSY:

Nothing! Is that nothing? It would be both a sin and a shame, doctor.

FOIGARD:

Here is twenty *louis d'ors*, joy, for your shame, and I will give you an absolution for the shin.

GIPSY:

But won't that money look like a bribe?

FOIGARD:

Dat is according as you shall tauk it. If you receive the money beforehand 'twill be *logicè* a bribe, but if you stay till afterwards 'twill be only a gratification.

GIPSY:

Well, doctor, I'll take it *logicè*. But what must I do with my conscience, sir?

FOIGARD:

Leave dat wid me, joy. I am your priest, gra, and your conscience is under my hands.

GIPSY:

But should I put the count into the closet—

FOIGARD:

Vel, is dere any shin for a man's being in a closhet? One may go to prayers in a closhet.

GIPSY:

But if the lady should come into her chamber and go to bed?

FOIGARD:

Vel, and is dere any shin in going to bed, joy?

GIPSY:

Ay, but if the parties should meet, doctor?

FOIGARD:

Vel den, the parties must be responsable. Do you be after putting the count in the closhet, and leave the shins wid themselves. I will come with the count to instruct you in your chamber.

GIPSY:

Well, doctor, your religion is so pure. Methinks I'm so easy after an absolution and can sin afresh with so much security that I'm resolved to die a martyr to't. Here's the key of the garden-door. Come in the back way when 'tis late. I'll be ready to receive you, but don't so much as whisper. Only take hold of my hand; I'll lead you, and do you lead the count and follow me. *Exeunt.*

Enter Scrub.

SCRUB:

What witchcraft now have these two imps of the devil been a-hatching here? There's twenty *louis d'ors*; I heard that and saw the purse. But I must give room to my betters. (*Exit.*)

Enter Aimwell *leading* Dorinda, *and making love in dumb show;* Mrs. Sullen *and* Archer.

MRS. SULLEN (*to* Archer):

Pray, sir, how d'ye like that piece?

ARCHER:

O, 'tis Leda. You find, madam, how Jupiter comes disguised to make love.

MRS. SULLEN:

But what think you there of Alexander's battles?

ARCHER:

We want only a Le Brun, madam, to draw greater battles and a greater general of our own. The Danube, madam, would make a greater figure in a picture than the Granicus, and we have our Ramillies to match their Arbela.

MRS. SULLEN:

Pray, sir, what head is that in the corner there?

ARCHER:

O, madam, 'tis poor Ovid in his exile.

MRS. SULLEN:

What was he banished for?

ARCHER:

His ambitious love, madam. (*Bowing.*) His misfortune touches me.

MRS. SULLEN:

Was he successful in his amours?

ARCHER:

There he has left us in the dark. He was too much a gentleman to tell.

MRS. SULLEN:

If he were secret I pity him.

ARCHER:

And if he were successful I envy him.

MRS. SULLEN:

How d'ye like that Venus over the chimney?

ARCHER:

Venus! I protest, madam, I took it for your picture, but now I look again 'tis not handsome enough.

MRS. SULLEN:

Oh, what a charm is flattery! If you would see my picture, there it is over that cabinet. How d'ye like it?

ARCHER:

I must admire anything, madam, that has the least resemblance of you. But, methinks, madam—

He looks at the picture and Mrs. Sullen *three or four times, by turns.*

Pray, madam, who drew it?

MRS. SULLEN:

A famous hand, sir.   *Here* Aimwell *and* Dorinda *go off.*

ARCHER:

A famous hand, madam! Your eyes, indeed, are featured there, but where's the sparkling moisture, shining fluid, in which they swim? The picture indeed has your dimples, but where's the swarm of killing Cupids that should ambush there? The lips too are figured out, but where's the carnation dew, the pouting ripeness that tempts the taste in the original?

MRS. SULLEN (*aside*):

Had it been my lot to have matched with such a man!

ARCHER:

Your breasts too. Presumptuous man! What, paint heaven! Apropos, madam, in the very next picture is Salmoneus, that was struck dead with lightning for offering to imitate Jove's thunder. I hope you served the painter so, madam?

MRS. SULLEN:

Had my eyes the power of thunder they should employ their lightning better.

ARCHER:

There's the finest bed in that room, madam. I suppose 'tis your ladyship's bedchamber.

MRS. SULLEN:

And what then, sir?

ARCHER:

I think that the quilt is the richest that ever I saw. I can't at this distance, madam, distinguish the figures of the embroidery. Will you give me leave, madam—

MRS. SULLEN (*aside*):

The devil take his impudence. Sure if I gave him an opportunity he durst not offer it. I have a great mind to try.   *Going.*

Returns.

S'death, what am I doing? And alone too!—Sister, sister?

Runs out.

ARCHER:

I'll follow her close,
>   For where a Frenchman durst attempt to storm,
>   A Briton sure may well the work perform.   *Going.*

Enter Scrub.

SCRUB:

Martin, Brother Martin.

ARCHER:

O, Brother Scrub, I beg your pardon, I was not a-going. Here's a guinea my master ordered you.

SCRUB:

A guinea, hi, hi, hi, a guinea! Eh, by this light it is a guinea, but I suppose you expect one and twenty shillings in change.

ARCHER:

Not at all; I have another for Gipsy.

SCRUB:

A guinea for her! Faggot and fire for the witch! Sir, give me that guinea, and I'll discover a plot.

ARCHER:

A plot!

SCRUB:

Ay, sir, a plot, and a horrid plot. First, it must be a plot because there's a woman in't. Secondly, it must be a plot because there's a priest in't. Thirdly, it must be a plot because there's French gold in't. And fourthly, it must be a plot because I don't know what to make on't.

ARCHER:

Nor anybody else, I'm afraid, Brother Scrub.

SCRUB:

Truly I'm afraid so too, for where there's a priest and a woman there's always a mystery and a riddle. This I know, that here has been the doctor with a temptation in one hand and an absolution in the other, and Gipsy has sold herself to the devil. I saw the price paid down; my eyes shall take their oath on't.

ARCHER:

And is all this bustle about Gipsy?

SCRUB:

That's not all. I could hear but a word here and there, but I remember they mentioned a count, a closet, a back door, and a key.

ARCHER:

The count! Did you hear nothing of Mrs. Sullen?

SCRUB:

I did hear some word that sounded that way, but whether it was Sullen or Dorinda I could not distinguish.

ARCHER:

You have told this matter to nobody, brother?

SCRUB:

Told! No, sir, I thank you for that. I'm resolved never to speak one word pro nor con till we have a peace.

ARCHER:

You're i'th'right, Brother Scrub. Here's a treaty a-foot between the count and the lady. The priest and the chambermaid are the plenipotentiaries. It shall go hard but I find a way to be included in the treaty. Where's the doctor now?

SCRUB:

He and Gipsy are this moment devouring my lady's marmalade in the closet.

AIMWELL (*from without*):

Martin, Martin.

ARCHER:

I come, sir, I come.

SCRUB:

But you forget the other guinea, Brother Martin.

ARCHER:

Here, I give it with all my heart.

SCRUB:

And I take it with all my soul.   (*Exit* Archer.)

Icod, I'll spoil your plotting, Mrs. Gipsy, and if you should set the captain upon me these two guineas will buy me off. *Exit.*

Enter Mrs. Sullen *and* Dorinda *meeting.*

MRS. SULLEN:
> Well, sister.

DORINDA:
> And well, sister.

MRS. SULLEN:
> What's become of my lord?

DORINDA:
> What's become of his servant?

MRS. SULLEN:
> Servant! He's a prettier fellow and a finer gentleman by fifty degrees than his master.

DORINDA:
> O' my conscience, I fancy you could beg that fellow at the gallows-foot.

MRS. SULLEN:
> O' my conscience, I could, provided I could put a friend of yours in his room.

DORINDA:
> You desired me, sister, to leave you when you transgressed the bounds of honor.

MRS. SULLEN:
> Thou dear censorious country girl. What dost mean? You can't think of the man without the bedfellow, I find.

DORINDA:
> I don't find anything unnatural in that thought; while the mind is conversant with flesh and blood it must conform to the humors of the company.

MRS. SULLEN:
> How a little love and good company improves a woman. Why, child, you begin to live. You never spoke before.

DORINDA:
> Because I was never spoke to. My lord has told me that I have more wit and beauty than any of my sex, and truly I begin to think the man is sincere.

MRS. SULLEN:
> You're in the right, Dorinda. Pride is the life of a woman, and flattery is our daily bread. And she's a fool that won't believe a man there as much as she that believes him in anything else. But I'll lay you a guinea that I had finer things said to me than you had.

DORINDA:
> Done. What did your fellow say to ye?

MRS. SULLEN:
My fellow took the picture of Venus for mine.

DORINDA:
But my lover took me for Venus herself.

MRS. SULLEN:
Common cant! Had my spark called me a Venus directly I
should have believed him a footman in good earnest.

DORINDA:
But my lover was upon his knees to me.

MRS. SULLEN:
And mine was upon his tiptoes to me.

DORINDA:
Mine vowed to die for me.

MRS. SULLEN:
Mine swore to die with me.

DORINDA:
Mine spoke the softest moving things.

MRS. SULLEN:
Mine had his moving things too.

DORINDA:
Mine kissed my hand ten thousand times.

MRS. SULLEN:
Mine has all that pleasure to come.

DORINDA:
Mine offered marriage.

MRS. SULLEN:
O Lard! D'ye call that a moving thing?

DORINDA:
The sharpest arrow in his quiver, my dear sister. Why, my ten
thousand pounds may lie brooding here this seven years and
hatch nothing at last but some ill-natured clown like yours.
Whereas, if I marry my Lord Aimwell there will be title, place,
and precedence, the park, the play, and the drawing-room, splendor, equipage, noise, and flambeaux.—"Hey, my Lady Aimwell's
servants there—Lights, lights to the stairs—My Lady Aimwell's
coach put forward—Stand by; make room for her Ladyship."—
Are not these things moving? What, melancholy of a sudden?

MRS. SULLEN:
Happy, happy sister! Your angel has been watchful for your
happiness whilst mine has slept regardless of his charge. Long
smiling years of circling joys for you but not one hour for me!
Weeps.

DORINDA:
Come, my dear, we'll talk of something else.

MRS. SULLEN:

O, Dorinda, I own myself a woman, full of my sex, a gentle, generous soul, easy and yielding to soft desires, a spacious heart where love and all his train might lodge. And must the fair apartment of my breast be made a stable for a brute to lie in?

DORINDA:

Meaning your husband, I suppose.

MRS. SULLEN:

Husband! No. Even husband is too soft a name for him. But, come, I expect my brother here tonight or tomorrow. He was abroad when my father married me. Perhaps he'll find a way to make me easy.

DORINDA:

Will you promise not to make yourself easy in the meantime with my lord's friend?

MRS. SULLEN:

You mistake me, sister. It happens with us, as among the men, the greatest talkers are the greatest cowards; and there's a reason for it: those spirits evaporate in prattle which might do more mischief if they took another course. Though to confess the truth, I do love that fellow. And if I met him dressed as he should be, and I undressed as I should be—look ye, sister, I have no supernatural gifts. I can't swear I could resist the temptation, though I can safely promise to avoid it; and that's as much as the best of us can do.

Exeunt Mrs. Sullen *and* Dorinda.

Act IV, Scene ii

Scene changes to the inn.
Enter Aimwell *and* Archer *laughing.*

ARCHER:

And the awkward kindness of the good motherly old gentlewoman—

AIMWELL:

And the coming easiness of the young one. S'death, 'tis pity to deceive her.

ARCHER:

Nay, if you adhere to those principles stop where you are.

AIMWELL:

I can't stop, for I love her to distraction.

ARCHER:

    S'death, if you love her a hair's breadth beyond discretion you must go no farther.

AIMWELL:

    Well, well, anything to deliver us from sauntering away our idle evenings at White's, Tom's, or Will's, and be stinted to bear looking at our old acquaintance, the cards, because our impotent pockets can't afford us a guinea for the mercenary drabs.

ARCHER:

    Or be obliged to some purse-proud coxcomb for a scandalous bottle, where we must not pretend to our share of the discourse because we can't pay our club o'th'reckoning. Damn it, I had rather sponge upon Morris and sup upon a dish of bohea scored behind the door.

AIMWELL:

    And there expose our want of sense by talking criticisms as we should our want of money by railing at the government.

ARCHER:

    Or be obliged to sneak into the side-box and between both houses steal two acts of a play, and because we han't money to see the other three we come away discontented and damn the whole five.

AIMWELL:

    And ten thousand such rascally tricks, had we outlived our fortunes among our acquaintance. But now—

ARCHER:

    Ay, now is the time to prevent all this. Strike while the iron is hot. This priest is the luckiest part of our adventure. He shall marry you and pimp for me.

AIMWELL:

    But I should not like a woman that can be so fond of a Frenchman.

ARCHER:

    Alas, sir, necessity has no law. The lady may be in distress. Perhaps she has a confounded husband, and her revenge may carry her farther than her love. Igad, I have so good an opinion of her, and of myself, that I begin to fancy strange things; and we must say this for the honor of our women, and indeed of ourselves, that they do stick to their men as they do to their Magna Charta. If the plot lies as I suspect I must put on the gentleman. But here comes the doctor. I shall be ready. *Exit.*

Enter Foigard.

FOIGARD:

Sauve you, noble friend.

AIMWELL:

O, sir, your servant. Pray, doctor, may I crave your name?

FOIGARD:

Fat naam is upon me? My naam is Foigard, joy.

AIMWELL:

Foigard, a very good name for a clergyman. Pray, Doctor Foigard, were you ever in Ireland?

FOIGARD:

Ireland! No, joy. Fat sort of plaace is dat saam Ireland? Dey say de people are catcht dere when dey are young.

AIMWELL:

And some of 'em when they're old, as for example—(*Takes* Foigard *by the shoulder.*) Sir, I arrest you as a traitor against the government. You're a subject of England and this morning showed me a commission by which you served as chaplain in the French army. This is death by our law, and your reverence must hang for't.

FOIGARD:

Upon my shoul, noble friend, dis is strange news you tell me— Fader Foigard a subject of England, de son of a burgomaster of Brussels, a subject of England! Ubooboo—

AIMWELL:

The son of a bogtrotter in Ireland. Sir, your tongue will condemn you before any bench in the kingdom.

FOIGARD:

And is my tongue all your evidensh, joy?

AIMWELL:

That's enough.

FOIGARD:

No, no, joy, for I vill never spake English no more.

AIMWELL:

Sir, I have other evidence.—Here, Martin, you know this fellow.

Enter Archer.

ARCHER (*in a brogue*):

Saave you, my dear cussen, how does your health?

FOIGARD (*aside*):

Ah, upon my shoul, dere is my countryman, and his brogue will hang mine.—*Mynheer, Ick wet neat watt hey zacht; Ick universton ewe neat, sacramant.*

AIMWELL:

Altering your language won't do, sir. This fellow knows your person and will swear to your face.

FOIGARD:

Faace, fey, is dere a brogue upon my faash, too?

ARCHER:

Upon my soulvation, dere ish, joy. But Cussen Mackshane, vil you not put a remembrance upon me?

FOIGARD (*aside*):

Mackshane! By St. Paatrick, dat is naame, shure enough.

AIMWELL:

I fancy, Archer, you have it.

FOIGARD:

The devil hang you, joy. By fat acquaintance are you my cussen?

ARCHER:

O, de devil hang yourshelf, joy. You know we were little boys togeder upon de school, and your foster moder's son was married upon my nurse's chister, joy, and so we are Irish cussens.

FOIGARD:

De devil taak the relation! Vel, joy, and fat school was it?

ARCHER:

I tinks is vas—aay—'twas Tipperary.

FOIGARD:

No, no, joy, it vas Kilkenny.

AIMWELL:

That's enough for us—self-confession. Come, sir, we must deliver you into the hands of the next magistrate.

ARCHER:

He sends you to jail, you're tried next assizes, and away you go swing into purgatory.

FOIGARD:

And is it so wid you, cussen?

ARCHER:

It vil be sho wid you, cussen, if you don't immediately confess the secret between you and Mrs. Gipsy. Look'ee, sir, the gallows or the secret; take your choice.

FOIGARD:

The gallows! Upon my shoul, I hate that saam gallow, for it is a diseash dat is fatal to our family.—Vel den, dere is nothing, shentlemens, but Mrs. Shullen would spaak wid the count in her chamber at midnight, and dere is no haarm, joy, for I am to conduct the count to the plash myshelf.

ARCHER:

As I guessed. Have you communicated the matter to the count?

FOIGARD:

I have not sheen him since.

ARCHER:

Right again. Why then, doctor, you shall conduct me to the lady instead of the count.

FOIGARD:

Fat, my cussen to the lady! Upon my shoul, gra, dat is too much upon the brogue.

ARCHER:

Come, come, doctor, consider we have got a rope about your neck, and if you offer to squeak we'll stop your windpipe most certainly. We shall have another job for you in a day or two, I hope.

AIMWELL:

Here's company coming this way. Let's into my chamber and there concert our affair farther.

ARCHER:

Come, my dear cussen, come along.   *Exeunt.*

Enter Boniface, Hounslow *and* Bagshot *at one door,* Gibbet *at the opposite.*

GIBBET:

Well, gentlemen, 'tis a fine night for our enterprise.

HOUNSLOW:

Dark as hell.

BAGSHOT:

And blows like the devil. Our landlord here has showed us the window where we must break in and tells us the plate stands in the wainscot cupboard in the parlor.

BONIFACE:

Ay, ay, Mr. Bagshot, as the saying is, knives and forks and cups and cans and tumblers and tankards. There's one tankard, as the saying is, that's near upon as big as me. It was a present to the squire from his godmother and smells of nutmeg and toast like an East India ship.

HOUNSLOW:

Then you say we must divide at the stairhead?

BONIFACE:

Yes, Mr. Hounslow, as the saying is. At one end of that gallery lies my Lady Bountiful and her daughter and at the other, Mrs. Sullen. As for the squire—

GIBBET:

He's safe enough. I have fairly entered him, and he's more than half seas over already. But such a parcel of scoundrels are got about him now that, Igad, I was ashamed to be seen in their company.

BONIFACE:

'Tis now twelve, as the saying is. Gentlemen, you must set out at one.

GIBBET:

Hounslow, do you and Bagshot see our arms fixed, and I'll come to you presently.

HOUNSLOW *and* BAGSHOT:

We will.   *Exeunt.*

GIBBET:

Well, my dear Bonny, you assure me that Scrub is a coward.

BONIFACE:

A chicken, as the saying is. You'll have no creature to deal with but the ladies.

GIBBET:

And I can assure you, friend, there's a great deal of address and good manners in robbing a lady. I am the most a gentleman that way that ever traveled the road. But, my dear Bonny, this prize will be a galleon, a Vigo business. I warrant you we shall bring off three or four thousand pound.

BONIFACE:

In plate, jewels, and money, as the saying is, you may.

GIBBET:

Why then, Tyburn, I defy thee. I'll get up to town, sell off my horse and arms, buy myself some pretty employment in the household, and be as snug and as honest as any courtier of 'um all.

BONIFACE:

And what think you then of my daughter Cherry for a wife?

GIBBET:

Look'ee, my dear Bonny, Cherry "is the goddess I adore," as the song goes, but it is a maxim that man and wife should never have it in their power to hang one another, for if they should the Lord have mercy on 'um both.   *Exeunt.*

Act V, Scene i

Scene continues. Knocking without.
Enter Boniface.

BONIFACE:

Coming, coming.—A coach and six foaming horses at this time o'night! Some great man, as the saying is, for he scorns to travel with other people.

Enter Sir Charles Freeman.

SIR CHARLES:

What, fellow, a public house, and a-bed when other people sleep?

BONIFACE:

Sir, I an't a-bed, as the saying is.

SIR CHARLES:

Is Mr. Sullen's family a-bed, think'ee?

BONIFACE:

All but the squire himself, sir, as the saying is; he's in the house.

SIR CHARLES:

What company has he?

BONIFACE:

Why, sir, there's the constable, Mr. Gage the exiseman, the hunchbacked barber, and two or three other gentlemen.

SIR CHARLES:

I find my sister's letters gave me the true picture of her spouse.

Enter Sullen *drunk*.

BONIFACE:

Sir, here's the squire.

SULLEN:

The puppies left me asleep.—Sir.

SIR CHARLES:

Well, sir.

SULLEN:

Sir, I'm an unfortunate man. I have three thousand pound a year, and I can't get a man to drink a cup of ale with me.

SIR CHARLES:

That's very hard.

SULLEN:

> Ay, sir, and unless you have pity upon me and smoke one pipe with me, I must e'en go home to my wife, and I had rather go to the devil by half.

SIR CHARLES:

> But I presume, sir, you won't see your wife tonight. She'll be gone to bed. You don't use to lie with your wife in that pickle?

SULLEN:

> What, not lie with my wife! Why, sir, do you take me for an atheist or a rake?

SIR CHARLES:

> If you hate her, sir, I think you had better lie from her.

SULLEN:

> I think so too, friend, but I'm a justice of peace and must do nothing against the law.

SIR CHARLES:

> Law! As I take it, Mr. Justice, nobody observes law for law's sake, only for the good of those for whom it was made.

SULLEN:

> But if the law orders me to send you to jail you must lie there, my friend.

SIR CHARLES:

> Not unless I commit a crime to deserve it.

SULLEN:

> A crime! Oons, an't I married?

SIR CHARLES:

> Nay, sir, if you call marriage a crime you must disown it for a law.

SULLEN:

> Eh! I must be acquainted with you, sir. But, sir, I should be very glad to know the truth of this matter.

SIR CHARLES:

> Truth, sir, is a profound sea, and few there be that dare wade deep enough to find out the bottom on't. Besides, sir, I'm afraid the line of your understanding mayn't be long enough.

SULLEN:

> Look'ee, sir, I have nothing to say to your sea of truth, but if a good parcel of land can intitle a man to a little truth I have as much as any he in the country.

BONIFACE:

> I never heard your worship, as the saying is, talk so much before.

SULLEN:

> Because I never met with a man that I liked before.

BONIFACE:

Pray, sir, as the saying is, let me ask you one question: are not man and wife one flesh?

SIR CHARLES:

You and your wife, Mr. Guts, may be one flesh because ye are nothing else, but rational creatures have minds that must be united.

SULLEN:

Minds!

SIR CHARLES:

Ay, minds, sir. Don't you think that the mind takes place of the body?

SULLEN:

In some people.

SIR CHARLES:

Then the interest of the master must be consulted before that of his servant.

SULLEN:

Sir, you shall dine with me tomorrow. Oons, I always thought that we were naturally one.

SIR CHARLES:

Sir, I know that my two hands are naturally one because they love one another, kiss one another, help one another in all the actions of life, but I could not say so much if they were always at cuffs.

SULLEN:

Then 'tis plain that we are two.

SIR CHARLES:

Why don't you part with her, sir?

SULLEN:

Will you take her, sir?

SIR CHARLES:

With all my heart.

SULLEN:

You shall have her tomorrow morning, and a venison pasty into the bargain.

SIR CHARLES:

You'll let me have her fortune too?

SULLEN:

Fortune! Why, sir, I have no quarrel at her fortune. I only hate the woman, sir, and none but the woman shall go.

SIR CHARLES:

But her fortune, sir—

SULLEN:

Can you play at whisk, sir?

SIR CHARLES:

No, truly, sir.

SULLEN:

Nor at all fours?

SIR CHARLES:

Neither!

SULLEN (*aside*):

Oons, where was this man bred?—Burn me, sir, I can't go home; 'tis but two o'clock.

SIR CHARLES:

For half an hour, sir, if you please. But you must consider 'tis late.

SULLEN:

Late! That's the reason I can't go to bed. Come, sir.

Exeunt.

Enter Cherry, *runs across the stage and knocks at Aimwell's chamber door. Enter* Aimwell *in his nightcap and gown.*

AIMWELL:

What's the matter? You tremble, child; you're frighted.

CHERRY:

No wonder, sir. But in short, sir, this very minute a gang of rogues are gone to rob my Lady Bountiful's house.

AIMWELL:

How!

CHERRY:

I dogged 'em to the very door and left 'em breaking in.

AIMWELL:

Have you alarmed anybody else with the news?

CHERRY:

No, no, sir, I wanted to have discovered the whole plot and twenty other things to your man Martin, but I have searched the whole house and can't find him. Where is he?

AIMWELL:

No matter, child. Will you guide me immediately to the house?

CHERRY:

With all my heart, sir. My Lady Bountiful is my godmother, and I love Mrs. Dorinda so well.

AIMWELL:

Dorinda! The name inspires me; the glory and the danger shall be all my own.—Come, my life, let me but get my sword.

Exeunt.

Act V, Scene ii

Scene changes to a bedchamber in Lady Bountiful's house.
Enter Mrs. Sullen, Dorinda *undressed; a table and lights.*

DORINDA:
'Tis very late, sister. No news of your spouse yet?

MRS. SULLEN:
No, I'm condemned to be alone till towards four, and then per-haps I may be executed with his company.

DORINDA:
Well, my dear, I'll leave you to your rest. You'll go directly to bed, I suppose.

MRS. SULLEN:
I don't know what to do, hey-hoe.

DORINDA:
That's a desiring sigh, sister.

MRS. SULLEN:
This is a languishing hour, sister.

DORINDA:
And might prove a critical minute if the pretty fellow were here.

MRS. SULLEN:
Here! What, in my bedchamber at two o'clock o'th' morning, I undressed, the family asleep, my hated husband abroad, and my lovely fellow at my feet? O, gad, sister!

DORINDA:
Thoughts are free, sister, and them I allow you. So, my dear, good night.

MRS. SULLEN:
A good rest to my dear Dorinda.—   (*Exit* Dorinda.)
Thoughts free! Are they so? Why then suppose him here, dressed like a youthful, gay, and burning bridegroom,

Here Archer *steals out of the closet.*

with tongue enchanting, eyes bewitching, knees imploring.

Turns a little o' one side, and sees Archer *in the posture she describes.*

Ah! (*Shrieks, and runs to the other side of the stage.*) Have my thoughts raised a spirit?—What are you, sir, a man or a devil?

ARCHER:
A man, a man, madam.   *Rising.*

MRS. SULLEN:

How shall I be sure of it?

ARCHER:

Madam, I'll give you demonstration this minute.

Takes her hand.

MRS. SULLEN:

What, sir, do you intend to be rude?

ARCHER:

Yes, madam, if you please.

MRS. SULLEN:

In the name of wonder, whence came ye?

ARCHER:

From the skies, madam. I'm a Jupiter in love, and you shall be my Alcmena.

MRS. SULLEN:

How came you in?

ARCHER:

I flew in at the window, madam. Your cousin Cupid lent me his wings, and your sister Venus opened the casement.

MRS. SULLEN:

I'm struck dumb with admiration.

ARCHER:

And I with wonder. *Looks passionately at her.*

MRS. SULLEN:

What will become of me?

ARCHER:

How beautiful she looks. The teeming jolly spring smiles in her blooming face, and when she was conceived her mother smelt to roses, looked on lilies.

Lilies unfold their white, their fragrant charms

When the warm sun thus darts into their arms.

Runs to her.

MRS. SULLEN (*shrieks*):

Ah!

ARCHER:

Oons, madam, what d'ye mean? You'll raise the house.

MRS. SULLEN:

Sir, I'll wake the dead before I bear this. What, approach me with the freedoms of a keeper! I'm glad on't. Your impudence has cured me.

ARCHER (*kneels*):

If this be impudence I leave to your partial self. No panting pilgrim after a tedious, painful voyage e'er bowed before his saint with more devotion.

MRS. SULLEN (*aside*):

Now, now, I'm ruined if he kneels!—(*To him.*) Rise, thou prostrate engineer. Not all thy undermining skill shall reach my heart. Rise, and know I am a woman without my sex. I can love to all the tenderness of wishes, sighs, and tears, but go no farther. Still to convince you that I'm more than woman, I can speak my frailty, confess my weakness even for you, but—

ARCHER:

For me! *Going to lay hold on her.*

MRS. SULLEN:

Hold, sir, build not upon that. For my most mortal hatred follows if you disobey what I command you. Now! Leave me this minute.—(*Aside.*) If he denies, I'm lost.

ARCHER:

Then you'll promise—

MRS. SULLEN:

Anything another time.

ARCHER:

When shall I come?

MRS. SULLEN:

Tomorrow when you will.

ARCHER:

Your lips must seal the promise.

MRS. SULLEN:

Pshaw!

ARCHER:

They must, they must. (*Kisses her.*) Raptures and paradise! And why not now, my angel? The time, the place, silence, and secrecy all conspire; and the now conscious stars have preordained this moment for my happiness. *Takes her in his arms.*

MRS. SULLEN:

You will not, cannot, sure.

ARCHER:

If the sun rides fast and disappoints not mortals of tomorrow's dawn, this night shall crown my joys.

MRS. SULLEN:

My sex's pride assist me.

ARCHER:

My sex's strength help me.

MRS. SULLEN:

You shall kill me first.

ARCHER:

I'll die with you. *Carrying her off.*

MRS. SULLEN:
 Thieves, thieves, murther!

Enter Scrub *in his breeches and one shoe.*

SCRUB:
 Thieves, thieves, murther, popery!
ARCHER:
 Ha, the very timorous stag will kill in rutting time.

Draws and offers to stab Scrub.

SCRUB (*kneeling*):
 O, pray, sir, spare all I have and take my life.
MRS. SULLEN (*holding Archer's hand*):
 What does the fellow mean?
SCRUB:
 O, madam, down upon your knees, your marrowbones. He's
 one of 'um.
ARCHER:
 Of whom?
SCRUB:
 One of the rogues—I beg your pardon, sir—one of the honest
 gentlemen that just now are broke into the house.
ARCHER:
 How!
MRS. SULLEN:
 I hope you did not come to rob me?
ARCHER:
 Indeed I did, madam, but I would have taken nothing but
 what you might ha' spared; but your crying thieves has waked
 this dreaming fool, and so he takes 'em for granted.
SCRUB:
 Granted! 'Tis granted, sir. Take all we have.
MRS. SULLEN:
 The fellow looks as if he were broke out of Bedlam.
SCRUB:
 Oons, madam, they're broke into the house with fire and
 sword; I saw them, heard them. They'll be here this minute.
ARCHER:
 What, thieves?
SCRUB:
 Under favor, sir, I think so.

MRS. SULLEN:

What shall we do, sir?

ARCHER:

Madam, I wish your ladyship a good night.

MRS. SULLEN:

Will you leave me?

ARCHER:

Leave you! Lord, madam, did you not command me to be gone just now upon pain of your immortal hatred?

MRS. SULLEN:

Nay, but pray, sir—   *Takes hold of him.*

ARCHER:

Ha, ha, ha, now comes my turn to be ravished. You see now, madam, you must use men one way or other. But take this by the way, good madam, that none but a fool will give you the benefit of his courage unless you'll take his love along with it.—How are they armed, friend?

SCRUB:

With sword and pistol, sir.

ARCHER:

Hush, I see a dark lanthorn coming through the gallery. Madam, be assured I will protect you or lose my life.

MRS. SULLEN:

Your life! No, sir, they can rob me of nothing that I value half so much. Therefore now, sir, let me intreat you to be gone.

ARCHER:

No, madam, I'll consult my own safety for the sake of yours. I'll work by stratagem. Have you courage enough to stand the appearance of 'em?

MRS. SULLEN:

Yes, yes. Since I have 'scaped your hands I can face anything.

ARCHER:

Come hither, Brother Scrub, don't you know me?

SCRUB:

Eh, my dear brother, let me kiss thee.   *Kisses* Archer.

ARCHER:

This way—here—

Archer *and* Scrub *hide behind the bed. Enter* Gibbet *with a dark lanthorn in one hand and a pistol in t'other.*

GIBBET:

Ay, ay, this is the chamber, and the lady alone.

MRS. SULLEN:

Who are you, sir? What would you have? D'ye come to rob me?

GIBBET:

Rob you! Alack a day, madam, I'm only a younger brother, madam, and so, madam, if you make a noise I'll shoot you through the head. But don't be afraid, madam. (*Laying his lanthorn and pistol upon the table.*) These rings, madam; don't be concerned, madam; I have a profound respect for you, madam; your keys, madam; don't be frighted, madam; I'm the most of a gentleman. (*Searching her pockets.*) This necklace, madam; I never was rude to a lady; I have a veneration—for this necklace—

Here Archer *having come round and seized the pistol, takes* Gibbet *by the collar, trips up his heels, and claps the pistol to his breast.*

ARCHER:

Hold, profane villain, and take the reward of thy sacrilege.

GIBBET:

Oh, pray, sir, don't kill me; I an't prepared.

ARCHER:

How many is there of 'em, Scrub?

SCRUB:

Five and forty, sir.

ARCHER:

Then I must kill the villain to have him out of the way.

GIBBET:

Hold, hold, sir, we are but three, upon my honor.

ARCHER:

Scrub, will you undertake to secure him?

SCRUB:

Not I, sir. Kill him, kill him!

ARCHER:

Run to Gipsy's chamber; there you'll find the doctor. Bring him hither presently.   *Exit* Scrub *running.*

Come, rogue, if you have a short prayer, say it.

GIBBET:

Sir, I have no prayer at all. The government has provided a chaplain to say prayers for us on these occasions.

MRS. SULLEN:

Pray, sir, don't kill him. You fright me as much as him.

ARCHER:

The dog shall die, madam, for being the occasion of my disappointment.—Sirrah, this moment is your last.

GIBBET:

Sir, I'll give you two hundred pound to spare my life.

ARCHER:

Have you no more, rascal?

GIBBET:

Yes, sir, I can command four hundred, but I must reserve two of 'em to save my life at the sessions.

Enter Scrub *and* Foigard.

ARCHER:

Here, doctor, I suppose Scrub and you between you may manage him. Lay hold of him, doctor.

Foigard *lays hold of* Gibbet.

GIBBET:

What, turned over to the priest already?—Look ye, doctor, you come before your time; I an't condemned yet, I thank ye.

FOIGARD:

Come, my dear joy, I vill secure your body and your shoul too. I vill make you a good Catholic and give you an absolution.

GIBBET:

Absolution! Can you procure me a pardon, doctor?

FOIGARD:

No, joy.

GIBBET:

Then you and your absolution may go to the devil.

ARCHER:

Convey him into the cellar; there bind him. Take the pistol, and if he offers to resist shoot him through the head. And come back to us with all the speed you can.

SCRUB:

Ay, ay, come, doctor. Do you hold him fast, and I'll guard him.

(*Exeunt* Foigard *and* Scrub *with* Gibbet.)

MRS. SULLEN:

But how came the doctor?

ARCHER:

In short, madam—(*Shrieking without.*) S'death, the rogues are at work with the other ladies. I'm vexed I parted with the pistol, but I must fly to their assistance.—Will you stay here, madam, or venture yourself with me?

MRS. SULLEN:

O, with you, dear sir, with you.

Takes him by the arm and exeunt.

Act V, Scene iii

Scene changes to another apartment in the same house. Enter Hounslow *dragging in* Lady Bountiful, *and* Bagshot *hauling in* Dorinda; *the rogues with swords drawn.*

HOUNSLOW:
> Come, come, your jewels, mistress.

BAGSHOT:
> Your keys, your keys, old gentlewoman.

Enter Aimwell *and* Cherry.

AIMWELL:
> Turn this way, villains. I durst engage an army in such a cause.
>> *He engages 'em both.*

DORINDA:
> O, madam, had I but a sword to help the brave man!

LADY BOUNTIFUL:
> There's three or four hanging up in the hall, but they won't draw. I'll go fetch one, however.   *Exit.*

Enter Archer *and* Mrs. Sullen.

ARCHER:
> Hold, hold, my lord; every man his bird, pray.

They engage man to man; the rogues are thrown and disarmed.

CHERRY:
> What, the rogues taken! Then they'll impeach my father. I must give him timely notice.   *Runs out.*

ARCHER:
> Shall we kill the rogues?

AIMWELL:
> No, no, we'll bind them.

ARCHER:
> Ay, ay.—(*To* Mrs. Sullen, *who stands by him.*) Here, madam, lend me your garter.

MRS. SULLEN (*aside*):
> The devil's in this fellow. He fights, loves, and banters, all in a breath.—Here's a cord that the rogues brought with 'em, I suppose.

ARCHER:

Right, right, the rogue's destiny, a rope to hang himself.—
Come, my lord. This is but a scandalous sort of an office (*binding the rogues together*) if our adventures should end in this sort of
hangman-work, but I hope there is something in prospect that—

Enter Scrub.

Well, Scrub, have you secured your tartar?

SCRUB:

Yes, sir, I left the priest and him disputing about religion.

AIMWELL:

And pray carry these gentlemen to reap the benefit of the
controversy.

> *Delivers the prisoners to* Scrub, *who leads 'em out.*

MRS. SULLEN:

Pray, sister, how came my lord here?

DORINDA:

And pray, how came the gentleman here?

MRS. SULLEN:

I'll tell you the greatest piece of villainy—

> *They talk in dumb show.*

AIMWELL:

I fancy, Archer, you have been more successful in your adventures than the housebreakers.

ARCHER:

No matter for my adventure; yours is the principal. Press her
this minute to marry you, now while she's hurried between the
palpitation of her fear and the joy of her deliverance, now
while the tide of her spirits are at high flood. Throw yourself at
her feet, speak some romantic nonsense or other, address her
like Alexander in the height of his victory, confound her senses,
bear down her reason, and away with her. The priest is now in
the cellar and dare not refuse to do the work.

Enter Lady Bountiful.

AIMWELL:

But how shall I get off without being observed?

ARCHER:

You a lover and not find a way to get off!—Let me see—

AIMWELL:

You bleed, Archer.

ARCHER:

S'death, I'm glad on't. This wound will do the business. I'll amuse the old lady and Mrs. Sullen about dressing my wound while you carry off Dorinda.

LADY BOUNTIFUL:

Gentlemen, could we understand how you would be gratified for the services—

ARCHER:

Come, come, my lady, this is no time for compliments. I'm wounded, madam.

LADY BOUNTIFUL *and* MRS. SULLEN:

How! Wounded!

DORINDA:

I hope, sir, you have received no hurt?

AIMWELL:

None but what you may cure.   *Makes love in dumb show.*

LADY BOUNTIFUL:

Let me see your arm, sir.—I must have some powder sugar to stop the blood.—O me, an ugly gash! Upon my word, sir, you must go into bed.

ARCHER:

Ay, my lady, a bed would do very well.—(*To* Mrs. Sullen.) Madam, will you do me the favor to conduct me to a chamber?

LADY BOUNTIFUL:

Do, do, daughter, while I get the lint and the probe and the plaster ready.

> *Runs out one way;* Aimwell *carries off* Dorinda *another.*

ARCHER:

Come, madam, why don't you obey your mother's commands?

MRS. SULLEN:

How can you, after what is past, have the confidence to ask me?

ARCHER:

And if you go to that, how can you, after what is past, have the confidence to deny me? Was not this blood shed in your defense and my life exposed for your protection? Look ye, madam, I'm none of your romantic fools that fight giants and monsters for nothing. My valor is downright Swiss. I'm a soldier of fortune and must be paid.

MRS. SULLEN:

'Tis ungenerous in you, sir, to upbraid me with your services.

ARCHER:

'Tis ungenerous in you, madam, not to reward 'em.

MRS. SULLEN:

How, at the expense of my honor?

ARCHER:

> Honor! Can honor consist with ingratitude? If you would deal like a woman of honor, do like a man of honor. D'ye think I would deny you in such a case?

Enter a Servant.

SERVANT:

> Madam, my lady ordered me to tell you that your brother is below at the gate. (*Exit* Servant.)

MRS. SULLEN:

> My brother? Heavens be praised.—Sir, he shall thank you for your services; he has it in his power.

ARCHER:

> Who is your brother, madam?

MRS. SULLEN:

> Sir Charles Freeman. You'll excuse me, sir, I must go and receive him. (*Exit.*)

ARCHER:

> Sir Charles Freeman! S'death and hell! My old acquaintance. Now unless Aimwell had made good use of his time, all our fair machine goes souse into the sea like the Eddystone. *Exit.*

Act V, Scene iv

Scene changes to the gallery in the same house.
Enter Aimwell *and* Dorinda.

DORINDA:

> Well, well, my lord, you have conquered. Your late generous action will, I hope, plead for my easy yielding, though I must own your lordship had a friend in the fort before.

AIMWELL:

> The sweets of Hybla dwell upon her tongue.—Here, doctor—

Enter Foigard *with a book.*

FOIGARD:

> Are you prepared boat?

DORINDA:

> I'm ready.—But first, my lord, one word. I have a frightful example of a hasty marriage in my own family. When I reflect upon't, it shocks me. Pray, my lord, consider a little.

AIMWELL:

Consider! Do you doubt my honor or my love?

DORINDA:

Neither. I do believe you equally just as brave. And were your whole sex drawn out for me to choose, I should not cast a look upon the multitude if you were absent. But, my lord, I'm a woman. Colors, concealments may hide a thousand faults in me; therefore know me better first. I hardly dare affirm I know myself in anything except my love.

AIMWELL (*aside*):

Such goodness who could injure? I find myself unequal to the task of villain; she has gained my soul and made it honest like her own. I cannot, cannot hurt her.—(*To* Foigard.) Doctor, retire.   *Exit* Foigard.

Madam, behold your lover and your proselyte, and judge of my passion by my conversion. I'm all a lie, nor dare I give a fiction to your arms. I'm all counterfeit except my passion.

DORINDA:

Forbid it, heaven! A counterfeit!

AIMWELL:

I am no lord, but a poor needy man come with a mean, a scandalous design to prey upon your fortune. But the beauties of your mind and person have so won me from myself that like a trusty servant I prefer the interest of my mistress to my own.

DORINDA:

Sure I have had the dream of some poor mariner, a sleepy image of a welcome port, and wake involved in storms.—Pray, sir, who are you?

AIMWELL:

Brother to the man whose title I usurped but stranger to his honor or his fortune.

DORINDA:

Matchless honesty! Once I was proud, sir, of your wealth and title but now am prouder that you want it. Now I can show my love was justly leveled and had no aim but love.—Doctor, come in.

Enter Foigard *at one door,* Gipsy *at another, who whispers* Dorinda.

Your pardon, sir, we shan't want you now.—(*To* Aimwell.) Sir, you must excuse me. I'll wait on you presently.

Exit with Gipsy.

FOIGARD:

Upon my shoul now, dis is foolish.   *Exit.*

AIMWELL:

Gone, and bid the priest depart! It has an ominous look.

Enter Archer.

ARCHER:

Courage, Tom. Shall I wish you joy?

AIMWELL:

No.

ARCHER:

Oons, man, what ha' you been doing?

AIMWELL:

O, Archer, my honesty I fear has ruined me.

ARCHER:

How!

AIMWELL:

I have discovered myself.

ARCHER:

Discovered! And without my consent? What, have I embarked my small remains in the same bottom with yours, and you dispose of all without my partnership?

AIMWELL:

O, Archer, I own my fault.

ARCHER:

After conviction—'tis then too late for pardon. You may remember, Mr. Aimwell, that you proposed this folly. As you begun, so end it. Henceforth I'll hunt my fortune single. So farewell.

AIMWELL:

Stay, my dear Archer, but a minute.

ARCHER:

Stay! What, to be despised, exposed, and laughed at? No, I would sooner change conditions with the worst of the rogues we just now bound than bear one scornful smile from the proud knight that once I treated as my equal.

AIMWELL:

What knight?

ARCHER:

Sir Charles Freeman, brother to the lady that I had almost— but no matter for that; 'tis a cursed night's work, and so I leave you to make your best on't. *Going*.

AIMWELL:

Freeman!—One word, Archer. Still I have hopes. Methought she received my confession with pleasure.

ARCHER:

S'death! Who doubts it?

AIMWELL:

She consented after to the match, and still I dare believe she will be just.

ARCHER:

To herself, I warrant her, as you should have been.

AIMWELL:

By all my hopes, she comes, and smiling comes.

Enter Dorinda *mighty gay.*

DORINDA:

Come, my dear lord, I fly with impatience to your arms. The minutes of my absence was a tedious year. Where's this tedious priest?

Enter Foigard.

ARCHER:

Oons, a brave girl.

DORINDA:

I suppose, my lord, this gentleman is privy to our affairs?

ARCHER:

Yes, yes, madam. I'm to be your father.

DORINDA:

Come, priest, do your office.

ARCHER:

Make haste, make haste, couple 'em any way. (*Takes Aimwell's hand.*) Come, madam, I'm to give you—

DORINDA:

My mind's altered. I won't.

ARCHER:

Eh—

AIMWELL:

I'm confounded.

FOIGARD:

Upon my shoul, and sho is myshelf.

ARCHER:

What's the matter now, madam?

DORINDA:

Look ye, sir, one generous action deserves another. This gentleman's honor obliged him to hide nothing from me; my justice engages me to conceal nothing from him. In short, sir, you are the person that you thought you counterfeited. You are the true Lord Viscount Aimwell, and I wish your lordship joy. Now, priest, you may be gone. If my lord is pleased now with the match let his lordship marry me in the face of the world.

AIMWELL *and* ARCHER:

What does she mean?

DORINDA:

Here's a witness for my truth.

Enter Sir Charles *and* Mrs. Sullen.

SIR CHARLES:

My dear Lord Aimwell, I wish you joy.

AIMWELL:

Of what?

SIR CHARLES:

Of your honor and estate. Your brother died the day before I left London, and all your friends have writ after you to Brussels; among the rest I did myself the honor.

ARCHER:

Hark ye, Sir Knight, don't you banter now?

SIR CHARLES:

'Tis truth, upon my honor.

AIMWELL:

Thanks to the pregnant stars that formed this accident.

ARCHER:

Thanks to the womb of time that brought it forth. Away with it.

AIMWELL:

Thanks to my guardian angel that led me to the prize.

Taking Dorinda's hand.

ARCHER:

And double thanks to the noble Sir Charles Freeman.—My lord, I wish you joy.—My lady, I wish you joy.—Igad, Sir Freeman, you're the honestest fellow living.—S'death, I'm grown strange airy upon this matter.—My lord, how d'ye? A word, my lord, how d'ye? A word, my lord: don't you remember something of a previous agreement that entitles me to the moiety of this lady's fortune, which I think will amount to five thousand pound?

AIMWELL:

Not a penny, Archer. You would ha' cut my throat just now because I would not deceive this lady.

ARCHER:

Ay, and I'll cut your throat again if you should deceive her now.

AIMWELL:

That's what I expected, and to end the dispute the lady's fortune is ten thousand pound. We'll divide stakes. Take the ten thousand pound or the lady.

DORINDA:

How! Is your lordship so indifferent?

ARCHER:

No, no, no, madam, his lordship knows very well that I'll take the money. I leave you to his lordship, and so we're both provided for.

Enter Count Bellair.

COUNT:

Mesdames et Messieurs, I am your servant trice humble. I hear you be rob here.

AIMWELL:

The ladies have been in some danger, sir.

COUNT:

And begar, our inn be rob too.

AIMWELL:

Our inn! By whom?

COUNT:

By the landlord, begar. Garzoon, he has rob himself and run away.

ARCHER:

Robbed himself!

COUNT:

Ay, begar, and me too of a hundre pound.

ARCHER:

A hundred pound.

COUNT:

Yes, that I owed him.

AIMWELL:

Our money's gone, Frank.

ARCHER:

Rot the money! My wench is gone. *Savez vous quelque chose de Mademoiselle Cherry?*

Enter a Fellow *with a strongbox and a letter.*

FELLOW:

Is there one Martin here?

ARCHER:

Ay, ay, who wants him?

FELLOW:

I have a box here and letter for him.

ARCHER (*taking the box*):

Ha, ha, ha, what's here? Legerdemain! By this light, my lord, our money again. But this unfolds the riddle. (*Opening the letter, reads.*) Hum, hum, hum. O, 'tis for the public good and must be communicated to the company.

"Mr. Martin,

My father being afraid of an impeachment by the rogues that are taken tonight is gone off, but if you can procure him a pardon he will make great discoveries that may be useful to the country. Could I have met you instead of your master tonight I would have delivered myself into your hands with a sum that much exceeds that in your strongbox, which I have sent you, with an assurance to my dear Martin that I shall ever be his most faithful friend till death.

CHERRY BONIFACE."

There's a billet-doux for you. As for the father, I think he ought to be encouraged, and for the daughter, pray, my lord, persuade your bride to take her into her service instead of Gipsy.

AIMWELL:

I can assure you, madam, your deliverance was owing to her discovery.

DORINDA:

Your command, my lord, will do without the obligation. I'll take care of her.

SIR CHARLES:

This good company meets opportunely in favor of a design I have in behalf of my unfortunate sister. I intend to part her from her husband. Gentlemen, will you assist me?

ARCHER:

Assist you! S'death, who would not?

COUNT:

Assist! Garzoon, we all assist.

Enter Sullen.

SULLEN:

What's all this? They tell me, spouse, that you had like to have been robbed.

MRS. SULLEN:

Truly, spouse, I was pretty near it, had not these two gentlemen interposed.

SULLEN:

How came these gentlemen here?

MRS. SULLEN:

That's his way of returning thanks, you must know.

COUNT:

Garzoon, the question be apropos for all dat.

SIR CHARLES:

You promised last night, sir, that you would deliver your lady to me this morning.

SULLEN:

Humph.

ARCHER:

Humph. What do you mean by humph? Sir, you shall deliver her. In short, sir, we have saved you and your family, and if you are not civil we'll unbind the rogues, join with 'um, and set fire to your house.—What does the man mean? Not part with his wife!

COUNT:

Ay, garzoon, de man no understan common justice.

MRS. SULLEN:

Hold, gentlemen, all things here must move by consent; compulsion would spoil us. Let my dear and I talk the matter over, and you shall judge it between us.

SULLEN:

Let me know first who are to be our judges.—Pray, sir, who are you?

SIR CHARLES:

I am Sir Charles Freeman, come to take away your wife.

SULLEN:

And you, good sir?

AIMWELL:

Thomas, Viscount Aimwell, come to take away your sister.

SULLEN:

And you, pray, sir?

ARCHER:

Francis Archer, Esquire, come—

SULLEN:

To take away my mother, I hope.—Gentlemen, you're heartily welcome. I never met with three more obliging people since I was born.—And now, my dear, if you please, you shall have the first word.

ARCHER:

And the last, for five pound.

MRS. SULLEN:

Spouse.

SULLEN:

Rib.

MRS. SULLEN:

How long have we been married?

SULLEN:

By the almanac fourteen months, but by my account fourteen
years.

MRS. SULLEN:

'Tis thereabout by my reckoning.

COUNT:

Garzoon, their account will agree.

MRS. SULLEN:

Pray, spouse, what did you marry for?

SULLEN:

To get an heir to my estate.

SIR CHARLES:

And have you succeeded?

SULLEN:

No.

ARCHER:

The condition fails of his side.—Pray, madam, what did you
marry for?

MRS. SULLEN:

To support the weakness of my sex by the strength of his and
to enjoy the pleasures of an agreeable society.

SIR CHARLES:

Are your expectations answered?

MRS. SULLEN:

No.

COUNT:

A clear case, a clear case.

SIR CHARLES:

What are the bars to your mutual contentment?

MRS. SULLEN:

In the first place I can't drink ale with him.

SULLEN:

Nor can I drink tea with her.

MRS. SULLEN:

I can't hunt with you.

SULLEN:
Nor can I dance with you.

MRS. SULLEN:
I hate cocking and racing.

SULLEN:
And I abhor ombre and piquet.

MRS. SULLEN:
Your silence is intolerable.

SULLEN:
Your prating is worse.

MRS. SULLEN:
Have we not been a perpetual offense to each other, a gnawing vulture at the heart?

SULLEN:
A frightful goblin to the sight.

MRS. SULLEN:
A porcupine to the feeling.

SULLEN:
Perpetual wormwood to the taste.

MRS. SULLEN:
Is there on earth a thing we could agree in?

SULLEN:
Yes—to part.

MRS. SULLEN:
With all my heart.

SULLEN:
Your hand.

MRS. SULLEN:
Here.

SULLEN:
These hands joined us; these shall part us—away—

MRS. SULLEN:
North.

SULLEN:
South.

MRS. SULLEN:
East.

SULLEN:
West—far as the poles asunder.

COUNT:
Begar, the ceremony be vera pretty.

SIR CHARLES:
Now, Mr. Sullen, there wants only my sister's fortune to make us easy.

SULLEN:

Sir Charles, you love your sister, and I love her fortune; every one to his fancy.

ARCHER:

Then you won't refund?

SULLEN:

Not a stiver.

ARCHER:

Then I find, madam, you must e'en go to your prison again.

COUNT:

What is the portion?

SIR CHARLES:

Ten thousand pound, sir.

COUNT:

Garzoon, I'll pay it, and she shall go home wid me.

ARCHER:

Ha, ha, ha, French all over.—Do you know, sir, what ten thousand pound English is?

COUNT:

No, begar, not *justement*.

ARCHER:

Why, sir, 'tis a hundred thousand livres.

COUNT:

A hundre tousand *livres*! A garzoon, me canno' do't. Your beauties and their fortunes are both too much for me.

ARCHER:

Then I will. This night's adventure has proved strangely lucky to us all, for Captain Gibbet in his walk had made bold, Mr. Sullen, with your study and escritoire and had taken out all the writings of your estate, all the articles of marriage with this lady, bills, bonds, leases, receipts to an infinite value. I took 'em from him, and I deliver them to Sir Charles.

> *Gives him a parcel of papers and parchments.*

SULLEN:

How, my writings! My head aches consumedly.—Well, gentlemen, you shall have her fortune—but I can't talk. If you have a mind, Sir Charles, to be merry and celebrate my sister's wedding and my divorce, you may command my house—but my head aches consumedly.—Scrub, bring me a dram.

ARCHER (*to* Mrs. Sullen):

Madam, there's a country dance to the trifle that I sung today. Your hand, and we'll lead it up.

Here a dance.

'Twould be hard to guess which of these parties is the better pleased, the couple joined or the couple parted: the one rejoicing in hopes of an untasted happiness and the other in their deliverance from an experienced misery.

Both happy in their several states we find,
Those parted by consent and those conjoined.
Consent, if mutual, saves the lawyer's fee;
Consent is law enough to set you free.

An Epilogue

(Designed to be spoke at end of play)

If to our play your judgment can't be kind,
Let its expiring author pity find;
Survey his mournful case with melting eyes,
Nor let the bard be damned before he dies.
Forbear you fair on his last scene to frown,
But his true exit with a plaudit crown;
Then shall the dying poet cease to fear
The dreadful knell while your applause he hears.
At Leuctra so, the conquering Theban died,
Claimed his friends' praises but their tears denied;
Pleased in the pangs of death he greatly thought
Conquest with loss of life but cheaply bought.
The difference this, the Greek was one would fight
As brave though not so gay as Sergeant Kite.
Ye sons of Will's, what's that to those who write?
To Thebes alone the Grecian owed his bays;
You may the bard above the hero raise,
Since yours is greater than Athenian praise.

OLIVER GOLDSMITH

Oliver Goldsmith was born on November 10, 1728, in Pallas, County Longford, Ireland. He was the second son in the large family of an Anglo-Irish clergyman. Sickly as a child, he was badly disfigured by smallpox at the age of seven. In school, he was considered idle and even stupid. Nevertheless, Goldsmith was sent to Trinity College, Dublin where as a sizar he did menial jobs for rich undergraduates to earn his place. He received an A.B. degree in 1749. In 1752, a wealthy uncle, the Reverend Thomas Contarine, gave him money to study medicine at the University of Edinburgh. But instead of completing his studies he used the money to wander the Continent, traveling through Holland, France, Italy, and Switzerland. When he settled in London four years later, he mysteriously procured a doctor's M.D. to support himself and also tried teaching. He also worked as a proofreader for novelist-printer Samuel Richardson, which led to employment with the *Monthly Review*, writing essays, reviews, and poems. In 1759, Goldsmith's *An Enquiry into the Present State of Polite Learning in Europe* was published to some success. Soon afterward he became a member of the Literary Club, where he met such illustrious personages as the painter Sir Joshua Reynolds, the politician Edmund Burke, the actor David Garrick, and, most importantly, the distinguished writer-critic Samuel Johnson.

Goldsmith, like his own creation Tony Lumpkin in *She Stoops to Conquer*, was an inveterate ne'er-do-well, someone who always lived beyond his means and preferred to eat, drink, and gamble away his money rather than work. When Goldsmith was about to be arrested for not paying his rent, his friend Samuel Johnson sent Goldsmith's novel *The Vicar of Wakefield*, even though unfinished, to a publisher for sixty pounds. Realizing how much money could be made from a successful play, Goldsmith finished his first, *The Good-Natured Man*, in 1768. It was produced two years later but was only a moderate success. He completed *She Stoops to Conquer*, his second play, in 1771, but the theater manager delayed production for more than a year. Again Samuel Johnson stepped in, convincing the theater manager to stage it. When the play finally opened on March 15, 1773, it was a huge success.

Even as a recognized novelist and playwright, Goldsmith continued writing furiously—hack writing that included essays, biographies, and histories like *The History of England*—until the very hour of his death, for he was never out of debt. He was working on the poem "Retaliation" when he died on April 4, 1774. It is not known which killed him, the fever or the wrong medication, which he had incompetently prescribed to himself as a "doctor," perhaps poisoning himself. Although he made five hundred pounds from *She Stoops to Conquer*, Goldsmith left a debt of two thousand pounds.

She Stoops to Conquer is a great comedy, a marvelously pure piece of entertainment. A review of the play on March 16, 1773, in the *Morning Chronicle* stated, "The audience are kept in a continual roar." Samuel Johnson wrote that the play "has answered . . . the great end of comedy—making an audience merry." It has been continually staged since, as actors and directors have found it to be a surefire crowd-pleaser. Goldsmith wrote the play in reaction to the Sentimental Comedy, the predominant genre of the day, which he considered a self-conscious and overly moral degradation of the comic form. He believed that it was his duty as a playwright to entertain and give pleasure, and to create what he termed "a laughing comedy." And he had that rare talent for consistently creating scenes and situations that hilariously exploit the humor in human folly. Farcical situations, mistaken identity, the contrast of high-class characters with low-class characters, and witty dialogue with characters speaking at cross-purposes are just some of the delightful devices he uses in *She Stoops to Conquer* that make it timeless and as funny today as when it was written.

She Stoops to Conquer

or,

The Mistakes of a Night

By Oliver Goldsmith

To Samuel Johnson, L.L.D.

Dear Sir,

By inscribing this slight performance to you, I do not mean so much to compliment you as myself. It may do me some honour to inform the public, that I have lived many years in intimacy with you. It may serve the interests of mankind also to inform them, that the greatest wit may be found in a character, without impairing the most unaffected piety.

I have, particularly, reason to thank you for your partiality to this performance. The undertaking a comedy, not merely sentimental, was very dangerous; and Mr Colman, who saw this piece in its various stages, always thought it so. However I ventured to trust it to the public; and though it was necessarily delayed till late in the season, I have every reason to be grateful.

I am Dear Sir,

Your most sincere friend,

And admirer,

OLIVER GOLDSMITH

Dramatis Personae

(As play was originally acted at the
Theatre Royal in Covent Garden, March 15, 1773)

Men

SIR CHARLES MARLOW	*Mr Gardner*
YOUNG MARLOW (*his Son*)	*Mr Lewes*
HARDCASTLE	*Mr Shuter*
HASTINGS	*Mr Dubellamy*
TONY LUMPKIN	*Mr Quick*
DIGGORY	*Mr Saunders*

Women

MRS HARDCASTLE	*Mrs Green*
MISS HARDCASTLE	*Mrs Bulkely*
MISS NEVILLE	*Mrs Kniveton*
MAID	*Miss Willems*
LANDLORD, SERVANTS, ETC. ETC.	

Prologue

By David Garrick, Esq.

Enter Mr Woodward,
Dressed in Black, and holding a Handkerchief to his Eyes

Excuse me, sirs, I pray—I can't yet speak—
I'm crying now—and have been all the week!
'Tis not alone this mourning suit, good masters;
I've that within—for which there are no plasters!
Pray would you know the reason why I'm crying?
The Comic muse, long sick, is now a-dying!
And if she goes, my tears will never stop;
For as a player, I can't squeeze out one drop:
I am undone, that's all—shall lose my bread—
I'd rather, but that's nothing—lose my head.
When the sweet maid is laid upon the bier,
Shuter and I shall be chief mourners here.
To *her* a mawkish drab of spurious breed,
Who deals in *sentimentals,* will succeed!
Poor *Ned* and *I* are dead to all intents,
We can as soon speak *Greek* as *sentiments!*
Both nervous grown, to keep our spirits up,
We now and then take down a hearty cup.
What shall we do?—If Comedy forsake us!
They'll turn us out, and no one else will take us;
But why can't I be moral?—Let me try—
My heart thus pressing—fixed my face and eye—
With a sententious look, that nothing means,
(Faces are blocks, in sentimental scenes)
Thus I begin—*All is not gold that glitters.*
Pleasure seems sweet, but proves a glass of bitters.
When ignorance enters, folly is at hand;
Learning is better far than house and land:
Let not your virtue trip, who trips may stumble,
And virtue is not virtue, if she tumble.

115

I give it up—morals won't do for me;
To make you laugh I must play tragedy.
One hope remains—hearing the maid was ill,
A *doctor* comes this night to show his skill.
To cheer her heart, and give your muscles motion,
He in *five draughts* prepared, presents a potion:
A kind of magic charm—for be assured,
If you will *swallow it,* the maid is cured:
But desperate the Doctor, and her case is,
If you reject the dose, and make wry faces!
This truth he boasts, will boast it while he lives,
No *poisonous drugs* are mixed in what he gives;
Should he succeed, you'll give him his degree;
If not, within he will receive no fee!
The college *you,* must his pretensions back,
Pronounce him *regular,* or dub him *quack.*

Act I, Scene i

Scene. A Chamber in an old fashioned House
Enter Mrs Hardcastle *and* Mr Hardcastle

MRS HARDCASTLE:

I vow, Mr Hardcastle, you're very particular. Is there a creature in the whole country, but ourselves, that does not take a trip to town now and then, to rub off the rust a little? There's the two Miss Hoggs, and our neighbour, Mrs Grigsby, go to take a month's polishing every winter.

HARDCASTLE:

Ay, and bring back vanity and affectation to last them the whole year. I wonder why London cannot keep its own fools at home? In my time, the follies of the town crept slowly among us, but now they travel faster than a stagecoach. Its fopperies come down, not only as inside passengers, but in the very basket.

MRS HARDCASTLE:

Ay, *your* times were fine times, indeed; you have been telling us of *them* for many a long year. Here we live in an old rumbling mansion, that looks for all the world like an inn, but that we never see company. Our best visitors are old Mrs Oddfish, the curate's wife, and little Cripplegate, the lame dancing-master: and all our entertainment your old stories of Prince Eugene and the Duke of Marlborough. I hate such old-fashioned trumpery.

HARDCASTLE:

And I love it. I love everything that's old: old friends, old times, old manners, old books, old wine; and I believe, Dorothy, (*Taking her hand*) you'll own I have been pretty fond of an old wife.

MRS HARDCASTLE:

Lord, Mr Hardcastle, you're for ever at your 'Dorothys' and your 'old wifes'. You may be a Darby, but I'll be no Joan, I promise you. I'm not so old as you'd make me, by more than one good year. Add twenty to twenty, and make money of that.

HARDCASTLE:

Let me see; twenty added to twenty, makes just fifty and seven.

117

MRS HARDCASTLE:

It's false, Mr Hardcastle: I was but twenty when I was brought to bed of Tony, that I had by Mr Lumpkin, my first husband; and he's not come to years of discretion yet.

HARDCASTLE:

Nor ever will, I dare answer for him. Ay, you have taught *him* finely.

MRS HARDCASTLE:

No matter, Tony Lumpkin has a good fortune. My son is not to live by his learning. I don't think a boy wants much learning to spend fifteen hundred a year.

HARDCASTLE:

Learning, quotha! A mere composition of tricks and mischief.

MRS HARDCASTLE:

Humour, my dear: nothing but humour. Come, Mr Hardcastle, you must allow the boy a little humour.

HARDCASTLE:

I'd sooner allow him an horse-pond. If burning the footmen's shoes, frighting the maids, and worrying the kittens, be humour, he has it. It was but yesterday he fastened my wig to the back of my chair, and when I went to make a bow, I popped my bald head in Mrs Frizzle's face.

MRS HARDCASTLE:

And am I to blame? The poor boy was always too sickly to do any good. A school would be his death. When he comes to be a little stronger, who knows what a year or two's Latin may do for him?

HARDCASTLE:

Latin for him! A cat and fiddle. No, no, the ale-house and the stable are the only schools he'll ever go to.

MRS HARDCASTLE:

Well, we must not snub the poor boy now, for I believe we shan't have him long among us. Anybody that looks in his face may see he's consumptive.

HARDCASTLE:

Ay, if growing too fat be one of the symptoms.

MRS HARDCASTLE:

He coughs sometimes.

HARDCASTLE:

Yes, when his liquor goes the wrong way.

MRS HARDCASTLE:

I'm actually afraid of his lungs.

HARDCASTLE:

And truly so am I; for he sometimes whoops like a speaking trumpet—(Tony *hallooing behind the Scenes*)—Oh there he goes—A very consumptive figure, truly.

Enter Tony, *crossing the Stage*

MRS HARDCASTLE:

Tony, where are you going, my charmer? Won't you give papa and I a little of your company, lovey?

TONY:

I'm in haste, mother, I cannot stay.

MRS HARDCASTLE:

You shan't venture out this raw evening, my dear: you look most shockingly.

TONY:

I can't stay, I tell you. The Three Pigeons expects me down every moment. There's some fun going forward.

HARDCASTLE:

Ay; the ale-house, the old place: I thought so.

MRS HARDCASTLE:

A low, paltry set of fellows.

TONY:

Not so low neither. There's Dick Muggins the exciseman, Jack Slang the horse doctor, Little Aminadab that grinds the music box, and Tom Twist that spins the pewter platter.

MRS HARDCASTLE:

Pray, my dear, disappoint them for one night at least.

TONY:

As for disappointing *them,* I should not so much mind; but I can't abide to disappoint *myself.*

MRS HARDCASTLE (*Detaining him*):

You shan't go.

TONY:

I will, I tell you.

MRS HARDCASTLE:

I say you shan't.

TONY:

We'll see which is strongest, you or I.

Exit, hauling her out

HARDCASTLE:

Ay, there goes a pair that only spoil each other. But is not the whole age in a combination to drive sense and discretion out of doors? There's my pretty darling Kate; the fashions of the times have almost infected her too. By living a year or two in town, she is come to be fond of gauze, and French frippery, as the best of them.

Enter Miss Hardcastle

HARDCASTLE:

Blessings on my pretty innocence! Dressed out as usual, my Kate. Goodness! What a quantity of superfluous silk hast thou got about thee, girl! I could never teach the fools of this age, that the indigent world could be clothed out of the trimmings of the vain.

MISS HARDCASTLE:

You know our agreement, sir. You allow me the morning to receive and pay visits, and to dress in my own manner; and in the evening, I put on my housewife's dress to please you.

HARDCASTLE:

Well, remember I insist on the terms of our agreement; and, by the bye, I believe I shall have occasion to try your obedience this very evening.

MISS HARDCASTLE:

I protest, sir, I don't comprehend your meaning.

HARDCASTLE:

Then, to be plain with you, Kate, I expect the young gentleman I have chosen to be your husband from town this very day. I have his father's letter, in which he informs me his son is set out, and that he intends to follow himself shortly after.

MISS HARDCASTLE:

Indeed! I wish I had known something of this before. Bless me, how shall I behave? It's a thousand to one I shan't like him; our meeting will be so formal, and so like a thing of business, that I shall find no room for friendship or esteem.

HARDCASTLE:

Depend upon it, child, I'll never control your choice; but Mr Marlow, whom I have pitched upon, is the son of my old friend, Sir Charles Marlow, of whom you have heard me talk so often. The young gentleman has been bred a scholar, and is designed for an employment in the service of his country. I am told he's a man of an excellent understanding.

MISS HARDCASTLE:

Is he?

HARDCASTLE:

Very generous.

MISS HARDCASTLE:

I believe I shall like him

HARDCASTLE:

Young and brave.

MISS HARDCASTLE:

I'm sure I shall like him.

HARDCASTLE:

And very handsome.

MISS HARDCASTLE:

My dear papa, say no more (*Kissing his hand*), he's mine, I'll have him.

HARDCASTLE:

And to crown all, Kate, he's one of the most bashful and reserved young fellows in all the world.

MISS HARDCASTLE:

Eh! you have frozen me to death again. That word reserved, has undone all the rest of his accomplishments. A reserved lover, it is said, always makes a suspicious husband.

HARDCASTLE:

On the contrary, modesty seldom resides in a breast that is not enriched with nobler virtues. It was the very feature in his character that first struck me.

MISS HARDCASTLE:

He must have more striking features to catch me, I promise you. However, if he be so young, so handsome, and so everything you mention, I believe he'll do still. I think I'll have him.

HARDCASTLE:

Ay, Kate, but there is still an obstacle. It's more than an even wager, he may not have *you*.

MISS HARDCASTLE:

My dear papa, why will you mortify one so?—Well, if he refuses, instead of breaking my heart at his indifference, I'll only break my glass for its flattery, set my cap to some newer fashion, and look out for some less difficult admirer.

HARDCASTLE:

Bravely resolved! In the meantime I'll go prepare the servants for his reception; as we seldom see company they want as much training as a company of recruits, the first day's muster.

Exit

MISS HARDCASTLE:

Lud, this news of papa's puts me all in a flutter. Young, handsome; these he put last; but I put them foremost. Sensible, good-natured; I like all that. But then reserved, and sheepish, that's much against him. Yet can't he be cured of his timidity, by being taught to be proud of his wife? Yes, and can't I—But I vow I'm disposing of the husband, before I have secured the lover.

Enter Miss Neville

MISS HARDCASTLE:

I'm glad you're come, Neville, my dear. Tell me, Constance, how do I look this evening? Is there anything whimsical about me? Is it one of my well-looking days, child? Am I in face today?

MISS NEVILLE:

Perfectly, my dear. Yet now I look again—bless me!—sure no accident has happened among the canary birds or the gold fishes? Has your brother or the cat been meddling? Or has the last novel been too moving?

MISS HARDCASTLE:

No; nothing of all this. I have been threatened—I can scarce get it out—I have been threatened with a lover.

MISS NEVILLE:

And his name—

MISS HARDCASTLE:

Is Marlow.

MISS NEVILLE:

Indeed!

MISS HARDCASTLE:

The son of Sir Charles Marlow.

MISS NEVILLE:

As I live, the most intimate friend of Mr Hastings, *my* admirer. They are never asunder. I believe you must have seen him when we lived in town.

MISS HARDCASTLE:

Never.

MISS NEVILLE:

He's a very singular character, I assure you. Among women of reputation and virtue, he is the modestest man alive; but his acquaintance give him a very different character among creatures of another stamp: you understand me.

MISS HARDCASTLE:

An odd character, indeed. I shall never be able to manage him. What shall I do? Pshaw, think no more of him, but trust to occurrences for success. But how goes on your own affair my dear, has my mother been courting you for my brother Tony, as usual?

MISS NEVILLE:

I have just come from one of our agreeable tête-à-têtes. She has been saying a hundred tender things, and setting off her pretty monster as the very pink of perfection.

MISS HARDCASTLE:

And her partiality is such, that she actually thinks him so. A fortune like yours is no small temptation. Besides, as she has the sole management of it, I'm not surprised to see her unwilling to let it go out of the family.

MISS NEVILLE:

A fortune like mine, which chiefly consists in jewels, is no such mighty temptation. But at any rate if my dear Hastings be but constant, I make no doubt to be too hard for her at last. However, I let her suppose that I am in love with her son, and she never once dreams that my affections are fixed upon another.

MISS HARDCASTLE:

My good brother holds out stoutly. I could almost love him for hating you so.

MISS NEVILLE:

It is a good-natured creature at bottom, and I'm sure would wish to see me married to anybody but himself. But my aunt's bell rings for our afternoon's walk round the improvements. *Allons*. Courage is necessary as our affairs are critical.

MISS HARDCASTLE:

Would it were bedtime and all were well.   *Exeunt*

Act I, Scene ii

Scene. An Alehouse Room. Several shabby fellows, with Punch and Tobacco. Tony at the head of the Table, a little higher than the rest: a mallet in his hand.

ALL:

Hurrah, hurrah, hurrah, bravo.

FIRST FELLOW:

Now, gentlemen, silence for a song. The Squire is going to knock himself down for a song.

ALL:

Ay, a song, a song.

TONY:

Then I'll sing you, gentlemen, a song I made upon this alehouse, the Three Pigeons.

Song

Let school-masters puzzle their brain,
    With grammar, and nonsense, and learning;
Good liquor, I stoutly maintain,
    Gives genus a better discerning.
Let them brag of their Heathenish Gods,
    Their Lethes, their Styxes, and Stygians;
Their Quis, and their Quæs, and their Quods,
    They're all but a parcel of Pigeons.
                Toroddle, toroddle, toroll.

When Methodist preachers come down,
    A preaching that drinking is sinful,
I'll wager the rascals a crown,
    They always preach best with a skinful.
But when you come down with your pence,
    For a slice of their scurvy religion,
I'll leave it to all men of sense,
    But you my good friend are the pigeon.
                Toroddle, toroddle, toroll.

Then come, put the jorum about,
    And let us be merry and clever,
Our hearts and our liquors are stout,
    Here's the Three Jolly Pigeons for ever.
Let some cry up woodcock or hare,
    Your bustards, your ducks, and your widgeons;
But of all the birds in the air,
    Here's a health to the Three Jolly Pigeons.
                Toroddle, toroddle, toroll.

ALL:
    Bravo, bravo.
FIRST FELLOW:
    The Squire has got spunk in him.
SECOND FELLOW:
    I love to hear him sing, bekeays he never gives us nothing that's *low.*
THIRD FELLOW:
    Oh damn anything that's *low,* I cannot bear it.
FOURTH FELLOW:
    The genteel thing is the genteel thing at any time. If so be that a gentleman bees in a concatenation accordingly.

THIRD FELLOW:

>I like the maxum of it, Master Muggins. What though I am obligated to dance a bear, a man may be a gentleman for all that. May this be my poison if my Bogie shall ever dance but to the very genteelest of tunes. 'Water parted,' or the minuet in *Ariadne*.

SECOND FELLOW:

>What a pity it is the Squire is not come to his own. It would be well for all the publicans within ten miles round of him.

TONY:

>Ecod and so it would Master Slang. I'd then show what it was to keep choice of company.

SECOND FELLOW:

>Oh he takes after his own father for that. To be sure old Squire Lumpkin was the finest gentleman I ever set my eyes on. For winding the straight horn, or beating a thicket for a hare, or a wench, he never had his fellow. It was a saying in the place, that he kept the best horses, dogs, and girls in the whole county.

TONY:

>Ecod, and when I'm of age I'll be no bastard I promise you. I have been thinking of Bet Bouncer and the miller's grey mare to begin with. But come, my boys, drink about and be merry, for you pay no reckoning. Well Stingo, what's the matter?

Enter Landlord

LANDLORD:

>There be two gentlemen in a post-chaise at the door. They have lost their way upo' the forest; and they are talking something about Mr Hardcastle.

TONY:

>As sure as can be one of them must be the gentleman that's coming down to court my sister. Do they seem to be Londoners?

LANDLORD:

>I believe they may. They look woundily like Frenchmen.

TONY:

>Then desire them to step this way, and I'll set them right in a twinkling. *Exit* Landlord
>Gentlemen, as they mayn't be good enough company for you, step down for a moment, and I'll be with you in the squeezing of a lemon. *Exeunt Mob*

TONY:

>Father-in-law has been calling me whelp, and hound, this half-year. Now if I pleased, I could be so revenged upon the old

grumbletonian. But then I'm afraid—afraid of what! I shall soon be worth fifteen hundred a year, and let him frighten me out of *that* if he can.

Enter Landlord, *conducting* Marlow *and* Hastings

MARLOW:

What a tedious uncomfortable day have we had of it! We were told it was but forty miles across the country, and we have come above threescore.

HASTINGS:

And all, Marlow, from that unaccountable reserve of yours, that would not let us enquire more frequently on the way.

MARLOW:

I own, Hastings, I am unwilling to lay myself under an obligation to everyone I meet; and often stand the chance of an unmannerly answer.

HASTINGS:

At present, however, we are not likely to receive any answer.

TONY:

No offence, gentlemen. But I'm told you have been enquiring for one Mr Hardcastle, in these parts. Do you know what part of the country you are in?

HASTINGS:

Not in the least, sir, but should thank you for information.

TONY:

Nor the way you came?

HASTINGS:

No, sir; but if you can inform us—

TONY:

Why, gentlemen, if you know neither the road you are going, nor where you are, nor the road you came, the first thing I have to inform you is, that—You have lost your way.

MARLOW:

We wanted no ghost to tell us that.

TONY:

Pray, gentlemen, may I be so bold as to ask the place from whence you came?

MARLOW:

That's not necessary towards directing us where we are to go.

TONY:

No offence; but question for question is all fair, you know. Pray, gentlemen, is not this same Hardcastle a cross-grained, old-fashioned, whimsical fellow, with an ugly face, a daughter, and a pretty son?

HASTINGS:

We have not seen the gentleman, but he has the family you mention.

TONY:

The daughter, a tall trapesing, trolloping, talkative maypole— The son, a pretty, well-bred, agreeable youth, that everybody is so fond of.

MARLOW:

Our information differs in this. The daughter is said to be well-bred and beautiful; the son, an awkward booby, reared up and spoiled at his mother's apron-string.

TONY:

He-he-hem!—Then, gentlemen, all I have to tell you is, that you won't reach Mr Hardcastle's house this night, I believe.

HASTINGS:

Unfortunate!

TONY:

It's a damned long, dark, boggy, dirty, dangerous way. Stingo, tell the gentlemen the way to Mr Hardcastle's; (*Winking upon the* Landlord) Mr Hardcastle's, of Quagmire Marsh, you understand me.

LANDLORD:

Master Hardcastle's! Lock-a-daisy, my masters, you're come a deadly deal wrong! When you came to the bottom of the hill, you should have crossed down Squash Lane.

MARLOW (*Noting it down*):

Cross down Squash Lane!

LANDLORD:

Then you were to keep straight forward, till you came to four roads.

MARLOW (*Still noting*):

Come to where four roads meet!

TONY:

Ay; but you must be sure to take only one of them.

MARLOW:

O sir, you're facetious.

TONY:

Then keeping to the right, you are to go sideways till you come upon Crack-skull Common: there you must look sharp for the track of the wheel, and go forward, till you come to farmer Murrain's barn. Coming to the farmer's barn, you are to turn to the right, and then to the left, and then to the right about again, till you find out the old mill—

MARLOW (*Who had been noting*):

Zounds, man! we could as soon find out the longitude!

HASTINGS:

What's to be done, Marlow?

MARLOW:

This house promises but a poor reception; though perhaps the Landlord can accommodate us.

LANDLORD:

Alack, master, we have but one spare bed in the whole house.

TONY:

And to my knowledge, that's taken up by three lodgers already. (*After a pause, in which the rest seem disconcerted*) I have hit it. Don't you think, Stingo, our landlady could accommodate the gentlemen by the fire-side, with—three chairs and a bolster?

HASTINGS:

I hate sleeping by the fire-side.

MARLOW:

And I detest your three chairs and a bolster.

TONY:

You do, do you?—then let me see—what if you go on a mile further, to the Buck's Head; the old Buck's Head on the hill, one of the best inns in the whole county?

HASTINGS:

O ho! so we have escaped an adventure for this night, however.

LANDLORD (*Apart to* Tony):

Sure, you ben't sending them to your father's as an inn, be you?

TONY:

Mum, you fool you. Let *them* find that out. (*To them*) You have only to keep on straight forward, till you come to a large old house by the roadside. You'll see a pair of large horns over the door. That's the sign. Drive up the yard, and call stoutly about you.

HASTINGS:

Sir, we are obliged to you. The servants can't miss the way?

TONY:

No, no: But I must tell you though, the landlord is rich, and going to leave off business; so he wants to be thought a gentleman, saving your presence, he! he! he! He'll be for giving you his company, and ecod if you mind him, he'll persuade you that his mother was an alderman, and his aunt a Justice of Peace.

LANDLORD:

A troublesome old blade to be sure; but a' keeps as good wines and beds as any in the whole country.

MARLOW:

Well, if he supplies us with these, we shall want no further connection. We are to turn to the right, did you say?

TONY:

No, no; straight forward. I'll just step myself, and show you a piece of the way. (*To the* Landlord) Mum.

LANDLORD:

Ah, bless your heart, for a sweet, pleasant—damned mischievous son of a whore.   *Exeunt*

Act II, Scene i

Scene. An old-fashioned House

Enter Hardcastle, *followed by three or four awkward* Servants

HARDCASTLE:

Well, I hope you're perfect in the table exercise I have been teaching you these three days. You all know your posts and your places, and can show that you have been used to good company, without ever stirring from home.

SERVANTS:

Ay, ay.

HARDCASTLE:

When company comes, you are not to pop out and stare, and then run in again, like frighted rabbits in a warren.

SERVANTS:

No, no.

HARDCASTLE:

You, Diggory, whom I have taken from the barn, are to make a show at the side-table; and you, Roger, whom I have advanced from the plough, are to place yourself behind *my* chair. But you're not to stand so, with your hands in your pockets. Take your hands from your pockets, Roger; and from your head, you blockhead you. See how Diggory carries his hands. They're a little too stiff, indeed, but that's no great matter.

DIGGORY:

Ay, mind how I hold them. I learned to hold my hands this way, when I was upon drill for the militia. And so being upon drill—

HARDCASTLE:

You must not be so talkative, Diggory. You must be all attention to the guests. You must hear us talk, and not think of talking; you must see us drink, and not think of drinking; you must see us eat, and not think of eating.

DIGGORY:

By the laws, your worship, that's parfectly unpossible. When ever Diggory sees yeating going forward, ecod he's always wishing for a mouthful himself.

HARDCASTLE:

Blockhead! Is not a belly-full in the kitchen as good as a belly-full in the parlour? Stay your stomach with that reflection.

DIGGORY:

Ecod I thank your worship, I'll make a shift to stay my stomach with a slice of cold beef in the pantry.

HARDCASTLE:

Diggory, you are too talkative. Then if I happen to say a good thing, or tell a good story at table, you must not all burst out a-laughing, as if you made part of the company.

DIGGORY:

Then ecod your worship must not tell the story of Ould Grouse in the gun-room: I can't help laughing at that—he! he! he!—for the soul of me. We have laughed at that these twenty years—ha! ha! ha!

HARDCASTLE:

Ha! ha! ha! The story is a good one. Well, honest Diggory, you may laugh at that—but still remember to be attentive. Suppose one of the company should call for a glass of wine, how will you behave? A glass of wine, sir, if you please—(*To* Diggory) Eh, why don't you move?

DIGGORY:

Ecod, your worship, I never have courage till I see the eatables and drinkables brought upo' the table, and then I'm as bauld as a lion.

HARDCASTLE:

What, will nobody move?

FIRST SERVANT:

I'm not to leave this pleace.

SECOND SERVANT:

I'm sure it's no pleace of mine.

THIRD SERVANT:

Nor mine, for sartain.

DIGGORY:

Wauns, and I'm sure it canna be mine.

HARDCASTLE:

You numbskulls! and so while, like your betters, you are quarrelling for places, the guests must be starved. Oh you dunces! I find I must begin all over again.———But don't I hear a coach drive into the yard? To your posts, you blockheads. I'll go in the meantime and give my old friend's son a hearty reception at the gate.

Exit Hardcastle

DIGGORY:

By the elevens, my pleace is gone quite out of my head.

ROGER:

I know that my pleace is to be everywhere.

FIRST SERVANT:

Where the devil is mine?

SECOND SERVANT:

My pleace is to be nowhere at all; and so Ize go about my business.

Exeunt Servants, *running about as if frighted, different ways*
Enter Servant *with Candles, showing in* Marlow *and* Hastings

SERVANT:

Welcome, gentlemen, very welcome. This way.

HASTINGS:

After the disappointments of the day, welcome once more, Charles, to the comforts of a clean room and a good fire. Upon my word, a very well-looking house; antique, but creditable.

MARLOW:

The usual fate of a large mansion. Having first ruined the master by good housekeeping, it at last comes to levy contributions as an inn.

HASTINGS:

As you say, we passengers are to be taxed to pay all these fineries. I have often seen a good sideboard, or a marble chimney-piece, though not actually put in the bill, inflame a reckoning confoundedly.

MARLOW:

Travellers, George, must pay in all places. The only difference is, that in good inns, you pay dearly for luxuries; in bad ones, you are fleeced and starved.

HASTINGS:

You have lived pretty much among them. In truth, I have been often surprised, that you who have seen so much of the world, with your natural good sense, and your many opportunities, could never yet acquire a requisite share of assurance.

MARLOW:

The Englishman's malady. But tell me, George, where could I have learned that assurance you talk of? My life has been chiefly spent in a college, or an inn, in seclusion from that lovely part of the creation that chiefly teach men confidence. I don't know that I was ever familiarly acquainted with a single modest woman—except my mother—But among females of another class you know—

HASTINGS:

Ay, among them you are impudent enough of all conscience.

MARLOW:

They are of *us* you know.

HASTINGS:

But in the company of women of reputation I never saw such an idiot, such a trembler; you look for all the world as if you wanted an opportunity of stealing out of the room.

MARLOW:

Why man that's because I *do* want to steal out of the room. Faith, I have often formed a resolution to break the ice, and rattle away at any rate. But I don't know how, a single glance from a pair of fine eyes has totally overset my resolution. An impudent fellow may counterfeit modesty, but I'll be hanged if a modest man can ever counterfeit impudence.

HASTINGS:

If you could but say half the fine things to them that I have heard you lavish upon the barmaid of an inn, or even a college bedmaker—

MARLOW:

Why, George, I can't say fine things to them. They freeze, they petrify me. They may talk of a comet, or a burning mountain, or some such bagatelle. But to me, a modest woman, dressed out in all her finery, is the most tremendous object of the whole creation.

HASTINGS:

Ha! ha! ha! At this rate, man, how can you ever expect to marry!

MARLOW:

Never, unless as among kings and princes, my bride were to be courted by proxy. If, indeed, like an Eastern bridegroom, one were to be introduced to a wife he never saw before, it might be endured. But to go through all the terrors of a formal courtship, together with the episode of aunts, grandmothers, and cousins, and at last to blurt out the broad staring question, of, 'Madam, will you marry me?' No, no, that's a strain much above me I assure you.

HASTINGS:

I pity you. But how do you intend behaving to the lady you are come down to visit at the request of your father?

MARLOW:

As I behave to all other ladies. Bow very low. Answer yes, or no, to all her demands—But for the rest, I don't think I shall venture to look in her face, till I see my father's again.

HASTINGS:

I'm surprised that one who is so warm a friend can be so cool a lover.

MARLOW:

To be explicit, my dear Hastings, my chief inducement down was to be instrumental in forwarding your happiness, not my own. Miss Neville loves you, the family don't know you, as my friend you are sure of a reception, and let honour do the rest.

HASTINGS:

My dear Marlow! But I'll suppress the emotion. Were I a wretch, meanly seeking to carry off a fortune, you should be the last man in the world I would apply to for assistance. But Miss Neville's person is all I ask, and that is mine, both from her deceased father's consent, and her own inclination.

MARLOW:

Happy man! You have talents and art to captivate any woman. I'm doomed to adore the sex, and yet to converse with the only part of it I despise. This stammer in my address, and this awkward professing visage of mine, can never permit me to soar above the reach of a milliner's 'prentice, or one of the duchesses of Drury Lane. Pshaw! this fellow here to interrupt us.

Enter Hardcastle

HARDCASTLE:

> Gentlemen, once more you are heartily welcome. Which is Mr
> Marlow? Sir, you're heartily welcome. It's not my way, you see,
> to receive my friends with my back to the fire. I like to give
> them a hearty reception in the old style at my gate. I like to see
> their horses and trunks taken care of.

MARLOW (*Aside*):

> He has got our names from the servants already. (*To him*) We
> approve your caution and hospitality, sir. (*To* Hastings) I have
> been thinking, George, of changing our travelling dresses in
> the morning. I am grown confoundedly ashamed of mine.

HARDCASTLE:

> I beg, Mr Marlow, you'll use no ceremony in this house.

HASTINGS:

> I fancy, Charles, you're right: the first blow is half the battle. I
> intend opening the campaign with the white and gold.

HARDCASTLE:

> Mr Marlow—Mr Hastings—gentlemen—pray be under no
> constraint in this house. This is Liberty-Hall, gentlemen. You
> may do just as you please here.

MARLOW:

> Yet, George, if we open the campaign too fiercely at first, we
> may want ammunition before it is over. I think to reserve the
> embroidery to secure a retreat.

HARDCASTLE:

> Your talking of a retreat, Mr Marlow, puts me in mind of the
> Duke of Marlborough, when we went to besiege Denain. He
> first summoned the garrison.

MARLOW:

> Don't you think the *ventre d'or* waistcoat will do with the plain
> brown?

HARDCASTLE:

> He first summoned the garrison, which might consist of about
> five thousand men——

HASTINGS:

> I think not: brown and yellow mix but very poorly.

HARDCASTLE:

> I say, gentlemen, as I was telling you, he summoned the garri-
> son, which might consist of about five thousand men——

MARLOW:

> The girls like finery.

HARDCASTLE:

> Which might consist of about five thousand men, well ap-
> pointed with stores, ammunition, and other implements of

war. Now, says the Duke of Marlborough, to George Brooks, that stood next to him—You must have heard of George Brooks; I'll pawn my Dukedom, says he, but I take that garrison without spilling a drop of blood. So——

MARLOW:

What, my good friend, if you gave us a glass of punch in the meantime, it would help us to carry on the siege with vigour.

HARDCASTLE:

Punch, sir! (*Aside*) This is the most unaccountable kind of modesty I ever met with.

MARLOW:

Yes, sir, punch. A glass of warm punch, after our journey, will be comfortable. This is Liberty-Hall, you know.

HARDCASTLE:

Here's Cup, sir.

MARLOW (*Aside*):

So this fellow, in his Liberty-Hall, will only let us have just what he pleases.

HARDCASTLE (*Taking the Cup*):

I hope you'll find it to your mind. I have prepared it with my own hands, and I believe you'll own the ingredients are tolerable. Will you be so good as to pledge me, sir? Here, Mr Marlow, here is to our better acquaintance.   *Drinks*

MARLOW (*Aside*):

A very impudent fellow this! but he's a character, and I'll humour him a little. Sir, my service to you.   *Drinks*

HASTINGS (*Aside*):

I see this fellow wants to give us his company, and forgets that he's an inn-keeper, before he has learned to be a gentleman.

MARLOW:

From the excellence of your Cup, my old friend, I suppose you have a good deal of business in this part of the country. Warm work, now and then, at elections, I suppose.

HARDCASTLE:

No, sir, I have long given that work over. Since our betters have hit upon the expedient of electing each other, there's no business for us that sell ale.

HASTINGS:

So, then you have no turn for politics I find.

HARDCASTLE:

Not in the least. There was a time, indeed, I fretted myself about the mistakes of government, like other people; but finding myself every day grow more angry, and the government growing no better, I left it to mend itself. Since that, I no more

trouble my head about Hyder Ali, or Ali Cawn, than about
Ally Croaker. Sir, my service to you.

HASTINGS:

So what with eating above stairs, and drinking below, with
receiving your friends without, and amusing them within, you
lead a good pleasant bustling life of it.

HARDCASTLE:

I do stir about a great deal, that's certain. Half the differences
of the parish are adjusted in this very parlour.

MARLOW (*After drinking*):

And you have an argument in your Cup, old gentleman, better
than any in Westminster-Hall.

HARDCASTLE:

Ay, young gentleman, that, and a little philosophy.

MARLOW (*Aside*):

Well, this is the first time I ever heard of an inn-keeper's philosophy.

HASTINGS:

So then, like an experienced general, you attack them on every
quarter. If you find their reason manageable, you attack it with
your philosophy; if you find they have no reason, you attack
them with this. Here's your health, my philosopher.   *Drinks*

HARDCASTLE:

Good, very good, thank you; ha! ha! Your Generalship puts me
in mind of Prince Eugene, when he fought the Turks at the battle of Belgrade. You shall hear.

MARLOW:

Instead of the battle of Belgrade, I believe it's almost time to
talk about supper. What has your philosophy got in the house
for supper?

HARDCASTLE:

For supper, sir! (*Aside*) Was ever such a request to a man in his
own house!

MARLOW:

Yes, sir, supper sir; I begin to feel an appetite. I shall make devilish work tonight in the larder, I promise you.

HARDCASTLE (*Aside*):

Such a brazen dog sure never my eyes beheld. (*To him*) Why
really, sir, as for supper I can't well tell. My Dorothy, and the
cook-maid, settle these things between them. I leave these kind
of things entirely to them.

MARLOW:

You do, do you?

HARDCASTLE:

Entirely. By the bye, I believe they are in actual consultation upon what's for supper this moment in the kitchen.

MARLOW:

Then I beg they'll admit *me* as one of their privy council. It's a way I have got. When I travel, I always choose to regulate my own supper. Let the cook be called. No offence I hope, sir.

HARDCASTLE:

O no, sir, none in the least; yet I don't know how: our Bridget, the cook-maid, is not very communicative upon these occasions. Should we send for her, she might scold us all out of the house.

HASTINGS:

Let's see your list of the larder then. I ask it as a favour. I always match my appetite to my bill of fare.

MARLOW (*To* Hardcastle, *who looks at them with surprise*):

Sir, he's very right, and it's my way too.

HARDCASTLE:

Sir, you have a right to command here. Here, Roger, bring us the bill of fare for tonight's supper. I believe it's drawn out. Your manner, Mr Hastings, puts me in mind of my uncle, Colonel Wallop. It was a saying of his, that no man was sure of his supper till he had eaten it.

Enter Roger, *who gives a Bill of Fare*

HASTINGS (*Aside*):

All upon the high ropes! His uncle a Colonel! We shall soon hear of his mother being a Justice of Peace. But let's hear the bill of fare.

MARLOW (*Perusing*):

What's here? For the first course; for the second course; for the dessert. The devil, sir, do you think we have brought down the whole Joiners Company, or the Corporation of Bedford, to eat up such a supper? Two or three little things, clean and comfortable, will do.

HASTINGS:

But, let's hear it.

MARLOW (*Reading*):

For the first course at the top, a pig's face, and prune sauce.

HASTINGS:

Damn your pig's face, I say.

MARLOW:

And damn your prune sauce, say I.

HARDCASTLE:

And yet, gentlemen, to men that are hungry, a pig's face, with prune sauce, is very good eating.

MARLOW:

At the bottom, a calf's tongue and brains.

HASTINGS:

Let your brains be knocked out, my good sir; I don't like them.

MARLOW:

Or you may clap them on a plate by themselves. I do.

HARDCASTLE (*Aside*):

Their impudence confounds me. (*To them*) Gentlemen, you are my guests, make what alterations you please. Is there anything else you wish to retrench or alter, gentlemen?

MARLOW:

Item. A pork pie, a boiled rabbit and sausages, a florentine, a shaking pudding, and a dish of tiff—tuff—taffety cream!

HASTINGS:

Confound your made dishes, I shall be as much at a loss in this house as at a green and yellow dinner at the French ambassador's table. I'm for plain eating.

HARDCASTLE:

I'm sorry, gentlemen, that I have nothing you like, but if there be anything you have a particular fancy to——

MARLOW:

Why, really, sir, your bill of fare is so exquisite, that any one part of it is full as good as another. Send us what you please. So much for supper. And now to see that our beds are aired, and properly taken care of.

HARDCASTLE:

I entreat you'll leave all that to me. You shall not stir a step.

MARLOW:

Leave that to you! I protest, sir, you must excuse me, I always look to these things myself.

HARDCASTLE:

I must insist, sir, you'll make yourself easy on that head.

MARLOW:

You see I'm resolved on it. (*Aside*) A very troublesome fellow this, as ever I met with.

HARDCASTLE:

Well, sir, I'm resolved at least to attend you. (*Aside*) This may be modern modesty, but I never saw anything look so like old-fashioned impudence.

Exeunt Marlow *and* Hardcastle

HASTINGS:

So I find this fellow's civilities begin to grow troublesome. But who can be angry at those assiduities which are meant to please him? Ha! what do I see? Miss Neville, by all that's happy!

Enter Miss Neville

MISS NEVILLE:

My dear Hastings! To what unexpected good fortune? to what accident am I to ascribe this happy meeting?

HASTINGS:

Rather let me ask the same question, as I could never have hoped to meet my dearest Constance at an inn.

MISS NEVILLE:

An inn! sure you mistake! my aunt, my guardian, lives here. What could induce you to think this house an inn?

HASTINGS:

My friend Mr Marlow, with whom I came down, and I, have been sent here as to an inn, I assure you. A young fellow whom we accidentally met at a house hard by directed us hither.

MISS NEVILLE:

Certainly it must be one of my hopeful cousin's tricks, of whom you have heard me talk so often, ha! ha! ha! ha!

HASTINGS:

He whom your aunt intends for you? He of whom I have such just apprehensions?

MISS NEVILLE:

You have nothing to fear from him, I assure you. You'd adore him if you knew how heartily he despises me. My aunt knows it too, and has undertaken to court me for him, and actually begins to think she has made a conquest.

HASTINGS:

Thou dear dissembler! You must know, my Constance, I have just seized this happy opportunity of my friend's visit here to get admittance into the family. The horses that carried us down are now fatigued with their journey, but they'll soon be refreshed; and then if my dearest girl will trust in her faithful Hastings, we shall soon be landed in France, where even among slaves the laws of marriage are respected.

MISS NEVILLE:

I have often told you, that though ready to obey you, I yet should leave my little fortune behind with reluctance. The greatest part of it was left me by my uncle, the India Director,

and chiefly consists in jewels. I have been for some time persuading my aunt to let me wear them. I fancy I'm very near
succeeding. The instant they are put into my possession you
shall find me ready to make them and myself yours.

HASTINGS:

Perish the baubles! Your person is all I desire. In the meantime,
my friend Marlow must not be let into his mistake. I know the
strange reserve of his temper is such, that if abruptly informed
of it, he would instantly quit the house before our plan was
ripe for execution.

MISS NEVILLE:

But how shall we keep him in the deception? Miss Hardcastle
is just returned from walking; what if we still continue to
deceive him?——This, this way——(*They confer*)

Enter Marlow

MARLOW:

The assiduities of these good people tease me beyond bearing.
My host seems to think it ill manners to leave me alone, and so
he claps not only himself but his old-fashioned wife on my
back. They talk of coming to sup with us too; and then, I suppose, we are to run the gauntlet through all the rest of the family.—What have we got here!—

HASTINGS:

My dear Charles! Let me congratulate you!—The most fortunate accident!—Who do you think is just alighted?

MARLOW:

Cannot guess.

HASTINGS:

Our mistresses my boy, Miss Hardcastle and Miss Neville. Give
me leave to introduce Miss Constance Neville to your acquaintance. Happening to dine in the neighbourhood, they called on
their return to take fresh horses here. Miss Hardcastle has just
stepped into the next room, and will be back in an instant.
Wasn't it lucky? eh?

MARLOW (*Aside*):

I have just been mortified enough of all conscience, and here
comes something to complete my embarrassment.

HASTINGS:

Well! but wasn't it the most fortunate thing in the world?

MARLOW:

Oh! yes. Very fortunate—a most joyful encounter——But our
dresses, George, you know, are in disorder——What if we
should postpone the happiness till tomorrow?——Tomorrow

at her own house——It will be every bit as convenient—And rather more respectful——Tomorrow let it be.   *Offering to go*

MISS NEVILLE:

By no means, sir. Your ceremony will displease her. The disorder of your dress will show the ardour of your impatience. Besides, she knows you are in the house, and will permit you to see her.

MARLOW:

Oh! the devil! how shall I support it? Hem! hem! Hastings, you must not go. You are to assist me, you know. I shall be confoundedly ridiculous.

HASTINGS:

Pshaw man! it's but the first plunge, and all's over. She's but a woman, you know.

MARLOW:

And of all women, she that I dread most to encounter! Yet, hang it! I'll take courage. Hem!

Enter Miss Hardcastle *as returned from walking, with a Bonnet on, etc.*

HASTINGS (*Introducing them*):

Miss Hardcastle, Mr Marlow, I'm proud of bringing two persons of such merit together, that only want to know, to esteem each other.

MISS HARDCASTLE (*Aside*):

Now for meeting my modest gentleman with a demure face, and quite in his own manner. (*After a pause, in which he appears very uneasy and disconcerted*) I'm glad of your safe arrival, sir——I'm told you had some accidents by the way.

MARLOW:

Only a few madam. Yet we had some. Yes, madam, a good many accidents, but should be sorry—madam—or rather glad of any accidents—that are so agreeably concluded. Hem!

HASTINGS (*To him*):

You never spoke better in your whole life. Keep it up, and I'll ensure you the victory.

MISS HARDCASTLE:

I'm afraid you flatter, sir. You that have seen so much of the finest company can find little entertainment in an obscure corner of the country.

MARLOW (*Gathering courage*):

I have lived, indeed, in the world, madam; but I have kept very little company. I have been but an observer upon life, madam, while others were enjoying it.

MISS NEVILLE:

But that, I am told, is the way to enjoy it at last.

HASTINGS (*To him*):

Cicero never spoke better. Once more, and you are confirmed in assurance for ever.

MARLOW (*To him*):

Hem! Stand by me then, and when I'm down, throw in a word or two to set me up again.

MISS HARDCASTLE:

An observer, like you, upon life, were, I fear, disagreeably employed, since you must have had much more to censure than to approve.

MARLOW:

Pardon me, madam. I was always willing to be amused. The folly of most people is rather an object of mirth than uneasiness.

HASTINGS (*To him*):

Bravo, Bravo. Never spoke so well in your whole life. Well! Miss Hardcastle, I see that you and Mr Marlow are going to be very good company. I believe our being here will but embarrass the interview.

MARLOW:

Not in the least, Mr Hastings. We like your company of all things. (*To him*) Zounds! George, sure you won't go? How can you leave us?

HASTINGS:

Our presence will but spoil conversation, so we'll retire to the next room. (*To him*) You don't consider, man, that we are to manage a little tête-à-tête of our own.

Exeunt Hastings *and* Miss Neville

MISS HARDCASTLE (*After a pause*):

But you have not been wholly an observer, I presume, sir: the ladies I should hope have employed some part of your addresses.

MARLOW (*Relapsing into timidity*):

Pardon me, madam, I—I—I—

MISS HARDCASTLE:

Then why take such pains to study and observe them?

MARLOW:

As yet I have studied—only—to—deserve them.

MISS HARDCASTLE:

And that some say is the very worst way to obtain them.

MARLOW:

Perhaps so, madam. But I love to converse only with the more grave and sensible part of the sex.——But I'm afraid I grow tiresome.

MISS HARDCASTLE:

Not at all, sir; there is nothing I like so much as grave conversation myself; I could hear it for ever. Indeed I have often been surprised how a man of sentiment could ever admire those light airy pleasures, where nothing reaches the heart.

MARLOW:

It's——a disease——of the mind, madam. In the variety of tastes there must be some who wanting a relish——for—— um-a-um.

MISS HARDCASTLE:

I understand you, sir. There must be some, who wanting a relish for refined pleasures, pretend to despise what they are incapable of tasting.

MARLOW:

My meaning, madam, but infinitely better expressed. And I can't help observing——a——

MISS HARDCASTLE (*Aside*):

Who could ever suppose this fellow impudent upon some occasions? (*To him*) You were going to observe, sir——

MARLOW:

I was observing, madam——I protest, madam, I forget what I was going to observe.

MISS HARDCASTLE (*Aside*):

I vow and so do I. (*To him*) You were observing, sir, that in this age of hypocrisy—something about hypocrisy, sir.

MARLOW:

Yes, madam. In this age of hypocrisy there are few who upon strict enquiry do not—a—a—a——

MISS HARDCASTLE:

I understand you perfectly, sir.

MARLOW (*Aside*):

Egad! and that's more than I do myself.

MISS HARDCASTLE:

You mean that in this hypocritical age there are few that do not condemn in public what they practise in private, and think they pay every debt to virtue when they praise it.

MARLOW:

True, madam; those who have most virtue in their mouths, have least of it in their bosoms. But I'm sure I tire you, madam.

MISS HARDCASTLE:

Not in the least, sir; there's something so agreeable and spirited in your manner, such life and force—pray, sir, go on.

MARLOW:

Yes, madam. I was saying——that there are some occasions——when a total want of courage, madam, destroys all the——and puts us——upon a——a——a——

MISS HARDCASTLE:

I agree with you entirely, a want of courage upon some occasions assumes the appearance of ignorance, and betrays us when we most want to excel. I beg you'll proceed.

MARLOW:

Yes, madam. Morally speaking, madam—but I see Miss Neville expecting us in the next room. I would not intrude for the world.

MISS HARDCASTLE:

I protest, sir, I never was more agreeably entertained in all my life. Pray go on.

MARLOW:

Yes, madam. I was——But she beckons us to join her. Madam, shall I do myself the honour to attend you?

MISS HARDCASTLE:

Well then, I'll follow.

MARLOW (*Aside*):

This pretty smooth dialogue has done for me.   *Exit*

MISS HARDCASTLE:

Ha! ha! ha! Was there ever such a sober sentimental interview? I'm certain he scarce looked in my face the whole time. Yet the fellow, but for his unaccountable bashfulness, is pretty well too. He has good sense, but then so buried in his fears, that it fatigues one more than ignorance. If I could teach him a little confidence, it would be doing somebody that I know of a piece of service. But who is that somebody?—that, faith, is a question I can scarce answer.   *Exit*

Enter Tony *and* Miss Neville, *followed by* Mrs Hardcastle *and* Hastings

TONY:

What do you follow me for, cousin Con? I wonder you're not ashamed to be so very engaging.

MISS NEVILLE:

I hope, cousin, one may speak to one's own relations, and not be to blame.

TONY:

>Ay, but I know what sort of a relation you want to make me though; but it won't do. I tell you, cousin Con, it won't do, so I beg you'll keep your distance, I want no nearer relationship.
>
>*She follows coqueting him to the Back Scene*

MRS HARDCASTLE:

>Well! I vow, Mr Hastings, you are very entertaining. There's nothing in the world I love to talk of so much as London, and the fashions, though I was never there myself.

HASTINGS:

>Never there! You amaze me! From your air and manner, I concluded you had been bred all your life either at Ranelagh, St James's, or Tower Wharf.

MRS HARDCASTLE:

>Oh! Sir, you're only pleased to say so. We country persons can have no manner at all. I'm in love with the town, and that serves to raise me above some of our neighbouring rustics; but who can have a manner, that has never seen the Pantheon, the Grotto Gardens, the Borough, and such places where the Nobility chiefly resort? All I can do, is to enjoy London at second-hand. I take care to know every tête-à-tête from the *Scandalous Magazine,* and have all the fashions, as they come out, in a letter from the two Miss Rickets of Crooked Lane. Pray how do you like this head, Mr Hastings?

HASTINGS:

>Extremely elegant and *dégagée,* upon my word, madam. Your *Friseur* is a Frenchman, I suppose?

MRS HARDCASTLE:

>I protest I dressed it myself from a print in the *Ladies Memorandum-book* for the last year.

HASTINGS:

>Indeed. Such a head in a side-box, at the Playhouse, would draw as many gazers as my Lady Mayoress at a City Ball.

MRS HARDCASTLE:

>I vow, since inoculation began, there is no such thing to be seen as a plain woman; so one must dress a little particular or one may escape in the crowd.

HASTINGS:

>But that can never be your case, madam, in any dress.
>
>*Bowing*

MRS HARDCASTLE:

>Yet, what signifies *my* dressing when I have such a piece of antiquity by my side as Mr Hardcastle: all I can say will never argue down a single button from his clothes. I have often

wanted him to throw off his great flaxen wig, and where he was
bald, to plaster it over like my Lord Pately, with powder.

HASTINGS:

You are right, madam; for, as among the ladies, there are none
ugly, so among the men there are none old.

MRS HARDCASTLE:

But what do you think his answer was? Why, with his usual
Gothic vivacity, he said I only wanted him to throw off his wig
to convert it into a *tête* for my own wearing.

HASTINGS:

Intolerable! At your age you may wear what you please, and it
must become you.

MRS HARDCASTLE:

Pray, Mr Hastings, what do you take to be the most fashionable age about town?

HASTINGS:

Some time ago, forty was all the mode; but I'm told the ladies
intend to bring up fifty for the ensuing winter.

MRS HARDCASTLE:

Seriously? Then I shall be too young for the fashion.

HASTINGS:

No lady begins now to put on jewels till she's past forty. For
instance, Miss there, in a polite circle, would be considered as a
child, as a mere maker of samplers.

MRS HARDCASTLE:

And yet Mrs Niece thinks herself as much a woman, and is as
fond of jewels as the oldest of us all.

HASTINGS:

Your niece, is she? And that young gentleman, a brother of
yours, I should presume?

MRS HARDCASTLE:

My son, sir. They are contracted to each other. Observe their
little sports. They fall in and out ten times a day, as if they were
man and wife already. (*To them*) Well Tony, child, what soft
things are you saying to your cousin Constance this evening?

TONY:

I have been saying no soft things; but that it's very hard to be
followed about so. Ecod! I've not a place in the house now
that's left to myself but the stable.

MRS HARDCASTLE:

Never mind him, Con my dear. He's in another story behind
your back.

MISS NEVILLE:

There's something generous in my cousin's manner. He falls out before faces to be forgiven in private.

TONY:

That's a damned confounded——crack.

MRS HARDCASTLE:

Ah! he's a sly one. Don't you think they're like each other about the mouth, Mr Hastings? The Blenkinsop mouth to a T. They're of a size too. Back to back, my pretties, that Mr Hastings may see you. Come Tony.

TONY:

You had as good not make me, I tell you.   *Measuring*

MISS NEVILLE:

O lud! he has almost cracked my head.

MRS HARDCASTLE:

Oh the monster! For shame, Tony. You a man, and behave so!

TONY:

If I'm a man, let me have my fortin. Ecod! I'll not be made a fool of no longer.

MRS HARDCASTLE:

Is this, ungrateful boy, all that I'm to get for the pains I have taken in your education? I that have rocked you in your cradle, and fed that pretty mouth with a spoon! Did not I work that waistcoat to make you genteel? Did not I prescribe for you every day, and weep while the receipt was operating?

TONY:

Ecod! you had reason to weep, for you have been dosing me ever since I was born. I have gone through every receipt in the *Complete Huswife* ten times over; and you have thoughts of coursing me through *Quincy* next spring. But, ecod! I tell you, I'll not be made a fool of no longer.

MRS HARDCASTLE:

Wasn't it all for your good, viper? Wasn't it all for your good?

TONY:

I wish you'd let me and my good alone then. Snubbing this way when I'm in spirits. If I'm to have any good, let it come of itself; not to keep dinging it, dinging it into one so.

MRS HARDCASTLE:

That's false; I never see you when you're in spirits. No, Tony, you then go to the alehouse or kennel. I'm never to be delighted with your agreeable, wild notes, unfeeling monster!

TONY:

Ecod! Mama, your own notes are the wildest of the two.

MRS HARDCASTLE:

Was ever the like? But I see he wants to break my heart, I see he does.

HASTINGS:

Dear madam, permit me to lecture the young gentleman a little. I'm certain I can persuade him to his duty.

MRS HARDCASTLE:

Well! I must retire. Come, Constance, my love. You see Mr Hastings, the wretchedness of my situation: was ever poor woman so plagued with a dear, sweet, pretty, provoking, undutiful boy.

Exeunt Mrs Hardcastle *and* Miss Neville

TONY (*Singing*):

'There was a young man riding by, and fain would have his will. Rang do didlo dee'. Don't mind her. Let her cry. It's the comfort of her heart. I have seen her and sister cry over a book for an hour together, and they said, they liked the book the better the more it made them cry.

HASTINGS:

Then you're no friend to the ladies, I find, my pretty young gentleman?

TONY:

That's as I find 'em.

HASTINGS:

Not to her of your mother's choosing, I dare answer? And yet she appears to me a pretty well-tempered girl.

TONY:

That's because you don't know her as well as I. Ecod! I know every inch about her; and there's not a more bitter cantankerous toad in all Christendom.

HASTINGS (*Aside*):

Pretty encouragement this for a lover!

TONY:

I have seen her since the height of that. She has as many tricks as a hare in a thicket, or a colt the first day's breaking.

HASTINGS:

To me she appears sensible and silent!

TONY:

Ay, before company. But when she's with her playmates she's as loud as a hog in a gate.

HASTINGS:

But there is a meek modesty about her that charms me.

TONY:

Yes, but curb her never so little, she kicks up, and you're flung in a ditch.

HASTINGS:

Well, but you must allow her a little beauty.—Yes, you must allow her some beauty.

TONY:

Bandbox! She's all a made up thing, mun. Ah! could you but see Bet Bouncer of these parts, you might then talk of beauty. Ecod, she has two eyes as black as sloes, and cheeks as broad and red as a pulpit cushion. She'd make two of she.

HASTINGS:

Well, what say you to a friend that would take this bitter bargain off your hands?

TONY:

Anon?

HASTINGS:

Would you thank him that would take Miss Neville and leave you to happiness and your dear Betsy?

TONY:

Ay; but where is there such a friend, for who would take *her*?

HASTINGS:

I am he. If you but assist me, I'll engage to whip her off to France, and you shall never hear more of her.

TONY:

Assist you! Ecod I will, to the last drop of my blood. I'll clap a pair of horses to your chaise that shall trundle you off in a twinkling, and maybe get you a part of her fortin beside, in jewels, that you little dream of.

HASTINGS:

My dear Squire, this looks like a lad of spirit.

TONY:

Come along then, and you shall see more of my spirit before you have done with me. (*Singing*) 'We are the boys that fears no noise where the thundering cannons roar'.

Exeunt

Act III, Scene i

Enter Hardcastle

HARDCASTLE:

What could my old friend Sir Charles mean by recommending his son as the modestest young man in town? To me he appears the most impudent piece of brass that ever spoke with a tongue. He has taken possession of the easy chair by the fireside already. He took off his boots in the parlour, and desired me to see them taken care of. I'm desirous to know how his impudence affects my daughter.—She will certainly be shocked at it.

Enter Miss Hardcastle, *plainly dressed*

HARDCASTLE:

Well, my Kate, I see you have changed your dress as I bid you; and yet, I believe, there was no great occasion.

MISS HARDCASTLE:

I find such a pleasure, sir, in obeying your commands, that I take care to observe them without ever debating their propriety.

HARDCASTLE:

And yet, Kate, I sometimes give you some cause, particularly when I recommended my *modest* gentleman to you as a lover today.

MISS HARDCASTLE:

You taught me to expect something extraordinary, and I find the original exceeds the description.

HARDCASTLE:

I was never so surprised in my life! He has quite confounded all my faculties!

MISS HARDCASTLE:

I never saw anything like it: and a man of the world too!

HARDCASTLE:

Ay, he learned it all abroad,—what a fool was I, to think a young man could learn modesty by travelling. He might as soon learn wit at a masquerade.

MISS HARDCASTLE:

It seems all natural to him.

HARDCASTLE:

A good deal assisted by bad company and a French dancing-master.

MISS HARDCASTLE:

Sure you mistake, papa! a French dancing-master could never have taught him that timid look,—that awkward address,—that bashful manner——

HARDCASTLE:

Whose look? whose manner? child!

MISS HARDCASTLE:

Mr Marlow's: his *mauvaise honte,* his timidity, struck me at the first sight.

HARDCASTLE:

Then your first sight deceived you; for I think him one of the most brazen first sights that ever astonished my senses.

MISS HARDCASTLE:

Sure, sir, you rally! I never saw anyone so modest.

HARDCASTLE:

And can you be serious! I never saw such a bouncing swaggering puppy since I was born. Bully Dawson was but a fool to him.

MISS HARDCASTLE:

Surprising! He met me with a respectful bow, a stammering voice, and a look fixed on the ground.

HARDCASTLE:

He met me with loud voice, a lordly air, and a familiarity that froze me to death.

MISS HARDCASTLE:

He treated me with diffidence and respect; censured the manners of the age; admired the prudence of girls that never laughed; tired me with apologies for being tiresome; then left the room with a bow, and, madam, I would not for the world detain you.

HARDCASTLE:

He spoke to me as if he knew me all his life before. Asked twenty questions, and never waited for an answer. Interrupted my best remarks with some silly pun, and when I was in my best story of the Duke of Marlborough and Prince Eugene, he asked if I had not a good hand at making punch. Yes, Kate, he asked your father if he was a maker of punch!

MISS HARDCASTLE:

One of us must certainly be mistaken.

HARDCASTLE:

If he be what he has shown himself, I'm determined he shall never have my consent.

MISS HARDCASTLE:

And if he be the sullen thing I take him, he shall never have mine.

HARDCASTLE:

In one thing then we are agreed—to reject him.

MISS HARDCASTLE:

Yes. But upon conditions. For if you should find him less impudent, and I more presuming; if you find him more respectful, and I more importunate——I don't know——the fellow is well enough for a man—certainly we don't meet many such at a horse race in the country.

HARDCASTLE:

If we should find him so——but that's impossible. The first appearance has done my business. I'm seldom deceived in that.

MISS HARDCASTLE:

And yet there may be many good qualities under that first appearance.

HARDCASTLE:

Ay, when a girl finds a fellow's outside to her taste, she then sets about guessing the rest of his furniture. With her, a smooth face stands for good sense, and a genteel figure for every virtue.

MISS HARDCASTLE:

I hope, sir, a conversation begun with a compliment to my good sense won't end with a sneer at my understanding?

HARDCASTLE:

Pardon me, Kate. But if young Mr Brazen can find the art of reconciling contradictions, he may please us both, perhaps.

MISS HARDCASTLE:

And as one of us must be mistaken, what if we go to make further discoveries?

HARDCASTLE:

Agreed. But depend on't I'm in the right.

MISS HARDCASTLE:

And depend on't I'm not much in the wrong. *Exeunt*

Enter Tony *running in with a Casket*

TONY:

Ecod! I have got them. Here they are. My cousin Con's necklaces, bobs and all. My mother shan't cheat the poor souls out of their fortune neither. Oh! my genus, is that you?

Enter Hastings

HASTINGS:

My dear friend, how have you managed with your mother? I hope you have amused her with pretending love for your cousin, and that you are willing to be reconciled at last? Our horses will be refreshed in a short time, and we shall soon be ready to set off.

TONY:

And here's something to bear your charges by the way (*Giving the Casket*). Your sweetheart's jewels. Keep them, and hang those, I say, that would rob you of one of them.

HASTINGS:

But how have you procured them from your mother?

TONY:

Ask me no questions, and I'll tell you no fibs. I procured them by the rule of thumb. If I had not a key to every drawer in mother's bureau, how could I go to the alehouse so often as I do? An honest man may rob himself of his own at any time.

HASTINGS:

Thousands do it every day. But to be plain with you; Miss Neville is endeavouring to procure them from her aunt this very instant. If she succeeds, it will be the most delicate way at least of obtaining them.

TONY:

Well, keep them, till you know how it will be. But I know how it will be well enough, she'd as soon part with the only sound tooth in her head.

HASTINGS:

But I dread the effects of her resentment, when she finds she has lost them.

TONY:

Never you mind her resentment, leave *me* to manage that. I don't value her resentment the bounce of a cracker. Zounds! here they are. Morris. Prance. *Exit* Hastings

Enter Mrs Hardcastle, Miss Neville

MRS HARDCASTLE:

Indeed, Constance, you amaze me. Such a girl as you want jewels? It will be time enough for jewels, my dear, twenty years hence, when your beauty begins to want repairs.

MISS NEVILLE:

But what will repair beauty at forty, will certainly improve it at twenty, madam.

MRS HARDCASTLE:

Yours, my dear, can admit of none. That natural blush is beyond a thousand ornaments. Besides, child, jewels are quite out at present. Don't you see half the ladies of our acquaintance, my Lady Kill-day-light, and Mrs Crump, and the rest of them, carry their jewels to town, and bring nothing but paste and marcasites back.

MISS NEVILLE:

But who knows, madam, but somebody that shall be nameless would like me best with all my little finery about me?

MRS HARDCASTLE:

> Consult your glass, my dear, and then see, if with such a pair of eyes, you want any better sparklers. What do you think, Tony, my dear, does your cousin Con want any jewels, in your eyes, to set off her beauty?

TONY:

> That's as thereafter may be.

MISS NEVILLE:

> My dear aunt, if you knew how it would oblige me.

MRS HARDCASTLE:

> A parcel of old-fashioned rose- and table-cut things. They would make you look like the court of King Solomon at a puppet-show. Besides, I believe I can't readily come at them. They may be missing for ought I know to the contrary.

TONY (*Apart to* Mrs Hardcastle):

> Then why don't you tell her so at once, as she's so longing for them. Tell her they're lost. It's the only way to quiet her. Say they're lost, and call me to bear witness.

MRS HARDCASTLE (*Apart to* Tony):

> You know, my dear, I'm only keeping them for you. So if I say they're gone, you'll bear me witness, will you? He! he! he!

TONY:

> Never fear me. Ecod! I'll say I saw them taken out with my own eyes.

MISS NEVILLE:

> I desire them but for a day, madam. Just to be permitted to show them as relics, and then they may be locked up again.

MRS HARDCASTLE:

> To be plain with you, my dear Constance; if I could find them, you should have them. They're missing, I assure you. Lost, for ought I know; but we must have patience wherever they are.

MISS NEVILLE:

> I'll not believe it; this is but a shallow pretence to deny me. I know they're too valuable to be so slightly kept, and as you are to answer for the loss.

MRS HARDCASTLE:

> Don't be alarmed, Constance. If they be lost, I must restore an equivalent. But my son knows they are missing, and not to be found.

TONY:

> That I can bear witness to. They are missing, and not to be found, I'll take my oath on't.

MRS HARDCASTLE:

You must learn resignation, my dear; for though we lose our fortune, yet we should not lose our patience. See me, how calm I am.

MISS NEVILLE:

Ay, people are generally calm at the misfortunes of others.

MRS HARDCASTLE:

Now, I wonder a girl of your good sense should waste a thought upon such trumpery. We shall soon find them; and, in the meantime, you shall make use of my garnets till your jewels be found.

MISS NEVILLE:

I detest garnets.

MRS HARDCASTLE:

The most becoming things in the world to set off a clear complexion. You have often seen how well they look upon me. You *shall* have them. *Exit*

MISS NEVILLE:

I dislike them of all things. You shan't stir.—Was ever anything so provoking to mislay my own jewels, and force me to wear her trumpery?

TONY:

Don't be a fool. If she gives you the garnets, take what you can get. The jewels are your own already. I have stolen them out of her bureau, and she does not know it. Fly to your spark, he'll tell you more of the matter. Leave me to manage *her*.

MISS NEVILLE:

My dear cousin. (*Exit*)

TONY:

Vanish. She's here, and has missed them already. Zounds! how she fidgets and spits about like a Catharine wheel.

Enter Mrs Hardcastle

MRS HARDCASTLE:

Confusion! thieves! robbers! We are cheated, plundered, broke open, undone.

TONY:

What's the matter, what's the matter, mama? I hope nothing has happened to any of the good family!

MRS HARDCASTLE:

We are robbed. My bureau has been broke open, the jewels taken out, and I'm undone.

TONY:

> Oh! is that all? Ha! ha! ha! By the laws, I never saw it better acted in my life. Ecod, I thought you was ruined in earnest, ha! ha! ha!

MRS HARDCASTLE:

> Why boy, I *am* ruined in earnest. My bureau has been broke open, and all taken away.

TONY:

> Stick to that; ha! ha! ha! Stick to that. I'll bear witness, you know, call me to bear witness.

MRS HARDCASTLE:

> I tell you, Tony, by all that's precious, the jewels are gone, and I shall be ruined for ever.

TONY:

> Sure I know they're gone, and I am to say so.

MRS HARDCASTLE:

> My dearest Tony, but hear me. They're gone, I say.

TONY:

> By the laws, mama, you make me for to laugh, ha! ha! I know who took them well enough, ha! ha! ha!

MRS HARDCASTLE:

> Was there ever such a blockhead, that can't tell the difference between jest and earnest? I tell you I'm not in jest, booby.

TONY:

> That's right, that's right: you must be in a bitter passion, and then nobody will suspect either of us. I'll bear witness that they are gone.

MRS HARDCASTLE:

> Was there ever such a cross-grained brute, that won't hear me! Can you bear witness that you're no better than a fool! Was ever poor woman so beset with fools on one hand, and thieves on the other?

TONY:

> I can bear witness to that.

MRS HARDCASTLE:

> Bear witness again, you blockhead you, and I'll turn you out of the room directly. My poor niece, what will become of *her!* Do you laugh, you unfeeling brute, as if you enjoyed my distress?

TONY:

> I can bear witness to that.

MRS HARDCASTLE:

> Do you insult me, monster? I'll teach you to vex your mother, I will.

TONY:

I can bear witness to that.   *He runs off, she follows him*

Enter Miss Hardcastle *and* Maid

MISS HARDCASTLE:

What an unaccountable creature is that brother of mine, to send them to the house as an inn, ha! ha! I don't wonder at his impudence.

MAID:

But what is more, madam, the young gentleman, as you passed by in your present dress, asked me, if you were the barmaid? He mistook you for the barmaid, madam.

MISS HARDCASTLE:

Did he? Then as I live I'm resolved to keep up the delusion. Tell me, Pimple, how do you like my present dress? Don't you think I look something like Cherry in *The Beaux' Stratagem?*

MAID:

It's the dress, madam, that every lady wears in the country, but when she visits or receives company.

MISS HARDCASTLE:

And are you sure he does not remember my face or person?

MAID:

Certain of it.

MISS HARDCASTLE:

I vow I thought so; for though we spoke for some time together, yet his fears were such, that he never once looked up during the interview. Indeed, if he had, my bonnet would have kept him from seeing me.

MAID:

But what do you hope from keeping him in his mistake?

MISS HARDCASTLE:

In the first place, I shall be *seen,* and that is no small advantage to a girl who brings her face to market. Then I shall perhaps make an acquaintance, and that's no small victory gained over one who never addresses any but the wildest of her sex. But my chief aim is to take my gentleman off his guard, and like an invisible champion of romance examine the giant's force before I offer to combat.

MAID:

But are you sure you can act your part, and disguise your voice, so that he may mistake that, as he has already mistaken your person?

MISS HARDCASTLE:

Never fear me. I think I have got the true bar cant.—Did your honour call?—Attend the Lion there.——Pipes and tobacco for the Angel.—The Lamb has been outrageous this half hour.

MAID:

It will do, madam. But he's here. *Exit* Maid

Enter Marlow

MARLOW:

What a bawling in every part of the house; I have scarce a moment's repose. If I go to the best room, there I find my host and his story. If I fly to the gallery, there we have my hostess with her curtsey down to the ground. I have at last got a moment to myself, and now for recollection.

Walks and muses

MISS HARDCASTLE:

Did you call, sir? Did your honour call?

MARLOW (*Musing*):

As for Miss Hardcastle, she's too grave and sentimental for me.

MISS HARDCASTLE:

Did your honour call?

She still places herself before him, he turning away

MARLOW:

No, child. (*Musing*) Besides from the glimpse I had of her, I think she squints.

MISS HARDCASTLE:

I'm sure, sir, I heard the bell ring.

MARLOW:

No, no. (*Musing*) I have pleased my father, however, by coming down, and I'll tomorrow please myself by returning.

Taking out his Tablets, and perusing

MISS HARDCASTLE:

Perhaps the other gentleman called, sir.

MARLOW:

I tell you, no.

MISS HARDCASTLE:

I should be glad to know, sir. We have such a parcel of servants.

MARLOW:

No, no, I tell you. (*Looks full in her face*) Yes, child, I think I did call. I wanted——I wanted——I vow, child, you are vastly handsome.

MISS HARDCASTLE:

O la, sir, you'll make one ashamed.

MARLOW:

Never saw a more sprightly malicious eye. Yes, yes, my dear, I did call. Have you got any of your—a—what-d'ye-call-it in the house?

MISS HARDCASTLE:

No, sir, we have been out of that these ten days.

MARLOW:

One may call in this house, I find, to very little purpose. Suppose I should call for a taste, just by way of trial, of the nectar of your lips; perhaps I might be disappointed of that too.

MISS HARDCASTLE:

Nectar! nectar! that's a liquor there's no call for in these parts. French, I suppose. We keep no French wines here, sir.

MARLOW:

Of true English growth, I assure you.

MISS HARDCASTLE:

Then it's odd I should not know it. We brew all sorts of wines in this house, and I have lived here these eighteen years.

MARLOW:

Eighteen years! Why one would think, child, you kept the bar before you were born. How old are you?

MISS HARDCASTLE:

Oh! sir, I must not tell my age. They say women and music should never be dated.

MARLOW:

To guess at this distance, you can't be much above forty (*Approaching*). Yet nearer I don't think so much (*Approaching*). By coming close to some women they look younger still; but when we come very close indeed (*Attempting to kiss her*).

MISS HARDCASTLE:

Pray, sir, keep your distance. One would think you wanted to know one's age as they do horses, by mark of mouth.

MARLOW:

I protest, child, you use me extremely ill. If you keep me at this distance, how is it possible you and I can be ever acquainted?

MISS HARDCASTLE:

And who wants to be acquainted with you? I want no such acquaintance, not I. I'm sure you did not treat Miss Hardcastle that was here a while ago in this obstropalous manner. I'll warrant me, before her you looked dashed, and kept bowing to the ground, and talked, for all the world, as if you was before a Justice of Peace.

MARLOW (*Aside*):

> Egad! she has hit it, sure enough. (*To her*) In awe of her, child?
> Ha! ha! ha! A mere, awkward, squinting thing, no, no. I find
> you don't know me. I laughed, and rallied her a little; but I
> was unwilling to be too severe. No, I could not be too severe,
> curse me!

MISS HARDCASTLE:

> Oh! then, sir, you are a favourite, I find, among the ladies?

MARLOW:

> Yes, my dear, a great favourite. And yet, hang me, I don't see
> what they find in me to follow. At the Ladies Club in town, I'm
> called their agreeable Rattle. Rattle, child, is not my real name,
> but one I'm known by. My name is Solomons. Mr Solomons,
> my dear, at your service.
>
> *Offering to salute her*

MISS HARDCASTLE:

> Hold, sir; you were introducing me to your club, not to your-
> self. And you're so great a favourite there you say?

MARLOW:

> Yes, my dear. There's Mrs Mantrap, Lady Betty Blackleg, the
> Countess of Sligo, Mrs Longhorns, old Miss Biddy Buckskin,
> and your humble servant, keep up the spirit of the place.

MISS HARDCASTLE:

> Then it's a very merry place, I suppose.

MARLOW:

> Yes, as merry as cards, suppers, wine, and old women can
> make us.

MISS HARDCASTLE:

> And their agreeable Rattle, ha! ha! ha!

MARLOW (*Aside*):

> Egad! I don't quite like this chit. She looks knowing, methinks.
> You laugh, child!

MISS HARDCASTLE:

> I can't but laugh to think what time they all have for minding
> their work or their family.

MARLOW (*Aside*):

> All's well, she don't laugh at me. (*To her*) Do *you* ever work,
> child?

MISS HARDCASTLE:

> Ay, sure. There's not a screen or a quilt in the whole house but
> what can bear witness to that.

MARLOW:

    Odso! Then you must show me your embroidery. I embroider and draw patterns myself a little. If you want a judge of your work you must apply to me.

         Seizing her hand

MISS HARDCASTLE:

    Ay, but the colours don't look well by candlelight. You shall see all in the morning.   *Struggling*

MARLOW:

    And why not now, my angel? Such beauty fires beyond the power of resistance.——Pshaw! the father here! My old luck: I never nicked seven that I did not throw ames ace three times following.   *Exit* Marlow

Enter Hardcastle, *who stands in surprise*

HARDCASTLE:

    So, madam! So I find *this* is your *modest* lover. This is your humble admirer that kept his eyes fixed on the ground, and only adored at humble distance. Kate, Kate, art thou not ashamed to deceive thy father so?

MISS HARDCASTLE:

    Never trust me, dear papa, but he's still the modest man I first took him for, you'll be convinced of it as well as I.

HARDCASTLE:

    By the hand of my body I believe his impudence is infectious! Didn't I see him seize your hand? Didn't I see him haul you about like a milkmaid? and now you talk of his respect and his modesty, forsooth!

MISS HARDCASTLE:

    But if I shortly convince you of his modesty, that he has only the faults that will pass off with time, and the virtues that will improve with age, I hope you'll forgive him.

HARDCASTLE:

    The girl would actually make one run mad! I tell you I'll not be convinced. I am convinced. He has scarcely been three hours in the house, and he has already encroached on all my prerogatives. You may like his impudence, and call it modesty. But my son-in-law, madam, must have very different qualifications.

MISS HARDCASTLE:

    Sir, I ask but this night to convince you.

HARDCASTLE:

> You shall not have half the time, for I have thoughts of turning him out this very hour.

MISS HARDCASTLE:

> Give me that hour then, and I hope to satisfy you.

HARDCASTLE:

> Well, an hour let it be then. But I'll have no trifling with your father. All fair and open, do you mind me?

MISS HARDCASTLE:

> I hope, sir, you have ever found that I considered your commands as my pride; for your kindness is such, that my duty as yet has been inclination.   *Exeunt*

Act IV, Scene i

Enter Hastings *and* Miss Neville

HASTINGS:

> You surprise me! Sir Charles Marlow expected here this night? Where have you had your information?

MISS NEVILLE:

> You may depend upon it. I just saw his letter to Mr Hardcastle, in which he tells him he intends setting out a few hours after his son.

HASTINGS:

> Then, my Constance, all must be completed before he arrives. He knows me; and should he find me here, would discover my name, and perhaps my designs, to the rest of the family.

MISS NEVILLE:

> The jewels, I hope, are safe.

HASTINGS:

> Yes, yes. I have sent them to Marlow, who keeps the keys of our baggage. In the meantime, I'll go to prepare matters for our elopement. I have had the Squire's promise of a fresh pair of horses; and, if I should not see him again, will write him further directions.   *Exit*

MISS NEVILLE:

> Well! success attend you. In the meantime, I'll go amuse my aunt with the old pretence of a violent passion for my cousin.
>
>   *Exit*

Enter Marlow, *followed by a* Servant

MARLOW:

> I wonder what Hastings could mean by sending me so valuable a thing as a casket to keep for him, when he knows the only place I have is the seat of a post-coach at an inn-door. Have you deposited the casket with the landlady, as I ordered you? Have you put it into her own hands?

SERVANT:

> Yes, your honour.

MARLOW:

> She said she'd keep it safe, did she?

SERVANT:

> Yes, she said she'd keep it safe enough; she asked me, how I came by it? and she said she had a great mind to make me give an account of myself. *Exit* Servant

MARLOW:

> Ha! ha! ha! They're safe however. What an unaccountable set of beings have we got amongst! This little barmaid though runs in my head most strangely, and drives out the absurdities of all the rest of the family. She's mine, she must be mine, or I'm greatly mistaken.

Enter Hastings

HASTINGS:

> Bless me! I quite forgot to tell her that I intended to prepare at the bottom of the garden. Marlow here, and in spirits too!

MARLOW:

> Give me joy, George! Crown me, shadow me with laurels! Well, George, after all, we modest fellows don't want for success among the women.

HASTINGS:

> Some women you mean. But what success has your honour's modesty been crowned with now, that it grows so insolent upon us?

MARLOW:

> Didn't you see the tempting, brisk, lovely, little thing that runs about the house with a bunch of keys to its girdle?

HASTINGS:

> Well! and what then?

MARLOW:

> She's mine, you rogue you. Such fire, such motion, such eyes, such lips——but, egad! she would not let me kiss them though.

HASTINGS:

But are you so sure, so very sure of her?

MARLOW:

Why man, she talked of showing me her work above-stairs, and I am to improve the pattern.

HASTINGS:

But how can *you*, Charles, go about to rob a woman of her honour?

MARLOW:

Pshaw! pshaw! we all know the honour of the barmaid of an inn. I don't intend to *rob* her, take my word for it, there's nothing in this house, I shan't honestly *pay* for.

HASTINGS:

I believe the girl has virtue.

MARLOW:

And if she has, I should be the last man in the world that would attempt to corrupt it.

HASTINGS:

You have taken care, I hope, of the casket I sent you to lock up? It's in safety?

MARLOW:

Yes, yes. It's safe enough. I have taken care of it. But how could you think the seat of a post-coach at an inn-door a place of safety? Ah! numbskull! I have taken better precautions for you than you did for yourself.——I have——

HASTINGS:

What!

MARLOW:

I have sent it to the landlady to keep for you.

HASTINGS:

To the landlady!

MARLOW:

The landlady.

HASTINGS:

You did.

MARLOW:

I did. She's to be answerable for its forthcoming, you know.

HASTINGS:

Yes, she'll bring it forth, with a witness.

MARLOW:

Wasn't I right? I believe you'll allow that I acted prudently upon this occasion?

HASTINGS (*Aside*):

He must not see my uneasiness.

MARLOW:

You seem a little disconcerted though, methinks. Sure nothing has happened?

HASTINGS:

No, nothing. Never was in better spirits in all my life. And so you left it with the landlady who, no doubt, very readily undertook the charge?

MARLOW:

Rather too readily. For she not only kept the casket; but, through her great precaution, was going to keep the messenger too. Ha! ha! ha!

HASTINGS:

He! he! he! They're safe however.

MARLOW:

As a guinea in a miser's purse.

HASTINGS (*Aside*):

So now all hopes of fortune are at an end, and we must set off without it. (*To him*) Well, Charles, I'll leave you to your meditations on the pretty barmaid, and, he! he! he! may you be as successful for yourself as you have been for me.

Exit

MARLOW:

Thank ye, George! I ask no more. Ha! ha! ha!

Enter Hardcastle

HARDCASTLE:

I no longer know my own house. It's turned all topsy-turvy. His servants have got drunk already. I'll bear it no longer, and yet, from my respect for his father, I'll be calm. (*To him*) Mr Marlow, your servant, I'm your very humble servant.

Bowing low

MARLOW:

Sir, your humble servant. (*Aside*) What's to be the wonder now?

HARDCASTLE:

I believe, sir, you must be sensible, sir, that no man alive ought to be more welcome than your father's son, sir. I hope you think so?

MARLOW:

I do from my soul, sir. I don't want much entreaty. I generally make my father's son welcome wherever he goes.

HARDCASTLE:

I believe you do, from my soul, sir. But though I say nothing to your own conduct, that of your servants is insufferable.

Their manner of drinking is setting a very bad example in this house, I assure you.

MARLOW:

I protest, my very good sir, that's no fault of mine. If they don't drink as they ought *they* are to blame. I ordered them not to spare the cellar. I did, I assure you. (*To the Side Scene*) Here, let one of my servants come up. (*To him*) My positive directions were, that as I did not drink myself, they should make up for my deficiencies below.

HARDCASTLE:

Then they had your orders for what they do! I'm satisfied!

MARLOW:

They had, I assure you. You shall hear from one of themselves.

Enter Servant *drunk*

MARLOW:

You, Jeremy! Come forward, sirrah! What were my orders? Were you not told to drink freely, and call for what you thought fit, for the good of the house?

HARDCASTLE (*Aside*):

I begin to lose my patience.

SERVANT:

Please your honour, liberty and Fleet Street for ever! Though I'm but a servant, I'm as good as another man. I'll drink for no man before supper, sir, damme! Good liquor will sit upon a good supper, but a good supper will not sit upon——hiccup——upon my conscience, sir.

MARLOW:

You see, my old friend, the fellow is as drunk as he can possibly be. I don't know what you'd have more, unless you'd have the poor devil soused in a beer-barrel.

HARDCASTLE:

Zounds! He'll drive me distracted if I contain myself any longer. Mr Marlow, sir; I have submitted to your insolence for more than four hours, and I see no likelihood of its coming to an end. I'm now resolved to be master here, sir, and I desire that you and your drunken pack may leave my house directly.

MARLOW:

Leave your house!——Sure you jest, my good friend? What, when I'm doing what I can to please you?

HARDCASTLE:

I tell you, sir, you don't please me; so I desire you'll leave my house.

MARLOW:

Sure you cannot be serious? At this time o'night, and such a night. You only mean to banter me?

HARDCASTLE:

I tell you, sir, I'm serious; and, now that my passions are roused, I say this house is mine, sir; this house is mine, and I command you to leave it directly.

MARLOW:

Ha! ha! ha! A puddle in a storm. I shan't stir a step, I assure you. (*In a serious tone*) This, your house, fellow! It's my house. This is my house. Mine, while I choose to stay. What right have you to bid me leave this house, sir? I never met with such impudence, curse me, never in my whole life before.

HARDCASTLE:

Nor I, confound me if ever I did. To come to my house, to call for what he likes, to turn me out of my own chair, to insult the family, to order his servants to get drunk, and then to tell me, 'This house is mine, sir'. By all that's impudent it makes me laugh. Ha! ha! ha! Pray, sir, (*Bantering*) as you take the house, what think you of taking the rest of the furniture? There's a pair of silver candlesticks, and there's a firescreen, and here's a pair of brazen-nosed bellows, perhaps you may take a fancy to them?

MARLOW:

Bring me your bill, sir, bring me your bill, and let's make no more words about it.

HARDCASTLE:

There are a set of prints too. What think you of the *Rake's Progress* for your own apartment?

MARLOW:

Bring me your bill, I say; and I'll leave you and your infernal house directly.

HARDCASTLE:

Then there's a mahogany table, that you may see your own face in.

MARLOW:

My bill, I say.

HARDCASTLE:

I had forgot the great chair, for your own particular slumbers, after a hearty meal.

MARLOW:

Zounds! bring me my bill, I say, and let's hear no more on't.

HARDCASTLE:

Young man, young man, from your father's letter to me, I was taught to expect a well-bred modest man as a visitor here, but now I find him no better than a coxcomb and a bully; but he will be down here presently, and shall hear more of it.   *Exit*

MARLOW:

How's this! Sure I have not mistaken the house! Everything looks like an inn. The servants cry, 'Coming'. The attendance is awkward; the barmaid too to attend us. But she's here, and will further inform me. Whither so fast, child? A word with you.

Enter Miss Hardcastle

MISS HARDCASTLE:

Let it be short then. I'm in a hurry. (*Aside*) I believe he begins to find out his mistake, but it's too soon quite to undeceive him.

MARLOW:

Pray, child, answer me one question. What are you, and what may your business in this house be?

MISS HARDCASTLE:

A relation of the family, sir.

MARLOW:

What? A poor relation?

MISS HARDCASTLE:

Yes, sir. A poor relation appointed to keep the keys, and to see that the guests want nothing in my power to give them.

MARLOW:

That is, you act as the barmaid of this inn.

MISS HARDCASTLE:

Inn! O law—What brought that in your head? One of the best families in the county keep an inn! Ha! ha! ha! old Mr Hardcastle's house an inn!

MARLOW:

Mr Hardcastle's house! Is this Mr Hardcastle's house, child!

MISS HARDCASTLE:

Ay, sure. Whose else should it be?

MARLOW:

So then all's out, and I have been damnably imposed on. Oh, confound my stupid head, I shall be laughed at over the whole town. I shall be stuck up in *caricatura* in all the print-shops. The *Dullissimo Macaroni*. To mistake this house of all others for an inn, and my father's old friend for an inn-keeper. What a swaggering puppy must he take me for! What a silly puppy do I find myself! There again, may I be hanged, my dear, but I mistook you for the barmaid.

MISS HARDCASTLE:

Dear me! dear me! I'm sure there's nothing in my behaviour to put me upon a level with one of that stamp.

MARLOW:

Nothing, my dear, nothing. But I was in for a list of blunders, and could not help making you a subscriber. My stupidity saw everything the wrong way. I mistook your assiduity for assurance, and your simplicity for allurement. But it's over—This house I no more show *my* face in.

MISS HARDCASTLE:

I hope, sir, I have done nothing to disoblige you. I'm sure I should be sorry to affront any gentleman who has been so polite, and said so many civil things to me. I'm sure I should be sorry (*Pretending to cry*) if he left the family upon my account. I'm sure I should be sorry people said anything amiss, since I have no fortune but my character.

MARLOW (*Aside*):

By heaven, she weeps. This is the first mark of tenderness I ever had from a modest woman, and it touches me; (*To her*) excuse me, my lovely girl, you are the only part of the family I leave with reluctance. But to be plain with you, the difference of our birth, fortune, and education, make an honourable connection impossible; and I can never harbour a thought of seducing simplicity that trusted in my honour, or bringing ruin upon one, whose only fault was being too lovely.

MISS HARDCASTLE (*Aside*):

Generous man! I now begin to admire him. (*To him*) But I'm sure my family is as good as Miss Hardcastle's, and though I'm poor, that's no great misfortune to a contented mind, and, until this moment, I never thought that it was bad to want fortune.

MARLOW:

And why now, my pretty simplicity?

MISS HARDCASTLE:

Because it puts me at a distance from one, that if I had a thousand pound I would give it all too.

MARLOW (*Aside*):

This simplicity bewitches me, so that if I stay I'm undone. I must make one bold effort, and leave her. (*To her*) Your partiality in my favour, my dear, touches me most sensibly, and were I to live for myself alone, I could easily fix my choice. But I owe too much to the opinion of the world, too much to the authority of a father, so that—I can scarcely speak it—it affects me. Farewell. *Exit*

MISS HARDCASTLE:

I never knew half his merit till now. He shall not go, if I have power or art to detain him. I'll still preserve the character in which I stooped to conquer, but will undeceive my papa, who, perhaps, may laugh him out of his resolution.   *Exit*

Enter Tony, Miss Neville

TONY:

Ay, you may steal for yourselves the next time. I have done my duty. She has got the jewels again, that's a sure thing; but she believes it was all a mistake of the servants.

MISS NEVILLE:

But, my dear cousin, sure you won't forsake us in this distress? If she in the least suspects that I am going off, I shall certainly be locked up, or sent to my aunt Pedigree's, which is ten times worse.

TONY:

To be sure, aunts of all kinds are damned bad things. But what can I do? I have got you a pair of horses that will fly like Whistlejacket, and I'm sure you can't say but I have courted you nicely before her face. Here she comes, we must court a bit or two more, for fear she should suspect us.

They retire, and seem to fondle

Enter Mrs Hardcastle

MRS HARDCASTLE:

Well, I was greatly fluttered, to be sure. But my son tells me it was all a mistake of the servants. I shan't be easy, however, till they are fairly married, and then let her keep her own fortune. But what do I see! Fondling together, as I'm alive. I never saw Tony so sprightly before. Ah! have I caught you, my pretty doves! What, billing, exchanging stolen glances, and broken murmurs? Ah!

TONY:

As for murmurs, mother, we grumble a little now and then, to be sure. But there's no love lost between us.

MRS HARDCASTLE:

A mere sprinkling, Tony, upon the flame, only to make it burn brighter.

MISS NEVILLE:

Cousin Tony promises to give us more of his company at home. Indeed, he shan't leave us any more. It won't leave us cousin Tony, will it?

TONY:

Oh! it's a pretty creature. No, I'd sooner leave a hare in her form, the dogs in full cry, or my horse in a pound, than leave you when you smile upon one so. Your laugh makes you so becoming.

MISS NEVILLE:

Agreeable cousin! Who can help admiring that natural humour, that pleasant, broad, red, thoughtless, (*Patting his cheek*) ah! it's a bold face.

MRS HARDCASTLE:

Pretty innocence.

TONY:

I'm sure I always loved cousin Con's hazel eyes, and her pretty long fingers, that she twists this way and that, over the haspicholls, like a parcel of bobbins.

MRS HARDCASTLE:

Ah, he would charm the bird from the tree. I was never so happy before. My boy takes after his father, poor Mr Lumpkin, exactly. The jewels, my dear Con, shall be yours incontinently. You shall have them. Isn't he a sweet boy, my dear? You shall be married tomorrow, and we'll put off the rest of his education, like Dr Drowsy's sermons, to a fitter opportunity.

Enter Diggory

DIGGORY:

Where's the Squire? I have got a letter for your worship.

TONY:

Give it to my mama. She reads all my letters first.

DIGGORY:

I had orders to deliver it into your own hands.

TONY:

Who does it come from?

DIGGORY:

Your worship mun ask that o' the letter itself.

TONY:

I could wish to know, though.

Turning the letter, and gazing on it

MISS NEVILLE (*Aside*):

Undone, undone. A letter to him from Hastings. I know the hand. If my aunt sees it, we are ruined for ever. I'll keep her employed a little if I can. (*To* Mrs Hardcastle) But I have not told you, madam, of my cousin's smart answer just now to Mr

Marlow. We so laughed—You must know, madam—this way a little, for he must not hear us. *They confer*

TONY (*Still gazing*):

A damned cramp piece of penmanship, as ever I saw in my life. I can read your print-hand very well. But here there are such handles, and shanks, and dashes, that one can scarce tell the head from the tail. 'To Anthony Lumpkin, Esquire'. It's very odd, I can read the outside of my letters, where my own name is, well enough. But when I come to open it, it's all—buzz. That's hard, very hard; for the inside of the letter is always the cream of the correspondence.

MRS HARDCASTLE:

Ha! ha! ha! Very well, very well. And so my son was too hard for the philosopher.

MISS NEVILLE:

Yes, madam; but you must hear the rest, madam. A little more this way, or he may hear us. You'll hear how he puzzled him again.

MRS HARDCASTLE:

He seems strangely puzzled now himself, methinks.

TONY (*Still gazing*):

A damned up and down hand, as if it was disguised in liquor. (*Reading*) 'Dear Squire'. Ay, that's that. Then there's an 'M', and a 'T', and an 'S', but whether the next be an 'izzard' or an 'R', confound me, I cannot tell.

MRS HARDCASTLE:

What's that, my dear? Can I give you any assistance?

MISS NEVILLE:

Pray, aunt, let me read it. Nobody reads a cramp hand better than I. (*Twitching the letter from her*) Do you know who it is from?

TONY:

Can't tell, except from Dick Ginger the feeder.

MISS NEVILLE:

Ay, so it is, (*Pretending to read*) 'Dear Squire, Hoping that you're in health, as I am at this present. The gentlemen of the Shake-bag club has cut the gentlemen of Goose-green quite out of feather. The odds—um—odd battle—um—long fighting'—um—here, here, it's all about cocks, and fighting; it's of no consequence, here, put it up, put it up.

Thrusting the crumpled letter upon him

TONY:

But I tell you, Miss, it's of all the consequence in the world. I would not lose the rest of it for a guinea. Here, mother, do you make it out. Of no consequence!

Giving Mrs Hardcastle *the letter*

MRS HARDCASTLE:

How's this! (*Reads*) 'Dear Squire, I'm now waiting for Miss Neville, with a post-chaise and pair, at the bottom of the garden, but I find my horses yet unable to perform the journey. I expect you'll assist us with a pair of fresh horses, as you promised. Dispatch is necessary, as the *hag* (ay the hag) your mother, will otherwise suspect us. Yours, Hastings. Grant me patience! I shall run distracted! My rage chokes me!

MISS NEVILLE:

I hope, madam, you'll suspend your resentment for a few moments, and not impute to me any impertinence, or sinister design that belongs to another.

MRS HARDCASTLE (*Curtseying very low*):

Fine spoken, madam, you are most miraculously polite and engaging, and quite the very pink of courtesy and circumspection, madam. (*Changing her tone*) And you, you great ill-fashioned oaf with scarce sense enough to keep your mouth shut. Were you too joined against me? But I'll defeat all your plots in a moment. As for you, madam, since you have got a pair of fresh horses ready, it would be cruel to disappoint them. So, if you please, instead of running away with your spark, prepare, this very moment, to run off with *me*. Your old aunt Pedigree will keep you secure, I'll warrant me. You too, sir, may mount your horse, and guard us upon the way. Here, Thomas, Roger, Diggory. I'll show you that I wish you better than you do yourselves. *Exit*

MISS NEVILLE:

So now I'm completely ruined.

TONY:

Ay, that's a sure thing.

MISS NEVILLE:

What better could be expected from being connected with such a stupid fool, and after all the nods and signs I made him.

TONY:

By the laws, Miss, it was your own cleverness, and not my stupidity, that did your business. You were so nice and so busy with your Shake-bags and Goose-greens, that I thought you could never be making believe.

Enter Hastings

HASTINGS:

So, sir, I find by my servant, that you have shown my letter, and betrayed us. Was this well done, young gentleman?

TONY:

Here's another. Ask Miss there who betrayed you. Ecod, it was her doing, not mine.

Enter Marlow

MARLOW:

So I have been finely used here among you. Rendered contemptible, driven into ill manners, despised, insulted, laughed at.

TONY:

Here's another. We shall have old Bedlam broke loose presently.

MISS NEVILLE:

And there, sir, is the gentleman to whom we all owe every obligation.

MARLOW:

What can I say to him, a mere boy, an idiot, whose ignorance and age are a protection?

HASTINGS:

A poor contemptible booby, that would but disgrace correction.

MISS NEVILLE:

Yet with cunning and malice enough to make himself merry with all our embarrassments.

HASTINGS:

An insensible cub.

MARLOW:

Replete with tricks and mischief.

TONY:

Baw! damme, but I'll fight you both one after the other,—— with baskets.

MARLOW:

As for him, he's below resentment. But your conduct, Mr Hastings, requires an explanation. You knew of my mistakes, yet would not undeceive me.

HASTINGS:

Tortured as I am with my own disappointments, is this a time for explanations! It is not friendly, Mr Marlow.

MARLOW:

But, sir—

MISS NEVILLE:

Mr Marlow, we never kept on your mistake, till it was too late to undeceive you. Be pacified.

Enter Servant

SERVANT:

My mistress desires you'll get ready immediately, madam. The horses are putting to. Your hat and things are in the next room. We are to go thirty miles before morning.

Exit Servant

MISS NEVILLE:

Well, well; I'll come presently.

MARLOW (*To* Hastings):

Was it well done, sir, to assist in rendering me ridiculous? To hang me out for the scorn of all my acquaintance? Depend upon it, sir, I shall expect an explanation.

HASTINGS:

Was it well done, sir, if you're upon that subject, to deliver what I entrusted to yourself, to the care of another, sir?

MISS NEVILLE:

Mr Hastings, Mr Marlow. Why will you increase my distress by this groundless dispute? I implore, I entreat you——

Enter Servant

SERVANT:

Your cloak, madam. My mistress is impatient.

MISS NEVILLE:

I come. Pray be pacified. If I leave you thus, I shall die with apprehension.

SERVANT:

Your fan, muff, and gloves, madam. The horses are waiting.

MISS NEVILLE:

Oh, Mr Marlow! if you knew what a scene of constraint and ill-nature lies before me, I'm sure it would convert your resentment into pity.

MARLOW:

I'm so distracted with a variety of passions, that I don't know what I do. Forgive me, madam. George, forgive me. You know my hasty temper, and should not exasperate it.

HASTINGS:

The torture of my situation is my only excuse.

MISS NEVILLE:

Well, my dear Hastings, if you have that esteem for me that I think, that I am sure you have, your constancy for three years will but increase the happiness of our future connection. If—

MRS HARDCASTLE (*Within*):

Miss Neville! Constance, why Constance, I say.

MISS NEVILLE:

I'm coming. Well, constancy. Remember, constancy is the word.

Exit

HASTINGS:

My heart! How can I support this? To be so near happiness, and such happiness.

MARLOW (*To* Tony):

You see now, young gentleman, the effects of your folly. What might be amusement to you, is here disappointment, and even distress.

TONY (*From a reverie*):

Ecod, I have hit it. It's here. Your hands. Yours and yours, my poor Sulky. My boots there, ho! Meet me two hours hence at the bottom of the garden; and if you don't find Tony Lumpkin a more good-natured fellow than you thought for, I'll give you leave to run me through the guts with a shoulder of mutton. Come along. My boots, ho!

Exeunt

Act V, Scene i

Scene Continues

Enter Hastings *and* Servant

HASTINGS:

You saw the old lady and Miss Neville drive off, you say.

SERVANT:

Yes, your honour. They went off in a post coach, and the young Squire went on horseback. They're thirty miles off by this time.

HASTINGS:

Then all my hopes are over.

SERVANT:

Yes, sir. Old Sir Charles is arrived. He and the old gentleman of the house have been laughing at Mr Marlow's mistake this half hour. They are coming this way.

HASTINGS:

Then I must not be seen. So now to my fruitless appointment at the bottom of the garden. This is about the time.

Exeunt

Enter Sir Charles *and* Hardcastle

HARDCASTLE:

Ha! ha! ha! The peremptory tone in which he sent forth his sublime commands.

SIR CHARLES:

And the reserve with which I suppose he treated all your advances.

HARDCASTLE:

And yet he might have seen something in me above a common inn-keeper, too.

SIR CHARLES:

Yes, Dick, but he mistook you for an uncommon inn-keeper, ha! ha! ha!

HARDCASTLE:

Well, I'm in too good spirits to think of anything but joy. Yes, my dear friend, this union of our families will make our personal friendship hereditary; and though my daughter's fortune is but small——

SIR CHARLES:

Why, Dick, will you talk of fortune to *me*? My son is possessed of more than a competence already, and can want nothing but a good and virtuous girl to share his happiness and increase it. If they like each other, as you say they do——

HARDCASTLE:

If, man? I tell you they *do* like each other. My daughter as good as told me so.

SIR CHARLES:

But girls are apt to flatter themselves, you know.

HARDCASTLE:

I saw him grasp her hand in the warmest manner myself; and here he comes to put you out of your 'ifs', I warrant him.

Enter Marlow

MARLOW:

    I come, sir, once more, to ask pardon for my strange conduct. I can scarce reflect on my insolence without confusion.

HARDCASTLE:

    Tut, boy, a trifle. You take it too gravely. An hour or two's laughing with my daughter will set all to rights again. She'll never like you the worse for it.

MARLOW:

    Sir, I shall be always proud of her approbation.

HARDCASTLE:

    Approbation is but a cold word, Mr Marlow; if I am not deceived, you have something more than approbation there-abouts. You take me.

MARLOW:

    Really, sir, I have not that happiness.

HARDCASTLE:

    Come, boy, I'm an old fellow, and know what's what, as well as you that are younger. I know what has passed between you; but mum.

MARLOW:

    Sure, sir, nothing has passed between us but the most profound respect on my side, and the most distant reserve on hers. You don't think, sir, that my impudence has been passed upon all the rest of the family?

HARDCASTLE:

    Impudence! No, I don't say that—Not quite impudence—Though girls like to be played with, and rumpled a little too sometimes. But she has told no tales, I assure you.

MARLOW:

    I never gave her the slightest cause.

HARDCASTLE:

    Well, well, I like modesty in its place well enough. But this is over-acting, young gentleman. You *may* be open. Your father and I will like you the better for it.

MARLOW:

    May I die, sir, if I ever——

HARDCASTLE:

    I tell you, she don't dislike you; and as I'm sure you like her——

MARLOW:

    Dear sir—I protest, sir——

HARDCASTLE:

    I see no reason why you should not be joined as fast as the parson can tie you.

MARLOW:

But hear me, sir——

HARDCASTLE:

Your father approves the match, I admire it, every moment's delay will be doing mischief, so——

MARLOW:

But why won't you hear me? By all that's just and true, I never gave Miss Hardcastle the slightest mark of my attachment, or even the most distant hint to suspect me of affection. We had but one interview, and that was formal, modest, and uninteresting.

HARDCASTLE (*Aside*):

This fellow's formal modest impudence is beyond bearing.

SIR CHARLES:

And you never grasped her hand, or made any protestations!

MARLOW:

As heaven is my witness, I came down in obedience to your commands. I saw the lady without emotion, and parted without reluctance. I hope you'll exact no further proofs of my duty, nor prevent me from leaving a house in which I suffer so many mortifications. *Exit*

SIR CHARLES:

I'm astonished at the air of sincerity with which he parted.

HARDCASTLE:

And I'm astonished at the deliberate intrepidity of his assurance.

SIR CHARLES:

I dare pledge my life and honour upon his truth.

HARDCASTLE:

Here comes my daughter, and I would stake my happiness upon her veracity.

Enter Miss Hardcastle

HARDCASTLE:

Kate, come hither, child. Answer us sincerely, and without reserve; has Mr Marlow made you any professions of love and affection.

MISS HARDCASTLE:

The question is very abrupt, sir! But since you require unreserved sincerity, I think he has.

HARDCASTLE (*To* Sir Charles):

You see.

SIR CHARLES:

And pray, madam, have you and my son had more than one interview?

MISS HARDCASTLE:

Yes, sir, several.

HARDCASTLE (*To* Sir Charles):

You see.

SIR CHARLES:

But did he profess any attachment?

MISS HARDCASTLE:

A lasting one.

SIR CHARLES:

Did he talk of love?

MISS HARDCASTLE:

Much, sir.

SIR CHARLES:

Amazing! And all this formally?

MISS HARDCASTLE:

Formally.

HARDCASTLE:

Now, my friend, I hope you are satisfied.

SIR CHARLES:

And how did he behave, madam?

MISS HARDCASTLE:

As most professed admirers do. Said some civil things of my face, talked much of his want of merit, and the greatness of mine; mentioned his heart, gave a short tragedy speech, and ended with pretended rapture.

SIR CHARLES:

Now I'm perfectly convinced, indeed. I know his conversation among women to be modest and submissive. This forward canting ranting manner by no means describes him, and I am confident, he never sat for the picture.

MISS HARDCASTLE:

Then what, sir, if I should convince you to your face of my sincerity? If you and my papa, in about half an hour, will place yourselves behind that screen, you shall hear him declare his passion to me in person.

SIR CHARLES:

Agreed. And if I find him what you describe, all my happiness in him must have an end. *Exit*

MISS HARDCASTLE:

And if you don't find him what I describe—I fear my happiness must never have a beginning. *Exeunt*

Act V, Scene ii

Scene changes to the Back of the Garden
Enter Hastings

HASTINGS:

What an idiot am I, to wait here for a fellow, who probably takes a delight in mortifying me. He never intended to be punctual, and I'll wait no longer. What do I see? It is he, and perhaps with news of my Constance.

Enter Tony, *booted and spattered*

HASTINGS:

My honest Squire! I now find you a man of your word. This looks like friendship.

TONY:

Ay, I'm your friend, and the best friend you have in the world, if you knew but all. This riding by night, by the bye, is cursedly tiresome. It has shook me worse than the basket of a stage-coach.

HASTINGS:

But how? Where did you leave your fellow travellers? Are they in safety? Are they housed?

TONY:

Five and twenty miles in two hours and a half is no such bad driving. The poor beasts have smoked for it: rabbit me, but I'd rather ride forty miles after a fox, than ten with such varment.

HASTINGS:

Well, but where have you left the ladies? I die with impatience.

TONY:

Left them? Why where should I leave them, but where I found them?

HASTINGS:

This is a riddle.

TONY:

Riddle me this then. What's that goes round the house, and round the house, and never touches the house?

HASTINGS:

I'm still astray.

TONY:

> Why that's it, mon. I have led them astray. By jingo, there's not a pond or slough within five miles of the place but they can tell the taste of.

HASTINGS:

> Ha! ha! ha! I understand; you took them in a round, while they supposed themselves going forward. And so you have at last brought them home again.

TONY:

> You shall hear. I first took them down Feather-bed Lane, where we stuck fast in the mud. I then rattled them crack over the stones of Up-and-down Hill—I then introduced them to the gibbet on Heavy-tree Heath, and from that, with a circumbendibus, I fairly lodged them in the horse-pond at the bottom of the garden.

HASTINGS:

> But no accident, I hope.

TONY:

> No, no. Only mother is confoundedly frightened. She thinks herself forty miles off. She's sick of the journey, and the cattle can scarce crawl. So if your own horses be ready, you may whip off with cousin, and I'll be bound that no soul here can budge a foot to follow you.

HASTINGS:

> My dear friend, how can I be grateful?

TONY:

> Ay, now it's dear friend, noble Squire. Just now, it was all idiot, cub, and run me through the guts. Damn *your* way of fighting, I say. After we take a knock in this part of the country, we kiss and be friends. But if you had run me through the guts, then I should be dead, and you might go kiss the hangman.

HASTINGS:

> The rebuke is just. But I must hasten to relieve Miss Neville; if you keep the old lady employed, I promise to take care of the young one.   *Exit* Hastings

TONY:

> Never fear me. Here she comes. Vanish. She's got from the pond, and draggled up to the waist like a mermaid.

Enter Mrs Hardcastle

MRS HARDCASTLE:

> Oh, Tony, I'm killed. Shook. Battered to death. I shall never survive it. That last jolt that laid us against the quickset hedge has done my business.

TONY:

> Alack, mama, it was all your own fault. You would be for running away by night, without knowing one inch of the way.

MRS HARDCASTLE:

> I wish we were at home again. I never met so many accidents in so short a journey. Drenched in the mud, overturned in a ditch, stuck fast in a slough, jolted to a jelly, and at last to lose our way. Whereabouts do you think we are, Tony?

TONY:

> By my guess we should be upon Crack-skull Common, about forty miles from home.

MRS HARDCASTLE:

> O lud! O lud! the most notorious spot in all the country. We only want a robbery to make a complete night on't.

TONY:

> Don't be afraid, mama, don't be afraid. Two of the five that kept here are hanged, and the other three may not find us. Don't be afraid. Is that a man that's galloping behind us? No; it's only a tree. Don't be afraid.

MRS HARDCASTLE:

> The fright will certainly kill me.

TONY:

> Do you see anything like a black hat moving behind the thicket?

MRS HARDCASTLE:

> O death!

TONY:

> No, it's only a cow. Don't be afraid, mama; don't be afraid.

MRS HARDCASTLE:

> As I'm alive, Tony, I see a man coming towards us. Ah! I'm sure on't. If he perceives us we are undone.

TONY (*Aside*):

> Father-in-law, by all that's unlucky, come to take one of his night walks. (*To her*) Ah, it's a highwayman, with pistols as long as my arm. A damned ill-looking fellow.

MRS HARDCASTLE:

> Good heaven defend us! He approaches.

TONY:

> Do you hide yourself in that thicket, and leave me to manage him. If there be any danger I'll cough and cry, Hem! When I cough be sure to keep close.

Mrs Hardcastle hides behind a tree in the Back Scene
Enter Hardcastle

HARDCASTLE:

> I'm mistaken, or I heard voices of people in want of help. Oh, Tony, is that you? I did not expect you so soon back. Are your mother and her charge in safety?

TONY:

> Very safe, sir, at my aunt Pedigree's. Hem!

MRS HARDCASTLE (*From behind*):

> Ah death! I find there's danger.

HARDCASTLE:

> Forty miles in three hours; sure, that's too much, my youngster.

TONY:

> Stout horses and willing minds make short journeys, as they say. Hem!

MRS HARDCASTLE (*From behind*):

> Sure he'll do the dear boy no harm.

HARDCASTLE:

> But I heard a voice here; I should be glad to know from whence it came?

TONY:

> It was I, sir, talking to myself, sir. I was saying that forty miles in four hours was very good going. Hem! As to be sure it was. Hem! I have got a sort of cold by being out in the air. We'll go in, if you please. Hem!

HARDCASTLE:

> But if you talked to yourself, you did not answer yourself. I am certain I heard two voices, and am resolved (*Raising his voice*) to find the other out.

MRS HARDCASTLE (*From behind*):

> Oh! he's coming to find me out. Oh!

TONY:

> What need you go, sir, if I tell you. Hem! I'll lay down my life for the truth—hem!—I'll tell you all, sir.
>
> *Detaining him*

HARDCASTLE:

> I tell you, I will not be detained. I insist on seeing. It's in vain to expect I'll believe you.

MRS HARDCASTLE (*Running forward from behind*):

O lud, he'll murder my poor boy, my darling. Here, good gentleman, whet your rage upon me. Take my money, my life, but
spare that young gentleman, spare my child, if you have any
mercy.

HARDCASTLE:

My wife! as I'm a Christian. From whence can she come, or
what does she mean!

MRS HARDCASTLE (*Kneeling*):

Take compassion on us, good Mr Highwayman. Take our
money, our watches, all we have, but spare our lives. We will
never bring you to justice, indeed we won't, good Mr Highwayman.

HARDCASTLE:

I believe the woman's out of her senses. What, Dorothy, don't
you know *me*?

MRS HARDCASTLE:

Mr Hardcastle, as I'm alive. My fears blinded me. But who, my
dear, could have expected to meet you here, in this frightful
place, so far from home? What has brought you to follow us?

HARDCASTLE:

Sure, Dorothy, you have not lost your wits? So far from home,
when you are within forty yards of your own door? (*To him*)
This is one of your old tricks, you graceless rogue you. (*To her*)
Don't you know the gate, and the mulberry-tree; and don't
you remember the horse-pond, my dear?

MRS HARDCASTLE:

Yes, I shall remember the horse-pond as long as I live; I have
caught my death in it. (*To Tony*) And it is to you, you graceless
varlet, I owe all this? I'll teach you to abuse your mother, I will.

TONY:

Ecod, mother, all the parish says you have spoiled me, and so
you may take the fruits on't.

MRS HARDCASTLE:

I'll spoil you, I will.   *Follows him off the stage. Exeunt*

HARDCASTLE:

There's morality, however, in his reply.   *Exit*

Enter Hastings *and* Miss Neville

HASTINGS:

My dear Constance, why will you deliberate thus? If we delay
a moment, all is lost for ever. Pluck up a little resolution, and
we shall soon be out of the reach of her malignity.

MISS NEVILLE:

> I find it impossible. My spirits are so sunk with the agitations I have suffered, that I am unable to face any new danger. Two or three years' patience will at last crown us with happiness.

HASTINGS:

> Such a tedious delay is worse than inconstancy. Let us fly, my charmer. Let us date our happiness from this very moment. Perish fortune. Love and content will increase what we possess beyond a monarch's revenue. Let me prevail.

MISS NEVILLE:

> No, Mr Hastings; no. Prudence once more comes to my relief, and I will obey its dictates. In the moment of passion, fortune may be despised, but it ever produces a lasting repentance. I'm resolved to apply to Mr Hardcastle's compassion and justice for redress.

HASTINGS:

> But though he had the will, he has not the power to relieve you.

MISS NEVILLE:

> But he has influence, and upon that I am resolved to rely.

HASTINGS:

> I have no hopes. But since you persist, I must reluctantly obey you. *Exeunt*

Act V, Scene iii

Enter Sir Charles *and* Miss Hardcastle

SIR CHARLES:

> What a situation am I in! If what you say appears, I shall then find a guilty son. If what he says be true, I shall then lose one that, of all others, I most wished for a daughter.

MISS HARDCASTLE:

> I am proud of your approbation, and to show I merit it, if you place yourselves as I directed, you shall hear his explicit declaration. But he comes.

SIR CHARLES:

> I'll to your father, and keep him to the appointment. *Exit* Sir Charles

Enter Marlow

MARLOW:

Though prepared for setting out, I come once more to take leave, nor did I, till this moment, know the pain I feel in the separation.

MISS HARDCASTLE (*In her own natural manner*):

I believe those sufferings cannot be very great, sir, which you can so easily remove. A day or two longer, perhaps, might lessen your uneasiness, by showing the little value of what you now think proper to regret.

MARLOW (*Aside*):

This girl every moment improves upon me. (*To her*) It must not be, madam. I have already trifled too long with my heart. My very pride begins to submit to my passion. The disparity of education and fortune, the anger of a parent, and the contempt of my equals, begin to lose their weight; and nothing can restore me to myself, but this painful effort of resolution.

MISS HARDCASTLE:

Then go, sir. I'll urge nothing more to detain you. Though my family be as good as hers you came down to visit, and my education, I hope, not inferior, what are these advantages without equal affluence? I must remain contented with the slight approbation of imputed merit; I must have only the mockery of your addresses, while all your serious aims are fixed on fortune.

Enter Hardcastle *and* Sir Charles *from behind*

SIR CHARLES:

Here, behind this screen.

HARDCASTLE:

Ay, ay, make no noise. I'll engage my Kate covers him with confusion at last.

MARLOW:

By heavens, madam, fortune was ever my smallest consideration. Your beauty at first caught my eye; for who could see that without emotion? But every moment that I converse with you, steals in some new grace, heightens the picture, and gives it stronger expression. What at first seemed rustic plainness, now appears refined simplicity. What seemed forward assurance, now strikes me as the result of courageous innocence, and conscious virtue.

SIR CHARLES:

What can it mean! He amazes me!

HARDCASTLE:

I told you how it would be. Hush!

MARLOW:

I am now determined to stay, madam, and I have too good an opinion of my father's discernment, when he sees you, to doubt his approbation.

MISS HARDCASTLE:

No, Mr Marlow, I will not, cannot detain you. Do you think I could suffer a connection, in which there is the smallest room for repentance? Do you think I would take the mean advantage of a transient passion, to load you with confusion? Do you think I could ever relish that happiness, which was acquired by lessening yours?

MARLOW:

By all that's good, I can have no happiness but what's in your power to grant me. Nor shall I ever feel repentance, but in not having seen your merits before. I will stay, even contrary to your wishes; and though you should persist to shun me, I will make my respectful assiduities atone for the levity of my past conduct.

MISS HARDCASTLE:

Sir, I must entreat you'll desist. As our acquaintance began, so let it end, in indifference. I might have given an hour or two to levity; but seriously, Mr Marlow, do you think I could ever submit to a connection, where *I* must appear mercenary, and *you* imprudent? Do you think I could ever catch at the confident addresses of a secure admirer?

MARLOW (*Kneeling*):

Does this look like security? Does this look like confidence? No, madam, every moment that shows me your merit, only serves to increase my diffidence and confusion. Here let me continue——

SIR CHARLES:

I can hold it no longer. Charles, Charles, how hast thou deceived me! Is this your indifference, your uninteresting conversation!

HARDCASTLE:

Your cold contempt; your formal interview? What have you to say now?

MARLOW:

That I'm all amazement! What can it mean!

HARDCASTLE:

It means that you can say and unsay things at pleasure. That you can address a lady in private, and deny it in public; that you have one story for us, and another for my daughter.

MARLOW:

Daughter!—this lady your daughter!

HARDCASTLE:

Yes, sir, my only daughter. My Kate, whose else should she be?

MARLOW:

Oh, the devil.

MISS HARDCASTLE:

Yes, sir, that very identical tall squinting lady you were pleased to take me for (*Curtseying*). She that you addressed as the mild, modest, sentimental man of gravity, and the bold forward agreeable Rattle of the Ladies Club; ha! ha! ha!

MARLOW:

Zounds, there's no bearing this; it's worse than death.

MISS HARDCASTLE:

In which of your characters, sir, will you give us leave to address you? As the faltering gentleman, with looks on the ground, that speaks just to be heard, and hates hypocrisy; or the loud confident creature, that keeps it up with Mrs Mantrap, and old Miss Biddy Buckskin, till three in the morning; ha! ha! ha!

MARLOW:

Oh, curse on my noisy head. I never attempted to be impudent yet, that I was not taken down. I must be gone.

HARDCASTLE:

By the hand of my body, but you shall not. I see it was all a mistake, and I am rejoiced to find it. You shall not stir, I tell you. I know she'll forgive you. Won't you forgive him, Kate? We'll all forgive you. Take courage, man.

They retire, she tormenting him, to the Back Scene

Enter Mrs Hardcastle, Tony

MRS HARDCASTLE:

So, so, they're gone off. Let them go, I care not.

HARDCASTLE:

Who gone?

MRS HARDCASTLE:

My dutiful niece and her gentleman, Mr Hastings, from Town. He who came down with our modest visitor here.

SIR CHARLES:

Who, my honest George Hastings? As worthy a fellow as lives, and the girl could not have made a more prudent choice.

HARDCASTLE:

Then, by the hand of my body, I'm proud of the connection.

MRS HARDCASTLE:

Well, if he has taken away the lady, he has not taken her fortune; that remains in this family to console us for her loss.

HARDCASTLE:

Sure Dorothy you would not be so mercenary?

MRS HARDCASTLE:

Ay, that's my affair, not yours.

HARDCASTLE:

But you know if your son, when of age, refuses to marry his cousin, her whole fortune is then at her own disposal.

MRS HARDCASTLE:

Ay, but he's not of age, and she has not thought proper to wait for his refusal.

Enter Hastings *and* Miss Neville

MRS HARDCASTLE (*Aside*):

What? returned so soon, I begin not to like it.

HASTINGS (*To* Hardcastle):

For my late attempt to fly off with your niece, let my present confusion be my punishment. We are now come back, to appeal from your justice to your humanity. By her father's consent, I first paid her my addresses, and our passions were first founded in duty.

MISS NEVILLE:

Since his death, I have been obliged to stoop to dissimulation to avoid oppression. In an hour of levity, I was ready even to give up my fortune to secure my choice. But I'm now recovered from the delusion, and hope from your tenderness what is denied me from a nearer connection.

MRS HARDCASTLE:

Pshaw, pshaw, this is all but the whining end of a modern novel.

HARDCASTLE:

Be it what it will, I'm glad they're come back to reclaim their due. Come hither, Tony boy. Do you refuse this lady's hand whom I now offer you?

TONY:

What signifies my refusing? You know I can't refuse her till I'm of age, father.

HARDCASTLE:

While I thought concealing your age, boy, was likely to conduce to your improvement, I concurred with your mother's desire to keep it secret. But since I find she turns it to a wrong use, I must now declare, you have been of age these last three months.

TONY:

Of age! Am I of age, father?

HARDCASTLE:

Above three months.

TONY:

Then you'll see the first use I'll make of my liberty. (*Taking* Miss Neville's *hand*) Witness all men by these presents, that I, Anthony Lumpkin, Esquire, of BLANK place, refuse you, Constantia Neville, spinster, of no place at all, for my true and lawful wife. So Constance Neville may marry whom she pleases, and Tony Lumpkin is his own man again.

SIR CHARLES:

O brave Squire.

HASTINGS:

My worthy friend.

MRS HARDCASTLE:

My undutiful offspring.

MARLOW:

Joy, my dear George, I give you joy sincerely. And could I prevail upon my little tyrant here to be less arbitrary, I should be the happiest man alive, if you would return me the favour.

HASTINGS (*To* Miss Hardcastle):

Come, madam, you are now driven to the very last scene of all your contrivances. I know you like him, I'm sure he loves you, and you must and shall have him.

HARDCASTLE (*Joining their hands*):

And I say so too. And Mr Marlow, if she makes as good a wife as she has a daughter, I don't believe you'll ever repent your bargain. So now to supper, tomorrow we shall gather all the poor of the parish about us, and the Mistakes of the Night shall be crowned with a merry morning; so, boy, take her; and as you have been mistaken in the mistress, my wish is, that you may never be mistaken in the wife.

Epilogue

By Dr Goldsmith

Well, having stooped to conquer with success,
And gained a husband without aid from dress,
Still as a Barmaid, I could wish it too,
As I have conquered him to conquer you:
And let me say, for all your resolution,
That pretty Barmaids have done execution.
Our life is all a play, composed to please,
We have our exits and our entrances.
The first act shows the simple country maid,
Harmless and young, of every thing afraid;
Blushes when hired, and with unmeaning action,
'I hopes as how to give you satisfaction.'
Her second act displays a livelier scene.—
Th'unblushing Barmaid of a country inn.
Who whisks about the house, at market caters,
Talks loud, coquets the guests, and scolds the waiters.
Next the scene shifts to town, and there she soars,
The chop house toast of ogling connoisseurs.
On Squires and Cits she there displays her arts,
And on the gridiron broils her lovers' hearts—
And as she smiles, her triumphs to complete,
Even Common Councilmen forget to eat.
The fourth act shows her wedded to the Squire,
And Madam now begins to hold it higher;
Pretends to taste, at Operas cries, *Caro,*
And quits her Nancy Dawson, for *Che faro.*
Dotes upon dancing, and in all her pride,
Swims round the room, the *Heinel* of Cheapside:
Ogles and leers with artificial skill,
Till having lost in age the power to kill,
She sits all night at cards, and ogles at spadille.
Such, through our lives, the eventful history—
The fifth and last act still remains for me.
The Barmaid now for your protection prays,
Turns Female Barrister, and pleads for Bayes.

RICHARD BRINSLEY SHERIDAN

Richard Brinsley Sheridan was born in Dublin, Ireland, on October 30, 1751. It might be said that he had the theater in his blood. He was the third son of Thomas Sheridan, who after graduating from Trinity College had become an actor and, for a time, a successful theater manager. Richard Sheridan's mother, the former Frances Chamberlaine, wrote plays and novels. While his family's theatrical background no doubt helped him in his career as a dramatist, their perennially shaky financial situation and lack of social status—being Irish and a theatrical family—left an enduring impression upon the young Sheridan, inspiring him with the ambition to overcome these obstacles and succeed. While Sheridan was a student at the exclusive English public school, Harrow, his family was forced to flee to France to escape creditors, leaving him alone and destitute, vulnerable to the condescension and cruel abuse of his teachers and schoolfellows—the blue-blooded scions of English nobility.

By 1770, the family returned to London and Sheridan rejoined them. A year later they moved to Bath, the fashionable resort town and spa where he was able to closely observe *le beau monde* that he would later satirize in his plays. He also met the beautiful young soprano Elizabeth Ann Linley, whom he would marry in 1773 after fighting two duels over her, the second of which almost resulted in his death. Sheridan's first play, *The Rivals*, opened in 1775 at the Covent Garden Theatre in London and was so successful that he decided to become a dramatist rather than a lawyer as his father had hoped. The next year he wrote the comic opera *The Duenna*, which was an even bigger hit, running for a record-breaking seventy-five nights. In 1778, Sheridan bought controlling interest in the Drury Lane Theatre. He wrote two more plays—*The School for Scandal* and *The Critic*—before he was elected to Parliament in 1780. Although the theater would remain a major source of income, his career as a dramatist essentially ended as he devoted his energies to his political career.

Sheridan's parliamentary career came to a close when he lost his seat in the election of 1812. His theater had burned down three years earlier, depleting his finances and leaving him unable to run an effective campaign. He started drinking heavily and was imprisoned several times for debt. He died on July 7, 1816, in poverty. Sheridan, nonetheless, received a lavish public funeral attended by dignitaries and peers of the realm when he was buried in Poets' Corner in Westminster Abbey. An intelligent and powerful speaker, he had had a distinguished political career and had even served as an adviser to the Prince of Wales (later George IV). Still, during his political years he had been condescendingly called "Poor Sherry," even by his supposed friends, and was always hindered by the fact that as a poor Irish actor's son he would never overcome the innate English suspicion and apprehension that he was a disreputable, self-interested Irish adventurer and an unreliable lightweight.

Sheridan was well aware of this bias, and in *The School for Scandal*, his finest play, he satirized the aristocracy, though very subtly and, since it is a comedy, good-naturedly. The characters in the play are, as one of them states, "all people of rank and fortune." But Sheridan portrayed them as scandalmongers, rotten to the core, who had nothing better to do with their time than to spread lies and gossip about each other out of vanity, malice, and fun. Inspired by the wit and satiric bite of the Restoration comedy of manners, he created a play that whimsically yet relentlessly uncovered high society's illusions and pretensions as well as its hypocrisy.

Although his dramatic career lasted only five years, Sheridan is considered one of the best playwrights of the eighteenth century and, along with William Shakespeare, Oscar Wilde, and George Bernard Shaw, ranks as one of the English language's best writers of comedy. *The School for Scandal* is a masterpiece that contains some of the literature's funniest scenes, as well as some of the wittiest dialogue ever written.

THE SCHOOL FOR SCANDAL

BY RICHARD BRINSLEY SHERIDAN

Dramatis Personae

(As play was originally acted at Drury Lane Theatre,
May 8, 1777)

Men

SIR PETER TEAZLE	*Mr King*
SIR OLIVER SURFACE	*Mr Yates*
JOSEPH SURFACE	*Mr Palmer*
CHARLES SURFACE	*Mr Smith*
CRABTREE	*Mr Parsons*
SIR BENJAMIN BACKBITE	*Mr Dodd*
ROWLEY	*Mr Aickin*
MOSES	*Mr Baddeley*
TRIP	*Mr La Mash*
SNAKE	*Mr Packer*
CARELESS	*Mr Farren*
SIR HARRY (*later* TOBY) BUMPER	*Mr Gaudry*

Women

LADY TEAZLE	*Mrs Abington*
MARIA	*Miss P. Hopkins*
LADY SNEERWELL	*Miss Sherry*
MRS CANDOUR	*Miss Pope*

Prologue

By David Garrick, Esq.

Spoken by Thomas King

A School for Scandal! Tell me, I beseech you,
Needs there a school this modish art to teach you?
No need of lessons *now,* the knowing think;
We might as well be taught to eat and drink.
Caused by a dearth of scandal, should the vapours
Distress our fair ones—let them read the papers.
Their powerful mixtures such disorders hit;
Crave what you will—there's *quantum sufficit.*
'Lord!' cries my Lady Wormwood (who loves tattle,
And puts much salt and pepper in her prattle),
Just risen at noon, all night at cards when threshing,
Strong tea and scandal—'Bless me, how refreshing!
Give me the papers, Lisp—how bold and free! (*sips*)
Last night Lord L. (*sips*) *was caught with Lady D.*
For aching heads what charming *sal volatile!* (*sips*)
If Mrs B. will still continue flirting,
We hope she'll draw, or we'll undraw *the curtain.*
Fine satire, poz—in public all abuse it,
But, by ourselves, (*sips*) our praise we can't refuse it.
Now, Lisp, read you—there, at that dash and star'.
'Yes, ma'am: *A certain lord had best beware,*
Who lives not twenty miles from Grosvenor Square;
For should he Lady W. find willing,
Wormwood is bitter—'Oh! that's me, the villain!
Throw it behind the fire and never more
Let that vile paper come within my door.'
Thus at our friends we laugh, who feel the dart;
To reach our feelings, we ourselves must smart.
Is our young bard so young to think that he
Can stop the full spring-tide of calumny?

Knows he the world so little, and its trade?
Alas! the devil's sooner raised than laid.
So strong, so swift, the monster there's no gagging;
Cut Scandal's head off, still the tongue is wagging.
Proud of your smiles once lavishly bestowed,
Again our young Don Quixote takes the road;
To show his gratitude he draws his pen
And seeks this hydra Scandal in his den.
For your applause all perils he would through—
He'll fight—that's write—a cavalliero true,
Till every drop of blood—that's ink—is spilt for you.

Act I, Scene i

A dressing-room in Lady Sneerwell's *house.* Lady Sneerwell (*on right*) *at her toilet;* Snake (*left*) *drinking chocolate*

LADY SNEERWELL:

The paragraphs, you say, Mr Snake, were all inserted?

SNAKE:

They were, madam, and as I copied them myself in a feigned hand, there can be no suspicion whence they came.

LADY SNEERWELL:

Did you circulate the report of Lady Brittle's intrigue with Captain Boastall?

SNAKE:

That's in as fine a train as your ladyship could wish. In the common course of things I think it must reach Mrs Clackitt's ears within four and twenty hours—and then, you know, the business is as good as done.

LADY SNEERWELL:

Why truly Mrs Clackitt has a very pretty talent—and a great deal of industry.

SNAKE:

True, madam, and has been tolerably successful in her day. To my knowledge she has been the cause of six matches being broken off and three sons disinherited, of four forced elopements, and as many close confinements, nine separate maintenances, and two divorces. Nay, I have more than once traced her causing a tête-à-tête in the *Town and Country Magazine,* when the parties perhaps had never seen each other's face before in the course of their lives.

LADY SNEERWELL:

She certainly has talents, but her *manner* is gross.

SNAKE:

'Tis very true. She generally designs well, has a free tongue, and a bold invention; but her colouring is too dark and her outlines often extravagant. She wants that delicacy of hint and mellowness of sneer which distinguishes your ladyship's scandal.

LADY SNEERWELL:

You are partial, Snake.

SNAKE:

Not in the least. Everybody allows that Lady Sneerwell can do more with a word or a look than many can with the most laboured detail, even when they happen to have a little truth on their side to support it.   *They rise*

LADY SNEERWELL:

Yes, my dear Snake, and I am no hypocrite to deny the satisfaction I reap from the success of my efforts. Wounded myself in the early part of my life by the envenomed tongue of slander, I confess I have since known no pleasure equal to the reducing others to the level of my own injured reputation.

SNAKE:

Nothing can be more natural. But, Lady Sneerwell, there is one affair in which you have lately employed me wherein, I confess, I am at a loss to guess your motives.

LADY SNEERWELL:

I conceive you mean with respect to my neighbour Sir Peter Teazle and his family?

SNAKE:

I do. Here are two young men, to whom Sir Peter has acted as a kind of guardian since their father's death—the elder possessing the most amiable character and universally well spoken of, the other the most dissipated and extravagant young fellow in the kingdom, without friends or character—the former an avowed admirer of your ladyship and apparently your favourite; the latter attached to Maria, Sir Peter's ward—and confessedly beloved by her. Now on the face of these circumstances it is utterly unaccountable to me why you, the widow of a City knight with a good jointure, should not close with the addresses of a man of such character and expectations as Mr Surface—and more so why you should be so uncommonly earnest to destroy the mutual attachment subsisting between his brother Charles and Maria.

LADY SNEERWELL:

Then at once to unravel this mystery I must inform you that love has no share whatever in the intercourse between Mr Surface and me.

SNAKE:

No!

LADY SNEERWELL:

His real attachment is to Maria—or her fortune. But finding in his brother a favoured rival he has been obliged to mask his pretensions and profit by my assistance.

SNAKE:

Yet still I am more puzzled why you should interest yourself in his success.

LADY SNEERWELL:

How dull you are! Cannot you surmise the weakness which I hitherto through shame have concealed even from you? Must I confess that Charles, that libertine, that extravagant, that bankrupt in fortune and reputation, that he it is for whom I am thus anxious and malicious—and to gain whom I would sacrifice everything?

SNAKE:

Now, indeed, your conduct appears consistent; but how came you and Mr Surface so confidential?

LADY SNEERWELL:

For our mutual interest. I have found him out a long time since. I know him to be artful, selfish, and malicious—in short, a sentimental knave, while with Sir Peter, and indeed with all his acquaintance, he passes for a youthful miracle of prudence, good sense, and benevolence.

SNAKE:

Yes, yet Sir Peter vows he has not his equal in England; and above all, he praises him as a Man of Sentiment.

LADY SNEERWELL:

True; and with the assistance of his sentiment and hypocrisy he has brought Sir Peter entirely into his interest with regard to Maria, while poor Charles has no friend in the house, though I fear he has a powerful one in Maria's heart, against whom we must direct our schemes.

Enter Servant (*left*)

SERVANT:

Mr Surface.

LADY SNEERWELL:

Show him up. He generally calls about this time. I don't wonder at people's giving him to me for a lover.

Exit Servant (*left*)

Enter Joseph Surface (*left*)

JOSEPH:

My dear Lady Sneerwell, how do you do today? Mr Snake, your most obedient.

LADY SNEERWELL:

Snake has just been arraigning me on our mutual attachment; but I have informed him of our real views. You know how useful he has been to us, and, believe me, the confidence is not ill placed.

JOSEPH:

Madam, it is impossible for me to suspect a man of Mr Snake's sensibility and discernment.

LADY SNEERWELL:

Well, well, no compliments now; but tell me when you saw your mistress, Maria—or what is more material to me, your brother.

JOSEPH:

I have not seen either since I left you; but I can inform you that they never meet. Some of your stories have taken a good effect on Maria.

LADY SNEERWELL:

Ah, my dear Snake, the merit of this belongs to you. But do your brother's distresses increase?

JOSEPH:

Every hour. I am told he has had another execution in the house yesterday. In short, his dissipation and extravagance exceed anything I have ever heard of.

LADY SNEERWELL:

Poor Charles!

JOSEPH:

True, madam, notwithstanding his vices, one can't help feeling for him. Poor Charles! I'm sure I wish it were in my power to be of any essential service to him, for the man who does not share in the distresses of a brother, even though merited by his own misconduct, deserves—

LADY SNEERWELL:

O lud, you are going to be moral and forget that you are among friends.

JOSEPH:

Egad, that's true. I'll keep that sentiment till I see Sir Peter. However, it is certainly a charity to rescue Maria from such a libertine, who, if he is to be reclaimed, can be so only by a person of your ladyship's superior accomplishments and understanding.

SNAKE:

I believe, Lady Sneerwell, here's company coming. I'll go and copy the letter I mentioned to you. Mr Surface, your most obedient.

JOSEPH:

> Sir, your very devoted.   *Exit* Snake (*right*)
> Lady Sneerwell, I am very sorry you have put any further confidence in that fellow.

LADY SNEERWELL:

> Why so?

JOSEPH:

> I have lately detected him in frequent conference with old Rowley, who was formerly my father's steward and has never, you know, been a friend of mine.

LADY SNEERWELL:

> And do you think he would betray us?

JOSEPH:

> Nothing more likely. Take my word for 't, Lady Sneerwell, that fellow hasn't virtue enough to be faithful even to his own villainy. Hah, Maria!

Enter Maria (*left*)

LADY SNEERWELL:

> Maria, my dear, how do you do? What's the matter?

MARIA:

> Oh, there's that disagreeable lover of mine, Sir Benjamin Backbite, has just called at my guardian's with his odious uncle Crabtree. So I slipped out and have run hither to avoid them.

LADY SNEERWELL:

> Is that all?

JOSEPH:

> If my brother Charles had been of the party, ma'am, perhaps you would not have been so much alarmed.

LADY SNEERWELL:

> Nay, now you are ill-natured; for I dare swear the truth of the matter is Maria heard you were here. But, my dear, what has Sir Benjamin done that you should avoid him so?

MARIA:

> Oh, he has *done* nothing; but 'tis for what he has said. His conversation is a perpetual libel on all his acquaintance.

JOSEPH:

> Aye, and the worst of it is there is no advantage in not knowing him, for he'll abuse a stranger just as soon as his best friend—and his uncle's as bad.

LADY SNEERWELL:

> Nay, but we should make allowance. Sir Benjamin is a wit and a poet.

MARIA:

> For my part, I confess, madam, wit loses its respect with me when I see it in company with malice. What do you think, Mr Surface?

JOSEPH:

> Certainly, madam. To smile at the jest which plants a thorn in another's breast is to become a principal in the mischief.

LADY SNEERWELL:

> Pshaw, there's no possibility of being witty without a little ill nature. The malice of a good thing is the barb that makes it stick. What's your opinion, Mr Surface?

JOSEPH:

> To be sure, madam, that conversation where the spirit of raillery is suppressed will ever appear tedious and insipid.

MARIA:

> Well, I'll not debate how far scandal may be allowable; but in a man, I am sure, it is always contemptible. We have pride, envy, rivalship, and a thousand motives to depreciate each other; but the male slanderer must have the cowardice of a woman before he can traduce one.

Enter Servant (*left*)

SERVANT:

> Madam, Mrs Candour is below and, if your ladyship's at leisure, will leave her carriage.

LADY SNEERWELL:

> Beg her to walk in. *Exit* Servant (*left*)
>
> Now, Maria, however, here is a character to your taste, for though Mrs Candour is a little talkative, everybody allows her to be the best-natured and best sort of woman.

MARIA:

> Yes, with a very gross affectation of good nature and benevolence, she does more mischief than the direct malice of old Crabtree.

JOSEPH:

> I' faith that's true, Lady Sneerwell. Whenever I hear the current running against the characters of my friends, I never think them in such danger as when Candour undertakes their defence.

LADY SNEERWELL:

> Hush! Here she is.

Enter Mrs Candour (*left*)

MRS CANDOUR:

My dear Lady Sneerwell, how have you been this century? Mr Surface, what news do you hear? Though indeed it is no matter, for I think one hears nothing else but scandal.

JOSEPH:

Just so, indeed, ma'am.

MRS CANDOUR:

Ah, Maria, child! What, is the whole affair off between you and Charles? His extravagance, I presume? The town talks of nothing else.

MARIA:

Indeed! I am very sorry, ma'am, the town is not better employed.

MRS CANDOUR:

True, true, child; but there's no stopping people's tongues. I own I was hurt to hear it, as indeed I was to learn from the same quarter that your guardian, Sir Peter, and Lady Teazle have not agreed lately as well as could be wished.

MARIA:

'Tis strangely impertinent for people to busy themselves so.

MRS CANDOUR:

Very true, child, but what's to be done? People *will* talk; there's no preventing it. Why is was but yesterday I was told that Miss Gadabout had eloped with Sir Filigree Flirt. But, Lord, there's no minding what one hears—though to be sure I had this from very good authority.

MARIA:

Such reports are highly scandalous.

MRS CANDOUR:

So they are, child—shameful, shameful! But the world is so censorious, no character escapes. Lord, now who would have suspected your friend Miss Prim of an indiscretion? Yet such is the ill nature of people that they say her uncle stopped her last week just as she was stepping into the York diligence with her dancing-master.

MARIA:

I'll answer for't there are no grounds for that report.

MRS CANDOUR:

Oh, no foundation in the world, I dare swear. No more probably than for the story circulated last month of Mrs Festino's affair with Colonel Cassino—though to be sure that matter was never rightly cleared up.

JOSEPH:

The licence of invention some people take is monstrous indeed.

MARIA:

'Tis so—but in my opinion those who report such things are equally culpable.

MRS CANDOUR:

To be sure they are. Tale-bearers are as bad as the tale-makers—'tis an old observation, and a very true one. But what's to be done, as I said before? How will you prevent people from talking? Today Mrs Clackitt assured me Mr and Mrs Honeymoon were at last become mere man and wife like the rest of their acquaintance. She likewise hinted that a certain widow in the next street had got rid of her dropsy and recovered her shape in a most surprising manner. And at the same time Miss Tattle, who was by, affirmed that Lord Buffalo had discovered his lady at a house of no extraordinary fame—and that Sir Harry Bouquet and Tom Saunter were to measure swords on a similar provocation. But, Lord, do you think I would report these things? No, no, tale-bearers, as I said before, are just as bad as the tale-makers.

JOSEPH:

Ah, Mrs Candour, if everybody had your forbearance and good nature!

MRS CANDOUR:

I confess, Mr Surface, I cannot bear to hear people attacked behind their backs, and when ugly circumstances come out against one's acquaintance, I own I always love to think the best. By the bye, I hope 'tis not true your brother is absolutely ruined?

JOSEPH:

I am afraid his circumstances are very bad indeed, ma'am.

MRS CANDOUR:

Ah, I heard so—but you must tell him to keep up his spirits. Everybody almost is in the same way—Lord Spindle, Sir Thomas Splint, Captain Quinze, and Mr Nickit. All up, I hear, within this week. So if Charles is undone, he'll find half his friends and acquaintance ruined too, and that, you know, is a consolation.

JOSEPH:

Doubtless, ma'am, a very great one.

Enter Servant (*left*)

SERVANT:

Mr Crabtree and Sir Benjamin Backbite.   *Exit* Servant (*left*)

LADY SNEERWELL:

So, Maria, you see your lover pursues you; positively you shan't escape.

Enter Crabtree *and* Sir Benjamin Backbite (*left*)

CRABTREE:

Lady Sneerwell, I kiss your hand. Mrs Candour, I don't believe you are acquainted with my nephew, Sir Benjamin Backbite? Egad! ma'am, he has a pretty wit—and is a pretty poet too, isn't he, Lady Sneerwell?

SIR BENJAMIN:

Oh, fie, uncle!

CRABTREE:

Nay, egad, it's true. I back him at a rebus or a charade against the best rhymer in the kingdom. Has your ladyship heard the epigram he wrote last week on Lady Frizzle's feather catching fire? Do, Benjamin, repeat it—or the charade you made last night extempore at Mrs Drowzie's conversazione. Come now: your first is the name of a fish, your second a great naval commander, and—

SIR BENJAMIN:

Uncle, now, prithee—

CRABTREE:

I' faith, ma'am, 'twould surprise you to hear how ready he is at all these fine sort of things.

LADY SNEERWELL:

I wonder, Sir Benjamin, you never publish anything.

SIR BENJAMIN:

To say truth, ma'am, 'tis very vulgar to print. And as my little productions are mostly satires and lampoons on particular people, I find they circulate more by giving copies in confidence to the friends of the parties. However, I have some love elegies, which, when favoured with this lady's smiles, I mean to give the public.

CRABTREE:

'Fore Heaven, ma'am, they'll immortalize you! You will be handed down to posterity, like Petrarch's Laura, or Waller's Sacharissa.

SIR BENJAMIN:

Yes, madam, I think you will like them when you shall see them on a beautiful quarto page, where a neat rivulet of text shall meander through a meadow of margin. 'Fore Gad, they will be the most elegant things of their kind!

CRABTREE:

But, ladies, that's true. Have you heard the news?

MRS CANDOUR:

What, sir, do you mean the report of—

CRABTREE:

No, ma'am, that's not it. Miss Nicely is going to be married to her own footman!

MRS CANDOUR:

Impossible!

CRABTREE:

Ask Sir Benjamin.

SIR BENJAMIN:

'Tis very true, ma'am. Everything is fixed and the wedding liveries bespoke.

CRABTREE:

Yes, and they do say there were *pressing* reasons for it.

LADY SNEERWELL:

Why, I have heard something of this before.

MRS CANDOUR:

It can't be. And I wonder anyone should believe such a story of so prudent a lady as Miss Nicely.

SIR BENJAMIN:

O lud, ma'am, that's the very reason 'twas believed at once. She has always been so cautious and so reserved that everybody was sure there was some reason for it at bottom.

MRS CANDOUR:

Why, to be sure, a tale of scandal is as fatal to the credit of a prudent lady of her stamp as a fever is generally to those of the strongest constitutions. But there is a sort of puny, sickly reputation that is always ailing, yet will outlive the robuster characters of a hundred prudes.

SIR BENJAMIN:

True, madam, there are valetudinarians in reputation as well as in constitution, who, being conscious of their weak part, avoid the least breath of air and supply their want of stamina by care and circumspection.

MRS CANDOUR:

Well, but this may be all a mistake. You know, Sir Benjamin, very trifling circumstances often give rise to the most injurious tales.

CRABTREE:

That they do, I'll be sworn, ma'am. Did you ever hear how Miss Piper came to lose her lover and her character last summer at Tunbridge? Sir Benjamin, you remember it?

SIR BENJAMIN:

Oh, to be sure—the most whimsical circumstance.

LADY SNEERWELL:

How was it, pray?

CRABTREE:

Why, one evening at Mrs Ponto's assembly the conversation happened to turn on the breeding Nova Scotia sheep in this country. Says a young lady in company, 'I have known instances of it, for Miss Letitia Piper, a first cousin of mine, had a Nova Scotia sheep that produced her twins'. 'What', cries the Lady Dowager Dundizzy, who you know is as deaf as a post, 'has Miss Piper had twins?' This mistake, as you may imagine, threw the whole company into a fit of laughter. However, 'twas next morning everywhere reported—and in a few days believed by the whole town—that Miss Letitia Piper had actually been brought to bed of a fine boy and a girl. And in less than a week there were some people who could name the father and the farm-house where the babies were put to nurse.

LADY SNEERWELL:

Strange indeed!

CRABTREE:

Matter of fact, I assure you. O lud, Mr Surface, pray is it true that your uncle Sir Oliver is coming home?

JOSEPH:

Not that I know of, indeed, sir.

CRABTREE:

He has been in the East Indies a long time. You can scarcely remember him, I believe? Sad comfort, whenever he returns, to hear how your brother has gone on.

JOSEPH:

Charles has been imprudent, sir, to be sure; but I hope no busy people have already prejudiced Sir Oliver against him. He may reform.

SIR BENJAMIN:

To be sure, he may. For my part I never believed him to be so utterly void of principle as people say, and, though he has lost all his friends, I am told nobody is better spoken of by the Jews.

CRABTREE:

That's true, egad, nephew. If the Old Jewry was a ward, I believe Charles would be an alderman. No man is more popular there, 'fore Gad! I hear he pays as many annuities as the Irish tontine—and that whenever he is sick they have prayers for the recovery of his health in the Synagogue.

SIR BENJAMIN:

Yet no man lives in greater splendour. They tell me when he entertains his friends he will sit down to dinner with a dozen of his own securities, have a score of tradesmen waiting in the antechamber, and an officer behind every guest's chair.

JOSEPH:

This may be entertainment to you, gentlemen, but you pay very little regard to the feelings of a brother.

MARIA:

Their malice is intolerable. Lady Sneerwell, I must wish you a good morning. I'm not very well.   *Exit* Maria (*left*)

MRS CANDOUR:

Oh dear, she changes colour very much.

LADY SNEERWELL:

Do, Mrs Candour, follow her: she may want assistance.

MRS CANDOUR:

That I will, with all my soul, ma'am. Poor dear girl, who knows what her situation may be?   *Exit* Mrs Candour (*left*)

LADY SNEERWELL:

'Twas nothing but that she could not bear to hear Charles reflected on, notwithstanding their difference.

SIR BENJAMIN:

The young lady's *penchant* is obvious.

CRABTREE:

But, Benjamin, you must not give up the pursuit for that.— Follow her, and put her into good humour. Repeat her some of your own verses. Come, I'll assist you.

SIR BENJAMIN:

Mr Surface, I did not mean to hurt you; but depend on't your brother is utterly undone.   *Going*

CRABTREE:

O lud, aye! Undone as ever man was. Can't raise a guinea!

Going

SIR BENJAMIN:

And everything sold, I'm told, that was movable.

Returning

CRABTREE:

I have seen one that was at his house. Not a thing left but some empty bottles that were overlooked—and the family pictures, which I believe are framed in the wainscots.   *Going*

SIR BENJAMIN:

And I'm very sorry, also, to hear some bad stories against him.

Returning

CRABTREE:

Oh, he has done many mean things, that's certain. *Going*

SIR BENJAMIN:

But, however, as he's your brother— *Returning*

CRABTREE:

We'll tell you all another opportunity.

Exeunt Crabtree *and* Sir Benjamin (*left*)

LADY SNEERWELL:

Ha, ha! 'tis very hard for them to leave a subject they have not quite run down.

JOSEPH:

And I believe the abuse was no more acceptable to your ladyship than Maria.

LADY SNEERWELL:

I doubt her affections are farther engaged than we imagined. But the family are to be here this evening, so you may as well dine where you are, and we shall have an opportunity of observing farther. In the meantime I'll go and plot mischief— and you shall study sentiment. *Exeunt* (*right*)

Act I, Scene ii

Sir Peter Teazle's *house*
Enter Sir Peter (*left*)

SIR PETER:

When an old bachelor marries a young wife, what is he to expect? 'Tis now six months since Lady Teazle made me the happiest of men—and I have been the miserablest dog ever since. We tifted a little going to church, and fairly quarrelled before the bells had done ringing. I was more than once nearly choked with gall during the honeymoon, and had lost all comfort in life before my friends had done wishing me joy. Yet I chose with caution—a girl bred wholly in the country, who never knew luxury beyond one silk gown, nor dissipation above the annual gala of a race ball. Yet now she plays her part in all the extravagant fopperies of the fashion and the town, with as ready a grace as if she had never seen a bush nor a grass plat out of Grosvenor Square. I am sneered at by all my acquaintance and paragraphed in the newspapers. She dissipates my fortune and contradicts all my humours. Yet the worst of it is, I doubt I love her, or I should never bear all this. However, I'll never be weak enough to own it.

Enter Rowley (*right*)

ROWLEY:

Oh, Sir Peter, your servant. How is it with you, sir?

SIR PETER:

Very bad, Master Rowley, very bad. I meet with nothing but crosses and vexations.

ROWLEY:

What can have happened to trouble you since yesterday?

SIR PETER:

A good question to a married man!

ROWLEY:

Nay, I'm sure your lady, Sir Peter, can't be the cause of your uneasiness.

SIR PETER:

Why, has anybody told you she was dead?

ROWLEY:

Come, come, Sir Peter, you love her, notwithstanding your tempers don't exactly agree.

SIR PETER:

But the fault is entirely hers, Master Rowley, I am myself the sweetest-tempered man alive and hate a teasing temper—and so I tell her a hundred times a day.

ROWLEY:

Indeed!

SIR PETER:

Aye—and what is very extraordinary in all our disputes she is always in the wrong. But Lady Sneerwell and the set she meets at her house encourage the perverseness of her disposition. Then, to complete my vexations, Maria, my ward, whom I ought to have the power of a father over, is determined to turn rebel too, and absolutely refuses the man whom I have long resolved on for her husband;—meaning, I suppose, to bestow herself on his profligate brother.

ROWLEY:

You know, Sir Peter, I have always taken the liberty to differ with you on the subject of these two young gentlemen. I only wish you may not be deceived in your opinion of the elder. For Charles (my life on't!), he will retrieve his errors yet. Their worthy father, once my honoured master, was at his years nearly as wild a spark; yet, when he died, he did not leave a more benevolent heart to lament his loss.

SIR PETER:

You are wrong, Master Rowley, you are wrong. On their father's death, you know, I acted as a kind of guardian to them both, till their uncle Sir Oliver's eastern liberality gave them an early independence. Of course, no person could have more opportunities of judging of their hearts, and I was never mistaken in my life. Joseph is indeed a model for the young men of the age. He is a Man of Sentiment, and acts up to the sentiments he professes; but for the other, take my word for't, if he had any grain of virtue by descent, he has dissipated it with the rest of his inheritance. Ah, my old friend Sir Oliver will be deeply mortified when he finds how part of his bounty has been misapplied.

ROWLEY:

I am sorry to find you so violent against the young man, because this may be the most critical period of his fortune. I came hither with news that will surprise you.

SIR PETER:

What? Let me hear.

ROWLEY:

Sir Oliver *is* arrived and at this moment in town.

SIR PETER:

How? You astonish me. I thought you did not expect him this month.

ROWLEY:

I did not; but his passage has been remarkably quick.

SIR PETER:

Egad, I shall rejoice to see my old friend. 'Tis fifteen years since we met. We have had many a day together. But does he still enjoin us not to inform his nephews of his arrival?

ROWLEY:

Most strictly. He means, before it is known, to make some trial of their dispositions.

SIR PETER:

Ah, there needs no art to discover their merits; however, he shall have his way. But pray does he know I am married?

ROWLEY:

Yes, and will soon wish you joy.

SIR PETER:

What, as we drink health to a friend in a consumption? Ah, Oliver will laugh at me. We used to rail at matrimony together, and he has been steady to his text. Well, he must be soon at my house, though. I'll instantly give orders for his reception. But,

Master Rowley, don't drop a word that Lady Teazle and I ever disagree.

ROWLEY:

By no means.

SIR PETER:

For I should never be able to stand Noll's jokes. So I'd have him think, Lord forgive me, that we are a very happy couple.

ROWLEY:

I understand you. But then you must be very careful not to differ while he is in the house with you.

SIR PETER:

Egad, and so we must—and that's impossible. Ah, Master Rowley, when an old bachelor marries a young wife, he deserves—no, the crime carries its punishment along with it.

Exeunt (Sir Peter *left and* Rowley *right*)

Act II, Scene i

Sir Peter Teazle*'s house*
Enter Sir Peter *and* Lady Teazle (*left*)

SIR PETER:

Lady Teazle, Lady Teazle, I'll not bear it!

LADY TEAZLE:

Sir Peter, Sir Peter, you may bear it or not as you please; but I ought to have my own way in everything—and what's more I will too. What, though I was educated in the country, I know very well that women of fashion in London are accountable to nobody after they are married.

SIR PETER:

Very well, ma'am, very well. So a husband is to have no influence, no authority?

LADY TEAZLE:

Authority? No, to be sure. If you wanted authority over me, you should have adopted me and not married me. I am sure you were old enough.

SIR PETER:

Old enough! Aye—there it is. Well, well, Lady Teazle, though my life may be made unhappy by your temper, I'll not be ruined by your extravagance.

LADY TEAZLE:

My extravagance! I'm sure I'm not more extravagant than a woman of fashion ought to be.

SIR PETER:

No, no, madam, you shall throw away no more sums on such unmeaning luxury. 'Slife, to spend as much to furnish your dressing-room with flowers in winter as would suffice to turn the Pantheon into a greenhouse and give a *fête champêtre* at Christmas!

LADY TEAZLE:

Lord, Sir Peter, am I to blame because flowers are dear in cold weather? You should find fault with the climate and not with me. For my part, I'm sure I wish it was spring all the year round and that roses grew under one's feet!

SIR PETER:

Oons, madam, if you had been born to this, I shouldn't wonder at your talking thus. But you forget what your situation was when I married you.

LADY TEAZLE:

No, no, I don't. 'Twas a very disagreeable one, or I should never have married you.

SIR PETER:

Yes, yes, madam, you were then in somewhat an humbler style—the daughter of a plain country squire. Recollect, Lady Teazle, when I saw you first, sitting at your tambour in a pretty figured linen gown with a bunch of keys by your side, your hair combed smooth over a roll, and your apartment hung round with fruits in worsted of your own working.

LADY TEAZLE:

Oh, yes! I remember it very well, and a curious life I led—my daily occupation to inspect the dairy, superintend the poultry, make extracts from the family receipt-book, and comb my aunt Deborah's lap-dog.

SIR PETER:

Yes, yes, ma'am, 'twas so indeed.

LADY TEAZLE:

And then, you know, my evening amusements—to play Pope Joan with the curate; to read a sermon to my aunt; or to be stuck down to an old spinet to strum my father to sleep after a fox-chase.

SIR PETER:

I am glad you have so good a memory. Yes, madam, these were the recreations I took you from; but now you must have your coach—*vis-à-vis*—and three powdered footmen before your chair, and in the summer a pair of white cats to draw you to Kensington Gardens. No recollection, I suppose, when you were content to ride double behind the butler on a docked coach-horse.

LADY TEAZLE:

No—I swear I never did that. I deny the butler and the coach-horse.

SIR PETER:

This, madam, *was* your situation; and what have I done for you? I have made you a woman of fashion, of fortune, of rank—in short, I have made you my wife.

LADY TEAZLE:

Well, then—and there is but one thing more you can make me to add to the obligation, and that is—

SIR PETER:

My widow, I suppose?

LADY TEAZLE:

Hem! Hem!

SIR PETER:

Thank you, madam. But don't flatter yourself; for, though your ill conduct may disturb my peace, it shall never break my heart, I promise you. However, I am equally obliged to you for the hint.

LADY TEAZLE:

Then why will you endeavour to make yourself so disagreeable to me and thwart me in every little elegant expense?

SIR PETER:

'Slife, madam, I say—had you any of these little elegant expenses when you married me?

LADY TEAZLE:

Lud, Sir Peter, would you have me be out of the fashion?

SIR PETER:

The fashion, indeed! What had you to do with the fashion before you married me?

LADY TEAZLE:

For my part, I should think you would like to have your wife thought a woman of taste.

SIR PETER:

Aye! There again! Taste! Zounds, madam, you had no taste when you married me.

LADY TEAZLE:

That's very true, indeed, Sir Peter; and after having married you I should never pretend to taste again, I allow. But now, Sir Peter, if we have finished our daily jangle, I presume I may go to my engagement at Lady Sneerwell's.

SIR PETER:

Aye, there's another precious circumstance. A charming set of acquaintance you have made there!

LADY TEAZLE:

Nay, Sir Peter, they are all people of rank and fortune, and remarkably tenacious of reputation.

SIR PETER:

Yes, egad, they are tenacious of reputation with a vengeance; for they don't choose anybody should have a character but themselves. Such a crew! Ah, many a wretch has rid on a hurdle who has done less mischief than these utterers of forged tales, coiners of scandal, and clippers of reputation.

LADY TEAZLE:

What, would you restrain the freedom of speech?

SIR PETER:

Oh, they have made you just as bad as any one of the society.

LADY TEAZLE:

Why, I believe I do bear a part with a tolerable grace. But I vow I bear no malice against the people I abuse. When I say an ill-natured thing, 'tis out of pure good humour, and I take it for granted they deal exactly in the same manner with me. But, Sir Peter, you know you promised to come to Lady Sneerwell's too.

SIR PETER:

Well, well, I'll call in just to look after my own character.

LADY TEAZLE:

Then, indeed, you must make haste after me, or you'll be too late. So good-bye to ye! *Exit (right)*

SIR PETER:

So I have gained much by my intended expostulation. Yet with what a charming air she contradicts everything I say—and how pleasingly she shows her contempt for my authority. Well, though I can't make her love me, there is great satisfaction in quarrelling with her. And I think she never appears to such advantage as when she is doing everything in her power to plague me. *Exit (through proscenium door left)*

Act II, Scene ii

At Lady Sneerwell's
Lady Sneerwell, Mrs Candour, Crabtree, Sir Benjamin Backbite,
and Joseph Surface

LADY SNEERWELL:

Nay, positively, we *will* hear it.

JOSEPH SURFACE:

Yes, yes, the epigram, by all means.

ALL:

Yes, the epigram if you please.

SIR BENJAMIN:

Oh, plague on't, uncle! 'Tis mere nonsense.

CRABTREE:

No, no. 'Fore Gad, very clever for an extempore.

SIR BENJAMIN:

But, ladies, you should be acquainted with the circumstance. You must know that one day last week as Lady Betty Curricle was taking the dust in Hyde Park in a sort of duodecimo phaeton, she desired me to write some verses on her ponies, upon which I took out my pocket-book and in one moment produced the following:

> Sure never were seen two such beautiful ponies;
> Other horses are clowns, but these macaronis.
> To give 'em this title I'm sure isn't wrong,
> Their legs are so slim and their tails are so long.

CRABTREE:

There, ladies, done in the smack of a whip and on horseback, too.

JOSEPH SURFACE:

A very Phoebus mounted. Indeed, Sir Benjamin!

SIR BENJAMIN:

Oh, dear sir! Trifles, trifles.

Enter (*left*) Lady Teazle *and* Maria

MRS CANDOUR:

I must have a copy.

LADY SNEERWELL:

Lady Teazle! I hope we shall see Sir Peter?

LADY TEAZLE:

I believe he'll wait on your ladyship presently.

LADY SNEERWELL:

Maria, my love, you look grave. Come, you shall sit down to piquet with Mr Surface.

MARIA:

I take very little pleasure in cards; however, I'll do as your lady-ship pleases.

LADY TEAZLE (*Aside*):

I am surprised Mr Surface should sit down with her; I thought he would have embraced this opportunity of speaking to me before Sir Peter came.

MRS CANDOUR:

Now, I'll die; but you are so scandalous I'll forswear your society.

LADY TEAZLE:

What's the matter, Mrs Candour?

MRS CANDOUR:

They'll not allow our friend Miss Vermilion to be handsome.

LADY SNEERWELL:

Oh, surely she is a pretty woman.

CRABTREE:

I am very glad you think so, ma'am.

MRS CANDOUR:

She has a charming fresh colour.

LADY TEAZLE:

Yes, when it is fresh put on.

MRS CANDOUR:

Oh, fie! I'll swear her colour is natural. I have seen it come and go.

LADY TEAZLE:

I daresay you have, ma'am: it goes off at night and comes again in the morning.

SIR BENJAMIN:

True, Lady Teazle, it not only comes and goes, but, what's more, egad—her maid can fetch and carry it.

MRS CANDOUR:

Ha, ha, ha! How I hate to hear you talk so. But surely now, her sister is—or *was*—very handsome.

CRABTREE:

Who—Mrs Evergreen? Oh, Lord, she's six and fifty if she's an hour.

MRS CANDOUR:

Now *positively* you wrong her. Fifty-two or fifty-three is the utmost—and I don't think she looks more.

SIR BENJAMIN:

Ah, there is no judging by her looks unless one could see her face.

LADY SNEERWELL:

Well, well, if Mrs Evergreen *does* take some pains to repair the ravages of time, you must allow she effects it with great ingenuity; and surely that's better than the careless manner in which the widow Ochre caulks her wrinkles.

SIR BENJAMIN:

Nay, now, Lady Sneerwell, you are severe upon the widow. Come, come, it is not that she paints so ill—but, when she has finished her face, she joins it on so badly to her neck that she looks like a mended statue, in which the connoisseur sees at once that the head's modern, though the trunk's antique.

CRABTREE:

Ha, ha, ha! Well said, nephew!

MRS CANDOUR:

Ha, ha, ha! Well, you make me laugh, but I vow I hate you for it. What do you think of Miss Simper?

SIR BENJAMIN:

Why, she has very pretty teeth.

LADY TEAZLE:

Yes; and on that account, when she is neither speaking nor laughing (which very seldom happens), she never absolutely shuts her mouth, but leaves it always on a jar, as it were thus.

(*Shows her teeth*)

MRS CANDOUR:

How can you be so ill-natured?

LADY TEAZLE:

Nay, I allow even that's better than the pains Mrs Prim takes to conceal her losses in front. She draws her mouth till it positively resembles the aperture of a poor's-box and all her words appear to slide out edgewise, as it were thus, *How do you do, madam?—Yes, madam.*

LADY SNEERWELL:

Very well, Lady Teazle; I see you can be a little severe.

LADY TEAZLE:

In defence of a friend it is but justice. But here comes Sir Peter to spoil our pleasantry.

Enter Sir Peter Teazle (*left proscenium door*)

SIR PETER:

Ladies, your most obedient. (*Aside*) Mercy on me, here is the whole set. A character dead at every word, I suppose.

MRS CANDOUR:

I am rejoiced you are come, Sir Peter. They have been *so* censorious—and Lady Teazle as bad as anyone.

SIR PETER:

It must be very distressing to *you*, Mrs Candour, I dare swear.

MRS CANDOUR:

Oh, they will allow good qualities to nobody—not even good nature to our friend Mrs Pursy.

LADY TEAZLE:

What, the fat dowager who was at Mrs Codille's last night?

MRS CANDOUR:

Nay, her bulk is her misfortune; and when she takes such pains to get rid of it, you ought not to reflect on her.

LADY SNEERWELL:

That's very true, indeed.

LADY TEAZLE:

Yes, I know she almost lives on acids and small whey; laces herself by pulleys; and often in the hottest noon of summer, you may see her on a little squat pony, with her hair plaited up behind like a drummer's, and puffing round the Ring on a full trot.

MRS CANDOUR:

I thank you, Lady Teazle, for defending her.

SIR PETER:

Yes, a good defence truly.

MRS CANDOUR:

But Sir Benjamin is as censorious as Miss Sallow.

CRABTREE:

Yes, and she is a curious being to pretend to be censorious—an awkward gawky without any one good point under Heaven!

MRS CANDOUR:

Positively you shall not be so very severe. Miss Sallow is a near relation of mine by marriage, and as for her person great allowance is to be made; for let me tell you a woman labours under many disadvantages who tries to pass for a girl at six and thirty.

LADY SNEERWELL:

Though surely she is handsome still—and for the weakness in her eyes, considering how much she reads by candlelight it is not to be wondered at.

MRS CANDOUR:

True, and then as to her manner—upon my word I think it is particularly graceful considering she never had the least education. For you know her mother was a Welsh milliner and her father a sugar-baker at Bristol.

SIR BENJAMIN:

Ah, you are both of you too good-natured.

SIR PETER (*Aside*):

Yes, damned good-natured! This their own relation! Mercy on me!

MRS CANDOUR:

For my part I own I cannot bear to hear a friend ill spoken of.

SIR PETER:

No, to be sure!

SIR BENJAMIN:

Oh, you are of a moral turn. Mrs Candour and I can sit for an hour and hear Lady Stucco talk sentiment.

LADY TEAZLE:

Nay, I vow Lady Stucco is very well with the dessert after dinner; for she's just like the French fruit one cracks for mottoes—made up of paint and proverb.

MRS CANDOUR:

Well, I never will join in ridiculing a friend—and so I constantly tell my cousin Ogle, and you all know what pretensions *she* has to be critical in beauty.

CRABTREE:

Oh, to be sure. She has herself the oddest countenance that ever was seen. 'Tis a collection of features from all the different countries of the globe.

SIR BENJAMIN:

So she has indeed. An Irish front . . .

CRABTREE:

Caledonian locks . . .

SIR BENJAMIN:

Dutch nose . . .

CRABTREE:

Austrian lip . . .

SIR BENJAMIN:

Complexion of a Spaniard . . .

CRABTREE:

And teeth *à la Chinoise*!

SIR BENJAMIN:

In short, her face resembles a *table d'hôte* at Spa, where no two guests are of a nation—

CRABTREE:

Or a Congress at the close of a general war—wherein all the members, even to her eyes, appear to have a different interest, and her nose and chin are the only parties likely to join issue.

MRS CANDOUR:

Ha, ha, ha!

SIR PETER (*Aside*):

Mercy on my life—a person they dine with twice a week!

LADY SNEERWELL:

Go, go; you are a couple of provoking toads.

MRS CANDOUR:

Nay, but I vow you shall not carry the laugh off so. For give me leave to say that Mrs Ogle—

SIR PETER:

Madam, madam, I beg your pardon. There's no stopping these good gentlemen's tongues. But when I tell *you,* Mrs Candour, that the lady they are abusing is a particular friend of mine, I hope you'll not take her part.

LADY SNEERWELL:

Ha, ha, ha! Well said, Sir Peter! But you are a cruel creature too phlegmatic yourself for a jest, and too peevish to allow wit in others.

SIR PETER:

Ah, madam, true wit is more nearly allied to good nature than your ladyship is aware of.

LADY TEAZLE:

True, Sir Peter. I believe they are so near akin that they can never be united.

SIR BENJAMIN:

Or rather, madam, suppose them to be man and wife, because one seldom sees them together.

LADY TEAZLE:

But Sir Peter is such an enemy to scandal I believe he would have it put down by Parliament.

SIR PETER:

'Fore Heaven, madam, if they were to consider the sporting with reputation of as much importance as poaching on manors and pass an Act for the Preservation of Fame, I believe there are many would thank them for the Bill.

LADY SNEERWELL:

O lud, Sir Peter, would you deprive us of our privileges?

SIR PETER:

Aye, madam; and then no person should be permitted to kill characters or run down reputations, but qualified old maids and disappointed widows.

LADY SNEERWELL:

Go, you monster!

MRS CANDOUR:

But sure you would not be quite so severe on those who only report what they hear?

SIR PETER:

Yes, madam, I would have law merchant for them too; and in all cases of slander currency, whenever the drawer of the lie was not to be found, the injured parties should have a right to come on any of the endorsers.

CRABTREE:

Well, for my part I believe there never was a scandalous tale without some foundation.

SIR PETER:

Oh, nine out of ten of the malicious inventions are founded on some ridiculous misrepresentation.

LADY SNEERWELL:

Come, ladies, shall we sit down to cards in the next room?

Enter a Servant *(left)*, *who whispers* Sir Peter

SIR PETER:

I'll be with them directly.   (*Exit* Servant)

(*Aside*) I'll get away unperceived.

LADY SNEERWELL:

Sir Peter, you are not leaving us?

SIR PETER:

Your ladyship must excuse me; I'm called away by particular business. But I leave my character behind me.

Exit Sir Peter (*left*)

SIR BENJAMIN:

Well, certainly, Lady Teazle, that lord of yours is a strange being. I could tell you some stories of him would make you laugh heartily if he were not your husband.

LADY TEAZLE:

Oh, pray don't mind that. Come, do let's hear them.

They join the rest of the company, all talking as they are going into the next room (i.e., *upper end stage*)

JOSEPH (*Rising with* Maria):

Maria, I see you have no satisfaction in this society.

MARIA:

How is it possible I should? If to raise malicious smiles at the infirmities or misfortunes of those who have never injured us be the province of wit or humour, Heaven grant me a double portion of dullness!

JOSEPH:

Yet they appear more ill-natured than they are. They have no malice at heart.

MARIA:

Then is their conduct still more contemptible, for, in my opinion, nothing could excuse the intemperance of their tongues but a natural and ungovernable bitterness of mind.

JOSEPH:

Undoubtedly, madam; and it has always been a sentiment of mine that to propagate a malicious truth wantonly is more despicable than to falsify from revenge. But can you, Maria, feel thus for others and be unkind to me alone? Is hope to be denied the tenderest passion?

MARIA:

Why will you distress me by renewing the subject?

JOSEPH:

Ah, Maria, you would not treat me thus and oppose your guardian Sir Peter's will, but that I see that profligate Charles is still a favoured rival.

MARIA:

Ungenerously urged! But whatever my sentiments are of that unfortunate young man, be assured I shall not feel more bound to give him up because his distresses have lost him the regard even of a brother.

JOSEPH:

Nay, but Maria, do not leave me with a frown. By all that's honest I swear—(*Kneels*)

Enter Lady Teazle

(*Aside*) Gad's life, here's Lady Teazle. (*Aloud*) You must not— no, you shall not—for though I have the greatest regard for Lady Teazle—

MARIA:

Lady Teazle!

JOSEPH:

Yet were Sir Peter to suspect—

Lady Teazle *comes forward*

LADY TEAZLE:

What is this, pray? (*Aside*) Does he take her for me?—(*Aloud*) Child, you are wanted in the next room.   *Exit* Maria What is all this, pray?

JOSEPH:

Oh, the most unlucky circumstance in nature. Maria has somehow suspected the tender concern I have for your happiness and threatened to acquaint Sir Peter with her suspicions, and I was just endeavouring to reason with her when you came in.

LADY TEAZLE:

Indeed! But you seemed to adopt a very tender mode of reasoning. Do you usually argue on your knees?

JOSEPH:

Oh, she's a child and I thought a little bombast—but, Lady Teazle, when are you to give me your judgment on my library, as you promised?

LADY TEAZLE:

No, no; I begin to think it would be imprudent, and you know I admit you as a lover no farther than fashion sanctions.

JOSEPH:

True—a mere Platonic *cicisbeo*—what every London wife is entitled to.

LADY TEAZLE:

Certainly one must not be out of the fashion. However, I have so much of my country prejudices left that, though Sir Peter's ill humour may vex me ever so, it shall never provoke me to—

JOSEPH:

The only revenge in your power. Well, I applaud your moderation.

LADY TEAZLE:

Go! You are an insinuating wretch! But we shall be missed. Let us join the company.

JOSEPH:

But we had best not return together.

LADY TEAZLE:

Well, don't stay, for Maria shan't come to hear any more of your reasoning, I promise you.   *Exit (back wing left)*

JOSEPH:

A curious dilemma my politics have run me into! I wanted at first only to ingratiate myself with Lady Teazle that she might not be my enemy with Maria; and I have, I don't know how, become her serious lover. Sincerely I begin to wish I had never made such a point of gaining so very good a character, for it has led me into so many cursed rogueries that I doubt I shall be exposed at last.

Exit (middle wing left)

Act II, Scene iii

Sir Peter Teazle's (*house*)
Enter Sir Oliver Surface *and* Rowley (*right door*)

SIR OLIVER:

Ha, ha, ha! So my old friend is married, hey? A young wife out of the country. Ha, ha, ha! That he should have stood bluff to old bachelor so long and sink into a husband at last.

ROWLEY:

But you must not rally him on the subject, Sir Oliver. 'Tis a tender point, I assure you, though he has been married only seven months.

SIR OLIVER:

Then he has been just half a year on the stool of repentance! Poor Peter! But you say he has entirely given up Charles— never sees him, hey?

ROWLEY:

His prejudice against him is astonishing, and I am sure greatly increased by a jealousy of him with Lady Teazle, which he has been industriously led into by a scandalous society in the neighbourhood, who have contributed not a little to Charles's ill name; whereas the truth is, I believe, if the lady is partial to either of them, his brother is the favourite.

SIR OLIVER:

Aye, I know there are a set of malicious, prating, prudent gossips, both male and female, who murder characters to kill time, and will rob a young fellow of his good name before he has years to know the value of it. But I am not to be prejudiced against my nephew by such, I promise you. No, no, if Charles has done nothing false or mean, I shall compound for his extravagance.

ROWLEY:

Then, my life on't, you will reclaim him. Ah, sir, it gives me new life to find that *your* heart is not turned against him, and that the son of my good old master has one friend however left.

SIR OLIVER:

What, shall I forget, Master Rowley, when I was at his years myself? Egad, my brother and I were neither of us very prudent youths—and yet, I believe, you have not seen many better men than your old master was.

ROWLEY:

Sir, 'tis this reflection gives me assurance that Charles may yet be a credit to his family. But here comes Sir Peter.

SIR OLIVER:

Egad, so he does! Mercy on me, he's greatly altered, and seems to have a settled married look. One may read husband in his face at this distance!

Enter Sir Peter Teazle (*right*)

SIR PETER:

Hah! Sir Oliver—my old friend. Welcome to England a thousand times!

SIR OLIVER:

Thank you—thank you, Sir Peter! And i'faith I am as glad to find you well, believe me.

SIR PETER:

Oh! 'tis a long time since we met—fifteen years, I doubt, Sir Oliver, and many a cross accident in the time.

SIR OLIVER:

Aye, I have had my share. But what—I find you are married, hey? Well, well, it can't be helped, and so I wish you joy with all my heart.

SIR PETER:

Thank you, thank you. Sir Oliver. Yes, I have entered into the happy state. But we'll not talk of that now.

SIR OLIVER:

True, true, Sir Peter. Old friends should not begin on grievances at first meeting. No, no, no.

ROWLEY (*To* Sir Oliver):

Take care, pray, sir.

SIR OLIVER:

Well—so one of my nephews is a wild rogue, hey?

SIR PETER:

Wild! Ah, my old friend, I grieve for your disappointment there; he's a lost young man, indeed. However, his brother will make you amends; Joseph is, indeed, what a youth should be. Everybody in the world speaks well of him.

SIR OLIVER:

I am sorry to hear it; he has too good a character to be an honest fellow. Everybody speaks well of him! Pshaw! Then he has bowed as low to knaves and fools as to the honest dignity of genius and virtue.

SIR PETER:

What, Sir Oliver, do you blame him for not making enemies?

SIR OLIVER:

Yes, if he has merit enough to deserve them.

SIR PETER:

> Well, well—you'll be convinced when you know him. 'Tis edification to hear him converse; he professes the noblest sentiments.

SIR OLIVER:

> Oh, plague of his sentiments! If he salutes me with a scrap of morality in his mouth, I shall be sick directly. But, however, don't mistake me, Sir Peter; I don't mean to defend Charles's errors. But before I form my judgment of either of them, I intend to make a trial of their hearts; and my friend Rowley and I have planned something for the purpose.

ROWLEY:

> And Sir Peter shall own for once he has been mistaken.

SIR PETER:

> Oh, my life on Joseph's honour!

SIR OLIVER:

> Well, come, give us a bottle of good wine, and we'll drink the lads' health, and tell you our scheme.

SIR PETER:

> *Allons,* then!

SIR OLIVER:

> And don't, Sir Peter, be so severe against your old friend's son. Odds my life! I am not sorry that he has run out of the course a little. For my part I hate to see prudence clinging to the green suckers of youth; 'tis like ivy round a sapling and spoils the growth of the tree.   *Exeunt (right)*

Act III, Scene i

Sir Peter Teazle's *house. Scene continues. Enter (right)* Sir Peter Teazle, Sir Oliver Surface, *and* Rowley (*Manservant in attendance*)

SIR PETER:

> Well then, we will see this fellow first and have our wine afterwards. But how is this, Master Rowley? I don't see the jet of your scheme.

ROWLEY:

> Why, sir, this Mr Stanley who I was speaking of is nearly related to them by their mother. He was once a merchant in Dublin but has been ruined by a series of undeserved misfortunes. He has applied by letter since his confinement to both Mr Surface and Charles. From the former he has received nothing but evasive promises of future service, while Charles has done all that his extravagance has left him power to do; and he

is at this time endeavouring to raise a sum of money, part of which, in the midst of his own distresses, I know he intends for the service of poor Stanley.

SIR OLIVER:

Ah, he is my brother's son.

SIR PETER:

Well, but how is Sir Oliver personally to—

ROWLEY:

Why, sir, I will inform Charles and his brother that Stanley has obtained permission to apply personally to his friends; and, as they have neither of them ever seen him, let Sir Oliver assume his character and he will have a fair opportunity of judging at least of the benevolence of their dispositions. And believe me, sir, you will find in the younger brother one who, in the midst of folly and dissipation, has still, as our immortal bard expresses it,

> a tear for pity and a hand
> Open as day for melting charity.

SIR PETER:

Pshaw! What signifies his having an open hand, or purse either, when he has nothing left to give? Well, well, make the trial if you please. But where is the fellow whom you brought for Sir Oliver to examine relative to Charles's affairs?

ROWLEY:

Below, waiting his commands, and no one can give him better intelligence. This, Sir Oliver, is a friendly Jew, who to do him justice has done everything in his power to bring your nephew to a proper sense of his extravagance.

SIR PETER:

Pray, let us have him in.

ROWLEY (*Apart to* Servant):

Desire Mr Moses to walk upstairs.

SIR PETER:

But, pray, why should you suppose he will speak the truth?

ROWLEY:

Oh, I have convinced him that he has no chance of recovering certain sums advanced to Charles but through the bounty of Sir Oliver, who he knows has arrived, so that you may depend on his fidelity to his own interest. I have also another evidence in my power, one Snake, whom I have detected in a matter little short of forgery and shall speedily produce to remove some of your prejudices.

SIR PETER:

I have heard too much on that subject.

ROWLEY:

Here comes the honest Israelite.

Enter Moses (*right*)

This is Sir Oliver.

SIR OLIVER:

Sir, I understand you have lately had great dealings with my nephew Charles.

MOSES:

Yes, Sir Oliver, I have done all I could for him; but he was ruined before he came to me for assistance.

SIR OLIVER:

That was unlucky truly, for you have had no opportunity of showing your talents.

MOSES:

None at all. I hadn't the pleasure of knowing his distresses till he was some thousands worse than nothing.

SIR OLIVER:

Unfortunate, indeed! But I suppose you have done all in your power for him, honest Moses?

MOSES:

Yes, he knows that. This very evening I was to have brought him a gentleman from the City, who does not know him and will, I believe, advance him some money.

SIR PETER:

What—one Charles has never had money from before?

MOSES:

Yes. Mr Premium of Crutched Friars, formerly a broker.

SIR PETER:

Egad, Sir Oliver, a thought strikes me. Charles, you say, does not know Mr Premium?

MOSES:

Not at all.

SIR PETER:

Now then, Sir Oliver, you may have a better opportunity of satisfying yourself than by an old romancing tale of a poor relation. Go with my friend Moses and represent Mr Premium, and then, I'll answer for it, you'll see your nephew in all his glory.

SIR OLIVER:

Egad, I like this idea better than the other, and I may visit Joseph afterwards as old Stanley.

SIR PETER:

True. So you may.

ROWLEY:

Well, this is taking Charles rather at a disadvantage, to be sure. However, Moses, you understand Sir Peter and will be faithful?

MOSES:

You may depend upon me. This is near the time I was to have gone.

SIR OLIVER:

I'll accompany you as soon as you please, Moses. But hold, I have forgot one thing. How the plague shall I be able to pass for a Jew?

MOSES:

There's no need. The principal is Christian.

SIR OLIVER:

Is he? I'm sorry to hear it. But then again, a'n't I rather too smartly dressed to look like a money-lender?

SIR PETER:

Not at all; 'twould not be out of character, if you went in your own carriage. Would it, Moses?

MOSES:

Not in the least.

SIR OLIVER:

Well, but how must I talk? There's certainly some cant of usury and mode of treating that I ought to know.

SIR PETER:

Oh, there's not much to learn. The great point, as I take it, is to be exorbitant enough in your demands—hey, Moses?

MOSES:

Yes, that's a very great point.

SIR OLIVER:

I'll answer for't I'll not be wanting in that. I'll ask him eight or ten per cent on the loan—at least.

MOSES:

If you ask him no more than that, you'll be discovered immediately.

SIR OLIVER:

Hey, what the plague! How much then?

MOSES:

That depends upon the circumstances. If he appears not very anxious for the supply, you should require only forty or fifty per cent. But if you find him in great distress and want the moneys very bad, you must ask double.

SIR PETER:

A good honest trade you're learning, Sir Oliver.

SIR OLIVER:

Truly, I think so—and not unprofitable.

MOSES:

Then, you know, you haven't the moneys yourself, but are forced to borrow them for him of an old friend.

SIR OLIVER:

Oh, I borrow it of a friend, do I?

MOSES:

Yes, and your friend is an unconscionable dog; but you can't help it.

SIR OLIVER:

My friend is an unconscionable dog, is he?

MOSES:

Yes, and he himself has not the moneys by him, but is forced to sell stock at a great loss.

SIR OLIVER:

He is forced to sell stock at a great loss, is he? Well, that's very kind of him.

SIR PETER:

I'faith, Sir Oliver—Mr Premium, I mean—you'll soon be master of the trade. But, Moses, wouldn't you have him run out a little against the Annuity Bill? That would be in character I should think.

MOSES:

Very much.

ROWLEY:

And lament that a young man now must be at years of discretion before he is suffered to ruin himself?

MOSES:

Aye, great pity!

SIR PETER:

And abuse the public for allowing merit to an Act whose only object is to snatch misfortune and imprudence from the rapacious relief of usury—and give the minor a chance of inheriting his estate without being undone by coming into possession.

SIR OLIVER:

So—so. Moses shall give me further instructions as we go together.

SIR PETER:

You will not have much time, for your nephew lives hard by.

SIR OLIVER:

Oh, never fear: my tutor appears so able, that though Charles lived in the next street, it must be my own fault if I am not a complete rogue before I turn the corner.

Exeunt Sir Oliver Surface *and* Moses (*left*)

SIR PETER:

So now I think Sir Oliver will be convinced. You are partial, Rowley, and would have prepared Charles for the other plot.

ROWLEY:

No, upon my word, Sir Peter.

SIR PETER:

Well, go bring me this Snake, and I'll hear what he has to say presently. I see Maria and want to speak with her.

Exit Rowley (*right*)

I should be glad to be convinced my suspicions of Lady Teazle and Charles were unjust. I have never yet opened my mind on this subject to my friend Joseph. I am determined I will do it; he will give me his opinion sincerely.

Enter Maria (*left*)

So, child, has Mr Surface returned with you?

MARIA:

No, sir. He was engaged.

SIR PETER:

Well, Maria, do you not reflect the more you converse with that amiable young man what return his partiality for you deserves?

MARIA:

Indeed, Sir Peter, your frequent importunity on this subject distresses me extremely. You compel me to declare that I know no man who has ever paid me a particular attention whom I would not prefer to Mr Surface.

SIR PETER:

So—here's perverseness! No, no, Maria, 'tis Charles only whom you would prefer. 'Tis evident his vices and follies have won your heart.

MARIA:

This is unkind, sir. You know I have obeyed you in neither seeing nor corresponding with him. I have heard enough to convince me that he is unworthy my regard. Yet I cannot think it culpable, if while my understanding severely condemns his vices, my heart suggests some pity for his distresses.

SIR PETER:

> Well, well, pity him as much as you please, but give your heart and hand to a worthier object.

MARIA:

> Never to his brother.

SIR PETER:

> Go, perverse and obstinate! But take care, madam; you have never yet known what the authority of a guardian is. Don't compel me to inform you of it.

MARIA:

> I can only say you shall not have just reason. 'Tis true, by my father's will I am for a short period bound to regard you as his substitute, but must cease to think you so when you would compel me to be miserable. *Exit (right)*

SIR PETER:

> Was ever man so crossed as I am?—everything conspiring to fret me! I had not been involved in matrimony a fortnight before her father, a hale and hearty man, died, on purpose I believe, for the pleasure of plaguing me with the care of his daughter. But here comes my helpmate. She appears in great good humour. How happy I should be if I could tease her into loving me, though but a little.

Enter Lady Teazle

LADY TEAZLE:

> Lud, Sir Peter, I hope you haven't been quarrelling with Maria? It is not using me well to be ill-humoured when I am not by.

SIR PETER:

> Ah, Lady Teazle, you might have the power to make me good-humoured at all times.

LADY TEAZLE:

> I am sure I wish I had, for I want you to be in a charming sweet temper at this moment. Do be good-humoured now and let me have two hundred pounds, will you?

SIR PETER:

> Two hundred pounds! What, a'n't I to be in a good humour without paying for it? But speak to me thus and i'faith there's nothing I could refuse you. You shall have it, but seal me a bond for the repayment.

LADY TEAZLE:

> Oh, no. There—my note of hand will do as well.

SIR PETER (*Kissing her hand*):

And you shall no longer reproach me with not giving you an independent settlement. I mean shortly to surprise you. But shall we always live thus, hey?

LADY TEAZLE:

If you please. I'm sure I don't care how soon we leave off quarrelling provided you'll own you were tired first.

SIR PETER:

Well, then let our future contest be who shall be most obliging.

LADY TEAZLE:

I assure you, Sir Peter, good nature becomes you. You look now as you did before we were married, when you used to walk with me under the elms and tell me stories of what a gallant you were in your youth and chuck me under the chin, you would, and ask me if I thought I could love an old fellow who would deny me nothing—didn't you?

SIR PETER:

Yes, yes, and you were as kind and attentive—

LADY TEAZLE:

Aye, so I was, and would always take your part when my acquaintance used to abuse you and turn you into ridicule.

SIR PETER:

Indeed!

LADY TEAZLE:

Aye, and when my cousin Sophy has called you a stiff, peevish old bachelor and laughed at me for thinking of marrying one who might be my father, I have always defended you and said I didn't think you so ugly by any means—and I dared say you'd make a very good sort of husband.

SIR PETER:

And you prophesied right. And we shall now be the happiest couple—

LADY TEAZLE:

And never differ again?

SIR PETER:

No, never. Though at the same time indeed, my dear Lady Teazle, you must watch your temper very narrowly, for in all our quarrels, my dear, if you recollect, my love, you always began first.

LADY TEAZLE:

I beg your pardon, my dear Sir Peter. Indeed you always gave the provocation.

SIR PETER:

Now see, my angel! Take care. Contradicting isn't the way to keep friends.

LADY TEAZLE:

Then don't you begin it, my love.

SIR PETER:

There, now, you—you—are going on. You don't perceive, my life, that you are just doing the very thing which you know always makes me angry.

LADY TEAZLE:

Nay, you know if you will be angry without any reason, my dear—

SIR PETER:

There now, you want to quarrel again.

LADY TEAZLE:

No, I'm sure I don't; but if you will be so peevish—

SIR PETER:

There now! Who begins first?

LADY TEAZLE:

Why, you to be sure. I said nothing; but there's no bearing your temper.

SIR PETER:

No, no, madam! The fault's in your own temper.

LADY TEAZLE:

Aye, you are just what my cousin Sophy said you would be.

SIR PETER:

Your cousin Sophy is a forward impertinent gipsy.

LADY TEAZLE:

You are a great bear, I'm sure, to abuse my relations.

SIR PETER:

Now may all the plagues of marriage be doubled on me if ever I try to be friends with you any more!

LADY TEAZLE:

So much the better.

SIR PETER:

No, no, madam. 'Tis evident you never cared a pin for me and I was a madman to marry you—a pert rural coquette that had refused half the honest squires in the neighbourhood.

LADY TEAZLE:

And I am sure I was a fool to marry you—an old dangling bachelor, who was single at fifty only because he never could meet with anyone who would have him.

SIR PETER:

> Aye, aye, madam; but you were pleased enough to listen to me. You never had such an offer before.

LADY TEAZLE:

> No? Didn't I refuse Sir Tivy Terrier, who everybody said would have been a better match, for his estate is just as good as yours and he has broke his neck since we have married?

SIR PETER:

> I have done with you, madam! You are an unfeeling, ungrateful—But there's an end of everything. I believe you capable of everything that is bad. Yes, madam, I now believe the reports relative to you and Charles, madam. Yes, madam, you and Charles are, not without grounds—

LADY TEAZLE:

> Take care, Sir Peter! You had better not insinuate any such thing. I'll not be suspected without cause, I promise you.

SIR PETER:

> Very well, madam, very well! A separate maintenance as soon as you please. Yes, madam, or a divorce! I'll make an example of myself for the benefit of all old bachelors. Let us separate, madam.

LADY TEAZLE:

> Agreed, agreed! And now, my dear Sir Peter, we are of a mind once more, we may be the happiest couple and never differ again, you know. Ha, ha, ha! Well, you are going to be in a passion, I see, and I shall only interrupt you; so bye, bye!
>
> *Exit* (*right*)

SIR PETER:

> Plagues and tortures! Can't I make her angry either? Oh, I am the miserablest fellow! But I'll not bear her presuming to keep her temper. No. She may break my heart, but she shan't keep her temper. *Exit* (*left*)

Act III, Scene ii

Charles Surface*'s house*
Enter Trip, Moses, *and* Sir Oliver Surface (*left*)

TRIP:

> Here, Master Moses! If you'll stay a moment, I'll try whether— What's the gentleman's name?

SIR OLIVER (*Aside* [*to* Moses]):

> Mr Moses, what is my name?

MOSES:

Mr Premium.

TRIP:

Premium. Very well.   *Exit, taking snuff* (*right*)

SIR OLIVER:

To judge by the servants one wouldn't believe the master was ruined. But what—sure, this was my brother's house?

MOSES:

Yes, sir; Mr Charles bought it of Mr Joseph, with the furniture, pictures, etc., just as the old gentleman left it. Sir Peter thought it a great piece of extravagance in him.

SIR OLIVER:

In my mind the other's economy in selling it to him was more reprehensible by half.

Enter Trip (*right*)

TRIP:

My master says you must wait, gentlemen; he has company and can't speak with you yet.

SIR OLIVER:

If he knew who it was wanted to see him, perhaps he wouldn't have sent such a message.

TRIP:

Yes, yes, sir; he knows *you* are here. I didn't forget little Premium. No, no, no.

SIR OLIVER:

Very well. And I pray, sir, what may be *your* name?

TRIP:

Trip, sir. My name is Trip, at your service.

SIR OLIVER:

Well, then, Mr Trip, you have a pleasant sort of place here, I guess?

TRIP:

Why, yes. Here are three or four of us pass our time agreeably enough, but then our wages are sometimes a little in arrear— and not very great either. But fifty pounds a year, and find our own bags and bouquets.

SIR OLIVER:

Bags and bouquets! Halters and bastinadoes!

TRIP:

But *à propos*, Moses, have you been able to get me that little bill discounted?

SIR OLIVER (*Aside*):

> Wants to raise money—mercy on me! Has his distresses too, I warrant, like a lord—and affects creditors and duns.

MOSES:

> 'Twas not to be done, indeed, Mr Trip.   *Gives the note*

TRIP:

> Good lack, you surprise me! My friend Brush has endorsed it, and I thought when he put his name at the back of a bill 'twas as good as cash.

MOSES:

> No, 'twouldn't do.

TRIP:

> A small sum—but twenty pounds. Hark'ee, Moses, do you think you couldn't get it me by way of annuity?

SIR OLIVER (*Aside*):

> An annuity! Ha, ha! A footman raise money by way of annuity! Well done, luxury, egad!

MOSES:

> Well, but you must insure your place.

TRIP:

> Oh, with all my heart! I'll insure my place, and my life too, if you please.

SIR OLIVER (*Aside*):

> It's more than I would your neck.

MOSES:

> But is there nothing you could deposit?

TRIP:

> Why, nothing capital of my master's wardrobe has dropped lately; but I could give you a mortgage on some of his winter clothes, with equity of redemption before November. Or you shall have the reversion of the French velvet, or a post-obit on the blue and silver. These, I should think, Moses, with a few pair of point ruffles, as a collateral security—hey, my little fellow?

MOSES:

> Well, well.   *Bell rings*

TRIP:

> Egad, I heard the bell. I believe, gentlemen, I can now introduce you. Don't forget the annuity, little Moses! This way, gentlemen. Insure my place, you know.

SIR OLIVER (*Aside*):

> If the man be a shadow of the master, this is the temple of dissipation indeed.   *Exeunt* (*right*)

Act III, Scene iii

Charles Surface, Careless, etc., at a table with wine, etc.

CHARLES:

'Fore Heaven, 'tis true—there's the great degeneracy of the age! Many of our acquaintance have taste, spirit, and politeness; but plague on't they won't *drink*.

CARELESS:

It is so, indeed, Charles. They give in to all the substantial luxuries of the table, and abstain from nothing but wine and wit.

CHARLES:

Oh, certainly society suffers by it intolerably. For now, instead of the social spirit of raillery that used to mantle over a glass of bright burgundy, their conversation is become just like the Spawater they drink, which has all the pertness and flatulence of champagne, without its spirit or flavour.

1ST GENTLEMAN:

But what are they to do who love play better than wine?

CARELESS:

True. There's Harry diets himself for gaming, and is now under a hazard regimen.

CHARLES:

Then he'll have the worst of it. What! You wouldn't train a horse for the course by keeping him from corn. For my part, egad, I am now never so successful as when I am a little merry. Let me throw on a bottle of champagne, and I never lose—at least I never feel my losses, which is exactly the same thing.

2ND GENTLEMAN:

Aye, that I believe.

CHARLES:

And then what man can pretend to be a believer in love, who is an abjurer of wine? 'Tis the test by which the lover knows his own heart. Fill a dozen bumpers to a dozen beauties, and she that floats atop is the maid that has bewitched you.

CARELESS:

Now then, Charles, be honest and give us your real favourite.

CHARLES:

Why, I have withheld her only in compassion to you. If I toast her, you must give a round of her peers, which is impossible—on earth.

CARELESS:

Oh, then we'll find some canonized vestals or heathen goddesses that will do, I warrant.

CHARLES:

Here then, bumpers, you rogues! Bumpers! Maria! Maria!

SIR TOBY:

Maria who?

CHARLES:

Oh, damn the surname! 'Tis too formal to be registered in love's calendar. But now, Sir Toby, beware! We must have beauty superlative.

CARELESS:

Nay, never study, Sir Toby. We'll stand to the toast though your mistress should want an eye, and you know you have a song will excuse you.

SIR TOBY:

Egad, so I have, and I'll give him the song instead of the lady. *Sings*

Song

Here's to the maiden of bashful fifteen;
Here's to the widow of fifty;
Here's to the flaunting, extravagant queen,
And here's to the housewife that's thrifty.

CHORUS   Let the toast pass,
           Drink to the lass,
I'll warrant she'll prove an excuse for the glass!

Here's to the charmer whose dimples we prize;
Now to the maid who has none, sir!
Here's to the girl with a pair of blue eyes,
And here's to the nymph with but *one,* sir!

CHORUS   Let the toast pass, etc.

Here's to the maid with a bosom of snow!
Now to her that's brown as a berry!
Here's to the wife with a face full of woe,
And now to the girl that is merry!

CHORUS   Let the toast pass, etc.

For let 'em be clumsy, or let 'em be slim,
Young or ancient, I care not a feather;
So fill a pint bumper quite up to the brim,
And let us e'en toast them together!

CHORUS   Let the toast pass, etc.

Enter Trip (*right*) *and whispers* Charles Surface

CHARLES:
Gentlemen, you must excuse me a little. Careless, take the chair, will you?

CARELESS:
Nay, prithee. Charles, what now? This is one of your peerless beauties, I suppose, has dropped in by chance?

CHARLES:
No, faith! To tell you the truth, 'tis a Jew and a broker, who are come by appointment.

CARELESS:
Oh, damn it, let's have the Jew in.

1ST GENTLEMAN:
Aye, and the broker too, by all means.

2ND GENTLEMAN:
Yes, yes, the Jew and the broker!

CHARLES:
Egad, with all my heart! Trip, bid the gentlemen walk in.
                                                  Exit Trip
Though there's one of them a stranger, I can tell you.

CARELESS:
Charles, let us give them some generous burgundy and perhaps they'll grow conscientious.

CHARLES:
Oh, hang 'em, no! Wine does but draw forth a man's natural qualities, and to make them drink would only be to whet their knavery.

Enter Trip, Sir Oliver, *and* Moses

CHARLES:
So, honest Moses! Walk in, pray, Mr Premium. That's the gentleman's name, isn't it, Moses?

MOSES:
Yes, sir.

CHARLES:

Set chairs, Trip. Sit down, Mr Premium. Glasses, Trip. Sit down, Moses. Come, Mr Premium, I'll give you a sentiment: here's *Success to usury!* Moses, fill the gentleman a bumper.

MOSES:

Success to usury!   *Drinks*

CARELESS:

Right, Moses! Usury is prudence and industry, and deserves to succeed.

SIR OLIVER:

Then here's—*all the success it deserves!*   *Drinks*

CARELESS:

No, no, that won't do. Mr Premium, you have demurred at the toast and must drink it in a pint bumper.

1ST GENTLEMAN:

A pint bumper at least.

MOSES:

Oh, pray, sir, consider. Mr Premium's a gentleman.

CARELESS:

And therefore loves good wine.

2ND GENTLEMAN:

Give Moses a quart glass. This is mutiny and a high contempt for the chair.

CARELESS:

Here, now for't. I'll see justice done to the last drop of my bottle.

SIR OLIVER:

Nay, pray, gentlemen. I did not expect this usage.

CHARLES:

No, hang it, you shan't. Mr Premium's a stranger.

SIR OLIVER (*Aside*):

Odd! I wish I was well out of their company.

CARELESS:

Plague on 'em, then! If they don't drink, we'll not sit down with 'em. Come, Harry, the dice are in the next room. Charles, you'll join us when you have finished your business with these gentlemen?

CHARLES:

I will! I will!   *Exeunt* (Charles's *friends right*)
Careless!

CARELESS (*Returning*):

Well?

CHARLES:

Perhaps I may want *you.*

CARELESS:

Oh, you know I am always ready: word, note, or bond, 'tis all the same to me. *Exit* (*right*)

MOSES:

Sir, this is Mr Premium, a gentleman of the strictest honour and secrecy—and always performs what he undertakes. Mr Premium, this is—

CHARLES:

Pshaw! Have done. Sir, my friend Moses is a very honest fellow, but a little slow at expression. He'll be an hour giving us our titles. Mr Premium, the plain state of the matter is this: I am an extravagant young fellow who wants to borrow money, you I take to be a prudent old fellow, who have got money to lend. I am blockhead enough to give fifty per cent sooner than not have it, and you, I presume, are rogue enough to take a hundred if you can get it. Now, sir, you see we are acquainted at once and may proceed to business without further ceremony.

SIR OLIVER:

Exceeding frank, upon my word. I see, sir, you are not a man of many compliments.

CHARLES:

Oh, no, sir. Plain dealing in business I always think best.

SIR OLIVER:

Sir, I like you the better for it. However, you are mistaken in one thing. I have no money to lend, but I believe I could procure some of a friend. But then he's an unconscionable dog, isn't he, Moses?

MOSES:

But you can't help that.

SIR OLIVER:

And must sell stock to accommodate you—mustn't he, Moses?

MOSES:

Yes, indeed! You know I always speak the truth, and I scorn to tell a lie!

CHARLES:

Right. People that speak the truth generally do: but these are trifles, Mr Premium. What! I know money isn't to be bought without paying for't.

SIR OLIVER:

Well—but what security could you give? You have no land, I suppose?

CHARLES:

Not a mole-hill, nor a twig, but what's in beau-pots out of the window!

SIR OLIVER:

Nor any stock, I presume?

CHARLES:

Nothing but live stock—and that's only a few pointers and ponies. But pray, Mr Premium, are you acquainted at all with any of my connections?

SIR OLIVER:

Why, to say truth, I am.

CHARLES:

Then you must know that I have a dev'lish rich uncle in the East Indies, Sir Oliver Surface, from whom I have the greatest expectations.

SIR OLIVER:

That you have a wealthy uncle I have heard, but how your expectations will turn out is more, I believe, than you can tell.

CHARLES:

Oh, no. There can be no doubt of it. They tell me I'm a prodigious favourite and that he talks of leaving me everything.

SIR OLIVER:

Indeed! This is the first I've heard on't.

CHARLES:

Yes, yes, 'tis just so. Moses knows 'tis true, don't you, Moses?

MOSES:

Oh, yes! I'll swear to't.

SIR OLIVER (*Aside*):

Egad, they'll persuade me presently I'm at Bengal.

CHARLES:

Now I propose, Mr Premium, if it's agreeable to you, a post-obit on Sir Oliver's life; though at the same time the old fellow has been so liberal to me that I give you my word I should be very sorry to hear that anything had happened to him.

SIR OLIVER:

Not more than *I* should, I assure you. But the bond you mention happens to be just the worst security you could offer me—for I might live to a hundred and never recover the principal.

CHARLES:

Oh, yes, you would. The moment Sir Oliver dies, you know, you would come on me for the money.

SIR OLIVER:

Then I believe I should be the most unwelcome dun you ever had in your life.

CHARLES:

What? I suppose you are afraid now that Sir Oliver is too good a life?

SIR OLIVER:

No, indeed I am not—though I have heard he is as hale and healthy as any man of his years in Christendom.

CHARLES:

There again you are misinformed. No, no, the climate has hurt him considerably, poor Uncle Oliver. Yes, yes, he breaks apace, I'm told—and so much altered lately that his nearest relations don't know him.

SIR OLIVER:

No? Ha, ha, ha!—so much altered lately that his nearest relations don't know him! Ha, ha, ha! That's droll, egad. Ha, ha, ha!

CHARLES:

Ha, ha! You're glad to hear that, little Premium.

SIR OLIVER:

No, no, I'm not.

CHARLES:

Yes, yes, you are. Ha, ha, ha! You know that mends your chance.

SIR OLIVER:

But I'm told Sir Oliver is coming over. Nay, some say he is actually arrived.

CHARLES:

Pshaw! Sure I must know better than you whether he's come or not. No, no, rely on't, he's at this moment at Calcutta, isn't he. Moses?

MOSES:

Oh, yes, certainly.

SIR OLIVER:

Very true, as you say, you must know better than I, though I have it from pretty good authority, haven't I, Moses?

MOSES:

Yes, most undoubted!

SIR OLIVER:

But, sir, as I understand you want a few hundreds immediately, is there nothing you could dispose of?

CHARLES:

How do you mean?

SIR OLIVER:

> For instance now, I have heard that your father left behind him a great quantity of massy old plate.

CHARLES:

> Oh, lud, that's gone long ago. Moses can tell you how better than I can.

SIR OLIVER (*Aside*):

> Good lack, all the family race-cups and corporation bowls! (*Aloud*) Then it was also supposed that his library was one of the most valuable and complete.

CHARLES:

> Yes, yes, so it was—vastly too much so for a private gentleman. For my part, I was always of a communicative disposition; so I thought it a shame to keep so much knowledge to myself.

SIR OLIVER (*Aside*):

> Mercy upon me! Learning that had run in the family like an heirloom! (*Aloud*) Pray what are become of the books?

CHARLES:

> You must inquire of the auctioneer, Master Premium, for I don't believe even Moses can direct you.

MOSES:

> I know nothing of books.

SIR OLIVER:

> So, so, nothing of the family property left, I suppose?

CHARLES:

> Not much, indeed, unless you have a mind to the family pictures. I have got a room full of ancestors above; and if you have a taste for paintings, egad, you shall have 'em a bargain.

SIR OLIVER:

> Hey! And the devil! Sure, you wouldn't sell your forefathers, would you?

CHARLES:

> Every man of them to the best bidder.

SIR OLIVER:

> What! Your great-uncles and aunts?

CHARLES:

> Aye, and my great-grandfathers and grandmothers too.

SIR OLIVER (*Aside*):

> Now I give him up! (*Aloud*) What the plague, have you no bowels for your own kindred? Odd's life, do you take me for Shylock in the play that you would raise money of me on your own flesh and blood?

CHARLES:

Nay, my little broker, don't be angry. What need you care if you have your money's worth?

SIR OLIVER:

Well, I'll be the purchaser. I think I can dispose of the family canvas. (*Aside*) Oh, I'll never forgive him this—never!

Enter Careless

CARELESS:

Come, Charles; what keeps you?

CHARLES:

I can't come yet. I' faith, we are going to have a sale above stairs. Here's little Premium will buy all my ancestors.

CARELESS:

Oh, burn your ancestors!

CHARLES:

No, he may do that afterwards if he pleases. Stay, Careless, we want you. Egad, you shall be auctioneer; so come along with us.

CARELESS:

Oh, have with you, if that's the case. I can handle a hammer as well as a dice-box.

SIR OLIVER (*Aside*):

Oh, the profligates!

CHARLES:

Come, Moses, you shall be appraiser if we want one. Gad's life, little Premium, you don't seem to like the business.

SIR OLIVER:

Oh, yes, I do, vastly. Ha, ha, ha! Yes, yes, I think it a rare joke to sell one's family by auction. Ha, ha! (*Aside*) Oh, the prodigal!

CHARLES:

To be sure! When a man wants money, where the plague should he get assistance if he can't make free with his own relations? *Exeunt* (*left*)

Act IV, Scene i

Picture room at Charles Surface's *house. Enter* (*left*) Charles Surface, Sir Oliver Surface, Moses, *and* Careless

CHARLES:

Walk in, gentlemen, pray walk in. Here they are, the family of the Surfaces, up to the Conquest.

SIR OLIVER:

> And, in my opinion, a goodly collection.

CHARLES:

> Aye, aye, these are done in the true spirit of portrait painting—
> no *volontière grace* and expression, not like the works of your
> modern Raphael, who gives you the strongest resemblance, yet
> contrives to make your own portrait independent of you, so
> that you may sink the original and not hurt the picture. No, no;
> the merit of these is the inveterate likeness—all stiff and awk-
> ward as the originals, and like nothing in human nature beside.

SIR OLIVER:

> Ah! we shall never see such figures of men again.

CHARLES:

> I hope not. Well, you see, Master Premium, what a domestic
> character I am. Here I sit of an evening surrounded by my fam-
> ily. But come, get to your pulpit, Mr Auctioneer. Here's an old
> gouty chair of my grandfather's will answer the purpose.

CARELESS:

> Aye, aye, this will do. But, Charles, I have ne'er a hammer—
> and what's an auctioneer without his hammer?

CHARLES:

> Egad, that's true. (*Reading a roll*) What parchment have we
> here? *Richard, heir to Thomas*. Oh, our genealogy in full. Here,
> Careless, you shall have no common bit of mahogany—here's
> the family tree for you, you rogue. This shall be your hammer,
> and now you may knock down my ancestors with their own
> pedigree.

SIR OLIVER (*Aside*):

> What an unnatural rogue—an *ex post facto* parricide!

CARELESS:

> Yes, yes, here's a list of your generation indeed. Faith, Charles,
> this is the most convenient thing you could have found for the
> business, for 'twill serve not only as a hammer but a catalogue
> into the bargain. But come, begin. A-going, a-going, a-going!

CHARLES:

> Bravo, Careless. Well, here's my great-uncle Sir Richard Rave-
> line, a marvellous good general in his day, I assure you. He
> served in all the Duke of Marlborough's wars, and got that cut
> over his eye at the Battle of Malplaquet. What say you, Mr Pre-
> mium? Look at him—there's a hero for you! Not cut out of his
> feathers, as your modern clipped captains are, but enveloped in
> wig and regimentals, as a general should be. What do you bid?

MOSES:

> Mr Premium would have *you* speak.

CHARLES:

Why, then, he shall have him for ten pounds, and I'm sure that's not dear for a staff-officer.

SIR OLIVER (*Aside*):

Heaven deliver me! His famous uncle Richard for ten pounds! (*Aloud*) Well, sir, I take him at that.

CHARLES:

Careless, knock down my uncle Richard. Here now is a maiden sister of his, my great-aunt Deborah, done by Kneller, thought to be in his best manner, and a very formidable likeness. There she is, you see, a shepherdess feeding her flock. You shall have her for five pounds ten—the sheep are worth the money.

SIR OLIVER (*Aside*):

Ah, poor Deborah—a woman who set such value on herself! (*Aloud*) Five pounds ten—she's mine.

CHARLES:

Knock down my aunt Deborah. Here now are two that were a sort of cousins of theirs. You see, Moses, these pictures were done some time ago, when beaux wore wigs, and the ladies their own hair.

SIR OLIVER:

Yes, truly, head-dresses appear to have been a little lower in those days.

CHARLES:

Well, take that couple for the same.

MOSES:

'Tis good bargain.

CHARLES:

Careless! This now is a grandfather of my mother's, a learned judge, well known on the western circuit. What do you rate him at, Moses?

MOSES:

Four guineas.

CHARLES:

Four guineas! Gad's life, you don't bid me the price of his wig. Mr Premium, you have more respect for the woolsack. Do let us knock his lordship down at fifteen.

SIR OLIVER:

By all means.

CARELESS:

Gone.

CHARLES:

And these are two brothers of his, William and Walter Blunt, Esquires, both Members of Parliament and noted speakers; and what's very extraordinary, I believe this is the first time they were ever bought and sold.

SIR OLIVER:

That is very extraordinary, indeed! I'll take them at your own price for the honour of Parliament.

CARELESS:

Well said, little Premium! I'll knock them down at forty.

CHARLES:

Here's a jolly fellow. I don't know what relation, but he was Mayor of Manchester. Take him at eight pounds.

SIR OLIVER:

No, no; six will do for the mayor.

CHARLES:

Come, make it guineas, and I'll throw you the two aldermen there into the bargain.

SIR OLIVER:

They're mine.

CHARLES:

Careless, knock down the Lord Mayor and aldermen. But, plague on't, we shall be all day retailing in this manner. Do let us deal wholesale, what say you, little Premium? Give us three hundred pounds for the rest of the family in the lump.

CARELESS:

Aye, aye, that will be the best way.

SIR OLIVER:

Well, well, anything to accommodate you. They are mine. But there is one portrait which you have always passed over.

CARELESS:

What, that ill-looking little fellow over the settee?

SIR OLIVER:

Yes, sir, I mean that, though I don't think him so ill-looking a little fellow by any means.

CHARLES:

What, that? Oh, that's my uncle Oliver. 'Twas done before he went to India.

CARELESS:

Your uncle Oliver! Gad, then you'll never be friends, Charles. That now to me is as stern a looking rogue as ever I saw—an unforgiving eye and a damned disinheriting countenance. An inveterate knave, depend on't, don't you think so, little Premium?

SIR OLIVER:

Upon my soul, sir, I do not. I think it is as honest a looking face as any in the room, dead or alive. But I suppose Uncle Oliver goes with the rest of the lumber?

CHARLES:

No, hang it! I'll not part with poor Noll. The old fellow has been very good to me, and egad I'll keep his picture while I've a room to put it in.

SIR OLIVER (*Aside*):

The rogue's my nephew after all! (*Aloud*) But, sir, I have somehow taken a fancy to that picture.

CHARLES:

I'm sorry for't, for you certainly will not have it. Oons, haven't you got enough of them?

SIR OLIVER (*Aside*):

I forgive him for everything! (*Aloud*) But, sir, when I take a whim in my head, I don't value money. I'll give you as much for that as for all the rest.

CHARLES:

Don't tease me, master broker. I tell you I'll not part with it, and there's an end of it.

SIR OLIVER (*Aside*):

How like his father the dog is! (*Aloud*) Well, well, I have done. (*Aside*) I did not perceive it before, but I think I never saw such a striking resemblance. (*Aloud*) Here's a draft for your sum.

CHARLES:

Why, 'tis for eight hundred pounds!

SIR OLIVER:

You will not let Sir Oliver go?

CHARLES:

Zounds, no! I tell you once more.

SIR OLIVER:

Then never mind the difference, we'll balance that another time. But give me your hand on the bargain. You are an honest fellow, Charles. I beg pardon, sir, for being so free. Come, Moses.

CHARLES (*Aside*):

Egad, this is a whimsical old fellow! (*Aloud*) But hark'ee, Premium, you'll prepare lodgings for these gentlemen.

SIR OLIVER:

Yes, yes, I'll send for them in a day or two.

CHARLES:

But hold! Do, now, send a genteel conveyance for them, for, I assure you, they were most of them used to ride in their own carriages.

SIR OLIVER:

I will, I will—for all but Oliver.

CHARLES:

Aye, all but the little nabob.

SIR OLIVER:

> You're fixed on that?

CHARLES:

> Peremptorily.

SIR OLIVER (*Aside*):

> A dear extravagant rogue! (*Aloud*) Good day! Come, Moses. (*Aside*) Let me hear now who calls him profligate!

Exeunt Sir Oliver *and* Moses (*left*)

CARELESS:

> Why, this is the oddest genius of the sort I ever saw.

CHARLES:

> Egad, he's the prince of brokers, I think. I wonder how the devil Moses got acquainted with so honest a fellow. Ha! here's Rowley. Do, Careless, say I'll join the company in a few moments.

CARELESS:

> I will; but don't let that old blockhead persuade you to squander any of that money on old musty debts, or any such nonsense; for tradesmen, Charles, are the most exorbitant fellows!

CHARLES:

> Very true, and paying them is only encouraging them.

CARELESS:

> Nothing else.

CHARLES:

> Aye, aye, never fear. *Exit* Careless
>
> So this was an odd old fellow, indeed! Let me see, two-thirds of this is mine by right—five hundred and thirty odd pounds. 'Fore Heaven! I find one's ancestors are more valuable relations than I took 'em for! Ladies and gentlemen, your most obedient and very grateful humble servant.

Enter Rowley

> Ha, old Rowley! Egad, you are just come in time to take leave of your old acquaintance.

ROWLEY:

> Yes, I heard they were a-going. But I wonder you can have such spirits under so many distresses.

CHARLES:

> Why, there's the point—my distresses are so many, that I can't afford to part with my spirits. But I shall be rich and splenetic all in good time. However, I suppose you are surprised that I am not more sorrowful at parting with so many near relations. To be sure, 'tis very affecting; but, rot 'em, you see they never move a muscle, so why should I?

ROWLEY:

There's no making you serious a moment.

CHARLES:

Yes, faith, I am so now. Hence, my honest Rowley. Here, get me this changed, and take a hundred pounds of it immediately to old Stanley.

ROWLEY:

A hundred pounds! Consider only—

CHARLES:

Gad's life, don't talk about it! Poor Stanley's wants are pressing, and if you don't make haste, we shall have someone call that has a better right to the money.

ROWLEY:

Ah, there's the point! I never will cease dunning you with the old proverb—

CHARLES:

'Be just before you're generous', hey? Why, so I would if I could; but Justice is an old lame hobbling beldame, and I can't get her to keep pace with Generosity for the soul of me.

ROWLEY:

Yet, Charles, believe me, one hour's reflection—

CHARLES:

Aye, aye, it's all very true, but, hark'ee, Rowley, while I have, by Heaven I'll give. So damn your economy, and now for hazard.

Exeunt (*left*)

Act IV, Scene ii

The Parlour at Charles Surface's *house*
Enter (*left*) Sir Oliver Surface *and* Moses

MOSES:

Well, sir, I think, as Sir Peter said, you have seen Mr Charles in high glory; 'tis great pity he's so extravagant.

SIR OLIVER:

True, but he wouldn't sell my picture.

MOSES:

And loves wine and women so much.

SIR OLIVER:

But he wouldn't sell my picture.

MOSES:

And games so deep.

SIR OLIVER:

But he wouldn't sell my picture. Oh, here's Rowley.

Enter Rowley (*left*)

ROWLEY:

So, Sir Oliver, I find you have made a purchase.

SIR OLIVER:

Yes, yes, our young rake has parted with his ancestors like old tapestry.

ROWLEY:

And here has he commissioned me to re-deliver you part of the purchase-money—I mean, though, in your necessitous character of old Stanley.

MOSES:

Ah, there is the pity of all. He is so damned charitable.

ROWLEY:

And I left a hosier and two tailors in the hall, who, I'm sure, won't be paid, and this hundred would satisfy them.

SIR OLIVER:

Well, well, I'll pay his debts—and his benevolence too. But now I am no more a broker and you shall introduce me to the elder brother as old Stanley.

ROWLEY:

Not yet awhile. Sir Peter I know means to call there about this time.

Enter Trip (*left*)

TRIP:

Oh, gentlemen, I beg pardon for not showing you out; this way. Moses, a word.   *Exeunt* Trip *and* Moses (*right*)

SIR OLIVER:

There's a fellow for you! Would you believe it, that puppy intercepted the Jew on our coming and wanted to raise money before he got to his master?

ROWLEY:

Indeed.

SIR OLIVER:

Yes, they are now planning an annuity business. Ah, Master Rowley, in my days servants were content with the follies of their masters, when they were worn a little threadbare; but now they have their vices, like their Birthday clothes, with the gloss on.   *Exeunt* (*right*)

Act IV, Scene iii

Joseph Surface and Servant (*in the*) *library in* Joseph's *house*

JOSEPH:

No letter from Lady Teazle?

SERVANT:

No, sir.

JOSEPH (*Aside*):

I am surprised she has not sent, if she is prevented from coming. Sir Peter certainly does not suspect me. Yet, I wish I may not lose the heiress, through the scrape I have drawn myself in with the wife; however, Charles's imprudence and bad character are great points in my favour.

Knocking heard without (*right*)

SERVANT:

Sir, I believe that must be Lady Teazle.

JOSEPH:

Hold! See whether it is or not before you go to the door; I have a particular message for you, if it should be my brother.

SERVANT:

'Tis her ladyship, sir; she always leaves her chair at the milliner's in the next street.

JOSEPH:

Stay, stay. Draw that screen before the window—that will do. My opposite neighbour is a maiden lady of so anxious a temper.

Servant draws the screen, and exit (*right*)

I have a difficult hand to play in this affair. Lady Teazle has lately suspected my views on Maria, but she must by no means be let into that secret—at least, not till I have her more in my power.

Enter Lady Teazle (*left*)

LADY TEAZLE:

What! Sentiment in soliloquy now? Have you been very impatient? O lud, don't pretend to look grave. I vow I couldn't come before.

JOSEPH:

Oh, madam, punctuality is a species of constancy, a very unfashionable quality in a lady.

LADY TEAZLE:

Upon my word, you ought to pity me. Do you know Sir Peter is grown so ill-tempered to me of late—and so jealous of Charles too! That's the best of the story, isn't it?

JOSEPH (*Aside*):

I am glad my scandalous friends keep that up.

LADY TEAZLE:

I am sure I wish he would let Maria marry him and then perhaps he would be convinced; don't you, Mr Surface?

JOSEPH (*Aside*):

Indeed I do not. (*Aloud*) Oh, certainly I do. For then my dear
Lady Teazle would also be convinced how wrong her suspicions were of my having any design on the silly girl.

(*They*) *sit*

LADY TEAZLE:

Well, well, I'm inclined to believe you. But isn't it provoking to
have the most ill-natured things said to one? And there's my
friend Lady Sneerwell has circulated I don't know how many
scandalous tales of me, and all without any foundation too.
That's what vexes me.

JOSEPH:

Aye, madam, to be sure, that's the provoking circumstance—
without foundation. Yes, yes, there's the mortification, indeed; for, when a scandalous story is believed against one,
there certainly is no comfort like the consciousness of having
deserved it.

LADY TEAZLE:

No, to be sure, then I'd forgive their malice. But to attack me,
who am really so innocent and who never say an ill-natured
thing of anybody—that is, of any friend; and then Sir Peter,
too, to have him so peevish and so suspicious, when I know the
integrity of my own heart—indeed, 'tis monstrous!

JOSEPH:

But, my dear Lady Teazle, 'tis your own fault if you suffer it.
When a husband entertains a groundless suspicion of his wife
and withdraws his confidence from her, the original compact is
broken; and she owes it to the honour of her sex to outwit him.

LADY TEAZLE:

Indeed! So that, if he suspects me without cause, it follows that
the best way of curing his jealousy is to give him reason for it?

JOSEPH:

Undoubtedly—for your husband should never be deceived in
you; and in that case it becomes you to be frail in compliment
to his discernment.

LADY TEAZLE:

To be sure, what you say is very reasonable, and when the consciousness of my own innocence—

JOSEPH:

Ah, my dear madam, there is the great mistake! 'Tis this very conscious innocence that is of the greatest prejudice to you. What is it makes you negligent of forms, and careless of the world's opinion? Why, the consciousness of your own innocence. What makes you thoughtless in your conduct, and apt to run into a thousand little imprudences? Why, the consciousness of your own innocence. What makes you impatient of Sir Peter's temper, and outrageous at his suspicions? Why, the consciousness of your innocence.

LADY TEAZLE:

'Tis very true.

JOSEPH:

Now, my dear Lady Teazle, if you would but once make a trifling *faux pas,* you can't conceive how cautious you would grow, and how ready to humour and agree with your husband.

LADY TEAZLE:

Do you think so?

JOSEPH:

Oh, I am sure on't; and then you would find all scandal would cease at once, for, in short, your character at present is like a person in a plethora, absolutely dying from too much health.

LADY TEAZLE:

So, so; then I perceive your prescription is that I must sin in my own defence, and part with my virtue to secure my reputation?

JOSEPH:

Exactly so, upon my credit, ma'am.

LADY TEAZLE:

Well, certainly this is the oddest doctrine, and the newest receipt for avoiding calumny.

JOSEPH:

An infallible one, believe me. Prudence, like experience, must be paid for.

LADY TEAZLE:

Why, if my understanding were once convinced—

JOSEPH:

Oh, certainly, madam, your understanding should be convinced. Yes, yes—Heaven forbid I should persuade you to do anything you *thought* wrong. No, no, I have too much honour to desire it.

LADY TEAZLE:

Don't you think we may as well leave *honour* out of the argument?

JOSEPH:

    Ah, the ill effects of your country education, I see, still remain with you.

LADY TEAZLE:

    I doubt they do indeed; and I will fairly own to you that if I could be persuaded to do wrong, it would be by Sir Peter's ill usage sooner than your *honourable logic* after all.

JOSEPH:

    Then, by this hand, which he is unworthy of—

Taking her hand

Enter Servant (*left*)

    'Sdeath, you blockhead—what do you want?

SERVANT:

    I beg your pardon, sir, but I thought you wouldn't choose Sir Peter to come up without announcing him.

JOSEPH:

    Sir Peter! Oons—the devil!   *Both rise*

LADY TEAZLE:

    Sir Peter! O lud, I'm ruined! I'm ruined!

SERVANT:

    Sir, 'twasn't I let him in.

LADY TEAZLE:

    Oh, I'm undone! What will become of me now, Mr Logic? Oh, mercy, he's on the stairs. I'll get behind here—and if ever I'm so imprudent again—   (*Hides behind screen*)

JOSEPH:

    Give me that book.

Sits down. Servant *pretends to adjust his hair*

Enter Sir Peter Teazle (*left*)

SIR PETER:

    Aye, ever improving himself! Mr Surface, Mr Surface—

JOSEPH:

    Oh, my dear Sir Peter, I beg your pardon. (*Gaping, and throws away the book*) I have been dozing over a stupid book. Well, I am much obliged to you for this call. You haven't been here, I believe, since I fitted up this room. Books, you know, are the only things I am a coxcomb in.

SIR PETER:

    'Tis very neat indeed. Well, well, that's proper; and you make even your screen a source of knowledge—hung, I perceive, with maps.

JOSEPH:

Oh, yes, I find great use in that screen.

SIR PETER:

I dare say you must. Certainly when you want to find anything in a hurry.

JOSEPH (*Aside*):

Aye, or to hide anything in a hurry either.

SIR PETER:

Well, I have a little private business—

JOSEPH (*To* Servant):

You needn't stay.

SERVANT:

No, sir.   *Exit* (*right*)

JOSEPH:

Here's a chair, Sir Peter. I beg—

SIR PETER:

Well, now we are alone, there is a subject, my dear friend, on which I wish to unburden my mind to you—a point of the greatest moment to my peace; in short, my dear friend, Lady Teazle's conduct of late has made me extremely unhappy.

JOSEPH:

Indeed! I am very sorry to hear it.

SIR PETER:

Aye, 'tis too plain she has not the least regard for me; but, what's worse, I have pretty good authority to suppose she must have formed an attachment to another.

JOSEPH:

Indeed! You astonish me!

SIR PETER:

Yes; and, between ourselves, I think I've discovered the person.

JOSEPH:

How! You alarm me exceedingly.

SIR PETER:

Aye, my dear friend, I knew you would sympathize with me.

JOSEPH:

Yes—believe me, Sir Peter, such a discovery would hurt me just as much as it would you.

SIR PETER:

I am convinced of it. Ah, it is a happiness to have a friend whom one can trust even with one's family secrets. But have you no guess who I mean?

JOSEPH:

I haven't the most distant idea. It can't be Sir Benjamin Back-bite?

SIR PETER:

Oh, no! What say you to Charles?

JOSEPH:

My brother! Impossible!

SIR PETER:

Ah, my dear friend, the goodness of your own heart misleads you. You judge of others by yourself.

JOSEPH:

Certainly, Sir Peter, the heart that is conscious of its own integrity is ever slow to credit another's treachery.

SIR PETER:

True, but your brother has no sentiment. You never hear him talk so.

JOSEPH:

Yet I can't but think Lady Teazle herself has too much principle.

SIR PETER:

Aye, but what is principle against the flattery of a handsome, lively young fellow?

JOSEPH:

That's very true.

SIR PETER:

And then, you know, the difference of our ages makes it very improbable that she should have any very great affection for me; and, if she were to be frail, and I were to make it public, why, the town would only laugh at me—the foolish old bachelor who had married a girl.

JOSEPH:

That's true, to be sure. They *would* laugh.

SIR PETER:

Laugh—aye, and make ballads and paragraphs and the devil knows what of me.

JOSEPH:

No, you must never make it public.

SIR PETER:

But then, again, that the nephew of my old friend, Sir Oliver, should be the person to attempt such a wrong, hurts me more nearly.

JOSEPH:

Aye, there's the point. When ingratitude barbs the dart of injury, the wound has double danger in it.

SIR PETER:

Aye. I that was, in a manner, left his guardian, in whose house he had been so often entertained—who never in my life denied him my advice!

JOSEPH:

Oh, 'tis not to be credited! There may be a man capable of such baseness, to be sure; but, for my part, till you can give me positive proofs, I cannot but doubt it. However, if it should be proved on him, he is no longer a brother of mine; I disclaim kindred with him; for the man who can break the laws of hospitality and attempt the wife of his friend, deserves to be branded as the pest of society.

SIR PETER:

What a difference there is between you. What noble sentiments!

JOSEPH:

Yet I cannot suspect Lady Teazle's honour.

SIR PETER:

I am sure I wish to think well of her and to remove all ground of quarrel between us. She has lately reproached me more than once with having made no settlement on her, and in our last quarrel she almost hinted that she should not break her heart if I was dead. Now, as we seem to differ in our ideas of expense, I have resolved she shall have her own way and be her own mistress in that respect for the future; and, if I were to die, she will find that I have not been inattentive to her interest while living. Here, my friend, are the drafts of two deeds, which I wish to have your opinion on. By one she will enjoy eight hundred a year independent while I live; and, by the other, the bulk of my fortune at my death.

JOSEPH:

This conduct, Sir Peter, is indeed truly generous. (*Aside*) I wish it may not corrupt my pupil.

SIR PETER:

Yes, I am determined she shall have no cause to complain, though I would not have her acquainted with the latter instance of my affection yet awhile.

JOSEPH (*Aside*):

Nor I, if I could help it.

SIR PETER:

And now, my dear friend, if you please, we will talk over the situation of your affairs with Maria.

JOSEPH (*Softly*):

Oh, no, Sir Peter! Another time, if you please.

SIR PETER:

I am sensibly chagrined at the little progress you seem to make in her affection.

JOSEPH (*Softly*):

> I beg you will not mention it. What are my disappointments when your happiness is in debate! (*Aside*) 'Sdeath, I shall be ruined every way.

SIR PETER:

> And though you are so averse to my acquainting Lady Teazle with your passion for Maria, I'm sure she's not your enemy in the affair.

JOSEPH:

> Pray, Sir Peter, now, oblige me. I am really too much affected by the subject we have been speaking of, to bestow a thought on my own concerns. The man who is entrusted with his friend's distresses can never—

Enter Servant (*left*)

> Well, sir?

SERVANT:

> Your brother, sir, is speaking to a gentleman in the street, and says he knows you are within.

JOSEPH:

> 'Sdeath, blockhead—I'm not within. I'm out for the day.

SIR PETER:

> Stay. Hold. A thought has struck me. You *shall* be at home.

JOSEPH:

> Well, well, let him up.   *Exit* Servant
>
> (*Aside*) He'll interrupt Sir Peter, however.

SIR PETER:

> Now, my good friend, oblige me, I entreat you. Before Charles comes, let me conceal myself somewhere; then do you tax him on the point we have been talking on, and his answers may satisfy me at once.

JOSEPH:

> Oh, fie, Sir Peter! Would you have me join in so mean a trick—to trepan my brother too?

SIR PETER:

> Nay, you tell me you are *sure* he is innocent; if so, you do him the greatest service by giving him an opportunity to clear himself, and you will set my heart at rest. Come, you shall not refuse me. Here, behind this screen will be— (*Goes to the screen*). Hey! What the devil! There seems to be *one* listener there already. I'll swear I saw a petticoat.

JOSEPH:

Ha, ha, ha! Well, this is ridiculous enough. I'll tell you, Sir Peter, though I hold a man of intrigue to be a most despicable character, yet you know it doesn't follow that one is to be an absolute Joseph either. Hark'ee, 'tis a little French milliner, a silly rogue that plagues me—and having some character on your coming, sir, she ran behind the screen.

SIR PETER:

Ah, you rogue! But, egad, she has overheard all I have been saying of my wife.

JOSEPH:

Oh, 'twill never go any farther, you may depend upon't.

SIR PETER:

No? Then i'faith let her hear it out. Here's a closet will do as well.

JOSEPH:

Well, go in then.

SIR PETER:

Sly rogue! sly rogue!   *Goes (right) into the closet*

JOSEPH:

A narrow escape, indeed, and a curious situation I'm in to part man and wife in this manner.

LADY TEAZLE (*Peeping from the screen*):

Couldn't I steal off?

JOSEPH:

Keep close, my angel.

SIR PETER (*Peeping (right)*):

Joseph, tax him home.

JOSEPH:

Back, my dear friend.

LADY TEAZLE (*Peeping*):

Couldn't you lock Sir Peter in?

JOSEPH:

Be still, my life.

SIR PETER (*Peeping*):

You're sure the little milliner won't blab?

JOSEPH:

In, in, my good Sir Peter. 'Fore Gad, I wish I had a key to the door.

Enter Charles Surface (*left*)

CHARLES:

> Hullo, brother, what has been the matter? Your fellow would not let me up at first. What, have you had a Jew or a wench with you?

JOSEPH:

> Neither, brother, I assure you.

CHARLES:

> But what has made Sir Peter steal off? I thought he had been with you.

JOSEPH:

> He *was* brother, but hearing *you* were coming he did not choose to stay.

CHARLES:

> What! Was the old gentleman afraid I wanted to borrow money of him?

JOSEPH:

> No, sir. But I am sorry to find, Charles, you have lately given that worthy man grounds for great uneasiness.

CHARLES:

> Yes, they tell me I do that to a great many worthy men. But how so, pray?

JOSEPH:

> To be plain with you, brother, he thinks you are endeavouring to gain Lady Teazle's affections from him.

CHARLES:

> Who, I? O lud, not I, upon my word. Ha, ha, ha! So the old fellow has found out that he has got a young wife, has he? Or, what is worse, her ladyship has found out she has an old husband?

JOSEPH:

> This is no subject to jest on, brother. He who can laugh—

CHARLES:

> True, true, as you were going to say. Then, seriously, I never had the least idea of what you charge me with, upon my honour.

JOSEPH (*Aloud*):

> Well, it will give Sir Peter great satisfaction to hear this.

CHARLES:

> To be sure, I once thought the lady seemed to have taken a fancy to me; but, upon my soul, I never gave her the least encouragement. Besides, you know my attachment to Maria.

JOSEPH:

> But sure, brother, even if Lady Teazle had betrayed the fondest partiality for you—

CHARLES:

> Why, look'ee, Joseph, I hope I shall never deliberately do a dishonourable action; but if a pretty woman was purposely to

throw herself in my way—and that pretty woman married to a man old enough to be her father—

JOSEPH:

Well?

CHARLES:

Why, I believe I should be obliged to borrow a little of your morality. That's all. But brother, do you know now that you surprise me exceedingly by naming *me* with Lady Teazle; for, faith, I always understood *you* were her favourite.

JOSEPH:

Oh, for shame, Charles! This retort is foolish.

CHARLES:

Nay, I swear I have seen you exchange such significant glances—

JOSEPH:

Nay, nay, sir, this is no jest—

CHARLES:

Egad, I'm serious. Don't you remember, one day, when I called here—

JOSEPH:

Nay, prithee, Charles—

CHARLES:

And found you together—

JOSEPH:

Zounds, sir, I insist—

CHARLES:

And another time, when your servant—

JOSEPH:

Brother, brother, a word with you. (*Aside*) Gad, I must stop him.

CHARLES:

Informed me, I say, that—

JOSEPH:

Hush! I beg your pardon, but Sir Peter has overheard all we have been saying. I knew you would clear yourself, or I should not have consented.

CHARLES:

How, Sir Peter! Where is he?

JOSEPH:

Softly. There! *Points to the closet*

CHARLES:

Oh, 'fore Heaven, I'll have him out. Sir Peter, come forth!

JOSEPH:

No, no—

CHARLES:

I say, Sir Peter, come into court. (*Pulls in* Sir Peter) What! My old guardian! What, turn inquisitor and take evidence *incog.*?

SIR PETER:

Give me your hand, Charles. I believe I have suspected you wrongfully; but you mustn't be angry with Joseph. 'Twas my plan.

CHARLES:

Indeed!

SIR PETER:

But I acquit you. I promise you I don't think near so ill of you as I did. What I have heard has given me great satisfaction.

CHARLES:

Egad, then, 'twas lucky you didn't hear any more. (*Apart to* Joseph) Wasn't it Joseph?

SIR PETER:

Ah, you would have retorted on him.

CHARLES:

Aye, aye, that was a joke.

SIR PETER:

Yes, yes, I know his honour too well.

CHARLES:

But you might as well have suspected him as me in this matter for all that. (*Apart to* Joseph) Mightn't he, Joseph?

SIR PETER:

Well, well, I believe you.

JOSEPH (*Aside*):

Would they were both out of the room!

Enter Servant (*left*) *and whispers* Joseph

SIR PETER:

And in future, perhaps, we may not be such strangers.

Exit Servant (*left*)

JOSEPH:

Gentlemen, I beg your pardon. I must wait on you downstairs. Here is a person come on particular business.

CHARLES:

Well, you can see him in another room. Sir Peter and I have not met a long time, and I have something to say to him.

JOSEPH (*Aside*):

They must not be left together. (*Aloud*) I'll send this man away and return directly. (*Apart to* Sir Peter *and goes out* (*left*)) Sir Peter, not a word of the French milliner.

SIR PETER (*Apart to* Joseph):

I? Not for the world. (*Aloud*) Ah, Charles, if you associated more with your brother, one might indeed hope for your reformation. He is a Man of Sentiment. Well, there is nothing in the world so noble as a Man of Sentiment.

CHARLES:

Pshaw, he is too moral by half—and so apprehensive of his good name, as he calls it, that I suppose he would as soon let a priest into his house as a girl.

SIR PETER:

No, no! Come, come! You wrong him. No, no, Joseph is no rake, but he is no saint either in that respect. (*Aside*) I have a great mind to tell him. We should have such a laugh.

CHARLES:

Oh, hang him, he's a very anchorite, a young hermit.

SIR PETER:

Hark'ee, you must not abuse him. He may chance to hear of it again, I promise you.

CHARLES:

Why, you won't tell him?

SIR PETER:

No. But this way. (*Aside*) Egad, I'll tell him. (*Aloud*) Hark'ee, have you a mind to have a good laugh at Joseph?

CHARLES:

I should like it of all things.

SIR PETER:

Then, i'faith, we will! (*Aside*) I'll be quit with him for discovering me. (*Aloud*) He had a girl with him when I called.

CHARLES:

What! Joseph? You jest.

SIR PETER:

Hush! A little French milliner. And the best of the jest is—she's in the room now.

CHARLES:

The devil she is!

SIR PETER:

Hush! I tell you. *Points* (*to the screen*)

CHARLES:

Behind the screen! 'Slife, let's unveil her.

SIR PETER:

No, no, he's coming—you shan't indeed.

CHARLES:

Oh, egad, we'll have a peep at the little milliner.

SIR PETER:

Not for the world! Joseph will never forgive me.

CHARLES:

I'll stand by you.

SIR PETER:

Odds, here he is!

Joseph *enters* (*left*) *just as* Charles *throws down the screen*

CHARLES:

Lady Teazle—by all that's wonderful!

SIR PETER:

Lady Teazle, by all that's damnable!

CHARLES:

Sir Peter, this is one of the smartest French milliners I ever saw. Egad, you seem all to have been diverting yourselves here at hide and seek—and I don't see who is out of the secret. Shall I beg your ladyship to inform me? Not a word! Brother, will you be pleased to explain this matter? What! Is morality dumb too? Sir Peter, though I *found* you in the dark, perhaps you are not so now? All mute. Well, though *I* can make nothing of the affair, I suppose you perfectly understand one another. So I'll leave you to yourselves. (*Going*) Brother, I'm sorry to find you have given that worthy man cause for so much uneasiness. Sir Peter, there's nothing in the world so noble as a Man of Sentiment!

Exit Charles (*left*). *They stand for some time looking at each other*

JOSEPH:

Sir Peter, notwithstanding I confess that appearances are against me, if you will afford me your patience, I make no doubt—but I shall explain everything to your satisfaction.

SIR PETER:

If you please, sir.

JOSEPH:

The fact is, sir, that Lady Teazle, knowing my pretensions to your ward, Maria—I say, sir—Lady Teazle, being apprehensive of the jealousy of your temper—and knowing my friendship to the family—she, sir, I say—called here—in order that—I might explain these pretensions—but on your coming—being apprehensive—as I said—of your jealousy—she withdrew—and this, you may depend on it, is the whole truth of the matter.

SIR PETER:

A very clear account, upon my word; and I dare swear the lady will vouch for every article of it.

LADY TEAZLE:

For not one word of it, Sir Peter.

SIR PETER:

How? Don't you even think it worth while to agree in the lie?

LADY TEAZLE:

There is not one syllable of truth in what that gentleman has told you.

SIR PETER:

I believe you, upon my soul, ma'am.

JOSEPH (*Aside* (*to* Lady Teazle)):

'Sdeath, madam, will you betray me?

LADY TEAZLE:

Good Mr Hypocrite, by your leave, I'll speak for myself.

SIR PETER:

Aye, let her alone, sir; you'll find she'll make out a better story than you without prompting.

LADY TEAZLE:

Hear me, Sir Peter! I came hither on no matter relating to your ward, and even ignorant of this gentleman's pretensions to her. But I came seduced by his insidious arguments, at least to listen to his pretended passion, if not to sacrifice your honour to his baseness.

SIR PETER:

Now I believe the truth is coming indeed!

JOSEPH:

The woman's mad!

LADY TEAZLE:

No, sir, she has recovered her senses, and your own arts have furnished her with the means. Sir Peter, I do not expect you to credit me, but the tenderness you expressed for me, when I am sure you could not think I was a witness to it, has penetrated so to my heart that had I left the place without the shame of this discovery, my future life should have spoken the sincerity of my gratitude. As for that smooth-tongued hypocrite, who would have seduced the wife of his too credulous friend, while he affected honourable addresses to his ward—I behold him now in a light so truly despicable that I shall never again respect myself for having listened to him.   *Exit* (*left*)

JOSEPH:

Notwithstanding all this, Sir Peter, Heaven knows—

SIR PETER:

> That you are a villain! And so I leave you to your conscience.

JOSEPH:

> You are too rash, Sir Peter; you *shall* hear me. The man who shuts out conviction by refusing to—
>
> > *Exeunt (left) Joseph Surface following and speaking*

Act V, Scene i

The library in Joseph Surface's *house*
Enter (left) Joseph Surface *and* Servant

JOSEPH:

> Mr Stanley! And why should you think I would see him? You must know he comes to ask something.

SERVANT:

> Sir, I should not have let him in, but that Mr Rowley came to the door with him.

JOSEPH:

> Pshaw, blockhead! To suppose that I should now be in a temper to receive visits from poor relations! Well, why don't you show the fellow up?

SERVANT:

> I will, sir. Why, sir, it was not my fault that Sir Peter discovered my lady—

JOSEPH:

> Go, fool! *Exit* Servant *(left)*
>
> Sure, Fortune never played a man of my policy such a trick before. My character with Sir Peter, my hopes with Maria, destroyed in a moment! I'm in a rare humour to listen to other people's distresses. I shan't be able to bestow even a benevolent sentiment on Stanley.—So here he comes and Rowley with him. I must try to recover myself and put a little charity into my face, however. *Exit (right)*

Enter Sir Oliver Surface *and* Rowley *(left)*

SIR OLIVER:

> What, does he avoid us? That was he, was it not?

ROWLEY:

> It was, sir. But I doubt you are come a little too abruptly. His nerves are so weak that the sight of a poor relation may be

too much for him. I should have gone first to break you to him.

SIR OLIVER:

Oh, plague of his nerves! Yet this is he whom Sir Peter extols as a man of the most benevolent way of thinking.

ROWLEY:

As to his way of thinking, I cannot pretend to decide; for, to do him justice, he appears to have as much speculative benevolence as any private gentleman in the kingdom, though he is seldom so sensual as to indulge himself in the exercise of it.

SIR OLIVER:

Yet he has a string of charitable sentiments, I suppose, at his fingers' ends.

ROWLEY:

Or, rather, at his tongue's end, Sir Oliver, for I believe there is no sentiment he has such faith in as that 'Charity begins at home'.

SIR OLIVER:

And his, I presume, is of that domestic sort which never stirs abroad at all.

ROWLEY:

I doubt you'll find it so. But he's coming. I mustn't seem to interrupt you; and you know immediately as you leave him, I come in to announce your arrival in your real character.

SIR OLIVER:

True, and afterwards you'll meet me at Sir Peter's.

ROWLEY:

Without losing a moment.   *Exit* (*left*)

SIR OLIVER:

I don't like the complaisance of his features.

Enter Joseph Surface (*right*)

JOSEPH:

Sir, I beg you ten thousand pardons for keeping you a moment waiting. Mr Stanley, I presume.

SIR OLIVER:

At your service.

JOSEPH:

Sir, I beg you will do me the honour to sit down.—I entreat you, sir.

SIR OLIVER:

Dear sir, there's no occasion. (*Aside*) Too civil by half.

JOSEPH:

I have not the pleasure of knowing you, Mr Stanley, but I am extremely happy to see you look so well. You were nearly related to my mother, I think, Mr Stanley?

SIR OLIVER:

I was, sir; so nearly that my present poverty, I fear, may do discredit to her wealthy children; else I should not have presumed to trouble you.

JOSEPH:

Dear sir, there needs no apology. He that is in distress, though a stranger, has a right to claim kindred with the wealthy. I am sure I wish I was of that class and had it in my power to offer you even a small relief.

SIR OLIVER:

If your uncle, Sir Oliver, were here, I should have a friend.

JOSEPH:

I wish he was, sir, with all my heart. You should not want an advocate with him, believe me, sir.

SIR OLIVER:

I should not need one—my distresses would recommend me. But I imagined his bounty had enabled you to become the agent of his charity.

JOSEPH:

My dear sir, you were strangely misinformed. Sir Oliver is a worthy man, a very worthy man; but avarice, Mr Stanley, is the vice of age. I will tell you, my good sir, in confidence, what he has done for me has been a mere nothing; though people, I know, have thought otherwise, and for my part I never chose to contradict the report.

SIR OLIVER:

What! Has he never transmitted you bullion—rupees, pagodas?

JOSEPH:

Oh, dear sir, nothing of the kind! No, no. A few presents now and then—china, shawls, congou tea, avadavats, and India crackers. Little more, believe me.

SIR OLIVER (*Aside*):

Here's gratitude for twelve thousand pounds! Avadavats and India crackers!

JOSEPH:

Then, my dear sir, you have heard, I doubt not, of the extravagance of my brother. There are very few would credit what I have done for that unfortunate young man.

SIR OLIVER (*Aside*):

Not I, for one!

JOSEPH:

The sums I have lent him! Indeed I have been exceedingly to blame. It was an amiable weakness; however, I don't pretend to defend it. And now I feel it doubly culpable, since it has deprived me of the pleasure of serving you, Mr Stanley, as my heart dictates.

SIR OLIVER (*Aside*):

Dissembler! (*Aloud*) Then, sir, you can't assist me?

JOSEPH:

At present, it grieves me to say, I cannot; but, whenever I have the ability, you may depend upon hearing from me.

SIR OLIVER:

I am extremely sorry—

JOSEPH:

Not more than I, believe me. To pity without the power to relieve is still more painful than to ask and be denied.

SIR OLIVER:

Kind sir, your most obedient humble servant.

JOSEPH:

You leave me deeply affected, Mr Stanley. William, be ready to open the door.

SIR OLIVER:

Oh, dear sir, no ceremony.

JOSEPH:

Your very obedient—

SIR OLIVER:

Sir, your most obsequious—

JOSEPH:

You may depend upon hearing from me, whenever I can be of service.

SIR OLIVER:

Sweet sir, you are too good!

JOSEPH:

In the meantime I wish you health and spirits.

SIR OLIVER:

Your ever grateful and perpetual humble servant.

JOSEPH:

Sir, yours as sincerely.

SIR OLIVER (*Aside*):

Charles, you are my heir!   *Exit* (*left*)

JOSEPH (*Alone*):

This is one bad effect of a good character; it invites application from the unfortunate, and there needs no small degree of address to gain the reputation of benevolence without incurring the expense. The silver ore of pure charity is an expensive article in the catalogue of a man's good qualities; whereas the sentimental French plate I use instead of it makes just as good a show and pays no tax.

Enter Rowley (*left*)

ROWLEY:

Mr Surface, your servant. I was apprehensive of interrupting you, though my business demands immediate attention—as this note will inform you.

JOSEPH:

Always happy to see Mr Rowley. (*Aside*) A rascal. (*Reads*) How? '*Oliver Surface!*'—my uncle arrived?

ROWLEY:

He is, indeed. We have just parted. Quite well after a speedy voyage, and impatient to embrace his worthy nephew.

JOSEPH:

I am astonished. William, stop Mr Stanley, if he's not gone.

ROWLEY:

Oh, he's out of reach, I believe.

JOSEPH:

Why didn't you let me know this when you came in together?

ROWLEY:

I thought you had particular business. But I must be gone to inform your brother and appoint him here to meet his uncle. He will be with you in a quarter of an hour.

JOSEPH:

So he says. Well, I am strangely overjoyed at his coming. (*Aside*) Never to be sure was anything so damned unlucky!

ROWLEY:

You will be delighted to see how well he looks.

JOSEPH:

Oh, I'm rejoiced to hear it. (*Aside*) Just at this time!

ROWLEY:

I'll tell him how impatiently you expect him.

JOSEPH:

Do, do. Pray give my best duty and affection. Indeed, I cannot express the sensation I feel at the thought of seeing him!

Exit Rowley (*left*)

JOSEPH (*Alone*):

Certainly his coming just at this time is the cruellest piece of ill fortune. *Exit* (*right*)

Act V, Scene ii

Sir Peter Teazle's
Enter Mrs Candour *and* Maid (*left*)

MAID:
Indeed, ma'am, my lady will see nobody at present.

MRS CANDOUR:
Did you tell her it was her friend Mrs Candour?

MAID:
Yes, ma'am; but she begs you will excuse her.

MRS CANDOUR:
Do go again. I shall be glad to see her if it be only for a moment, for I am sure she must be in great distress.

Exit Maid (*right*)

Dear heart, how provoking! I'm not mistress of half the circumstances. We shall have the whole affair in the newspapers with the names of the parties at length before I have dropped the story at a dozen houses.

Enter Sir Benjamin Backbite (*left*)

Oh, Sir Benjamin, you have heard, I suppose—

SIR BENJAMIN:
Of Lady Teazle and Mr Surface—

MRS CANDOUR:
And Sir Peter's discovery—

SIR BENJAMIN:
Oh, the strangest piece of business, to be sure!

MRS CANDOUR:
Well, I never was so surprised in my life. I am so sorry for all parties, indeed I am.

SIR BENJAMIN:
Now, I don't pity Sir Peter at all; he was so extravagantly partial to Mr Surface.

MRS CANDOUR:
Mr Surface! Why, 'twas with Charles Lady Teazle was detected.

SIR BENJAMIN:
No, no, I tell you; Mr Surface is the gallant.

MRS CANDOUR:
No such thing! Charles is the man. 'Twas Mr Surface brought Sir Peter on purpose to discover them.

SIR BENJAMIN:

    I tell you I had it from one—

MRS CANDOUR:

    And I have it from one—

SIR BENJAMIN:

    Who had it from one, who had it—

MRS CANDOUR:

    From one immediately. But here comes Lady Sneerwell; perhaps she knows the whole affair.

Enter Lady Sneerwell (*left*)

LADY SNEERWELL:

    So, my dear Mrs Candour, here's a sad affair of our friend Lady Teazle.

MRS CANDOUR:

    Aye, my dear friend, who would have thought—

LADY SNEERWELL:

    Well, there is no trusting appearances, though indeed she was always too lively for me.

MRS CANDOUR:

    To be sure, her manners were a little too free; but then she was so young!

LADY SNEERWELL:

    And had, indeed, some good qualities.

MRS CANDOUR:

    So she had, indeed. But have you heard the particulars?

LADY SNEERWELL:

    No; but everybody says that Mr Surface—

SIR BENJAMIN:

    Aye, there I told you Mr Surface was the man.

MRS CANDOUR:

    No, no; indeed, the assignation was with Charles.

LADY SNEERWELL:

    With Charles? You alarm me, Mrs Candour!

MRS CANDOUR:

    Yes, yes; he was the lover. Mr Surface, do him justice, was only the informer.

SIR BENJAMIN:

    Well, I'll not dispute with you, Mrs Candour; but, be it which it may, I hope that Sir Peter's wound will not—

MRS CANDOUR:

    Sir Peter's wound! Oh, mercy! I didn't hear a word of their fighting.

LADY SNEERWELL:

Nor I, not a syllable.

SIR BENJAMIN:

No? What, no mention of the duel?

MRS CANDOUR:

Not a word.

SIR BENJAMIN:

Oh, Lord, yes. They fought before they left the room.

LADY SNEERWELL:

Pray let us hear.

MRS CANDOUR:

Aye, do oblige us with the duel.

SIR BENJAMIN:

'Sir,' says Sir Peter, immediately after the discovery, 'you are a most ungrateful fellow.'

MRS CANDOUR:

Aye, to Charles—

SIR BENJAMIN:

No, no, to Mr Surface. 'A most ungrateful fellow; and old as I am, sir,' says he, 'I insist on immediate satisfaction.'

MRS CANDOUR:

Aye, that must have been to Charles; for 'tis very unlikely Mr Surface should go to fight in his own house.

SIR BENJAMIN:

Gad's life, ma'am, not at all—'Giving me immediate satisfaction.' On this, ma'am, Lady Teazle, seeing Sir Peter in such danger, ran out of the room in strong hysterics, and Charles after her, calling out for hartshorn and water. Then, madam, they began to fight with swords—

Enter Crabtree (*left*)

CRABTREE:

With pistols, nephew—pistols. I have it from undoubted authority.

MRS CANDOUR:

Oh, Mr Crabtree, then it is all true?

CRABTREE:

Too true, indeed, madam, and Sir Peter is dangerously wounded—

SIR BENJAMIN:

By a thrust in segoon quite through his left side—

CRABTREE:

By a bullet lodged in the thorax.

MRS CANDOUR:

Mercy on me! Poor Sir Peter!

CRABTREE:

Yes, madam; though Charles would have avoided the matter, if he could.

MRS CANDOUR:

I knew Charles was the person.

SIR BENJAMIN:

My uncle, I see, knows nothing of the matter.

CRABTREE:

But Sir Peter taxed him with the basest ingratitude.

SIR BENJAMIN:

That I told you, you know—

CRABTREE:

Do, nephew, let me speak—and insisted on immediate—

SIR BENJAMIN:

Just as I said—

CRABTREE:

Odds life, nephew, allow others to know something too. A pair of pistols lay on the bureau (for Mr Surface, it seems, had come home the night before late from Salthill, where he had been to see the Montem with a friend, who has a son at Eton). So, unluckily, the pistols were left charged.

SIR BENJAMIN:

I heard nothing of this.

CRABTREE:

Sir Peter forced Charles to take one, and they fired, it seems, pretty nearly together. Charles's shot took effect, as I told you, and Sir Peter's missed; but, what is very extraordinary, the ball struck against a little bronze Pliny that stood over the fireplace, grazed out of the window at a right angle, and wounded the postman, who was just coming to the door with a double letter from Northamptonshire.

SIR BENJAMIN:

My uncle's account is more circumstantial, I confess; but I believe mine is the true one, for all that.

LADY SNEERWELL (*Aside*):

I am more interested in this affair than they imagine and must have better information. *Exit* Lady Sneerwell (*left*)

SIR BENJAMIN (*After a pause looking at each other*):

Ah, Lady Sneerwell's alarm is very easily accounted for.

CRABTREE:

Yes, yes, they certainly *do* say—but that's neither here nor there.

MRS CANDOUR:

But, pray, where is Sir Peter at present?

CRABTREE:

Oh, they brought him home, and he is now in the house, though the servants are ordered to deny it.

MRS CANDOUR:

I believe so, and Lady Teazle, I suppose, attending him.

CRABTREE:

Yes, yes. I saw one of the faculty enter just before me.

SIR BENJAMIN:

Hey! Who comes here?

CRABTREE:

Oh, this is he—the physician, depend on't.

MRS CANDOUR:

Oh, certainly. It must be the physician; and now we shall know.

Enter Sir Oliver Surface (*left*)

CRABTREE:

Well, doctor, what hopes?

MRS CANDOUR:

Aye, doctor, how's your patient?

SIR BENJAMIN:

Now, doctor, isn't it a wound with a small sword?

CRABTREE:

A bullet lodged in the thorax, for a hundred!

SIR OLIVER:

Doctor! A wound with a small sword! And a bullet in the thorax? Oons! Are you mad, good people?

SIR BENJAMIN:

Perhaps, sir, you are not a doctor?

SIR OLIVER:

Truly, I am to thank you for my degree, if I am.

CRABTREE:

Only a friend of Sir Peter's, then, I presume. But, sir, you must have heard of his accident?

SIR OLIVER:

Not a word!

CRABTREE:

Not of his being dangerously wounded?

SIR OLIVER:

The devil he is!

SIR BENJAMIN:

Run through the body—

CRABTREE:

Shot in the breast—

SIR BENJAMIN:

By one Mr Surface—

CRABTREE:

Aye, the younger.

SIR OLIVER:

Hey! What the plague! You seem to differ strangely in your accounts. However you agree that Sir Peter is dangerously wounded.

SIR BENJAMIN:

Oh, yes, we agree there.

CRABTREE:

Yes, yes, I believe there can be no doubt of that.

SIR OLIVER:

Then, upon my word, for a person in that situation he is the most imprudent man alive; for here he comes, walking as if nothing at all was the matter.

Enter Sir Peter Teazle (*left*)

Odds heart, Sir Peter, you are come in good time, I promise you; for we had just given you over.

SIR BENJAMIN:

Egad, uncle, this is the most sudden recovery!

SIR OLIVER:

Why, man, what do you out of bed with a small sword through your body, and a bullet lodged in your thorax?

SIR PETER:

A small sword, and a bullet!

SIR OLIVER:

Aye, these gentlemen would have killed you without law or physic, and wanted to dub me a doctor to make me an accomplice.

SIR PETER:

Why, what is all this?

SIR BENJAMIN:

We rejoice, Sir Peter, that the story of the duel is not true and are sincerely sorry for your other misfortune.

SIR PETER (*Aside*):

So, so. All over the town already.

CRABTREE:

Though, Sir Peter, you were certainly vastly to blame to marry at all at your years.

SIR PETER:

Sir, what business is that of yours?

MRS CANDOUR:

Though, indeed, as Sir Peter made so good a husband, he's very much to be pitied.

SIR PETER:

Plague on your pity, ma'am! I desire none of it.

SIR BENJAMIN:

However, Sir Peter, you must not mind the laughing and jests you will meet on this occasion.

SIR PETER:

Sir, I desire to be master in my own house.

CRABTREE:

'Tis no uncommon case; that's one comfort.

SIR PETER:

I insist on being left to myself. Without ceremony I insist on your leaving my house directly!

MRS CANDOUR:

Well, well, we are going—and depend on't, we'll make the best report of you we can.

SIR PETER:

Leave my house!

CRABTREE:

And tell how hardly you have been treated.

SIR PETER:

Leave my house!

SIR BENJAMIN:

And how patiently you bear it.

SIR PETER:

Fiends! Vipers! Furies! Oh, that their own venom would choke them!

Exeunt Mrs Candour, Sir Benjamin Backbite, Crabtree (*left*)

SIR OLIVER:

They are very provoking indeed, Sir Peter.

Enter Rowley (*left*)

ROWLEY:

I heard high words—what has ruffled you, Sir Peter?

SIR PETER:

Pshaw! What signifies asking? Do I ever pass a day without my vexations?

ROWLEY:

Well, I'm not inquisitive.

SIR OLIVER:

Well, Sir Peter, I have seen both my nephews in the manner we proposed.

SIR PETER:

A precious couple they are!

ROWLEY:

Yes, and Sir Oliver is convinced that your judgment was right, Sir Peter.

SIR OLIVER:

Yes, I find Joseph is indeed the man, after all.

ROWLEY:

Aye, as Sir Peter says, he is a Man of Sentiment.

SIR OLIVER:

And acts up to the sentiments he professes.

ROWLEY:

It certainly is edification to hear him talk.

SIR OLIVER:

Oh, he's a model for the young men of the age! But how's this, Sir Peter, you don't join us in your friend Joseph's praise, as I expected.

SIR PETER:

Sir Oliver, we live in a damned wicked world, and the fewer we praise the better.

ROWLEY:

What? Do you say so, Sir Peter, who were never mistaken in your life?

SIR PETER:

Pshaw! Plague on you both! I see by your sneering you have heard the whole affair. I shall go mad among you.

ROWLEY:

Then, to fret you no longer, Sir Peter, we are indeed acquainted with it all. I met Lady Teazle coming from Mr Surface's so humbled that she deigned to request *me* to be her advocate with you.

SIR PETER:

And does Sir Oliver know all this?

SIR OLIVER:

Every circumstance.

SIR PETER:

What? Of the closet and the screen, hey?

SIR OLIVER:

Yes, yes, and the little French milliner. Oh, I have been vastly diverted with the story! Ha, ha, ha!

SIR PETER:

'Twas very pleasant.

SIR OLIVER:

    I never laughed more in my life, I assure you. Ha, ha, ha!

SIR PETER:

    Oh, vastly diverting. Ha, ha, ha!

ROWLEY:

    To be sure, Joseph with his sentiments! Ha, ha, ha!

SIR PETER:

    Yes, yes, his sentiments! Ha, ha, ha! Hypocritical villain.

SIR OLIVER:

    Aye, and that rogue Charles to pull Sir Peter out of the closet! Ha, ha, ha!

SIR PETER:

    Ha, ha! 'Twas devilish entertaining, to be sure.

SIR OLIVER:

    Ha, ha, ha! Egad, Sir Peter, I should like to have seen your face when the screen was thrown down. Ha, ha!

SIR PETER:

    Yes, yes, my face when the screen was thrown down. Ha, ha, ha! Oh, I must never show my head again.

SIR OLIVER:

    But, come, come, it isn't fair to laugh at you neither, my old friend, though, upon my soul, I can't help it.

SIR PETER:

    Oh, pray don't restrain your mirth on my account. It does not hurt me at all. I laugh at the whole affair myself. Yes, yes, I think being a standing jest for all one's acquaintance a very happy situation. Oh, yes, and then of a morning to read the paragraphs about Mr S—, Lady T—, and Sir P— will be so entertaining.

ROWLEY:

    Without affectation, Sir Peter, you may despise the ridicule of fools. But I see Lady Teazle going towards the next room. I am sure you must desire a reconciliation as earnestly as she does.

SIR OLIVER:

    Perhaps my being here prevents her coming to you. Well, I'll leave honest Rowley to mediate between you; but he must bring you all presently to Mr Surface's, where I am now returning, if not to reclaim a libertine, at least to expose hypocrisy.

SIR PETER:

    Ah, I'll be present at your discovering yourself there with all my heart, though 'tis a vile unlucky place for discoveries.

ROWLEY:

    We'll follow.   *Exit* Sir Oliver (*left*)

SIR PETER:

    She is not coming here, you see, Rowley.

ROWLEY:

    No, but she has left the door of that room open, you perceive. See, she is in tears.

SIR PETER:

    Certainly a little mortification appears very becoming in a wife. Don't you think it will do her good to let her pine a little?

ROWLEY:

    Oh this is ungenerous in you.

SIR PETER:

    Well, I know not what to think. You remember, Rowley, the letter I found of hers evidently intended for Charles?

ROWLEY:

    A mere forgery, Sir Peter, laid in your way on purpose. This is one of the points which I intend Snake shall give you conviction on.

SIR PETER:

    I wish I were once satisfied of that. She looks this way. What a remarkably elegant turn of the head she has! Rowley, I'll go to her.

ROWLEY:

    Certainly.

SIR PETER:

    Though, when it is known that we are reconciled, people will laugh at me ten times more.

ROWLEY:

    Let them laugh and retort their malice only by showing them you are happy in spite of it.

SIR PETER:

    I'faith, so I will! And, if I'm not mistaken, we may yet be the happiest couple in the country.

ROWLEY:

    Nay, Sir Peter, he who once lays aside suspicion—

SIR PETER:

    Hold, Master Rowley! If you have any regard for me, never let me hear you utter anything like a sentiment. I have had enough of them to serve me the rest of my life.

Exeunt (right)

Act V, Scene iii

The library in Joseph Surface's *house*
Enter Joseph Surface *and* Lady Sneerwell (*left*)

LADY SNEERWELL:

> Impossible! Will not Sir Peter immediately be reconciled to Charles and, of course, no longer oppose his union with Maria? The thought is distraction to me.

JOSEPH:

> Can passion furnish a remedy?

LADY SNEERWELL:

> No, nor cunning neither. Oh, I was a fool, an idiot, to league with such a blunderer!

JOSEPH:

> Sure, Lady Sneerwell, I am the greatest sufferer; yet you see I bear the accident with calmness.

LADY SNEERWELL:

> Because the disappointment doesn't reach your heart; your interest only attached you to Maria. Had you felt for her what I have for that ungrateful libertine, neither your temper nor hypocrisy could prevent your showing the sharpness of your vexation.

JOSEPH:

> But why should your reproaches fall on me for this disappointment?

LADY SNEERWELL:

> Are you not the cause of it? What had you to do to bate in your pursuit of Maria to pervert Lady Teazle by the way? Had you not a sufficient field for your roguery in imposing upon Sir Peter, and supplanting your brother but you must endeavour to seduce his wife? I hate such an avarice of crimes; 'tis an unfair monopoly, and never prospers.

JOSEPH:

> Well, I admit I have been to blame. I confess I deviated from the direct road of wrong, but I don't think we're so totally defeated neither.

LADY SNEERWELL:

> No!

JOSEPH:

> You tell me you have made a trial of Snake since we met, and that you still believe him faithful to us?

LADY SNEERWELL:

> I do believe so.

JOSEPH:

> And that he has undertaken, should it be necessary, to swear and prove that Charles is at this time contracted by vows and honour to your ladyship—which some of his former letters to you will serve to support.

LADY SNEERWELL:

> This, indeed, might have assisted.

JOSEPH:

> Come, come; it is not too late yet. (*Knocking at the door* (*left*)) But hark! This is probably my uncle, Sir Oliver: retire to that room; we'll consult farther when he's gone.

LADY SNEERWELL:

> Well, but if he should find you out too?

JOSEPH:

> Oh, I have no fear of that. Sir Peter will hold his tongue for his own credit's sake—and you may depend on't I shall soon discover Sir Oliver's weak side!

LADY SNEERWELL:

> I have no diffidence of your abilities. Only be constant to one roguery at a time.   *Exit* (*right*)

JOSEPH:

> I will, I will! So! 'tis confounded hard, after such bad fortune, to be baited by one's confederate in evil. Well, at all events my character is so much better than Charles's that I certainly—hey! What? This is not Sir Oliver but old Stanley again. Plague on't that he should return to tease me just now. We shall have Sir Oliver come and find him here and—

Enter Sir Oliver Surface (*left*)

> Gad's life, Mr Stanley, why have you come back to plague me just at this time? You must not stay now, upon my word.

SIR OLIVER:

> Sir, I hear your uncle Oliver is expected here, and though he has been so penurious to you I'll try what he'll do for me.

JOSEPH:

> Sir, 'tis impossible for you to stay now, so I must beg—come any other time, and I promise you, you shall be assisted.

SIR OLIVER:

> No. Sir Oliver and I must be acquainted.

JOSEPH:

> Zounds, sir! Then I insist on your quitting the room directly.

SIR OLIVER:

> Nay, sir—

JOSEPH:

Sir, I insist on't. Here, William! Show this gentleman out. Since you compel me, sir, not one moment. This is such inso-lence. *Going to push him out*

Enter Charles Surface (*left*)

CHARLES:

Hey day! what's the matter now? What the devil have you got hold of my little broker here? Zounds, brother, don't hurt little Premium. What's the matter, my little fellow?

JOSEPH:

So! he has been with you too, has he?

CHARLES:

To be sure he has. Why, he's as honest a little—but sure, Joseph, you have not been borrowing money too, have you?

JOSEPH:

Borrowing? No. But, brother, you know we expect Sir Oliver here every—

CHARLES:

O Gad, that's true! Noll mustn't find the little broker here, to be sure.

JOSEPH:

Yet, Mr Stanley insists—

CHARLES:

Stanley! Why his name is Premium.

JOSEPH:

No, no, Stanley.

CHARLES:

No, no, Premium.

JOSEPH:

Well, no matter which. But—

CHARLES:

Aye, aye, Stanley or Premium, 'tis the same thing, as you say; for I suppose he goes by half a hundred names, besides A.B. at the coffee-houses.

JOSEPH:

Death! here's Sir Oliver at the door. *Knocking again* (*left*) Now I beg, Mr Stanley—

CHARLES:

Aye, aye, and I beg, Mr Premium—

SIR OLIVER:

Gentlemen—

JOSEPH:

Sir, by Heaven you shall go.

CHARLES:

Aye, out with him, certainly.

SIR OLIVER:

This violence—

JOSEPH:

Sir, 'tis your own fault.

CHARLES:

Out with him, to be sure. *Both forcing* Sir Oliver *out*

Enter Sir Peter *and* Lady Teazle, Maria, *and* Rowley (*left*)

SIR PETER:

My old friend, Sir Oliver—hey! What in the name of wonder?
Here are dutiful nephews—assault their uncle at a first visit.

LADY TEAZLE:

Indeed, Sir Oliver, 'twas well we came in to rescue you.

ROWLEY:

Truly it was; for I perceive, Sir Oliver, the character of old
Stanley was no protection to you.

SIR OLIVER:

Nor of Premium either. The necessities of the *former* could not
extort a shilling from *that* benevolent gentleman: and now,
egad, I stood a chance of faring worse than my ancestors and
being knocked down without being bid for.

After a pause, Joseph *and* Charles *turning to each other*

JOSEPH:

Charles!

CHARLES:

Joseph!

JOSEPH:

'Tis now complete.

CHARLES:

Very!

SIR OLIVER:

Sir Peter, my friend, and Rowley, too, look on that elder
nephew of mine. You know what he has already received from
my bounty; and you know also how gladly I would have
regarded half my fortune as held in trust for him. Judge then
my disappointment in discovering him to be destitute of truth,
charity, and gratitude.

SIR PETER:

> Sir Oliver, I should be more surprised at this declaration if I had not myself found him to be mean, treacherous, and hypocritical.

LADY TEAZLE:

> And if the gentleman pleads not guilty to these, pray let him call *me* to his character.

SIR PETER:

> Then, I believe, we need add no more. If he knows himself, he will consider it as the most perfect punishment that he is known to the world.

CHARLES (*Aside*):

> If they talk this way to Honesty, what will they say to *me* by and by?

SIR OLIVER:

> As for that prodigal, his brother there—

CHARLES (*Aside*):

> Aye, now comes my turn. The damned family pictures will ruin me.

JOSEPH:

> Sir Oliver, Uncle, will you honour me with a hearing?

CHARLES (*Aside*):

> Now, if Joseph makes one of his long speeches, and I might recollect myself a little.

SIR OLIVER (*To* Joseph):

> I suppose you would undertake to justify yourself entirely?

JOSEPH:

> I trust I could.

SIR OLIVER:

> Pshaw! (*To* Charles) Well, sir, and you could justify yourself too, I suppose?

CHARLES:

> Not that I know of, Sir Oliver.

SIR OLIVER:

> What? Little Premium has been let too much into the secret, I suppose?

CHARLES:

> True, sir; but they were *family secrets* and should not be mentioned again, you know.

ROWLEY:

> Come, Sir Oliver, I know you cannot speak of Charles's follies with anger.

SIR OLIVER:

> Odd's heart, no more I can—nor with gravity either. Sir Peter, do you know the rogue bargained with me for all his ancestors,

sold me judges and generals by the foot and maiden aunts as cheap as broken china?

CHARLES:

To be sure, Sir Oliver, I did make a little free with the family canvas, that's the truth on't. My ancestors may certainly rise in judgment against me, there's no denying it. But believe me sincere when I tell you, and upon my soul I would not say it if I was not, that if I do not appear mortified at the exposure of my follies, it is because I feel at this moment the warmest satisfaction in seeing you, my liberal benefactor.

SIR OLIVER:

Charles, I believe you. Give me your hand again. The ill-looking little fellow over the settee has made your peace.

CHARLES:

Then, sir, my gratitude to the original is still increased.

LADY TEAZLE:

Yet I believe, Sir Oliver, here is one whom Charles is still more anxious to be reconciled to.

SIR OLIVER:

Oh, I have heard of his attachment there; and, with the young lady's pardon, if I construe right that blush—

SIR PETER:

Well, child, speak your sentiments!

MARIA:

Sir, I have little to say, but that I shall rejoice to hear that he is happy. For me, whatever claim I had to his affection, I willingly resign to one who has a better title.

CHARLES:

How, Maria!

SIR PETER:

Hey day! What's the mystery now? When he appeared an incorrigible rake, you would give your hand to no one else; and now that he is likely to reform, I warrant you won't have him.

MARIA:

His own heart and Lady Sneerwell know the cause.

CHARLES:

Lady Sneerwell!

JOSEPH:

Brother, it is with great concern I am obliged to speak on this point, but my regard to justice compels me, and Lady Sneerwell's injuries can no longer be concealed.

Opens the door (*right*)

Enter Lady Sneerwell (*right*)

SIR PETER:

So another French milliner! Egad, he has one in every room in the house, I suppose.

LADY SNEERWELL:

Ungrateful Charles! Well may you be surprised, and feel for the indelicate situation which your perfidy has forced me into.

CHARLES:

Pray, Uncle, is this another plot of yours? For, as I have life, I don't understand it.

JOSEPH:

I believe, sir, there is but the evidence of one person more necessary to make it extremely clear.

SIR PETER:

And that person, I imagine, is Mr Snake. Rowley, you were perfectly right to bring him with us, and pray let him appear.

ROWLEY:

Walk in, Mr Snake.

Enter Snake (*left*)

I thought his testimony might be wanted; however, it happens unluckily, that he comes to confront Lady Sneerwell, not to support her.

LADY SNEERWELL:

Villain! Treacherous to me at last! (*Aside*) Speak, fellow, have *you* too conspired against me?

SNAKE:

I beg your ladyship ten thousand pardons. You paid me extremely liberally for the lie in question; but I unfortunately have been offered double to speak the truth.

SIR PETER:

Plot and counterplot, egad!

LADY SNEERWELL:

The torments of shame and disappointment on you all!

LADY TEAZLE:

Hold, Lady Sneerwell. Before you go, let me thank you for the trouble you and that gentleman have taken in writing letters from me to Charles, and answering them yourself. And let me also request you to make my respects to the scandalous college of which you are president, and inform them, that Lady Teazle, licentiate, begs leave to return the diploma they gave her, as she leaves off practice and kills characters no longer.

LADY SNEERWELL:

You too, madam! Provoking insolent! May your husband live these fifty years. *Exit (left)*

SIR PETER:

Oons! what a Fury!

LADY TEAZLE:

What a malicious creature it is!

SIR PETER:

Hey! Not for her last wish?

LADY TEAZLE:

Oh, no!

SIR OLIVER:

Well, sir, and what have you to say now?

JOSEPH:

Sir, I am so confounded to find that Lady *Sneerwell* could be guilty of suborning Mr *Snake* in this manner, to impose on us all that I know not what so say. However, lest her revengeful spirit should prompt her to injure my brother I had certainly better follow her directly. *Exit (left)*

SIR PETER:

Moral to the last drop!

SIR OLIVER:

Aye, and marry her, Joseph, if you can. Oil and vinegar, egad! You'll do very well together.

ROWLEY:

I believe we have no more occasion for Mr Snake at present.

SNAKE:

Before I go, I beg your pardon once for all for whatever uneasiness I have been the humble instrument of causing to the parties present.

SIR PETER:

Well, well, you have made atonement by a good deed at last.

SNAKE:

But I must request of the company that it shall never be known.

SIR PETER:

Hey! What the plague! Are you ashamed of having done a right thing once in your life?

SNAKE:

Ah, sir, consider. I live by the badness of my character. I have nothing but my infamy to depend on, and, if it were once known that I had been betrayed into an honest action, I should lose every friend I have in the world.

SIR OLIVER:

Well, well, we'll not traduce you by saying anything in your praise, never fear. *Exit* Snake (*left*)

SIR PETER:

There's a precious rogue! Yet that fellow is a writer and a critic.

LADY TEAZLE:

See, Sir Oliver. There needs no persuasion now to reconcile your nephew and Maria. Charles *and* Maria *apart*

SIR OLIVER:

Aye, aye, that's as it should be, and, egad, we'll have the wedding tomorrow morning.

CHARLES:

Thank you, dear Uncle.

SIR PETER:

What, you rogue, don't you ask the girl's consent first?

CHARLES:

Oh, I have done that a long time—above a minute ago—and she has looked *yes*.

MARIA:

For shame, Charles! I protest, Sir Peter, there has not been a word.

SIR OLIVER:

Well then, the fewer the better. May your love for each other never know abatement!

SIR PETER:

And may you live as happily together as Lady Teazle and I intend to do!

CHARLES:

Rowley, my old friend, I am sure you congratulate me; and I suspect that I owe you much.

SIR OLIVER:

You do, indeed, Charles.

ROWLEY:

If my efforts to serve you had not succeeded, you would have been in my debt for the attempt; but deserve to be happy and you overpay me.

SIR PETER:

Aye, honest Rowley always said you would reform.

CHARLES:

Why, as to reforming, Sir Peter, I'll make no promises, and that I take to be a proof that I intend to set about it. But here shall

be my monitor, my gentle guide. Ah, can I leave the virtuous
path those eyes illumine?

Though thou, dear maid, shouldst waive thy beauty's
    sway,
Thou still must rule, because I will obey.
An humbled fugitive from folly view,
No sanctuary near but love and you.

                                   (*To the audience*)

You can, indeed, each anxious fear remove,
For even Scandal dies, if you approve!

Epilogue

By Mr Colman

Spoken by Lady Teazle

I, who was late so volatile and gay,
Like a trade-wind must now blow all one way,
Blend all my cares, my studies, and my vows,
To one dull rusty weathercock—my spouse!
So wills our virtuous bard—the motley Bayes
Of crying epilogues and laughing plays.
Old bachelors who marry smart young wives
Learn from our play to regulate your lives.
Each bring his dear to town, all faults upon her—
London will prove the very source of honour.
Plunged fairly in, like a cold bath it serves,
When principles relax, to brace the nerves.
Such is my case; and yet I must deplore
That the gay dream of dissipation's o'er.
And say, ye fair, was ever lively wife,
Born with a genius for the highest life,
Like me untimely blasted in her bloom,
Like me condemned to such a dismal doom?
Save money, when I just knew how to waste it!
Leave London, just as I began to taste it!
Must I then watch the early-crowing cock,
The melancholy ticking of a clock
In a lone rustic hall forever pounded,
With dogs, cats, rats, and squalling brats surrounded?
With humble curate can I now retire
(While good Sir Peter boozes with the squire)
And at backgammon mortify my soul,
That pants for loo or flutters at a vole?
'Seven's the main!'—dear sound that must expire,
Lost at hot cockles round a Christmas fire.

The transient hour of fashion too soon spent,
Farewell the tranquil mind, farewell content!
Farewell the plumèd head, the cushioned *tête*,
That takes the cushion from its proper seat!
That spirit-stirring drum! (card drums, I mean—
Spadille, odd trick, pam, basto, king and queen!)
And you, ye knockers that with brazen throat
The welcome visitors' approach denote.
Farewell all quality of high renown,
Pride, pomp, and circumstance of glorious town!
Farewell! Your revels I partake no more,
And Lady Teazle's occupation's o'er!
All this I told our bard; he smiled and said 'twas clear,
I ought to play deep tragedy next year.
Meanwhile he drew wise morals from his play
And in these solemn periods stalked away:
'Blessed were the fair like you, her faults who stopped,
And closed her follies when the curtain dropped—
No more in vice or error to engage
Or play the fool at large on life's great stage.'

DION BOUCICAULT

Although almost completely forgotten today, Dion Boucicault was one of the nineteenth-century's most popular and influential playwrights—he wrote or adapted more than a hundred plays—as well as an actor, director, and manager. He was born Dionysius Lardner Boursiquot in Dublin, Ireland, on December 27, 1820. His mother was Anne Darley, sister of the poet and editor George and of the Reverend Charles Darley, who was also a minor playwright. She married Samuel Smith Boursiquot, a Dublin wine merchant; the couple separated in 1819. Although Boursiquot acknowledged Dion as his legitimate son, it is believed that Dr. Dionysius Lardner, who lived with Anne from 1820, and who was the boy's guardian, was most likely his real father. Around 1833, Boucicault moved to London, where Lardner paid for his education. Five years later Boucicault started his acting career under the name Lee Moreton, and in 1841 his play *London Assurance*, a comedy of manners inspired by such eighteenth-century playwrights as Sheridan, was a big success at Covent Garden. As a *bon vivant* and a lady's man, he led a colorful and lavish life. However, after the failure of his next few plays he was soon bankrupt.

In 1845, Boucicault married Anne Guiot, a French widow who was twenty years his senior. She died soon after in the Swiss Alps—rumor had it that he had pushed her off a mountain—leaving him with an inheritance that enabled him to live in Paris and study the French plays that were becoming popular in England. By 1848 he was broke again; and two years later he was back in London, where he joined Charles Kean's acting company, writing sensational, melodramatic blockbusters to great commercial success, including a stage adaptation of Alexander Dumas's *The Corsican Brothers*. Around the same time he met the actress Agnes Robertson, who would be his companion and partner for the next thirty years—although it seems they were never officially married—and with whom he would have six children. In 1853, Agnes and Boucicault began a theatrical tour and a long stay in the United States. In New York in 1860, he wrote

The Colleen Bawn, which was loosely based on the novel *The Colle-
gians* by Gerald Griffin. It was a huge success in New York, and
when it opened in London later that September, it ran for a record
278 performances.

For the rest of his career, Boucicault's fortunes rose and fell. He
made huge sums of money that he spent just as fast on grandiose
schemes that failed, while continually writing plays and touring the
world with his acting company. In 1885, while on tour in Australia,
he married Louise Thorndyke, the young ingenue star of one of his
last successful plays, *The Jilt*. In retaliation Agnes sued and was
granted a divorce in England. Although their marriage had been
legally doubtful, she was publicly acknowledged and known as his
wife. Three years later, however, again almost broke, he was forced
to disband his acting company. In his last years he taught acting in
New York, where he died of a heart attack, complicated by pneumonia, on September 18, 1890.

Today, Boucicault is remembered chiefly for his three best Irish
plays: *The Colleen Bawn* (1860), *Arrah-na-Pogue* (1864), and *The
Shaughraun* (1874). While he was not a "great" playwright, he was
a superb theatrical craftsman. He was a practical man of the theater
and gave the audience what it wanted—entertainment. Boucicault
never had any literary pretensions or illusions about his craft; as he
wrote: "More money has been made out of guano than out of
poetry." But he influenced and earned the admiration of such
renowned figures as George Bernard Shaw and Oscar Wilde.

In *The Colleen Bawn* Boucicault synthesizes his gift for comedy
with his mastery of melodrama to create a dazzling and memorable
romantic comedy. But it is in his lifelike and, for the time, realistic
portrayals of his Irish characters that he is most successful. With
Miles na Coppaleen—a part Boucicault wrote for himself to play—
he transformed the stereotyped image of the stage Irishman into a
sharp-tongued heroic rogue who became the forerunner of John
Millington Synge's and Sean O'Casey's greatest characters. In this
and his other Irish plays, Boucicault successfully presented for the
first time on stage—albeit in a slightly sanitized fashion—Ireland's
peasant life and culture, as well as touched upon its troubling social
and political issues.

The Colleen Bawn

or, the brides of Garryowen

By Dion Boucicault

Dramatis Personae

(As play was originally performed at
Miss Laura Keene's Theatre, New York, March 27th, 1860)

MYLES-NA-COPPALEEN	*Mr. Dion Boucicault*
HARDRESS CREGAN, *Son of Mrs. Cregan*	*Mr. H. F. Daly*
DANNY MANN, *the Hunchbacked Servant*	*Mr. Charles Wheatleigh*
KYRLE DALY, *College Friend to Hardress*	*Mr. Charles Fisher*
FATHER TOM, *Parish Priest of Garryowen*	*Mr. D. W. Leeson*
MR. CORRIGAN, *a Pettifogging Attorney*	*Mr. J. G. Burnett*
BERTIE O'MOORE	*Mr. Henry*
HYLAND CREAGH	*Mr. Levick*
SERVANT	*Mr. Goodrich*
CORPORAL	*Mr. Clarke*
EILY O'CONNOR, *the Colleen Bawn*	*Miss Agnes Robertson*
ANNE CHUTE, *the Colleen Ruadh*	*Miss Laura Keene*
MRS. CREGAN	*Madam Ponisi*
SHEELAH	*Miss Mary Wells*
KATHLEEN CREAGH	*Miss Josephine Henry*
DUCIE BLENNERHASSET	*Miss Hamilton*

Act I, Scene i

Night—Torc Cregan—the Residence of Mrs. Cregan on the Banks of Killarney. House; window facing Audience—stage open at back. Music—seven bars before curtain. Enter Hardress Cregan, *from house.*

HARDRESS (*going up*):

Hist! Danny, are you there?

Danny *appearing from below, at back.*

DANNY:

Is it yourself, Masther Hardress?

HARDRESS:

Is the boat ready?

DANNY:

Snug under the blue rock, sir.

HARDRESS:

Does Eily expect me tonight?

DANNY:

Expict is it? Here is a lether she bade me give yuz; sure the young thing is never aisy when you are away. Look, masther, dear, do ye see that light, no bigger than a star beyant on Muckross Head?

HARDRESS:

Yes, it is the signal which my dear Eily leaves burning in our chamber.

DANNY:

All night long she sits beside that light, wid her face fixed on that lamp in your windy above.

HARDRESS:

Dear, dear Eily, after all here's asleep, I will leap from my window, and we'll cross the lake.

DANNY (*searching*):

Where did I put that lether?

Enter Kyrle Daly *from house.*

303

KYRLE:

Hardress, who is that with you?

HARDRESS:

Only Danny Mann, my boatman.

KYRLE:

That fellow is like your shadow.

DANNY:

Is it a cripple like me, that would be the shadow of an illegant gintleman like Mr. Hardress Cregan?

KYRLE:

Well, I mean that he never leaves your side.

HARDRESS:

And he never *shall* leave me. Ten years ago he was a fine boy— we were foster-brothers and playmates—in a moment of passion, while we were struggling, I flung him from the gap rock into the reeks below, and thus he was maimed for life.

DANNY:

Arrah! whist aroon! wouldn't I die for yez? didn't the same mother foster us? Why, wouldn't ye brake my back if it plazed ye, and welkim! Oh, Masther Kyrle, if ye'd seen him nursin' me for months, and cryin' over me, and keenin'! Sin' that time, sir, my body's been crimpin' up smaller and smaller every year, but my heart is gettin' bigger for him every day.

HARDRESS:

Go along, Danny.

DANNY:

Long life t'ye sir! I'm off.

Runs up and descends rocks.

KYRLE:

Hardress, a word with you. Be honest with me—do you love Anne Chute?

HARDRESS:

Why do you ask?

KYRLE:

Because we have been fellow-collegians and friends through life, and the five years that I have passed at sea have strengthened, but have not cooled, my feelings towards you. (*offers hand*).

Enter Mrs. Cregan, *from house.*

HARDRESS:

Nor mine for you, Kyrle. You are the same noble fellow as ever. You ask me if I love my cousin Anne?

MRS. CREGAN (*between them*):

And I will answer you, Mr. Daly.

HARDRESS:

My mother!

MRS. CREGAN:

My son and Miss Chute are engaged. Excuse me, Kyrle, for intruding on your secret, but I have observed your love for Anne with some regret. I hope your heart is not so far gone as to be beyond recovery.

KYRLE:

Forgive me, Mrs. Cregan, but are you certain that Miss Chute really is in love with Hardress?

MRS. CREGAN:

Look at him! I'm sure no girl could do that and doubt it.

KYRLE:

But I'm not a girl, ma'am; and sure, if you are mistaken—

HARDRESS:

My belief is that Anne does not care a token for me, and likes Kyrle better.

MRS. CREGAN:

You are an old friend of my son, and I may confide to you a family secret. The extravagance of my husband left this estate deeply involved. By this marriage with Anne Chute we redeem every acre of our barony. My son and she have been brought up as children together, and don't know their true feelings yet.

HARDRESS:

Stop, mother, I know this: I would not wed my cousin if she did not love me, not if she carried the whole county Kerry in her pocket, and the barony of Kenmare in the crown of her hat.

MRS. CREGAN:

Do you hear the proud blood of the Cregans?

HARDRESS:

Woo her, Kyrle, if you like, and win her if you can. I'll back you.

Enter Anne Chute, *from house.*

ANNE:

So will I—what's the bet?

MRS. CREGAN:

Hush!

ANNE:

I'd like to have a bet on Kyrle.

HARDRESS:

Well, Anne, I'll tell you what it was.

MRS. CREGAN:

>Hardress!

ANNE:

>Pull in one side, aunt, and let the boy go on.

HARDRESS:

>Kyrle wanted to know if the dark brown colt, Hardress Cregan, was going to walk over the course for the Anne Chute Stakes, or whether it was a scrub-race open to all.

ANNE:

>I'm free-trade—coppleens, mules and biddys.

MRS. CREGAN:

>How can you trifle with a heart like Kyrle's?

ANNE:

>Trifle! his heart can be no trifle, if he's all in proportion.

Enter Servant *from house.*

SERVANT:

>Squire Corrigan, ma'am, begs to see you.

MRS. CREGAN:

>At this hour, what can the fellow want? Show Mr. Corrigan here. *Exit* Servant *into house.* I hate this man; he was my husband's agent, or what the people here call a middle-man—vulgarly polite, and impudently obsequious.

HARDRESS:

>Genus squireen—a half sir, and a whole scoundrel.

ANNE:

>I know—a potatoe on a silver plate: I'll leave you to peel him. Come, Mr. Daly, take me for a moonlight walk, and be funny.

KYRLE:

>Funny, ma'am, I'm afraid I am—

ANNE:

>You are heavy, you mean; you roll through the world like a hogshead of whiskey; but you only want tapping for pure spirits to flow out spontaneously. Give me your arm. Hold that glove now. You are from Ballinasloe, I think?

KYRLE:

>I'm Connaught to the core of my heart.

ANNE:

>To the roots of your hair, you mean. I bought a horse at Ballinasloe fair that deceived me; I hope you won't turn out to belong to the same family.

KYRLE:

>What did he do?

ANNE:

Oh! like you, he looked well enough—deep in the chest as a pool—a-dhiol, and broad in the back, as the Gap of Dunloe—but after two days' warm work he came all to pieces, and Larry, my groom, said he'd been stuck together with glue.

KYRLE:

Really, Miss Chute! *Music—Exeunt*.

HARDRESS (*advancing, laughing*):

That girl is as wild as a coppleen—she won't leave him a hair on the head. (*goes up*).

Enter Servant, *showing in* Corrigan *from house*.
Exit Servant.

CORRIGAN:

Your humble servant, Mrs. Cregan—my service t'ye, 'Squire—it's a fine night entirely.

MRS. CREGAN:

May I ask to what business, sir, we have the honour of your call?

CORRIGAN (*aside*):

Proud as Lady Beelzebub, and as grand as a queen. (*aloud*) True for you, ma'am; I would not have come but for a divil of a pinch I'm in entirely. I've got to pay £8,000 tomorrow, or lose the Knockmakilty farms.

MRS. CREGAN:

Well, sir?

CORRIGAN:

And I wouldn't throuble ye—

MRS. CREGAN:

Trouble me, sir?

CORRIGAN:

Iss, m'am—ye'd be forgettin' now that mortgage I have on this property. It ran out last May, and by rights—

MRS. CREGAN:

It will be paid next month.

CORRIGAN:

Are you reckonin' on the marriage of Mister Hardress and Miss Anne Chute?

HARDRESS (*advancing*):

Mr. Corrigan, you forget yourself.

MRS. CREGAN:

Leave us, Hardress, awhile. (Hardress *retires*). Now, Mr. Corrigan, state, in as few words as possible, what you demand.

CORRIGAN:

Mrs. Cregan, ma'am, you depend on Miss Anne Chute's fortune to pay me the money, but your son does not love the lady, or, if he does, he has a mighty quare way of shewing it. He has another girl on hand, and betune the two he'll come to the ground, and so bedad will I.

MRS. CREGAN:

That is false—it is a calumny, sir!

CORRIGAN:

I wish it was, ma'am. D'ye see that light over the lake?—your son's eyes are fixed on it. What would Anne Chute say if she knew that her husband, that is to be, had a mistress beyant—that he slips out every night after you're all in bed, and like Leandher, barrin' the wettin', he sails across to his sweetheart?

MRS. CREGAN:

Is this the secret of his aversion to the marriage? Fool! fool! what madness, and at such a moment.

CORRIGAN:

That's what I say, and no lie in it.

MRS. CREGAN:

He shall give up this girl—he must!

CORRIGAN:

I would like to have some security for that. I want by tomorrow Anne Chute's written promise to marry him or my £8,000.

MRS. CREGAN:

It is impossible, sir; you hold ruin over our heads.

CORRIGAN:

Madam, it's got to hang over your head or mine.

MRS. CREGAN:

Stay, you know that what you ask is out of our power—you know it—therefore this demand only covers the true object of your visit.

CORRIGAN:

'Pon my honour! and you are as 'cute, ma'am, as you are beautiful!

MRS. CREGAN:

Go on, sir.

CORRIGAN:

Mrs. Cregan, I'm goin' to do a foolish thing—now, by gorra I am! I'm richer than ye think, maybe, and if you'll give me your *personal* security, I'll take it.

MRS. CREGAN:

What do you mean?

CORRIGAN:

    I mean that I'll take a lien for life on *you,* instead of the mortgage I hold on the Cregan property. (*aside*) That's nate, I'm thinkin'.

MRS. CREGAN:

    Are you mad?

CORRIGAN:

    I am—mad in love with yourself, and that's what I've been these fifteen years. (*Music through dialogue till* Anne Chute *is off.*)

MRS. CREGAN:

    Insolent wretch! my son shall answer and chastize you. (*calls*) Hardress!

HARDRESS (*advancing*):

    Madam.

Enter Anne Chute *and* Kyrle.

CORRIGAN:

    Miss Chute!

HARDRESS:

    Well, mother?   (*together*)

ANNE:

    Well, sir?

MRS. CREGAN (*aside*):

    Scoundrel! he will tell her all and ruin us! (*aloud*) Nothing. (*turns aside*).

CORRIGAN:

    Your obedient.

ANNE:

    Oh! *Crosses with* Kyrle *and exit—Music ceases.*

CORRIGAN:

    You are in my power, ma'am. See, now, not a sowl but myself knows of this secret love of Hardress Cregan, and I'll keep it as snug as a bug in a rug, if you'll only say the word.

MRS. CREGAN:

    Contemptible hound, I loathe and despise you!

CORRIGAN:

    I've known that fifteen years, but it hasn't cured my heart ache.

MRS. CREGAN:

    And you would buy my aversion and disgust!

CORRIGAN:

    Just as Anne Chute buys your son, if she knew but all. Can he love his girl beyant, widout haten this heiress he's obliged to swallow?—ain't you sthriven to sell him? But you didn't feel the hardship of being sold till you tried it on yourself.

MRS. CREGAN:

    I beg you, sir, to leave me.

CORRIGAN:

    That's right, ma'am—think over it, sleep on it. Tomorrow I'll call for your answer. Good evenin' kindly.

Music—Exit Corrigan *in house.*

MRS. CREGAN:

    Hardress.

HARDRESS:

    What did he want?

MRS. CREGAN:

    He came to tell me the meaning of yonder light upon Muckross Head.

HARDRESS:

    Ah! has it been discovered. Well, mother, now you know the cause of my coldness, my indifference for Anne.

MRS. CREGAN:

    Are you in your senses, Hardress? Who is this girl?

HARDRESS:

    She is known at every fair and pattern in Munster as the Colleen Bawn—her name is Eily O'Connor.

MRS. CREGAN:

    A peasant girl—a vulgar barefooted beggar.

HARDRESS:

    Whatever she is, love has made her my equal, and when you set your foot upon her you tread upon my heart.

MRS. CREGAN:

    'Tis well, Hardress. I feel that perhaps I have no right to dispose of your life and your happiness—no, my dear son—I would not wound you—heaven knows how well I love my darling boy, and you shall feel it. Corrigan has made me an offer by which you may regain the estate, and without selling yourself to Anne Chute.

HARDRESS:

    What is it? Of course you accepted it?

MRS. CREGAN:

    No, but I will accept, yes, for your sake—I—I will. He offers to cancel this mortgage if—if—I will consent to—become his wife.

HARDRESS:

    You—you, mother? Has he dared—

MRS. CREGAN:

    Hush! he is right. A sacrifice must be made—either you or I must suffer. Life is before you—my days are well nigh past—

and for your sake, Hardress—for yours; my pride, my only one. Oh! I would give you more than my life.

HARDRESS:

Never—never! I will not, cannot accept it. I'll tear that dog's tongue from his throat that dared insult you with the offer.

MRS. CREGAN:

Foolish boy, before tomorrow night we shall be beggars—outcasts from this estate. Humiliation and poverty stand like spectres at yonder door—tomorrow they will be realities. Can you tear out the tongues that will wag over our fallen fortunes? You are a child, you cannot see beyond your happiness.

HARDRESS:

Oh! mother, mother, what can be done? My marriage with Anne is impossible.

Enter Danny Mann, *up rock, at back.*

DANNY:

Whisht, if ye plaze—ye're talkin' so loud she'll hear ye say that—she's comin'.

MRS. CREGAN:

Has this fellow overheard us?

HARDRESS:

If he has, he is mine, body and soul. I'd rather trust him with a secret than keep it myself.

MRS. CREGAN:

I cannot remain to see Anne; excuse me to my friends. The night perhaps will bring counsel, or at least resolution to hear the worst! Good night, my son.

Music—Exit into house.

DANNY:

Oh! masther, she doesn't know the worst! She doesn't know that you are married to the Colleen Bawn.

HARDRESS:

Hush! what fiend prompts you to thrust that act of folly in my face.

DANNY:

Thrue for ye, masther! I'm a dirty mane scut to remind ye of it.

HARDRESS:

What will my haughty, noble mother say, when she learns the truth! how can I ask her to receive Eily as a daughter? Eily, with her awkward manners, her Kerry brogue, her ignorance of the usages of society. Oh! what have I done?

DANNY:

Oh! vo—vo, has the ould family come to this! Is it the daughter of Mihil-na-Thradrucha, the ould rope-maker of Garryowen, that 'ud take the flure as your wife?

HARDRESS:

Be silent, scoundrel! How dare you speak thus of my love?—wretch that I am to blame her?—poor, beautiful, angelhearted Eily.

DANNY:

Beautiful is it! Och—wurra—wurra, deelish! The looking-glass was never made that could do her justice; and if St. Patrick wanted a wife, where would he find an angel that 'ud compare with the Colleen Bawn. As I row her on the lake, the little fishes come up to look at her; and the wind from heaven lifts up her hair to see what the devil brings her down here at all—at all.

HARDRESS:

The fault is mine—mine alone—I alone will suffer!

DANNY:

Oh! why isn't it mine? Why can't I suffer for yez, masther dear? Wouldn't I swally every tear in your body, and every bit of bad luck in your life, and then wid a stone round my neck, sink myself and your sorrows in the bottom of the lower lake.

HARDRESS (*placing hand on* Danny):

Good Danny, away with you to the boat—be ready in a few moments, we will cross to Muckross Head. (*looks at light at back*).

Music—Exit Hardress *into house.*

DANNY:

Never fear, sir. Oh! it isn't that spalpeen, Corrigan, that shall bring ruin on that ould place. Lave Danny alone. Danny, the fox, will lade yez round and about, and cross the scint. (*takes off his hat—sees letter*). Bedad, here's the letter from the Colleen Bawn that I couldn't find awhile ago—it's little use now. (*goes to lower window, and reads by light from house*). "Come to your own Eily, that has not seen you for two long days. Come, acushla agrah machree. I have forgotten how much you love me—Shule, shule agrah.—Colleen Bawn." Divil an address is on it.

Enter Kyrle *and* Anne.

ANNE:

Have they gone?

KYRLE:

It is nearly midnight.

ANNE:

Before we go in, I insist on knowing who is this girl that possesses your heart. You confess that you are in love—deeply in love.

KYRLE:

I do confess it—but not even your power can extract that secret from me—do not ask me, for I could not be false, yet dare not be true. *Exit* Kyrle *into house.*

ANNE:

He loves me—oh! he loves me—the little bird is making a nest in my heart. Oh! I'm faint with joy.

DANNY (*as if calling after him*):

Sir, sir!

ANNE:

Who is that?

DANNY:

I'm the boatman below, an' I'm waitin' for the gintleman.

ANNE:

What gentleman?

DANNY:

Him that's jist left ye, ma'am—I'm waitin' on him.

ANNE:

Does Mr. Kyrle Daly go out boating at this hour?

DANNY:

It's not for me to say, ma'am, but every night at twelve o'clock I'm here wid my boat under the blue rock below, to put him across the lake to Muckross Head. I beg your pardon, ma'am, but here's a paper ye droppped on the walk beyant—if it's no vally I'd like to light my pipe wid it. (*gives it*).

ANNE:

A paper I dropped! (*goes to window—reads*).

DANNY (*aside*):

Oh, Misther Corrigan, you'll ruin masther will ye? asy now, and see how I'll put the cross on ye.

ANNE:

A love-letter from some peasant girl to Kyrle Daly! Can this be the love of which he spoke? have I deceived myself?

DANNY:

I must be off, ma'am; here comes the signal. *Music.*

ANNE:

The signal?

DANNY:

D'ye see yonder light upon Muckross Head? It is in a cottage windy; that light goes in and out three times winkin' that way, as much as to say, "Are ye comin'?" Then if the light in that room there (*points at house above*) answers by a wink, it manes No! but if it goes out entirely, his honour jumps from the parlour windy into the garden behind and we're off. Look! (*light in cottage disappears*). That's one. (*light appears*) Now again. (*light disappears*) That's two. (*light appears*) What did I tell you? (*light disappears*) That's three, and here it comes again. (*light appears*) Wait now, and ye'll see the answer. (*light disappears from window*) That's my gentleman. (*Music change*) You see he's goin'—good night, ma'am.

ANNE:

Stay, here's money; do not tell Mr. Daly that I know of this.

DANNY:

Divil a word—long life t'ye. (*goes up*)

ANNE:

I was not deceived; he meant me to understand that he loved me! Hark! I hear the sound of some one who leaped heavily on the garden walk. (*goes to house—looking at back*)

Enter Hardress *wrapped in a boat cloak.*

DANNY (*going down*):

All right, yer honour.

ANNE (*hiding*):

It is he, 'tis he. (*mistaking* Hardress *for* Daly—*closed in*)

Act I, Scene ii

The Gap of Dunloe. Hour before sunrise.
Enter Corrigan.

CORRIGAN:

From the rock above I saw the boat leave Torc Cregan. It is now crossing the lake to the cottage. Who is this girl? What is this mysterious misthress of young Cregan?—that I'll find out.

Myles *sings outside*

"Oh! Charley Mount is a pretty place,
In the month of July—"

CORRIGAN:

Who's that?—'Tis that poaching scoundrel—that horse stealer, Myles-na-Coppaleen. Here he comes with a keg of illicit whiskey, as bould as Nebuckadezzar.

Enter Myles *singing, with keg on his shoulder.*

CORRIGAN:
Is that you, Myles?

MYLES:
No! it's my brother.

CORRIGAN:
I know ye, my man.

MYLES:
Then why the divil did ye ax?

CORRIGAN:
You may as well answer me kindly—civility costs nothing.

MYLES:
Ow now! don't it? Civility to a lawyer manes six-and-eight-pence about.

CORRIGAN:
What's that on your shoulder?

MYLES:
What's that to you?

CORRIGAN:
I am a magistrate, and can oblige you to answer.

MYLES:
Well! it's a boulster belongin' to my mother's feather bed.

CORRIGAN:
Stuff'd with whiskey!

MYLES:
Bedad! how would I know what it's stuff'd wid? I'm not an upholsterer.

CORRIGAN:
Come, Myles, I'm not so bad a fellow as ye may think.

MYLES:
To think of that now!

CORRIGAN:
I am not the mane creature you imagine!

MYLES:
Ain't ye now, sir? You keep up appearances mighty well, indeed.

CORRIGAN:
No, Myles! I am not that blackguard I've been represented.

MYLES (*sits on keg*):
See that now—how people take away a man's character. You are another sort of blackguard entirely.

CORRIGAN:
You shall find me a gentleman—liberal, and ready to protect you.

MYLES:

Long life t'ye, sir.

CORRIGAN:

Myles, you have come down in the world lately; a year ago you were a thriving horse-dealer, now you are a lazy, ragged fellow.

MYLES:

Ah, it's the bad luck, sir, that's in it.

CORRIGAN:

No, it's the love of Eily O'Connor that's in it—it's the pride of Garryowen that took your heart away, and made ye what ye are—a smuggler and a poacher.

MYLES:

Thim's hard words.

CORRIGAN:

But they are true. You live like a wild beast in some cave or hole in the rocks above; by night your gun is heard shootin' the otter as they lie out on the stones, or you snare the salmon in your nets; on a cloudy night your whiskey still is going—you see, I know your life.

MYLES:

Better than the priest, and devil a lie in it.

CORRIGAN:

Now, if I put ye in a snug farm—stock ye with pigs and cattle, and rowl you up comfortable—d'ye think the Colleen Bawn wouldn't jump at ye?

MYLES:

Bedad, she'd make a lape I b'leve—and what would I do for all this luck?

CORRIGAN:

Find out for me who it is that lives at the cottage on Muckross Head.

MYLES:

That's asy—it's Danny Mann—no less and his ould mother Sheelah.

CORRIGAN:

Yes, Myles, but there's another—a girl who is hid there.

MYLES:

Ah, now!

CORRIGAN:

She only goes out at night.

MYLES:

Like the owls.

CORRIGAN:

She's the misthress of Hardress Cregan.

MYLES (*seizing* Corrigan):

Thurra mon dhiol, what's that?

CORRIGAN:

Oh, lor! Myles—Myles—what's the matter—are you mad?

MYLES:

No—that is—why—why did ye raise your hand at me in that way?

CORRIGAN:

I didn't.

MYLES:

I thought ye did—I'm mighty quick at takin' thim hints, bein' on me keepin' agin' the gaugers—go on—I didn't hurt ye.

CORRIGAN:

Not much.

MYLES:

You want to find out who this girl is?

CORRIGAN:

I'll give £20 for the information—there's ten on account. (*gives money*)

MYLES:

Long life t'ye; that's the first money I iver got from a lawyer, and bad luck to me but there's a cure for the evil eye in thim pieces.

CORRIGAN:

You will watch tonight?

MYLES:

In five minutes I'll be inside the cottage itself.

CORRIGAN:

That's the lad.

MYLES (*aside*):

I was goin' there.

CORRIGAN:

And tomorrow you will step down to my office with the particulars?

MYLES:

Tomorrow you shall breakfast on them.

CORRIGAN:

Good night, entirely. *Exit* Corrigan.

MYLES:

I'll give ye a cowstail to swally, and make ye think it's a chapter in St. Patrick, ye spalpeen! When he called Eily the misthress of Hardress Cregan, I nearly sthretched him—begorra, I was full of sudden death that minute! Oh, Eily! acushla agrah asthore machree! as the stars watch over Innisfallen, and as the wathers go round it and keep it, so I watch and keep round you, avourneen!

Song—Myles

Oh, Limerick is beautiful, as everybody knows,
The river Shannon's full of fish, beside that city flows;
But it is not the river, nor the fish that preys upon my mind,
Nor with the town of Limerick have I any fault to find.
The girl I love is beautiful, she's fairer than the dawn;
She lives in Garryowen, and she's called the Colleen Bawn.
As the river, proud and bold, goes by that famed city,
So proud and cold, widout a word, that Colleen goes by me!
Oh, hone! Oh, hone!

Oh, if I was the Emperor of Russia to command,
Or Julius Caesar, or the Lord Lieutenant of the land,
I'd give up all my wealth, my manes, I'd give up my army,
Both the horse, the fut, and the Royal Artillery;
I'd give the crown from off my head, the people on their knees,
I'd give my fleet of sailing ships upon the briny seas,
And a beggar I'd go to sleep, a happy man at dawn,
If by my side, fast for my bride, I'd the darlin' Colleen Bawn.
Oh, hone! Oh, hone!

I must reach the cottage before the masther arrives; Father Tom is there waitin' for this keg o' starlight—it's my tithe; I call every tenth keg "his riverince". It's worth money to see the way it does the old man good, and brings the wather in his eyes; it's the only place I ever see any about him—heaven bless him! (*sings*) *Exit* Myles—*Music*

Act I, Scene iii

Interior of Eily's Cottage on Muckross Head—fire burning; table; armchair; stools; basin, sugar spoon, two jugs, tobacco, plate, knife, and lemon on table. Father Tom *discovered smoking in armchair,* Eily *in balcony, watching over lake.*

FATHER TOM (*sings*):
"Tobacco is an Injun weed." And every weed wants wathering to make it come up; but tobacco bein' an Injun weed that is accustomed to a hot climate, water is entirely, too cold for its

warrum nature—it's whiskey and water it wants. I wonder if Myles has come; I'll ask Eily. (*calls*) Eily alanna! Eily a suilish machree!

EILY (*turning*):

Is it me, Father Tom?

FATHER TOM:

Has he come?

EILY:

No, his boat is half a mile off yet.

FATHER TOM:

Half a mile! I'll choke before he's here.

EILY:

Do you mean Hardress?

FATHER TOM:

No, dear! Myles-na-Coppaleen—cum spiritu Hiberneuse—which manes in Irish, wid a keg of poteen.

Enter Myles

MYLES:

Here I am, your riverince, never fear. I tould Sheelah to hurry up with the materials, knowin' ye'd be dhry and hasty.

Enter Sheelah, *with kettle of water*

SHEELAH:

Here's the hot water.

MYLES:

Lave it there till I brew Father Tom a pint of mother's milk.

SHEELAH:

We'ell thin, ye'll do your share of the work, and not a ha'porth more.

MYLES:

Didn't I bring the sperrits from two miles and more? and I deserve to have the pref'rence to make the punch for his riverince.

SHEELAH:

And didn't I watch the kettle all night, not to let it off the boil?—there now.

MYLES (*quarrelling with* Sheelah):

No, you didn't, &c.

SHEELAH (*quarrelling*):

Yes, I did, &c.

EILY:

No, no; I'll make it, and nobody else.

FATHER TOM:

Asy now, ye bocauns, and whist; Myles shall put in the whiskey, Sheelah shall put in the hot water, and Eily, my Colleen, shall put the sugar in the cruiskeen. A blessin' on ye all three that loves the ould man. (Myles *takes off hat*—Women *curtsey*—*they make punch*) See now, my children, there's a moral in everything, e'en in a jug of punch. There's the sperrit, which is the sowl and strength of the man. (Myles *pours spirit from keg*) That's the whiskey. There's the sugar, which is the smile of woman; (Eily *puts sugar*) without that, life is without taste or sweetness. Then there's the lemon, (Eily *puts lemon*) which is love; a squeeze now and again does a boy no harm; but not too much. And the hot water (Sheelah *pours water*) which is adversity—as little as possible if ye plaze—that makes the good things better still.

MYLES:

And it's complate, ye see, for it's a woman that gets into hot wather all the while. (*pours from jug to jug*)

SHEELAH:

Myles, if I hadn't the kettle, I'd bate ye.

MYLES:

Then, why didn't ye let me make the punch? There's a guinea for your riverince that's come t'ye—one in ten I got awhile ago—it's your tithe—put a hole in it, and hang it on your watch chain, for it's a mighty grate charm entirely. (*they sit, Sheelah near fire, Colleen on stool beside her, Father Tom in chair, Myles on stool*)

FATHER TOM:

Eily, look at that boy, and tell me, haven't ye a dale to answer for?

EILY:

He isn't as bad about me as he used to be; he's getting over it.

MYLES:

Yes, darlin', the storm has passed over, and I've got into settled bad weather.

FATHER TOM:

Maybe, afther all, ye'd have done better to have married Myles there, than be the wife of a man that's ashamed to own ye.

EILY:

He isn't—he's proud of me. It's only when I spake like the poor people, and say or do anything wrong, that he's hurt; but I'm gettin' clane of the brogue, and learnin' to do nothing—I'm to be changed entirely.

MYLES:

Oh! if he'd lave me yer own self, and only take away wid him his improvements. Oh! murder—Eily, aroon, why wasn't ye twins, an' I could have one of ye, only nature couldn't make two like ye—it would be onreasonable to ax it.

EILY:

Poor Myles, do you love me still so much?

MYLES:

Didn't I lave the world to folly ye, and since then there's been neither night nor day in my life—I lay down on Glenna Point above, where I see this cottage, and I lived on the sight of it. Oh! Eily, if tears were pison to the grass there wouldn't be a green blade on Glenna Hill this day.

EILY:

But you knew I was married, Myles.

MYLES:

Not thin, aroon—Father Tom found me that way, and sat beside, and lifted up my soul. Then I confessed to him, and, sez he, "Myles, go to Eily, she has something to say to you—say I sent you." I came, and yet tould me ye were Hardress Cregan's wife, and that was a great comfort entirely. Since I knew that (*drinks—voice in cup*) I haven't been the blackguard I was.

FATHER TOM:

See the beauty of the priest, my darlin'—*videte et admirate*—see and admire it. It was at confession that Eily tould me she loved Cregan, and what did I do?—sez I, "Where did you meet your sweetheart?" "At Garryowen," sez she. "Well," says I; "that's not the place." "Thrue, your riverince, it's too public entirely," sez she. "Ye'll mate him only in one place," sez I; "and that's the stile that's behind my chapel," for, d'ye see, her mother's grave was forenint the spot, and there's a sperrit round the place, (Myles *drinks*) that kept her pure and strong. Myles, ye thafe, drink fair.

SHEELAH:

Come now, Eily, couldn't ye cheer up his riverince wid the tail of a song?

EILY:

Hardress bid me not sing any ould Irish songs, he says the words are vulgar.

SHEELAH:

Father Tom will give ye absolution.

FATHER TOM:

Put your lips to that jug; there's only the sthrippens left. Drink! and while that thrue Irish liquor warms your heart, take this wid it. May the brogue of ould Ireland niver forsake your tongue—may her music niver lave yer voice—and may a true Irishwoman's virtue niver die in your heart!

MYLES:

Come, Eily, it's my liquor—haven't ye a word to say for it?

Song, Eily—*"Cruiskeen Lawn"*

Let the farmer praise his grounds
As the huntsman doth his hounds,
And the shepherd his fresh and dewy morn;
But I, more blest than they,
Spend each night and happy day,
With my smilin' little Cruiskeen Lawn, Lawn, Lawn.

Chorus (repeat) Gramachree, mavourneen, slanta gal avourneen,
Gramachree ma Cruiskeen Lawn, Lawn, Lawn,
With my smiling little Cruiskeen Lawn.

(*chorussed by* Myles, Father Tom *and* Sheelah)

Myles

And when grim Death appears
In long and happy years,
To tell me that my glass is run,
I'll say, begone, you slave,
For great Bacchus gave me lave
To have another Cruiskeen Lawn—Lawn—Lawn.

Chorus—Repeat.

Gramachree, etc., etc.

HARDRESS (*without*):

Ho! Sheelah—Sheelah!

SHEELAH (*rising*):

Whist! it's the master.

EILY (*frightened*):

Hardress! oh, my! what will he say if he finds us here—run, Myles—quick, Sheelah—clear away the things.

FATHER TOM:

Hurry now, or we'll get Eily in throuble. (*takes keg*—Myles *takes jugs*—Sheelah *kettle*)

HARDRESS:

Sheelah, I say!

Exeunt Father Tom *and* Myles *quickly*

SHEELAH:

Comin', Sir, I'm puttin' on my petticoat.

Exit Sheelah *quickly*

Enter Hardress *and* Danny—Danny *immediately goes off*

EILY:

Oh, Hardress, asthore!

HARDRESS:

Don't call me by those confounded Irish words—what's the matter? you're trembling like a bird caught in a trap.

EILY:

Am I, mavou—no I mean—is it tremblin' I am, dear?

HARDRESS:

What a dreadful smell of tobacco there is here, and the fumes of whiskey punch too, the place smells like a shebeen. Who has been here?

EILY:

There was Father Tom an' Myles dhropped in.

HARDRESS:

Nice company for my wife—a vagabond.

EILY:

Ah! who made him so but me, dear? Before I saw you, Hardress, Myles coorted me, and I was kindly to the boy.

HARDRESS:

Damn it, Eily, why will you remind me that my wife was ever in such a position?

EILY:

I won't see him again—if yer angry, dear, I'll tell him to go away, and he will, because the poor boy loves me.

HARDRESS:

Yes, better than I do you mean?

EILY:

No, I don't—oh! why do you spake so to your poor Eily?

HARDRESS:

Spake so! Can't you say speak?

EILY:

I'll thry, aroon—I'm sthrivin'—'tis mighty hard, but what wouldn't I undert-tee-ta—undergo for your sa-se—for your seek.

HARDRESS:

Sake—sake!

EILY:

Sake—seek—oh, it is to bother people entirely they mixed 'em up! Why didn't they make them all one way?

HARDRESS (*aside*):

It is impossible! How can I present her as my wife? Oh! what an act of madness to tie myself to one so much beneath me—beautiful—good as she is—

EILY:

Hardress, you are pale—what has happened?

HARDRESS:

Nothing—that is nothing but what you will rejoice at.

EILY:

What d'ye mane?

HARDRESS:

What do I mane! Mean—mean!

EILY:

I beg your pardon, dear.

HARDRESS:

Well; I mean that after tomorrow there will be no necessity to hide our marriage, for I shall be a beggar, my mother will be an outcast, and amidst all the shame, who will care what wife a Cregan takes?

EILY:

And d'ye think I'd like to see you dhragged down to my side—ye don't know me—see now—never all me life again—don't let on to mortal that we're married—I'll go as a servant in your mother's house—I'll work for the smile ye'll give me in passing, and I'll be happy, if ye'll only let me stand outside and hear your voice.

HARDRESS:

You're a fool. I told you that I was bethrothed to the richest heiress in Kerry; her fortune alone can save us from ruin. Tonight my mother discovered my visits here, and I told her who you were.

EILY:

Oh! what did she say?

HARDRESS:

It broke her heart.

EILY:

Hardress! is there no hope?

HARDRESS:

None. That is none—that—that I can name.

EILY:

There is one—I see it.

HARDRESS:

There is. We were children when we were married, and I could get no priest to join our hands but one, and he had been disgraced by his bishop. He is dead. There was no witness to the ceremony but Danny Mann—no proof but his word, and your certificate.

EILY (*takes paper from her breast*):

This!

HARDRESS:

Eily! if you doubt my eternal love keep that security, it gives you the right to the shelter of my roof; but oh! if you would be content with the shelter of my heart.

EILY:

And will it save ye, Hardress? and will your mother forgive me?

HARDRESS:

She will bless you—she will take you to her breast.

EILY:

But you—another will take you to her breast.

HARDRESS:

Oh! Eily, darling—d'ye think I could forget you, machree—forget the sacrifice more than blood you give me.

EILY:

Oh! when you talk that way to me, ye might take my life, and heart, and all. Oh! Hardress, I love you—take the paper and tare it. (Hardress *takes paper*)

Enter Myles

MYLES:

No. I'll be damned if he shall.

HARDRESS:

Scoundrel! you have been listening?

MYLES:

To every word. I saw Danny wid his ear agin that dure, so as there was only one kay-hole I adopted the windy. Eily, aroon, Mr. Cregan will giv' ye back that paper; you can't tare up an oath; will ye help him then to cheat this other girl, and to make her his mistress, for that's what she'll be if ye are his wife. An' after all, what is there agin' the crature? Only the money she's got. Will you stop lovin' him when his love belongs to another? No! I know it by myself; but if ye jine their hands together your love will be an adultery.

EILY:

Oh, no!

HARDRESS:

Vagabond! outcast! jail bird! dare you prate of honour to me?

MYLES:

> I am an outlaw, Mr. Cregan—a felon may be—but if you do this thing to that poor girl that loves you so much—had I my neck in the rope—or my fut on the deck of a convict ship—I'd turn round and say to ye, "Hardress Cregan, I make ye a present of the contimpt of a rogue." (*snaps fingers*)

Music till end of Act—Enter Father Tom, Sheelah *and* Danny— Hardress *throws down paper—goes to table—takes hat.*

HARDRESS:

> Be it so, Eily, farewell! until my house is clear of these vermin— (Danny *appears at back*)—you will see me no more.
>
> (*Exit* Hardress *followed by* Danny)

EILY:

> Hardress—Hardress! (*going up*) Don't leave me, Hardress!

FATHER TOM (*intercepts her*):

> Stop, Eily! (Danny *returns and listens*)

EILY:

> He's gone—he's gone!

FATHER TOM:

> Give me that paper, Myles. (Myles *picks it up, gives it*) Kneel down there, Eily, before me—put that paper in your breast.

EILY (*kneeling*):

> Oh! what will I do—what will I do!

FATHER TOM:

> Put your hand upon it now.

EILY:

> Oh, my heart—my heart!

FATHER TOM:

> Be the hush, and spake after me—by my mother that's in heaven.

EILY:

> By my mother that's in heaven.

FATHER TOM:

> By the light and the word.

EILY:

> By the light and the word.

FATHER TOM:

> Sleepin' or wakin'.

EILY:

> Sleepin' or wakin'.

FATHER TOM:

> This proof of my truth.

EILY:

This proof of my truth.

FATHER TOM:

Shall never again quit my breast.

EILY:

Shall never again quit my breast (Eily *utters a cry and falls—Tableau*)

Act II, Scene i

Gap of Dunloe; same as Second Scene, Act I—Music.
Enter Hardress *and* Danny

HARDRESS:

Oh! what a giddy fool I've been. What would I give to recall this fatal act which bars my fortune?

DANNY:

There's something throublin' yez, Masther Hardress. Can't Danny do something to aise ye?—spake the word and I'll die for ye.

HARDRESS:

Danny, I *am* troubled. I was a fool when I refused to listen to you at the chapel of Castle Island.

DANNY:

When I warned ye to have no call to Eily O'Connor.

HARDRESS:

I was mad to marry her.

DANNY:

I knew she was no wife for you. A poor thing widout manners, or money, or book larnin', or a ha'porth of fortin'. Oh! worra. I told ye dat, but ye bate me off, and here now is the way of it.

HARDRESS:

Well, it's done, and can't be undone.

DANNY:

Bedad, I dun know that. Wouldn't she untie the knot herself—couldn't ye coax her?

HARDRESS:

No.

DANNY:

Is that her love for you? You that give' up the divil an all for her. What's *her* ruin to yours? Ruin—goredoutha—ruin is it? Don't I pluck a shamrock and wear it a day for the glory of St. Patrick, and then throw it away when it's gone by my likin'. What, is *she* to be ruined by a gentleman? Whoo! Mighty good, for the likes o' her.

HARDRESS:

She would have yielded, but—

DANNY:

Asy now, an' I'll tell ye. Pay her passage out to Quaybec, and put her aboord a three-master widout sayin' a word. Lave it to me. Danny will clare the road forenint ye.

HARDRESS:

Fool, if she still possesses that certificate—the proof of my first marriage—how can I dare to wed another? Commit bigamy— disgrace my wife—bastardize my children!

DANNY:

Den' by the powers, I'd do by Eily as wid the glove there on her hand; make it come off, as it come on—an' if it fits too tight, take the knife to it.

HARDRESS (*turning to him*):

What do you mean?

DANNY:

Only gi' me the word, an' I'll engage that the Colleen Bawn will never throuble ye any more; don't ax me any questions at all. Only—if you're agreeable, take off that glove from yer hand and give it me for a token—that's enough.

HARDRESS (*throws off cloak—seizes him—throws him down*):

Villain! Dare you utter a word or meditate a thought of violence towards that girl—

DANNY:

Oh! murder—may I never die in sin, if—

HARDRESS:

Begone! away, at once, and quit my sight. I have chosen my doom; I must learn to endure it—but, blood! and hers! Shall I make cold and still that heart that beats alone for me?—quench those eyes, that look so tenderly in mine? Monster! am I so vile that you dare to whisper such a thought?

DANNY:

Oh! masther, divil burn me if I meant any harm.

HARDRESS:

Mark me well, now. Respect my wife as you would the queen of the land—whisper a word such as those you uttered to me, and it will be your last. I warn ye—remember and obey.

Exit Hardress

DANNY (*rises—picks up cloak*):

> Oh! the darlin' crature! would I harrum a hair of her blessed head?—no! Not unless you gave me that glove, and den I'd jump into the bottomless pit for ye.

Exit Danny—*Music—change*

Act II, Scene ii

Room in Mrs. Cregan's house; window, backed by landscape; door, backed by interior; (lights up). Enter Anne Chute.

ANNE:

> That fellow runs in my head. (*looking at window*) There he is in the garden, smoking like a chimney-pot. (*calls*) Mr. Daly!

KYRLE (*outside window*):

> Good morning!

ANNE (*aside*):

> To think he'd smile that way, after going Leandering all night like a dissipated young owl. (*aloud*) Did you sleep well? (*aside*) Not a wink, you villain, and you know it.

KYRLE:

> I slept like a top.

ANNE (*aside*):

> I'd like to have the whipping of ye. (*aloud*) When did you get back?

KYRLE:

> Get back! I've not been out.

ANNE (*aside*):

> He's not been out! This is what men come to after a cruise at sea—they get sunburnt with love. Those foreign donnas teach them to make fire-places of their hearts, and chimney-pots of their mouths. (*aloud*) What are you doing down there? (*aside*) As if he was stretched out to dry. (Kyrle *puts down pipe outside*)

Enter Kyrle *through window*

KYRLE:

> I have been watching Hardress coming over from Divil's Island in his boat—the wind was dead against him.

ANNE:

> It was fair for going to Divil's Island last night, I believe.

KYRLE:

> Was it?

ANNE:

You were up late, I think?

KYRLE:

I was. I watched by my window for hours, thinking of her I loved—slumber overtook me and I dreamed of a happiness I never can hope for.

ANNE:

Look me straight in the face.

KYRLE:

Oh! if some fairy could strike us into stone now—and leave us looking for ever into each other's faces, like the blue lake below and the sky above it.

ANNE:

Kyrle Daly! What would you say to a man who had two loves, one to whom he escaped at night and the other to whom he devoted himself during the day, what would you say?

KYRLE:

I'd say he had no chance.

ANNE:

Oh! Captain Cautious! Well answered. Isn't he fit to take care of anybody?—his cradle was cut out of a witness box.

Enter Hardress *through window*

KYRLE:

Anne! I don't know what you mean, but that I know that I love you, and you are sporting with a wretchedness you cannot console. I was wrong to remain here so long, but I thought my friendship for Hardress would protect me against your invasion—now I will go. (Hardress *advancing*)

HARDRESS:

No. Kyrle, you will stay. Anne, he loves you, and I more than suspect you prefer him to me. From this moment you are free; I release you from all troth to me; in his presence I do this.

ANNE:

Hardress!

HARDRESS:

There is a bar between us which you should have known before, but I could not bring myself to confess. Forgive me, Anne—you deserve a better man than I am. *Exit*

ANNE:

A bar between us! What does he mean?

KYRLE:

> He means that he is on the verge of ruin: he did not know how bad things were till last night. His generous noble heart recoils from receiving anything from you but love.

ANNE:

> And does he think I'd let him be ruined any way? Does he think I wouldn't sell the last rood o' land—the gown off my back, and the hair off my head before the boy that protected and loved me, the child, years ago, should come to a hap'orth of harrum.

KYRLE:

> Miss Chute!

ANNE:

> Well, I can't help it. When I am angry the brogue comes out, and my Irish heart will burst through manners, and graces, and twenty stay-laces. I'll give up my fortune, that I will.

KYRLE:

> You can't—you've got a guardian who cannot consent to such a sacrifice.

ANNE:

> Have I? then I'll find a husband that will.

KYRLE (*aside*):

> She means me—I see it in her eyes.

ANNE (*aside*):

> He's trying to look unconscious. (*aloud*) Kyrle Daly, on your honour and word as a gentleman, do you love me and nobody else?

KYRLE:

> Do you think me capable of contaminating your image by admitting a meaner passion into my breast?

ANNE:

> Yes, I do.

KYRLE:

> Then you wrong me.

ANNE:

> I'll prove that in one word. Take care now—it's coming.

KYRLE:

> Go on.

ANNE (*aside*):

> Now I'll astonish him. (*aloud*) Eily!

KYRLE:

> What's that?

ANNE:

> "Shule, shule, agrah!"

KYRLE:

Where to?

ANNE:

Three winks, as much as to say, "Are you coming?" and an extinguisher above here means "Yes". Now you see I know all about it.

KYRLE:

You have the advantage of me.

ANNE:

Confess now, and I'll forgive you.

KYRLE:

I will—tell me what to confess, and I'll confess it—I don't care what it is.

ANNE (*aside*):

If I hadn't eye-proof he'd brazen it out of me. Isn't he cunning? He's one of those that would get fat where a fox would starve.

KYRLE:

That was a little excursion into my past life—a sudden descent on my antecedents, to see if you could not surprise an infidelity—but I defy you.

ANNE:

You do? I accept that defiance, and mind me, Kyrle, if I find you true, as I once thought, there's my hand; but if you are false in this, Anne Chute will never change her name for yours. (*he kissed her hand*) Leave me now.

KYRLE:

Oh! the lightness you have given to my heart. The number of pipes I'll smoke this afternoon will make them think we've got a haystack on fire.   *Exit* Kyrle *through window*

ANNE (*rings bell on table*):

Here, Pat—Barney—someone.

Enter Servant

Tell Larry Dolan, my groom, to saddle the black mare, Fireball, but not bring her round the house—I'll mount in the stables.

Exit Servant

I'll ride over to Muckross Head, and draw that cottage; I'll know what's there. It mayn't be right, but I haven't a big brother to see after me—and self-protection is the first law of nature.   *Exit* Anne

Music—Enter Mrs. Cregan *and* Hardress

MRS. CREGAN:

What do you say, Hardress?

HARDRESS:

I say, mother, that my heart and faith are both already pledged to another, and I cannot break my engagement.

MRS. CREGAN:

And this is the end of all our pride!

HARDRESS:

Repining is useless—thought and contrivance are of no avail—the die is cast.

MRS. CREGAN:

Hardress—I speak not for myself, but for you—and I would rather see you in your coffin than married to this poor, low-born, silly, vulgar creature. I know you, my son, you will be miserable, when the infatuation of first love is past; when you turn from her and face the world, as one day you must do, you will blush to say, "This is my wife." Every word from her mouth will be a pang to your pride—you will follow her movements with terror—the contempt and derision she excites will rouse you first to remorse, and then to hatred—and from the bed to which you go with a blessing, you will rise with a curse.

HARDRESS:

Mother! mother! (*throws himself in chair*)

MRS. CREGAN:

To Anne you have acted a heartless and dishonourable part—her name is already coupled with yours at every fireside in Kerry.

Enter Servant

SERVANT:

Mr. Corrigan, ma'am.

MRS. CREGAN:

He comes for his answer. Shew him in. *Exit* Servant The hour has come, Hardress—what answer shall I give him?

HARDRESS:

Refuse him—let him do his worst.

MRS. CREGAN:

And face beggary! On what shall we live? I tell you the prison for debt is open before us. Can you work? No! Will you enlist as a soldier and send your wife into service? We are ruined—d'ye hear—ruined. I must accept this man only to give you and yours a shelter, and under Corrigan's roof I may not be ashamed perhaps to receive your wife.

Enter Servant, *shewing in* Mr. Corrigan

CORRIGAN:
Good morning, ma'am; I am punctual you perceive.

MRS. CREGAN:
We have considered your offer, sir, and we see no alternative—but—but—

CORRIGAN:
Mrs. Cregan, I'm proud, ma'am, to take your hand.

HARDRESS (*starting up*):
Begone—begone, I say—touch her and I'll brain you.

CORRIGAN:
Squire! Sir! Mr. Hardress.

HARDRESS:
Must I hurl you from the house?

Enter two Servants

MRS. CREGAN:
Hardress, my darling boy, restrain yourself.

CORRIGAN:
Good morning ma'am. I have my answer. (*to* Servant) Is Miss Chute within?

SERVANT:
No, sir, she's just galloped out of the stable yard.

CORRIGAN:
Say I called to see her. I will wait upon her at this hour tomorrow. (*looking at the Cregans*) Tomorrow! tomorrow!

Exit followed by Servants

MRS. CREGAN:
Tomorrow will see us in Limerick Jail, and this house in the hands of the sheriff.

HARDRESS:
Mother! heaven guide and defend me; let me rest for awhile—you don't know all yet, and I have not the heart to tell you.

MRS. CREGAN:
With you, Hardress, I can bear anything—anything—but your humiliation and your unhappiness—

HARDRESS:
I know it, mother, I know it. *Exit—Music*

Danny *appears at window*

DANNY:
Whisht—missiz—whisht.

MRS. CREGAN:

Who's there?

DANNY:

It's me sure, Danny—that is—I know the throuble that's in it. I've been through it all wid him.

MRS. CREGAN:

You know, then—?

DANNY:

Everything, ma'am; and, shure, I sthruv hard and long to impache him from doing id.

MRS. CREGAN:

Is he, indeed, so involved with this girl that he will not give her up?

DANNY:

No; he's got over the worst of it, but she holds him tight, and he feels kindly and soft-hearted for her, and darn't do what another would.

MRS. CREGAN:

Dare not?

DANNY:

Sure she might be packed off across the wather to Ameriky, or them parts beyant? Who'd ever ax a word afther her?—barrin' the masther, who'd murdher me if he knew I whispered such a thing.

MRS. CREGAN:

But would she go?

DANNY:

Ow, ma'am, wid a taste of persuasion, we'd mulvather her abo- ord. But there's another way again, and if ye'd only coax the masther to send me his glove, he'd know the manin' of that token, and so would I.

MRS. CREGAN:

His glove?

DANNY:

Sorra a haporth else. If he'll do that, I'll take my oath ye'll hear no more of the Colleen Bawn.

MRS. CREGAN:

I'll see my son.   *Exit*

DANNY:

Tare an' 'ouns, that lively girl, Miss Chute, has gone the road to Muckross Head; I've watched her—I've got my eye on all of them. If she sees Eily—ow, ow, she'll get the ring itself in that helpin' of kale-canon. Be the piper, I'll run across the lake, and, maybe, get there first; she's got a long round to go, and the wind rising—a purty blast entirely. (*goes to window—Music*)

Re-enter Mrs. Cregan, *with glove*

MRS. CREGAN (*aside*):
 I found his gloves in the hall, where he had thrown them in his hat.
DANNY:
 Did ye ax him, ma'am?
MRS. CREGAN:
 I did—and here is the reply. (*holds out glove*)
DANNY:
 He has changed his mind, then?
MRS. CREGAN:
 He has entirely.
DANNY:
 And—and—I am—to—do it?
MRS. CREGAN:
 That is the token.
DANNY:
 I know it—I'll keep my promise. I'm to make away with her?
MRS. CREGAN:
 Yes, yes—take her away—away with her! *Exit* Mrs. Cregan
DANNY:
 Never fear, ma'am. (*going to window*) He shall never see or hear again of the Colleen Bawn. *Exit* Danny *through window*

Act II, Scene iii

Exterior of Eily's Cottage; Cottage, set pieces, backed by Lake; table and two seats. Sheelah *and* Eily *discovered knitting.*

SHEELAH:
 Don't cry, darlin'—don't alaina!
EILY:
 He'll never come back to me—I'll never see him again, Sheelah!
SHEELAH:
 Is it lave his own wife?
EILY:
 I've sent him a letther by Myles, and Myles has never come back—I've got no answer—he won't spake to me—I am

standin' betune him and fortune—I'm in the way of his happiness. I wish I was dead!

SHEELAH:

Whisht! be the husht! what talk is that? when I'm tuk sad that way, I go down to the chapel and pray a turn—it lifts the cloud off my heart.

EILY:

I can't pray; I've tried, but unless I pray for him, I can't bring my mind to it.

SHEELAH:

I never saw a colleen that loved as you love; sorra come to me, but I b'lieve you've got enough to supply all Munster, and more left over than would choke ye if you wern't azed of it.

EILY:

He'll come back—I'm sure he will; I was wicked to doubt. Oh! Sheelah! what becomes of the girls he doesn't love. Is there anything goin' on in the world where he isn't?

SHEELAH:

There now—you're smilin' again.

EILY:

I'm like the first mornin' when he met me—there was dew on the young day's eye—a smile on the lips o' the lake. Hardress will come back—oh! yes; he'll never leave his poor Eily all alone by herself in this place. Whisht!, now, an' I'll tell you. (*Music*)

Song—Air, "Pretty Girl Milking her Cow."

'Twas on a bright morning in summer,
I first heard his voice speaking low,
As he said to a colleen beside me,
"Who's that pretty girl milking her cow?"
And many times after he met me,
And vow'd that I always should be
His own little darling alanna,
Mavourneen a sweelish machree.
I haven't the manners or graces
Of the girls in the world where ye move,
I haven't their beautiful faces,
But I have a heart that can love.
If it plase ye, I'll dress in satins,
And jewels I'll put on my brow,
But don't ye be after forgettin'
Your pretty girl milking her cow.

SHEELAH:

Ah, the birds sit still on the boughs to listen to her, and the trees stop whisperin'; she leaves a mighty big silence behind her voice, that nothin' in nature wants to break. My blessin' on the path before her—there's an angel at the other end of it.

Exit Sheelah *in cottage*

EILY (*repeats last line of song*)

Enter Anne Chute

ANNE:

There she is.

EILY (*sings till facing* Anne—stops—*they examine each other*)

ANNE:

My name is Anne Chute.

EILY:

I am Eily O'Connor.

ANNE:

You are the Colleen Bawn—the pretty girl.

EILY:

And you are the Colleen Ruaidh.

ANNE (*aside*):

She is beautiful.

EILY (*aside*):

How lovely she is.

ANNE:

We are rivals.

EILY:

I am sorry for it.

ANNE:

So am I, for I feel that I could have loved you.

EILY:

That's always the way of it; everybody want to love me, but there's something spoils them off.

ANNE (*showing letter*):

Do you know that writing?

EILY:

I do, ma'am, well, though I don't know how you came by it.

ANNE:

I saw your signals last night—I saw his departure, and I have come here to convince myself of his falsehood to me. But now that I have seen you, you have no longer a rival in his love, for I despise him with all my heart, who could bring one so beautiful and simple as you are to ruin and shame!

EILY:

> He didn't—no—I am his wife! Oh, what have I said!

ANNE:

> What?

EILY:

> Oh, I didn't mane to confess it—no, I didn't! but you wrung it from me in defence of him.

ANNE:

> You his wife?

Enter Danny

DANNY (*at back—aside*):

> The divil! they're at it—an' I'm too late!

ANNE:

> I cannot believe this—shew me your certificate.

EILY:

> Here it is.

DANNY (*advances between them*):

> Didn't you swear to the priest that it should niver lave your breast?

ANNE:

> Oh! you're the boatman.

DANNY:

> Iss, ma'am!

ANNE:

> Eily, forgive me for doubting your goodness, and your purity. I believe you. Let me take your hand. (*crosses to her*) While the heart of Anne Chute beats you have a friend that won't be spoiled off, but you have no longer a rival, mind that. All I ask of you is that you will never mention this visit to Mr. Daly— and for you (*to* Danny) this will purchase your silence. (*gives money*) Good-bye! *Exit* Anne

DANNY:

> Long life t'ye. (*aside*) What does it mane? Hasn't she found me out.

EILY:

> Why did she ask me never to spake to Mr. Daly of her visit here? Sure I don't know any Mr. Daly.

DANNY:

> Didn't she spake of him before, dear?

EILY:

> Never!

DANNY:

    Nor didn't she name Master Hardress?

EILY:

    Well, I don't know; she spoke of him and of the letter I wrote to him, but I b'lieve she never named him intirely.

DANNY (*aside*):

    The divil's in it for sport; She's got 'em mixed yet.

Enter Sheelah *from cottage*

SHEELAH:

    What bring you back, Danny?

DANNY:

    Nothing! but a word I have from the masther for the Colleen here.

EILY:

    Is it the answer to the letter I sent by Myles?

DANNY:

    That's it, jewel, he sent me wid a message.

SHEELAH:

    Somethin' bad has happened. Danny, you are as pale as milk, and your eye is full of blood—yez been drinkin'.

DANNY:

    Maybe I have.

SHEELAH:

    You thrimble, and can't spake straight to me. Oh! Danny, what is it, avick?

DANNY:

    Go on now, an' stop yer keenin'.

EILY:

    Faith, it isn't yourself that's in it, Danny; sure there's nothing happened to Hardress.

DANNY:

    Divil a word, good or bad, I'll say while the mother's there.

SHEELAH:

    I'm goin'. (*aside*) What's come to Danny this day, at all, at all; bedad, I don't know my own flesh and blood.

                               (*runs into cottage*)

DANNY:

    Sorro' and ruin has come on the Cregans; they're broke intirely.

EILY:

    Oh, Danny.

DANNY:

    Whisht, now! You are to meet Masther Hardress this evenin', at a place on the Divil's Island, beyant. Ye'll niver breath a word to mortal to where yer goin', d'ye mind, now; but slip down, unbeknown, to the landin' below, where I'll have the boat waitin' for yez.

EILY:

At what hour?

DANNY:

Just after dark, there's no moon tonight, an' no one will see us crossin' the water. (*music till end of scene*)

EILY:

I will be there; I'll go down only to the little chapel by the shore, and pray there 'till ye come. *Exit* Eily *into cottage*.

DANNY:

I'm wake and cowld! What's this come over me? Mother, mother acushla.

Enter Sheelah

SHEELAH:

What is it, Danny?

DANNY (*staggering to table*):

Give me a glass of spirits! *Falls in chair.*

Act II, Scene iv

The old Weir Bridge, or a Wood on the verge of the Lake.
Enter Anne Chute

ANNE:

Married! the wretch is married! and with that crime already on his conscience he was ready for another and similar piece of villany. It's the Navy that does it. It's my belief those sailors have a wife in every place they stop at.

MYLES (*sings outside*)

"Oh! Eily astoir, my love is all crost,
Like a bud in the frost."

ANNE:

Here's a gentleman who has got my complaint—his love is all crost, like a bud in the frost.

Enter Myles

MYLES:

"And there's no use at all in my goin' to bed,
For it's drames, and not sleep, that comes into my head,
And it's all about you," etc., etc.

ANNE:

My good friend, since you can't catch your love, d'ye think you could catch my horse? (*distant thunder*)

MYLES:

Is it a black mare wid a white stockin' on the fore off leg?

ANNE:

I dismounted to unhook a gate—a peal of thunder frightened her, and she broke away.

MYLES:

She's at Torc Cregan stables by this time—it was an admiration to watch her stride across the Phil Dolan's bit of plough.

ANNE:

And how am I to get home?

MYLES:

If I had four legs, I wouldn't ax betther than to carry ye, an' a proud baste I'd be. (*thunder—rain*)

ANNE:

The storm is coming down to the mountain—is there no shelter near?

MYLES:

There may be a corner in this ould chapel. (*rain*) Here comes the rain—murdher! ye'll be wet through. (*Music—pulls off coat*) Put this round yez.

ANNE:

What will you do? You'll catch your death of cold.

MYLES (*taking out bottle*):

Cowld is it. Here's a wardrobe of top coats. (*thunder*) Whoo! this is a fine time for the water—this way, ma'am.

Exeunt Myles *and* Anne

Enter Eily, *cloak and hood*

EILY:

Here's the place where Danny was to meet me with the boat. Oh! here he is.

Enter Danny

How pale you are!

DANNY:

The thunder makes me sick.

EILY:

Shall we not wait till the storm is over?

DANNY:

If it comes on bad we can put into the Divil's Island Cave.

EILY:

> I feel so happy that I am going to see him, yet there is a weight about my heart that I can't account for.

DANNY:

> I can. (*aside*) Are you ready now?

EILY:

> Yes; come—come.

DANNY (*staggering*):

> I'm wake yet. My throat is dry—if I'd a draught of whiskey now.

EILY:

> Sheelah gave you a bottle.

DANNY:

> I forgot—it's in the boat. (*rain*)

EILY:

> Here comes the rain—we shall get wet.

DANNY:

> There's the masther's boat cloak below.

EILY:

> Come, Danny, lean on me. I'm afraid you are not sober enough to sail the skiff.

DANNY:

> Sober! The dhrunker I am the better I can do the work I've got to do.

EILY:

> Come, Danny, come—come!

> > *Exeunt* Eily *and* Danny—*Music ceases*

> > *Re-enter* Anne Chute *and* Myles

MYLES:

> It was only a shower, I b'lieve—are ye wet, ma'am?

ANNE:

> Dry as a biscuit.

MYLES:

> Ah! then it's yerself is the brave and beautiful lady—as bould an' proud as a ship before the blast. (Anne *looks off*)

ANNE:

> Why, there is my mare, and who comes with—

MYLES:

> It's Mr. Hardress Cregan himself.

ANNE:

> Hardress here?

MYLES:

> Eily gave me a letter for him this morning.

Enter Hardress

HARDRESS:

Anne, what has happened? Your horse galloped wildly into the stable—we thought you had been thrown.

MYLES:

Here is the letther Eily told me to give him. (*to* Hardress) I beg your pardon, sir, but here's the taste of a letther—I was axed to give your honor. (*gives letter*)

HARDRESS (*aside*):

From Eily!

ANNE:

Thanks, my good fellow, for your assistance.

MYLES:

Not at all, ma'am. Sure, there isn't a boy in the County Kerry that would not give two thumbs off his hands to do a service to the Colleen Ruaidh, as you are called among us—iss indeed, ma'am. (*going—aside*) Ah! then it's the purty girl she is in them long clothes.   *Exit* Myles

HARDRESS (*reads, aside*):

"I am the cause of your ruin; I can't live with that thought killin' me. If I do not see you before night you will never again be throubled with your poor Eily". Little simpleton! she is capable of doing herself an injury.

ANNE:

Hardress! I have been very blind and very foolish, but today I have learned to know my own heart. There's my hand, I wish to seal my fate at once. I know the delicacy which prompted you to release me from my engagement to you. I don't accept that release; I am yours.

HARDRESS:

Anne, you don't know all.

ANNE:

I know more than I wanted, that's enough. I forbid you ever to speak on this subject.

HARDRESS:

You don't know my past life.

ANNE:

And I don't want to know. I've had enough of looking into past lives; don't tell me anything you wish to forget.

HARDRESS:

Oh, Anne—my dear cousin; if I could forget—if silence could be oblivion.   *Exeunt* Hardress *and* Anne

Act II, Scene v

Exterior of Myles's Hut.
Enter Myles *singing "Brian O' Linn"*

"Brian o' Linn had no breeches to wear,
So he bought him a sheepskin to make him a pair;
The skinny side out, the woolly side in,
'They are cool and convanient,' said Brian O' Linn."

(*locks door of cabin*) Now I'll go down to my whiskey-still. It is under my feet this minute, bein' in a hole in the rocks they call O'Donoghue's stables, a sort of water cave; the people around here think that the cave is haunted with bad spirits, and they say that of a dark stormy night strange onearthly noises is heard comin' out of it—it is me singing "The Night before Larry was stretched." Now I'll go down to that cave, and wid a sod of live turf under a kettle of worty, I'll invoke them sperrits—and what's more they'll come.

Exit Myles *singing—Music till* Myles *begins to speak next scene.*

Act II, Scene vi

A Cave; through large opening at back is seen the Lake and moon; rocks—flat rock; gauze waters all over stage; rope hanging. Enter Myles *singing, top of rock.*

MYLES:
And this is a purty night for my work! The smoke of my whiskey-still will not be seen; there's my distillery beyant in a snug hole up there, (*unfastens rope*) and here's my bridge to cross over to it. I think it would puzzle a gauger to folly me; this is a patent of my own—a tight-rope bridge. (*swings across*) Now I tie up my drawbridge at this side till I want to go back—what's that—it was an otter I woke from a nap he was taken on that bit of rock there—ow! ye divil! if I had my gun I'd give ye a leaden supper. I'll go up and load it, maybe I'll get a shot; them stones is the place where they lie out of a night, and many a one I've shot of them. *Music—disappears up rock.*

A small boat with Danny *and* Eily *appears and works on to rock.*

EILY:
What place is this you have brought me to?

DANNY:

> Never fear—I know where I'm goin'—step out on that rock—mind yer footin'; 'tis wet there.

EILY:

> I don't like this place—it's like a tomb.

DANNY:

> Step out, I say; the boat is laking. (Eily *steps on to rock*)

EILY:

> Why do you spake to me so rough and cruel?

DANNY:

> Eily, I have a word to say t'ye, listen now, and don't thrimble that way.

EILY:

> I won't, Danny—I won't.

DANNY:

> Wonst, Eily, I was a fine brave boy, the pride of my ould mother, her white haired darlin'—you wouldn't think it to look at me now. D'ye know how I got changed to this?

EILY:

> Yes, Hardress told me.

DANNY:

> He done it—but I loved him before it, an' I loved him afther it—not a dhrop of blood I have, but I'd pour out like wather for the masther.

EILY:

> I know what you mean—as he has deformed your body—ruined your life—made ye what ye are.

DANNY:

> Have you, a woman, less love for him than I, that you wouldn't give him what he wants of you, even if he broke your heart as he broke my back, both in a moment of passion? Did I ax him to ruin himself and his ould family, and all to mend my bones? No! I loved him, and I forgave him that.

EILY:

> Danny, what d'ye want me to do?

>   (Danny *steps out on to rock*)

DANNY:

> Give me that paper in your breast? (*boat floats off slowly*)

EILY:

> I can't—I've sworn never to part with it! You know I have!

DANNY:

> Eily, that paper stands between Hardress Cregan and his fortune; that paper is the ruin of him. Give it, I tell yez.

EILY:

Take me to the priest; let him lift the oath off me. Oh! Danny, I swore a blessed oath on my two knees, and ye would ax me to break that?

DANNY (*seizes her hands*):

Give it up, and don't make me hurt ye.

EILY:

I swore by my mother's grave, Danny. Oh! Danny, dear, don't. Don't, acushla, and I'll do anything. See now, what good would it be; sure, while I live I'm his wife. (*Music changes*)

DANNY:

Then you've lived too long. Take your marriage lines wid ye to the bottom of the lake. (*he throws her from rock backwards into the water, with a cry; she reappears, clinging to rock*)

EILY:

No! save me. Don't kill me. Don't, Danny, I'll—do any thing, only let me live.

DANNY:

He wants ye dead. (*pushes her off*)

EILY:

Oh! Heaven help me. Danny—Dan—(*sinks*)

DANNY (*looking down*):

I've done it. She's gone. (*shot is fired; he falls—rolls from the rock into the water*)

Myles *appears with gun on rock*

MYLES:

I hit one of them bastes that time. I could see well, though it was so dark. But there was somethin' moving on that stone. (*swings across*) Divil a sign of him. Stop! (*looks down*) What's this? it's a woman—there's something white there. (*figure rises near rock—kneels down; tries to take the hand of figure*) Ah! that dress; it's Eily. My own darlin' Eily. (*pulls off waistcoat—jumps off rock. Eily rises—then Myles and Eily rise up—he turns, and seizes rock—Eily across left arm.*)

Act III, Scene i

Interior of an Irish Hut; door and small opening; Truckle bed and bedding, on which Danny Mann *is discovered; table with jug of water; lighted candle stuck in bottle; two stools—Sheelah at table—Music.*

DANNY (*in his sleep*):

Gi'me the paper, thin—screeching won't save ye—down, down! (*wakes*) Oh, mother, darlin'—mother!

SHEELAH (*waking*):

Eh! did ye call me, Danny?

DANNY:

Gi'me a dhrop of wather—it's the thirst that's killin' me.

SHEELAH (*takes jug*):

The fever's on ye mighty bad.

DANNY (*drinks, falls back, groans*):

Oh, the fire in me won't go out! How long have I been here?

SHEELAH:

Ten days this night.

DANNY:

Ten days dis night! have I been all that time out of my mind?

SHEELAH:

Iss, Danny. Ten days ago, that stormy night, ye crawled in at that dure, wake an' like a ghost.

DANNY:

I remind me now.

SHEELAH:

Ye tould me that ye'd been poachin' salmon, and had been shot by the keepers.

DANNY:

Who said I hadn't?

SHEELAH:

Divil a one! Why did ye make me promise not to say a word about it? didn't ye refuse even to see a doctor itself?

DANNY:

Has any one axed after me?

SHEELAH:

No one but Mr. Hardress.

DANNY:

Heaven bless him.

SHEELAH:

I told him I hadn't seen ye, and here ye are this day groanin' when there's great doin's up at Castle Chute. Tomorrow the masther will be married to Miss Anne.

DANNY:

Married! but—the—his—

SHEELAH:

Poor Eily, ye mane?

DANNY:

> Hide the candle from my eyes, it's painin' me, shade it off. Go on, mother.

SHEELAH:

> The poor Colleen! Oh, vo, Danny, I knew she'd die of the love that was chokin' her. He didn't know how tindher she was, when he give her the hard word. What was that message the masther sent to her, that ye wouldn't let me hear? It was cruel, Danny, for it broke her heart entirely; she went away that night, and, two days after, a cloak was found floatin' in the reeds, under Brikeen Bridge; nobody knew it but me. I turned away, and never said—. The crature is drowned, Danny, and wo to them as dhruv her to it. She has no father, no mother to put a curse on him, but there's the Father above that niver spakes till the last day, and then—(*she turns and sees* Danny *gasping, his eyes fixed on her, supporting himself on his arm*) Danny! Danny! he's dyin'—he's dyin'. (*runs to him*)

DANNY:

> Who said that? Ye lie! I never killed her—sure he sent me the glove—where is it?

SHEELAH:

> He's ravin' again.

DANNY:

> The glove, he sent it to me full of blood. Oh! master, dear, there's your token. I tould ye I would clear the path forenist ye.

SHEELAH:

> Danny, what d'ye mane?

DANNY:

> I'll tell ye how I did it, masther; 'twas dis way, but don't smile like dat, don't, sir! She wouldn't give me de marriage lines, so I sunk her, and her proofs wid her! She's gone! she came up wonst, but I put her down agin! Never fear—she'll never throuble yer agin, never, never. (*lies down, mutters*—Sheelah *on her knees, in horror and prayer*)

SHEELAH:

> 'Twas he! he!—my own son—he's murdered her, and he's dyin'— dyin', wid blood on his hands! Danny! Danny! Spake to me!

DANNY:

> A docther! will dey let me die like a baste, and never a docther?

SHEELAH:

> I'll run for one that'll cure ye. Oh! weerasthrue, Danny! Is it for this I've loved ye? No, forgive me, acushla, it isn't your own mother that 'ud add to yer heart-breakin' and pain. I'll fetch the

docther, avick. (*Music—puts on cloak and pulls hood over her head*) Oh! hone—oh! hone!

Exit Sheelah—*a pause—knock—pause—knock*
Enter Corrigan

CORRIGAN:

Sheelah! Nobody here?—I'm bothered entirely. The cottage on Muckross Head is empty—not a sowl in it but a cat. Myles has disappeared, and Danny gone—vanished, bedad, like a fog. Sheelah is the only one remaining. I called to see Miss Chute; I was kicked out. I sent her a letther; it was returned to me unopened. Her lawyer has paid off the mortgage, and taxed my bill of costs—the spalpeen! (Danny *groans*) What's that? Some one asleep there. 'Tis Danny!

DANNY:

A docther—gi'me a doctor!

CORRIGAN:

Danny here—concealed, too! Oh! there's something going on that's worth peepin' into. Whist! there's footsteps comin'. If I could hide a bit. I'm a magistrate, an' I ought to know what's goin' on—here's a turf hole wid a windy in it.

Exit Corrigan.

Enter Sheelah *and* Father Tom

SHEELAH (*goes to* Danny):

Danny!

DANNY:

Is that you, mother?

SHEELAH:

I've brought the docther, asthore. (Danny *looks up*)

DANNY:

The priest!

SHEELAH (*on her knees*):

Oh! my darlin', don't be angry wid me, but dis is the docther you want; it isn't in your body where the hurt is; the wound is in your poor sowl—there's all the harrum.

FATHER TOM:

Danny, my son—(*sits*)—it's sore-hearted I am to see you down this way.

SHEELAH:

And so good a son he was to his ould mother.

DANNY:

Don't say that—don't. (*covering his face*)

SHEELAH:

I will say it—my blessin' on ye—see that, now, he's cryin'.

FATHER TOM:

Danny, the hand of death is on ye. Will ye lave your sins behind ye here below, or will ye take them with ye above, to show them on ye? Is there anything ye can do that'll mend a wrong? leave that legacy to your friend, and he'll do it. Do ye want pardon of any one down here—tell me, avick; I'll get it for ye, and send it after you—may be ye'll want it.

DANNY (*rising up on arm*):

I killed Eily O'Connor.

SHEELAH (*covers her face with her hands*):

Oh! oh!

FATHER TOM:

What harrum had ye agin the poor Colleen Bawn? (Corrigan *takes notes*)

DANNY:

She stud in *his* way, and he had my heart and sowl in his keeping.

FATHER TOM:

Hardress!

DANNY:

Hisself! I said I'd do it for him, if he'd give me the token.

FATHER TOM:

Did Hardress employ you to kill the girl?

DANNY:

He sent me the glove; that was to be the token that I was to put her away, and I did—I—in the Pool a Dhiol. She wouldn't gi'me the marriage lines; I threw her in and then I was kilt.

FATHER TOM:

Killed! by whose hand?

DANNY:

I don't know, unless it was the hand of heaven.

FATHER TOM (*rising, goes down—aside*):

Myles-na-Coppaleen is at the bottom of this; his whiskey still is in that cave, and he has not been seen for ten days past. (*aloud— goes to* Danny) Danny, after ye fell, how did ye get home?

DANNY:

I fell in the wather; the current carried me to a rock; how long I was there half drowned I don't know, but on wakin' I found my boat floatin' close by, an' it was still dark, I got in and crawled here.

FATHER TOM (*aside*):

I'll go and see Myles—there's more in this than has come out.

SHEELAH:

Won't yer riverince say a word of comfort to the poor boy?—he's in great pain entirely.

FATHER TOM:

Keep him quiet, Sheelah. (*Music*) I'll be back again with the comfort for him. Danny, your time is short; make the most of it. (*aside*) I'm off to Myles-na-Coppaleen. Oh, Hardress (*going up*) Cregan, ye little think what a bridal day ye'll have! *Exit.*

CORRIGAN (*who has been writing in note-book, comes out—at back*):

I've got down every word of the confession. Now, Hardress Cregan, there will be guests at your weddin' tonight ye little dhrame of. *Exit*

DANNY (*rising up*):

Mother, mother! the pain is on me. Wather—quick—wather!

(Sheelah *runs to table—takes jug—gives it to* Danny—*he drinks—*Sheelah *takes jug—*Danny *struggles—falls back on bed—close on picture*)

Act III, Scene ii

Chamber in Castle Chute.
Enter Kyrle Daly *and* Servant

KYRLE:

Inform Mrs. Cregan that I am waiting upon her.

Enter Mrs. Cregan

MRS. CREGAN:

I am glad to see you, Kyrle.   *Exit* Servant.

KYRLE:

You sent for me, Mrs. Cregan. My ship sails from Liverpool tomorrow. I never thought I could be so anxious to quit my native land.

MRS. CREGAN:

I want you to see Hardress. For ten days past he shuns the society of his bride. By night he creeps out alone in his boat on the lake—by day he wanders round the neighbourhood pale as death. He is heartbroken.

KYRLE:

Has he asked to see me?

MRS. CREGAN:

Yesterday he asked where you were.

KYLE:

> Did he forget that I left your house when Miss Chute, without a word of explanation, behaved so unkindly to me?

MRS. CREGAN:

> She is not the same girl since she accepted Hardress. She quarrels—weeps—complains, and has lost her spirits.

KYRLE:

> She feels the neglect of Hardress.

ANNE (*without*):

> Don't answer me. Obey! and hold your tongue.

MRS. CREGAN:

> Do you hear? she is rating one of the servants.

ANNE (*without*):

> No words—I'll have no sulky looks neither!

Enter Anne, *dressed as a bride, with veil and wreath in her hand*

ANNE:

> Is that the veil and wreath I ordered? How dare you tell me that. (*throws it off*)

MRS. CREGAN:

> Anne! (Anne *sees* Kyrle—*stands confused*)

KYRLE:

> You are surprised to see me in your house, Miss Chute?

ANNE:

> You are welcome, sir.

KYRLE (*aside*):

> She looks pale! She's not happy—that's gratifying.

ANNE:

> He doesn't look well—that's some comfort.

MRS. CREGAN:

> I'll try to find Hardress. *Exit* Mrs. Cregan

KYRLE:

> I hope you don't think I intrude—that is—I came to see Mrs. Cregan.

ANNE (*sharply*):

> I don't flatter myself you wished to see me, why should you?

KYRLE:

> Anne, I am sorry I offended you; I don't know what I did, but no matter.

ANNE:

> Not the slightest.

KYRLE:

> I released your neighbourhood of my presence.

ANNE:

Yes, and you released the neighbourhood of the presence of somebody else—she and you disappeared together.

KYRLE:

She!

ANNE:

Never mind.

KYRLE:

But I do mind. I love Hardress Cregan as a brother, and I hope the time may come, Anne, when I can love you as a sister.

ANNE:

Do you? I don't.

KYRLE:

I don't want the dislike of my friend's wife to part my friend and me.

ANNE:

Why should it? I'm nobody.

KYRLE:

If you were my wife, and asked me to hate any one, I'd do it— I couldn't help it.

ANNE:

I believed words like that once when you spoke them, but I have been taught how basely you can deceive.

KYRLE:

Who taught you?

ANNE:

Who?—your wife.

KYRLE:

My what?

ANNE:

Your wife—the girl you concealed in the cottage on Muckross Head. Stop now, don't speak—save a falsehood, however many ye have to spare. I saw the girl—she confessed.

KYRLE:

Confessed that she was my wife?

ANNE:

Made a clean breast of it in a minute, which is more than you could do with a sixteen-foot waggon and a team of ten in a week.

KYRLE:

Anne, hear me; this is a frightful error—the girl will not repeat it.

ANNE:

Bring her before me and let her speak.

KYRLE:

How do I know where she is?

ANNE:

Well, bring your boatman then, who told me the same.

KYRLE:

I tell you it is false; I never saw—never knew the girl!

ANNE:

You did not? (*shows* Eily's *letter*) Do you know that? You dropped it, and I found it.

KYRLE (*takes letter*):

This! (*reads*).

Enter Hardress

ANNE:

Hardress! (*turns aside*)

KYRLE:

Oh! (*suddenly struck with the truth—glances towards* Anne— *finding her looking away, places letter to* Hardress) Do you know that? you dropped it.

HARDRESS (*conceals letter*):

Eh?—Oh!

KYRLE:

'Twas he. (*looks from one to the other*) She thinks me guilty; but if I stir to exculpate myself, he is in for it.

HARDRESS:

You look distressed, Kyrle. Anne, what is the matter?

KYRLE:

Nothing, Hardress. I was about to ask Miss Chute to forget a subject which was painful to her, and to beg of her never to mention it again—not even to you, Hardress.

HARDRESS:

I am sure she will deny you nothing.

ANNE:

I will forget, sir; (*aside*) but I will never forgive him—never.

KYRLE (*aside*):

She loves me still, and he loves another, and I am the most miserable dog that ever was kicked. Hardress, a word with you.

Exit Kyrle *and* Hardress.

ANNE:

And this is my wedding day. There goes the only man I ever loved. When he's here near by me, I could give him the worst treatment a man could desire, and when he goes he takes the heart and all of me off with him, and I feel like an unfurnished house. This is pretty feelings for a girl to have, and she in her regimentals. Oh! if he wasn't married—but he is, and he'd have married me as well—the malignant! Oh! if he had, how I'd have made him swing for it—it would have afforded me the happiest moment of my life. (*Music*) *Exit* Anne

Act III, Scene iii

Exterior of Myles's Hut.
Enter Father Tom

FATHER TOM:

Here's Myles's shanty. I'm nearly killed with climbin' the hill. I wonder is he at home? Yes, the door is locked inside. (*knocks*) Myles—Myles, are ye at home?

MYLES (*outside*):

No—I'm out.

Enter Myles

Arrah! is it yourself, Father Tom, that's in it?

FATHER TOM:

Let us go inside, Myles—I've a word to say t'ye.

MYLES:

I—I've lost the key.

FATHER TOM:

Sure it's sticken inside.

MYLES:

Iss—I always lock the dure inside and lave it there when I go out, for fear on losin' it.

FATHER TOM:

Myles, come here to me. It's lyin' ye are. Look me in the face. What's come to ye these tin days past—three times I've been to your door and it was locked, but I heard ye stirrin' inside.

MYLES:

It was the pig, yer riverince.

FATHER TOM:

Myles, why did yer shoot Danny Mann?

MYLES:

Oh, murther, who tould you that?

FATHER TOM:

Himself.

MYLES:

Oh, Father Tom, have ye seen him?

FATHER TOM:

 I've just left him.

MYLES:

 Is it down there ye've been?

FATHER TOM:

 Down where?

MYLES:

 Below, where he's gone to—where would he be, afther murthering a poor crature?

FATHER TOM:

 How d'ye know that?

MYLES:

 How! How did I?—whisht, Father Tom, it was his ghost.

FATHER TOM:

 He is not dead, but dyin' fast, from the wound ye gave him.

MYLES:

 I never knew 'twas himself 'till I was tould.

FATHER TOM:

 Who tould you?

MYLES:

 Is it who?

FATHER TOM:

 Who? who?—not Danny, for he doesn't know who killed him.

MYLES:

 Wait, an' I'll tell you. It was nigh twelve that night, I was comin' home—I know the time, betoken Murty Dwyer made me step in his shebeen, bein' the wake of the ould Callaghan, his wife's uncle—and a dacent man he was. "Murty," ses I—

FATHER TOM:

 Myles, you're desavin' me.

MYLES:

 Is it afther desavin' yer riverence I'd be?

FATHER TOM:

 I see the lie in yer mouth. Who tould ye it was Danny Mann ye killed?

MYLES:

 You said so awhile ago.

FATHER TOM:

 Who tould ye it was Danny Mann?

MYLES:

 I'm comin' to it. While I was at Murty's, yer riverince, as I was a-tellin' you—Dan Dayley was there—he had just kim'd in. "Good morrow,—good day"—ses he. "Good morrow, good Dan, ses

I,"—jest that ways entirely—"it's an opening to the heart to see you." Well, yer riverince, as I ware sayin',—"long life an' good wife to ye, Masther Dan," ses I. "Thank ye, ses he, and the likes to ye, anyway." The moment I speck them words, Dan got heart, an' up an' tould Murty about his love for Murty's darter—the Colleen Rue. The moment he heard that, he puts elbows in himself, an' stood lookin' at him out on the flure. "You flog Europe, for boldness," ses he—"get out of my sight," ses he,—"this moment," ses he,—"or I'll give yer a kick that will rise you from poverty to the highest pitch of affluence," ses he—"away out o' that, you notorious delinquent; single yer freedom and double yer distance," ses he. Well, Dan was forced to cut an' run. Poor boy, I was sorry for his trouble; there isn't a better son nor brother this moment goin' the road than what he is—said—said—there wasn't a better, an', an'—oh! Father Tom, don't ax me; I've got an oath on my lips. (*music*) Don't be hard on a poor boy.

FATHER TOM:

I lift the oath from ye. Tell me, avich, oh! tell me. Did ye search for the poor thing—the darlin' soft-eyed Colleen? Oh! Myles, could ye lave her to lie in the cowld lake all alone?

Enter Eily *from door*

MYLES:

No, I couldn't.

FATHER TOM (*turns—sees* Eily):

Eily! Is it yerself, and alive—an' not—not—Oh! Eily, mavourneen. Come to my heart. (*embraces* Eily)

MYLES:

D'ye think ye'd see me alive if she wasn't? I thought ye knew better—it's at the bottom of the Pool a Dhiol I'd be this minute if she wasn't to the fore.

FATHER TOM:

Speak to me—let me hear your voice.

EILY:

Oh! father, father, won't ye take me, far far away from this place.

FATHER TOM:

Why, did ye hide yourself, this way?

EILY:

For fear *he'd* see me.

FATHER TOM:

Hardress. You knew then that he instigated Danny to get rid of ye?

EILY:

Why didn't I die—why am I alive now for him to hate me?

FATHER TOM:

D'ye know that in a few hours he is going to marry another.

EILY:

I know it, Myles tould me—that's why I'm hiding myself away.

FATHER TOM:

What does she mean?

MYLES:

She loves him still—that's what she manes.

FATHER TOM:

Love the wretch who sought your life!

EILY:

Isn't it his own? It isn't his fault if his love couldn't last as long as mine. I was a poor, mane creature—not up to him any way; but if he's only said, "Eily, put the grave between us and make me happy," sure I'd lain down, wid a big heart, in the loch.

FATHER TOM:

And you are willing to pass a life of seclusion that he may live in his guilty joy?

EILY:

If I was alive wouldn't I be a shame to him an' a ruin—ain't I in his way? Heaven help me—why would I trouble him? Oh! he was in great pain o' mind entirely when he let them put a hand on me—the poor darlin'.

FATHER TOM:

And you mean to let him believe you dead?

EILY:

Dead an' gone: then perhaps, his love for me will come back, and the thought of his poor, foolish little Eily that worshipped the ground he stood on, will fill his heart awhile.

FATHER TOM:

And where will you go?

EILY:

I don't know. Anywhere. What matters?

MYLES:

Love makes all places alike.

EILY:

I'm alone in the world now.

FATHER TOM:

The villain—the monster! He sent her to heaven because he wanted her there to blot out with her tears the record of his iniquity. Eily, ye have but one home, and that's my poor house. You are not alone in the world—there's one beside ye, your father, and that's myself.

MYLES:

Two—bad luck to me, two. I am her mother; sure I brought her into the world a second time.

FATHER TOM:

Whist! look down there, Myles—what's that on the road?

MYLES:

It's the sogers—a company of red-coats. What brings the army out?—who's that wid them?—it is ould Corrigan, and they are going towards Castle Chute. There's mischief in the wind.

FATHER TOM:

In with you, an' keep close awhile; I'll go down to the castle and see what's the matter.

EILY:

Promise me that you'll not betray me—that none but yourself and Myles shall ever know I'm livin'; promise me that, before you go.

FATHER TOM:

I do, Eily; I'll never breathe a word of it—it is as sacred as an oath. *Exit—music*

EILY (*going to cottage*):

Shut me in, Myles, and take the key wid ye, this time.

Exit in cottage

MYLES (*locks door*):

There ye are like a pearl in an oyster; now I'll go to my bed as usual on the mountain above—the bolster is stuffed wid rocks, and I'll have a cloud round me for a blanket.

Exit Myles

Act III, Scene iv

Outside of Castle Chute.
Enter Corrigan *and six* Soldiers

CORRIGAN:

Quietly, boys; sthrew yourselves round the wood—some of ye at the gate beyant—two more this way—watch the windies; if he's there to escape at all, he'll jump from a windy. The house is surrounded.

Quadrille music under stage—Air, "The Boulanger"

Oh, oh! they're dancin'—dancin' and merry-making, while the net is closin' around 'em. Now Masther Hardress Cregan—I was kicked out, was I; but I'll come this time wid a call that ye'll answer wid your head instead of your foot. My letters were returned unopened; but here's a bit of writin' that ye'll not be able to hand back so easy.

Enter Corporal

CORPORAL:

All right, sir.

CORRIGAN:

Did you find the woman, as I told ye?

CORPORAL:

Here she is, sir.

Enter Sheelah, *guarded by two* Soldiers

SHEELAH (*crying*):

What's this? Why am I thrated this way—what have I done?

CORRIGAN:

You are wanted awhile—it's your testimony we require. Bring her this way. Follow me! *Exit*

SHEELAH (*struggling*):

Let me go back to my boy. Ah! good luck t'ye, don't kape me from my poor boy! (*struggling*) Oh! you dirty blackguards, let me go—let me go! *Exit* Sheelah *and* Soldiers

Act III, Scene v

Ballroom in Castle Chute. Steps; platform—balustrades on top; backed by moonlight landscape; doors; table; writing materials, books, papers on; chairs; chandeliers lighted.

Ladies *and* Gentlemen, Wedding Guests *discovered,* Hyland Creagh, Bertie O'Moore, Ducie, Kathleen Creagh, Ada Creagh, Patsie O'Moore, Bridesmaids *and* Servants *discovered.*—*Music going on under stage.*

HYLAND:

Ducie, they are dancing the Boulanger, and they can't see the figure unless you lend them the light of your eyes.

KATHLEEN:

>We have danced enough; it is nearly seven o'clock.

DUCIE:

>Mr. O'Moore; when is the ceremony to commence?

O'MOORE:

>The execution is fixed for seven—here's the scaffold, I presume. (*points to table*)

HYLAND:

>Hardress looks like a criminal. I've seen him fight three duels, and he never showed such a pale face as he exhibits tonight.

DUCIE:

>He looks as if he was frightened at being so happy.

HYLAND:

>And Kyrle Daly wears as gay an appearance.

Enter Kyrle Daly, *down steps*

DUCIE:

>Hush! here he is.

KYRLE:

>That need not stop your speech, Hyland. I don't hide my love for Anne Chute, and it is my pride, and no fault of mine if she has found a better man.

HYLAND:

>He is not a better man.

KYRLE:

>He is—she thinks so—what she says becomes the truth.

Enter Mrs. Cregan

MRS. CREGAN:

>Who says the days of chivalry are over? Come, gentlemen, the bridesmaids must attend the bride. The guests will assemble in the hall.

Enter Servant *with letter and card on salver*

SERVANT:

>Mr. Bertie O'Moore, if you plase. A gentleman below asked me to hand you this card.

O'MOORE:

>A gentleman; what can he want (*reads card*) Ah! indeed; this is a serious matter, and excuses the intrusion.

HYLAND:
>   What's the matter?

O'MOORE:
>   A murder has been committed.

ALL:
>   A murder?

O'MOORE:
>   The perpetrator of the deed has been discovered, and the warrant for his arrest requires my signature.

HYLAND:
>   Hang the rascal. (*goes up with* Ducie)

O'MOORE:
>   A magistrate, like a doctor, is called on at all hours.

MRS. CREGAN:
>   We can excuse you for such a duty, Mr. O'Moore.

O'MOORE:
>   This is the result of some brawl at a fair I suppose. Is Mr. Corrigan below?

MRS. CREGAN (*starting*):
>   Corrigan?

O'MOORE:
>   Show me to him.

Exit O'Moore *and* Servant—Guests *go up and off*

MRS. CREGAN:
>   Corrigan here! What brings that man to this house?
>
>   *Exit* Mrs. Cregan

Enter Hardress, *down steps, pale*

HARDRESS (*sits*):
>   It is in vain—I cannot repress the terror with which I approach these nuptials—yet, what have I to fear? Oh! my heart is bursting with its load of misery.

Enter Anne, *down steps*

ANNE:
>   Hardress! what is the matter with you?

HARDRESS (*rising*):
>   I will tell you—yes, it may take this horrible oppression from my heart. At one time I thought you knew my secret: I was mistaken.—The girl you saw at Muckross Head—

ANNE:

Eily O'Connor.

HARDRESS:

Was my wife!

ANNE:

Your wife?

HARDRESS:

Hush! Maddened with the miseries this act brought upon me, I treated her with cruelty—she committed suicide.

ANNE:

Merciful powers!

HARDRESS:

She wrote to me bidding me farewell for ever, and the next day her cloak was found floating in the lake. (Anne *sinks in chair*) Since then I have neither slept nor waked—I have but one thought, one feeling; my love for her, wild and maddened, has come back upon my heart like a vengeance.

Music—tumult heard

ANNE:

Heaven defend our hearts, what is that?

Enters Mrs. Cregan, *deadly pale—locks door behind her*

MRS. CREGAN:

Hardress! my child!

HARDRESS:

Mother!

ANNE:

Mother, he is here. Look on him—speak to him—do not gasp and stare on your son in that horrid way. Oh! mother, speak, or you will break my heart.

MRS. CREGAN:

Fly—fly! (Hardress *going*) Not that way. No—the doors are defended! there is a soldier placed at every entrance! You—you are trapped and caught—what shall we do?—the window in my chamber—come—come—quick—

ANNE:

Of what is he accused?

HARDRESS:

Of murder. I see it in her face. (*noise*)

MRS. CREGAN:

Hush! they come—begone! Your boat is below that window. Don't speak! when oceans are between you and danger— write! Till then not a word. (*forcing him off,—noise*)

ANNE:

Accused of murder! He is innocent!

MRS. CREGAN:

Go to your room! Go quickly to your room, you will betray him—you can't command your features.

ANNE:

Dear mother, I will.

MRS. CREGAN:

Away, I say—you will drive me frantic, girl. My brain is stretched to cracking. Ha! (*noise*)

ANNE:

There is a tumult in the drawingroom.

MRS. CREGAN:

They come! You tremble! Go—take away your puny love— hide it where it will not injury him—leave me to face this danger!

ANNE:

He is not guilty.

MRS. CREGAN:

What's that to me, woman? I am his mother—the hunters are after my blood! Sit there—look away from this door. They come!

Knocking loudly—crash—door opened—enter Corporal *and* Soldiers *who cross stage, facing up to charge—*Gentlemen *with drawn swords on steps;* Ladies *on at back—*O'Moore,*—enter* Corrigan—Kyrle *on steps.*

CORRIGAN:

Gentlemen, put up your swords, the house is surrounded by a military force, and we are here in the king's name.

ANNE:

Gentlemen, come on, there was a time in Ireland when neither king nor faction could call on Castle Chute without a bloody welcome.

GUESTS:

Clear them out!

KYRLE (*interposing*):

Anne, are you mad. Put up your swords—stand back there— speak—O'Moore, what does this strange outrage mean?

Soldiers *fall back*—Gentlemen *on steps*—Kyrle *comes forward*

O'MOORE:

Mrs. Cregan, a fearful charge is made against your son; I know—I believe he is innocent. I suggest, then, that the matter be investigated here at once, amongst his friends, so that this scandal may be crushed in its birth.

KYRLE:

Where is Hardress?

CORRIGAN:

Where?—why he's escaping while we are jabbering here. Search the house.   *Exit two* Soldiers

MRS. CREGAN:

Must we submit to this, sir? Will you, a magistrate, permit—

O'MOORE:

I regret, Mrs. Cregan, but as a form—

MRS. CREGAN:

Go on, sir!

CORRIGAN (*at door*):

What room is this? 'tis locked—

MRS. CREGAN:

That is my sleeping chamber.

CORRIGAN:

My duty compels me.

MRS. CREGAN (*throws key down on grond*):

Be it so, sir.

CORRIGAN (*picks up key—unlocks door*):

She had the key—he's there.

Exit Corrigan, Corporal *and two* Soldiers

MRS. CREGAN:

He has escaped by this time.

O'MOORE:

I hope Miss Chute will pardon me for my share in this transaction—believe me, I regret—

ANNE:

Don't talk to me of your regret, while you are doing your worst. It is hate, not justice, that brings this accusation against Hardress, and this disgrace upon me.

KYRLE:

Anne!

ANNE:

Hold *your* tongue—his life's in danger, and if I can't love him, I'll fight for him, and that's more than any of you men can do. (*to* O'Moore) Go on with your dirty work. You have done the worst now—you have dismayed our guests, scattered terror amid our festival, and made the remembrance of this night, which should have been a happy one, a thought of gloom and shame.

MRS. CREGAN:

Hark! I hear—I hear his voice. It cannot be.

Re-enter Corrigan

CORRIGAN:

The prisoner is here!

MRS. CREGAN:

Ah, (*utters a cry*) is he? Dark bloodhound, have you found him? May the tongue that tells me so be withered from the roots, and the eye that first detected him be darkened in its socket!

KYRLE:

Oh, madam! for heaven's sake!

ANNE:

Mother! mother!

MRS. CREGAN:

What! shall it be for nothing he has stung the mother's heart, and set her brain on fire?

Enter Hardress, *handcuffed, and two* Soldiers

I tell you that my tongue may hold its peace, but there is not a vein in all my frame but curses him. (*turns—sees* Hardress; *falls on his breast*) My boy! my boy!

HARDRESS:

Mother, I entreat you to be calm. Kyrle, there are my hands, do you think there is blood upon them?

Kyrle *seizes his hand*—Gentlemen *press around him, take his hand, and retire up*

HARDRESS:

I thank you, gentlemen; your hands acquit me. Mother, be calm—sit there. (*points to chair*)

ANNE:

Come here, Hardress; your place is here by me.

HARDRESS:

Now, sir, I am ready.

CORRIGAN:

I will lay before you, sir, the deposition upon which the warrant issues against the prisoner. Here is the confession of

Daniel or Danny Mann, a person in the service of the accused, taken on his death-bed; in articulo mortis, you'll observe.

O'MOORE:

But not witnessed.

CORRIGAN (*calling*):

Bring in that woman.

Enter Sheelah *and two* Soldiers

I have witnesses. Your worship will find the form of law in perfect shape.

O'MOORE:

Read the confession, sir.

CORRIGAN (*reads*):

"The deponent being on his death-bed, in the presence of Sheelah Mann and Thomas O'Brien, parish priest of Kinmare, deposed and said—"

Enter Father Tom

Oh, you are come in time, sir.

FATHER TOM:

I hope I am.

CORRIGAN:

We may have to call your evidence.

FATHER TOM:

I have brought it with me.

CORRIGAN:

"Deposed and said, that he, deponent, killed Eily O'Connor; that said Eily was the wife of Hardress Cregan and stood in the way of his marriage with Miss Anne Chute; deponent offered to put away the girl, and his master employed him to do so."

O'MOORE:

Sheelah, did Danny confess this crime?

SHEELAH:

Divil a word—it's a lie from end to end, that ould thief was niver in my cabin—he invented the whole of it—sure you're the divil's own parverter of the truth!

CORRIGAN:

Am I? Oh, oh! Father Tom will scarcely say as much? (*to him*) Did Danny Mann confess this in your presence?

FATHER TOM:

I decline to answer that question!

CORRIGAN:

Aha! you must—the law will compel you!

FATHER TOM:

I'd like to see the law that can unseal the lips of the priest, and make him reveal the secrets of heaven.

ANNE:

So much for your two witnesses. Ladies stand close. Gentlemen, give us room here. (Bridesmaids *down*) *Exit* Father Tom

CORRIGAN:

We have abundant proof, your worship—enough to hang a whole county. Danny isn't dead yet. Deponent agreed with Cregan that if the deed was to be done, that he, Cregan, should give his glove as a token.

MRS. CREGAN:

Ah!

HARDRESS:

Hold! I confess that what he has read is true. Danny did make the offer, and I repelled his horrible proposition.

CORRIGAN:

Aha! but you gave him the glove?

HARDRESS:

Never, by my immortal soul—never!

MRS. CREGAN (*advancing*):

But *I—I* did! (*movement of surprise*) I, your wretched mother— I gave it to him—I am guilty! thank heaven for that! remove those bonds from his hands and put them here on mine.

HARDRESS:

'Tis false, mother, you did not know his purpose—you could not know it. (Corporal *takes off handcuffs*)

MRS. CREGAN:

I will not say anything that takes the welcome guilt from off me.

Enter Myles *from steps*

MYLES:

Won't ye, ma'am? Well; if ye won't, I will.

ALL:

Myles!

MYLES:

Save all here. If you plaze, I'd like to say a word; there's been a murder done, and I done it.

ALL:

You!

MYLES:

    Myself. Danny was killed by my hand. (*to* Corrigan) Wor yez any way nigh that time?

CORRIGAN (*quickly*):

    No.

MYLES (*quickly*):

    That's lucky; then take down what I'm sayin'. I shot the poor boy—but widout manin' to hurt him. It's lucky I killed him that time, for it's lifted a mighty sin off the sowl of the crature.

O'MOORE:

    What does he mean?

MYLES:

    I mane, that if you found one witness to Eily O'Connor's death, I found another that knows a little more about it, and here she is.

Enter Eily *and* Father Tom *down steps*

ALL:

    Eily!

MYLES:

    The Colleen Bawn herself!

EILY:

    Hardress!

HARDRESS:

    My wife—my own Eily.

EILY:

    Here, darlin', take the paper, and tear it if you like. (*offers him the certificate*)

HARDRESS:

    Eily, I could not live without you.

MRS. CREGAN:

    If ever he blamed you, it was my foolish pride spoke in his hard words—he loves you with all his heart. Forgive me, Eily.

EILY:

    Forgive.

MRS. CREGAN:

    Forgive your mother, Eily.

EILY (*embracing her*):

    Mother!

Mrs. Cregan, Hardress, Eily, Father Tom *group together*—Anne, Kyrle, *and* Gentlemen—Ladies *together—their backs to* Corrigan—Corrigan *takes bag, puts in papers, looks about, puts on hat, buttons coat, slinks up stage, runs up stairs and off*—Myles *points off after him*—*several* Gentlemen *run after* Corrigan

ANNE:

But what's to become of me, is all my emotion to be summoned for nothing? Is my wedding dress to go to waste, and here's all my blushes ready? I must have a husband.

HYLAND *and* GENTLEMEN:

Take me.

O'MOORE:

Take me.

ANNE:

Don't all speak at once! Where's Mr. Daly!

KYRLE:

Here I am, Anne!

ANNE:

Kyrle, come here! You said you loved me, and I think you do.

KYRLE:

Oh!

ANNE:

Behave yourself now. If you'll ask me, I'll have you.

KYRLE (*embracing* Anne):

Anne! (*shouts outside*)

ALL:

What's that?

MYLES (*looking off at back*):

Don't be uneasy! it's only the boys outside that's caught ould Corrigan thryin' to get off, and they've got him in the horsepond.

KYRLE:

They'll drown him.

MYLES:

Nivir fear, he wasn't born to be drownded—he won't sink—he'll rise out of the world, and divil a fut nearer heaven he'll get than the top o' the gallows.

EILY (*to* Hardress):

And ye won't be ashamed of me?

ANNE:

I'll be ashamed of him if he does.

EILY:

And when I spake—no—speak—

ANNE:

Spake is the right sound. Kyrle Daly, pronounce that word.

KYRLE:

That's right; if you ever spake it any other way I'll divorce ye—mind that.

FATHER TOM:

Eily, darlin', in the middle of your joy, sure you would not forget one who never forsook you in your sorrow.

EILY:

Oh, Father Tom!

FATHER TOM:

Oh, it's not myself I mane.

ANNE:

No, it's that marauder there, that lent me his top coat in the thunder storm. (*pointing to* Myles)

MYLES:

Bedad, ma'am, your beauty left a linin' in it that has kept me warm ever since.

EILY:

Myles, you saved my life—it belongs to you. There's my hand, what will you do with it?

MYLES (*takes her hand and* Hardress's):

Take her, wid all my heart. I may say that, for ye can't take her widout. I am like the boy who had a penny to put in the poor-box—I'd rather keep it for myself. It's a shamrock itself ye have got, sir; and like that flower she'll come up every year fresh and green forenent ye. When he cease to love her may dyin' become ye, and when ye *do* die, lave yer money to the poor, your widdy to me, and we'll both forgive ye. (*joins hands*)

EILY:

I'm only a poor simple girl, and it's frightened I am to be surrounded by so many—

ANNE:

Friends, Eily, friends.

EILY:

Oh, if I could think so—if I could hope that I had established myself in a little corner of their hearts, there wouldn't be a happier girl alive than THE COLLEEN BAWN.

OSCAR WILDE

Oscar Fingal O'Flahertie Wills Wilde was born in Dublin, Ireland, on October 16, 1854. He was the second son of Sir William and Lady Wilde, one of the Irish gentry's most colorful couples. Sir William was a famed surgeon as well as an amateur archaeologist and infamous philanderer. Lady Wilde, the former Jane Francesca Elgee, was a renowned Irish nationalist and poet who wrote under the pseudonym "Speranza." Oscar Wilde started writing verse at the early age of thirteen with the poem "Requiescat," written in memory of the death of his sister Isola. He graduated from Trinity College and then continued his brilliant academic career at Magdalen College, Oxford, in 1874, after winning an academic scholarship. There he came under the tutelage of two of the Victorian era's most eminent and influential figures, John Ruskin, then a professor of art, and Walter Pater. Pater's latter-day epicurean philosophy, encapsulated in his famous phrase "To burn always with this hard, gem-like flame to maintain this ecstasy, is success in life," had a profound effect on Wilde.

After graduating in 1878, Wilde moved to London, where his flamboyant manner—he wore colorful velvet coats, knee-breeches, and green carnations—and his intellectual gifts made him the spokesman of the Aesthetic ("Art for Art's sake") movement. From all accounts he was a brilliant and witty conversationalist. W. B. Yeats wrote: "I never before heard a man talking with perfect sentences, as if he had written them all overnight with labor and yet all spontaneous." In 1881, he undertook a very successful lecture tour of the United States that made him famous. Wilde's public celebrity was such that Gilbert and Sullivan caricatured him with the character of Bunthorne in their operetta *Patience*. In January 1885, Wilde married Constance Lloyd and they had two sons, Cyril and Vyvyan. At the time of his marriage he was working primarily as a journalist, contributing articles and reviews to such magazines as the *Pall Mall Gazette*. In 1891, his novel *The Picture of Dorian Gray* and a collection of short stories, *Lord Arthur Saville's Crime and Other Stories*, established his literary reputation. To earn more money to support his family and his extravagant lifestyle, he began to write plays. Between 1892 and 1895 he wrote four successful comedies—*Lady Windemere's Fan, A Woman of No Importance, An Ideal Husband,* and *The Importance of Being Earnest*—and *Salomé*, an experimental poetic drama that was not allowed to be staged in London, where the Lord Chamberlain banned it in 1892.

In the spring of 1895, at the height of his commercial success and fame, Wilde was arrested. His homosexual relationship with Lord Alfred Douglas, a handsome young poet, was the cause. Douglas's father, the Marquis of Queensberry, publicly accused Wilde of homosexuality, and Wilde sued for libel. For his defense the Marquis gathered a series of witnesses—blackmailers and male prostitutes—who testified to Wilde's proclivities. Wilde lost the case and was sentenced to two years of hard labor. At the time sodomy was a serious criminal offense. His reputation and his career were in ruins. When he was released, he moved to France under an assumed name, divorced and financially bankrupt. *De Profundis* and *The Ballad of Reading Gaol*, two major late works about his unfortunate experiences, were published shortly after his release. He died of cerebral meningitis on November 30, 1900.

Although Wilde did not have much regard for his comedies—which he wrote primarily for financial gain—*The Importance of Being Earnest* is now considered his masterpiece. As suggested by the paradoxical subtitle, *A Trivial Comedy for Serious People*, Wilde intended the play to "treat all the trivial things in life seriously, and all the serious things in life with sincere and studied triviality." Though frivolous, the play succeeds with witty wordplay and effervescent humor at being a perfect entertainment. When the play opened, theater critic A. B. Walkley wrote that Wilde had "'found himself' at last, as an artist in sheer nonsense." The plot follows the progress of two friends, Algernon and Jack—the latter also has an alter ego called Ernest—through the entertaining twists and confusions that lead to their respective marriages. It contains some of Wilde's best dialogue and shows why he remains, next to Shakespeare, the most quoted dramatist in English literature.

THE IMPORTANCE OF BEING EARNEST

A TRIVIAL COMEDY FOR SERIOUS PEOPLE

BY OSCAR WILDE

Dramatis Personae

(As play was originally performed at St. James's Theatre, February 14th, 1895)

JOHN WORTHING, J.P., *of the Manor House, Woolton, Hertfordshire*	*Mr. George Alexander*
ALGERNON MONCRIEFF, *his friend*	*Mr. Allen Aynesworth*
REV. CANON CHASUBLE, D.D., *Rector of Woolton*	*Mr. H. H. Vincent*
MERRIMAN, *butler to Mr. Worthing*	*Mr. Frank Dyall*
LANE, *Mr. Moncrieff's manservant*	*Mr. F. Kinsey Peile*
LADY BRACKNELL	*Miss Rose Leclercq*
HON. GWENDOLEN FAIRFAX, *her daughter*	*Miss Irene Vanbrugh*
CECILY CARDEW, *John Worthing's Ward*	*Miss Evelyn Millard*
MISS PRISM, *her governess*	*Mrs. George Canninge*

The Scenes of the Play

Act I   *Algernon Moncrieff's Flat in Half Moon Street, W.*

Act II   *The Garden at the Manor House, Woolton*

Act III   *Morning-Room at the Manor House, Woolton*

Time—The Present

First Act

SCENE—*Morning room in* Algernon's *flat in Half-Moon Street. The room is luxuriously and artistically furnished. The sound of a piano is heard in the adjoining room.*

Lane *is arranging afternoon tea on the table, and after the music has ceased,* Algernon *enters.*

ALGERNON:

Did you hear what I was playing, Lane?

LANE:

I didn't think it polite to listen, sir.

ALGERNON:

I'm sorry for that, for your sake. I don't play accurately—anyone can play accurately—but I play with wonderful expression. As far as the piano is concerned, sentiment is my forte. I keep science for Life.

LANE:

Yes, sir.

ALGERNON:

And, speaking of the science of Life, have you got the cucumber sandwiches cut for Lady Bracknell?

LANE:

Yes, sir. (*Hands them on a salver.*)

ALGERNON (*inspects them, takes two, and sits down on the sofa*):

Oh! . . . by the way, Lane, I see from your book that on Thursday night, when Lord Shoreman and Mr. Worthing were dining with me, eight bottles of champagne are entered as having been consumed.

LANE:

Yes, sir; eight bottles and a pint.

ALGERNON:

Why is it that at a bachelor's establishment the servants invariably drink the champagne? I ask merely for information.

LANE:

> I attribute it to the superior quality of the wine, sir. I have often observed that in married households the champagne is rarely of a first-rate brand.

ALGERNON:

> Good Heavens! Is marriage so demoralizing as that?

LANE:

> I believe it *is* a very pleasant state, sir. I have had very little experience of it myself up to the present. I have only been married once. That was in consequence of a misunderstanding between myself and a young person.

ALGERNON (*languidly*):

> I don't know that I am much interested in your family life, Lane.

LANE:

> No, sir; it is not a very interesting subject. I never think of it myself.

ALGERNON:

> Very natural, I am sure. That will do, Lane, thank you.

LANE:

> Thank you, sir.   (Lane *goes out.*)

ALGERNON:

> Lane's views on marriage seem somewhat lax. Really, if the lower orders don't set us a good example, what on earth is the use of them? They seem, as a class, to have absolutely no sense of moral responsibility.

Enter Lane.

LANE:

> Mr. Ernest Worthing.

Enter Jack.   Lane *goes out.*

ALGERNON:

> How are you, my dear Ernest? What brings you up to town?

JACK:

> Oh, pleasure, pleasure! What else should bring one anywhere? Eating as usual, I see, Algy!

ALGERNON (*stiffy*):

> I believe it is customary in good society to take some slight refreshment at five o'clock. Where have you been since last Thursday?

JACK (*sitting down on the sofa*):

In the country.

ALGERNON:

What on earth do you do there?

JACK (*pulling off his gloves*):

When one is in town one amuses oneself. When one is in the country one amuses other people. It is excessively boring.

ALGERNON:

And who are the people you amuse?

JACK (*airily*):

Oh, neighbors, neighbors.

ALGERNON:

Got nice neighbors in your part of Shropshire?

JACK:

Perfectly horrid! Never speak to one of them.

ALGERNON:

How immensely you must amuse them! (*Goes over and takes sandwich.*) By the way, Shropshire is your county, is it not?

JACK:

Eh? Shropshire? Yes, of course. Hallo! Why all these cups? Why cucumber sandwiches? Why such reckless extravagance in one so young? Who is coming to tea?

ALGERNON:

Oh! merely Aunt Augusta and Gwendolen.

JACK:

How perfectly delightful!

ALGERNON:

Yes, that is all very well; but I am afraid Aunt Augusta won't quite approve of your being here.

JACK:

May I ask why?

ALGERNON:

My dear fellow, the way you flirt with Gwendolen is perfectly disgraceful. It is almost as bad as the way Gwendolen flirts with you.

JACK:

I am in love with Gwendolen. I have come up to town expressly to propose to her.

ALGERNON:

I thought you had come up for pleasure? . . . I call that business.

JACK:

How utterly unromantic you are!

ALGERNON:

> I really don't see anything romantic in proposing. It is very romantic to be in love. But there is nothing romantic about a definite proposal. Why, one may be accepted. One usually is, I believe. Then the excitement is all over. The very essence of romance is uncertainty. If ever I get married, I'll certainly try to forget the fact.

JACK:

> I have no doubt about that, dear Algy. The Divorce Court was specially invented for people whose memories are so curiously constituted.

ALGERNON:

> Oh! there is no use speculating on that subject. Divorces are made in Heaven—(Jack *puts out his hand to take a sandwich.* Algernon *at once interferes.*) Please don't touch the cucumber sandwiches. They are ordered specially for Aunt Augusta. (*Takes one and eats it.*)

JACK:

> Well, you have been eating them all the time.

ALGERNON:

> That is quite a different matter. She is my aunt. (*Takes plate from below.*) Have some bread and butter. The bread and butter is for Gwendolen. Gwendolen is devoted to bread and butter.

JACK (*advancing to table and helping himself*):

> And very good bread and butter it is too.

ALGERNON:

> Well, my dear fellow, you need not eat as if you were going to eat it all. You behave as if you were married to her already. You are not married to her already, and I don't think you ever will be.

JACK:

> Why on earth do you say that?

ALGERNON:

> Well, in the first place girls never marry the men they flirt with. Girls don't think it right.

JACK:

> Oh, that is nonsense!

ALGERNON:

> It isn't. It is a great truth. It accounts for the extraordinary number of bachelors that one sees all over the place. In the second place, I don't give my consent.

JACK:

> Your consent!

ALGERNON:

My dear fellow, Gwendolen is my first cousin. And before I allow you to marry her, you will have to clear up the whole question of Cecily. (*Rings bell.*)

JACK:

Cecily! What on earth do you mean? What do you mean, Algy, by Cecily? I don't know anyone of the name of Cecily.

Enter Lane.

ALGERNON:

Bring me that cigarette case Mr. Worthing left in the smoking-room the last time he dined here.

LANE:

Yes, sir. (Lane *goes out.*)

JACK:

Do you mean to say you have had my cigarette case all this time? I wish to goodness you had let me know. I have been writing frantic letters to Scotland Yard about it. I was very nearly offering a large reward.

ALGERNON:

Well, I wish you would offer one. I happen to be more than usually hard up.

JACK:

There is no good offering a large reward now that the thing is found.

Enter Lane *with the cigarette case on a salver.* Algernon *takes it at once.* Lane *goes out.*

ALGERNON:

I think that is rather mean of you, Ernest, I must say. (*Opens case and examines it.*) However, it makes no matter, for, now that I look at the inscription inside, I find that the thing isn't yours after all.

JACK:

Of course it's mine. (*Moving to him.*) You have seen me with it a hundred times, and you have no right whatsoever to read what is written inside. It is a very ungentlemanly thing to read a private cigarette case.

ALGERNON:

Oh! it is absurd to have a hard-and-fast rule about what one should read and what one shouldn't. More than half of modern culture depends on what one shouldn't read.

JACK:

I am quite aware of the fact, and I don't propose to discuss modern culture. It isn't the sort of thing one should talk of in private. I simply want my cigarette case back.

ALGERNON:

Yes; but this isn't your cigarette case. This cigarette case is a present from someone of the name of Cecily, and you said you didn't know anyone of that name.

JACK:

Well, if you want to know, Cecily happens to be my aunt.

ALGERNON:

Your aunt!

JACK:

Yes. Charming old lady she is, too. Lives at Tunbridge Wells. Just give it back to me, Algy.

ALGERNON (*retreating to back of sofa*):

But why does she call herself Cecily if she is your aunt and lives at Tunbridge Wells? (*Reading.*) "From little Cecily with her fondest love."

JACK (*moving to sofa and kneeling upon it*):

My dear fellow, what on earth is there in that? Some aunts are tall, some aunts are not tall. That is a matter that surely an aunt may be allowed to decide for herself. You seem to think that every aunt should be exactly like your aunt! That is absurd! For Heaven's sake give me back my cigarette case. (*Follows Algy round the room.*)

ALGERNON:

Yes. But why does your aunt call you her uncle? "From little Cecily, with her fondest love to her dear Uncle Jack." There is no objection, I admit, to an aunt being a small aunt, but why an aunt, no matter what her size may be, should call her own nephew her uncle, I can't quite make out. Besides, your name isn't Jack at all; it is Ernest.

JACK:

It isn't Ernest; it's Jack.

ALGERNON:

You have always told me it was Ernest. I have introduced you to everyone as Ernest. You answer to the name of Ernest. You look as if your name was Ernest. You are the most earnest look-ing person I ever saw in my life. It is perfectly absurd your say-ing that your name isn't Ernest. It's on your cards. Here is one of them. (*Taking it from case.*) "Mr. Ernest Worthing, B. 4, The Albany." I'll keep this as a proof that your name is Ernest if ever you attempt to deny it to me, or to Gwendolen, or to anyone else. (*Puts the card in his pocket.*)

JACK:

Well, my name is Ernest in town and Jack in the country, and the cigarette case was given to me in the country.

ALGERNON:

Yes, but that does not account for the fact that your small Aunt Cecily, who lives at Tunbridge Wells, calls you her dear uncle. Come, old boy, you had much better have the thing out at once.

JACK:

My dear Algy, you talk exactly as if you were a dentist. It is very vulgar to talk like a dentist when one isn't a dentist. It produces a false impression.

ALGERNON:

Well, that is exactly what dentists always do. Now, go on! Tell me the whole thing. I may mention that I have always suspected you of being a confirmed and secret Bunburyist; and I am quite sure of it now.

JACK:

Bunburyist? What on earth do you mean by a Bunburyist?

ALGERNON:

I'll reveal to you the meaning of that incomparable expression as soon as you are kind enough to inform me why you are Ernest in town and Jack in the country.

JACK:

Well, produce my cigarette case first.

ALGERNON:

Here it is. (*Hands cigarette case.*) Now produce your explanation, and pray make it improbable. (*Sits on sofa.*)

JACK:

My dear fellow, there is nothing improbable about my explanation at all. In fact it's perfectly ordinary. Old Mr. Thomas Cardew, who adopted me when I was a little boy, made me in his will guardian to his granddaughter, Miss Cecily Cardew. Cecily, who addresses me as her uncle from motives of respect that you could not possibly appreciate, lives at my place in the country under the charge of her admirable governess, Miss Prism.

ALGERNON:

Where is that place in the country, by the way?

JACK:

That is nothing to you, dear boy. You are not going to be invited. . . . I may tell you candidly that the place is not in Shropshire.

ALGERNON:

I suspected that, my dear fellow! I have Bunburyed all over Shropshire on two separate occasions. Now, go on. Why are you Earnest in town and Jack in the country?

JACK:

My dear Algy, I don't know whether you will be able to understand my real motives. You are hardly serious enough. When one is placed in the position of guardian, one has to adopt a very high moral tone on all subjects. It's one's duty to do so. And as a high moral tone can hardly be said to conduce very much to either one's health or one's happiness, in order to get up to town I have always pretended to have a younger brother of the name of Ernest, who lives in the Albany, and gets into the most dreadful scrapes. That, my dear Algy, is the whole truth pure and simple.

ALGERNON:

The truth is rarely pure and never simple. Modern life would be very tedious if it were either, and modern literature a complete impossibility!

JACK:

That wouldn't be at all a bad thing.

ALGERNON:

Literary criticism is not your forte, my dear fellow. Don't try it. You should leave that to people who haven't been at a University. They do it so well in the daily papers. What you really are is a Bunburyist. I was quite right in saying you were a Bunburyist. You are one of the most advanced Bunburyists I know.

JACK:

What on earth do you mean?

ALGERNON:

You have invented a very useful young brother called Ernest, in order that you may be able to come up to town as often as you like. I have invented an invaluable permanent invalid called Bunbury, in order that I may be able to go down into the country whenever I choose. Bunbury is perfectly invaluable. If it wasn't for Bunbury's extraordinary bad health, for instance, I wouldn't be able to dine with you at Willis's tonight, for I have been really engaged to Aunt Augusta for more than a week.

JACK:

I haven't asked you to dine with me anywhere tonight.

ALGERNON:

I know. You are absurdly careless about sending out invitations. It is very foolish of you. Nothing annoys people so much as not receiving invitations.

JACK:

You had much better dine with your Aunt Augusta.

ALGERNON:

I haven't the smallest intention of doing anything of the kind. To begin with, I dined there on Monday, and once a week is quite enough to dine with one's own relations. In the second place, whenever I do dine there I am always treated as a member of the family, and sent down with either no woman at all, or two. In the third place, I know perfectly well whom she will place me next to, tonight. She will place me next Mary Farquhar, who always flirts with her own husband across the dinner table. That is not very pleasant. Indeed, it is not even decent . . . and that sort of thing is enormously on the increase. The amount of women in London who flirt with their own husbands is perfectly scandalous. It looks so bad. It is simply washing one's clean linen in public. Besides, now that I know you to be a confirmed Bunburyist, I naturally want to talk to you about Bunburying. I want to tell you the rules.

JACK:

I'm not a Bunburyist at all. If Gwendolen accepts me, I am going to kill my brother, indeed I think I'll kill him in any case. Cecily is a little too much interested in him. It is rather a bore. So I am going to get rid of Ernest. And I strongly advise you to do the same with Mr. . . . with your invalid friend who has the absurd name.

ALGERNON:

Nothing will induce me to part with Bunbury, and if you ever get married, which seems to me extremely problematic, you will be very glad to know Bunbury. A man who marries without knowing Bunbury has a very tedious time of it.

JACK:

That is nonsense. If I marry a charming girl like Gwendolen, and she is the only girl I ever saw in my life that I would marry, I certainly won't want to know Bunbury.

ALGERNON:

Then your wife will. You don't seem to realize, that in married life three is company and two is none.

JACK (*sententiously*):

That, my dear young friend, is the theory that the corrupt French Drama has been propounding for the last fifty years.

ALGERNON:

Yes; and that the happy English home has proved in half the time.

JACK:

> For heaven's sake, don't try to be cynical. It's perfectly easy to be cynical.

ALGERNON:

> My dear fellow, it isn't easy to be anything nowadays. There's such a lot of beastly competition about. (*The sound of an electric bell is heard.*) Ah! that must be Aunt Augusta. Only relatives, or creditors, ever ring in that Wagnerian manner. Now, if I get her out of the way for ten minutes, so that you can have an opportunity for proposing to Gwendolen, may I dine with you tonight at Willis's?

JACK:

> I suppose so, if you want to.

ALGERNON:

> Yes, but you must be serious about it. I hate people who are not serious about meals. It is so shallow of them.

Enter Lane.

LANE:

> Lady Bracknell and Miss Fairfax.

Algernon *goes forward to meet them. Enter* Lady Bracknell *and* Gwendolen.

LADY BRACKNELL:

> Good afternoon, dear Algernon, I hope you are behaving very well.

ALGERNON:

> I'm feeling very well, Aunt Augusta.

LADY BRACKNELL:

> That's not quite the same thing. In fact the two things rarely go together. (*Sees* Jack *and bows to him with icy coldness.*)

ALGERNON (*to* Gwendolen):

> Dear me, you are smart!

GWENDOLEN:

> I am always smart! Aren't I, Mr. Worthing?

JACK:

> You're quite perfect, Miss Fairfax.

GWENDOLEN:

> Oh! I hope I am not that. It would leave no room for developments, and I intend to develop in many directions. (Gwendolen *and* Jack *sit down together in the corner.*)

LADY BRACKNELL:

I'm sorry if we are a little late, Algernon, but I was obliged to call on dear Lady Harbury. I hadn't been there since her poor husband's death. I never saw a woman so altered; she looks quite twenty years younger. And now I'll have a cup of tea, and one of those nice cucumber sandwiches you promised me.

ALGERNON:

Certainly, Aunt Augusta. (*Goes over to teatable.*)

LADY BRACKNELL:

Won't you come and sit here, Gwendolen?

GWENDOLEN:

Thanks, mamma, I'm quite comfortable where I am.

ALGERNON (*picking up empty plate in horror*):

Good heavens! Lane! Why are there no cucumber sandwiches? I ordered them specially.

LANE (*gravely*):

There were no cucumbers in the market this morning, sir. I went down twice.

ALGERNON:

No cucumbers!

LANE:

No, sir. Not even for ready money.

ALGERNON:

That will do, Lane, thank you.

LANE:

Thank you, sir.

ALGERNON:

I am greatly distressed, Aunt Augusta, about there being no cucumbers, not even for ready money.

LADY BRACKNELL:

It really makes no matter, Algernon. I had some crumpets with Lady Harbury, who seems to me to be living entirely for pleasure now.

ALGERNON:

I hear her hair has turned quite gold from grief.

LADY BRACKNELL:

It certainly has changed its color. From what cause I, of course, cannot say. (Algernon *crosses and hands tea.*) Thank you. I've quite a treat for you tonight, Algernon. I am going to send you down with Mary Farquhar. She is such a nice woman, and so attentive to her husband. It's delightful to watch them.

ALGERNON:

I am afraid, Aunt Augusta, I shall have to give up the pleasure of dining with you tonight after all.

LADY BRACKNELL (*frowning*):

I hope not, Algernon. It would put my table completely out. Your uncle would have to dine upstairs. Fortunately he is accustomed to that.

ALGERNON:

It is a great bore, and, I need hardly say, a terrible disappointment to me, but the fact is I have just had a telegram to say that my poor friend Bunbury is very ill again. (*Exchanges glances with* Jack.) They seem to think I should be with him.

LADY BRACKNELL:

It is very strange. This Mr. Bunbury seems to suffer from curiously bad health.

ALGERNON:

Yes; poor Bunbury is a dreadful invalid.

LADY BRACKNELL:

Well, I must say, Algernon, that I think it is high time that Mr. Bunbury made up his mind whether he was going to live or to die. This shilly-shallying with the question is absurd. Nor do I in any way approve of the modern sympathy with invalids. I consider it morbid. Illness of any kind is hardly a thing to be encouraged in others. Health is the primary duty of life. I am always telling that to your poor uncle, but he never seems to take much notice . . . as far as any improvement in his ailments goes. I should be obliged if you would ask Mr. Bunbury, from me, to be kind enough not to have a relapse on Saturday, for I rely on you to arrange my music for me. It is my last reception, and one wants something that will encourage conversation, particularly at the end of the season when everyone has practically said whatever they had to say, which, in most cases, was probably not much.

ALGERNON:

I'll speak to Bunbury, Aunt Augusta, if he is still conscious, and I think I can promise you he'll be all right by Saturday. Of course the music is a great difficulty. You see, if one plays good music, people don't listen, and if one plays bad music, people don't talk. But I'll run over the program I've drawn out, if you will kindly come into the next room for a moment.

LADY BRACKNELL:

Thank you, Algernon. It is very thoughtful of you. (*Rising, and following* Algernon.) I'm sure the program will be delightful, after a few expurgations. French songs I cannot possibly allow. People always seem to think that they are improper, and either look shocked, which is vulgar, or laugh, which is worse. But

German sounds a thoroughly respectable language, and indeed, I believe is so. Gwendolen, you will accompany me.

GWENDOLEN:

Certainly, mamma.

Lady Bracknell and Algernon go into the music room, Gwendolen remains behind.

JACK:

Charming day it has been, Miss Fairfax.

GWENDOLEN:

Pray don't talk to me about the weather, Mr. Worthing. Whenever people talk to me about the weather, I always feel quite certain that they mean something else. And that makes me so nervous.

JACK:

I do mean something else.

GWENDOLEN:

I thought so. In fact, I am never wrong.

JACK:

And I would like to be allowed to take advantage of Lady Bracknell's temporary absence . . .

GWENDOLEN:

I would certainly advise you to do so. Mamma has a way of coming back suddenly into a room that I have often had to speak to her about.

JACK (*nervously*):

Miss Fairfax, ever since I met you I have admired you more than any girl . . . I have ever met since . . . I met you.

GWENDOLEN:

Yes, I am quite aware of the fact. And I often wish that in public, at any rate, you had been more demonstrative. For me you have always had an irresistible fascination. Even before I met you I was far from indifferent to you. (Jack *looks at her in amazement.*) We live, as I hope you know, Mr. Worthing, in an age of ideals. The fact is constantly mentioned in the more expensive monthly magazines, and has reached the provincial pulpits, I am told: and my ideal has always been to love someone of the name of Ernest. There is something in that name that inspires absolute confidence. The moment Algernon first mentioned to me that he had a friend called Ernest, I knew I was destined to love you.

JACK:

You really love me, Gwendolen?

GWENDOLEN:

Passionately!

JACK:

Darling! You don't know how happy you've made me.

GWENDOLEN:

My own Ernest!

JACK:

But you don't really mean to say that you couldn't love me if my name wasn't Ernest?

GWENDOLEN:

But your name is Ernest.

JACK:

Yes, I know it is. But supposing it was something else? Do you mean to say you couldn't love me then?

GWENDOLEN (*glibly*):

Ah! that is clearly a metaphysical speculation, and like most metaphysical speculations has very little reference at all to the actual facts of real life, as we know them.

JACK:

Personally, darling, to speak quite candidly, I don't much care about the name of Ernest . . . I don't think the name suits me at all.

GWENDOLEN:

It suits you perfectly. It is a divine name. It has a music of its own. It produces vibrations.

JACK:

Well, really, Gwendolen, I must say that I think there are lots of other much nicer names. I think Jack, for instance, a charming name.

GWENDOLEN:

Jack? . . . No, there is very little music in the name Jack, if any at all, indeed. It does not thrill. It produces absolutely no vibrations. . . . I have known several Jacks, and they all, without exception, were more than usually plain. Besides, Jack is a notorious domesticity for John! And I pity any woman who is married to a man called John. She would probably never be allowed to know the entrancing pleasure of a single moment's solitude. The only really safe name is Ernest.

JACK:

Gwendolen, I must get christened at once—I mean we must get married at once. There is no time to be lost.

GWENDOLEN:

Married, Mr. Worthing?

JACK (*astounded*):

Well . . . surely. You know that I love you, and you led me to believe, Miss Fairfax, that you were not absolutely indifferent to me.

GWENDOLEN:

I adore you. But you haven't proposed to me yet. Nothing has been said at all about marriage. The subject has not even been touched on.

JACK:

Well . . . may I propose to you now?

GWENDOLEN:

I think it would be an admirable opportunity. And to spare you any possible disappointment, Mr. Worthing, I think it only fair to tell you quite frankly beforehand that I am fully determined to accept you.

JACK:

Gwendolen!

GWENDOLEN:

Yes, Mr. Worthing, what have you got to say to me?

JACK:

You know what I have got to say to you.

GWENDOLEN:

Yes, but you don't say it.

JACK:

Gwendolen, will you marry me? (*Goes on his knees.*)

GWENDOLEN:

Of course I will, darling. How long you have been about it! I am afraid you have had very little experience in how to propose.

JACK:

My own one, I have never loved anyone in the world but you.

GWENDOLEN:

Yes, but men often propose for practice. I know my brother Gerald does. All my girlfriends tell me so. What wonderfully blue eyes you have, Ernest! They are quite, quite blue. I hope you will always look at me just like that, especially when there are other people present.

Enter Lady Bracknell.

LADY BRACKNELL:

Mr. Worthing! Rise, sir, from this semi-recumbent posture. It is most indecorous.

GWENDOLEN:

Mamma! (*He tries to rise; she restrains him.*) I must beg you to retire. This is no place for you. Besides, Mr. Worthing has not quite finished yet.

LADY BRACKNELL:

Finished what, may I ask?

GWENDOLEN:

I am engaged to Mr. Worthing, mamma.

They rise together.

LADY BRACKNELL:

Pardon me, you are not engaged to anyone. When you do become engaged to someone, I, or your father, should his health permit him, will inform you of the fact. An engagement should come on a young girl as a surprise, pleasant or unpleasant, as the case may be. It is hardly a matter that she could be allowed to arrange for herself. . . . And now I have a few questions to put to you, Mr. Worthing. While I am making these inquiries, you, Gwendolen, will wait for me below in the carriage.

GWENDOLEN (*reproachfully*):

Mamma!

LADY BRACKNELL:

In the carriage, Gwendolen! (Gwendolen *goes to the door. She and* Jack *blow kisses to each other behind* Lady Bracknell's *back.* Lady Bracknell *looks vaguely about as if she could not understand what the noise was. Finally turns round.*) Gwendolen, the carriage!

GWENDOLEN:

Yes, mamma. (*Goes out, looking back at* Jack.)

LADY BRACKNELL (*sitting down*):

You can take a seat, Mr. Worthing.

Looks in her pocket for notebook and pencil.

JACK:

Thank you, Lady Bracknell, I prefer standing.

LADY BRACKNELL (*pencil and notebook in hand*):

I feel bound to tell you that you are not down on my list of eligible young men, although I have the same list as the dear Duchess of Bolton has. We work together, in fact. However, I am quite ready to enter your name, should your answers be what a really affectionate mother requires. Do you smoke?

JACK:

Well, yes, I must admit I smoke.

LADY BRACKNELL:

I am glad to hear it. A man should always have an occupation of some kind. There are far too many idle men in London as it is. How old are you?

JACK:

Twenty-nine.

LADY BRACKNELL:

A very good age to be married at. I have always been of opinion that a man who desires to get married should know either everything or nothing. Which do you know?

JACK (*after some hesitation*):

I know nothing, Lady Bracknell.

LADY BRACKNELL:

I am pleased to hear it. I do not approve of anything that tampers with natural ignorance. Ignorance is like a delicate exotic fruit; touch it and the bloom is gone. The whole theory of modern education is radically unsound. Fortunately in England, at any rate, education produces no effect whatsoever. If it did, it would prove a serious danger to the upper classes, and probably lead to acts of violence in Grosvenor Square. What is your income?

JACK:

Between seven and eight thousand a year.

LADY BRACKNELL (*makes a note in her book*):

In land, or in investments?

JACK:

In investments, chiefly.

LADY BRACKNELL:

That is satisfactory. What between the duties expected of one during one's lifetime, and the duties exacted from one after one's death, land has ceased to be either a profit or a pleasure. It gives one position, and prevents one from keeping it up. That's all that can be said about land.

JACK:

I have a country house with some land, of course, attached to it, about fifteen hundred acres, I believe; but I don't depend on that for my real income. In fact, as far as I can make out, the poachers are the only people who make anything out of it.

LADY BRACKNELL:

A country house! How many bedrooms? Well, that point can be cleared up afterwards. You have a town house, I hope? A girl with a simple, unspoiled nature, like Gwendolen, could hardly be expected to reside in the country.

JACK:

Well, I own a house in Belgrave Square, but it is let by the year to Lady Bloxham. Of course, I can get it back whenever I like, at six months' notice.

LADY BRACKNELL:

Lady Bloxham? I don't know her.

JACK:

Oh, she goes about very little. She is a lady considerably advanced in years.

LADY BRACKNELL:

Ah, nowadays that is no guarantee of respectability of character. What number in Belgrave Square?

JACK:

149.

LADY BRACKNELL (*shaking her head*):

The unfashionable side. I thought there was something. However, that could easily be altered.

JACK:

Do you mean the fashion, or the side?

LADY BRACKNELL (*sternly*):

Both, if necessary, I presume. What are your politics?

JACK:

Well, I am afraid I really have none. I am a Liberal Unionist.

LADY BRACKNELL:

Oh, they count as Tories. They dine with us. Or come in the evening, at any rate. Now to minor matters. Are your parents living?

JACK:

I have lost both my parents.

LADY BRACKNELL:

Both? . . . That seems like carelessness. Who was your father? He was evidently a man of some wealth. Was he born in what the Radical papers call the purple of commerce, or did he rise from the ranks of aristocracy?

JACK:

I am afraid I really don't know. The fact is, Lady Bracknell, I said I had lost my parents. It would be nearer the truth to say that my parents seem to have lost me. . . . I don't actually know who I am by birth. I was . . . well, I was found.

LADY BRACKNELL:

Found!

JACK:

> The late Mr. Thomas Cardew, an old gentleman of a very charitable and kindly disposition, found me, and gave me the name of Worthing, because he happened to have a first-class ticket for Worthing in his pocket at the time. Worthing is a place in Sussex. It is a seaside resort.

LADY BRACKNELL:

> Where did the charitable gentleman who had a first-class ticket for this seaside resort find you?

JACK (*gravely*):

> In a handbag.

LADY BRACKNELL:

> A handbag?

JACK (*very seriously*):

> Yes, Lady Bracknell. I was in a handbag—a somewhat large, black leather handbag, with handles to it—an ordinary handbag, in fact.

LADY BRACKNELL:

> In what locality did this Mr. James, or Thomas, Cardew come across this ordinary handbag?

JACK:

> In the cloak room at Victoria Station. It was given to him in mistake for his own.

LADY BRACKNELL:

> The cloak room at Victoria Station?

JACK:

> Yes. The Brighton line.

LADY BRACKNELL:

> The line is immaterial. Mr. Worthing, I confess I feel somewhat bewildered by what you have just told me. To be born, or at any rate, bred in a handbag, whether it had handles or not, seems to me to display a contempt for the ordinary decencies of family life that remind one of the worst excesses of the French Revolution. And I presume you know what that unfortunate movement led to? As for the particular locality in which the handbag was found, a cloak room at a railway station might serve to conceal a social indiscretion—has probably, indeed, been used for that purpose before now—but it could hardly be regarded as an assured basis for a recognized position in good society.

JACK:

> May I ask you then what you would advise me to do? I need hardly say I would do anything in the world to ensure Gwendolen's happiness.

LADY BRACKNELL:

> I would strongly advise you, Mr. Worthing, to try and acquire some relations as soon as possible, and to make a definite effort to produce at any rate one parent, of either sex, before the season is quite over.

JACK:

> Well, I don't see how I could possibly manage to do that. I can produce the handbag at any moment. It is in my dressing room at home. I really think that should satisfy you, Lady Bracknell.

LADY BRACKNELL:

> Me, sir! What has it to do with me? You can hardly imagine that I and Lord Bracknell would dream of allowing our only daughter—a girl brought up with the utmost care—to marry into a clock room, and form an alliance with a parcel? Good morning, Mr. Worthing!

> Lady Bracknell *sweeps out in majestic indignation.*

JACK:

> Good morning! (Algernon, *from the other room, strikes up the Wedding March.* Jack *looks perfectly furious, and goes to the door.*) For goodness' sake don't play that ghastly tune, Algy! How idiotic you are!

> *The music stops, and* Algernon *enters cheerily.*

ALGERNON:

> Didn't it go off all right, old boy? You don't mean to say Gwendolen refused you? I know it is a way she has. She is always refusing people. I think it is most ill-natured of her.

JACK:

> Oh, Gwendolen is as right as a trivet. As far as she is concerned, we are engaged. Her mother is perfectly unbearable. Never met such a Gorgon . . . I don't really know what a Gorgon is like, but I am quite sure that Lady Bracknell is one. In any case, she is a monster, without being a myth, which is rather unfair . . . I beg your pardon, Algy, I suppose I shouldn't talk about your own aunt in that way before you.

ALGERNON:

> My dear boy, I love hearing my relations abused. It is the only thing that makes me put up with them at all. Relations are simply a tedious pack of people who haven't got the remotest knowledge of how to live, nor the smallest instinct about when to die.

JACK:

Oh, that is nonsense!

ALGERNON:

It isn't!

JACK:

Well, I won't argue about the matter. You always want to argue about things.

ALGERNON:

That is exactly what things were originally made for.

JACK:

Upon my word, if I thought that, I'd shoot myself . . . (*A pause.*) You don't think there is any chance of Gwendolen becoming like her mother in about a hundred and fifty years, do you, Algy?

ALGERNON:

All women become like their mothers. That is their tragedy. No man does. That's his.

JACK:

Is that clever?

ALGERNON:

It is perfectly phrased! and quite as true as any observation in civilized life should be.

JACK:

I am sick to death of cleverness. Everybody is clever nowadays. You can't go anywhere without meeting clever people. The thing has become an absolute public nuisance. I wish to goodness we had a few fools left.

ALGERNON:

We have.

JACK:

I should extremely like to meet them. What do they talk about?

ALGERNON:

The fools? Oh! about the clever people, of course.

JACK:

What fools!

ALGERNON:

By the way, did you tell Gwendolen the truth about your being Ernest in town, and Jack in the country?

JACK (*in a very patronizing manner*):

My dear fellow, the truth isn't quite the sort of thing one tells to a nice sweet refined girl. What extraordinary ideas you have about the way to behave to a woman!

ALGERNON:

The only way to behave to a woman is to make love to her, if she is pretty, and to someone else if she is plain.

JACK:

Oh, that is nonsense.

ALGERNON:

What about your brother? What about the profligate Ernest?

JACK:

Oh, before the end of the week I shall have got rid of him. I'll say he died in Paris of apoplexy. Lots of people die of apoplexy, quite suddenly, don't they?

ALGERNON:

Yes, but it's hereditary, my dear fellow. It's a sort of thing that runs in families. You had much better say a severe chill.

JACK:

You are sure a severe chill isn't hereditary, or anything of that kind?

ALGERNON:

Of course it isn't!

JACK:

Very well, then. My poor brother Ernest is carried off suddenly in Paris, by a severe chill. That gets rid of him.

ALGERNON:

But I thought you said that . . . Miss Cardew was a little too much interested in your poor brother Ernest? Won't she feel his loss a good deal?

JACK:

Oh, that is all right. Cecily is not a silly romantic girl, I am glad to say. She has got a capital appetite, goes on long walks, and pays no attention at all to her lessons.

ALGERNON:

I would rather like to see Cecily.

JACK:

I will take very good care you never do. She is excessively pretty, and she is only just eighteen.

ALGERNON:

Have you told Gwendolen yet that you have an excessively pretty ward who is only just eighteen?

JACK:

Oh! one doesn't blurt these things out to people. Cecily and Gwendolen are perfectly certain to be extremely great friends. I'll bet you anything you like that half an hour after they have met, they will be calling each other sister.

ALGERNON:

Women only do that when they have called each other a lot of other things first. Now, my dear boy, if we want to get a good

table at Willis's, we really must go and dress. Do you know it
is nearly seven?

JACK (*irritably*):

Oh! it always is nearly seven.

ALGERNON:

Well, I'm hungry.

JACK:

I never knew you when you weren't. . . .

ALGERNON:

What shall we do after dinner? Go to the theater?

JACK:

Oh no! I loathe listening.

ALGERNON:

Well, let us go to the club?

JACK:

Oh, no! I hate talking.

ALGERNON:

Well, we might trot around to the Empire at ten?

JACK:

Oh no! I can't bear looking at things. It is so silly.

ALGERNON:

Well, what shall we do?

JACK:

Nothing!

ALGERNON:

It is awfully hard work doing nothing. However, I don't mind
hard work where there is no definite object of any kind.

Enter Lane.

LANE:

Miss Fairfax.

Enter Gwendolen. Lane *goes out*.

ALGERNON:

Gwendolen, upon my word!

GWENDOLEN:

Algy, kindly turn your back. I have something very particular
to say to Mr. Worthing.

ALGERNON:

Really, Gwendolen, I don't think I can allow this at all.

GWENDOLEN:

Algy, you always adopt a strictly immoral attitude towards life. You are not quite old enough to do that. (Algernon *retires to the fireplace.*)

JACK:

My own darling!

GWENDOLEN:

Ernest, we may never be married. From the expression on mamma's face I fear we never shall. Few parents nowadays pay any regard to what their children say to them. The old-fashioned respect for the young is fast dying out. Whatever influence I ever had over mamma, I lost at the age of three. But although she may prevent us from becoming man and wife, and I may marry someone else, and marry often, nothing that she can possibly do can alter my eternal devotion to you.

JACK:

Dear Gwendolen!

GWENDOLEN:

The story of your romantic origin, as related to me by mamma, with unpleasing comments, has naturally stirred the deeper fibers of my nature. Your Christian name has an irresistible fascination. The simplicity of your character makes you exquisitely incomprehensible to me. Your town address at the Albany I have. What is your address in the country?

JACK:

The Manor House, Woolton, Hertfordshire.

(Algernon, *who has been carefully listening, smiles to himself, and writes the address on his shirt-cuff. Then picks up the Railway Guide.*)

GWENDOLEN:

There is a good postal service, I suppose? It may be necessary to do something desperate. That of course will require serious consideration. I will communicate with you daily.

JACK:

My own one!

GWENDOLEN:

How long do you remain in town?

JACK:

Till Monday.

GWENDOLEN:

Good! Algy, you may turn round now.

ALGERNON:

Thanks, I've turned round already.

GWENDOLEN:

You may also ring the bell.

JACK:

You will let me see you to your carriage, my own darling?

GWENDOLEN:

Certainly.

JACK (*to* Lane, *who now enters*):

I will see Miss Fairfax out.

LANE:

Yes, sir. (Jack *and* Gwendolen *go off.*)

Lane *presents several letters on a salver to* Algernon. *It is to be surmised that they are bills, as* Algernon *after looking at the envelopes, tears them up.*

ALGERNON:

A glass of sherry, Lane.

LANE:

Yes, sir.

ALGERNON:

Tomorrow, Lane, I'm going Bunburying.

LANE:

Yes, sir.

ALGERNON:

I shall probably not be back till Monday. You can put up my dress clothes, my smoking jacket, and all the Bunbury suits . . .

LANE:

Yes, sir. (*Handing sherry.*)

ALGERNON:

I hope tomorrow will be a fine day, Lane.

LANE:

It never is, sir.

ALGERNON:

Lane, you're a perfect pessimist.

LANE:

I do my best to give satisfaction, sir.

Enter Jack. Lane *goes off.*

JACK:

There's a sensible, intellectual girl! the only girl I ever cared for in my life. (Algernon *is laughing immoderately.*) What on earth are you so amused at?

ALGERNON:

Oh, I'm a little anxious about poor Bunbury, that is all.

JACK:

> If you don't take care, your friend Bunbury will get you into a serious scrape some day.

ALGERNON:

> I love scrapes. They are the only things that are never serious.

JACK:

> Oh, that's nonsense, Algy. You never talk anything but nonsense.

ALGERNON:

> Nobody ever does.

Jack *looks indignantly at him, and leaves the room.* Algernon *lights a cigarette, reads his shirt-cuff, and smiles.*

Second Act

SCENE—*Garden at the Manor House. A flight of gray stone steps leads up to the house. The garden, an old-fashioned one, full of roses. Time of year, July. Basket chairs, and a table covered with books, are set under a large yew tree.*

Miss Prism *discovered seated at the table.* Cecily *is at the back watering flowers.*

MISS PRISM (*calling*):

> Cecily, Cecily! Surely such a utilitarian occupation as the watering of flowers is rather Moulton's duty than yours? Especially at a moment when intellectual pleasures await you. Your German grammar is on the table. Pray open it at page fifteen. We will repeat yesterday's lesson.

CECILY (*coming over very slowly*):

> But I don't like German. It isn't at all a becoming language. I know perfectly well that I look quite plain after my German lesson.

MISS PRISM:

> Child, you know how anxious your guardian is that you should improve yourself in every way. He laid particular stress on your German, as he was leaving for town yesterday. Indeed, he always lays stress on your German when he is leaving for town.

CECILY:

> Dear Uncle Jack is so very serious! Sometime he is so serious that I think he cannot be quite well.

MISS PRISM (*drawing herself up*):

Your guardian enjoys the best of health, and his gravity of demeanor is especially to be commended in one so comparatively young as he is. I know no one who has a higher sense of duty and responsibility.

CECILY:

I suppose that is why he often looks a little bored when we three are together.

MISS PRISM:

Cecily! I am surprised at you. Mr. Worthing has many troubles in his life. Idle merriment and triviality would be out of place in his conversation. You must remember his constant anxiety about that unfortunate young man his brother.

CECILY:

I wish Uncle Jack would allow that unfortunate young man, his brother, to come down here sometimes. We might have a good influence over him, Miss Prism. I am sure you certainly would. You know German, and geology, and things of that kind influence a man very much. (Cecily *begins to write in her diary.*)

MISS PRISM (*shaking her head*):

I do not think that even I could produce any effect on a character that according to his own brother's admission is irretrievably weak and vacillating. Indeed I am not sure that I would desire to reclaim him. I am not in favor of this modern mania for turning bad people into good people at a moment's notice. As a man sows so let him reap. You must put away your diary, Cecily. I really don't see why you should keep a diary at all.

CECILY:

I keep a diary in order to enter the wonderful secrets of my life. If I didn't write them down I should probably forget all about them.

MISS PRISM:

Memory, my dear Cecily, is the diary that we all carry about with us.

CECILY:

Yes, but it usually chronicles the things that have never happened, and couldn't possibly have happened. I believe that Memory is responsible for nearly all the three-volume novels that Mudie sends us.

MISS PRISM:

Do not speak slightingly of the three-volume novel, Cecily. I wrote one myself in earlier days.

CECILY:

> Did you really, Miss Prism? How wonderfully clever you are! I hope it did not end happily? I don't like novels that end happily. They depress me so much.

MISS PRISM:

> The good ended happily, and the bad unhappily. That is what Fiction means.

CECILY:

> I suppose so. But it seems very unfair. And was your novel ever published?

MISS PRISM:

> Alas! no. The manuscript unfortunately was abandoned. I use the word in the sense of lost or mislaid. To your work, child, these speculations are profitless.

CECILY (*smiling*):

> But I see dear Dr. Chasuble coming up through the garden.

MISS PRISM (*rising and advancing*):

> Dr. Chasuble! This is indeed a pleasure.

Enter Canon Chasuble.

CHASUBLE:

> And how are we this morning? Miss Prism, you are, I trust, well?

CECILY:

> Miss Prism has just been complaining of a slight headache. I think it would do her so much good to have a short stroll with you in the Park, Dr. Chasuble.

MISS PRISM:

> Cecily, I have not mentioned anything about a headache.

CECILY:

> No, dear Miss Prism, I know that, but I felt instinctively that you had a headache. Indeed I was thinking about that, and not about my German lesson, when the Rector came in.

CHASUBLE:

> I hope Cecily, you are not inattentive.

CECILY:

> Oh, I am afraid I am.

CHASUBLE:

> That is strange. Were I fortunate enough to be Miss Prism's pupil, I would hang upon her lips. (Miss Prism *glares*.) I spoke metaphorically.—My metaphor was drawn from bees. Ahem! Mr. Worthing I suppose, has not returned from town yet?

MISS PRISM:

We do not expect him till Monday afternoon.

CHASUBLE:

Ah yes, he usually likes to spend his Sunday in London. He is not one of those whose sole aim is enjoyment, as, by all accounts, that unfortunate young man his brother seems to be. But I must not disturb Egeria and her pupil any longer.

MISS PRISM:

Egeria? My name is Laetitia, Doctor.

CHASUBLE (*bowing*):

A classical allusion merely, drawn from the Pagan authors. I shall see you both no doubt at Evensong?

MISS PRISM:

I think, dear Doctor, I will have a stroll with you. I find I have a headache after all, and a walk might do it good.

CHASUBLE:

With pleasure, Miss Prism, with pleasure. We might go as far as the schools and back.

MISS PRISM:

That would be delightful. Cecily, you will read your Political Economy in my absence. The chapter on the Fall of the Rupee you may omit. It is somewhat too sensational. Even these metallic problems have their melodramatic side.

(*Goes down the garden with* Dr. Chasuble.)

CECILY (*picks up books and throws them back on table*):

Horrid Political Economy! Horrid Geography! Horrid, horrid German!

Enter Merriman *with a card on a salver.*

MERRIMAN:

Mr. Ernest Worthing has just driven over from the station. He has brought his luggage with him.

CECILY (*takes the card and reads it.*):

"Mr. Ernest Worthing, B. 4, The Albany, W." Uncle Jack's brother! Did you tell him Mr. Worthing was in town?

MERRIMAN:

Yes, Miss. He seemed very much disappointed. I mentioned that you and Miss Prism were in the garden. He said he was anxious to speak to you privately for a moment.

CECILY:

Ask Mr. Ernest Worthing to come here. I suppose you had better talk to the housekeeper about a room for him.

MERRIMAN:

Yes, Miss.   (Merriman *goes off.*)

CECILY:

I have never met any really wicked person before. I feel rather frightened. I am so afraid he will look just like everyone else.

Enter Algernon, *very gay and debonair.*

He does!

ALGERNON (*raising his hat.*):

You are my little cousin Cecily, I'm sure.

CECILY:

You are under some strange mistake. I am not little. In fact, I believe I am more than usually tall for my age. (Algernon *is rather taken aback.*) But I am your cousin Cecily. You, I see from your card, are Uncle Jack's brother, my cousin Ernest, my wicked cousin Ernest.

ALGERNON:

Oh! I am not really wicked at all, cousin Cecily. You mustn't think that I am wicked.

CECILY:

If you are not, then you have certainly been deceiving us all in a very inexcusable manner. I hope you have not been leading a double life, pretending to be wicked and being really good all the time. That would be hypocrisy.

ALGERNON (*looks at her in amazement*):

Oh! Of course I have been rather reckless.

CECILY:

I am glad to hear it.

ALGERNON:

In fact, now you mention the subject, I have been very bad in my own small way.

CECILY:

I don't think you should be so proud of that, though I am sure it must have been very pleasant.

ALGERNON:

It is much pleasanter being here with you.

CECILY:

I can't understand how you are here at all. Uncle Jack won't be back till Monday afternoon.

ALGERNON:

That is a great disappointment. I am obliged to go up by the first train on Monday morning. I have a business appointment that I am anxious . . . to miss.

CECILY:

Couldn't you miss it anywhere but in London?

ALGERNON:

No: the appointment is in London.

CECILY:

Well, I know, of course, how important it is not to keep a business engagement, if one wants to retain any sense of the beauty of life, but still I think you had better wait till Uncle Jack arrives. I know he wants to speak to you about your emigrating.

ALGERNON:

About my what?

CECILY:

Your emigrating. He has gone up to buy your outfit.

ALGERNON:

I certainly wouldn't let Jack buy my outfit. He has no taste in neckties at all.

CECILY:

I don't think you will require neckties. Uncle Jack is sending you to Australia.

ALGERNON:

Australia? I'd sooner die.

CECILY:

Well, he said at dinner on Wednesday night, that you would have to choose between this world, the next world, and Australia.

ALGERNON:

Oh, well! The accounts I have received of Australia and the next world are not particularly encouraging. This world is good enough for me, cousin Cecily.

CECILY:

Yes, but are you good enough for it?

ALGERNON:

I'm afraid I'm not that. That is why I want you to reform me. You might make that your mission, if you don't mind, cousin Cecily.

CECILY:

I'm afraid I've no time, this afternoon.

ALGERNON:

Well, would you mind my reforming myself this afternoon?

CECILY:

It is rather Quixotic of you. But I think you should try.

ALGERNON:

I will. I feel better already.

CECILY:

You are looking a little worse.

ALGERNON:

That is because I am hungry.

CECILY:

How thoughtless of me. I should have remembered that when
one is going to lead an entirely new life, one requires regular
and wholesome meals. Won't you come in?

ALGERNON:

Thank you. Might I have a buttonhole first? I never have any
appetite unless I have a buttonhole first.

CECILY:

A Maréchale Niel? (*Picks up scissors.*)

ALGERNON:

No, I'd sooner have a pink rose.

CECILY:

Why? (*Cuts a flower.*)

ALGERNON:

Because you are like a pink rose, cousin Cecily.

CECILY:

I don't think it can be right for you to talk to me like that. Miss
Prism never says such things to me.

ALGERNON:

Then Miss Prism is shortsighted old lady. (Cecily *puts the rose in
his buttonhole.*) You are the prettiest girl I ever saw.

CECILY:

Miss Prism says that all good looks are a snare.

ALGERNON:

They are a snare that every sensible man would like to be
caught in.

CECILY:

Oh! I don't think I would care to catch a sensible man. I
shouldn't know what to talk to him about.

(*They pass into the house.* Miss Prism *and* Dr. Chasuble *return.*)

MISS PRISM:

You are too much alone, dear Dr. Chasuble. You should get
married. A misanthrope I can understand—a womanthrope,
never!

CHASUBLE (*with a scholar's shudder*):

Believe me, I do not deserve so neologistic a phrase. The pre-
cept as well as the practice of the Primitive Church was dis-
tinctly against matrimony.

MISS PRISM (*sententiously*):

That is obviously the reason why the Primitive Church has
not lasted up to the present day. And you do not seem to realize, dear Doctor, that by persistently remaining single, a man

converts himself into a permanent public temptation. Men should be more careful; this very celibacy leads weaker vessels astray.

CHASUBLE:

But is a man not equally attractive when married?

MISS PRISM:

No married man is ever attractive except to his wife.

CHASUBLE:

And often, I've been told, not even to her.

MISS PRISM:

That depends on the intellectual sympathies of the woman. Maturity can always be depended on. Ripeness can be trusted. Young women are green. (*Dr. Chasuble starts.*) I spoke horticulturally. My metaphor was drawn from fruits. But where is Cecily?

CHASUBLE:

Perhaps she followed us to the schools.

Enter Jack *slowly from the back of the garden. He is dressed in the deepest mourning, with crêpe hat-band and black gloves.*

MISS PRISM:

Mr. Worthing!

CHASUBLE:

Mr. Worthing?

MISS PRISM:

This is indeed a surprise. We did not look for you till Monday afternoon.

JACK (*shakes* Miss Prism*'s hand in a tragic manner*):

I have returned sooner than I expected. Dr. Chasuble, I hope you are well?

CHASUBLE:

Dear Mr. Worthing, I trust this garb of woe does not betoken some terrible calamity?

JACK:

My brother.

MISS PRISM:

More shameful debts and extravagance?

CHASUBLE:

Still leading his life of pleasure?

JACK (*shaking his head*):

Dead!

CHASUBLE:

Your brother Ernest dead?

JACK:

Quite dead.

MISS PRISM:

What a lesson for him! I trust he will profit by it.

CHASUBLE:

Mr. Worthing, I offer you my sincere condolence. You have at least the consolation of knowing that you were always the most generous and forgiving of brothers.

JACK:

Poor Ernest! He had many faults, but it is a sad, sad blow.

CHASUBLE:

Very sad indeed. Were you with him at the end?

JACK:

No. He died abroad; in Paris, in fact. I had a telegram last night from the manager of the Grand Hotel.

CHASUBLE:

Was the cause of death mentioned?

JACK:

A severe chill, it seems.

MISS PRISM:

As a man sows, so shall he reap.

CHASUBLE (*raising his hand*):

Charity, dear Miss Prism, charity! None of us are perfect. I myself am peculiarly susceptible to drafts. Will the interment take place here?

JACK:

No. He seemed to have expressed a desire to be buried in Paris.

CHASUBLE:

In Paris! (*Shakes his head.*) I fear that hardly points to any very serious state of mind at the last. You would no doubt wish me to make some slight allusion to this tragic domestic affliction next Sunday. (Jack *presses his hand convulsively.*) My sermon on the meaning of the manna in the wilderness can be adapted to almost any occasion, joyful, or, as in the present case, distressing. (*All sigh.*) I have preached it at harvest celebrations, christenings, confirmations, on days of humiliation and festal days. The last time I delivered it was in the Cathedral, as a charity sermon on behalf of the Society for the Prevention of Discontent among the Upper Orders. The Bishop, who was present, was much struck by some of the analogies I drew.

JACK:

Ah! That reminds me, you mentioned christenings, I think, Dr. Chasuble? I suppose you know how to christen all right? (Dr.

Chasuble *looks astounded*.) I mean, of course, you are continually christening, aren't you?

MISS PRISM:

It is, I regret to say, one of the Rector's most constant duties in this parish. I have often spoken to the poorer classes on the subject. But they don't seem to know what thrift is.

CHASUBLE:

But is there any particular infant in whom you are interested, Mr. Worthing? Your brother was, I believe, unmarried, was he not?

JACK:

Oh yes.

MISS PRISM (*bitterly*):

People who live entirely for pleasure usually are.

JACK:

But it is not for any child, dear Doctor. I am very fond of children. No! the fact is, I would like to be christened myself, this afternoon, if you have nothing better to do.

CHASUBLE:

But surely, Mr. Worthing, you have been christened already?

JACK:

I don't remember anything about it.

CHASUBLE:

But have you any grave doubts on the subject?

JACK:

I certainly intend to have. Of course I don't know if the thing would bother you in any way, or if you think I am a little too old now.

CHASUBLE:

Not at all. The sprinkling, and, indeed, the immersion of adults is a perfectly canonical practice.

JACK:

Immersion!

CHASUBLE:

You need have no apprehensions. Sprinkling is all that is necessary, or indeed I think advisable. Our weather is so changeable. At what hour would you wish the ceremony performed?

JACK:

Oh, I might trot round about five if that would suit you.

CHASUBLE:

Perfectly, perfectly! In fact I have two similar ceremonies to perform at that time. A case of twins that occurred recently in one of the outlying cottages on your own estate. Poor Jenkins the carter, a most hard-working man.

JACK:

Oh! I don't see much fun in being christened along with other babies. It would be childish. Would half-past five do?

CHASUBLE:

Admirably! Admirably! (*Takes out watch.*) And now, dear Mr. Worthing, I will not intrude any longer into a house of sorrow. I would merely beg you not to be too much bowed down by grief. What seem to us bitter trials are often blessings in disguise.

MISS PRISM:

This seems to me a blessing of an extremely obvious kind.

Enter Cecily *from the house.*

CECILY:

Uncle Jack! Oh, I am pleased to see you back. But what horrid clothes you have got on! Do go and change them.

MISS PRISM:

Cecily!

CHASUBLE:

My child! my child! (Cecily *goes towards* Jack; *he kisses her brow in a melancholy manner.*)

CECILY:

What is the matter, Uncle Jack? Do look happy! You look as if you had toothache, and I have got such a surprise for you. Who do you think is in the dining room? Your brother!

JACK:

Who?

CECILY:

Your brother Ernest. He arrived about half an hour ago.

JACK:

What nonsense! I haven't got a brother!

CECILY:

Oh, don't say that. However badly he may have behaved to you in the past he is still your brother. You couldn't be so heartless as to disown him. I'll tell him to come out. And you will shake hands with him, won't you, Uncle Jack? (*Runs back into the house.*)

CHASUBLE:

These are very joyful tidings.

MISS PRISM:

After we had all been resigned to his loss, his sudden return seems to me peculiarly distressing.

JACK:

>My brother is in the dining room? I don't know what it all means. I think it is perfectly absurd.

Enter Algernon *and* Cecily *hand in hand. They come slowly up to* Jack.

JACK:

>Good heavens! (*Motions* Algernon *away.*)

ALGERNON:

>Brother John, I have come down from town to tell you that I am very sorry for all the trouble I have given you, and that I intend to lead a better life in the future. (Jack *glares at him and does not take his hand.*)

CECILY:

>Uncle Jack, you are not going to refuse your own brother's hand?

JACK:

>Nothing will induce me to take his hand. I think his coming down here disgraceful. He knows perfectly well why.

CECILY:

>Uncle Jack, do be nice. There is some good in everyone. Ernest has just been telling me about his poor invalid friend Mr. Bunbury whom he goes to visit so often. And surely there must be much good in one who is kind to an invalid, and leaves the pleasures of London to sit by a bed of pain.

JACK:

>Oh! he has been talking about Bunbury, has he?

CECILY:

>Yes, he has told me all about poor Mr. Bunbury, and his terrible state of health.

JACK:

>Bunbury! Well, I won't have him talk to you about Bunbury or about anything else. It is enough to drive one perfectly frantic.

ALGERNON:

>Of course I admit that the faults were all on my side. But I must say that I think that Brother John's coldness to me is peculiarly painful. I expected a more enthusiastic welcome, especially considering it is the first time I have come here.

CECILY:

>Uncle Jack, if you don't shake hands with Ernest, I will never forgive you.

JACK:

>Never forgive me?

CECILY:

Never, never, never!

JACK:

Well, this is the last time I shall ever do it. (*Shakes hands with* Algernon *and glares.*)

CHASUBLE:

It's pleasant, is it not, to see so perfect a reconciliation? I think we might leave the two brothers together.

MISS PRISM:

Cecily, you will come with us.

CECILY:

Certainly, Miss Prism. My little task of reconciliation is over.

CHASUBLE:

You have done a beautiful action today, dear child.

MISS PRISM:

We must not be premature in our judgments.

CECILY:

I feel very happy. (*They all go off.*)

JACK:

You young scoundrel, Algy, you must get out of this place as soon as possible. I don't allow any Bunburying here.

Enter Merriman.

MERRIMAN:

I have put Mr. Ernest's things in the room next to yours, sir. I suppose that is all right?

JACK:

What?

MERRIMAN:

Mr. Ernest's luggage, sir. I have unpacked it and put it in the room next to your own.

JACK:

His luggage?

MERRIMAN:

Yes, sir. Three portmanteaus, a dressing case, two hatboxes, and a large luncheon basket.

ALGERNON:

I am afraid I can't stay more than a week this time.

JACK:

Merriman, order the dogcart at once. Mr. Ernest has been suddenly called back to town.

MERRIMAN:

Yes, sir. (*Goes back into the house.*)

ALGERNON:

What a fearful liar you are, Jack. I have not been called back to town at all.

JACK:

Yes, you have.

ALGERNON:

I haven't heard anyone call me.

JACK:

Your duty as a gentleman calls you back.

ALGERNON:

My duty as a gentleman has never interfered with my pleasures in the smallest degree.

JACK:

I can quite understand that.

ALGERNON:

Well, Cecily is a darling.

JACK:

You are not to talk of Miss Cardew like that. I don't like it.

ALGERNON:

Well, I don't like your clothes. You look perfectly ridiculous in them. Why on earth don't you go up and change? It is perfectly childish to be in deep mourning for a man who is actually staying for a whole week with you in your house as a guest. I call it grotesque.

JACK:

You are certainly not staying with me for a whole week as a guest or anything else. You have got to leave . . . by the four-five train.

ALGERNON:

I certainly won't leave you so long as you are in mourning. It would be most unfriendly. If I were in mourning you would stay with me, I suppose. I should think it very unkind if you didn't.

JACK:

Well, will you go if I change my clothes?

ALGERNON:

Yes, if you are not too long. I never saw anybody take so long to dress, and with such little result.

JACK:

Well, at any rate, that is better than being always overdressed as you are.

ALGERNON:

If I am occasionally a little overdressed, I make up for it by being always immensely overeducated.

JACK:

> Your vanity is ridiculous, your conduct an outrage, and your presence in my garden utterly absurd. However, you have got to catch the four-five, and I hope you will have a pleasant journey back to town. This Bunburying, as you call it, has not been a great success for you. (*Goes into the house.*)

ALGERNON:

> I think it has been a great success. I'm in love with Cecily, and that is everything.

Enter Cecily *at the back of the garden. She picks up the can and begins to water the flowers.*

> But I must see her before I go, and make arrangements for another Bunbury. Ah, there she is.

CECILY:

> Oh, I merely came back to water the roses. I thought you were with Uncle Jack.

ALGERNON:

> He's gone to order the dogcart for me.

CECILY:

> Oh, is he going to take you for a nice drive?

ALGERNON:

> He's going to send me away.

CECILY:

> Then have we got to part?

ALGERNON:

> I am afraid so. It's very painful parting.

CECILY:

> It is always painful to part from people whom one has known for a very brief space of time. The absence of old friends one can endure with equanimity. But even a momentary separation from anyone to whom one has just been introduced is almost unbearable.

ALGERNON:

> Thank you.

Enter Merriman.

MERRIMAN:

> The dogcart is at the door, sir. (Algernon *looks appealingly at* Cecily.)

CECILY:

> It can wait, Merriman . . . for . . . five minutes.

MERRIMAN:

Yes, Miss. (*Exit* Merriman.)

ALGERNON:

I hope, Cecily, I shall not offend you if I state quite frankly and openly that you seem to me to be in every way the visible personification of absolute perfection.

CECILY:

I think your frankness does you great credit, Ernest. If you will allow me I will copy your remarks into my diary. (*Goes over to table and begins writing in diary.*)

ALGERNON:

Do you really keep a diary? I'd give anything to look at it. May I?

CECILY:

Oh no. (*Puts her hand over it.*) You see, it is simply a very young girl's record of her own thoughts and impressions, and consequently meant for publication. When it appears in volume form I hope you will order a copy. But pray, Ernest, don't stop. I delight in taking down from dictation. I have reached "absolute perfection." You can go on. I am quite ready for more.

ALGERNON (*somewhat taken aback*):

Ahem! Ahem!

CECILY:

Oh, don't cough, Ernest. When one is dictating one should speak fluently and not cough. Besides, I don't know how to spell a cough. (*Writes as* Algernon *speaks.*)

ALGERNON (*speaking very rapidly*):

Cecily, ever since I first looked upon your wonderful and incomparable beauty, I have dared to love you wildly, passionately, devotedly, hopelessly.

CECILY:

I don't think that you should tell me that you love me wildly, passionately, devotedly, hopelessly. Hopelessly doesn't seem to make much sense, does it?

ALGERNON:

Cecily!

Enter Merriman.

MERRIMAN:

The dogcart is waiting, sir.

ALGERNON:

Tell it to come round next week, at the same hour.

MERRIMAN (*looks at* Cecily, *who makes no sign*):

Yes, sir.   (Merriman *retires.*)

CECILY:

Uncle Jack would be very much annoyed if he knew you were staying on till next week, at the same hour.

ALGERNON:

Oh, I don't care about Jack. I don't care for anybody in the whole world but you. I love you, Cecily. You will marry me, won't you?

CECILY:

You silly boy! Of course. Why, we have been engaged for the last three months.

ALGERNON:

For the last three months?

CECILY:

Yes, it will be exactly three months on Thursday.

ALGERNON:

But how did we become engaged?

CECILY:

Well, ever since dear Uncle Jack first confessed to us that he had a younger brother who was very wicked and bad, you of course have formed the chief topic of conversation between myself and Miss Prism. And of course a man who is much talked about is always very attractive. One feels there must be something in him after all. I daresay it was foolish of me, but I fell in love with you, Ernest.

ALGERNON:

Darling! And when was the engagement actually settled?

CECILY:

On the 14th of February last. Worn out by your entire ignorance of my existence, I determined to end the matter one way or the other, and after a long struggle with myself I accepted you under this dear old tree here. The next day I bought this little ring in your name, and this is the little bangle with the true lovers' knot I promised you always to wear.

ALGERNON:

Did I give you this? It's very pretty, isn't it?

CECILY:

Yes, you've wonderfully good taste, Ernest. It's the excuse I've always given for your leading such a bad life. And this is the box in which I keep all your dear letters. (*Kneels at table, opens box, and produces letters tied up with blue ribbon.*)

ALGERNON:

My letters! But my own sweet Cecily, I have never written you any letters.

CECILY:

You need hardly remind me of that, Ernest. I remember only too well that I was forced to write your letters for you. I always wrote three times a week, and sometimes oftener.

ALGERNON:

Oh, do let me read them, Cecily?

CECILY:

Oh, I couldn't possibly. They would make you far too conceited. (*Replaces box.*) The three you wrote me after I had broken off the engagement are so beautiful, and so badly spelled, that even now I can hardly read them without crying a little.

ALGERNON:

But was our engagement ever broken off?

CECILY:

Of course it was. On the 22nd of last March. You can see the entry if you like. (*Shows diary.*) "Today I broke off my engagement with Ernest. I feel it is better to do so. The weather still continues charming."

ALGERNON:

But why on earth did you break it off? What had I done? I had done nothing at all. Cecily, I am very much hurt indeed to hear you broke it off. Particularly when the weather was so charming.

CECILY:

It would hardly have been a really serious engagement if it hadn't been broken off at least once. But I forgave you before the week was out.

ALGERNON (*crossing to her, and kneeling*):

What a perfect angel you are, Cecily.

CECILY:

You dear romantic boy. (*He kisses her, she puts her fingers through his hair.*) I hope your hair curls naturally, does it?

ALGERNON:

Yes, darling, with a little help from others.

CECILY:

I am so glad.

ALGERNON:

You'll never break off our engagement again, Cecily?

CECILY:

> I don't think I could break it off now that I have actually met you. Besides, of course, there is the question of your name.

ALGERNON:

> Yes, of course. (*Nervously.*)

CECILY:

> You must not laugh at me, darling, but it had always been a girlish dream of mine to love someone whose name was Ernest. (Algernon *rises*, Cecily *also*.) There is something in that name that seems to inspire absolute confidence. I pity any poor married woman whose husband is not called Ernest.

ALGERNON:

> But, my dear child, do you mean to say you could not love me if I had some other name?

CECILY:

> But what name?

ALGERNON:

> Oh, any name you like—Algernon—for instance . . .

CECILY:

> But I don't like the name of Algernon.

ALGERNON:

> Well, my own dear, sweet, loving little darling, I really can't see why you should object to the name of Algernon. It is not at all a bad name. In fact, it is rather an aristocratic name. Half of the chaps who get into the Bankruptcy Court are called Algernon. But seriously, Cecily . . . (*Moving to her*) . . . if my name was Algy, couldn't you love me?

CECILY (*rising*):

> I might respect you, Ernest, I might admire your character, but I fear that I should not be able to give you my undivided attention.

ALGERNON:

> Ahem! Cecily! (*Picking up hat.*) Your Rector here is, I suppose, thoroughly experienced in the practice of all the rites and ceremonials of the Church?

CECILY:

> Oh, yes. Dr. Chasuble is a most learned man. He has never written a single book, so you can imagine how much he knows.

ALGERNON:

> I must see him at once on a most important christening—I mean on most important business.

CECILY:

> Oh!

ALGERNON:

I shan't be away more than half an hour.

CECILY:

Considering that we have been engaged since February the 14th, and that I only met you today for the first time, I think it is rather hard that you should leave me for so long a period as half an hour. Couldn't you make it twenty minutes?

ALGERNON:

I'll be back in no time.

(*Kisses her and rushes down the garden.*)

CECILY:

What an impetuous boy he is! I like his hair so much. I must enter his proposal in my diary.

Enter Merriman.

MERRIMAN:

A Miss Fairfax has just called to see Mr. Worthing. On very important business, Miss Fairfax states.

CECILY:

Isn't Mr. Worthing in his library?

MERRIMAN:

Mr. Worthing went over in the direction of the Rectory some time ago.

CECILY:

Pray ask the lady to come out here; Mr. Worthing is sure to be back soon. And you can bring tea.

MERRIMAN:

Yes, Miss.   (*Goes out.*)

CECILY:

Miss Fairfax! I suppose one of the many good elderly women who are associated with Uncle Jack in some of his philanthropic work in London. I don't quite like women who are interested in philanthropic work. I think it is so forward of them.

Enter Merriman.

MERRIMAN:

Miss Fairfax.

Enter Gwendolen.
Exit Merriman.

CECILY (*advancing to meet her*):

Pray let me introduce myself to you. My name is Cecily Cardew.

GWENDOLEN:

Cecily Cardew? (*Moving to her and shaking hands.*) What a very sweet name! Something tells me that we are going to be great friends. I like you already more than I can say. My first impressions of people are never wrong.

CECILY:

How nice of you to like me so much after we have known each other such a comparatively short time. Pray sit down.

GWENDOLEN (*still standing up*):

I may call you Cecily, may I not?

CECILY:

With pleasure!

GWENDOLEN:

And you will always call me Gwendolen, won't you?

CECILY:

If you wish.

GWENDOLEN:

Then that is all quite settled, is it not?

CECILY:

I hope so. (*A pause. They both sit down together.*)

GWENDOLEN:

Perhaps this might be a favorable opportunity for my mentioning who I am. My father is Lord Bracknell. You have never heard of papa, I suppose?

CECILY:

I don't think so.

GWENDOLEN:

Outside the family circle, papa, I am glad to say, is entirely unknown. I think that is quite as it should be. The home seems to me to be the proper sphere for the man. And certainly once a man begins to neglect his domestic duties he becomes painfully effeminate, does he not? And I don't like that. It makes men so very attractive. Cecily, mamma, whose views on education are remarkably strict, has brought me up to be extremely shortsighted; it is part of her system; so do you mind my looking at you through my glasses?

CECILY:

Oh! not at all, Gwendolen. I am very fond of being looked at.

GWENDOLEN (*after examining* Cecily *carefully through a lorgnette*):

You are here on a short visit, I suppose.

CECILY:

Oh no! I live here.

GWENDOLEN (*severely*):

Really? Your mother, no doubt, or some female relative of advanced years, resides here also?

CECILY:

Oh no! I have no mother, nor, in fact, any relations.

GWENDOLEN:

Indeed?

CECILY:

My dear guardian, with the assistance of Miss Prism, has the arduous task of looking after me.

GWENDOLEN:

Your guardian?

CECILY:

Yes, I am Mr. Worthing's ward.

GWENDOLEN:

Oh! It is strange he never mentioned to me that he had a ward. How secretive of him! He grows more interesting hourly. I am not sure, however, that the news inspires me with feelings of unmixed delight. (*Rising and going to her.*) I am very fond of you, Cecily; I have liked you ever since I met you! But I am bound to state that now that I know that you are Mr. Worthing's ward, I cannot help expressing a wish you were—well just a little older than you seem to be—and not quite so very alluring in appearance. In fact, if I may speak candidly—

CECILY:

Pray do! I think that whenever one has anything unpleasant to say, one should always be quite candid.

GWENDOLEN:

Well, to speak with perfect candor, Cecily, I wish that you were fully forty-two, and more than usually plain for your age. Ernest has a strong upright nature. He is the very soul of truth and honor. Disloyalty would be as impossible to him as deception. But even men of the noblest possible moral character are extremely susceptible to the influence of the physical charms of others. Modern, no less than Ancient History, supplies us with many most painful examples of what I refer to. If it were not so, indeed, History would be quite unreadable.

CECILY:

I beg your pardon, Gwendolen, did you say Ernest?

GWENDOLEN:

Yes.

CECILY:

Oh, but it is not Mr. Ernest Worthing who is my guardian. It is his brother—his elder brother.

GWENDOLEN (*sitting down again*):

Ernest never mentioned to me that he had a brother.

CECILY:

I am sorry to say they have not been on good terms for a long time.

GWENDOLEN:

Ah! that accounts for it. And now that I think of it I have never heard any man mention his brother. The subject seems distasteful to most men. Cecily, you have lifted a load from my mind. I was growing almost anxious. It would have been terrible if any cloud had come across a friendship like ours, would it not? Of course you are quite, quite sure that it is not Mr. Ernest Worthing who is your guardian?

CECILY:

Quite sure. (*A pause.*) In fact, I am going to be his.

GWENDOLEN (*inquiringly*):

I beg your pardon?

CECILY (*rather shy and confidingly*):

Dearest Gwendolen, there is no reason why I should make a secret of it to you. Our little county newspaper is sure to chronicle the fact next week. Mr. Ernest Worthing and I are engaged to be married.

GWENDOLEN (*quite politely, rising*):

My darling Cecily, I think there must be some slight error. Mr. Ernest Worthing is engaged to me. The announcement will appear in the *Morning Post* on Saturday at the latest.

CECILY (*very politely, rising*):

I am afraid you must be under some misconception. Ernest proposed to me exactly ten minutes ago. (*Shows diary.*)

GWENDOLEN (*examines diary through her lorgnette carefully*):

It is certainly very curious, for he asked me to be his wife yesterday afternoon at 5:30. If you would care to verify the incident, pray do so. (*Produces diary of her own.*) I never travel without my diary. One should always have something sensational to read in the train. I am so sorry, dear Cecily, if it is any disappointment to you, but I am afraid *I* have the prior claim.

CECILY:

It would distress me more than I can tell you, dear Gwendolen, if it caused you any mental or physical anguish, but I feel bound to point out that since Ernest proposed to you he clearly has changed his mind.

GWENDOLEN (*meditatively*):

> If the poor fellow has been entrapped into any foolish promise I shall consider it my duty to rescue him at once, and with a firm hand.

CECILY (*thoughtfully and sadly*):

> Whatever unfortunate entanglement my dear boy may have got into, I will never reproach him with it after we are married.

GWENDOLEN:

> Do you allude to me, Miss Cardew, as an entanglement? You are presumptuous. On an occasion of this kind it becomes more than a moral duty to speak one's mind. It becomes a pleasure.

CECILY:

> Do you suggest, Miss Fairfax, that I entrapped Ernest into an engagement? How dare you? This is no time for wearing the shallow mask of manners. When I see a spade I call it a spade.

GWENDOLEN (*satirically*):

> I am glad to say that I have never seen a spade. It is obvious that our social spheres have been widely different.

Enter Merriman, *followed by the footman. He carries a salver, tablecloth, and plate stand.* Cecily *is about to retort. The presence of the servants exercises a restraining influence, under which both girls chafe.*

MERRIMAN:

> Shall I lay tea here as usual, Miss?

CECILY (*sternly, in a calm voice*):

> Yes, as usual.

Merriman *begins to clear table and lay cloth. A long pause.* Cecily *and* Gwendolen *glare at each other.*

GWENDOLEN:

> Are there many interesting walks in the vicinity, Miss Cardew?

CECILY:

> Oh! yes! a great many. From the top of one of the hills quite close one can see five counties.

GWENDOLEN:

> Five counties! I don't think I should like that. I hate crowds.

CECILY (*sweetly*):

> I suppose that is why you live in town?

Gwendolen *bites her lip, and beats her foot nervously with her parasol.*

GWENDOLEN (*looking round*):

    Quite a well-kept garden this is, Miss Cardew.

CECILY:

    So glad you like it, Miss Fairfax.

GWENDOLEN:

    I had no idea there were any flowers in the country.

CECILY:

    Oh, flowers are as common here, Miss Fairfax, as people are in London.

GWENDOLEN:

    Personally I cannot understand how anybody manages to exist in the country, if anybody who is anybody does. The country always bores me to death.

CECILY:

    Ah! This is what the newspapers call agricultural depression, is it not? I believe the aristocracy are suffering very much from it just at present. It is almost an epidemic amongst them, I have been told. May I offer you some tea, Miss Fairfax?

GWENDOLEN (*with elaborate politeness*):

    Thank you. (*Aside.*) Detestable girl! But I require tea!

CECILY (*sweetly*):

    Sugar?

GWENDOLEN (*superciliously*):

    No, thank you. Sugar is not fashionable any more. (Cecily *looks angrily at her, takes up the tongs and puts four lumps of sugar into the cup.*)

CECILY (*severely*):

    Cake or bread and butter?

GWENDOLEN (*in a bored manner*):

    Bread and butter, please. Cake is rarely seen at the best houses nowadays.

CECILY (*cuts a very large slice of cake, and puts it on the tray*):

    Hand that to Miss Fairfax.

Merriman *does so, and goes out with footman.* Gwendolen *drinks the tea and makes a grimace. Puts down cup at once, reaches out her hand to the bread and butter, looks at it, and finds it is cake. Rises in indignation.*

GWENDOLEN:

    You have filled my tea with lumps of sugar, and though I asked most distinctly for bread and butter, you have given me cake. I am known for the gentleness of my disposition, and the extraordinary sweetness of my nature, but I warn you, Miss Cardew, you may go too far.

CECILY (*rising*):

> To save my poor, innocent, trusting boy from the machinations of any other girl there are no lengths to which I would not go.

GWENDOLEN:

> From the moment I saw you I distrusted you. I felt that you were false and deceitful. I am never deceived in such matters. My first impressions of people are invariably right.

CECILY:

> It seems to me, Miss Fairfax, that I am trespassing on your valuable time. No doubt you have many other calls of a similar character to make in the neighborhood.

Enter Jack.

GWENDOLEN (*catching sight of him*):

> Ernest! My own Ernest!

JACK:

> Gwendolen! Darling! (*Offers to kiss her.*)

GWENDOLEN (*drawing back*):

> A moment! May I ask if you are engaged to be married to this young lady? (*Points to* Cecily.)

JACK (*laughing*):

> To dear little Cecily! Of course not! What could have put such an idea into your pretty little head?

GWENDOLEN:

> Thank you. You may! (*Offers her cheek.*)

CECILY (*very sweetly*):

> I knew there must be some misunderstanding, Miss Fairfax. The gentleman whose arm is at present round your waist is my dear guardian, Mr. John Worthing.

GWENDOLEN:

> I beg your pardon?

CECILY:

> This is Uncle Jack.

GWENDOLEN (*receding*):

> Jack! Oh!

Enter Algernon.

CECILY:

> Here is Ernest.

ALGERNON (*goes straight over to* Cecily *without noticing anyone else*):

> My own love! (*Offers to kiss her.*)

CECILY (*drawing back*):

> A moment, Ernest! May I ask you—are you engaged to be married to this young lady?

ALGERNON (*looking round*):

>   To what young lady? Good heavens! Gwendolen!

CECILY:

>   Yes! to good heavens, Gwendolen, I mean to Gwendolen.

ALGERNON (*laughing*):

>   Of course not! What could have put such an idea into your
>   pretty little head?

CECILY:

>   Thank you. (*Presenting her cheek to be kissed.*) You may. (*Alger-
>   non kisses her.*)

GWENDOLEN:

>   I felt there was some slight error, Miss Cardew. The gentleman
>   who is now embracing you is my cousin, Mr. Algernon Mon-
>   crieff.

CECILY (*breaking away from* Algernon):

>   Algernon Moncrieff! Oh! (*The two girls move towards each other
>   and put their arms round each other's waists as if for protection.*)

CECILY:

>   Are you called Algernon?

ALGERNON:

>   I cannot deny it.

CECILY:

>   Oh!

GWENDOLEN:

>   Is your name really John?

JACK (*standing rather proudly*):

>   I could deny it if I liked, I could deny anything if I liked. But
>   my name certainly is John. It has been John for years.

CECILY (*to* Gwendolen):

>   A gross deception has been practiced on both of us.

GWENDOLEN:

>   My poor wounded Cecily!

CECILY:

>   My sweet wronged Gwendolen!

GWENDOLEN (*slowly and seriously*):

>   You will call me sister, will you not? (*They embrace.* Jack *and*
>   Algernon *groan and walk up and down.*)

CECILY (*rather brightly*):

>   There is just one question I would like to be allowed to ask my
>   guardian.

GWENDOLEN:

>   An admirable idea! Mr. Worthing, there is just one question I
>   would like to be permitted to put to you. Where is your
>   brother Ernest? We are both engaged to be married to your

brother Ernest, so it is a matter of some importance to us to know where your brother Ernest is at present.

JACK (*slowly and hesitatingly*):

Gwendolen—Cecily—it is very painful for me to be forced to speak the truth. It is the first time in my life that I have ever been reduced to such a painful position, and I am really quite inexperienced in doing anything of the kind. However I will tell you quite frankly that I have no brother Ernest. I have no brother at all. I never had a brother in my life, and I certainly have not the smallest intention of ever having one in the future.

CECILY (*surprised*):

No brother at all?

JACK (*cheerily*):

None!

GWENDOLEN(*severely*):

Had you never a brother of any kind?

JACK (*pleasantly*):

Never. Not even of any kind.

GWENDOLEN:

I am afraid it is quite clear, Cecily, that neither of us is engaged to be married to anyone.

CECILY:

It is not a very pleasant position for a young girl suddenly to find herself in. Is it?

GWENDOLEN:

Let us go into the house. They will hardly venture to come after us there.

CECILY:

No, men are so cowardly, aren't they?

They retire into the house with scornful looks.

JACK:

This ghastly state of things is what you call Bunburying, I suppose?

ALGERNON:

Yes, and a perfectly wonderful Bunbury it is. The most wonderful Bunbury I have ever had in my life.

JACK:

Well, you've no right whatsoever to Bunbury here.

ALGERNON:

That is absurd. One has a right to Bunbury anywhere one chooses. Every serious Bunburyist knows that.

JACK:

Serious Bunburyist! Good heavens!

ALGERNON:

Well, one must be serious about something, if one wants to have any amusement in life. I happen to be serious about Bunburying. What on earth you are serious about I haven't got the remotest idea. About everything, I should fancy. You have such an absolutely trivial nature.

JACK:

Well, the only small satisfaction I have in the whole of this wretched business is that your friend Bunbury is quite exploded. You won't be able to run down to the country quite so often as you used to do, dear Algy. And a very good thing too.

ALGERNON:

Your brother is a little off-color, isn't he, dear Jack? You won't be able to disappear to London quite so frequently as your wicked custom was. And not a bad thing either.

JACK:

As for your conduct towards Miss Cardew, I must say that your taking in a sweet, simple, innocent girl like that is quite inexcusable. To say nothing of the fact that she is my ward.

ALGERNON:

I can see no possible defense at all for your deceiving a brilliant, clever, thoroughly experienced young lady like Miss Fairfax. To say nothing of the fact that she is my cousin.

JACK:

I wanted to be engaged to Gwendolen, that is all. I love her.

ALGERNON:

Well, I simply wanted to be engaged to Cecily. I adore her.

JACK:

There is certainly no chance of your marrying Miss Cardew.

ALGERNON:

I don't think there is much likelihood, Jack, of you and Miss Fairfax being united.

JACK:

Well, that is no business of yours.

ALGERNON:

If it was my business, I wouldn't talk about it. (*Begins to eat muffins.*) It is very vulgar to talk about one's business. Only people like stockbrokers do that, and then merely at dinner parties.

JACK:

How you can sit there, calmly eating muffins when we are in this horrible trouble, I can't make out. You seem to me to be perfectly heartless.

ALGERNON:

Well, I can't eat muffins in an agitated manner. The butter would probably get on my cuffs. One should always eat muffins quite calmly. It is the only way to eat them.

JACK:

I say it's perfectly heartless your eating muffins at all, under the circumstances.

ALGERNON:

When I am in trouble, eating is the only thing that consoles me. Indeed, when I am in really great trouble, as anyone who knows me intimately will tell you, I refuse everything except food and drink. At the present moment I am eating muffins because I am unhappy. Besides, I am particularly fond of muffins. (*Rising.*)

JACK (*rising*):

Well, that is no reason why you should eat them all in that greedy way. (*Takes muffins from* Algernon.)

ALGERNON (*offering tea cake*):

I wish you would have tea cake instead. I don't like tea cake.

JACK:

Good heavens! I suppose a man may eat his own muffins in his own garden.

ALGERNON:

But you have just said it was perfectly heartless to eat muffins.

JACK:

I said it was perfectly heartless of you, under the circumstances. That is a very different thing.

ALGERNON:

That may be. But the muffins are the same. (*He seizes the muffin dish from* Jack.)

JACK:

Algy, I wish to goodness you would go.

ALGERNON:

You can't possibly ask me to go without having some dinner. It's absurd. I never go without my dinner. No one ever does, except vegetarians and people like that. Besides I have just made arrangements with Dr. Chasuble to be christened at a quarter to six under the name of Ernest.

JACK:

My dear fellow, the sooner you give up that nonsense the better. I made arrangements this morning with Dr. Chasuble to be christened myself at 5:30, and I naturally will take the name of Ernest. Gwendolen would wish it. We can't both be christened Ernest. It's absurd. Besides, I have a perfect right to be christened if I like. There is no evidence at all that I ever have been

christened by anybody. I should think it extremely probable I
never was, and so does Dr. Chasuble. It is entirely different in
your case. You have been christened already.

ALGERNON:

Yes, but I have not been christened for years.

JACK:

Yes, but you have been christened. That is the important thing.

ALGERNON:

Quite so. So I know my constitution can stand it. If you are not
quite sure about your ever having been christened, I must say I
think it rather dangerous your venturing on it now. It might
make you very unwell. You can hardly have forgotten that
someone very closely connected with you was very nearly carried off this week in Paris by a severe chill.

JACK:

Yes, but you said yourself that a severe chill was not hereditary.

ALGERNON:

It usen't to be, I know—but I daresay it is now. Science is
always making wonderful improvements in things.

JACK (*picking up the muffin dish*):

Oh, that is nonsense; you are always talking nonsense.

ALGERNON:

Jack, you are at the muffins again! I wish you wouldn't. There
are only two left. (*Takes them.*) I told you I was particularly
fond of muffins.

JACK:

But I hate tea cake.

ALGERNON:

Why on earth then do you allow tea cake to be served up for
your guests? What ideas you have of hospitality!

JACK:

Algernon! I have already told you to go. I don't want you here.
Why don't you go!

ALGERNON:

I haven't quite finished my tea yet! and there is still one muffin
left. (Jack *groans, and sinks into a chair.* Algernon *still continues
eating.*)

Third Act

SCENE—*Morning room at the Manor House.*

Gwendolen *and* Cecily *are at the window, looking out into the garden.*

GWENDOLEN:
> The fact that they did not follow us at once into the house, as anyone else would have done, seems to me to show that they have some sense of shame left.

CECILY:
> They have been eating muffins. That looks like repentance.

GWENDOLEN (*after a pause*):
> They don't seem to notice us at all. Couldn't you cough?

CECILY:
> But I haven't got a cough.

GWENDOLEN:
> They're looking at us. What effrontery!

CECILY:
> They're approaching. That's very forward of them.

GWENDOLEN:
> Let us preserve a dignified silence.

CECILY:
> Certainly. It's the only thing to do now.

Enter Jack *followed by* Algernon. *They whistle some dreadful popular air from a British Opera.*

GWENDOLEN:
> This dignified silence seems to produce an unpleasant effect.

CECILY:
> A most distasteful one.

GWENDOLEN:
> But we will not be the first to speak.

CECILY:
> Certainly not.

GWENDOLEN:
> Mr. Worthing, I have something very particular to ask you. Much depends on your reply.

CECILY:
> Gwendolen, your common sense is invaluable. Mr. Moncrieff, kindly answer me the following question. Why did you pretend to be my guardian's brother?

ALGERNON:

In order that I might have an opportunity of meeting you.

CECILY (*To* Gwendolen):

That certainly seems a satisfactory explanation, does it not?

GWENDOLEN:

Yes, dear, if you can believe him.

CECILY:

I don't. But that does not affect the wonderful beauty of his answer.

GWENDOLEN:

True. In matters of grave importance, style, not sincerity is the vital thing. Mr. Worthing, what explanation can you offer to me for pretending to have a brother? Was it in order that you might have an opportunity of coming up to town to see me as often as possible?

JACK:

Can you doubt it, Miss Fairfax?

GWENDOLEN:

I have the gravest doubts upon the subject. But I intend to crush them. This is not the moment for German skepticism. (*Moving to* Cecily.) Their explanations appear to be quite satisfactory, especially Mr. Worthing's. That seems to me to have the stamp of truth upon it.

CECILY:

I am more than content with what Mr. Moncrieff said. His voice alone inspires one with absolute credulity.

GWENDOLEN:

Then you think we should forgive them?

CECILY:

Yes. I mean no.

GWENDOLEN:

True! I had forgotten. There are principles at stake that one cannot surrender. Which of us should tell them? The task is not a pleasant one.

CECILY:

Could we not both speak at the same time?

GWENDOLEN:

An excellent idea! I nearly always speak at the same time as other people. Will you take the time from me?

CECILY:

Certainly. (Gwendolen *beats time with uplifted finger.*)

GWENDOLEN AND CECILY (*speaking together*):

Your Christian names are still an insuperable barrier. That is all!

JACK AND ALGERNON (*speaking together*):

> Our Christian names! Is that all? But we are going to be christened this afternoon.

GWENDOLEN (*to* Jack):

> For my sake you are prepared to do this terrible thing?

JACK:

> I am.

CECILY (*to* Algernon):

> To please me you are ready to face this fearful ordeal?

ALGERNON:

> I am!

GWENDOLEN:

> How absurd to talk of the equality of the sexes! Where questions of self-sacrifice are concerned, men are infinitely beyond us.

JACK:

> We are. (*Clasps hands with* Algernon.)

CECILY:

> They have moments of physical courage of which we women know absolutely nothing.

GWENDOLEN (*to* Jack):

> Darling!

ALGERNON (*to* Cecily):

> Darling. (*They fall into each other's arms.*)

Enter Merriman. *When he enters he coughs loudly, seeing the situation.*

MERRIMAN:

> Ahem! Ahem! Lady Bracknell!

JACK:

> Good heavens!

Enter Lady Bracknell. *The couples separate in alarm. Exit* Merriman.

LADY BRACKNELL:

> Gwendolen! What does this mean?

GWENDOLEN:

> Merely that I am engaged to be married to Mr. Worthing, mamma.

LADY BRACKNELL:

> Come here. Sit down. Sit down immediately. Hesitation of any kind is a sign of mental decay in the young, of physical weakness in the old. (*Turns to* Jack.) Apprised, sir, of my daughter's sudden flight by her trusty maid, whose confidence I pur-

chased by means of a small coin, I followed her at once by a luggage train. Her unhappy father is, I am glad to say, under the impression that she is attending a more than usually lengthy lecture by the University Extension Scheme on the Influence of a permanent income on Thought. I do not propose to undeceive him. Indeed I have never undeceived him on any question. I would consider it wrong. But of course, you will clearly understand that all communication between yourself and my daughter must cease immediately from this moment. On this point, as indeed on all points, I am firm.

JACK:

I am engaged to be married to Gwendolen, Lady Bracknell!

LADY BRACKNELL:

You are nothing of the kind, sir. And now, as regards Algernon! . . . Algernon!

ALGERNON:

Yes, Aunt Augusta.

LADY BRACKNELL:

May I ask if it is in this house that your invalid friend Mr. Bunbury resides?

ALGERNON (*stammering*):

Oh! No! Bunbury doesn't live here. Bunbury is somewhere else at present. In fact, Bunbury is dead.

LADY BRACKNELL:

Dead! When did Mr. Bunbury die? His death must have been extremely sudden.

ALGERNON (*airily*):

Oh! I killed Bunbury this afternoon. I mean poor Bunbury died this afternoon.

LADY BRACKNELL:

What did he die of?

ALGERNON:

Bunbury? Oh, he was quite exploded.

LADY BRACKNELL:

Exploded! Was he the victim of a revolutionary outrage? I was not aware that Mr. Bunbury was interested in social legislation. If so, he is well punished for his morbidity.

ALGERNON:

My dear Aunt Augusta, I mean he was found out! The doctors found out that Bunbury could not live, that is what I mean—so Bunbury died.

LADY BRACKNELL:

He seems to have had great confidence in the opinion of his physicians. I am glad, however, that he made up his mind at the last to some definite course of action, and acted under proper medical advice. And now that we have finally got rid of this Mr. Bunbury, may I ask, Mr. Worthing, who is that young person whose hand my nephew Algernon is now holding in what seems to me a peculiarly unnecessary manner?

JACK:

That lady is Miss Cecily Cardew, my ward.

Lady Bracknell *bows coldly to* Cecily.

ALGERNON:

I am engaged to be married to Cecily, Aunt Augusta.

LADY BRACKNELL:

I beg your pardon?

CECILY:

Mr. Moncrieff and I are engaged to be married, Lady Bracknell.

LADY BRACKNELL (*with a shiver, crossing to the sofa and sitting down*):

I do not know whether there is anything peculiarly exciting in the air of this particular part of Hertfordshire, but the number of engagements that go on seems to me considerably above the proper average that statistics have laid down for our guidance. I think some preliminary inquiry on my part would not be out of place. Mr. Worthing, is Miss Cardew at all connected with any of the larger railway stations in London? I merely desire information. Until yesterday I had no idea that there were any families or persons whose origin was a Terminus. (Jack *looks perfectly furious, but restrains himself.*)

JACK (*in a clear, cold voice*):

Miss Cardew is the granddaughter of the late Mr. Thomas Cardew of 149, Belgrave Square, S.W.; Gervase Park, Dorking, Surrey; and the Sporran, Fifeshire, N.B.

LADY BRACKNELL:

That sounds not unsatisfactory. Three addresses always inspire confidence, even in tradesmen. But what proof have I of their authenticity?

JACK:

I have carefully preserved the Court Guides of the period. They are open to your inspection, Lady Bracknell.

LADY BRACKNELL (*grimly*):

I have known strange errors in that publication.

JACK:

Miss Cardew's family solicitors are Messrs. Markby, Markby, and Markby.

LADY BRACKNELL:

> Markby, Markby, and Markby? A firm of the very highest position in their profession. Indeed I am told that one of the Mr. Markbys is occasionally to be seen at dinner parties. So far I am satisfied.

JACK (*very irritably*):

> How extremely kind of you, Lady Bracknell! I have also in my possession, you will be pleased to hear, certificates of Miss Cardew's birth, baptism, whooping cough, registration, vaccination, confirmation, and the measles; both the German and the English variety.

LADY BRACKNELL:

> Ah! A life crowded with incident, I see; though perhaps somewhat too exciting for a young girl. I am not myself in favor of premature experiences. (*Rises, looks at her watch.*) Gwendolen! the time approaches for our departure. We have not a moment to lose. As a matter of form, Mr. Worthing, I had better ask you if Miss Cardew has any little fortune?

JACK:

> Oh! about a hundred and thirty thousand pounds in the Funds. That is all. Good-bye, Lady Bracknell. So pleased to have seen you.

LADY BRACKNELL (*sitting down again*):

> A moment, Mr. Worthing. A hundred and thirty thousand pounds! And in the Funds! Miss Cardew seems to me a most attractive young lady, now that I look at her. Few girls of the present day have any really solid qualities, any of the qualities that last, and improve with time. We live, I regret to say, in an age of surfaces. (*To* Cecily.) Come over here, dear (Cecily *goes across.*) Pretty child! your dress is sadly simple, and your hair seems almost as Nature might have left it. But we can soon alter all that. A thoroughly experienced French maid produces a really marvelous result in a very brief space of time. I remember recommending one to young Lady Lancing, and after three months her own husband did not know her.

JACK (*aside*):

> And after six months nobody knew her.

LADY BRACKNELL (*glares at* Jack *for a few moments. Then bends, with a practiced smile, to* Cecily.):

> Kindly turn round, sweet child (Cecily *turns completely round.*) No, the side view is what I want. (Cecily *presents her profile.*) Yes, quite as I expected. There are distinct social possibilities in your profile. The two weak points in our age are its want of

principle and its want of profile. The chin a little higher, dear. Style largely depends on the way the chin is worn. They are worn very high, just at present. Algernon!

ALGERNON:

Yes, Aunt Augusta!

LADY BRACKNELL:

There are distinct social possibilities in Miss Cardew's profile.

ALGERNON:

Cecily is the sweetest, dearest, prettiest girl in the whole world. And I don't care twopence about social possibilities.

LADY BRACKNELL:

Never speak disrespectfully of Society, Algernon. Only people who can't get into it do that. (*To* Cecily.) Dear child, of course you know that Algernon has nothing but his debts to depend upon. But I do not approve of mercenary marriages. When I married Lord Bracknell I had no fortune of any kind. But I never dreamed for a moment of allowing that to stand in my way. Well, I suppose I must give my consent.

ALGERNON:

Thank you, Aunt Augusta.

LADY BRACKNELL:

Cecily, you may kiss me!

CECILY (*kisses her*):

Thank you, Lady Bracknell.

LADY BRACKNELL:

You may also address me as Aunt Augusta for the future.

CECILY:

Thank you, Aunt Augusta.

LADY BRACKNELL:

The marriage, I think, had better take place quite soon.

ALGERNON:

Thank you, Aunt Augusta.

CECILY:

Thank you, Aunt Augusta.

LADY BRACKNELL:

To speak frankly, I am not in favor of long engagements. They give people the opportunity of finding out each other's character before marriage, which I think is never advisable.

JACK:

I beg your pardon for interrupting you, Lady Bracknell, but this engagement is quite out of the question. I am Miss Cardew's guardian, and she cannot marry without my consent until she comes of age. That consent I absolutely decline to give.

LADY BRACKNELL:

> Upon what grounds may I ask? Algernon is an extremely, I may almost say an ostentatiously, eligible young man. He has nothing, but he looks everything. What more can one desire?

JACK:

> It pains me very much to have to speak frankly to you, Lady Bracknell, about your nephew, but the fact is that I do not approve at all of his moral character. I suspect him of being untruthful. (Algernon *and* Cecily *look at him in indignant amazement.*)

LADY BRACKNELL:

> Untruthful! My nephew Algernon? Impossible! He is an Oxonian.

JACK:

> I fear there can be no possible doubt about the matter. This afternoon, during my temporary absence in London on an important question of romance, he obtained admission to my house by means of the false pretense of being my brother. Under an assumed name he drank, I've just been informed by my butler, an entire pint bottle of my Perrier-Jouet, Brut, '89; a wine I was specially reserving for myself. Continuing his disgraceful deception, he succeeded in the course of the afternoon in alienating the affections of my only ward. He subsequently stayed to tea, and devoured every single muffin. And what makes his conduct all the more heartless is, that he was perfectly well aware from the first that I have no brother, that I never had a brother, and that I don't intend to have a brother, not even of any kind. I distinctly told him so myself yesterday afternoon.

LADY BRACKNELL:

> Ahem! Mr. Worthing, after careful consideration I have decided entirely to overlook my nephew's conduct to you.

JACK:

> That is very generous of you, Lady Bracknell. My own decision, however, is unalterable. I decline to give my consent.

LADY BRACKNELL (*to* Cecily):

> Come here, sweet child. (Cecily *goes over.*) How old are you, dear?

CECILY:

> Well, I am really only eighteen, but I always admit to twenty when I go to evening parties.

LADY BRACKNELL:

> You are perfectly right in making some slight alteration. Indeed, no woman should ever be quite accurate about her

age. It looks so calculating. . . . (*In a meditative manner.*) Eighteen, but admitting to twenty at evening parties. Well, it will not be very long before you are of age and free from the restraints of tutelage. So I don't think your guardian's consent is, after all, a matter of any importance.

JACK:

Pray excuse me, Lady Bracknell, for interrupting you again, but it is only fair to tell you that according to the terms of her grandfather's will Miss Cardew does not come legally of age till she is thirty-five.

LADY BRACKNELL:

That does not seem to me to be a grave objection. Thirty-five is a very attractive age. London society is full of women of the very highest birth who have, of their own free choice, remained thirty-five for years. Lady Dumbleton is an instance in point. To my own knowledge she has been thirty-five ever since she arrived at the age of forty, which was many years ago now. I see no reason why our dear Cecily should not be even still more attractive at the age you mention than she is at present. There will be a large accumulation of property.

CECILY:

Algy, could you wait for me till I was thirty-five?

ALGERNON:

Of course I could, Cecily. You know I could.

CECILY:

Yes, I felt it instinctively, but I couldn't wait all that time. I hate waiting even five minutes for anybody. It always makes me rather cross. I am not punctual myself, I know, but I do like punctuality in others, and waiting, even to be married, is quite out of the question.

ALGERNON:

Then what is to be done, Cecily?

CECILY:

I don't know, Mr. Moncrieff.

LADY BRACKNELL:

My dear Mr. Worthing, as Miss Cardew states positively that she cannot wait till she is thirty-five—a remark which I am bound to say seems to me to show a somewhat impatient nature—I would beg of you to reconsider your decision.

JACK:

But my dear Lady Bracknell, the matter is entirely in your own hands. The moment you consent to my marriage with Gwendolen, I will most gladly allow your nephew to form an alliance with my ward.

LADY BRACKNELL (*rising and drawing herself up.*):

You must be quite aware that what you propose is out of the question.

JACK:

Then a passionate celibacy is all that any of us can look forward to.

LADY BRACKNELL:

This is not the destiny I propose for Gwendolen. Algernon, of course, can choose for himself. (*Pulls out her watch.*) Come, dear; (Gwendolen *rises.*) we have already missed five, if not six, trains. To miss any more might expose us to comment on the platform.

Enter Dr. Chasuble.

CHASUBLE:

Everything is quite ready for the christenings.

LADY BRACKNELL:

The christenings, sir! Is not that somewhat premature!

CHASUBLE (*looking rather puzzled, and pointing to* Jack *and* Algernon):

Both these gentlemen have expressed a desire for immediate baptism.

LADY BRACKNELL:

At their age? The idea is grotesque and irreligious! Algernon, I forbid you to be baptized. I will not hear of such excesses. Lord Bracknell would be highly displeased if he learned that that was the way in which you wasted your time and money.

CHASUBLE:

Am I to understand then that there are to be no christenings at all this afternoon?

JACK:

I don't think that, as things are now, it would be of much practical value to either of us, Dr. Chasuble.

CHASUBLE:

I am grieved to hear such sentiments from you, Mr. Worthing. They savor of the heretical views of the Anabaptists, views that I have completely refuted in four of my unpublished sermons. However, as your present mood seems to be one peculiarly secular, I will return to the church at once. Indeed, I have just been informed by the pew-opener that for the last hour and a half Miss Prism has been waiting for me in the vestry.

LADY BRACKNELL (*starting*):

Miss Prism! Did I hear you mention a Miss Prism?

CHASUBLE:

Yes, Lady Bracknell. I am on my way to join her.

LADY BRACKNELL:

Pray allow me to detain you for a moment. This matter may prove to be one of vital importance to Lord Bracknell and myself. Is this Miss Prism a female of repellent aspect, remotely connected with education?

CHASUBLE (*somewhat indignantly*):

She is the most cultivated of ladies, and the very picture of respectability.

LADY BRACKNELL:

It is obviously the same person. May I ask what position she holds in your household?

CHASUBLE (*severely*):

I am a celibate, madam.

JACK (*interposing*):

Miss Prism, Lady Bracknell, has been for the last three years Miss Cardew's esteemed governess and valued companion.

LADY BRACKNELL:

In spite of what I hear of her, I must see her at once. Let her be sent for.

CHASUBLE (*looking off*):

She approaches; she is nigh.

Enter Miss Prism *hurriedly.*

MISS PRISM:

I was told you expected me in the vestry, dear Canon. I have been waiting for you there for an hour and three quarters. (*Catches sight of* Lady Bracknell *who has fixed her with a stony glare,* Miss Prism *grows pale and quails. She looks anxiously round as if desirous to escape.*)

LADY BRACKNELL (*in a severe, judicial voice*):

Prism! (Miss Prism *bows her head in shame.*) Come here, Prism! (Miss Prism *approaches in a humble manner.*) Prism! Where is that baby? (*General consternation. The Canon starts back in horror.* Algernon *and* Jack *pretend to be anxious to shield* Cecily *and* Gwendolen *from hearing the details of a terrible public scandal.*) Twenty-eight years ago, Prism, you left Lord Bracknell's house, Number 104, Upper Grosvenor Street, in charge of a perambulator that contained a baby, of the male sex. You never returned. A few weeks later, through the elaborate investigations of the Metropolitan police, the perambulator was discovered at midnight, standing by itself in a remote corner of Bayswater. It contained the manuscript of a three-volume novel of more than usually revolting sentimentality. (Miss Prism *starts in involuntary indignation*.) But the baby was not there! (*Everyone looks at* Miss Prism.) Prism! Where is that baby? (*A pause*.)

MISS PRISM:

Lady Bracknell, I admit with shame that I do not know. I only wish I did. The plain facts of the case are these. On the morning of the day you mention, a day that is forever branded on my memory, I prepared as usual to take the baby out in its perambulator. I had also with me a somewhat old, but capacious handbag, in which I had intended to place the manuscript of a work of fiction that I had written during my few unoccupied hours. In a moment of mental abstraction, for which I never can forgive myself, I deposited the manuscript in the bassinette, and placed the baby in the handbag.

JACK (*who has been listening attentively*):

But where did you deposit the handbag?

MISS PRISM:

Do not ask me, Mr. Worthing.

JACK:

Miss Prism, this is a matter of no small importance to me. I insist on knowing where you deposited the handbag that contained that infant.

MISS PRISM:

I left it in the cloak room of one of the larger railway stations in London.

JACK:

What railway station?

MISS PRISM (*quite crushed*):

Victoria. The Brighton line. (*Sinks into a chair*.)

JACK:

I must retire to my room for a moment. Gwendolen, wait here for me.

GWENDOLEN:

If you are not too long, I will wait here for you all my life.

(*Exit* Jack *in great excitement*.)

CHASUBLE:

What do you think this means, Lady Bracknell?

LADY BRACKNELL:

I dare not even suspect, Dr. Chasuble. I need hardly tell you that in families of high position strange coincidences are not supposed to occur. They are hardly considered the thing.

Noises heard overhead as if someone was throwing trunks about. Everyone looks up.

CECILY:
Uncle Jack seems strangely agitated.
CHASUBLE:
Your guardian has a very emotional nature.
LADY BRACKNELL:
This noise is extremely unpleasant. It sounds as if he was having an argument. I dislike arguments of any kind. They are always vulgar, and often convincing.
CHASUBLE (*looking up*):
It has stopped now. (*The noise is redoubled.*)
LADY BRACKNELL:
I wish he would arrive at some conclusion.
GWENDOLEN:
This suspense is terrible. I hope it will last.

Enter Jack *with a handbag of black leather in his hand.*

JACK (*rushing over to* Miss Prism):
Is this the handbag, Miss Prism? Examine it carefully before you speak. The happiness of more than one life depends on your answer.
MISS PRISM (*calmly*):
It seems to be mine. Yes, here is the injury it received through the upsetting of a Gower Street omnibus in younger and happier days. Here is the stain on the lining caused by the explosion of a temperance beverage, an incident that occurred at Leamington. And here, on the lock, are my initials. I had forgotten that in an extravagant mood I had had them placed there. The bag is undoubtedly mine. I am delighted to have it so unexpectedly restored to me. It has been a great inconvenience being without it all these years.
JACK (*in a pathetic voice*):
Miss Prism, more is restored to you than this handbag. I was the baby you placed in it.
MISS PRISM (*amazed*):
You!
JACK (*embracing her*):
Yes . . . mother!
MISS PRISM (*recoiling in indignant astonishment*):
Mr. Worthing! I am unmarried!

JACK:

> Unmarried! I do not deny that is a serious blow. But after all, who has the right to cast a stone against one who has suffered? Cannot repentance wipe out an act of folly? Why should there be one law for men, and another for women? Mother, I forgive you. (*Tries to embrace her again.*)

MISS PRISM (*still more indignant*):

> Mr. Worthing, there is some error. (*Pointing to* Lady Bracknell.) There is the lady who can tell you who you really are.

JACK (*after a pause*):

> Lady Bracknell, I hate to seem inquisitive, but would you kindly inform me who I am?

LADY BRACKNELL:

> I am afraid that the news I have to give you will not altogether please you. You are the son of my poor sister, Mrs. Moncrieff, and consequently Algernon's elder brother.

JACK:

> Algy's elder brother! Then I have a brother after all. I knew I had a brother! I always said I had a brother! Cecily—how could you have ever doubted that I had a brother? (*Seizes hold of* Algernon.) Dr. Chasuble, my unfortunate brother. Miss Prism, my unfortunate brother. Gwendolen, my unfortunate brother. Algy, you young scoundrel, you will have to treat me with more respect in the future. You have never behaved to me like a brother in all your life.

ALGERNON:

> Well, not till today, old boy, I admit. I did my best, however, though I was out of practice. (*Shakes hands.*)

GWENDOLEN (*to* Jack):

> My own! But what own are you? What is your Christian name, now that you have become someone else?

JACK:

> Good heavens! . . . I had quite forgotten that point. Your decision on the subject of my name is irrevocable, I suppose?

GWENDOLEN:

> I never change, except in my affections.

CECILY:

> What a noble nature you have, Gwendolen!

JACK:

> Then the question had better be cleared up at once. Aunt Augusta, a moment. At the time when Miss Prism left me in the handbag, had I been christened already?

LADY BRACKNELL:

Every luxury that money could buy, including christening, had been lavished on you by your fond and doting parents.

JACK:

Then I was christened! That is settled. Now, what name was I given? Let me know the worst.

LADY BRACKNELL:

Being the eldest son you were naturally christened after your father.

JACK (*irritably*):

Yes, but what was my father's christian name?

LADY BRACKNELL (*meditatively*):

I cannot at the present moment recall what the General's christian name was. But I have no doubt he had one. He was eccentric, I admit. But only in later years. And that was the result of the Indian climate, and marriage, and indigestion, and other things of that kind.

JACK:

Algy! Can't you recollect what our father's christian name was?

ALGERNON:

My dear boy, we were never even on speaking terms. He died before I was a year old.

JACK:

His name would appear in the Army Lists of the period, I suppose, Aunt Augusta?

LADY BRACKNELL:

The General was essentially a man of peace, except in his domestic life. But I have no doubt his name would appear in any military directory.

JACK:

The Army Lists of the last forty years are here. These delightful records should have been my constant study. (*Rushes to bookcase and tears the books out.*) M. Generals . . . Mallam, Maxbohm, Magley, what ghastly names they have—Markby, Migsby, Mobbs, Moncrieff! Lieutenant 1840, Captain, Lieutenant Colonel, Colonel, General 1869, christian names, Ernest John. (*Puts book very quietly down and speaks quite calmly.*) I always told you, Gwendolen, my name was Ernest, didn't I? Well it is Ernest after all. I mean it naturally is Ernest.

LADY BRACKNELL:

Yes, I remember now that the General was called Ernest. I knew I had some particular reason for disliking the name.

GWENDOLEN:

Ernest! My own Ernest! I felt from the first that you could have no other name!

JACK:

Gwendolen, it is a terrible thing for a man to find out suddenly that all his life he has been speaking nothing but the truth. Can you forgive me?

GWENDOLEN:

I can. For I feel that you are sure to change.

JACK:

My own one!

CHASUBLE (*to* Miss Prism):

Laetitia! (*Embraces her.*)

MISS PRISM (*enthusiastically*):

Frederick! At last!

ALGERNON:

Cecily! (*Embraces her.*) At last!

JACK:

Gwendolen! (*Embraces her.*) At last!

LADY BRACKNELL:

My nephew, you seem to be displaying signs of triviality.

JACK:

On the contrary, Aunt Augusta, I've now realized for the first time in my life the vital Importance of Being Earnest.

GEORGE BERNARD SHAW

George Bernard Shaw was born in Dublin, Ireland, on July 26, 1856. He was the third child of George Carr Shaw and Lucinda Elizabeth Shaw. His mother was a talented singer and financially supported the family by giving voice lessons. His father was unsuccessful in his business affairs and an alcoholic. Shaw left school at the age of thirteen out of boredom and, in 1871, became a clerk at the C. Uniack Townshend and Company real-estate office. Although he hated the job, he remained there for four and a half years. In 1876, Shaw moved to London, where his sister Lucy and his mother—who had left her husband behind—had relocated three years earlier, in part, to help Lucy's singing career. For a brief period of time in 1879 he worked for the Edison Company, which made and installed telephones. However, Shaw soon quit and attempted to become a novelist. He wrote five unsuccessful novels and began a sixth before giving up in 1883. During this time he spent much of his time at the reading room of the British Museum, where he read voraciously on a variety of subjects, including economics and art. There he read *Das Kapital* by Karl Marx, which influenced his conversion to socialism. In 1884, he joined a group of radicals that included Beatrix Potter and helped found the Fabian Society, a Socialist organization that later included the writer H. G. Wells. Shaw began writing essays and, although rather shy at the time, made public speeches on the society's behalf.

In 1885, Shaw began a career in journalism, writing art criticism for *The World*, a job he obtained with the help of William Archer, the drama critic for the paper, whom he had met at the British Museum. Three years later he was writing music reviews under the pseudonym "Corno di Bassetto," and in 1894 he became the drama critic for the *Saturday Review*, a position he held for three years. By then, however, he had already begun his career as a dramatist. He finished writing his first play, *Widower's House*, in 1892. Although it caused controversy with its depiction of a slum landlord, it was a commercial failure. However, delighted at the uproar he had caused, Shaw continued to write, undeterred. He was greatly influenced by the Norwegian playwright Henrik Ibsen, whose plays emphasized the provocative social issues of the day. Following in Ibsen's footsteps, Shaw wrote *Mrs. Warren's Profession* in 1893. The play focused on prostitution and was banned in London by the Lord Chamberlain.

A steady stream of plays followed in a career that spanned almost sixty years, most notably *Caesar and Cleopatra* (1901), *Man and Superman* (1904), *Major Barbara* (1907), *Heartbreak House* (1917), and *Saint Joan* (1923). In 1925, Shaw was awarded the Nobel Prize for Literature, which he at first refused, but finally accepted after he found out that he could donate the money that accompanied the prize to a fund popularizing Scandinavian literature. Shaw died at the age of ninety-four on November 2, 1950, after succumbing to injuries sustained from falling off a ladder while pruning an apple tree.

All of Shaw's plays reflect his zeal for political, social, and economic reform. His goal was to shock audiences out of their complacency and their hypocrisy. Unlike Oscar Wilde's wit, which was an end unto itself, Shaw's comedy and humor were used to entertain the audience, and to overturn people's preconceived, middle-brow expectations. He wrote, "I must warn my readers that my attacks are directed against themselves not against my stage figures." At the core of his beliefs was what he called the Life Force, a sort of immanent Holy Spirit. Shaw was convinced that the human race, guided by the Life Force, was moving toward a self-willed evolution to improve and perfect humankind and the world. With an end to educate his audience toward greater awareness, his plays preached, among other things, socialism, the abolition of prisons, women's equality, and the stupidity of war. Shaw brought serious themes and issues back to English drama, and he remains one of the great playwrights of the twentieth century.

Pygmalion, written in 1913, is probably Shaw's most popular play. The story of Professor Higgins, a speech teacher, and the transformation he works upon his student Eliza Doolittle, a Cockney flowergirl, was immortalized in *My Fair Lady*, the musical version of the play by Lerner and Loewe. The original comedy is a penetrating and amusing investigation into the correlation between accent and social class in England.

PYGMALION

A ROMANCE IN FIVE ACTS

BY GEORGE BERNARD SHAW

Act I

Covent Garden at 11.15 p.m. Torrents of heavy summer rain. Cab whistles blowing frantically in all directions. Pedestrians running for shelter into the market and under the portico of St Paul's Church, where there are already several people, among them a lady and her daughter in evening dress. They are all peering out gloomily at the rain, except one man with his back turned to the rest, who seems wholly preoccupied with a notebook in which he is writing busily.

The church clock strikes the first quarter.

THE DAUGHTER (*in the space between the central pillars, close to the one on her left*):
> I'm getting chilled to the bone. What can Freddy be doing all this time? He's been gone twenty minutes.

THE MOTHER (*on her daughter's right*):
> Not so long. But he ought to have got us a cab by this.

A BYSTANDER (*on the lady's right*):
> He won't get no cab not until half-past eleven, missus, when they come back after dropping their theatre fares.

THE MOTHER:
> But we must have a cab. We can't stand here until half-past eleven. It's too bad.

THE BYSTANDER:
> Well, it ain't my fault, missus.

THE DAUGHTER:
> If Freddy had a bit of gumption, he would have got one at the theatre door.

THE MOTHER:
> What could he have done, poor boy?

THE DAUGHTER:
> Other people got cabs. Why couldn't he?

Freddy *rushes in out of the rain from the Southampton Street side, and comes between them closing a dripping umbrella. He is a young man of twenty, in evening dress, very wet round the ankles.*

THE DAUGHTER:

Well, haven't you got a cab?

FREDDY:

There's not one to be had for love or money.

THE MOTHER:

Oh, Freddy, there must be one. You can't have tried.

THE DAUGHTER:

It's too tiresome. Do you expect us to go and get one ourselves?

FREDDY:

I tell you they're all engaged. The rain was so sudden: nobody
was prepared; and everybody had to take a cab. I've been to
Charing Cross one way and nearly to Ludgate Circus the
other; and they were all engaged.

THE MOTHER:

Did you try Trafalgar Square?

FREDDY:

There wasn't one at Trafalgar Square.

THE DAUGHTER:

Did you try?

FREDDY:

I tried as far as Charing Cross Station. Did you expect me to
walk to Hammersmith?

THE DAUGHTER:

You haven't tried at all.

THE MOTHER:

You really are very helpless, Freddy. Go again; and don't come
back until you have found a cab.

FREDDY:

I shall simply get soaked for nothing.

THE DAUGHTER:

And what about us? Are we to stay here all night in this
draught, with next to nothing on? You selfish pig—

FREDDY:

Oh, very well: I'll go, I'll go. (*He opens his umbrella and dashes
off Strandwards, but comes into collision with a flower girl, who is
hurrying in for shelter, knocking her basket out of her hands. A
blinding flash of lightning, followed instantly by a rattling peal of
thunder, orchestrates the incident*).

THE FLOWER GIRL:

Nah then, Freddy: look wh' y' gowin, deah.

FREDDY:

Sorry (*he rushes off*).

THE FLOWER GIRL (*picking up her scattered flowers and replacing them in the basket*):

There's menners f' yer! Te-oo banches o voylets trod into the mad. (*She sits down on the plinth of the column, sorting her flowers, on the lady's right. She is not at all an attractive person. She is perhaps eighteen, perhaps twenty, hardly older. She wears a little sailor hat of black straw that has long been exposed to the dust and soot of London and has seldom if ever been brushed. Her hair needs washing rather badly: its mousy color can hardly be natural. She wears a shoddy black coat that reaches nearly to her knees and is shaped to her waist. She has a brown skirt with a coarse apron. Her boots are much the worse for wear. She is no doubt as clean as she can afford to be; but compared to the ladies she is very dirty. Her features are no worse than theirs; but their condition leaves something to be desired; and she needs the services of a dentist*).

THE MOTHER:

How do you know that my son's name is Freddy, pray?

THE FLOWER GIRL:

Ow, eez ye-ooa san, is e? Wal, fewd dan y' de-ooty bawmz a mather should, eed now bettern to spawl a pore gel's flahrzn than ran awy athaht pyin. Will ye-oo py me f'them? (*Here, with apologies, this desperate attempt to represent her dialect without a phonetic alphabet must be abandoned as unintelligible outside London*).

THE DAUGHTER:

Do nothing of the sort, mother. The idea!

THE MOTHER:

Please allow me, Clara. Have you any pennies?

THE DAUGHTER:

No. I've nothing smaller than sixpence.

THE FLOWER GIRL (*hopefully*):

I can give you change for a tanner, kind lady.

THE MOTHER (*to* Clara):

Give it to me. (Clara *parts reluctantly*). Now (*to the girl*) this is for your flowers.

THE FLOWER GIRL:

Thank you kindly, lady.

THE DAUGHTER:

Make her give you the change. These things are only a penny a bunch.

THE MOTHER:

Do hold your tongue, Clara. (*To the girl*) You can keep the change.

THE FLOWER GIRL:

Oh, thank you, lady.

THE MOTHER:

Now tell me how you know that young gentleman's name.

THE FLOWER GIRL:

I didn't.

THE MOTHER:

I heard you call him by it. Don't try to deceive me.

THE FLOWER GIRL (*protesting*):

Who's trying to deceive you? I called him Freddy or Charlie same as you might yourself if you was talking to a stranger and wished to be pleasant. (*She sits down beside her basket*).

THE DAUGHTER:

Sixpence thrown away! Really, mamma, you might have spared Freddy that. (*She retreats in disgust behind the pillar*).

An elderly gentleman of the amiable military type rushes into the shelter, and closes a dripping umbrella. He is in the same plight as Freddy, *very wet about the ankles. He is in evening dress, with a light overcoat. He takes the place left vacant by* The Daughter's *retirement.*

THE GENTLEMAN:

Phew!

THE MOTHER (*to* The Gentleman):

Oh, sir, is there any sign of its stopping?

THE GENTLEMAN:

I'm afraid not. It started worse than ever about two minutes ago (*he goes to the plinth beside* The Flower Girl; *puts up his foot on it; and stoops to turn down his trouser ends*).

THE MOTHER:

Oh dear! (*She retires sadly and joins her daughter*).

THE FLOWER GIRL (*taking advantage of the military gentleman's proximity to establish friendly relations with him*):

If it's worse, it's a sign it's nearly over. So cheer up, Captain; and buy a flower off a poor girl.

THE GENTLEMAN:

I'm sorry. I haven't any change.

THE FLOWER GIRL:

I can give you change, Captain.

THE GENTLEMAN:

For a sovereign? I've nothing less.

THE FLOWER GIRL:

Garn! Oh do buy a flower off me, Captain. I can change half-a-crown. Take this for tuppence.

THE GENTLEMAN:

Now don't be troublesome: there's a good girl. (*Trying his pockets*) I really haven't any change—Stop: here's three hapence, if that's any use to you (*he retreats to the other pillar*).

THE FLOWER GIRL (*disappointed, but thinking three half-pence better than nothing*):

Thank you, sir.

THE BYSTANDER (*to the girl*):

You be careful: give him a flower for it. There's a bloke here behind taking down every blessed word you're saying. (*All turn to the man who is taking notes*).

THE FLOWER GIRL (*springing up terrified*):

I ain't done nothing wrong by speaking to the gentleman. I've a right to sell flowers if I keep off the kerb. (*Hysterically*) I'm a respectable girl: so help me, I never spoke to him except to ask him to buy a flower off me. (*General hubbub, mostly sympathetic to* The Flower Girl, *but deprecating her excessive sensibility. Cries of* Don't start hollerin'. Who's hurting you? Nobody's going to touch you. What's the good of fussing? Steady on. Easy easy, etc., *come from the elderly staid spectators, who pat her comfortingly. Less patient ones bid her shut her head, or ask her roughly what is wrong with her. A remoter group, not knowing what the matter is, crowd in and increase the noise with question and answer:* What's the row? What she do? Where is he? A tec taking her down. What! him? Yes: him over there: Took money off the gentleman, etc. The Flower Girl, *distraught and mobbed, breaks through them to* The Gentleman, *crying wildly*) Oh, sir, don't let him charge me. You dunno what it means to me. They'll take away my character and drive me on the streets for speaking to gentlemen. They—

THE NOTE TAKER (*coming forward on her right, the rest crowding after him*):

There, there, there, there! who's hurting you, you silly girl? What do you take me for?

THE BYSTANDER:

It's all right: he's a gentleman: look at his boots. (*Explaining to* The Note Taker) She thought you was a copper's nark, sir.

THE NOTE TAKER (*with quick interest*):

What's a copper's nark?

THE BYSTANDER (*inapt at definition*):

It's a—well, it's a copper's nark, as you might say. What else would you call it? A sort of informer.

THE FLOWER GIRL (*still hysterical*):

I take my Bible oath I never said a word—

THE NOTE TAKER (*overbearing but good-humored*):

Oh, shut up, shut up. Do I look like a policeman?

THE FLOWER GIRL (*far from reassured*):

Then what did you take down my words for? How do I know whether you took me down right? You just show me what you've wrote about me. (The Note Taker *opens his book and holds it steadily under her nose, though the pressure of the mob trying to read it over his shoulders would upset a weaker man*). What's that? That ain't proper writing. I can't read that.

THE NOTE TAKER:

I can. (*Reads, reproducing her pronunciation exactly*) "Cheer ap, Keptin; n' baw ya flahr orf a pore gel."

THE FLOWER GIRL (*much distressed*):

It's because I called him Captain. I meant no harm. (*To* The Gentleman) Oh, sir, don't let him lay a charge agen me for a word like that. You—

THE GENTLEMAN:

Charge! I make no charge. (*To* The Note Taker) Really, sir, if you are a detective, you need not begin protecting me against molestation by young women until I ask you. Anybody could see that the girl meant no harm.

THE BYSTANDERS GENERALLY (*demonstrating against police espionage*):

Course they could. What business is it of yours? You mind your own affairs. He wants promotion, he does. Taking down people's words! Girl never said a word to him. What harm if she did? Nice thing a girl can't shelter from the rain without being insulted, etc., etc., etc. (*She is conducted by the more sympathetic demonstrators back to her plinth, where she resumes her seat and struggles with her emotion*).

THE BYSTANDER:

He ain't a tec. He's a blooming busybody: that's what he is. I tell you, look at his boots.

THE NOTE TAKER (*turning on him genially*):

And how are all your people down at Selsey?

THE BYSTANDER (*suspiciously*):

Who told you my people come from Selsey?

THE NOTE TAKER:

Never you mind. They did. (*To the girl*) How do you come to be up so far east? You were born in Lisson Grove.

THE FLOWER GIRL (*appalled*):

Oh, what harm is there in my leaving Lisson Grove? It wasn't fit for a pig to live in; and I had to pay four-and-six a week. (*In tears*) Oh, boo—hoo—oo—

THE NOTE TAKER:

Live where you like; but stop that noise.

THE GENTLEMAN (*to the girl*):

Come, come! he can't touch you: you have a right to live where you please.

A SARCASTIC BYSTANDER (*thrusting himself between* The Note Taker *and* The Gentleman):

Park Lane, for instance. I'd like to go into the Housing Question with you, I would.

THE FLOWER GIRL (*subsiding into a brooding melancholy over her basket, and talking very low-spiritedly to herself*):

I'm a good girl, I am.

THE SARCASTIC BYSTANDER (*not attending to her*):

Do you know where *I* come from?

THE NOTE TAKER (*promptly*):

Hoxton.

Titterings. Popular interest in The Note Taker's *performance increases.*

THE SARCASTIC ONE (*amazed*):

Well, who said I didn't? Bly me! You know everything, you do.

THE FLOWER GIRL (*still nursing her sense of injury*):

Ain't no call to meddle with me, he ain't.

THE BYSTANDER (*to her*):

Of course he ain't. Don't you stand it from him. (*To* The Note Taker) See here: what call have you to know about people what never offered to meddle with you? Where's your warrant?

SEVERAL BYSTANDERS (*encouraged by this seeming point of law*):

Yes: where's your warrant?

THE FLOWER GIRL:

Let him say what he likes. I don't want to have no truck with him.

THE BYSTANDER:

You take us for dirt under your feet, don't you? Catch you taking liberties with a gentleman!

THE SARCASTIC BYSTANDER:

Yes: tell him where he come from if you want to go fortune-telling.

THE NOTE TAKER:

Cheltenham, Harrow, Cambridge, and India.

THE GENTLEMAN:

Quite right. (*Great laughter. Reaction in* The Note Taker's *favor. Exclamations of* He knows all about it. Told him proper. Hear him tell the toff where he come from? etc.). May I ask, sir, do you do this for your living at a music hall?

THE NOTE TAKER:

I've thought of that. Perhaps I shall some day.

The rain has stopped; and the persons on the outside of the crowd begin to drop off.

THE FLOWER GIRL (*resenting the reaction*):

He's no gentleman, he ain't, to interfere with a poor girl.

THE DAUGHTER (*out of patience, pushing her way rudely to the front and displacing* The Gentleman, *who politely retires to the other side of the pillar*):

What on earth is Freddy doing? I shall get pneumonia if I stay in this draught any longer.

THE NOTE TAKER (*to himself, hastily making a note of her pronunciation of "monia"*):

Earlscourt.

THE DAUGHTER (*violently*):

Will you please keep your impertinent remarks to yourself.

THE NOTE TAKER:

Did I say that out loud? I didn't mean to. I beg your pardon. Your mother's Epsom, unmistakeably.

THE MOTHER (*advancing between her daughter and* The Note Taker):

How very curious! I was brought up in Largelady Park, near Epsom.

THE NOTE TAKER (*uproariously amused*):

Ha! ha! What a devil of a name! Excuse me. (*To* The Daughter) You want a cab, do you?

THE DAUGHTER:

Don't dare speak to me.

THE MOTHER:

Oh please, please, Clara. (*Her daughter repudiates her with an angry shrug and retires haughtily*). We should be so grateful to you, sir, if you found us a cab. (The Note Taker *produces a whistle*). Oh, thank you. (*She joins her daughter*).

The Note Taker *blows a piercing blast.*

THE SARCASTIC BYSTANDER:

There! I knowed he was a plain-clothes copper.

THE BYSTANDER:

That ain't a police whistle: that's a sporting whistle.

THE FLOWER GIRL (*still preoccupied with her wounded feelings*):

    He's no right to take away my character. My character is the same to me as any lady's.

THE NOTE TAKER:

    I don't know whether you've noticed it; but the rain stopped about two minutes ago.

THE BYSTANDER:

    So it has. Why didn't you say so before? and us losing our time listening to your silliness! (*He walks off towards the Strand*).

THE SARCASTIC BYSTANDER:

    I can tell where you come from. You come from Anwell. Go back there.

THE NOTE TAKER (*helpfully*):

    *H*anwell.

THE SARCASTIC BYSTANDER (*affecting great distinction of speech*):

    Thenk you, teacher. Haw haw! So long (*he touches his hat with mock respect and strolls off*).

THE FLOWER GIRL:

    Frightening people like that! How would he like it himself?

THE MOTHER:

    It's quite fine now, Clara. We can walk to a motor bus. Come. (*She gathers her skirts above her ankles and hurries off towards the Strand*).

THE DAUGHTER:

    But the cab—(*her mother is out of hearing*). Oh, how tiresome! (*She follows angrily*).

All the rest have gone except The Note Taker, The Gentleman, *and* The Flower Girl, *who sits arranging her basket and still pitying herself in murmurs.*

THE FLOWER GIRL:

    Poor girl! Hard enough for her to live without being worrited and chivied.

THE GENTLEMAN (*returning to his former place on* The Note Taker's *left*):

    How do you do it, if I may ask?

THE NOTE TAKER:

    Simply phonetics. The science of speech. That's my profession: also my hobby. Happy is the man who can make a living by his hobby! You can spot an Irishman or a Yorkshireman by his brogue. *I* can place any man within six miles. I can place him within two miles in London. Sometimes within two streets.

THE FLOWER GIRL:

Ought to be ashamed of himself, unmanly coward!

THE GENTLEMAN:

But is there a living in that?

THE NOTE TAKER:

Oh yes. Quite a fat one. This is an age of upstarts. Men begin in Kentish Town with £80 a year, and end in Park Lane with a hundred thousand. They want to drop Kentish Town; but they give themselves away every time they open their mouths. Now I can teach them—

THE FLOWER GIRL:

Let him mind his own business and leave a poor girl—

THE NOTE TAKER (*explosively*):

Woman: cease this detestable boohooing instantly; or else seek the shelter of some other place of worship.

THE FLOWER GIRL (*with feeble defiance*):

I've a right to be here if I like, same as you.

THE NOTE TAKER:

A woman who utters such depressing and disgusting sounds has no right to be anywhere—no right to live. Remember that you are a human being with a soul and the divine gift of artic- ulate speech: that your native language is the language of Shakespeare and Milton and The Bible: and don't sit there crooning like a bilious pigeon.

THE FLOWER GIRL (*quite overwhelmed, looking up at him in mingled wonder and deprecation without daring to raise her head*):

Ah-ah-ah-ow-ow-ow-oo!

THE NOTE TAKER (*whipping out his book*):

Heavens! what a sound! (*He writes; then holds out the book and reads, reproducing her vowels exactly*) Ah-ah-ah-ow-ow-ow-oo!

THE FLOWER GIRL (*tickled by the performance, and laughing in spite of herself*):

Garn!

THE NOTE TAKER:

You see this creature with her kerbstone English: the English that will keep her in the gutter to the end of her days. Well, sir, in three months I could pass that girl off as a duchess at an ambassador's garden party. I could even get her a place as lady's maid or shop assistant, which requires better English. That's the sort of thing I do for commercial millionaires. And on the profits of it I do genuine scientific work in phonetics, and a lit- tle as a poet on Miltonic lines.

THE GENTLEMAN:

I am myself a student of Indian dialects; and—

THE NOTE TAKER (*eagerly*):

> Are you? Do you know Colonel Pickering, the author of *Spoken Sanscrit*?

THE GENTLEMAN:

> I am Colonel Pickering. Who are you?

THE NOTE TAKER:

> Henry Higgins, author of *Higgins's Universal Alphabet*.

PICKERING (*with enthusiasm*):

> I came from India to meet you.

HIGGINS:

> I was going to India to meet you.

PICKERING:

> Where do you live?

HIGGINS:

> 27A Wimpole Street. Come and see me tomorrow.

PICKERING:

> I'm at the Carlton. Come with me now and let's have a jaw over some supper.

HIGGINS:

> Right you are.

THE FLOWER GIRL (*to* Pickering, *as he passes her*):

> Buy a flower, kind gentleman. I'm short for my lodging.

PICKERING:

> I really haven't any change. I'm sorry (*he gets away*).

HIGGINS (*shocked at the girl's mendacity*):

> Liar. You said you could change half-a-crown.

THE FLOWER GIRL (*rising in desperation*):

> You ought to be stuffed with nails, you ought. (*Flinging the basket at his feet*) Take the whole blooming basket for sixpence.

The church clock strikes the second quarter.

HIGGINS (*hearing in it the voice of God, rebuking him for his Pharisaic want of charity to the poor girl*):

> A reminder. (*He raises his hat solemnly; then throws a handful of money into the basket and follows* Pickering).

THE FLOWER GIRL (*picking up a half-crown*):

> Ah-ow-ooh! (*Picking up a couple of florins*) Aaah-ow-ooh! (*Picking up several coins*) Aaaaaah-ow-ooh! (*Picking up a half-sovereign*) Aaaaaaaaaaaah-ow-ooh!!!

FREDDY (*springing out of a taxicab*):

> Got one at last. Hallo! (*To the girl*) Where are the two ladies that were here?

THE FLOWER GIRL:

They walked to the bus when the rain stopped.

FREDDY:

And left me with a cab on my hands! Damnation!

THE FLOWER GIRL (*with grandeur*):

Never mind, young man. I'm going home in a taxi. (*She sails off to the cab. The driver puts his hand behind him and holds the door firmly shut against her. Quite understanding his mistrust, she shows him her handful of money*). Eightpence ain't no object to me, Charlie. (*He grins and opens the door*). Angel Court, Drury Lane, round the corner of Micklejohn's oil shop. Let's see how fast you can make her hop it. (*She gets in and pulls the door to with a slam as the taxicab starts*).

FREDDY:

Well, I'm dashed!

Act II

Next day at 11 a.m. Higgins's laboratory in Wimpole Street. It is a room on the first floor, looking on the street, and was meant for the drawing room. The double doors are in the middle of the back wall; and persons entering find in the corner to their right two tall file cabinets at right angles to one another against the walls. In this corner stands a flat writing-table, on which are a phonograph, a laryngoscope, a row of tiny organ pipes with bellows, a set of lamp chimneys for singing flames with burners attached to a gas plug in the wall by an indiarubber tube, several tuning-forks of different sizes, a life-size image of half a human head, showing in section the vocal organs, and a box containing a supply of wax cylinders for the phonograph.

Further down the room, on the same side, is a fireplace, with a comfortable leather-covered easy-chair at the side of the hearth nearest the door, and a coal-scuttle. There is a clock on the mantelpiece. Between the fireplace and the phonograph table is a stand for newspapers.

On the other side of the central door, to the left of the visitor, is a cabinet of shallow drawers. On it is a telephone and the telephone directory. The corner beyond, and most of the side wall, is occupied by a grand piano, with the keyboard at the end furthest from the door, and a bench for the player extending the full length of the keyboard. On the piano is a dessert dish heaped with fruit and sweets, mostly chocolates.

The middle of the room is clear. Besides the easy-chair, the piano bench, and two chairs at the phonograph table, there is one stray chair. It stands near the fireplace. On the walls, engravings: mostly Piranesis and mezzotint portraits. No paintings.

Pickering *is seated at the table, putting down some cards and a tuning-fork which he has been using.* Higgins *is standing up near him, closing two or three file drawers which are hanging out. He appears in the morning light as a robust, vital, appetizing sort of man of forty or thereabouts, dressed in a professional-looking black frock-coat with a white linen collar and black silk tie. He is of the energetic, scientific type, heartily, even violently interested in everything that can be studied as a scientific subject, and careless about himself and other people, including their feelings. He is, in fact, but for his years and size, rather like a very impetuous baby "taking notice" eagerly and loudly, and requiring almost as much watching to keep him out of unintended mischief. His manner varies from genial bullying when he is in a good humor to stormy petulance when anything goes wrong; but he is so entirely frank and void of malice that he remains likeable even in his least reasonable moments.*

HIGGINS (*as he shuts the last drawer*):
    Well, I think that's the whole show.
PICKERING:
    It's really amazing. I haven't taken half of it in, you know.
HIGGINS:
    Would you like to go over any of it again?
PICKERING (*rising and coming to the fireplace, where he plants himself with his back to the fire*):
    No, thank you; not now. I'm quite done up for this morning.
HIGGINS (*following him, and standing beside him on his left*):
    Tired of listening to sounds?
PICKERING:
    Yes. It's a fearful strain. I rather fancied myself because I can pronounce twenty-four distinct vowel sounds; but your hundred and thirty beat me. I can't hear a bit of difference between most of them.
HIGGINS (*chuckling, and going over to the piano to eat sweets*):
    Oh, that comes with practice. You hear no difference at first; but you keep on listening, and presently you find they're all as different as A from B. (Mrs Pearce *looks in: she is* Higgins's *housekeeper*). What's the matter?
MRS PEARCE (*hesitating, evidently perplexed*):
    A young woman wants to see you sir.
HIGGINS:
    A young woman! What does she want?
MRS PEARCE:
    Well, sir, she says you'll be glad to see her when you know what she's come about. She's quite a common girl, sir. Very common indeed. I should have sent her away, only I thought perhaps

you wanted her to talk into your machines. I hope I've not done wrong; but really you see such queer people sometimes— you'll excuse me, I'm sure, sir—

HIGGINS:

Oh, that's all right, Mrs Pearce. Has she an interesting accent?

MRS PEARCE:

Oh, something dreadful, sir, really. I don't know how you can take an interest in it.

HIGGINS (*to* Pickering):

Lets have her up. Show her up, Mrs Pearce (*he rushes across to his working table and picks out a cylinder to use on the phonograph*).

MRS PEARCE (*only half resigned to it*):

Very well, sir. It's for you to say. (*She goes downstairs*).

HIGGINS:

This is rather a bit of luck. I'll show you how I make records. We'll set her talking; and I'll take it down first in Bell's visible Speech; then in broad Romic; and then we'll get her on the phonograph so that you can turn her on as often as you like with the written transcript before you.

MRS PEARCE (*returning*):

This is the young woman, sir.

The Flower Girl *enters in state. She has a hat with three ostrich feathers, orange, sky-blue, and red. She has a nearly clean apron, and the shoddy coat has been tidied a little. The pathos of this deplorable figure, with its innocent vanity and consequential air, touches* Pickering, *who has already straightened himself in the presence of* Mrs Pearce. *But as to* Higgins, *the only distinction he makes between men and women is that when he is neither bullying nor exclaiming to the heavens against some feather-weight cross, he coaxes women as a child coaxes its nurse when it wants to get anything out of her.*

HIGGINS (*brusquely, recognizing her with unconcealed disappointment, and at once, babylike, making an intolerable grievance of it*):

Why, this is the girl I jotted down last night. She's no use: I've got all the records I want of the Lisson Grove lingo; and I'm not going to waste another cylinder on it. (*To the girl*) Be off with you: I don't want you.

THE FLOWER GIRL:

Don't you be so saucy. You ain't heard what I come for yet. (*To* Mrs Pearce, *who is waiting at the door for further instructions*) Did you tell him I come in a taxi?

MRS PEARCE:

> Nonsense, girl! what do you think a gentleman like Mr Higgins cares what you came in?

THE FLOWER GIRL:

> Oh, we are proud! He ain't above giving lessons, not him: I heard him say so. Well, I ain't come here to ask for any compliment; and if my money's not good enough I can go elsewhere.

HIGGINS:

> Good enough for what?

THE FLOWER GIRL:

> Good enough for ye-oo. Now you know, don't you? I'm come to have lessons, I am. And to pay for em too: make no mistake.

HIGGINS (*stupent*):

> Well!!! (*Recovering his breath with a gasp*) What do you expect me to say to you?

THE FLOWER GIRL:

> Well, if you was a gentleman, you might ask me to sit down, I think. Don't I tell you I'm bringing you business?

HIGGINS:

> Pickering: shall we ask this baggage to sit down, or shall we throw her out of the window?

THE FLOWER GIRL (*running away in terror to the piano, where she turns at bay*):

> Ah-ah-oh-ow-ow-ow-oo! (*Wounded and whimpering*) I won't be called a baggage when I've offered to pay like any lady.

Motionless, the two men stare at her from the other side of the room, amazed.

PICKERING (*gently*):

> What is it you want, my girl?

THE FLOWER GIRL:

> I want to be a lady in a flower shop stead of selling at the corner of Tottenham Court Road. But they won't take me unless I can talk more genteel. He said he could teach me. Well, here I am ready to pay him—not asking any favor—and he treats me as if I was dirt.

MRS PEARCE:

> How can you be such a foolish ignorant girl as to think you could afford to pay Mr Higgins?

THE FLOWER GIRL:

> Why shouldn't I? I know what lessons cost as well as you do; and I'm ready to pay.

HIGGINS:

How much?

THE FLOWER GIRL (*coming back to him, triumphant*):

Now you're talking! I thought you'd come off it when you saw a chance of getting back a bit of what you chucked at me last night. (*Confidentially*) You'd had a drop in, hadn't you?

HIGGINS (*peremptorily*):

Sit down.

THE FLOWER GIRL:

Oh, if you're going to make a compliment of it—

HIGGINS (*thundering at her*):

Sit down.

MRS PEARCE (*severely*):

Sit down, girl. Do as you're told. (*She places the stray chair near the hearthrug between* Higgins *and* Pickering, *and stands behind it waiting for the girl to sit down*).

THE FLOWER GIRL:

Ah-ah-ah-ow-ow-oo! (*She stands, half rebellious, half bewildered*).

PICKERING (*very courteous*):

Won't you sit down?

LIZA (*coyly*):

Don't mind if I do. (*She sits down.* Pickering *returns to the hearthrug*).

HIGGINS:

What's your name?

THE FLOWER GIRL:

Liza Doolittle.

HIGGINS (*declaiming gravely*):

Eliza, Elizabeth, Betsy and Bess,
They went to the woods to get a bird's nes':

PICKERING:

They found a nest with four eggs in it:

HIGGINS:

They took one apiece, and left three in it.

They laugh heartily at their own wit.

LIZA:

Oh, don't be silly.

MRS PEARCE:

You mustn't speak to the gentleman like that.

LIZA:

Well, why won't he speak sensible to me?

HIGGINS:

> Come back to business. How much do you propose to pay me for the lessons?

LIZA:

> Oh, I know what's right. A lady friend of mine gets French lessons for eighteenpence an hour from a real French gentleman. Well, you wouldn't have the face to ask me the same for teaching me my own language as you would for French; so I won't give more than a shilling. Take it or leave it.

HIGGINS (*walking up and down the room, rattling his keys and his cash in his pockets*):

> You know, Pickering, if you consider a shilling, not as a simple shilling, but as a percentage of this girl's income, it works out as fully equivalent to sixty or seventy guineas from a millionaire.

PICKERING:

> How so?

HIGGINS:

> Figure it out. A millionaire has about £150 a day. She earns about half-a-crown.

LIZA (*haughtily*):

> Who told you I only—

HIGGINS (*continuing*):

> She offers me two-fifths of her day's income for a lesson. Two-fifths of a millionaire's income for a day would be somewhere about £60. It's handsome. By George, it's enormous! it's the biggest offer I ever had.

LIZA (*rising, terrified*):

> Sixty pounds! What are you talking about? I never offered you sixty pounds. Where would I get—

HIGGINS:

> Hold your tongue.

LIZA (*weeping*):

> But I ain't got sixty pounds. Oh—

MRS PEARCE:

> Don't cry, you silly girl. Sit down. Nobody is going to touch your money.

HIGGINS:

> Somebody is going to touch you, with a broomstick, if you don't stop snivelling. Sit down.

LIZA (*obeying slowly*):

> Ah-ah-ah-ow-oo-o! One would think you was my father.

HIGGINS:

If I decide to teach you, I'll be worse than two fathers to you. Here (*he offers her his silk handkerchief*)!

LIZA:

What's this for?

HIGGINS:

To wipe your eyes. To wipe any part of your face that feels moist. Remember: that's your handkerchief; and that's your sleeve. Don't mistake the one for the other if you wish to become a lady in a shop.

Liza, *utterly bewildered, stares helplessly at him.*

MRS PEARCE:

It's no use talking to her like that, Mr Higgins: she doesn't understand you. Besides, you're quite wrong: she doesn't do it that way at all (*she takes the handkerchief*).

LIZA (*snatching it*):

Here! You give me that handkerchief. He give it to me, not to you.

PICKERING (*laughing*):

He did. I think it must be regarded as her property, Mrs Pearce.

MRS PEARCE (*resigning herself*):

Serve you right, Mr Higgins.

PICKERING:

Higgins: I'm interested. What about the ambassador's garden party? I'll say you're the greatest teacher alive if you make that good. I'll bet you all the expenses of the experiment you can't do it. And I'll pay for the lessons.

LIZA:

Oh, you are real good. Thank you, Captain.

HIGGINS (*tempted, looking at her*):

It's almost irresistible. She's so deliciously low—so horribly dirty—

LIZA (*protesting extremely*):

Ah-ah-ah-ah-ow-ow-oo-oo!!! I ain't dirty: I washed my face and hands afore I come, I did.

PICKERING:

You're certainly not going to turn her head with flattery, Higgins.

MRS PEARCE (*uneasy*):

Oh, don't say that, sir: there's more ways than one of turning a girl's head; and nobody can do it better than Mr Higgins, though he may not always mean it. I do hope, sir, you won't encourage him to do anything foolish.

HIGGINS (*becoming excited as the idea grows on him*):

What is life but a series of inspired follies? The difficulty is to find them to do. Never lose a chance: it doesn't come every day. I shall make a duchess of this draggletailed guttersnipe.

LIZA (*strongly deprecating this view of her*):

Ah-ah-ah-ow-ow-oo!

HIGGINS (*carried away*):

Yes: in six months—in three if she has a good ear and a quick tongue—I'll take her anywhere and pass her off as anything. We'll start today: now! this moment! Take her away and clean her, Mrs Pearce. Monkey Brand, if it won't come off any other way. Is there a good fire in the kitchen?

MRS PEARCE (*protesting*):

Yes; but—

HIGGINS (*storming on*):

Take all her clothes off and burn them. Ring up Whiteley or somebody for new ones. Wrap her up in brown paper till they come.

LIZA:

You're no gentleman, you're not, to talk of such things. I'm a good girl, I am; and I know what the like of you are, I do.

HIGGINS:

We want none of your Lisson Grove prudery here, young woman. You've got to learn to behave like a duchess. Take her away, Mrs Pearce. If she gives you any trouble, wallop her.

LIZA (*springing up and running between* Pickering *and* Mrs Pearce *for protection*):

No! I'll call the police, I will.

MRS PEARCE:

But I've no place to put her.

HIGGINS:

Put her in the dustbin.

LIZA:

Ah-ah-ah-ow-ow-oo!

PICKERING:

Oh come, Higgins! be reasonable.

MRS PEARCE (*resolutely*):

You must be reasonable, Mr Higgins: really you must. You can't walk over everybody like this.

Higgins, *thus scolded, subsides. The hurricane is succeeded by a zephyr of amiable surprise.*

HIGGINS (*with professional exquisiteness of modulation*):

I walk over everybody! My dear Mrs Pearce, my dear Pickering, I never had the slightest intention of walking over anyone. All I propose is that we should be kind to this poor girl. We must help her to prepare and fit herself for her new station in life. If I did not express myself clearly it was because I did not wish to hurt her delicacy, or yours.

Liza, *reassured, steals back to her chair.*

MRS PEARCE (*to* Pickering):

Well, did you ever hear anything like that, sir?

PICKERING (*laughing heartily*):

Never, Mrs Pearce: never.

HIGGINS (*patiently*):

What's the matter?

MRS PEARCE:

Well, the matter is, sir, that you can't take a girl up like that as if you were picking up a pebble on the beach.

HIGGINS:

Why not?

MRS PEARCE:

Why not! But you don't know anything about her. What about her parents? She may be married.

LIZA:

Garn!

HIGGINS:

There! As the girl very properly says, Garn! Married indeed! Don't you know that a woman of that class looks a worn out drudge of fifty a year after she's married?

LIZA:

Who'od marry me?

HIGGINS (*suddenly resorting to the most thrillingly beautiful low tones in his best elocutionary style*):

By George, Eliza, the streets will be strewn with the bodies of men shooting themselves for your sake before I've done with you.

MRS PEARCE:

Nonsense, sir. You mustn't talk like that to her.

LIZA (*rising and squaring herself determinedly*):

I'm going away. He's off his chump, he is. I don't want no balmies teaching me.

HIGGINS (*wounded in his tenderest point by her insensibility to his elocution*):

Oh, indeed! I'm mad, am I? Very well, Mrs Pearce: you needn't order the new clothes for her. Throw her out.

LIZA (*whimpering*):

Nah-ow. You got no right to touch me.

MRS PEARCE:

You see now what comes of being saucy. (*Indicating the door*) This way, please.

LIZA (*almost in tears*):

I didn't want no clothes. I wouldn't have taken them (*she throws away the handkerchief*). I can buy my own clothes.

HIGGINS (*deftly retrieving the handkerchief and intercepting her on her reluctant way to the door*):

You're an ungrateful wicked girl. This is my return for offering to take you out of the gutter and dress you beautifully and make a lady of you.

MRS PEARCE:

Stop, Mr Higgins. I won't allow it. It's you that are wicked. Go home to your parents, girl; and tell them to take better care of you.

LIZA:

I ain't got no parents. They told me I was big enough to earn my own living and turned me out.

MRS PEARCE:

Where's your mother?

LIZA:

I ain't got no mother. Her that turned me out was my sixth stepmother. But I done without them. And I'm a good girl, I am.

HIGGINS:

Very well, then, what on earth is all this fuss about? The girl doesn't belong to anybody—is no use to anybody but me. (*He goes to* Mrs Pearce *and begins coaxing*). You can adopt her, Mrs Pearce: I'm sure a daughter would be a great amusement to you. Now don't make any more fuss. Take her downstairs; and—

MRS PEARCE:

But what's to become of her? Is she to be paid anything? Do be sensible, sir.

HIGGINS:

Oh, pay her whatever is necessary: put it down in the house-keeping book. (*Impatiently*) What on earth will she want with money? She'll have her food and her clothes. She'll only drink if you give her money.

LIZA (*turning on him*):

Oh you are a brute. It's a lie: nobody ever saw the sign of liquor on me. (*She goes back to her chair and plants herself there defiantly*).

PICKERING (*in good-humored remonstrance*):

Does it occur to you, Higgins, that the girl has some feelings?

HIGGINS (*looking critically at her*):

Oh no, I don't think so. Not any feelings that we need bother about. (*Cheerily*) Have you, Eliza?

LIZA:

I got my feelings same as anyone else.

HIGGINS (*to Pickering, reflectively*):

You see the difficulty?

PICKERING:

Eh? What difficulty?

HIGGINS:

To get her to talk grammar. The mere pronunciation is easy enough.

LIZA:

I don't want to talk grammar. I want to talk like a lady.

MRS PEARCE:

Will you please keep to the point, Mr Higgins? I want to know on what terms the girl is to be here. Is she to have any wages? And what is to become of her when you've finished your teaching? You must look ahead a little.

HIGGINS (*impatiently*):

What's to become of her if I leave her in the gutter? Tell me that, Mrs Pearce.

MRS PEARCE:

That's her own business, not yours, Mr Higgins.

HIGGINS:

Well, when I've done with her, we can throw her back into the gutter; and then it will be her own business again; so that's all right.

LIZA:

Oh, you've no feeling heart in you: you don't care for nothing but yourself (*she rises and takes the floor resolutely*). Here! I've had enough of this. I'm going (*making for the door*). You ought to be ashamed of yourself, you ought.

HIGGINS (*snatching a chocolate cream from the piano, his eyes suddenly beginning to twinkle with mischief*):

Have some chocolates, Eliza.

LIZA (*halting, tempted*):

How do I know what might be in them? I've heard of girls being drugged by the like of you.

Higgins *whips out his penknife; cuts a chocolate in two; puts one half into his mouth and bolts it; and offers her the other half.*

HIGGINS:

Pledge of good faith, Eliza. I eat one half: you eat the other. (Liza *opens her mouth to retort: he pops the half chocolate into it*). You shall have boxes of them, barrels of them, every day. You shall live on them. Eh?

LIZA (*who has disposed of the chocolate after being nearly choked by it*):

I wouldn't have ate it, only I'm too ladylike to take it out of my mouth.

HIGGINS:

Listen, Eliza. I think you said you came in a taxi.

LIZA:

Well, what if I did? I've as good a right to take a taxi as anyone else.

HIGGINS:

You have, Eliza; and in future you shall have as many taxis as you want. You shall go up and down and round the town in a taxi every day. Think of that, Eliza.

MRS PEARCE:

Mr Higgins: you're tempting the girl. It's not right. She should think of the future.

HIGGINS:

At her age! Nonsense! Time enough to think of the future when you haven't any future to think of. No, Eliza: do as this lady does: think of other people's futures; but never think of your own. Think of chocolates, and taxis, and gold, and diamonds.

LIZA:

No: I don't want no gold and no diamonds. I'm a good girl, I am. (*She sits down again, with an attempt at dignity*).

HIGGINS:

You shall remain so, Eliza, under the care of Mrs Pearce. And you shall marry an officer in the Guards, with a beautiful moustache: the son of a marquis, who will disinherit him for marrying you, but will relent when he sees your beauty and goodness—

PICKERING:

Excuse me, Higgins; but I really must interfere. Mrs Pearce is quite right. If this girl is to put herself in your hands for six months for an experiment in teaching, she must understand thoroughly what she's doing.

HIGGINS:

How can she? She's incapable of understanding anything. Besides, do any of us understand what we are doing? If we did, would we ever do it?

PICKERING:

Very clever, Higgins; but not sound sense. (*To* Eliza) Miss Doolittle—

LIZA (*overwhelmed*):

Ah-ah-ow-oo!

HIGGINS:

There! That's all you'll get out of Eliza. Ah-ah-ow-oo! No use explaining. As a military man you ought to know that. Give her her orders: that's what she wants. Eliza: you are to live here for the next six months, learning how to speak beautifully, like a lady in a florist's shop. If you're good and do whatever you're told, you shall sleep in a proper bedroom, and have lots to eat, and money to buy chocolates and take rides in taxis. If you're naughty and idle you will sleep in the back kitchen among the black beetles, and be walloped by Mrs Pearce with a broom-stick. At the end of six months you shall go to Buckingham Palace in a carriage, beautifully dressed. If the King finds out you're not a lady, you will be taken by the police to the Tower of London, where your head will be cut off as a warning to other presumptuous flower girls. If you are not found out, you shall have a present of seven-and-sixpence to start life with as a lady in a shop. If you refuse this offer you will be a most ungrateful and wicked girl; and the angels will weep for you. (*To* Pickering) Now are you satisfied, Pickering? (*To* Mrs Pearce) Can I put it more plainly and fairly, Mrs Pearce?

MRS PEARCE (*patiently*):

I think you'd better let me speak to the girl properly in private. I don't know that I can take charge of her or consent to the arrangement at all. Of course I know you don't mean her any harm; but when you get what you call interested in people's accents, you never think or care what may happen to them or you. Come with me, Eliza.

HIGGINS:

That's all right. Thank you, Mrs Pearce. Bundle her off to the bath-room.

LIZA (*rising reluctantly and suspiciously*):

You're a great bully, you are. I won't stay here if I don't like. I won't let nobody wallop me. I never asked to go to Buck'n'am

Palace, I didn't. I was never in trouble with the police, not me. I'm a good girl—

MRS PEARCE:

Don't answer back, girl. You don't understand the gentleman. Come with me. (*She leads the way to the door, and holds it open for Eliza*).

LIZA (*as she goes out*):

Well, what I say is right. I won't go near the King, not if I'm going to have my head cut off. If I'd known what I was letting myself in for, I wouldn't have come here. I always been a good girl; and I never offered to say a word to him; and I don't owe him nothing; and I don't care; and I won't be put upon; and I have my feelings the same as anyone else—

Mrs Pearce *shuts the door; and* Eliza's *plaints are no longer audible.* Pickering *comes from the hearth to the chair and sits astride it with his arms on the back.*

PICKERING:

Excuse the straight question, Higgins. Are you a man of good character where women are concerned?

HIGGINS (*moodily*):

Have you ever met a man of good character where women are concerned?

PICKERING:

Yes: very frequently.

HIGGINS (*dogmatically, lifting himself on his hands to the level of the piano, and sitting on it with a bounce*):

Well, I haven't. I find that the moment I let a woman make friends with me, she becomes jealous, exacting, suspicious, and a damned nuisance. I find that the moment I let myself make friends with a woman, I become selfish and tyrannical. Women upset everything. When you let them into your life, you find that the woman is driving at one thing and you're driving at another.

PICKERING:

At what, for example?

HIGGINS (*coming off the piano restlessly*):

Oh, Lord knows! I suppose the woman wants to live her own life; and the man wants to live his; and each tries to drag the other on to the wrong track. One wants to go north and the other south; and the result is that both have to go east, though they both hate the east wind. (*He sits down on the bench at the keyboard*). So here I am, a confirmed old bachelor, and likely to remain so.

PICKERING (*rising and standing over him gravely*):

Come, Higgins! You know what I mean. If I'm to be in this business I shall feel responsible for that girl. I hope it's understood that no advantage is to be taken of her position.

HIGGINS:

What! That thing! Sacred, I assure you. (*Rising to explain*) You see, she'll be a pupil; and teaching would be impossible unless pupils were sacred. I've taught scores of American millionairesses how to speak English: the best looking women in the world. I'm seasoned. They might as well be blocks of wood. *I* might as well be a block of wood. It's—

Mrs Pearce *opens the door. She has* Eliza's *hat in her hand.* Pickering *retires to the easy-chair at the hearth and sits down.*

HIGGINS (*eagerly*):

Well, Mrs Pearce: is it all right?

MRS PEARCE (*at the door*):

I just wish to trouble you with a word, if I may, Mr Higgins.

HIGGINS:

Yes, certainly. Come in. (*She comes forward*). Don't burn that, Mrs Pearce. I'll keep it as a curiosity. (*He takes the hat*).

MRS PEARCE:

Handle it carefully, sir, please. I had to promise her not to burn it; but I had better put it in the oven for a while.

HIGGINS (*putting it down hastily on the piano*):

Oh! thank you. Well, what have you to say to me?

PICKERING:

Am I in the way?

MRS PEARCE:

Not at all, sir. Mr Higgins: will you please be very particular what you say before the girl?

HIGGINS (*sternly*):

Of course. I'm always particular about what I say. Why do you say this to me?

MRS PEARCE (*unmoved*):

No, sir: you're not at all particular when you've mislaid anything or when you get a little impatient. Now it doesn't matter before me: I'm used to it. But you really must not swear before the girl.

HIGGINS (*indignantly*):

    I swear! (*Most emphatically*) I never swear. I detest the habit. What the devil do you mean?

MRS PEARCE (*stolidly*):

    That's what I mean, sir. You swear a great deal too much. I don't mind your damning and blasting, and what the devil and where the devil and who the devil—

HIGGINS:

    Mrs Pearce: this language from your lips! Really!

MRS PEARCE (*not to be put off*):

    —but there is a certain word I must ask you not to use. The girl has just used it herself because the bath was too hot. It begins with the same letter as bath. She knows no better: she learnt it at her mother's knee. But she must not hear it from your lips.

HIGGINS (*loftily*):

    I cannot charge myself with having ever uttered it, Mrs Pearce. (*She looks at him steadfastly. He adds, hiding an uneasy conscience with a judicial air*) Except perhaps in a moment of extreme and justifiable excitement.

MRS PEARCE:

    Only this morning, sir, you applied it to your boots, to the butter, and to the brown bread.

HIGGINS:

    Oh, that! Mere alliteration, Mrs Pearce, natural to a poet.

MRS PEARCE:

    Well, sir, whatever you choose to call it, I beg you not to let the girl hear you repeat it.

HIGGINS:

    Oh, very well, very well. Is that all?

MRS PEARCE:

    No, sir. We shall have to be very particular with this girl as to personal cleanliness.

HIGGINS:

    Certainly. Quite right. Most important.

MRS PEARCE:

    I mean not to be slovenly about her dress or untidy in leaving things about.

HIGGINS (*going to her solemnly*):

    Just so. I intended to call your attention to that. (*He passes on to* Pickering, *who is enjoying the conversation immensely*). It is these little things that matter, Pickering. Take care of the pence and the pounds will take care of themselves is as true of personal habits as of money. (*He comes to anchor on the hearthrug, with the air of a man in an unassailable position*).

MRS PEARCE:

Yes, sir. Then might I ask you not to come down to breakfast in your dressing-gown, or at any rate not to use it as a napkin to the extent you do, sir. And if you would be so good as not to eat everything off the same plate, and to remember not to put the porridge saucepan out of your hand on the clean table-cloth, it would be a better example to the girl. You know you nearly choked yourself with a fishbone in the jam only last week.

HIGGINS (*routed from the hearthrug and drifting back to the piano*):

I may do these things sometimes in absence of mind; but surely I don't do them habitually. (*Angrily*) By the way: my dressing-gown smells most damnably of benzine.

MRS PEARCE:

No doubt it does, Mr Higgins. But if you will wipe your fingers—

HIGGINS (*yelling*):

Oh very well, very well: I'll wipe them in my hair in future.

MRS PEARCE:

I hope you're not offended, Mr Higgins.

HIGGINS (*shocked at finding himself thought capable of an unamiable sentiment*):

Not at all, not at all. You're quite right, Mrs Pearce: I shall be particularly careful before the girl. Is that all?

MRS PEARCE:

No, sir. Might she use some of those Japanese dresses you brought from abroad? I really can't put her back into her old things.

HIGGINS:

Certainly. Anything you like. Is that all?

MRS PEARCE:

Thank you, sir. That's all. (*She goes out*).

HIGGINS:

You know, Pickering, that woman has the most extraordinary ideas about me. Here I am, a shy, diffident sort of man. I've never been able to feel really grown-up and tremendous, like other chaps. And yet she's firmly persuaded that I'm an arbitrary overbearing bossing kind of person. I can't account for it.

Mrs Pearce *returns*.

MRS PEARCE:

> If you please, sir, the trouble's beginning already. There's a dustman downstairs, Alfred Doolittle, wants to see you. He says you have his daughter here.

PICKERING (*rising*):

> Phew! I say! (*He retreats to the hearthrug*).

HIGGINS (*promptly*):

> Send the blackguard up.

MRS PEARCE:

> Oh, very well, sir. (*She goes out*).

PICKERING:

> He may not be a blackguard, Higgins.

HIGGINS:

> Nonsense. Of course he's a blackguard.

PICKERING:

> Whether he is or not, I'm afraid we shall have some trouble with him.

HIGGINS (*confidently*):

> Oh no: I think not. If there's any trouble he shall have it with me, not I with him. And we are sure to get something interesting out of him.

PICKERING:

> About the girl?

HIGGINS:

> No. I mean his dialect.

PICKERING:

> Oh!

MRS PEARCE (*at the door*):

> Doolittle, sir. (*She admits* Doolittle *and retires*).

Alfred Doolittle *is an elderly but vigorous dustman, clad in the costume of his profession, including a hat with a back brim covering his neck and shoulders. He has well marked and rather interesting features, and seems equally free from fear and conscience. He has a remarkably expressive voice, the result of a habit of giving vent to his feelings without reserve. His present pose is that of wounded honor and stern resolution.*

DOOLITTLE (*at the door, uncertain which of the two gentlemen is his man*):

> Professor Higgins?

HIGGINS:

> Here. Good morning. Sit down.

DOOLITTLE:

> Morning, Governor. (*He sits down magisterially*) I come about a very serious matter, Governor.

HIGGINS (*to* Pickering):

> Brought up in Hounslow. Mother Welsh, I should think. (Doolittle *opens his mouth, amazed.* Higgins *continues*) What do you want, Doolittle?

DOOLITTLE (*menacingly*):

> I want my daughter: that's what I want. See?

HIGGINS:

> Of course you do. You're her father, aren't you? You don't suppose anyone else wants her, do you? I'm glad to see you have some spark of family feeling left. She's upstairs. Take her away at once.

DOOLITTLE (*rising, fearfully taken aback*):

> What!

HIGGINS:

> Take her away. Do you suppose I'm going to keep your daughter for you?

DOOLITTLE (*remonstrating*):

> Now, now, look here, Governor. Is this reasonable? Is it fairity to take advantage of a man like this? The girl belongs to me. You got her. Where do I come in? (*He sits down again*).

HIGGINS:

> Your daughter had the audacity to come to my house and ask me to teach her how to speak properly so that she could get a place in a flower-shop. This gentleman and my housekeeper have been here all the time. (*Bullying him*) How dare you come here and attempt to blackmail me? You sent her here on purpose.

DOOLITTLE (*protesting*):

> No, Governor.

HIGGINS:

> You must have. How else could you possibly know that she is here?

DOOLITTLE:

> Don't take a man up like that, Governor.

HIGGINS:

> The police shall take you up. This is a plant—a plot to extort money by threats. I shall telephone for the police. (*He goes resolutely to the telephone and opens the directory*).

DOOLITTLE:

> Have I asked you for a brass farthing? I leave it to the gentleman here: have I said a word about money?

HIGGINS (*throwing the book aside and marching down on* Doolittle *with a poser*):

What else did you come for?

DOOLITTLE (*sweetly*):

Well, what would a man come for? Be human, Governor.

HIGGINS (*disarmed*):

Alfred: did you put her up to it?

DOOLITTLE:

So help me, Governor, I never did. I take my Bible oath I ain't seen the girl these two months past.

HIGGINS:

Then how did you know she was here?

DOOLITTLE ("*most musical, most melancholy*"):

I'll tell you, Governor, if you'll only let me get a word in. I'm willing to tell you. I'm wanting to tell you. I'm waiting to tell you.

HIGGINS:

Pickering: this chap has a certain natural gift of rhetoric. Observe the rhythm of his native woodnotes wild. "I'm willing to tell you: I'm wanting to tell you: I'm waiting to tell you." Sentimental rhetoric! that's the Welsh strain in him. It also accounts for his mendacity and dishonesty.

PICKERING:

Oh, please, Higgins: I'm west-country myself. (*To* Doolittle) How did you know the girl was here if you didn't send her?

DOOLITTLE:

It was like this, Governor. The girl took a boy in the taxi to give him a jaunt. Son of her landlady, he is. He hung about on the chance of her giving him another ride home. Well, she sent him back for her luggage when she heard you was willing for her to stop here. I met the boy at the corner of Long Acre and Endell Street.

HIGGINS:

Public house. Yes?

DOOLITTLE:

The poor man's club, Governor: why shouldn't I?

PICKERING:

Do let him tell his story, Higgins.

DOOLITTLE:

He told me what was up. And I ask you, what was my feelings and my duty as a father? I says to the boy, "You bring me the luggage," I says—

PICKERING:

> Why didn't you go for it yourself?

DOOLITTLE:

> Landlady wouldn't have trusted me with it, Governor. She's that kind of woman: you know. I had to give the boy a penny afore he trusted me with it, the little swine. I brought it to her just to oblige you like, and make myself agreeable. That's all.

HIGGINS:

> How much luggage?

DOOLITTLE:

> Musical instrument, Governor. A few pictures, a trifle of jewellery, and a bird-cage. She said she didn't want no clothes. What was I to think from that, Governor? I ask you as a parent what was I to think?

HIGGINS:

> So you came to rescue her from worse than death, eh?

DOOLITTLE (*appreciatively: relieved at being so well understood*):

> Just so, Governor. That's right.

PICKERING:

> But why did you bring her luggage if you intended to take her away?

DOOLITTLE:

> Have I said a word about taking her away? Have I now?

HIGGINS (*determinedly*):

> You're going to take her away, double quick. (*He crosses to the hearth and rings the bell*).

DOOLITTLE (*rising*):

> No, Governor. Don't say that. I'm not the man to stand in my girl's light. Here's a career opening for her, as you might say; and—

Mrs Pearce *opens the door and awaits orders.*

HIGGINS:

> Mrs Pearce: this is Eliza's father. He has come to take her away. Give her to him. (*He goes back to the piano, with an air of washing his hands of the whole affair*).

DOOLITTLE:

> No. This is a misunderstanding. Listen here—

MRS PEARCE:

> He can't take her away, Mr Higgins: how can he? You told me to burn her clothes.

DOOLITTLE:

> That's right. I can't carry the girl through the streets like a blooming monkey, can I? I put it to you.

HIGGINS:

> You have put it to me that you want your daughter. Take your daughter. If she has no clothes go out and buy her some.

DOOLITTLE (*desperate*):

> Where's the clothes she come in? Did I burn them or did your missus here?

MRS PEARCE:

> I am the housekeeper, if you please. I have sent for some clothes for your girl. When they come you can take her away. You can wait in the kitchen. This way, please.

Doolittle, much troubled, accompanies her to the door; then hesitates; finally turns confidentially to Higgins.

DOOLITTLE:

> Listen here, Governor. You and me is men of the world, ain't we?

HIGGINS:

> Oh! Men of the world, are we? You'd better go, Mrs Pearce.

MRS PEARCE:

> I think so, indeed, sir. (*She goes, with dignity*).

PICKERING:

> The floor is yours, Mr Doolittle.

DOOLITTLE (*to* Pickering):

> I thank you, Governor. (*To* Higgins, *who takes refuge on the piano bench, a little overwhelmed by the proximity of his visitor; for* Doolittle *has a professional flavor of dust about him*). Well, the truth is, I've taken a sort of fancy to you, Governor; and if you want the girl, I'm not so set on having her back home again but what I might be open to an arrangement. Regarded in the light of a young woman, she's a fine handsome girl. As a daughter she's not worth her keep; and so I tell you straight. All I ask is my rights as a father; and you're the last man alive to expect me to let her go for nothing; for I can see you're one of the straight sort, Governor. Well, what's a five-pound note to you? And what's Eliza to me? (*He returns to his chair and sits down judicially*).

PICKERING:

> I think you ought to know, Doolittle, that Mr Higgins's intentions are entirely honorable.

DOOLITTLE:

Course they are, Governor. If I thought they wasn't, I'd ask fifty.

HIGGINS (*revolted*):

Do you mean to say, you callous rascal, that you would sell your daughter for £50?

DOOLITTLE:

Not in a general way I wouldn't; but to oblige a gentleman like you I'd do a good deal, I do assure you.

PICKERING:

Have you no morals, man?

DOOLITTLE (*unabashed*):

Can't afford them, Governor. Neither could you if you was as poor as me. Not that I mean any harm, you know. But if Liza is going to have a bit out of this, why not me too?

HIGGINS (*troubled*):

I don't know what to do, Pickering. There can be no question that as a matter of morals it's a positive crime to give this chap a farthing. And yet I feel a sort of rough justice in his claim.

DOOLITTLE:

That's it, Governor. That's all I say. A father's heart, as it were.

PICKERING:

Well, I know the feeling; but really it seems hardly right—

DOOLITTLE:

Don't say that, Governor. Don't look at it that way. What am I, Governors both? I ask you, what am I? I'm one of the undeserving poor: that's what I am. Think of what that means to a man. It means that he's up agen middle class morality all the time. If there's anything going, and I put in for a bit of it, it's always the same story: "You're undeserving; so you can't have it." But my needs is as great as the most deserving widow's that ever got money out of six different charities in one week for the death of the same husband. I don't need less than a deserving man: I need more. I don't eat less hearty than him; and I drink a lot more. I want a bit of amusement, cause I'm a thinking man. I want cheerfulness and a song and a band when I feel low. Well, they charge me just the same for everything as they charge the deserving. What is middle class morality? Just an excuse for never giving me anything. Therefore, I ask you, as two gentlemen, not to play that game on me. I'm playing straight with you. I ain't pretending to be deserving. I'm undeserving; and I mean to go on being undeserving. I like it; and that's the truth. Will you take advantage of a man's nature to do him out of the price of his own daughter what he's brought up and fed and clothed by the sweat of his brow until she's growed big enough to be interesting to you two gentlemen? Is five pounds unreasonable? I put it to you; and I leave it to you.

HIGGINS (*rising, and going over to* Pickering):

Pickering: if we were to take this man in hand for three months, he could choose between a seat in the Cabinet and a popular pulpit in Wales.

PICKERING:

What do you say to that, Doolittle?

DOOLITTLE:

Not me, Governor, thank you kindly. I've heard all the preachers and all the prime ministers—for I'm a thinking man and game for politics or religion or social reform same as all the other amusements—and I tell you it's a dog's life any way you look at it. Undeserving poverty is my line. Taking one station in society with another, it's—it's—well, it's the only one that has any ginger in it, to my taste.

HIGGINS:

I suppose we must give him a fiver.

PICKERING:

He'll make a bad use of it, I'm afraid.

DOOLITTLE:

Not me, Governor, so help me I won't. Don't you be afraid that I'll save it and spare it and live idle on it. There won't be a penny of it left by Monday: I'll have to go to work same as if I'd never had it. It won't pauperize me, you bet. Just one good spree for myself and the missus, giving pleasure to ourselves and employment to others, and satisfaction to you to think it's not been throwed away. You couldn't spend it better.

HIGGINS (*taking out his pocket book and coming between* Doolittle *and the piano*):

This is irresistible. Let's give him ten. (*He offers two notes to the dustman*).

DOOLITTLE:

No, Governor. She wouldn't have the heart to spend ten; and perhaps I shouldn't neither. Ten pounds is a lot of money: it makes a man feel prudent like; and then goodbye to happiness. You give me what I ask you, Governor: not a penny more, and not a penny less.

PICKERING:

Why don't you marry that missus of yours? I rather draw the line at encouraging that sort of immorality.

DOOLITTLE:

Tell her so, Governor: tell her so. I'm willing. It's me that suffers by it. I've no hold on her. I got to be agreeable to her. I got to give her presents. I got to buy her clothes something sinful. I'm a slave to that woman, Governor, just because I'm not her lawful husband. And she knows it too. Catch her marrying me! Take my advice, Governor: marry Eliza while she's young and don't know no better. If you don't you'll be sorry for it after. If you do, she'll be sorry for it after; but better her than you, because you're a man, and she's only a woman and don't know how to be happy anyhow.

HIGGINS:

Pickering: if we listen to this man another minute, we shall have no convictions left. (*To* Doolittle) Five pounds I think you said.

DOOLITTLE:

Thank you kindly, Governor.

HIGGINS:

You're sure you won't take ten?

DOOLITTLE:

Not now. Another time, Governor.

HIGGINS (*handing him a five-pound note*):

Here you are.

DOOLITTLE:

Thank you, Governor. Good morning. (*He hurries to the door, anxious to get away with his booty. When he opens it he is confronted with a dainty and exquisitely clean young* Japanese Lady *in a simple blue cotton kimono printed cunningly with small white jasmine blossoms. Mrs Pearce is with her. He gets out of her way deferentially and apologizes*). Beg pardon, miss.

THE JAPANESE LADY:

Garn! Don't you know your own daughter?

DOOLITTLE, HIGGINS *and* PICKERING (*exclaiming simultaneously*):

Bly me! it's Eliza! What's that! This! By Jove!

LIZA:

Don't I look silly?

HIGGINS:

Silly?

MRS PEARCE (*at the door*):

Now, Mr Higgins, please don't say anything to make the girl conceited about herself.

HIGGINS (*conscientiously*):

Oh! Quite right, Mrs Pearce. (*To* Eliza) Yes: damned silly.

MRS PEARCE:

Please, sir.

HIGGINS (*correcting himself*):

I mean extremely silly.

LIZA:

> I should look all right with my hat on. (*She takes up her hat; puts it on; and walks across the room to the fireplace with a fashionable air*).

HIGGINS:

> A new fashion, by George! And it ought to look horrible!

DOOLITTLE (*with fatherly pride*):

> Well, I never thought she'd clean up as good looking as that, Governor. She's a credit to me, ain't she?

LIZA:

> I tell you, it's easy to clean up here. Hot and cold water on tap, just as much as you like, there is. Woolly towels, there is; and a towel horse so hot, it burns your fingers. Soft brushes to scrub yourself, and a wooden bowl of soap smelling like primroses. Now I know why ladies is so clean. Washing's a treat for them. Wish they saw what it is for the like of me!

HIGGINS:

> I'm glad the bathroom met with your approval.

LIZA:

> It didn't: not all of it; and I don't care who hears me say it. Mrs Pearce knows.

HIGGINS:

> What was wrong, Mrs Pearce?

MRS PEARCE (*blandly*):

> Oh, nothing, sir. It doesn't matter.

LIZA:

> I had a good mind to break it. I didn't know which way to look. But I hung a towel over it, I did.

HIGGINS:

> Over what?

MRS PEARCE:

> Over the looking-glass, sir.

HIGGINS:

> Doolittle: you have brought your daughter up too strictly.

DOOLITTLE:

> Me! I never brought her up at all, except to give her a lick of a strap now and again. Don't put it on me, Governor. She ain't accustomed to it, you see: that's all. But she'll soon pick up your free-and-easy ways.

LIZA:

> I'm a good girl, I am; and I won't pick up no free-and-easy ways.

HIGGINS:

> Eliza: if you say again that you're a good girl, your father shall take you home.

LIZA:

Not him. You don't know my father. All he come here for was to touch you for some money to get drunk on.

DOOLITTLE:

Well, what else would I want money for? To put into the plate in church, I suppose. (*She puts out her tongue at him. He is so incensed by this that* Pickering *presently finds it necessary to step between them*). Don't you give me none of your lip; and don't let me hear you giving this gentleman any of it neither, or you'll hear from me about it. See?

HIGGINS:

Have you any further advice to give her before you go, Doolittle? Your blessing, for instance.

DOOLITTLE:

No, Governor: I ain't such a mug as to put up my children to all I know myself. Hard enough to hold them in without that. If you want Eliza's mind improved, Governor, you do it yourself with a strap. So long, gentlemen. (*He turns to go*).

HIGGINS (*impressively*):

Stop. You'll come regularly to see your daughter. It's your duty, you know. My brother is a clergyman; and he could help you in your talks with her.

DOOLITTLE (*evasively*):

Certainly. I'll come, Governor. Not just this week, because I have a job at a distance. But later on you may depend on me. Afternoon, gentlemen. Afternoon, ma'am. (*He takes off his hat to* Mrs Pearce, *who disdains the salutation and goes out. He winks at* Higgins, *thinking him probably a fellow-sufferer from* Mrs Pearce's *difficult disposition, and follows her*).

LIZA:

Don't you believe the old liar. He'd as soon you set a bull-dog on him as a clergyman. You won't see him again in a hurry.

HIGGINS:

I don't want to, Eliza. Do you?

LIZA:

Not me. I don't want never to see him again, I don't. He's a disgrace to me, he is, collecting dust, instead of working at his trade.

PICKERING:

What is his trade, Eliza?

LIZA:

Taking money out of other people's pockets into his own. His proper trade's a navvy; and he works at it sometimes too—for exercise—and earns good money at it. Ain't you going to call me Miss Doolittle any more?

PICKERING:

> I beg your pardon, Miss Doolittle. It was a slip of the tongue.

LIZA:

> Oh, I don't mind; only it sounded so genteel. I should just like to take a taxi to the corner of Tottenham Court Road and get out there and tell it to wait for me, just to put the girls in their place a bit. I wouldn't speak to them, you know.

PICKERING:

> Better wait till we get you something really fashionable.

HIGGINS:

> Besides, you shouldn't cut your old friends now that you have risen in the world. That's what we call snobbery.

LIZA:

> You don't call the like of them my friends now, I should hope. They've took it out of me often enough with their ridicule when they had the chance; and now I mean to get a bit of my own back. But if I'm to have fashionable clothes, I'll wait. I should like to have some. Mrs Pearce says you're going to give me some to wear in bed at night different to what I wear in the daytime; but it do seem a waste of money when you could get something to show. Besides, I never could fancy changing into cold things on a winter night.

MRS PEARCE (*coming back*):

> Now, Eliza. The new things have come for you to try on.

LIZA:

> Ah-ow-oo-ooh! (*She rushes out*).

MRS PEARCE (*following her*):

> Oh, don't rush about like that, girl. (*She shuts the door behind her*).

HIGGINS:

> Pickering: we have taken on a stiff job.

PICKERING (*with conviction*):

> Higgins: we have.

Act III

It is Mrs Higgins's *at-home day. Nobody has yet arrived. Her drawing room, in a flat on Chelsea Embankment, has three windows looking on the river; and the ceiling is not so lofty as it would be in an older house of the same pretension. The windows are open, giving access to a balcony with flowers in pots. If you stand with your face to the windows, you have the fireplace on your left and the door in the right-hand wall close to the corner nearest the windows.*

Mrs Higgins *was brought up on Morris and Burne Jones; and her room, which is very unlike her son's room in Wimpole Street, is not crowded with furniture and little tables and nick-nacks. In the middle of the room there is a big ottoman; and this, with the carpet, the Morris wall-papers, and the Morris chintz window curtains and brocade covers of the ottoman and its cushions, supply all the ornament, and are much too handsome to be hidden by odds and ends of useless things. A few good oil-paintings from the exhibitions in the Grosvenor Gallery thirty years ago (the Burne Jones, not the Whistler side of them) are on the walls. The only landscape is a Cecil Lawson on the scale of a Rubens. There is a portrait of* Mrs Higgins *as she was when she defied fashion in her youth in one of the beautiful Rossettian costumes which, when caricatured by people who did not understand, led to the absurdities of popular estheticism in the eighteen-seventies.*

In the corner diagonally opposite the door Mrs Higgins, *now over sixty and long past taking the trouble to dress out of the fashion, sits writing at an elegantly simple writing-table with a bell button within reach of her hand. There is a Chippendale chair further back in the room between her and the window nearest her side. At the other side of the room, further forward, is an Elizabethan chair roughly carved in the taste of Inigo Jones. On the same side a piano in a decorated case. The corner between the fireplace and the window is occupied by a divan cushioned in Morris chintz.*

It is between four and five in the afternoon.

The door is opened violently; and Higgins *enters with his hat on.*

MRS HIGGINS (*dismayed*):

Henry (*scolding him*)! What are you doing here to-day? It is my at-home day: you promised not to come. (*As he bends to kiss her, she takes his hat off, and presents it to him*).

HIGGINS:

Oh bother! (*He throws the hat down on the table*).

MRS HIGGINS:

Go home at once.

HIGGINS (*kissing her*):

I know, mother. I came on purpose.

MRS HIGGINS:

But you mustn't. I'm serious, Henry. You offend all my friends: they stop coming whenever they meet you.

HIGGINS:

Nonsense! I know I have no small talk; but people don't mind. (*He sits on the settee*).

MRS HIGGINS:

Oh! don't they? Small talk indeed! What about your large talk? Really, dear, you mustn't stay.

HIGGINS:

I must. I've a job for you. A phonetic job.

MRS HIGGINS:

No use, dear. I'm sorry; but I can't get round your vowels; and though I like to get pretty postcards in your patent shorthand, I always have to read the copies in ordinary writing you so thoughtfully send me.

HIGGINS:

Well, this isn't a phonetic job.

MRS HIGGINS:

You said it was.

HIGGINS:

Not your part of it. I've picked up a girl.

MRS HIGGINS:

Does that mean that some girl has picked you up?

HIGGINS:

Not at all. I don't mean a love affair.

MRS HIGGINS:

What a pity!

HIGGINS:

Why?

MRS HIGGINS:

Well, you never fall in love with anyone under forty-five. When will you discover that there are some rather nice-looking young women about?

HIGGINS:

Oh, I can't be bothered with young women. My idea of a lovable woman is something as like you as possible. I shall never get into the way of seriously liking young women: some habits lie too deep to be changed. (*Rising abruptly and walking about, jingling his money and his keys in his trouser pockets*) Besides, they're all idiots.

MRS HIGGINS:

Do you know what you would do if you really loved me, Henry?

HIGGINS:

Oh bother! What? Marry, I suppose?

MRS HIGGINS:

No. Stop fidgeting and take your hands out of your pockets. (*With a gesture of despair, he obeys and sits down again.*) That's a good boy. Now tell me about the girl.

HIGGINS:

She's coming to see you.

MRS HIGGINS:

> I don't remember asking her.

HIGGINS:

> You didn't. *I* asked her. If you'd known her you wouldn't have asked her.

MRS HIGGINS:

> Indeed! Why?

HIGGINS:

> Well, it's like this. She's a common flower girl. I picked her off the kerbstone.

MRS HIGGINS:

> And invited her to my at-home!

HIGGINS (*rising and coming to her to coax her*):

> Oh, that'll be all right. I've taught her to speak properly; and she has strict orders as to her behavior. She's to keep to two subjects: the weather and everybody's health—Fine day and How do you do, you know—and not to let herself go on things in general. That will be safe.

MRS HIGGINS:

> Safe! To talk about our health! about our insides! perhaps about our outsides! How could you be so silly, Henry?

HIGGINS (*impatiently*):

> Well, she must talk about something. (*He controls himself and sits down again*). Oh, she'll be all right: don't you fuss. Pickering is in it with me. I've a sort of bet on that I'll pass her off as a duchess in six months. I started on her some months ago; and she's getting on like a house on fire. I shall win my bet. She has a quick ear; and she's been easier to teach than my middle-class pupils because she's had to learn a complete new language. She talks English almost as you talk French.

MRS HIGGINS:

> That's satisfactory, at all events.

HIGGINS:

> Well, it is and it isn't.

MRS HIGGINS:

> What does that mean?

HIGGINS:

> You see, I've got her pronunciation all right; but you have to consider not only how a girl pronounces, but what she pronounces; and that's where—

They are interrupted by The Parlor-Maid, *announcing guests.*

THE PARLOR-MAID:

Mrs and Miss Eynsford Hill. (*She withdraws*).

HIGGINS:

Oh Lord! (*He rises; snatches his hat from the table; and makes for the door; but before he reaches it his mother introduces him*).

Mrs and Miss Eynsford Hill are the mother and daughter who sheltered from the rain in Covent Garden. The mother is well bred, quiet, and has the habitual anxiety of straitened means. The daughter has acquired a gay air of being very much at home in society: the bravado of genteel poverty.

MRS EYNSFORD HILL (*to Mrs Higgins*):

How do you do? (*They shake hands*).

MISS EYNSFORD HILL:

How d'you do? (*She shakes*).

MRS HIGGINS (*introducing*):

My son Henry.

MRS EYNSFORD HILL:

Your celebrated son! I have so longed to meet you, Professor Higgins.

HIGGINS (*glumly, making no movement in her direction*):

Delighted. (*He backs against the piano and bows brusquely*).

MISS EYNSFORD HILL (*going to him with confident familiarity*):

How do you do?

HIGGINS (*staring at her*):

I've seen you before somewhere. I haven't the ghost of a notion where; but I've heard your voice. (*Drearily*) It doesn't matter. You'd better sit down.

MRS HIGGINS:

I'm sorry to say that my celebrated son has no manners. You mustn't mind him.

MISS EYNSFORD HILL (*gaily*):

I don't. (*She sits in the Elizabethan chair*).

MRS EYNSFORD HILL (*a little bewildered*):

Not at all. (*She sits on the ottoman between her daughter and Mrs Higgins, who has turned her chair away from the writing-table*).

HIGGINS:

Oh, have I been rude? I didn't mean to be.

He goes to the central window, through which, with his back to the company, he contemplates the river and the flowers in Battersea Park on the opposite bank as if they were a frozen desert.

The Parlor-Maid *returns, ushering in* Pickering.

THE PARLOR-MAID:
> Colonel Pickering. (*She withdraws*).

PICKERING:
> How do you do, Mrs Higgins?

MRS HIGGINS:
> So glad you've come. Do you know Mrs Eynsford Hill—Miss Eynsford Hill? (*Exchange of bows. The Colonel brings the Chippendale chair a little forward between* Mrs Hill *and* Mrs Higgins, *and sits down*).

PICKERING:
> Has Henry told you what we've come for?

HIGGINS (*over his shoulder*):
> We were interrupted: damn it!

MRS HIGGINS:
> Oh Henry, Henry, really!

MRS EYNSFORD HILL (*half rising*):
> Are we in the way?

MRS HIGGINS (*rising and making her sit down again*):
> No, no. You couldn't have come more fortunately: we want you to meet a friend of ours.

HIGGINS (*turning hopefully*):
> Yes, by George! We want two or three people. You'll do as well as anybody else.

The Parlor-Maid *returns, ushering* Freddy.

THE PARLOR-MAID:
> Mr Eynsford Hill.

HIGGINS (*almost audibly, past endurance*):
> God of Heaven! another of them.

FREDDY (*shaking hands with* Mrs Higgins):
> Ahdedo?

MRS HIGGINS:
> Very good of you to come. (*Introducing*) Colonel Pickering.

FREDDY (*bowing*):
> Ahdedo?

MRS HIGGINS:
> I don't think you know my son, Professor Higgins.

FREDDY (*going to* Higgins):
> Ahdedo?

HIGGINS (*looking at him much as if he were a pickpocket*):

I'll take my oath I've met you before somewhere. Where was it?

FREDDY:

I don't think so.

HIGGINS (*resignedly*):

It don't matter, anyhow. Sit down.

He shakes Freddy's *hand, and almost slings him on to the ottoman with his face to the windows; then comes round to the other side of it.*

HIGGINS:

Well, here we are, anyhow! (*He sits down on the ottoman next* Mrs Eynsford Hill, *on her left*). And now, what the devil are we going to talk about until Eliza comes?

MRS HIGGINS:

Henry: you are the life and soul of the Royal Society's soirées; but really you're rather trying on more commonplace occasions.

HIGGINS:

Am I? Very sorry. (*Beaming suddenly*) I suppose I am, you know. (*Uproariously*) Ha, ha!

MISS EYNSFORD HILL (*who considers* Higgins *quite eligible matrimonially*):

I sympathize. *I* haven't any small talk. If people would only be frank and say what they really think!

HIGGINS (*relapsing into gloom*):

Lord forbid!

MRS EYNSFORD HILL (*taking up her daughter's cue*):

But why?

HIGGINS:

What they think they ought to think is bad enough, Lord knows; but what they really think would break up the whole show. Do you suppose it would be really agreeable if I were to come out now with what *I* really think?

MISS EYNSFORD HILL (*gaily*):

Is it so very cynical?

HIGGINS:

Cynical! Who the dickens said it was cynical? I mean it wouldn't be decent.

MRS EYNSFORD HILL (*seriously*):

Oh! I'm sure you don't mean that, Mr Higgins.

HIGGINS:

You see, we're all savages, more or less. We're supposed to be civilized and cultured—to know all about poetry and philosophy and art and science, and so on; but how many of us know even the meanings of these names? (*To* Miss Hill) What do you know of poetry? (*To* Mrs Hill) What do you know of science? (*Indicating* Freddy) What does he know of art or science or anything else? What the devil do you imagine I know of philosophy?

MRS HIGGINS (*warningly*):

Or of manners, Henry?

THE PARLOR-MAID (*opening the door*):

Miss Doolittle. (*She withdraws*).

HIGGINS (*rising hastily and running to* Mrs Higgins):

Here she is, mother. (*He stands on tiptoe and makes signs over his mother's head to* Eliza *to indicate to her which lady is her hostess*).

Eliza, *who is exquisitely dressed, produces an impression of such remarkable distinction and beauty as she enters that they all rise, quite fluttered. Guided by* Higgins's *signals, she comes to* Mrs Higgins *with studied grace.*

LIZA (*speaking with pedantic correctness of pronunciation and great beauty of tone*):

How do you do, Mrs Higgins? (*She gasps slightly in making sure of the H in* Higgins, *but is quite successful*). Mr Higgins told me I might come.

MRS HIGGINS (*cordially*):

Quite right: I'm very glad indeed to see you.

PICKERING:

How do you do, Miss Doolittle?

LIZA (*shaking hands with him*):

Colonel Pickering, is it not?

MRS EYNSFORD HILL:

I feel sure we have met before, Miss Doolittle. I remember your eyes.

LIZA:

How do you do? (*She sits down on the ottoman gracefully in the place just left vacant by* Higgins).

MRS EYNSFORD HILL (*introducing*):

My daughter Clara.

LIZA:

How do you do?

CLARA (*impulsively*):

How do you do? (*She sits down on the ottoman beside* Eliza, *devouring her with her eyes*).

FREDDY (*coming to their side of the ottoman*):

I've certainly had the pleasure.

MRS EYNSFORD HILL (*introducing*):

My son Freddy.

LIZA:

How do you do?

Freddy *bows and sits down in the Elizabethan chair, infatuated.*

HIGGINS (*suddenly*):

By George, yes: it all comes back to me! (*They stare at him*). Covent Garden! (*Lamentably*) What a damned thing!

MRS HIGGINS:

Henry, please! (*He is about to sit on the edge of the table*) Don't sit on my writing-table: you'll break it.

HIGGINS (*sulkily*):

Sorry.

He goes to the divan, stumbling into the fender and over the fire-irons on his way; extricating himself with muttered imprecations; and finishing his disastrous journey by throwing himself so impatiently on the divan that he almost breaks it. Mrs Higgins *looks at him, but controls herself and says nothing.*

A long and painful pause ensues.

MRS HIGGINS (*at last, conversationally*):

Will it rain, do you think?

LIZA:

The shallow depression in the west of these islands is likely to move slowly in an easterly direction. There are no indications of any great change in the barometrical situation.

FREDDY:

Ha! ha! how awfully funny!

LIZA:

What is wrong with that, young man? I bet I got it right.

FREDDY:

Killing!

MRS EYNSFORD HILL:

I'm sure I hope it won't turn cold. There's so much influenza about. It runs right through our whole family regularly every spring.

LIZA (*darkly*):

My aunt died of influenza: so they said.

MRS EYNSFORD HILL (*clicks her tongue sympathetically*):

!!!

LIZA (*in the same tragic tone*):

But it's my belief they done the old woman in.

MRS HIGGINS (*puzzled*):

Done her in?

LIZA:

Y-e-e-e-es, Lord love you! Why should she die of influenza? She come through diphtheria right enough the year before. I saw her with my own eyes. Fairly blue with it, she was. They all thought she was dead; but my father he kept ladling gin down her throat till she came to so sudden that she bit the bowl off the spoon.

MRS EYNSFORD HILL (*startled*):

Dear me!

LIZA (*piling up the indictment*):

What call would a woman with that strength in her have to die of influenza? What become of her new straw hat that should have come to me? Somebody pinched it; and what I say is, them as pinched it done her in.

MRS EYNSFORD HILL:

What does doing her in mean?

HIGGINS (*hastily*):

Oh, that's the new small talk. To do a person in means to kill them.

MRS EYNSFORD HILL (*to* Eliza, *horrified*):

You surely don't believe that your aunt was killed?

LIZA:

Do I not! Them she lived with would have killed her for a hat-pin, let alone a hat.

MRS EYNSFORD HILL:

But it can't have been right for your father to pour spirits down her throat like that. It might have killed her.

LIZA:

Not her. Gin was mother's milk to her. Besides, he'd poured so much down his own throat that he knew the good of it.

MRS EYNSFORD HILL:

Do you mean that he drank?

LIZA:

Drank! My word! Something chronic.

MRS EYNSFORD HILL:

How dreadful for you!

LIZA:

Not a bit. It never did him no harm what I could see. But then he did not keep it up regular. (*Cheerfully*) On the burst, as you might say, from time to time. And always more agreeable when he had a drop in. When he was out of work, my mother used to give him fourpence and tell him to go out and not come back until he'd drunk himself cheerful and loving-like. There's lots of women has to make their husbands drunk to make them fit to live with. (*Now quite at her ease*) You see, it's like this. If a man has a bit of a conscience, it always takes him when he's sober; and then it makes him low-spirited. A drop of booze just takes that off and makes him happy. (*To* Freddy, *who is in convulsions of suppressed laughter*) Here! what are you sniggering at?

FREDDY:

The new small talk. You do it so awfully well.

LIZA:

If I was doing it proper, what was you laughing at? (*To* Higgins) Have I said anything I oughtn't?

MRS HIGGINS (*interposing*):

Not at all, Miss Doolittle.

LIZA:

Well, that's a mercy, anyhow. (*Expansively*) What I always say is—

HIGGINS (*rising and looking at his watch*):

Ahem!

LIZA (*looking round at him; taking the hint; and rising*):

Well: I must go. (*They all rise.* Freddy *goes to the door*). So pleased to have met you. Goodbye. (*She shakes hands with* Mrs Higgins).

MRS HIGGINS:

Goodbye.

LIZA:

Goodbye, Colonel Pickering.

PICKERING:

Goodbye, Miss Doolittle. (*They shake hands*).

LIZA (*nodding to the others*):

Goodbye, all.

FREDDY (*opening the door for her*):

Are you walking across the Park, Miss Doolittle? If so—

LIZA:

Walk! Not bloody likely. (*Sensation*). I am going in a taxi. (*She goes out*).

Pickering *gasps and sits down.* Freddy *goes out on the balcony to catch another glimpse of* Eliza.

MRS EYNSFORD HILL (*suffering from shock*):

Well, I really can't get used to the new ways.

CLARA (*throwing herself discontentedly into the Elizabethan chair*):

Oh, it's all right, mamma, quite right. People will think we never go anywhere or see anybody if you are so old-fashioned.

MRS EYNSFORD HILL:

I daresay I am very old-fashioned; but I do hope you won't begin using that expression, Clara. I have got accustomed to hear you talking about men as rotters, and calling everything filthy and beastly; though I do think it horrible and unladylike. But this last is really too much. Don't you think so, Colonel Pickering?

PICKERING:

Don't ask me. I've been away in India for several years; and manners have changed so much that I sometimes don't know whether I'm at a respectable dinner-table or in a ship's forecastle.

CLARA:

It's all a matter of habit. There's no right or wrong in it. Nobody means anything by it. And it's so quaint, and gives such a smart emphasis to things that are not in themselves very witty. I find the new small talk delightful and quite innocent.

MRS EYNSFORD HILL (*rising*):

Well, after that, I think it's time for us to go.

Pickering *and* Higgins *rise*.

CLARA (*rising*):

Oh yes: we have three at-homes to go to still. Goodbye, Mrs Higgins. Goodbye, Colonel Pickering. Goodbye, Professor Higgins.

HIGGINS (*coming grimly at her from the divan, and accompanying her to the door*):

Goodbye. Be sure you try on that small talk at the three at-homes. Don't be nervous about it. Pitch it in strong.

CLARA (*all smiles*):

I will. Goodbye. Such nonsense, all this early Victorian prudery!

HIGGINS (*tempting her*):

Such damned nonsense!

CLARA:

Such bloody nonsense!

MRS EYNSFORD HILL (*convulsively*):

Clara!

CLARA:

> Ha! ha! (*She goes out radiant, conscious of being thoroughly up to date, and is heard descending the stairs in a stream of silvery laughter*).

FREDDY (*to the heavens at large*):

> Well, I ask you—(*He gives it up, and comes to* Mrs Higgins). Goodbye.

MRS HIGGINS (*shaking hands*):

> Goodbye. Would you like to meet Miss Doolittle again?

FREDDY (*eagerly*):

> Yes, I should, most awfully.

MRS HIGGINS:

> Well, you know my days.

FREDDY:

> Yes. Thanks awfully. Goodbye. (*He goes out*).

MRS EYNSFORD HILL:

> Goodbye, Mr Higgins.

HIGGINS:

> Goodbye. Goodbye.

MRS EYNSFORD HILL (*to* Pickering):

> It's no use. I shall never be able to bring myself to use that word.

PICKERING:

> Don't. It's not compulsory, you know. You'll get on quite well without it.

MRS EYNSFORD HILL:

> Only, Clara is so down on me if I am not positively reeking with the latest slang. Goodbye.

PICKERING:

> Goodbye (*They shake hands*).

MRS EYNSFORD HILL (*to* Mrs Higgins):

> You mustn't mind Clara. (Pickering, *catching from her lowered tone that this is not meant for him to hear, discreetly joins* Higgins *at the window*). We're so poor! and she gets so few parties, poor child! She doesn't quite know. (Mrs Higgins, *seeing that her eyes are moist, takes her hand sympathetically and goes with her to the door*). But the boy is nice. Don't you think so?

MRS HIGGINS:

> Oh, quite nice. I shall always be delighted to see him.

MRS EYNSFORD HILL:

> Thank you, dear. Goodbye. (*She goes out*).

HIGGINS (*eagerly*):

> Well? Is Eliza presentable? (*He swoops on his mother and drags her to the ottoman, where she sits down in* Eliza's *place with her son on her left*).

Pickering *returns to his chair on her right.*

MRS HIGGINS:

You silly boy, of course she's not presentable. She's a triumph of your art and of her dressmaker's; but if you suppose for a moment that she doesn't give herself away in every sentence she utters, you must be perfectly cracked about her.

PICKERING:

But don't you think something might be done? I mean something to eliminate the sanguinary element from her conversation.

MRS HIGGINS:

Not as long as she is in Henry's hands.

HIGGINS (*aggrieved*):

Do you mean that my language is improper?

MRS HIGGINS:

No, dearest: it would be quite proper—say on a canal barge; but it would not be proper for her at a garden party.

HIGGINS (*deeply injured*):

Well I must say—

PICKERING (*interrupting him*):

Come, Higgins: you must learn to know yourself. I haven't heard such language as yours since we used to review the volunteers in Hyde Park twenty years ago.

HIGGINS (*sulkily*):

Oh, well, if you say so, I suppose I don't always talk like a bishop.

MRS HIGGINS (*quieting Henry with a touch*):

Colonel Pickering: will you tell me what is the exact state of things in Wimpole Street?

PICKERING (*cheerfully: as if this completely changed the subject*):

Well, I have come to live there with Henry. We work together at my Indian Dialects; and we think it more convenient—

MRS HIGGINS:

Quite so. I know all about that: it's an excellent arrangement. But where does this girl live?

HIGGINS:

With us, of course. Where should she live?

MRS HIGGINS:

But on what terms? Is she a servant? If not, what is she?

PICKERING (*slowly*):

I think I know what you mean, Mrs Higgins.

HIGGINS:

Well, dash me if *I* do! I've had to work at the girl every day for months to get her to her present pitch. Besides, she's useful.

She knows where my things are, and remembers my appointments and so forth.

MRS HIGGINS:

How does your housekeeper get on with her?

HIGGINS:

Mrs Pearce? Oh, she's jolly glad to get so much taken off her hands; for before Eliza came, she used to have to find things and remind me of my appointments. But she's got some silly bee in her bonnet about Eliza. She keeps saying "You don't think, sir": doesn't she, Pick?

PICKERING:

Yes: that's the formula. "You don't think, sir." That's the end of every conversation about Eliza.

HIGGINS:

As if I ever stop thinking about the girl and her confounded vowels and consonants. I'm worn out, thinking about her, and watching her lips and her teeth and her tongue, not to mention her soul, which is the quaintest of the lot.

MRS HIGGINS:

You certainly are a pretty pair of babies, playing with your live doll.

HIGGINS:

Playing! The hardest job I ever tackled: make no mistake about that, mother. But you have no idea how frightfully interesting it is to take a human being and change her into a quite different human being by creating a new speech for her. It's filling up the deepest gulf that separates class from class and soul from soul.

PICKERING (*drawing his chair closer to* Mrs Higgins *and bending over to her eagerly*):

Yes: it's enormously interesting. I assure you, Mrs Higgins, we take Eliza very seriously. Every week—every day almost—there is some new change. (*Closer again*) We keep records of every stage—dozens of gramophone disks and photographs—

HIGGINS (*assailing her at the other ear*):

Yes, by George: it's the most absorbing experiment I ever tackled. She regularly fills our lives up: doesn't she, Pick?

PICKERING:

We're always talking Eliza.

HIGGINS:

Teaching Eliza.

PICKERING:

Dressing Eliza.

MRS HIGGINS:

What!

HIGGINS:

    Inventing new Elizas.

HIGGINS: *(speaking* You know, she has the most extraordinary
                       quickness of ear:
PICKERING: *together)* I assure you, my dear Mrs Higgins,
                       that girl

HIGGINS: just like a parrot. I've tried her
                       with every
PICKERING: is a genius. She can play the piano quite
                       beautifully.

HIGGINS: possible sort of sound that a human
                       being can make—
PICKERING: We have taken her to classical concerts
                       and to music

HIGGINS: Continental dialects, African dialects,
                       Hottentot
PICKERING: halls; and it's all the same to her: she
                       plays everything

HIGGINS: clicks, things it took me years to get hold
                       of; and
PICKERING: she hears right off when she comes home,
                       whether it's

HIGGINS: she picks them up like a shot, right away,
                       as if she had
PICKERING: Beethoven and Brahms or Lehar and
                       Lionel Monckton;

HIGGINS: been at it all her life.
PICKERING: though six months ago, she'd
                       never as much as touched
                       a piano—

MRS HIGGINS (*putting her fingers in her ears, as they are by this time
    shouting one another down with an intolerable noise*):
    Sh-sh-sh—sh! (*They stop*).

PICKERING:

    I beg your pardon. (*He draws his chair back apologetically*).

HIGGINS:

    Sorry. When Pickering starts shouting nobody can get a word
    in edgeways.

MRS HIGGINS:

    Be quiet, Henry. Colonel Pickering: don't you realize that when
    Eliza walked into Wimpole Street, something walked in with her?

PICKERING:

Her father did. But Henry soon got rid of him.

MRS HIGGINS:

It would have been more to the point if her mother had. But as her mother didn't something else did.

PICKERING:

But what?

MRS HIGGINS (*unconsciously dating herself by the word*):

A problem.

PICKERING:

Oh, I see. The problem of how to pass her off as a lady.

HIGGINS:

I'll solve that problem. I've half solved it already.

MRS HIGGINS:

No, you two infinitely stupid male creatures: the problem of what is to be done with her afterwards.

HIGGINS:

I don't see anything in that. She can go her own way, with all the advantages I have given her.

MRS HIGGINS:

The advantages of that poor woman who was here just now! The manners and habits that disqualify a fine lady from earning her own living without giving her a fine lady's income! Is that what you mean?

PICKERING (*indulgently, being rather bored*):

Oh, that will be all right, Mrs Higgins. (*He rises to go*).

HIGGINS (*rising also*):

We'll find her some light employment.

PICKERING:

She's happy enough. Don't you worry about her. Goodbye. (*He shakes hands as if he were consoling a frightened child, and makes for the door*).

HIGGINS:

Anyhow, there's no good bothering now. The thing's done. Goodbye, mother. (*He kisses her, and follows* Pickering).

PICKERING (*turning for a final consolation*):

There are plenty of openings. We'll do what's right. Goodbye.

HIGGINS (*to* Pickering *as they go out together*):

Let's take her to the Shakespeare exhibition at Earls Court.

PICKERING:

Yes: let's. Her remarks will be delicious.

HIGGINS:

She'll mimic all the people for us when we get home.

PICKERING:
>   Ripping. (*Both are heard laughing as they go downstairs*).

MRS HIGGINS (*rises with an impatient bounce, and returns to her work at the writing-table. She sweeps a litter of disarranged papers out of her way; snatches a sheet of paper from her stationery case; and tries resolutely to write. At the third line she gives it up; flings down her pen; grips the table angrily and exclaims*):
>   Oh, men! men!! men!!!

Act IV

The Wimpole Street laboratory. Midnight. Nobody in the room. The clock on the mantelpiece strikes twelve. The fire is not alight: it is a summer night. Presently Higgins *and* Pickering *are heard on the stairs.*

HIGGINS (*calling down to* Pickering):
>   I say, Pick: lock up, will you? I shan't be going out again.

PICKERING:
>   Right. Can Mrs Pearce go to bed? We don't want anything more, do we?

HIGGINS:
>   Lord, no!

Eliza *opens the door and is seen on the lighted landing in opera cloak, brilliant evening dress, and diamonds, with fan, flowers, and all accessories. She comes to the hearth, and switches on the electric lights there. She is tired: her pallor contrasts strongly with her dark eyes and hair; and her expression is almost tragic. She takes off her cloak; puts her fan and flowers on the piano; and sits down on the bench, brooding and silent.* Higgins, *in evening dress, with overcoat and hat, comes in, carrying a smoking jacket which he has picked up downstairs. He takes off the hat and overcoat; throws them carelessly on the newspaper stand; disposes of his coat in the same way; puts on the smoking jacket; and throws himself wearily into the easy-chair at the hearth.* Pickering, *similarly attired, comes in. He also takes off his hat and overcoat, and is about to throw them on* Higgins's *when he hesitates.*

PICKERING:
>   I say: Mrs Pearce will row if we leave these things lying about in the drawing room.

HIGGINS:
>   Oh, chuck them over the bannisters into the hall. She'll find them there in the morning and put them away all right. She'll think we were drunk.

PICKERING:

    We are, slightly. Are there any letters?

HIGGINS:

    I didn't look. (Pickering *takes the overcoats and hats and goes downstairs.* Higgins *begins half singing half yawning an air from "La Fanciulla del Golden West." Suddenly he stops and exclaims*) I wonder where the devil my slippers are!

Eliza *looks at him darkly; then rises suddenly and leaves the room.* Higgins *yawns again, and resumes his song.* Pickering *returns, with the contents of the letter-box in his hand.*

PICKERING:

    Only circulars, and this coroneted billet-doux for you. (*He throws the circulars into the fender, and posts himself on the hearthrug, with his back to the grate*).

HIGGINS (*glancing at the billet-doux*):

    Money-lender. (*He throws the letter after the circulars*).

Eliza *returns with a pair of large down-at-heel slippers. She places them on the carpet before* Higgins, *and sits as before without a word.*

HIGGINS (*yawning again*):

    Oh Lord! What an evening! What a crew! What a silly tom-foolery! (*He raises his shoe to unlace it, and catches sight of the slippers. He stops unlacing and looks at them as if they had appeared there of their own accord*). Oh! they're there, are they?

PICKERING (*stretching himself*):

    Well, I feel a bit tired. It's been a long day. The garden party, a dinner party, and the opera! Rather too much of a good thing. But you've won your bet, Higgins. Eliza did the trick, and something to spare, eh?

HIGGINS (*fervently*):

    Thank God it's over!

Eliza *flinches violently; but they take no notice of her; and she recovers herself and sits stonily as before.*

PICKERING:

    Were you nervous at the garden party? *I* was. Eliza didn't seem a bit nervous.

HIGGINS:

    Oh, she wasn't nervous. I knew she'd be all right. No: it's the strain of putting the job through all these months that has told on me. It was interesting enough at first, while we were at the phonetics; but after that I got deadly sick of it. If I hadn't backed myself to do it I should have chucked the whole thing up two months ago. It was a silly notion: the whole thing has been a bore.

PICKERING:

Oh come! the garden party was frightfully exciting. My heart began beating like anything.

HIGGINS:

Yes, for the first three minutes. But when I saw we were going to win hands down, I felt like a bear in a cage, hanging about doing nothing. The dinner was worse: sitting gorging there for over an hour, with nobody but a damned fool of a fashionable woman to talk to! I tell you, Pickering, never again for me. No more artificial duchesses. The whole thing has been simple purgatory.

PICKERING:

You've never been broken in properly to the social routine. (*Strolling over to the piano*) I rather enjoy dipping into it occasionally myself: it makes me feel young again. Anyhow, it was a great success: an immense success. I was quite frightened once or twice because Eliza was doing it so well. You see, lots of the real people can't do it at all: they're such fools that they think style comes by nature to people in their position; and so they never learn. There's always something professional about doing a thing superlatively well.

HIGGINS:

Yes: that's what drives me mad: the silly people don't know their own silly business. (*Rising*) However, it's over and done with; and now I can go to bed at last without dreading tomorrow.

Eliza's beauty becomes murderous.

PICKERING:

I think I shall turn in too. Still, it's been a great occasion: a triumph for you. Goodnight. (*He goes*).

HIGGINS (*following him*):

Goodnight. (*Over his shoulder, at the door*) Put out the lights, Eliza; and tell Mrs Pearce not to make coffee for me in the morning: I'll take tea. (*He goes out*).

Eliza *tries to control herself and feel indifferent as she rises and walks across to the hearth to switch off the lights. By the time she gets there she is on the point of screaming. She sits down in* Higgins's *chair and holds on hard to the arms. Finally she gives way and flings herself furiously on the floor, raging.*

HIGGINS (*in despairing wrath outside*):

What the devil have I done with my slippers? (*He appears at the door*).

LIZA (*snatching up the slippers, and hurling them at him one after the other with all her force*):

There are your slippers. And there. Take your slippers; and may you never have a day's luck with them!

HIGGINS (*astounded*):

What on earth—! (*He comes to her*). What's the matter? Get up. (*He pulls her up*). Anything wrong?

LIZA (*breathless*):

Nothing wrong—with you. I've won your bet for you, haven't I? That's enough for you. *I* don't matter, I suppose.

HIGGINS:

You won my bet! You! Presumptuous insect! *I* won it. What did you throw those slippers at me for?

LIZA:

Because I wanted to smash your face. I'd like to kill you, you selfish brute. Why didn't you leave me where you picked me out of—in the gutter? You thank God it's all over, and that now you can throw me back again there, do you? (*She crisps her fingers frantically*).

HIGGINS (*looking at her in cool wonder*):

The creature is nervous, after all.

LIZA (*gives a suffocated scream of fury, and instinctively darts her nails at his face*):!!

HIGGINS (*catching her wrists*):

Ah! would you? Claws in, you cat. How dare you show your temper to me? Sit down and be quiet. (*He throws her roughly into the easy-chair*).

LIZA (*crushed by superior strength and weight*):

What's to become of me? What's to become of me?

HIGGINS:

How the devil do I know what's to become of you? What does it matter what becomes of you?

LIZA:

You don't care. I know you don't care. You wouldn't care if I was dead. I'm nothing to you—not so much as them slippers.

HIGGINS (*thundering*):

Those slippers.

LIZA (*with bitter submission*):

Those slippers. I didn't think it made any difference now.

A pause. Eliza *hopeless and crushed.* Higgins *a little uneasy.*

HIGGINS (*in his loftiest manner*):

Why have you begun going on like this? May I ask whether you complain of your treatment here?

LIZA:

No.

HIGGINS:

Has anybody behaved badly to you? Colonel Pickering? Mrs Pearce? Any of the servants?

LIZA:

No.

HIGGINS:

I presume you don't pretend that *I* have treated you badly?

LIZA:

No.

HIGGINS:

I am glad to hear it. (*He moderates his tone*). Perhaps you're tired after the strain of the day. Will you have a glass of champagne? (*He moves towards the door*).

LIZA:

No. (*Recollecting her manners*) Thank you.

HIGGINS (*good-humored again*):

This has been coming on you for some days. I suppose it was natural for you to be anxious about the garden party. But that's all over now. (*He pats her kindly on the shoulder. She writhes*). There's nothing more to worry about.

LIZA:

No. Nothing more for you to worry about. (*She suddenly rises and gets away from him by going to the piano bench, where she sits and hides her face*). Oh God! I wish I was dead.

HIGGINS (*staring after her in sincere surprise*):

Why? In heaven's name, why? (*Reasonably, going to her*) Listen to me, Eliza. All this irritation is purely subjective.

LIZA:

I don't understand. I'm too ignorant.

HIGGINS:

It's only imagination. Low spirits and nothing else. Nobody's hurting you. Nothing's wrong. You go to bed like a good girl and sleep it off. Have a little cry and say your prayers: that will make you comfortable.

LIZA:

I heard your prayers. "Thank God it's all over!"

HIGGINS (*impatiently*):

Well, don't you thank God it's all over? Now you are free and can do what you like.

LIZA (*pulling herself together in desperation*):

What am I fit for? What have you left me fit for? Where am I to go? What am I to do? What's to become of me?

HIGGINS (*enlightened, but not at all impressed*):

Oh that's what's worrying you, is it? (*He thrusts his hands into his pockets, and walks about in his usual manner, rattling the contents of his pockets, as if condescending to a trivial subject out of pure kindness*). I shouldn't bother about it if I were you. I should imagine you won't have much difficulty in settling yourself somewhere or other, though I hadn't quite realized that you were going away. (*She looks quickly at him: he does not look at her, but examines the dessert stand on the piano and decides that he will eat an apple*). You might marry, you know. (*He bites a large piece out of the apple and munches it noisily*). You see, Eliza, all men are not confirmed old bachelors like me and the Colonel. Most men are the marrying sort (poor devils!); and you're not bad-looking: it's quite a pleasure to look at you sometimes—not now, of course, because you're crying and looking as ugly as the very devil; but when you're all right and quite yourself, you're what I should call attractive. That is, to the people in the marrying line, you understand. You go to bed and have a good nice rest; and then get up and look at yourself in the glass; and you won't feel so cheap.

Eliza *again looks at him, speechless, and does not stir. The look is quite lost on him: he eats his apple with a dreamy expression of happiness, as it is quite a good one.*

HIGGINS (*a genial afterthought occurring to him*):

I daresay my mother could find some chap or other who would do very well.

LIZA:

We were above that at the corner of Tottenham Court Road.

HIGGINS (*waking up*):

What do you mean?

LIZA:

I sold flowers. I didn't sell myself. Now you've made a lady of me I'm not fit to sell anything else. I wish you'd left me where you found me.

HIGGINS (*slinging the core of the apple decisively into the grate*):

Tosh, Eliza. Don't you insult human relations by dragging all this can't about buying and selling into it. You needn't marry the fellow if you don't like him.

LIZA:

What else am I to do?

HIGGINS:

Oh, lots of things. What about your old idea of a florist's shop? Pickering could set you up in one: he's lots of money. (*Chuckling*) He'll have to pay for all those togs you have been wearing today; and that, with the hire of the jewellery, will make a big hole in two hundred pounds. Why, six months ago you would have thought it the millennium to have a flower shop of your own. Come! you'll be all right. I must clear off to bed: I'm devilish sleepy. By the way, I came down for something: I forget what it was.

LIZA:

Your slippers.

HIGGINS:

Oh yes, of course. You shied them at me. (*He picks them up, and is going out when she rises and speaks to him*).

LIZA:

Before you go, sir—

HIGGINS (*dropping the slippers in his surprise at her calling him Sir*): Eh?

LIZA:

Do my clothes belong to me or to Colonel Pickering?

HIGGINS (*coming back into the room as if her question were the very climax of unreason*):

What the devil use would they be to Pickering?

LIZA:

He might want them for the next girl you pick up to experiment on.

HIGGINS (*shocked and hurt*):

Is that the way you feel towards us?

LIZA:

I don't want to hear anything more about that. All I want to know is whether anything belongs to me. My own clothes were burnt.

HIGGINS:

But what does it matter? Why need you start bothering about that in the middle of the night?

LIZA:

> I want to know what I may take away with me. I don't want to be accused of stealing.

HIGGINS (*now deeply wounded*):

> Stealing! You shouldn't have said that, Eliza. That shows a want of feeling.

LIZA:

> I'm sorry. I'm only a common ignorant girl; and in my station I have to be careful. There can't be any feelings between the like of you and the like of me. Please will you tell me what belongs to me and what doesn't?

HIGGINS (*very sulky*):

> You may take the whole damned houseful if you like. Except the jewels. They're hired. Will that satisfy you? (*He turns on his heel and is about to go in extreme dudgeon*).

LIZA (*drinking in his emotion like nectar, and nagging him to provoke a further supply*):

> Stop, please. (*She takes off her jewels*). Will you take these to your room and keep them safe? I don't want to run the risk of their being missing.

HIGGINS (*furious*):

> Hand them over. (*She puts them into his hands*). If these belonged to me instead of to the jeweller, I'd ram them down your ungrateful throat. (*He perfunctorily thrusts them into his pockets, unconsciously decorating himself with the protruding ends of the chains*).

LIZA (*taking a ring off*):

> This ring isn't the jeweller's: it's the one you bought me in Brighton. I don't want it now. (Higgins *dashes the ring violently into the fireplace, and turns on her so threateningly that she crouches over the piano with her hands over her face, and exclaims*) Don't you hit me.

HIGGINS:

> Hit you! You infamous creature, how dare you accuse me of such a thing? It is you who have hit me. You have wounded me to the heart.

LIZA (*thrilling with hidden joy*):

> I'm glad. I've got a little of my own back, anyhow.

HIGGINS (*with dignity, in his finest professional style*):

> You have caused me to lose my temper: a thing that has hardly ever happened to me before. I prefer to say nothing more tonight. I am going to bed.

LIZA (*pertly*):

> You'd better leave a note for Mrs Pearce about the coffee; for she won't be told by me.

HIGGINS (*formally*):

Damn Mrs Pearce; and damn the coffee; and damn you; and damn my own folly in having lavished hard-earned knowledge and the treasure of my regard and intimacy on a heartless guttersnipe. (*He goes out with impressive decorum, and spoils it by slamming the door savagely*).

Eliza *smiles for the first time; expresses her feelings by a wild pantomime in which an imitation of* Higgins's *exit is confused with her own triumph; and finally goes down on her knees on the hearthrug to look for the ring.*

Act V

Mrs Higgins's *drawing room. She is at her writing-table as before.* The Parlor-Maid *comes in.*

THE PARLOR-MAID (*at the door*):

Mr Henry, ma'am, is downstairs with Colonel Pickering.

MRS HIGGINS:

Well, show them up.

THE PARLOR-MAID:

They're using the telephone, ma'am. Telephoning to the police, I think.

MRS HIGGINS:

What!

THE PARLOR-MAID (*coming further in and lowering her voice*):

Mr Henry is in a state, ma'am. I thought I'd better tell you.

MRS HIGGINS:

If you had told me that Mr Henry was not in a state it would have been more surprising. Tell them to come up when they've finished with the police. I suppose he's lost something.

THE PARLOR-MAID:

Yes, ma'am (*going*).

MRS HIGGINS:

Go upstairs and tell Miss Doolittle that Mr Henry and the Colonel are here. Ask her not to come down till I send for her.

THE PARLOR-MAID:

Yes, ma'am.

Higgins *bursts in. He is, as* The Parlor-Maid *has said, in a state.*

HIGGINS:

Look here, mother: here's a confounded thing!

MRS HIGGINS:

Yes, dear. Good morning. (*He checks his impatience and kisses her, whilst* The Parlor-Maid *goes out*). What is it?

HIGGINS:

Eliza's bolted.

MRS HIGGINS (*calmly continuing her writing*):

You must have frightened her.

HIGGINS:

Frightened her! nonsense! She was left last night, as usual, to turn out the lights and all that; and instead of going to bed she changed her clothes and went right off: her bed wasn't slept in. She came in a cab for her things before seven this morning; and that fool Mrs Pearce let her have them without telling me a word about it. What am I to do?

MRS HIGGINS:

Do without, I'm afraid, Henry. The girl has a perfect right to leave if she chooses.

HIGGINS (*wandering distractedly across the room*):

But I can't find anything. I don't know what appointments I've got. I'm—(Pickering *comes in.* Mrs Higgins *puts down her pen and turns away from the writing-table*).

PICKERING (*shaking hands*):

Good morning, Mrs Higgins. Has Henry told you? (*He sits down on the ottoman*).

HIGGINS:

What does that ass of an inspector say? Have you offered a reward?

MRS HIGGINS (*rising in indignant amazement*):

You don't mean to say you have set the police after Eliza.

HIGGINS:

Of course. What are the police for? What else could we do? (*He sits in the Elizabethan chair*).

PICKERING:

The inspector made a lot of difficulties. I really think he suspected us of some improper purpose.

MRS HIGGINS:

Well, of course he did. What right have you to go to the police and give the girl's name as if she were a thief, or a lost umbrella, or something? Really! (*She sits down again, deeply vexed*).

HIGGINS:

But we want to find her.

PICKERING:

We can't let her go like this, you know, Mrs Higgins. What were we to do?

MRS HIGGINS:

You have no more sense, either of you, than two children. Why—

The Parlor-Maid comes in and breaks off the conversation.

THE PARLOR-MAID:

Mr Henry: a gentleman wants to see you very particular. He's been sent on from Wimpole Street.

HIGGINS:

Oh, bother! I can't see anyone now. Who is it?

THE PARLOR-MAID:

A Mr Doolittle, sir.

PICKERING:

Doolittle! Do you mean the dustman?

THE PARLOR-MAID:

Dustman! Oh no, sir: a gentleman.

HIGGINS (*springing up excitedly*):

By George, Pick, it's some relative of hers that she's gone to. Somebody we know nothing about. (*To* The Parlor-Maid) Send him up, quick.

THE PARLOR-MAID:

Yes, sir. (*She goes*).

HIGGINS (*eagerly, going to his mother*):

Genteel relatives! now we shall hear something. (*He sits down in the Chippendale chair*).

MRS HIGGINS:

Do you know any of her people?

PICKERING:

Only her father: the fellow we told you about.

THE PARLOR-MAID (*announcing*):

Mr Doolittle. (*She withdraws*).

Doolittle *enters. He is brilliantly dressed in a new fashionable frock-coat, with white waistcoat and grey trousers. A flower in his buttonhole, a daz-zling silk hat, and patent leather shoes complete the effect. He is too con-cerned with the business he has come on to notice* Mrs Higgins. *He walks straight to* Higgins, *and accosts him with vehement reproach.*

DOOLITTLE (*indicating his own person*):

See here! Do you see this? You done this.

HIGGINS:

> Done what, man?

DOOLITTLE:

> This, I tell you. Look at it. Look at this hat. Look at this coat.

PICKERING:

> Has Eliza been buying you clothes?

DOOLITTLE:

> Eliza! not she. Not half. Why would she buy me clothes?

MRS HIGGINS:

> Good morning, Mr Doolittle. Won't you sit down?

DOOLITTLE (*taken aback as he becomes conscious that he has forgotten his hostess*):

> Asking your pardon, ma'am. (*He approaches her and shakes her proffered hand*). Thank you. (*He sits down on the ottoman, on* Pickering's *right*). I am that full of what has happened to me that I can't think of anything else.

HIGGINS:

> What the dickens has happened to you?

DOOLITTLE:

> I shouldn't mind if it had only happened to me: anything might happen to anybody and nobody to blame but Providence, as you might say. But this is something that you done to me: yes, you, Henry Higgins.

HIGGINS:

> Have you found Eliza? that's the point.

DOOLITTLE:

> Have you lost her?

HIGGINS:

> Yes.

DOOLITTLE:

> You have all the luck, you have. I ain't found her; but she'll find me quick enough now after what you done to me.

MRS HIGGINS:

> But what has my son done to you, Mr Doolittle?

DOOLITTLE:

> Done to me! Ruined me. Destroyed my happiness. Tied me up and delivered me into the hands of middle class morality.

HIGGINS (*rising intolerantly and standing over* Doolittle):

> You're raving. You're drunk. You're mad. I gave you five pounds. After that I had two conversations with you, at half a-crown an hour. I've never seen you since.

DOOLITTLE:

> Oh! Drunk! am I? Mad! am I? Tell me this. Did you or did you not write a letter to an old blighter in America that was giving

five million to found Moral Reform Societies all over the world, and that wanted you to invent a universal language for him?

HIGGINS:

What! Ezra D. Wannafeller! He's dead. (*He sits down again carelessly*).

DOOLITTLE:

Yes: he's dead; and I'm done for. Now did you or did you not write a letter to him to say that the most original moralist at present in England, to the best of your knowledge, was Alfred Doolittle, a common dustman.

HIGGINS:

Oh, after your last visit I remember making some silly joke of the kind.

DOOLITTLE:

Ah! you may well call it a silly joke. It put the lid on me right enough. Just give him the chance he wanted to show that Americans is not like us: that they recognize and respect merit in every class of life, however humble. Them words is in his blooming will, in which, Henry Higgins, thanks to your silly joking, he leaves me a share in his Pre-digested Cheese Trust worth three thousand a year on condition that I lecture for his Wannafeller Moral Reform World League as often as they ask me up to six times a year.

HIGGINS:

The devil he does! Whew! (*Brightening suddenly*) What a lark!

PICKERING:

A safe thing for you, Doolittle. They won't ask you twice.

DOOLITTLE:

It ain't the lecturing I mind. I'll lecture them blue in the face, I will, and not turn a hair. It's making a gentleman of me that I object to. Who asked him to make a gentleman of me? I was happy. I was free. I touched pretty nigh everybody for money when I wanted it, same as I touched you, Henry Higgins. Now I am worrited; tied neck and heels; and everybody touches me for money. It's a fine thing for you, says my solicitor. Is it? says I. You mean it's a good thing for you, I says. When I was a poor man and had a solicitor once when they found a pram in the dust cart, he got me off, and got shut of me and got me shut of him as quick as he could. Same with the doctors: used to shove me out of the hospital before I could hardly stand on my legs, and nothing to pay. Now they finds out that I'm not a healthy man and can't live unless they looks after me twice a day. In the house I'm not let do a hand's turn for myself: somebody else must do it and touch me for it. A year ago I hadn't a relative in the world except two or three that wouldn't speak to me. Now I've fifty, and not a decent week's wages among the lot of them. I have to live for others and not for myself: that's middle class morality. You talk of losing Eliza. Don't you be anxious: I bet she's on my doorstep by this: she that could support herself easy by selling flowers if I wasn't respectable. And the next one to touch me will be you, Henry Higgins. I'll have to learn to speak middle class language from you, instead of speaking proper English. That's where you'll come in; and I daresay that's what you done it for.

MRS HIGGINS:

But, my dear Mr Doolittle, you need not suffer all this if you are really in earnest. Nobody can force you to accept this bequest. You can repudiate it. Isn't that so, Colonel Pickering?

PICKERING:

I believe so.

DOOLITTLE (*softening his manner in deference to her sex*):

That's the tragedy of it, ma'am. It's easy to say chuck it; but I haven't the nerve. Which of us has? We're all intimidated. Intimidated, ma'am: that's what we are. What is there for me if I chuck it but the workhouse in my old age? I have to dye my hair already to keep my job as a dustman. If I was one of the deserving poor, and had put by a bit, I could chuck it; but then why should I, acause the deserving poor might as well be millionaires for all the happiness they ever has. They don't know what happiness is. But I, as one of the undeserving poor, have nothing between me and the pauper's uniform but this here blasted three thousand a year that shoves me into the middle class. (Excuse the expression, ma'am: you'd use it yourself if you had my provocation.) They've got you every way you turn: it's a choice between the Skilly of the workhouse and the Char Bydis of the middle class; and I haven't the nerve for the workhouse. Intimidated: that's what I am. Broke. Bought up. Happier men than me will call for my dust, and touch me for their tip; and I'll look on helpless, and envy them. And that's what your son has brought me to. (*He is overcome by emotion*).

MRS HIGGINS:

Well, I'm very glad you're not going to do anything foolish, Mr Doolittle. For this solves the problem of Eliza's future. You can provide for her now.

DOOLITTLE (*with melancholy resignation*):

Yes, ma'am: I'm expected to provide for everyone now, out of three thousand a year.

HIGGINS (*jumping up*):

Nonsense! he can't provide for her. He shan't provide for her. She doesn't belong to him. I paid him five pounds for her. Doolittle: either you're an honest man or a rogue.

DOOLITTLE (*tolerantly*):

A little of both, Henry, like the rest of us: a little of both.

HIGGINS:

Well, you took that money for the girl; and you have no right to take her as well.

MRS HIGGINS:

Henry: don't be absurd. If you want to know where Eliza is, she is upstairs.

HIGGINS (*amazed*):

Upstairs!!! Then I shall jolly soon fetch her downstairs. (*He makes resolutely for the door*).

MRS HIGGINS (*rising and following him*):

Be quiet, Henry. Sit down.

HIGGINS:

I—

MRS HIGGINS:

Sit down, dear; and listen to me.

HIGGINS:

Oh very well, very well, very well. (*He throws himself ungraciously on the ottoman, with his face towards the windows*). But I think you might have told us this half an hour ago.

MRS HIGGINS:

Eliza came to me this morning. She passed the night partly walking about in a rage, partly trying to throw herself into the river and being afraid to, and partly in the Carlton Hotel. She told me of the brutal way you two treated her.

HIGGINS (*bounding up again*):

What!

PICKERING (*rising also*):

My dear Mrs Higgins, she's been telling you stories. We didn't treat her brutally. We hardly said a word to her; and we parted on particularly good terms. (*Turning on* Higgins). Higgins: did you bully her after I went to bed?

HIGGINS:

Just the other way about. She threw my slippers in my face. She behaved in the most outrageous way. I never gave her the slightest provocation. The slippers came bang into my face the moment I entered the room—before I had uttered a word. And used perfectly awful language.

PICKERING (*astonished*):

> But why? What did we do to her?

MRS HIGGINS:

> I think I know pretty well what you did. The girl is naturally rather affectionate, I think. Isn't she, Mr Doolittle?

DOOLITTLE:

> Very tender-hearted, ma'am. Takes after me.

MRS HIGGINS:

> Just so. She had become attached to you both. She worked very hard for you, Henry! I don't think you quite realize what anything in the nature of brain work means to a girl like that. Well, it seems that when the great day of trial came, and she did this wonderful thing for you without making a single mistake, you two sat there and never said a word to her, but talked together of how glad you were that it was all over and how you had been bored with the whole thing. And then you were surprised because she threw your slippers at you! *I* should have thrown the fire-irons at you.

HIGGINS:

> We said nothing except that we were tired and wanted to go to bed. Did we, Pick?

PICKERING (*shrugging his shoulders*):

> That was all.

MRS HIGGINS (*ironically*):

> Quite sure?

PICKERING:

> Absolutely. Really, that was all.

MRS HIGGINS:

> You didn't thank her, or pet her, or admire her, or tell her how splendid she'd been.

HIGGINS (*impatiently*):

> But she knew all about that. We didn't make speeches to her, if that's what you mean.

PICKERING (*conscience stricken*):

> Perhaps we were a little inconsiderate. Is she very angry?

MRS HIGGINS (*returning to her place at the writing-table*):

> Well, I'm afraid she won't go back to Wimpole Street, especially now that Mr Doolittle is able to keep up the position you have thrust on her; but she says she is quite willing to meet you on friendly terms and to let bygones be bygones.

HIGGINS (*furious*):

> Is she, by George? Ho!

MRS HIGGINS:

If you promise to behave yourself, Henry, I'll ask her to come down. If not, go home; for you have taken up quite enough of my time.

HIGGINS:

Oh, all right. Very well. Pick: you behave yourself. Let us put on our best Sunday manners for this creature that we picked out of the mud. (*He flings himself sulkily into the Elizabethan chair*).

DOOLITTLE (*remonstrating*):

Now, now, Henry Higgins! have some consideration for my feelings as a middle class man.

MRS HIGGINS:

Remember your promise, Henry. (*She presses the bell-button on the writing-table*). Mr Doolittle: will you be so good as to step out on the balcony for a moment. I don't want Eliza to have the shock of your news until she has made it up with these two gentlemen. Would you mind?

DOOLITTLE:

As you wish, lady. Anything to help Henry to keep her off my hands. (*He disappears through the window*).

The parlor-maid *answers the bell*. Pickering *sits down in* Doolittle's *place*.

MRS HIGGINS:

Ask Miss Doolittle to come down, please.

THE PARLOR-MAID:

Yes, ma'am. (*She goes out*).

MRS HIGGINS:

Now, Henry: be good.

HIGGINS:

I am behaving myself perfectly.

PICKERING:

He is doing his best, Mrs Higgins.

A pause. Higgins *throws back his head; stretches out his legs; and begins to whistle*.

MRS HIGGINS:

Henry, dearest, you don't look at all nice in that attitude.

HIGGINS (*pulling himself together*):

I was not trying to look nice, mother.

MRS HIGGINS:

It doesn't matter, dear. I only wanted to make you speak.

HIGGINS:

> Why?

MRS HIGGINS:

> Because you can't speak and whistle at the same time.

Higgins *groans. Another very trying pause.*

HIGGINS (*springing up, out of patience*):

> Where the devil is that girl? Are we to wait here all day?

Eliza *enters, sunny, self-possessed, and giving a staggeringly convincing exhibition of ease of manner. She carries a little work-basket, and is very much at home.* Pickering *is too much taken aback to rise.*

LIZA:

> How do you do, Professor Higgins? Are you quite well?

HIGGINS (*choking*):

> Am I—(*He can say no more*).

LIZA:

> But of course you are: you are never ill. So glad to see you again, Colonel Pickering. (*He rises hastily; and they shake hands*). Quite chilly this morning, isn't it? (*She sits down on his left. He sits beside her*).

HIGGINS:

> Don't you dare try this game on me. I taught it to you; and it doesn't take me in. Get up and come home; and don't be a fool.

Eliza *takes a piece of needlework from her basket, and begins to stitch at it, without taking the least notice of this outburst.*

MRS HIGGINS:

> Very nicely put, indeed, Henry. No woman could resist such an invitation.

HIGGINS:

> You let her alone, mother. Let her speak for herself. You will jolly soon see whether she has an idea that I haven't put into her head or a word that I haven't put into her mouth. I tell you I have created this thing out of the squashed cabbage leaves of Covent Garden; and now she pretends to play the fine lady with me.

MRS HIGGINS (*placidly*):

> Yes, dear; but you'll sit down, won't you?

Higgins *sits down again, savagely.*

LIZA (*to* Pickering, *taking no apparent notice of* Higgins, *and working away deftly*):

Will you drop me altogether now that the experiment is over, Colonel Pickering?

PICKERING:

Oh don't. You mustn't think of it as an experiment. It shocks me, somehow.

LIZA:

Oh, I'm only a squashed cabbage leaf—

PICKERING (*impulsively*):

No.

LIZA (*continuing quietly*):

—but I owe so much to you that I should be very unhappy if you forgot me.

PICKERING:

It's very kind of you to say so, Miss Doolittle.

LIZA:

It's not because you paid for my dresses. I know you are generous to everybody with money. But it was from you that I learnt really nice manners; and that is what makes one a lady, isn't it? You see it was so very difficult for me with the example of Professor Higgins always before me. I was brought up to be just like him, unable to control myself, and using bad language on the slightest provocation. And I should never have known that ladies and gentlemen didn't behave like that if you hadn't been there.

HIGGINS:

Well!!

PICKERING:

Oh, that's only his way, you know. He doesn't mean it.

LIZA:

Oh, *I* didn't mean it either, when I was a flower girl. It was only my way. But you see I did it; and that's what makes the difference after all.

PICKERING:

No doubt. Still, he taught you to speak; and I couldn't have done that, you know.

LIZA (*trivially*):

Of course: that is his profession.

HIGGINS:

Damnation!

LIZA (*continuing*):

It was just like learning to dance in the fashionable way: there was nothing more than that in it. But do you know what began my real education?

PICKERING:

> What?

LIZA (*stopping her work for a moment*):

> Your calling me Miss Doolittle that day when I first came to Wimpole Street. That was the beginning of self-respect for me. (*She resumes her stitching*). And there were a hundred little things you never noticed, because they came naturally to you. Things about standing up and taking off your hat and opening doors—

PICKERING:

> Oh, that was nothing.

LIZA:

> Yes: things that showed you thought and felt about me as if I were something better than a scullery-maid; though of course I know you would have been just the same to a scullery-maid if she had been let into the drawing room. You never took off your boots in the dining room when I was there.

PICKERING:

> You mustn't mind that. Higgins takes off his boots all over the place.

LIZA:

> I know. I am not blaming him. It is his way, isn't it? But it made such a difference to me that you didn't do it. You see, really and truly, apart from the things anyone can pick up (the dressing and the proper way of speaking, and so on), the difference between a lady and a flower girl is not how she behaves, but how she's treated. I shall always be a flower girl to Professor Higgins, because he always treats me as a flower girl, and always will; but I know I can be a lady to you, because you always treat me as a lady, and always will.

MRS HIGGINS:

> Please don't grind your teeth, Henry.

PICKERING:

> Well, this is really very nice of you, Miss Doolittle.

LIZA:

> I should like you to call me Eliza, now, if you would.

PICKERING:

> Thank you. Eliza, of course.

LIZA:

> And I should like Professor Higgins to call me Miss Doolittle.

HIGGINS:

> I'll see you damned first.

MRS HIGGINS:

> Henry! Henry!

PICKERING (*laughing*):

Why don't you slang back at him? Don't stand it. It would do him a lot of good.

LIZA:

I can't. I could have done it once; but now I can't go back to it. Last night, when I was wandering about, a girl spoke to me; and I tried to get back into the old way with her; but it was no use. You told me, you know, that when a child is brought to a foreign country, it picks up the language in a few weeks, and forgets its own. Well, I am a child in your country. I have forgotten my own language, and can speak nothing but yours. That's the real break-off with the corner of Tottenham Court Road. Leaving Wimpole Street finishes it.

PICKERING (*much alarmed*):

Oh! but you're coming back to Wimpole Street, aren't you? You'll forgive Higgins?

HIGGINS (*rising*):

Forgive! Will she, by George! Let her go. Let her find out how she can get on without us. She will relapse into the gutter in three weeks without me at her elbow.

Doolittle *appears at the centre window. With a look of dignified reproach at* Higgins, *he comes slowly and silently to his daughter, who, with her back to the window, is unconscious of his approach.*

PICKERING:

He's incorrigible, Eliza. You won't relapse, will you?

LIZA:

No: not now. Never again. I have learnt my lesson. I don't believe I could utter one of the old sounds if I tried. (Doolittle *touches her on her left shoulder. She drops her work, losing her self-possession utterly at the spectacle of her father's splendor*) A-a-a-a-a-ah-ow-ooh!

HIGGINS (*with a crow of triumph*):

Aha! Just so. A-a-a-a-ahowooh! A-a-a-a-ahowooh! A-a-a-a-ahowooh! Victory! Victory! (*He throws himself on the divan, folding his arms, and spraddling arrogantly*).

DOOLITTLE:

Can you blame the girl? Don't look at me like that, Eliza. It ain't my fault. I've come into some money.

LIZA:

You must have touched a millionaire this time, dad.

DOOLITTLE:

> I have. But I'm dressed something special today. I'm going to St George's, Hanover Square. Your stepmother is going to marry me.

LIZA (*angrily*):

> You're going to let yourself down to marry that low common woman!

PICKERING (*quietly*):

> He ought to, Eliza. (*To* Doolittle) Why has she changed her mind?

DOOLITTLE (*sadly*):

> Intimidated, Governor. Intimidated. Middle class morality claims its victim. Won't you put on your hat, Liza, and come and see me turned off?

LIZA:

> If the Colonel says I must, I—I'll (*almost sobbing*) I'll demean myself. And get insulted for my pains, like enough.

DOOLITTLE:

> Don't be afraid: she never comes to words with anyone now, poor woman! respectability has broke all the spirit out of her.

PICKERING (*squeezing* Eliza's *elbow gently*):

> Be kind to them, Eliza. Make the best of it.

LIZA (*forcing a little smile for him through her vexation*):

> Oh well, just to show there's no ill feeling. I'll be back in a moment. (*She goes out*).

DOOLITTLE (*sitting down beside* Pickering):

> I feel uncommon nervous about the ceremony, Colonel. I wish you'd come and see me through it.

PICKERING:

> But you've been through it before, man. You were married to Eliza's mother.

DOOLITTLE:

> Who told you that, Colonel?

PICKERING:

> Well, nobody told me. But I concluded—naturally—

DOOLITTLE:

> No: that ain't the natural way, Colonel: it's only the middle class way. My way was always the undeserving way. But don't say nothing to Eliza. She don't know: I always had a delicacy about telling her.

PICKERING:

> Quite right. We'll leave it so, if you don't mind.

DOOLITTLE:

> And you'll come to the church, Colonel, and put me through straight?

PICKERING:

> With pleasure. As far as a bachelor can.

MRS HIGGINS:

> May I come, Mr Doolittle? I should be very sorry to miss your wedding.

DOOLITTLE:

> I should indeed be honored by your condescension, ma'am; and my poor old woman would take it as a tremenjous compliment. She's been very low, thinking of the happy days that are no more.

MRS HIGGINS (*rising*):

> I'll order the carriage and get ready. (*The men rise, except* Higgins). I shan't be more than fifteen minutes. (*As she goes to the door* Eliza *comes in, hatted and buttoning her gloves*). I'm going to the church to see your father married, Eliza. You had better come in the brougham with me. Colonel Pickering can go on with the bridegroom.

Mrs Higgins *goes out.* Eliza *comes to the middle of the room between the centre window and the ottoman.* Pickering *joins her.*

DOOLITTLE:

> Bridegroom! What a word! It makes a man realize his position, somehow. (*He takes up his hat and goes towards the door*).

PICKERING:

> Before I go, Eliza, do forgive him and come back to us.

LIZA:

> I don't think papa would allow me. Would you, dad?

DOOLITTLE (*sad but magnanimous*):

> They played you off very cunning, Eliza, them two sportsmen. If it had been only one of them, you could have nailed him. But you see, there was two; and one of them chaperoned the other, as you might say. (*To* Pickering) It was artful of you, Colonel; but I bear no malice: I should have done the same myself. I been the victim of one woman after another all my life; and I don't grudge you two getting the better of Eliza. I shan't interfere. It's time for us to go, Colonel. So long, Henry. See you in St George's, Eliza. (*He goes out*).

PICKERING (*coaxing*):

> Do stay with us, Eliza. (*He follows* Doolittle).

Eliza goes out on the balcony to avoid being alone with Higgins. *He rises and joins her there. She immediately comes back into the room and makes for the door; but he goes along the balcony quickly and gets his back to the door before she reaches it.*

HIGGINS:

Well, Eliza, you've had a bit of your own back, as you call it. Have you had enough? and are you going to be reasonable? Or do you want any more?

LIZA:

You want me back only to pick up your slippers and put up with your tempers and fetch and carry for you.

HIGGINS:

I haven't said I wanted you back at all.

LIZA:

Oh, indeed. Then what are we talking about?

HIGGINS:

About you, not about me. If you come back I shall treat you just as I have always treated you. I can't change my nature; and I don't intend to change my manners. My manners are exactly the same as Colonel Pickering's.

LIZA:

That's not true. He treats a flower girl as if she was a duchess.

HIGGINS:

And I treat a duchess as if she was a flower girl.

LIZA:

I see. (*She turns away composedly, and sits on the ottoman, facing the window*). The same to everybody.

HIGGINS:

Just so.

LIZA:

Like father.

HIGGINS (*grinning, a little taken down*):

Without accepting the comparison at all points, Eliza, it's quite true that your father is not a snob, and that he will be quite at home in any station of life to which his eccentric destiny may call him. (*Seriously*) The great secret, Eliza, is not having bad manners or good manners or any other particular sort of manners, but having the same manner for all human souls: in short, behaving as if you were in Heaven, where there are no third-class carriages, and one soul is as good as another.

LIZA:

Amen. You are a born preacher.

HIGGINS (*irritated*):

The question is not whether I treat you rudely, but whether you ever heard me treat anyone else better.

LIZA (*with sudden sincerity*):

I don't care how you treat me. I don't mind your swearing at me. I don't mind a black eye: I've had one before this. But (*standing up and facing him*) I won't be passed over.

HIGGINS:

Then get out of my way; for I won't stop for you. You talk about me as if I were a motor bus.

LIZA:

So you are a motor bus: all bounce and go, and no consideration for anyone. But I can do without you: don't think I can't.

HIGGINS:

I know you can. I told you you could.

LIZA (*wounded, getting away from him to the other side of the ottoman with her face to the hearth*):

I know you did, you brute. You wanted to get rid of me.

HIGGINS:

Liar.

LIZA:

Thank you. (*She sits down with dignity*).

HIGGINS:

You never asked yourself, I suppose, whether *I* could do without you.

LIZA (*earnestly*):

Don't you try to get round me. You'll have to do without me.

HIGGINS (*arrogant*):

I can do without anybody. I have my own soul: my own spark of divine fire. But (*with sudden humility*) I shall miss you, Eliza. (*He sits down near her on the ottoman*). I have learnt something from your idiotic notions: I confess that humbly and gratefully. And I have grown accustomed to your voice and appearance. I like them, rather.

LIZA:

Well, you have both of them on your gramophone and in your book of photographs. When you feel lonely without me, you can turn the machine on. It's got no feelings to hurt.

HIGGINS:

I can't turn your soul on. Leave me those feelings; and you can take away the voice and the face. They are not you.

LIZA:

Oh, you are a devil. You can twist the heart in a girl as easy as some could twist her arms to hurt her. Mrs Pearce warned me. Time and again she has wanted to leave you; and you always got round her at the last minute. And you don't care a bit for her. And you don't care a bit for me.

HIGGINS:

I care for life, for humanity; and you are a part of it that has come my way and been built into my house. What more can you or anyone ask?

LIZA:

I won't care for anybody that doesn't care for me.

HIGGINS:

Commercial principles, Eliza. Like (*reproducing her Covent Garden pronunciation with professional exactness*) s'yollin voylets (selling violets), isn't it?

LIZA:

Don't sneer at me. It's mean to sneer at me.

HIGGINS:

I have never sneered in my life. Sneering doesn't become either the human face or the human soul. I am expressing my righteous contempt for Commercialism. I don't and won't trade in affection. You call me a brute because you couldn't buy a claim on me by fetching my slippers and finding my spectacles. You were a fool: I think a woman fetching a man's slippers is a disgusting sight: did I ever fetch your slippers? I think a good deal more of you for throwing them in my face. No use slaving for me and then saying you want to be cared for: who cares for a slave? If you come back, come back for the sake of good fellowship; for you'll get nothing else. You've had a thousand times as much out of me as I have out of you; and if you dare to set up your little dog's tricks of fetching and carrying slippers against my creation of a Duchess Eliza, I'll slam the door in your silly face.

LIZA:

What did you do it for if you didn't care for me?

HIGGINS (*heartily*):

Why, because it was my job.

LIZA:

You never thought of the trouble it would make for me.

HIGGINS:

Would the world ever have been made if its maker had been afraid of making trouble? Making life means making trouble.

There's only one way of escaping trouble; and that's killing things. Cowards, you notice, are always shrieking to have troublesome people killed.

LIZA:

I'm no preacher: I don't notice things like that. I notice that you don't notice me.

HIGGINS (*jumping up and walking about intolerantly*):

Eliza: you're an idiot. I waste the treasures of my Miltonic mind by spreading them before you. Once for all, understand that I go my way and do my work without caring two-pence what happens to either of us. I am not intimidated, like your father and your stepmother. So you can come back or go to the devil: which you please.

LIZA:

What am I to come back for?

HIGGINS (*bouncing up on his knees on the ottoman and leaning over it to her*):

For the fun of it. That's why I took you on.

LIZA (*with averted face*):

And you may throw me out to-morrow if I don't do everything you want me to?

HIGGINS:

Yes; and you may walk out tomorrow if I don't do everything you want me to.

LIZA:

And live with my stepmother?

HIGGINS:

Yes, or sell flowers.

LIZA:

Oh! if I only could go back to my flower basket! I should be independent of both you and father and all the world! Why did you take my independence from me? Why did I give it up? I'm a slave now, for all my fine clothes.

HIGGINS:

Not a bit. I'll adopt you as my daughter and settle money on you if you like. Or would you rather marry Pickering?

LIZA (*looking fiercely round at him*):

I wouldn't marry you if you asked me; and you're nearer my age than what he is.

HIGGINS (*gently*):

Than he is: not "than what he is."

LIZA (*losing her temper and rising*):

I'll talk as I like. You're not my teacher now.

HIGGINS (*reflectively*):

I don't suppose Pickering would, though. He's as confirmed an old bachelor as I am.

LIZA:

That's not what I want; and don't you think it. I've always had chaps enough wanting me that way. Freddy Hill writes to me twice and three times a day, sheets and sheets.

HIGGINS (*disagreeably surprised*):

Damn his impudence! (*He recoils and finds himself sitting on his heels*).

LIZA:

He has a right to if he likes, poor lad. And he does love me.

HIGGINS (*getting off the ottoman*):

You have no right to encourage him.

LIZA:

Every girl has a right to be loved.

HIGGINS:

What! By fools like that?

LIZA:

Freddy's not a fool. And if he's weak and poor and wants me, may be he'd make me happier than my betters that bully me and don't want me.

HIGGINS:

Can he make anything of you? That's the point.

LIZA:

Perhaps I could make something of him. But I never thought of us making anything of one another; and you never think of anything else. I only want to be natural.

HIGGINS:

In short, you want me to be as infatuated about you as Freddy? Is that it?

LIZA:

No I don't. That's not the sort of feeling I want from you. And don't you be too sure of yourself or of me. I could have been a bad girl if I'd liked. I've seen more of some things than you, for all your learning. Girls like me can drag gentlemen down to make love to them easy enough. And they wish each other dead the next minute.

HIGGINS:

Of course they do. Then what in thunder are we quarrelling about?

LIZA (*much troubled*):

I want a little kindness. I know I'm a common ignorant girl, and you a book-learned gentleman; but I'm not dirt under

your feet. What I done (*correcting herself*) what I did was not
for the dresses and the taxis: I did it because we were pleasant
together and I come—came—to care for you; not to want you
to make love to me, and not forgetting the difference between
us, but more friendly like.

HIGGINS:

Well, of course. That's just how I feel. And how Pickering feels.
Eliza: you're a fool.

LIZA:

That's not a proper answer to give me (*she sinks on the chair at
the writing-table in tears*).

HIGGINS:

It's all you'll get until you stop being a common idiot. If you're
going to be a lady, you'll have to give up feeling neglected if the
men you know don't spend half their time snivelling over you
and the other half giving you black eyes. If you can't stand the
coldness of my sort of life, and the strain of it, go back to the
gutter. Work till you are more a brute than a human being; and
then cuddle and squabble and drink till you fall asleep. Oh, it's
a fine life, the life of the gutter. It's real: it's warm: it's violent:
you can feel it through the thickest skin: you can taste it and
smell it without any training or any work. Not like Science and
Literature and Classical Music and Philosophy and Art. You
find me cold, unfeeling, selfish, don't you? Very well: be off
with you to the sort of people you like. Marry some sentimental hog or other with lots of money, and a thick pair of lips to
kiss you with and a thick pair of boots to kick you with. If you
can't appreciate what you've got, you'd better get what you can
appreciate.

LIZA (*desperate*):

Oh, you are a cruel tyrant. I can't talk to you: you turn everything against me: I'm always in the wrong. But you know very
well all the time that you're nothing but a bully. You know I can't
go back to the gutter, as you call it, and that I have no real friends
in the world but you and the Colonel. You know well I couldn't
bear to live with a low common man after you two; and it's
wicked and cruel of you to insult me by pretending I could. You
think I must go back to Wimpole Street because I have nowhere
else to go but father's. But don't you be too sure that you have
me under your feet to be trampled on and talked down. I'll
marry Freddy, I will, as soon as he's able to support me.

HIGGINS (*sitting down beside her*):

Rubbish! you shall marry an ambassador. You shall marry the
Governor-General of India or the Lord-Lieutenant of Ireland,

or somebody who wants a deputy-queen. I'm not going to
have my masterpiece thrown away on Freddy.

LIZA:

You think I like you to say that. But I haven't forgot what you
said a minute ago; and I won't be coaxed round as if I was a
baby or a puppy. If I can't have kindness, I'll have independence.

HIGGINS:

Independence? That's middle class blasphemy. We are all
dependent on one another, every soul of us on earth.

LIZA (*rising determinedly*):

I'll let you see whether I'm dependent on you. If you can
preach, I can teach. I'll go and be a teacher.

HIGGINS:

What'll you teach, in heaven's name?

LIZA:

What you taught me. I'll teach phonetics.

HIGGINS:

Ha! ha! ha!

LIZA:

I'll offer myself as an assistant to Professor Nepean.

HIGGINS (*rising in a fury*):

What! That impostor! that humbug! that toadying ignoramus!
Teach him my methods! my discoveries! You take one step in
his direction and I'll wring your neck. (*He lays hands on her*).
Do you hear?

LIZA (*defiantly non-resistant*):

Wring away. What do I care? I knew you'd strike me some day.
(*He let's her go, stamping with rage at having forgotten himself, and
recoils so hastily that he stumbles back into his seat on the ottoman*).
Aha! Now I know how to deal with you. What a fool I was not
to think of it before! You can't take away the knowledge you
gave me. You said I had a finer ear than you. And I can be civil
and kind to people, which is more than you can. Aha! That's
done you, Henry Higgins, it has. Now I don't care that (*snapping her fingers*) for your bullying and your big talk. I'll adver-
tize it in the papers that your duchess is only a flower girl that
you taught, and that she'll teach anybody to be a duchess just
the same in six months for a thousand guineas. Oh, when I
think of myself crawling under your feet and being trampled on
and called names, when all the time I had only to lift up my finger to be as good as you, I could just kick myself.

HIGGINS (*wondering at her*):

You damned impudent slut, you! But it's better than snivelling;
better than fetching slippers and finding spectacles, isn't it?

(*Rising*) By George, Eliza, I said I'd make a woman of you; and I have. I like you like this.

LIZA:

Yes: you turn round and make up to me now that I'm not afraid of you, and can do without you.

HIGGINS:

Of course I do, you little fool. Five minutes ago you were like a millstone round my neck. Now you're a tower of strength: a consort battleship. You and I and Pickering will be three old bachelors together instead of only two men and a silly girl.

Mrs Higgins *returns, dressed for the wedding.* Eliza *instantly becomes cool and elegant.*

MRS HIGGINS:

The carriage is waiting, Eliza. Are you ready?

LIZA:

Quite. Is the Professor coming?

MRS HIGGINS:

Certainly not. He can't behave himself in church. He makes remarks out loud all the time on the clergyman's pronunciation.

LIZA:

Then I shall not see you again, Professor. Goodbye. (*She goes to the door*).

MRS HIGGINS (*coming to* Higgins):

Goodbye, dear.

HIGGINS:

Goodbye, mother. (*He is about to kiss her, when he recollects something*). Oh, by the way, Eliza, order a ham and a Stilton cheese, will you? And buy me a pair of reindeer gloves, number eights, and a tie to match that new suit of mine, at Eale & Binman's. You can choose the color. (*His cheerful, careless, vigorous voice shows that he is incorrigible*).

LIZA (*disdainfully*):

Buy them yourself. (*She sweeps out*).

MRS HIGGINS:

I'm afraid you've spoiled that girl, Henry. But never mind, dear: I'll buy you the tie and gloves.

HIGGINS (*sunnily*):

Oh, don't bother. She'll buy 'em all right enough. Goodbye.

They kiss. Mrs Higgins *runs out.* Higgins, *left alone, rattles his cash in his pocket; chuckles; and disports himself in a highly self-satisfied manner.*

The rest of the story need not be shown in action, and indeed, would hardly need telling if our imaginations were not so enfeebled by their lazy dependence on the ready-mades and reach-me-downs of the ragshop in which Romance keeps its stock of "happy endings" to misfit all stories. Now, the history of Eliza Doolittle, though called a romance because the transfiguration it records seems exceedingly improbable, is common enough. Such transfigurations have been achieved by hundreds of resolutely ambitious young women since Nell Gwynne set them the example by playing queens and fascinating kings in the theatre in which she began by selling oranges. Nevertheless, people in all directions have assumed, for no other reason than that she became the heroine of a romance, that she must have married the hero of it. This is unbearable, not only because her little drama, if acted on such a thoughtless assumption, must be spoiled, but because the true sequel is patent to anyone with a sense of human nature in general, and of feminine instinct in particular.

Eliza, in telling Higgins she would not marry him if he asked her, was not coquetting: she was announcing a well-considered decision. When a bachelor interests, and dominates, and teaches, and becomes important to a spinster, as Higgins with Eliza, she always, if she has character enough to be capable of it, considers very seriously indeed whether she will play for becoming that bachelor's wife, especially if he is so little interested in marriage that a determined and devoted woman might capture him if she set herself resolutely to do it. Her decision will depend a good deal on whether she is really free to choose; and that, again, will depend on her age and income. If she is at the end of her youth, and has no security for her livelihood, she will marry him because she must marry anybody who will provide for her. But at Eliza's age a good-looking girl does not feel that pressure: she feels free to pick and choose. She is therefore guided by her instinct in the matter. Eliza's instinct tells her not to marry Higgins. It does not tell her to give him up. It is not in the slightest doubt as to his remaining one of the strongest personal interests in her life. It would be very sorely strained if there was another woman likely to supplant her with him. But as she feels sure of him on that last point, she has not doubt at all as to her course, and would not have any, even if the difference of twenty years in age, which seems so great to youth, did not exist between them.

As our own instincts are not appealed to by her conclusion, let us see whether we cannot discover some reason in it. When Higgins excused his indifference to young women on the ground that they had an irresistible rival in his mother, he gave the clue to his inveterate old-bachelordom. The case is uncommon only to the extent that remarkable mothers are uncommon. If an imaginative boy has a sufficiently rich mother who has intelligence, personal grace, dignity of character without harshness, and a cultivated sense of the best art of her time to enable her to make her house beautiful, she sets a standard for him against which very few women can struggle, besides effecting for him a disengagement, of his affections, his sense of beauty, and his idealism from his specifically sexual impulses. This makes him a standing puzzle to the huge number of uncultivated people who have been brought up in tasteless homes by commonplace or disagreeable parents, and to whom, consequently, literature, painting, sculpture, music, and affectionate personal relations come as modes of sex if they come at all. The word passion means nothing else to them; and that Higgins could have a passion for phonetics and idealize his mother instead of Eliza, would seem to them absurd and unnatural. Nevertheless, when we look round and see that hardly anyone is too ugly or disagreeable to find a wife or a husband if he or she wants one, whilst many old maids and bachelors are above the average in quality and culture, we cannot help suspecting that the disentanglement of sex from the associations with which it is so commonly confused, a disentanglement which persons of genius achieve by sheer intellectual analysis, is sometimes produced or aided by parental fascination.

Now, though Eliza was incapable of thus explaining to herself Higgins's formidable powers of resistance to the charm that prostrated Freddy at the first glance, she was instinctively aware that she could never obtain a complete grip of him, or come between him and his mother (the first necessity of the married woman). To put it shortly, she knew that for some mysterious reason he had not the makings of a married man in him, according to her conception of a husband as one to whom she would be his nearest and fondest and warmest interest. Even had there been no mother-rival, she would still have refused to accept an interest in herself that was secondary to philosophic interests. Had Mrs Higgins died, there would still have been Milton and the Universal Alphabet. Landor's remark that to those who have the greatest power of loving, love is a secondary affair, would not have recommended Landor to Eliza. Put that along with her resentment of Higgins's domineering superiority, and her mistrust of his coaxing cleverness in getting round her and evading her wrath when he had gone too far with his impetuous bullying, and you will see that Eliza's instinct had good grounds for warning her not to marry her Pygmalion.

And now, whom did Eliza marry? For if Higgins was a predestinate old bachelor, she was most certainly not a predestinate old maid. Well, that can be told very shortly to those who have not guessed it from the indications she has herself given them.

Almost immediately after Eliza is stung into proclaiming her considered determination not to marry Higgins, she mentions the fact that young Mr Frederick Eynsford Hill is pouring out his love for her daily through the post. Now Freddy is young, practically twenty years younger than Higgins: he is a gentleman (or, as Eliza would qualify him, a toff), and speaks like one; he is nicely dressed, is treated by the Colonel as an equal, loves her unaffectedly, and is not her master, nor ever likely to dominate her in spite of his advantage of social standing. Eliza has no use for the foolish romantic tradition that all women love to be mastered, if not actually bullied and beaten. "When you go to women," says Nietzsche, "take your whip with you." Sensible despots have never confined that precaution to women: they have taken their whips with them when they have dealt with men, and been slavishly idealized by the men over whom they have flourished the whip much more than by women. No doubt there are slavish women as well as slavish men; and women, like men, admire those that are stronger than themselves. But to admire a strong person and to live under that strong person's thumb are two different things. The weak may not be admired and hero-worshipped; but they are by no means disliked or shunned; and they never seem to have the least difficulty in marrying people who are too good for them. They may fail in emergencies; but life is not one long emergency: it is mostly a string of situations for which no exceptional strength is needed, and with which even rather weak people can cope if they have a stronger partner to help them out. Accordingly, it is a truth everywhere in evidence that strong people, masculine or feminine, not only do not marry stronger people, but do not show any preference for them in selecting their friends. When a lion meets another with a louder roar "the first lion thinks the last a bore." The man or woman who feels strong enough for two, seeks for every other quality in a partner than strength.

The converse is also true. Weak people want to marry strong people who do not frighten them too much; and this often leads them to make the mistake we describe metaphorically as "biting off more than they can chew." They want too much for too little; and when the bargain is unreasonable beyond all bearing, the union becomes impossible: it ends in the weaker party being either discarded or borne as a cross, which is worse. People who are not only weak, but silly or obtuse as well, are often in these difficulties.

This being the state of human affairs, what is Eliza fairly sure to do when she is placed between Freddy and Higgins? Will she look forward to a lifetime of fetching Higgins's slippers or to a lifetime of Freddy fetching hers? There can be no doubt about the answer. Unless Freddy is biologically repulsive to her, and Higgins biologically attractive to a degree that overwhelms all her other instincts, she will, if she marries either of them, marry Freddy.

And that is just what Eliza did.

Complications ensued; but they were economic, not romantic. Freddy had no money and no occupation. His mother's jointure, a last relic of the opulence of Largelady Park, had enabled her to struggle along in Earlscourt with an air of gentility, but not to procure any serious secondary education for her children, much less give the boy a profession. A clerkship at thirty shillings a week was beneath Freddy's dignity, and extremely distasteful to him besides. His prospects consisted of a hope that if he kept up appearances somebody would do something for him. The something appeared vaguely to his imagination as a private secretaryship or a sinecure of some sort. To his mother it perhaps appeared as a marriage to some lady of means who could not resist her boy's niceness. Fancy her feelings when he married a flower girl who had become déclassée under extraordinary circumstances which were now notorious!

It is true that Eliza's situation did not seem wholly ineligible. Her father, though formerly a dustman, and now fantastically disclassed, had become extremely popular in the smartest society by a social talent which triumphed over every prejudice and every disadvantage. Rejected by the middle class, which he loathed, he had shot up at once into the highest circles by his wit, his dustmanship (which he carried like a banner), and his Nietzschean transcendence of good and evil. At intimate ducal dinners he sat on the right hand of the Duchess; and in country houses he smoked in the pantry and was made much of by the butler when he was not feeding in the dining room and being consulted by cabinet ministers. But he found it almost as hard to do all this on four thousand a year as Mrs Eynsford Hill to live in Earlscourt on an income so pitiably smaller that I have not the heart to disclose its exact figure. He absolutely refused to add the last straw to his burden by contributing to Eliza's support.

Thus Freddy and Eliza, now Mr and Mrs Eynsford Hill, would have spent a penniless honeymoon but for a wedding present of £500 from the Colonel to Eliza. It lasted a long time because Freddy did not know how to spend money, never having had any to spend, and Eliza, socially trained by a pair of old bachelors, wore her clothes as long as they held together and looked pretty, without the least regard to their being many months out of fashion. Still, £500 will not last two young people forever; and they both knew, and Eliza felt as well, that they must shift for themselves in the end. She could quarter herself on Wimpole Street because it had come to be her home; but she was quite aware that she ought not to quarter Freddy there, and that it would not be good for his character if she did.

Not that the Wimpole Street bachelors objected. When she consulted them, Higgins declined to be bothered about her housing problem when that solution was so simple. Eliza's desire to have Freddy in the house with her seemed of no more importance than if she had wanted an extra piece of bedroom furniture. Pleas as to Freddy's character, and the moral obligation on him to earn his own living, were lost on Higgins. He denied that Freddy had any character, and declared that if he tried to do any useful work some competent person would have the trouble of undoing it: a procedure involving a net loss to the community, and great unhappiness to Freddy himself, who was obviously intended by Nature for such light work as amusing Eliza, which, Higgins declared, was a much more useful and honorable occupation than working in the city. When Eliza referred again to her project of teaching phonetics, Higgins abated not a jot of his violent opposition to it. He said she was not within ten years of being qualified to meddle with his pet subject; and as it was evident that the Colonel agreed with him, she felt she could not go against them in this grave matter, and that she had no right, without Higgins's consent, to exploit the knowledge he had given her; for his knowledge seemed to her as much his private property as his watch: Eliza was no communist. Besides, she was superstitiously devoted to them both, more entirely and frankly after her marriage than before it.

It was the Colonel who finally solved the problem, which had cost him much perplexed cogitation. He one day asked Eliza, rather shyly, whether she had quite given up her notion of keeping a flower shop. She replied that she had thought of it, but had put it out of her head, because the Colonel had said, that day at Mrs Higgins's, that it would never do. The Colonel confessed that when he said that, he had not quite recovered from the dazzling impression of the day before. They broke the matter to Higgins that evening. The sole comment vouchsafed by him very nearly led to a serious quarrel with Eliza. It was to the effect that she would have in Freddy an ideal errand boy.

Freddy himself was next sounded on the subject. He said he had been thinking of a shop himself; though it had presented itself to his pennilessness as a small place in which Eliza should sell tobacco at one counter whilst he sold newspapers at the opposite one. But he agreed that it would be extraordinarily jolly to go early every morning with Eliza to Covent Garden and buy flowers on the scene of their first meeting: a sentiment which earned him many kisses from his wife. He added that he had always been afraid to propose anything of the sort, because Clara would make an awful row about a step that must damage her matrimonial chances, and his mother could not be expected to like it after clinging for so many years to that step of the social ladder on which retail trade is impossible.

This difficulty was removed by an event highly unexpected by Freddy's mother. Clara, in the course of her incursions into those artistic circles which were the highest within her reach, discovered that her conversational qualifications were expected to include a grounding in the novels of Mr H. G. Wells. She borrowed them in various directions so energetically that she swallowed them all within two months. The result was a conversion of a kind quite common today. A modern Acts of the Apostles would fill fifty whole Bibles if anyone were capable of writing it.

Poor Clara, who appeared to Higgins and his mother as a disagreeable and ridiculous person, and to her own mother as in some inexplicable way a social failure, had never seen herself in either light; for, though to some extent ridiculed and mimicked in West Kensington like everybody else there, she was accepted as a rational and normal—or shall we say inevitable?—sort of human being. At worst they called her The Pusher; but to them no more than to herself had it ever occurred that she was pushing the air, and pushing it in a wrong direction. Still, she was not happy. She was growing desperate. Her one asset, the fact that her mother was what the Epsom greengrocer called a carriage lady, had no exchange value, apparently. It had prevented her from getting educated, because the only education she could have afforded was education with the Earlscourt greengrocer's daughter. It had led her to seek the society of her mother's class; and that class simply would not have her, because she was much poorer than the greengrocer, and, far from being able to afford a maid, could not afford even a housemaid, and had to scrape along at home with an illiberally treated general servant. Under such circumstances nothing could give her an air of being a genuine product of Largelady Park. And yet its tradition made her regard a marriage with anyone within her reach as an unbearable humiliation. Commercial people and professional people in a small way were odious to her. She ran after painters and novelists; but she did not charm them; and her bold attempts to pick up and practise artistic and literary talk irritated them. She was, in short, an utter failure, an ignorant, incompetent, pretentious, unwelcome, penniless, useless little snob; and though she did not admit these disqualifications (for nobody ever faces unpleasant truths of this kind until the possibility of a way out dawns on them) she felt their effects too keenly to be satisfied with her position.

Clara had a startling eyeopener when, on being suddenly wakened to enthusiasm by a girl of her own age who dazzled her and produced in her a gushing desire to take her for a model, and gain her friendship, she discovered that this exquisite apparition had graduated from the gutter in a few months time. It shook her so violently, that when Mr H. G. Wells lifted her on the point of his puissant pen, and placed her at the angle of view from which the life she was leading and the society to which she clung appeared in its true relation to real human needs and worthy social structure, he effected a conversion and a conviction of sin comparable to the most sensational feats of General Booth or Gypsy Smith. Clara's snobbery went bang. Life suddenly began to move with her. Without knowing how or why, she began to make friends and enemies. Some of the acquaintances to whom she had been a tedious or indifferent or ridiculous affliction, dropped her: others became cordial. To her amazement she found that some "quite nice" people were saturated with Wells, and that this accessibility to ideas was the secret of their niceness. People she had thought deeply religious, and had tried to conciliate on that tack with disastrous results, suddenly took an interest in her, and revealed a hostility to conventional religion which she had never conceived possible except among the most desperate characters. They made her read Galsworthy; and Galsworthy exposed the vanity of Largelady Park and finished her. It exasperated her to think that the dungeon in which she had languished for so many unhappy years had been unlocked all the time, and that the impulses she had so carefully struggled with and stifled for the sake of keeping well with society, were precisely those by which alone she could have come into any sort of sincere human contact. In the radiance of these discoveries, and the tumult of their reaction, she made a fool of herself as freely and conspicuously as when she so rashly adopted Eliza's expletive in Mrs Higgins's drawing room; for the newborn Wellsian had to find her bearings almost as ridiculously as a baby; but nobody hates a baby for its ineptitudes, or thinks the worse of it for trying to eat the matches; and Clara lost no friends by her follies. They laughed at her to her face this time; and she had to defend herself and fight it out as best she could.

When Freddy paid a visit to Earlscourt (which he never did when he could possibly help it) to make the desolating announcement that he and his Eliza were thinking of blackening the Largelady scutcheon by opening a shop, he found the little household already convulsed by a prior announcement from Clara that she also was going to work in an old furniture shop in Dover Street, which had been started by a fellow Wellsian. This appointment Clara owed, after all, to her old social accomplishment of Push. She had made up her mind that, cost what it might, she would see Mr Wells in the flesh; and she had achieved her end at a garden party. She had better luck than so rash an enterprise deserved. Mr Wells came up to her expectations. Age had not withered him, nor could custom stale his

infinite variety in half an hour. His pleasant neatness and compact-
ness, his small hands and feet, his teeming ready brain, his unaffected
accessibility, and a certain fine apprehensiveness which stamped him
as susceptible from his topmost hair to his tipmost toe, proved irresistible. Clara talked of nothing else for weeks and weeks afterwards.
And as she happened to talk to the lady of the furniture shop, and
that lady also desired above all things to know Mr Wells and sell
pretty things to him, she offered Clara a job on the chance of achiev-
ing that end through her.

And so it came about that Eliza's luck held, and the expected
opposition to the flower shop melted away. The shop is in the arcade
of a railway station not very far from the Victoria and Albert
Museum; and if you live in that neighborhood you may go there any
day and buy a buttonhole from Eliza.

Now here is a last opportunity for romance. Would you not like
to be assured that the shop was an immense success, thanks to Eliza's
charms and her early business experience in Covent Garden? Alas!
the truth is the truth: the shop did not pay for a long time, simply
because Eliza and her Freddy did not know how to keep it. True,
Eliza had not to begin at the very beginning: she knew the names
and prices of the cheaper flowers; and her elation was unbounded
when she found that Freddy, like all youths educated at cheap, pretentious, and thoroughly inefficient schools, knew a little Latin. It
was very little, but enough to make him appear to her a Porson or
Bentley, and to put him at his ease with botanical nomenclature.
Unfortunately he knew nothing else; and Eliza, though she could
count money up to eighteen shillings or so, and had acquired a certain familiarity with the language of Milton from her struggles to
qualify herself for winning Higgins's bet, could not write out a bill
without utterly disgracing the establishment. Freddy's power of stat-
ing in Latin that Balbus built a wall and that Gaul was divided into
three parts did not carry with it the slightest knowledge of accounts
or business: Colonel Pickering had to explain to him what a cheque
book and a bank account meant. And the pair were by no means easily teachable. Freddy backed up Eliza in her obstinate refusal to
believe that they could save money by engaging a bookkeeper with
some knowledge of the business. How, they argued, could you possibly save money by going to extra expense when you already could
not make both ends meet? But the Colonel, after making the ends
meet over and over again, at last gently insisted; and Eliza, humbled
to the dust by having to beg from him so often, and stung by the
uproarious derision of Higgins, to whom the notion of Freddy succeeding at anything was a joke that never palled, grasped the fact
that business, like phonetics, has to be learned.

On the piteous spectacle of the pair spending their evenings in shorthand schools and polytechnic classes, learning bookkeeping and typewriting with incipient junior clerks, male and female, from the elementary schools, let me not dwell. There were even classes at the London School of Economics, and a humble personal appeal to the director of that institution to recommend a course bearing on the flower business. He, being a humorist, explained to them the method of the celebrated Dickensian essay on Chinese Metaphysics by the gentleman who read an article on China and an article on Metaphysics and combined the information. He suggested that they should combine the London School with Kew Gardens. Eliza, to whom the procedure of the Dickensian gentleman seemed perfectly correct (as in fact it was) and not in the least funny (which was only her ignorance) took his advice with entire gravity. But the effort that cost her the deepest humiliation was a request to Higgins, whose pet artistic fancy, next to Milton's verse, was caligraphy, and who himself wrote a most beautiful Italian hand, that he would teach her to write. He declared that she was congenitally incapable of forming a single letter worthy of the least of Milton's words; but she persisted; and again he suddenly threw himself into the task of teaching her with a combination of stormy intensity, concentrated patience, and occasional bursts of interesting disquisition on the beauty and nobility, the august mission and destiny, of human handwriting. Eliza ended by acquiring an extremely uncommercial script which was a positive extension of her personal beauty, and spending three times as much on stationery as anyone else because certain qualities and shapes of paper became indispensable to her. She could not even address an envelope in the usual way because it made the margins all wrong.

Their commercial schooldays were a period of disgrace and despair for the young couple. They seemed to be learning nothing about flower shops. At last they gave it up as hopeless, and shook the dust of the shorthand schools, and the polytechnics, and the London School of Economics from their feet forever. Besides, the business was in some mysterious way beginning to take care of itself. They had somehow forgotten their objections to employing other people. They came to the conclusion that their own way was the best, and that they had really a remarkable talent for business. The Colonel, who had been compelled for some years to keep a sufficient sum on current account at his bankers to make up their deficits, found that the provision was unnecessary: the young people were prospering. It is true that there was not quite fair play between them and their competitors in trade. Their weekends in the country cost them nothing, and saved them the price of their Sunday dinners; for the motor car was the Colonel's; and he and Higgins paid the hotel bills. Mr F. Hill, florist and greengrocer (they soon discovered that there was money in asparagus; and asparagus led to other vegetables), had an air which stamped the business as classy; and in private life he was still Frederick Eynsford Hill, Esquire. Not that there was any swank about him: nobody but Eliza knew that he had been christened Frederick Challoner. Eliza herself swanked like anything.

That is all. That is how it has turned out. It is astonishing how much Eliza still manages to meddle in the housekeeping at Wimpole Street in spite of the shop and her own family. And it is notable that though she never nags her husband, and frankly loves the Colonel as if she were his favorite daughter, she has never got out of the habit of nagging Higgins that was established on the fatal night when she won his bet for him. She snaps his head off on the faintest provocation, or on none. He no longer dares to tease her by assuming an abysmal inferiority of Freddy's mind to his own. He storms and bullies and derides; but she stands up to him so ruthlessly that the Colonel has to ask her from time to time to be kinder to Higgins; and it is the only request of his that brings a mulish expression into her face. Nothing but some emergency or calamity great enough to break down all likes and dislikes, and throw them both back on their common humanity—and may they be spared any such trial!—will ever alter this. She knows that Higgins does not need her, just as her father did not need her. The very scrupulousness with which he told her that day that he had become used to having her there, and dependent on her for all sorts of little services, and that he should miss her if she went away (it would never have occurred to Freddy or the Colonel to say anything of the sort) deepens her inner certainty that she is "no more to him than them slippers"; yet she has a sense, too, that his indifference is deeper than the infatuation of commoner souls. She is immensely interested in him. She has even secret mischievous moments in which she wishes she could get him alone, on a desert island, away from all ties and with nobody else in the world to consider, and just drag him off his pedestal and see him making love like any common man. We all have private imaginations of that sort. But when it comes to business, to the life that she really leads as distinguished from the life of dreams and fancies, she likes Freddy and she likes the Colonel; and she does not like Higgins and Mr Doolittle. Galatea never does quite like Pygmalion; his relation to her is too godlike to be altogether agreeable.

LADY AUGUSTA GREGORY

Born Isabella Augusta Persee on March 15, 1852, in Roxborough, Ireland, Lady Gregory was the twelfth of sixteen children in a family whose Protestant forebears first came to Ireland in the seventeenth century. In 1880, she married Sir William Gregory, the former governor of Ceylon. She did not begin to write until the death of her husband in 1892, when she began to gather and translate the myths and legends of Ireland. She traveled through the country's rural villages recording stories from Ireland's rich oral tradition, which she feared was disappearing and which she believed was central to the future of Irish culture. She published several volumes, from *Cuchulain of Muirthemne*, in 1902, to her last book, *Visions and Beliefs of West Ireland*, in 1920.

Lady Gregory's literary work was only part of her contribution. She dedicated her life and fortune to, in her words, "add dignity to Ireland." With the poet and playwright William Butler Yeats, she was one of the founders of the Irish Literary Renaissance, the movement to revitalize Ireland's literature and culture. In 1897, Yeats discussed with her the idea of starting a theater devoted to the Irish writers and plays. In January 1899, the Irish Literary Theatre—later to become the famed Abbey Theatre—opened in Dublin. She worked tirelessly with Yeats and another cofounder, the playwright Edward Martyn, to keep the theater afloat, doing whatever job was needed: typist, fundraiser, director, and eventually playwright. She selflessly defended the theater through its constant artistic, political, and financial battles, as in 1907 when J. M. Synge's *The Playboy of the Western World* opened to riots. Although she personally disliked the play, she publicly supported it against zealous Irish nationalists who decried it as a slur against Ireland and against charges by the Catholic Church that it was immoral.

Lady Gregory's career as a playwright grew out of helping Yeats with his myth-based plots and realistic dialogue for his plays. She then started to write one-act plays to provide comic relief for Yeats's more serious-minded poetic dramas. Her plays, however, turned out to be more popular with the Dublin theatergoers and helped the Abbey through its lean times. Inspired by the people who lived near Coole Park, her estate in Gort, she created the fictional rural community of Cloon, a recurring locale in her plays. She had an unerring ear for capturing the speech mannerisms and rhythms of poor peasants and townsfolk, and was also able to accurately and realistically portray the quality of their lives in an entertaining and dramatic way on the stage. Her characters are not romanticized or heroic, but common folk and ne'er-do-wells. Included here are two of her most popular one-act plays: *Spreading the News* and *The Rising of the Moon*, both from 1904.

In *Spreading the News*, Lady Gregory explores how the Irish love of talk, one of the culture's most charming aspects, can also be a weakness—feeding the thirst for gossip and the Irish predilection for exaggeration and misrepresentation—as rumors of Bartley Fallon's attempt to do a good deed evolve into the tangled and universally believed story that he had murdered his neighbor and is about to run off with the deceased man's wife. *The Rising of the Moon*, the encounter between an escaping political prisoner and a police sergeant, effectively encapsulated the fervent hope of Irish patriotism and nationalism that inspired Lady Gregory and the nation.

Lady Gregory died at the age of eighty at her estate on May 22, 1932. She made a lasting contribution to the rebirth and revitalization of Irish culture for future generations. As the playwright Sean O'Casey wrote, she was the "mother of many books, Daughter of Ireland, daughter of wise words, of good deeds, of great humour . . . "

SPREADING THE NEWS

BY LADY AUGUSTA GREGORY

Dramatis Personae

Bartley Fallon
Mrs Fallon
Jack Smith
Shawn Early
Tim Casey
James Ryan
Mrs Tarpey
Mrs Tully
Jo Muldoon, a Policeman
A Removable Magistrate

SCENE: *The outskirts of a Fair. An Apple Stall.* Mrs Tarpey *sitting at it.* Magistrate *and* Policeman *enter.*

MAGISTRATE:

So that is the Fair Green. Cattle and sheep and mud. No system. What a repulsive sight!

POLICEMAN:

That is so, indeed.

MAGISTRATE:

I suppose there is a good deal of disorder in this place?

POLICEMAN:

There is.

MAGISTRATE:

Common assault?

POLICEMAN:

It's common enough.

MAGISTRATE:

Agrarian crime, no doubt?

POLICEMAN:

That is so.

MAGISTRATE:

Boycotting? Maiming of cattle? Firing into houses?

POLICEMAN:

There was one time, and there might be again.

MAGISTRATE:

That is bad. Does it go any farther than that?

POLICEMAN:

Far enough, indeed.

MAGISTRATE:

Homicide, then! This district has been shamefully neglected! I will change all that. When I was in the Andaman Islands, my system never failed. Yes, yes, I will change all that. What has that woman on her stall?

POLICEMAN:

Apples mostly—and sweets.

MAGISTRATE:

Just see if there are any unlicensed goods underneath—spirits or the like. We had evasions of the salt tax in the Andaman Islands.

POLICEMAN (*Sniffing cautiously and upsetting a heap of apples.*):

> I see no spirits here—or salt.

MAGISTRATE (*To Mrs Tarpey.*):

> Do you know this town well, my good woman?

MRS TARPEY (*Holding out some apples.*):

> A penny the half-dozen, your honour.

POLICEMAN (*Shouting.*):

> The gentleman is asking do you know the town! He's the new magistrate!

MRS TARPEY (*Rising and ducking.*):

> Do I know the town? I do, to be sure.

MAGISTRATE (*Shouting.*):

> What is its chief business?

MRS TARPEY:

> Business, is it? What business would the people here have but to be minding one another's business?

MAGISTRATE:

> I mean what trade have they?

MRS TARPEY:

> Not a trade. No trade at all but to be talking.

MAGISTRATE:

> I shall learn nothing here.

James Ryan *comes in, pipe in mouth. Seeing* Magistrate *he retreats quickly, taking pipe from mouth.*

MAGISTRATE:

> The smoke from that man's pipe had a greenish look; he may be growing unlicensed tobacco at home. I wish I had brought my telescope to this district. Come to the post-office, I will telegraph for it. I found it very useful in the Andaman Islands.

Magistrate *and* Policeman *go out left.*

MRS TARPEY:

> Bad luck to Jo Muldoon, knocking my apples this way and that way. (*Begins arranging them.*) Showing off he was to the new magistrate.

Enter Bartley Fallon *and* Mrs Fallon.

BARTLEY:

> Indeed it's a poor country and a scarce country to be living in. But I'm thinking if I went to America it's long ago the day I'd be dead!

MRS FALLON:

> So you might, indeed.

She puts her basket on a barrel and begins putting parcels in it, taking them from under her cloak.

BARTLEY:

> And it's a great expense for a poor man to be buried in America.

MRS FALLON:

> Never fear, Bartley Fallon, but I'll give you a good burying the day you'll die.

BARTLEY:

> Maybe it's yourself will be buried in the graveyard of Cloonmara before me, Mary Fallon, and I myself that will be dying unbeknownst some night, and no one a-near me. And the cat itself may be gone straying through the country, and the mice squealing over the quilt.

MRS FALLON:

> Leave off talking of dying. It might be twenty years you'll be living yet.

BARTLEY (*With a deep sigh.*):

> I'm thinking if I'll be living at the end of twenty years, it's a very old man I'll be then!

MRS TARPEY (*Turns and sees them.*):

> Good morrow, Bartley Fallon; good morrow, Mrs Fallon. Well, Bartley, you'll find no cause for complaining today; they are all saying it was a good fair.

BARTLEY (*Raising his voice.*):

> It was not a good fair, Mrs Tarpey. It was a scattered sort of a fair. If we didn't expect more, we got less. That's the way with me always; whatever I have to sell goes down and whatever I have to buy goes up. If there's ever any misfortune coming to this world, it's on myself it pitches, like a flock of crows on seed potatoes.

MRS FALLON:

> Leave off talking of misfortunes, and listen to Jack Smith that is coming the way, and he singing.

Voice of Jack Smith *heard singing—*

I thought, my first love,
    There'd be but one house between you and me,
And I thought I would find
    Yourself coaxing my child on your knee.
Over the tide
    I would leap with the leap of a swan,
Till I came to the side
    Of the wife of the Red-haired man!

Jack Smith *comes in; he is a red-haired man, and is carrying a hayfork.*

MRS TARPEY:
    That should be a good song if I had my hearing.

MRS FALLON (*Shouting.*):
    It's 'The Red-haired Man's Wife.'

MRS TARPEY:
    I know it well. That's the song that has a skin on it!

She turns her back to them and goes on arranging her apples.

MRS FALLON:
    Where's herself, Jack Smith?

JACK SMITH:
    She was delayed with her washing; bleaching the clothes on the hedge she is, and she daren't leave them, with all the tinkers that do be passing to the fair. It isn't to the fair I came myself, but up to the Five Acre Meadow I'm going, where I have a contract for the hay. We'll get a share of it into tramps today.
                (*He lays down hayfork and lights his pipe.*)

BARTLEY:
    You will not get it into tramps today. The rain will be down on it by evening, and on myself too. It's seldom I ever started on a journey but the rain would come down on me before I'd find any place of shelter.

JACK SMITH:
    If it didn't itself, Bartley, it is my belief you would carry a leaky pail on your head in place of a hat, the way you'd not be without some cause of complaining.

A voice heard, 'Go on, now, go on out o' that. Go on I say.'

JACK SMITH:
    Look at that young mare of Pat Ryan's that is backing into Shaughnessy's bullocks with the dint of the crowd! Don't be daunted, Pat, I'll give you a hand with her.

He goes out, leaving his hayfork.

MRS FALLON:

It's time for ourselves to be going home. I have all I bought put in the basket. Look at there, Jack Smith's hayfork he left after him! He'll be wanting it. (*Calls.*) Jack Smith! Jack Smith!—He's gone through the crowd—hurry after him, Bartley, he'll be wanting it.

BARTLEY:

I'll do that. This is no safe place to be leaving it. (*He takes up fork awkwardly and upsets the basket.*) Look at that now! If there is any basket in the fair upset, it must be our own basket!

(*He goes out to right.*)

MRS FALLON:

Get out of that! It is your own fault, it is. Talk of misfortunes and misfortunes will come. Glory be! Look at my new egg-cups rolling in every part—and my two pound of sugar with the paper broke—

MRS TARPEY (*Turning from stall.*):

God help us, Mrs Fallon, what happened your basket?

MRS FALLON:

It's himself that knocked it down, bad manners to him. (*Putting things up.*) My grand sugar that's destroyed, and he'll not drink his tea without it. I had best go back to the shop for more, much good may it do him!

Enter Tim Casey.

TIM CASEY:

Where is Bartley Fallon, Mrs Fallon? I want a word with him before he'll leave the fair. I was afraid he might have gone home by this, for he's a temperate man.

MRS FALLON:

I wish he did go home! It'd be best for me if he went home straight from the fair green, or if he never came with me at all! Where is he, is it? He's gone up the road (*jerks elbow*) following Jack Smith with a hayfork.

She goes out to left.

TIM CASEY:

Following Jack Smith with a hayfork! Did ever anyone hear the like of that. (*Shouts.*) Did you hear that news, Mrs Tarpey?

MRS TARPEY:

I heard no news at all.

TIM CASEY:

Some dispute I suppose it was that rose between Jack Smith and Bartley Fallon, and it seems Jack made off, and Bartley is following him with a hayfork!

MRS TARPEY:

Is he now? Well, that was quick work! It's not ten minutes since the two of them were here, Bartley going home and Jack going to the Five Acre Meadow; and I had my apples to settle up, that Jo Muldoon of the police had scattered, and when I looked round again Jack Smith was gone, and Bartley Fallon was gone, and Mrs Fallon's basket upset, and all in it strewed upon the ground—the tea here—the two pound of sugar there—the egg-cups there—Look, now, what a great hardship the deafness puts upon me, that I didn't hear the commencement of the fight! Wait till I tell James Ryan that I see below; he is a neighbour of Bartley's, it would be a pity if he wouldn't hear the news!

She goes out. Enter Shawn Early *and* Mrs Tully.

TIM CASEY:

Listen, Shawn Early! Listen, Mrs Tully, to the news! Jack Smith and Bartley Fallon had a falling out, and Jack knocked Mrs Fallon's basket into the road, and Bartley made an attack on him with a hayfork, and away with Jack, and Bartley after him. Look at the sugar here yet on the road!

SHAWN EARLY:

Do you tell me so? Well, that's a queer thing, and Bartley Fallon so quiet a man!

MRS TULLY:

I wouldn't wonder at all. I would never think well of a man that would have that sort of a mouldering look. It's likely he has overtaken Jack by this.

Enter James Ryan *and* Mrs Tarpey.

JAMES RYAN:

That is great news Mrs Tarpey was telling me! I suppose that's what brought the police and the magistrate up this way. I was wondering to see them in it a while ago.

SHAWN EARLY:

The police after them? Bartley Fallon must have injured Jack so. They wouldn't meddle in a fight that was only for show!

MRS TULLY:

> Why wouldn't he injure him? There was many a man killed with no more of a weapon than a hayfork.

JAMES RYAN:

> Wait till I run north as far as Kelly's bar to spread the news!
>
> *(He goes out.)*

TIM CASEY:

> I'll go tell Jack Smith's first cousin that is standing there south of the church after selling his lambs. *(Goes out.)*

MRS TULLY:

> I'll go telling a few of the neighbours I see beyond to the west.
>
> *(Goes out.)*

SHAWN EARLY:

> I'll give word of it beyond at the east of the green.

> *Is going out when* Mrs Tarpey *seizes hold of him.*

MRS TARPEY:

> Stop a minute, Shawn Early, and tell me did you see red Jack Smith's wife, Kitty Keary, in any place?

SHAWN EARLY:

> I did. At her own house she was, drying clothes on the hedge as I passed.

MRS TARPEY:

> What did you say she was doing?

SHAWN EARLY (*Breaking away.*):

> Laying out a sheet on the hedge. *(He goes.)*

MRS TARPEY:

> Laying out a sheet for the dead! The Lord have mercy on us! Jack Smith dead, and his wife laying out a sheet for his burying! (*Calls out.*) Why didn't you tell me that before, Shawn Early? Isn't the deafness the great hardship? Half the world might be dead without me knowing of it or getting word of it at all! (*She sits down and rocks herself.*) O my poor Jack Smith! To be going to his work so nice and so hearty, and to be left stretched on the ground in the full light of the day!

> *Enter* Tim Casey.

TIM CASEY:

> What is it, Mrs Tarpey? What happened since?

MRS TARPEY:

> O my poor Jack Smith!

TIM CASEY:

Did Bartley overtake him?

MRS TARPEY:

O the poor man!

TIM CASEY:

Is it killed he is?

MRS TARPEY:

Stretched in the Five Acre Meadow!

TIM CASEY:

The Lord have mercy on us! Is that a fact?

MRS TARPEY:

Without the rites of the Church or a ha'porth!

TIM CASEY:

Who was telling you?

MRS TARPEY:

And the wife laying out a sheet for his corpse. (*Sits up and wipes her eyes.*) I suppose they'll wake him the same as another?

Enter Mrs Tully, Shawn Early, *and* James Ryan.

MRS TULLY:

There is great talk about this work in every quarter of the fair.

MRS TARPEY:

Ochone! cold and dead. And myself maybe the last he was speaking to!

JAMES RYAN:

The Lord save us! Is it dead he is?

TIM CASEY:

Dead surely, and the wife getting provision for the wake.

SHAWN EARLY:

Well, now, hadn't Bartley Fallon great venom in him?

MRS TULLY:

You may be sure he had some cause. Why would he have made an end of him if he had not? (*To* Mrs Tarpey, *raising her voice.*) What was it rose the dispute at all, Mrs Tarpey?

MRS TARPEY:

Not a one of me knows. The last I saw of them, Jack Smith was standing there, and Bartley Fallon was standing there, quiet and easy, and he listening to 'The Red-haired Man's Wife.'

MRS TULLY:

Do you hear that, Tim Casey? Do you hear that, Shawn Early and James Ryan? Bartley Fallon was here this morning listening to red Jack Smith's wife, Kitty Keary that was! Listening to her and whispering with her! It was she started the fight so!

SHAWN EARLY:

> She must have followed him from her own house. It is likely some person roused him.

TIM CASEY:

> I never knew, before, Bartley Fallon was great with Jack Smith's wife.

MRS TULLY:

> How would you know it? Sure it's not in the streets they would be calling it. If Mrs Fallon didn't know of it, and if I that have the next house to them didn't know of it, and if Jack Smith himself didn't know of it, it is not likely you would know of it, Tim Casey.

SHAWN EARLY:

> Let Bartley Fallon take charge of her from this out so, and let him provide for her. It is little pity she will get from any person in this parish.

TIM CASEY:

> How can he take charge of her? Sure he has a wife of his own. Sure you don't think he'd turn souper and marry her in a Protestant church?

JAMES RYAN:

> It would be easy for him to marry her if he brought her to America.

SHAWN EARLY:

> With or without Kitty Keary, believe me it is for America he's making at this minute. I saw the new magistrate and Jo Muldoon of the police going into the post-office as I came up—there was hurry on them—you may be sure it was to telegraph they went, the way he'll be stopped in the docks at Queenstown!

MRS TULLY:

> It's likely Kitty Keary is gone with him, and not minding a sheet or a wake at all. The poor man, to be deserted by his own wife, and the breath hardly gone out yet from his body that is lying bloody in the field!

Enter Mrs Fallon.

MRS FALLON:

> What is it the whole of the town is talking about? And what is it you yourselves are talking about? Is it about my man Bartley Fallon you are talking? Is it lies about him you are telling, saying that he went killing Jack Smith? My grief that ever he came into this place at all!

JAMES RYAN:

> Be easy now, Mrs Fallon. Sure there is no one at all in the whole fair but is sorry for you!

MRS FALLON:

> Sorry for me, is it? Why would anyone be sorry for me? Let you be sorry for yourselves, and that there may be shame on you for ever and at the day of judgment, for the words you are saying and the lies you are telling to take away the character of my poor man, and to take the good name off of him, and to drive him to destruction! That is what you are doing!

SHAWN EARLY:

> Take comfort now, Mrs Fallon. The police are not so smart as they think. Sure he might give them the slip yet, the same as Lynchehaun.

MRS TULLY:

> If they do get him, and if they do put a rope around his neck, there is no one can say he does not deserve it!

MRS FALLON:

> Is that what you are saying, Bridget Tully, and is that what you think? I tell you it's too much talk you have, making yourself out to be such a great one, and to be running down every respectable person! A rope, is it? It isn't much of a rope was needed to tie up your own furniture the day you came into Martin Tully's house, and you never bringing as much as a blanket, or a penny, or a suit of clothes with you and I myself bringing seventy pounds and two feather beds. And now you are stiffer than a woman would have a hundred pounds! It is too much talk the whole of you have. A rope is it? I tell you the whole of this town is full of liars and schemers that would hang you up for half a glass of whisky. (*Turning to go.*) People they are you wouldn't believe as much as daylight from without you'd get up to have a look at it yourself. Killing Jack Smith indeed! Where are you at all, Bartley, till I bring you out of this? My nice quiet little man! My decent comrade! He that is as kind and as harmless as an innocent beast of the field! He'll be doing no harm at all if he'll shed the blood of some of you after this day's work! That much would be no harm at all. (*Calls out.*) Bartley! Bartley Fallon! Where are you? (*Going out.*) Did anyone see Bartley Fallon?

All turn to look after her.

JAMES RYAN:

> It is hard for her to believe any such a thing, God help her!

Enter Bartley Fallon *from right, carrying hayfork.*

BARTLEY:

It is what I often said to myself, if there is ever any misfortune coming to this world it is on myself it is sure to come!

All turn round and face him.

BARTLEY:

To be going about with this fork and to find no one to take it, and no place to leave it down, and I wanting to be gone out of this—Is that you, Shawn Early? (*Holds out fork.*) It's well I met you. You have no call to be leaving the fair for a while the way I have, and how can I go till I'm rid of this fork? Will you take it and keep it until such time as Jack Smith—

SHAWN EARLY (*Backing.*):

I will not take it, Bartley Fallon, I'm very thankful to you!

BARTLEY (*Turning to apple stall.*):

Look at it now, Mrs Tarpey, it was here I got it; let me thrust it in under the stall. It will lie there safe enough, and no one will take notice of it until such time as Jack Smith—

MRS TARPEY:

Take your fork out of that! Is it to put trouble on me and to destroy me you want? Putting it there for the police to be rooting it out maybe. (*Thrusts him back.*)

BARTLEY:

That is a very unneighbourly thing for you to do, Mrs Tarpey. Hadn't I enough care on me with that fork before this, running up and down with it like the swinging of a clock, and afeard to lay it down in any place! I wish I never touched it or meddled with it at all!

JAMES RYAN:

It is a pity, indeed, you ever did.

BARTLEY:

Will you yourself take it, James Ryan? You were always a neighbourly man.

JAMES RYAN (*Backing.*):

There is many a thing I would do for you, Bartley Fallon, but I won't do that!

SHAWN EARLY:

I tell you there is no man will give you any help or any encouragement for this day's work. If it was something agrarian now—

BARTLEY:

If no one at all will take it, maybe it's best to give it up to the police.

TIM CASEY:

There'd be a welcome for it with them surely!

Laughter.

MRS TULLY:

And it is to the police Kitty Keary herself will be brought.

MRS TARPEY (*Rocking to and fro.*):

I wonder now who will take the expense of the wake for poor Jack Smith?

BARTLEY:

The wake for Jack Smith!

TIM CASEY:

Why wouldn't he get a wake as well as another? Would you begrudge him that much?

BARTLEY:

Red Jack Smith dead! Who was telling you?

SHAWN EARLY:

The whole town knows of it by this.

BARTLEY:

Do they say what way did he die?

JAMES RYAN:

You don't know that yourself, I suppose, Bartley Fallon? You don't know he was followed and that he was laid dead with the stab of a hayfork?

BARTLEY:

The stab of a hayfork!

SHAWN EARLY:

You don't know, I suppose, that the body was found in the Five Acre Meadow?

BARTLEY:

The Five Acre Meadow!

TIM CASEY:

It is likely you don't know that the police are after the man that did it?

BARTLEY:

The man that did it!

MRS TULLY:

You don't know, maybe, that he was made away with for the sake of Kitty Keary, his wife?

BARTLEY:

Kitty Keary, his wife!

Sits down bewildered.

MRS TULLY:

And what have you to say now, Bartley Fallon?

BARTLEY (*Crossing himself.*):

I to bring that fork here, and to find that news before me! It is much if I can ever stir from this place at all, or reach as far as the road!

TIM CASEY:

Look, boys, at the new magistrate, and Jo Muldoon along with him! It's best for us to quit this.

SHAWN EARLY:

That is so. It is best not to be mixed in this business at all.

JAMES RYAN:

Bad as he is, I wouldn't like to be an informer against any man.

All hurry away except Mrs Tarpey, *who remains behind her stall. Enter* Magistrate *and* Policeman.

MAGISTRATE:

I knew the district was in a bad state, but I did not expect to be confronted with a murder at the first fair I came to.

POLICEMAN:

I am sure you did not, indeed.

MAGISTRATE:

It was well I had not gone home. I caught a few words here and there that roused my suspicions.

POLICEMAN:

So they would, too.

MAGISTRATE:

You heard the same story from everyone you asked?

POLICEMAN:

The same story—or if it was not altogether the same, anyway it was no less than the first story.

MAGISTRATE:

What is that man doing? He is sitting alone with a hayfork. He has a guilty look. The murder was done with a hayfork!

POLICEMAN (*In a whisper.*):

That's the very man they say did the act; Bartley Fallon himself!

MAGISTRATE:

> He must have found escape difficult—he is trying to brazen it out. A convict in the Andaman Islands tried the same game, but he could not escape my system! Stand aside—Don't go far—have the handcuffs ready. (*He walks up to* Bartley, *folds his arms, and stands before him.*) Here, my man, do you know anything of John Smith?

BARTLEY:

> Of John Smith! Who is he, now?

POLICEMAN:

> Jack Smith, sir—Red Jack Smith!

MAGISTRATE (*Coming a step nearer and tapping him on the shoulder.*):

> Where is Jack Smith?

BARTLEY (*With a deep sigh, and shaking his head slowly.*):

> Where is he, indeed?

MAGISTRATE:

> What have you to tell?

BARTLEY:

> It is where he was this morning, standing in this spot, singing his share of songs—no, but lighting his pipe—scraping a match on the sole of his shoe—

MAGISTRATE:

> I ask you, for the third time, where is he?

BARTLEY:

> I wouldn't like to say that. It is a great mystery, and it is hard to say of any man, did he earn hatred or love.

MAGISTRATE:

> Tell me all you know.

BARTLEY:

> All that I know—Well, there are the three estates; there is Limbo, and there is Purgatory, and there is—

MAGISTRATE:

> Nonsense! This is trifling! Get to the point.

BARTLEY:

> Maybe you don't hold with the clergy so? That is the teaching of the clergy. Maybe you hold with the old people. It is what they do be saying, that the shadow goes wandering, and the soul is tired, and the body is taking a rest—The shadow! (*Starts up.*) I was nearly sure I saw Jack Smith not ten minutes ago at the corner of the forge, and I lost him again—Was it his ghost I saw, do you think?

MAGISTRATE(*To* Policeman.):

> Conscience-struck! He will confess all now!

BARTLEY:

His ghost to come before me! It is likely it was on account of the fork! I to have it and he to have no way to defend himself the time he met with his death!

MAGISTRATE (*To* Policeman.):

I must note down his words. (*Takes out notebook.*) (*To* Bartley.) I warn you that your words are being noted.

BARTLEY:

If I had ha' run faster in the beginning, this terror would not be on me at the latter end! Maybe he will cast it up against me at the day of judgment—I wouldn't wonder at all at that.

MAGISTRATE (*Writing.*):

At the day of judgment—

BARTLEY:

It was soon for his ghost to appear to me—is it coming after me always by day it will be, and stripping the clothes off in the night time?—I wouldn't wonder at all at that, being as I am an unfortunate man!

MAGISTRATE (*Sternly.*):

Tell me this truly. What was the motive of this crime?

BARTLEY:

The motive, is it?

MAGISTRATE:

Yes, the motive; the cause.

BARTLEY:

I'd sooner not say that.

MAGISTRATE:

You had better tell me truly. Was it money?

BARTLEY:

Not at all! What did poor Jack Smith ever have in his pockets unless it might be his hands that would be in them?

MAGISTRATE:

Any dispute about land?

BARTLEY (*Indignantly.*):

Not at all! He never was a grabber or grabbed from any one!

MAGISTRATE:

You will find it better for you if you tell me at once.

BARTLEY:

I tell you I wouldn't for the whole world wish to say what it was—it is a thing I would not like to be talking about.

MAGISTRATE:

There is no use in hiding it. It will be discovered in the end.

BARTLEY:

Well, I suppose it will, seeing that mostly everybody knows it before. Whisper here now. I will tell no lie; where would be the use? (*Puts his hand to his mouth, and* Magistrate *stoops.*) Don't be putting the blame on the parish, for such a thing was never done in the parish before—it was done for the sake of Kitty Keary, Jack Smith's wife.

MAGISTRATE (*To* Policeman.):

Put on the handcuffs. We have been saved some trouble. I knew he would confess if taken in the right way.

Policeman *puts on handcuffs.*

BARTLEY:

Handcuffs now! Glory be! I always said, if there was ever any misfortune coming to this place it was on myself it would fall. I to be in handcuffs! There's no wonder at all in that.

Enter Mrs Fallon, *followed by the rest. She is looking back at them as she speaks.*

MRS FALLON:

Telling lies the whole of the people of this town are; telling lies, telling lies as fast as a dog will trot! Speaking against my poor respectable man! Saying he made an end of Jack Smith! My decent comrade! There is no better man and no kinder man in the whole of the five parishes! It's little annoyance he ever gave to anyone! (*Turns and sees him.*) What in the earthly world do I see before me? Bartley Fallon in charge of the police! Handcuffs on him! O Bartley, what did you do at all at all?

BARTLEY:

O Mary, there has a great misfortune come upon me! It is what I always said, that if there is ever any misfortune—

MRS FALLON:

What did he do at all, or is it bewitched I am?

MAGISTRATE:

This man has been arrested on a charge of murder.

MRS FALLON:

Whose charge is that? Don't believe them! They are all liars in this place! Give me back my man!

MAGISTRATE:

It is natural you should take his part, but you have no cause of complaint against your neighbours. He has been arrested for the murder of John Smith, on his own confession.

MRS FALLON:

> The saints of heaven protect us! And what did he want killing Jack Smith?

MAGISTRATE:

> It is best you should know all. He did it on account of a love affair with the murdered man's wife.

MRS FALLON (*Sitting down.*):

> With Jack Smith's wife! With Kitty Keary!—Ochone, the traitor!

THE CROWD:

> A great shame, indeed. He is a traitor, indeed.

MRS TULLY:

> To America he was bringing her, Mrs Fallon.

BARTLEY:

> What are you saying, Mary? I tell you—

MRS FALLON:

> Don't say a word! I won't listen to any word you'll say! (*Stops her ears.*) O, isn't he the treacherous villain? Ohone go deo!

BARTLEY:

> Be quiet till I speak! Listen to what I say!

MRS FALLON:

> Sitting beside me on the ass-car coming to the town, so quiet and so respectable, and treachery like that in his heart!

BARTLEY:

> Is it your wits you have lost or is it I myself that have lost my wits?

MRS FALLON:

> And it's hard I earned you, slaving, slaving—and you grumbling, and sighing, and coughing, and discontented, and the priest wore out anointing you, with all the times you threatened to die!

BARTLEY:

> Let you be quiet till I tell you!

MRS FALLON:

> You to bring such a disgrace into the parish. A thing that was never heard of before!

BARTLEY:

> Will you shut your mouth and hear me speaking?

MRS FALLON:

> And if it was for any sort of a fine handsome woman, but for a little fistful of a woman like Kitty Keary, that's not four feet high hardly, and not three teeth in her head unless she got new ones! May God reward you, Bartley Fallon, for the black treachery in your heart and the wickedness in your mind, and the red blood of poor Jack Smith that is wet upon your hand!

Voice of Jack Smith *heard singing*—

> The sea shall be dry,
>> The earth under mourning and ban!
> Then loud shall he cry
>> For the wife of the red-haired man!

BARTLEY:

It's Jack Smith's voice—I never knew a ghost to sing before—
It is after myself and the fork he is coming! (*Goes back. Enter*
Jack Smith.) Let one of you give him the fork and I will be
clear of him now and for eternity!

MRS TARPEY:

The Lord have mercy on us! Red Jack Smith! The man that
was going to be waked!

JAMES RYAN:

Is it back from the grave you are come?

SHAWN EARLY:

Is it alive you are, or is it dead you are?

TIM CASEY:

Is it yourself at all that's in it?

MRS TULLY:

Is it letting on you were to be dead?

MRS FALLON:

Dead or alive, let you stop Kitty Keary, your wife, from bringing my man away with her to America!

JACK SMITH:

It is what I think, the wits are gone astray on the whole of you.
What would my wife want bringing Bartley Fallon to America?

MRS FALLON:

To leave yourself, and to get quit of you she wants, Jack Smith,
and to bring him away from myself. That's what the two of
them has settled together.

JACK SMITH:

I'll break the head of any man that says that! Who is it says it? (*To*
Tim Casey:) Was it you said it? (*To* Shawn Early:) Was it you?

ALL TOGETHER (*Backing and shaking their heads.*):

It wasn't I said it!

JACK SMITH:

Tell me the name of any man that said it!

ALL TOGETHER (*Pointing to* Bartley):

It was *him* that said it!

JACK SMITH:

Let me at him till I break his head!

Bartley *backs in terror. Neighbours hold* Jack Smith *back.*

JACK SMITH (*Trying to free himself.*):

Let me at him! Isn't he the pleasant sort of a scarecrow for any woman to be crossing the ocean with! It's back from the docks of New York he'd be turned (*trying to rush at him again*), with a lie in his mouth and treachery in his heart, and another man's wife by his side, and he passing her off as his own! Let me at him can't you.

Makes another rush, but is held back.

MAGISTRATE (*Pointing to* Jack Smith.):

Policeman, put the handcuffs on this man. I see it all now. A case of false impersonation, a conspiracy to defeat the ends of justice. There was a case in the Andaman Islands, a murderer of the Mopsa tribe, a religious enthusiast—

POLICEMAN:

So he might be, too.

MAGISTRATE:

We must take both these men to the scene of the murder. We must confront them with the body of the real Jack Smith.

JACK SMITH:

I'll break the head of any man that will find my dead body!

MAGISTRATE:

I'll call more help from the barracks. (*Blows* Policeman's *whistle.*)

BARTLEY:

It is what I am thinking, if myself and Jack Smith are put together in the one cell for the night, the handcuffs will be taken off him, and his hands will be free, and murder will be done that time surely!

MAGISTRATE:

Come on! (*They turn to the right.*)

THE RISING
OF THE MOON

BY LADY AUGUSTA GREGORY

Dramatis Personae

Sergeant
Policeman X
Policeman B
A Ragged Man

SCENE: *Side of a quay in a seaport town. Some posts and chains. A large barrel. Enter three policemen. Moonlight.*

Sergeant, *who is older than the others, crosses the stage to right and looks down steps. The others put down a pastepot and unroll a bundle of placards.*

POLICEMAN B:

 I think this would be a good place to put up a notice. (*He points to barrel.*)

POLICEMAN X:

 Better ask him. (*Calls to* Sergeant.) Will this be a good place for a placard?

 (*No answer.*)

POLICEMAN B:

 Will we put up a notice here on the barrel?

 (*No answer.*)

SERGEANT:

 There's a flight of steps here that leads to the water. This is a place that should be minded well. If he got down here, his friends might have a boat to meet him; they might send it in here from outside.

POLICEMAN B:

 Would the barrel be a good place to put a notice up?

SERGEANT:

 It might; you can put it there.

They paste the notice up.

SERGEANT (*Reading it.*):

 Dark hair—dark eyes, smooth face, height, five feet five—there's not much to take hold of in that—It's a pity I had no chance of seeing him before he broke out of jail. They say he's a wonder, that it's he makes all the plans for the whole organization. There isn't another man in Ireland would have broken jail the way he did. He must have some friends among the jailers.

575

POLICEMAN B:

A hundred pounds is little enough for the Government to offer for him. You may be sure any man in the force that takes him will get promotion.

SERGEANT:

I'll mind this place myself. I wouldn't wonder at all if he came this way. He might come slipping along there (*points to side of quay*), and his friends might be waiting for him there (*points down steps*), and once he got away it's little chance we'd have of finding him; it's maybe under a load of kelp he'd be in a fishing boat, and not one to help a married man that wants it to the reward.

POLICEMAN X:

And if we get him itself, nothing but abuse on our heads for it from the people, and maybe from our own relations.

SERGEANT:

Well, we have to do our duty in the force. Haven't we the whole country depending on us to keep law and order? It's those that are down would be up and those that are up would be down, if it wasn't for us. Well, hurry on, you have plenty of other places to placard yet, and come back here then to me. You can take the lantern. Don't be too long now. It's very lonesome here with nothing but the moon.

POLICEMAN B:

It's a pity we can't stop with you. The Government should have brought more police into the town, with *him* in jail, and at assize time too. Well, good luck to your watch.

They go out.

SERGEANT (*Walks up and down once or twice and looks at placard.*):

A hundred pounds and promotion sure. There must be a great deal of spending in a hundred pounds. It's a pity some honest man not to be the better of that.

A ragged man appears at left and tries to slip past. Sergeant *suddenly turns.*

SERGEANT:

Where are you going?

MAN:

I'm a poor ballad-singer, your honour. I thought to sell some of these (*holds out bundle of ballads*) to the sailors. (*He goes on.*)

SERGEANT:

    Stop! Didn't I tell you to stop? You can't go on there.

MAN:

    Oh, very well. It's a hard thing to be poor. All the world's against the poor!

SERGEANT:

    Who are you?

MAN:

    You'd be as wise as myself if I told you, but I don't mind. I'm one Jimmy Walsh, a ballad-singer.

SERGEANT:

    Jimmy Walsh? I don't know that name.

MAN:

    Ah, sure they know it well enough in Ennis. Were you ever in Ennis, sergeant?

SERGEANT:

    What brought you here?

MAN:

    Sure, it's to the assizes I came, thinking I might make a few shillings here or there. It's in the one train with the judges I came.

SERGEANT:

    Well, if you came so far, you may as well go farther, for you'll walk out of this.

MAN:

    I will, I will; I'll just go on where I was going.

Goes towards steps.

SERGEANT:

    Come back from those steps; no one has leave to pass down them tonight.

MAN:

    I'll just sit on the top of the steps till I see will some sailor buy a ballad off me that would give me my supper. They do be late going back to the ship. It's often I saw them in Cork carried down the quay in a hand-cart.

SERGEANT:

    Move on, I tell you. I won't have anyone lingering about the quay tonight.

MAN:

    Well, I'll go. It's the poor have the hard life! Maybe yourself might like one, sergeant. Here's a good sheet now. (*Turns one over.*) 'Content and a pipe'—that's not much. 'The Peeler and the goat'—you wouldn't like that. 'Johnny Hart'—that's a lovely song.

SERGEANT:

Move on.

MAN:

Ah, wait till you hear it. (*Sings*)—

There was a rich farmer's daughter lived near the town of Ross;
She courted a Highland soldier, his name was Johnny Hart;
Says the mother to her daughter, 'I'll go distracted mad
If you marry that Highland soldier dressed up in Highland plaid.'

SERGEANT:

Stop that noise.

Man *wraps up his ballads and shuffles towards the steps.*

SERGEANT:

Where are you going?

MAN:

Sure you told me to be going, and I am going.

SERGEANT:

Don't be a fool. I didn't tell you to go that way; I told you to go back to the town.

MAN:

Back to the town, is it?

SERGEANT (*Taking him by the shoulder and shoving him before him.*):

Here, I'll show you the way. Be off with you. What are you stopping for?

MAN (*Who has been keeping his eye on the notice, points to it.*):

I think I know what you're waiting for, sergeant.

SERGEANT:

What's that to you?

MAN:

And I know well the man you're waiting for—I know him well—I'll be going.

He shuffles on.

SERGEANT:

You know him? Come back here. What sort is he?

MAN:

Come back is it, sergeant? Do you want to have me killed?

SERGEANT:

Why do you say that?

MAN:

Never mind. I'm going. I wouldn't be in your shoes if the reward was ten times as much. (*Goes on off stage to left.*) Not if it was ten times as much.

SERGEANT (*Rushing after him.*):

Come back here, come back. (*Drags him back.*) What sort is he? Where did you see him?

MAN:

I saw him in my own place, in the County Clare. I tell you you wouldn't like to be looking at him. You'd be afraid to be in the one place with him. There isn't a weapon he doesn't know the use of, and as to strength, his muscles are as hard as that board (*slaps barrel*)

SERGEANT:

Is he as bad as that?

MAN:

He is then.

SERGEANT:

Do you tell me so?

MAN:

There was a poor man in our place, a sergeant from Bally-vaughan—It was with a lump of stone he did it.

SERGEANT:

I never heard of that.

MAN:

And you wouldn't, sergeant. It's not everything that happens gets into the papers. And there was a policeman in plain clothes, too . . . It is in Limerick he was. . . . It was after the time of the attack on the police barrack at Kilmallock. . . . Moonlight . . . just like this . . . waterside. . . . Nothing was known for certain.

SERGEANT:

Do you say so? It's a terrible county to belong to.

MAN:

That's so, indeed! You might be standing there, looking out that way, thinking you saw him coming up this side of the quay (*points*), and he might be coming up this other side (*points*), and he might be coming up this other (*points*), and he'd be on you before you knew where you were.

SERGEANT:

> It's a whole troop of police they ought to put here to stop a man like that.

MAN:

> But if you'd like me to stop with you, I could be looking down this side. I could be sitting up here on this barrel.

SERGEANT:

> And you know him well, too?

MAN:

> I'd know him a mile off, sergeant.

SERGEANT:

> But you wouldn't want to share the reward?

MAN:

> Is it a poor man like me, that has to be going the roads and singing in fairs, to have the name on him that he took a reward? But you don't want me. I'll be safer in the town.

SERGEANT:

> Well, you can stop.

MAN (*Getting up on barrel.*):

> All right, sergeant. I wonder, now, you're not tired out, sergeant, walking up and down the way you are.

SERGEANT:

> If I'm tired I'm used to it.

MAN:

> You might have hard work before you tonight yet. Take it easy while you can. There's plenty of room up here on the barrel, and you see farther when you're higher up.

SERGEANT:

> Maybe so. (*Gets up beside him on barrel, facing right. They sit back to back, looking different ways.*) You made me feel a bit queer with the way you talked.

MAN:

> Give me a match, sergeant (*he gives it, and man lights pipe*); take a draw yourself? It'll quiet you. Wait now till I give you a light, but you needn't turn round. Don't take your eye off the quay for the life of you.

SERGEANT:

> Never fear, I won't. (*Lights pipe. They both smoke.*) Indeed it's a hard thing to be in the force, out at night and no thanks for it, for all the danger we're in. And it's little we get but abuse from the people, and no choice but to obey our orders, and never asked when a man is sent into danger, if you are a married man with a family.

MAN (*Sings*)—

As through the hills I walked to view the hills and shamrock plain,
I stood awhile where nature smiles to view the rocks and streams,
On a matron fair I fixed my eyes beneath a fertile vale,
As she sang her song it was on the wrong of poor old Granuaile.

SERGEANT:
   Stop that; that's no song to be singing in these times.
MAN:
   Ah, sergeant, I was only singing to keep my heart up. It sinks
   when I think of him. To think of us two sitting here, and he
   creeping up the quay, maybe, to get to us.
SERGEANT:
   Are you keeping a good lookout?
MAN:
   I am; and for no reward too. Amn't I the foolish man? But
   when I saw a man in trouble, I never could help trying to get
   him out of it. What's that? Did something hit me?

Rubs his heart.

SERGEANT (*Patting him on the shoulder.*):
   You will get your reward in heaven.
MAN:
   I know that, I know that, sergeant, but life is precious.
SERGEANT:
   Well, you can sing if it gives you more courage.
MAN (*Sings*)—

Her head was bare, her hands and feet with iron bands were bound,
Her pensive strain and plaintive wail mingles with the evening gale,
And the song she sang with mournful air, I am old Granuaile.
Her lips so sweet that monarchs kissed . . .

SERGEANT:
   That's not it. . . . 'Her gown she wore was stained with
   gore.' . . . That's it—you missed that.
MAN:
   You're right, sergeant, so it is; I missed it. (*Repeats line.*) But to
   think of a man like you knowing a song like that.
SERGEANT:
   There's many a thing a man might know and might not have
   any wish for.

MAN:

Now, I daresay, sergeant, in your youth, you used to be sitting up on a wall, the way you are sitting up on this barrel now, and the other lads beside you, and you singing 'Granuaile'? . . .

SERGEANT:

I did then.

MAN:

And the 'Shan Bhean Bhocht'? . . .

SERGEANT:

I did then.

MAN:

And the 'Green on the Cape?'

SERGEANT:

That was one of them.

MAN:

And maybe the man you are watching for tonight used to be sitting on the wall, when he was young, and singing those same songs. . . . It's a queer world. . . .

SERGEANT:

Whisht! . . . I think I see something coming. . . . It's only a dog.

MAN:

And isn't it a queer world? . . . Maybe it's one of the boys you used to be singing with that time you will be arresting today or tomorrow, and sending into the dock. . . .

SERGEANT:

That's true indeed.

MAN:

And maybe one night, after you had been singing, if the other boys had told you some plan they had, some plan to free the country, you might have joined with them . . . and maybe it is you might be in trouble now.

SERGEANT:

Well, who knows but I might? I had a great spirit in those days.

MAN:

It's a queer world, sergeant, and it's little any mother knows when she sees her child creeping on the floor what might happen to it before it has gone through its life, or who will be who in the end.

SERGEANT:

That's a queer thought now, and a true thought. Wait now till I think it out. . . . If it wasn't for the sense I have, and for my wife and family, and for me joining the force the time I did, it might be myself now would be after breaking jail and hiding in the dark, and it might be him that's hiding in the dark and that got out of jail would be sitting up where I am on this barrel. . . . And it might be myself would be creeping up trying to make my escape from himself, and it might be himself would be keeping the law, and myself would be breaking it, and myself would be trying maybe to put a bullet in his head, or to take up a lump of a stone the way you said he did . . . no, that myself did. . . . Oh! (*Gasps. After a pause.*) What's that? (*Grasps man's arm.*)

MAN (*Jumps off barrel and listens, looking out over water.*):
It's nothing, sergeant.

SERGEANT:
I thought it might be a boat. I had a notion there might be friends of his coming about the quays with a boat.

MAN:
Sergeant, I am thinking it was with the people you were, and not with the law you were, when you were a young man.

SERGEANT:
Well, if I was foolish then, that time's gone.

MAN:
Maybe, sergeant, it comes into your head sometimes, in spite of your belt and your tunic, that it might have been as well for you to have followed Granuaile.

SERGEANT:
It's no business of yours what I think.

MAN:
Maybe, sergeant, you'll be on the side of the country yet.

SERGEANT (*Gets off barrel.*):
Don't talk to me like that. I have my duties and I know them. (*Looks round.*) That was a boat; I hear the oars.

Goes to the steps and looks down.

MAN (*Sings*):

> O, then, tell me, Shawn O'Farrell,
>   Where the gathering is to be.
> In the old spot by the river
>   Right well known to you and me!

SERGEANT:
Stop that! Stop that, I tell you!

MAN (*Sings louder*):

> One word more, for signal token,
> Whistle up the marching tune,
> With your pike upon your shoulder,
> At the Rising of the Moon.

SERGEANT:

If you don't stop that, I'll arrest you.

A whistle from below answers, repeating the air.

SERGEANT:

That's a signal. (*Stands between him and steps.*) You must not pass this way. . . . Step farther back. . . . Who are you? You are no ballad-singer.

MAN:

You needn't ask who I am; that placard will tell you.

Points to placard.

SERGEANT:

You are the man I am looking for.

MAN (*Takes off hat and wig. Sergeant seizes them.*):

I am. There's a hundred pounds on my head. There is a friend of mine below in a boat. He knows a safe place to bring me to.

SERGEANT (*Looking still at hat and wig.*):

It's a pity! It's a pity. You deceived me. You deceived me well.

MAN:

I am a friend of Granuaile. There is a hundred pounds on my head.

SERGEANT:

It's a pity, it's a pity!

MAN:

Will you let me pass, or must I make you let me?

SERGEANT:

I am in the force. I will not let you pass.

MAN:

I thought to do it with my tongue. (*Puts hand in breast.*) What is that?

(*Voice of* Policeman X *outside:*)

Here, this is where we left him.

SERGEANT:

It's my comrades coming.

MAN:
> You won't betray me . . . the friend of Granuaile.

Slips behind barrel.

(*Voice of* Policeman B:)
> That was the last of the placards.

POLICEMAN X (*As they come in.*):
> If he makes his escape it won't be unknown he'll make it.

Sergeant puts hat and wig behind his back.

POLICEMAN B:
> Did any one come this way?

SERGEANT (*After a pause.*):
> No one.

POLICEMAN B:
> No one at all?

SERGEANT:
> No one at all.

POLICEMAN B:
> We had no orders to go back to the station; we can stop along with you.

SERGEANT:
> I don't want you. There is nothing for you to do here.

POLICEMAN B:
> You bade us to come back here and keep watch with you.

SERGEANT:
> I'd sooner be alone. Would any man come this way and you making all that talk? It is better the place to be quiet.

POLICEMAN B:
> Well, we'll leave you the lantern anyhow.

Hands it to him.

SERGEANT:
> I don't want it. Bring it with you.

POLICEMAN B:
> You might want it. There are clouds coming up and you have the darkness of the night before you yet. I'll leave it over here on the barrel.

Goes to barrel.

SERGEANT:

Bring it with you I tell you. No more talk.

POLICEMAN B:

Well, I thought it might be a comfort to you. I often think when I have it in my hand and can be flashing it about into every dark corner (*doing so*) that it's the same as being beside the fire at home, and the bits of bogwood blazing up now and again.

Flashes it about, now on the barrel, now on Sergeant.

SERGEANT (*Furious.*):

Be off the two of you, yourselves and your lantern!

They go out. Man comes from behind barrel. He and Sergeant *stand looking at one another.*

SERGEANT:

What are you waiting for?

MAN:

For my hat, of course, and my wig. You wouldn't wish me to get my death of cold?

Sergeant gives them.

MAN (*Going towards steps.*):

Well, good-night, comrade, and thank you. You did me a good turn tonight, and I'm obliged to you. Maybe I'll be able to do as much for you when the small rise up and the big fall down . . . when we all change places at the Rising (*waves his hand and disappears*) of the Moon.

SERGEANT (*Turning his back to audience and reading placard.*):

A hundred pounds reward! A hundred pounds! (*Turns towards audience.*) I wonder, now, am I as great a fool as I think I am?

WILLIAM BUTLER YEATS

William Butler Yeats was born in Sandymount, near Dublin, Ireland, on June 13, 1865. He was the eldest of four children of John Butler Yeats, the painter, and the former Susan Pollexfen. Although the Yeats family was of English descent, by the time of William's birth they had been in Ireland for over two hundred years. At the age of nine, he moved with his family to London, but continued to spend summers with his grandparents in County Sligo, in the rural part of West Ireland. In 1880, the family returned to Dublin and after finishing high school in 1883, Yeats attended art school for a brief time before deciding to become a poet.

Yeats came of age in the turbulent era of growing Irish nationalism and rebellion against English rule and he became actively involved in the struggle for Irish independence. By the early 1890s he had helped form the Irish Literary Society of London and the National Literary Society in Dublin to promote Irish cultural awareness. In 1896, he became a member of the Irish Republican Brotherhood, an organization that actively sought independence, by violent means if necessary. In 1922, to reward his patriotic efforts, he was appointed Senator in the newly formed Irish Free State.

Yeats believed that political and economic independence for Ireland were not enough, and that just as important, or more so, was freedom from the materialistic culture of England. He felt that the richness and vitality of the Irish way of life were to be found in its myths, legends, and folklore. Through the cultivation of its native art, he believed Ireland could rejuvenate its unique culture and "preserve an ancient ideal of life." Along with his patron, Lady Gregory, Yeats became one of the leaders in a movement that came to be known as the Irish Literary Renaissance. Their major project was the establishment in 1899 of the Irish National Theatre (later the Abbey Theatre), a showcase for talented Irish playwrights, including Yeats, Lady Gregory, and John Millington Synge.

But Yeats's greatest contribution to Ireland was his own lyric poetry and plays. In 1923, Yeats became the first Irishman to win the

Nobel Prize for literature. He is today considered one of English literature's greatest poets. In the elegy "In Memory of W. B. Yeats"—Yeats died on January 28, 1939—the poet W. H. Auden wrote that "mad Ireland hurt you into poetry." Yeats's involvement and experiences in the country's bitter struggle for independence greatly influenced his writing. His desire to more effectively communicate the realities of Irish life and aspirations led him to believe "that the element of strength in poetic language is common idiom. . . ." While Yeats drew from Ireland's oral tradition of mythology and folklore for sources of his plots and language, his plays are for the most part experimental. His conception of drama differed from that of his contemporaries, who, for the most part, wrote realistic plays. Yeats was influenced by the Japanese Nōh plays and by Classical Greek and Medieval drama. In his plays he combined verse, dance, the use of masks, and symbolic action to create a formal, sophisticated, and ritualized drama that prefigured the Absurdist drama of Samuel Beckett.

In *The Land of Heart's Desire* (1894) Yeats depicts the conflict of a young bride who must choose between the material world and the supernatural fairy world that haunts her imagination. *On Baile's Strand* (1904) is one of five plays Yeats based on the exploits of Cuchulain, the hero of the Red Branch Ulster cycle of Celtic myth. The play focuses on the episode in which Cuchulain, defending the domain of his king, Conchobar, unknowingly kills his own son.

The Land of Heart's Desire

By W. B. Yeats

Dramatis Personae

MAURTEEN BRUIN
SHAWN BRUIN
FATHER HART
BRIDGET BRUIN
MAIRE BRUIN
A FAERY CHILD

The scene is laid in the Barony of Kilmacowen, in the County of Sligo, and the characters are supposed to speak in Gaelic. They wear the costume of a century ago.

The kitchen of Maurteen Bruin's *house. An open grate with a turf fire is at the left side of the room, with a table in front of it. There is a door leading to the open air at the back, and another door a little to its left, leading into an inner room. There is a window, a settle, and a large dresser on the right side of the room, and a great bowl of primroses on the sill of the window.* Maurteen Bruin, Father Hart, *and* Bridget Bruin *are sitting at the table.* Shawn Bruin *is setting the table for supper.* Maire Bruin *sits on the settle reading a yellow manuscript.*

BRIDGET BRUIN:

> Because I bade her go and feed the calves,
> She took that old book down out of the thatch
> And has been doubled over it all day.
> We would be deafened by her groans and moans
> Had she to work as some do, Father Hart,
> Get up at dawn like me, and mend and scour;
> Or ride abroad in the boisterous night like you,
> The pyx and blessed bread under your arm.

SHAWN BRUIN:

> You are too cross.

BRIDGET BRUIN:

> The young side with the young.

MAURTEEN BRUIN:

> She quarrels with my wife a bit at times,
> And is too deep just now in the old book!
> But do not blame her greatly; she will grow
> As quiet as a puff-ball in a tree
> When but the moons of marriage dawn and die
> For half a score of times.

FATHER HART:

> Their hearts are wild
> As be the hearts of birds, till children come.

BRIDGET BRUIN:

> She would not mind the griddle, milk the cow,
> Or even lay the knives and spread the cloth.

FATHER HART:

> I never saw her read a book before;
> What may it be?

MAURTEEN BRUIN:

> I do not rightly know;
> It has been in the thatch for fifty years.
> My father told me my grandfather wrote it,
> Killed a red heifer and bound it with the hide.
> But draw your chair this way—supper is spread;
> And little good he got out of the book,
> Because it filled his house with roaming bards,
> And roaming ballad-makers and the like,
> And wasted all his goods.—Here is the wine:
> The griddle bread's beside you, Father Hart.
> Colleen, what have you got there in the book
> That you must leave the bread to cool? Had I,
> Or had my father, read or written books
> There were no stocking full of silver and gold
> To come, when I am dead, to Shawn and you.

FATHER HART:

> You should not fill your head with foolish dreams.
> What are you reading?

MAIRE BRUIN:

> How a Princess Edane,
> A daughter of a King of Ireland, heard
> A voice singing on a May Eve like this,
> And followed, half awake and half asleep,
> Until she came into the land of faery,
> Where nobody gets old and godly and grave,
> Where nobody gets old and crafty and wise,
> Where nobody gets old and bitter of tongue;
> And she is still there, busied with a dance,
> Deep in the dewy shadow of a wood,
> Or where stars walk upon a mountain-top.

MAURTEEN BRUIN:

> Persuade the colleen to put by the book:
> My grandfather would mutter just such things,
> And he was no judge of a dog or horse,
> And any idle boy could blarney him:
> Just speak your mind.

FATHER HART:

> Put it away, my colleen.

Maire Bruin *goes over to the window and takes flowers from the bowl and strews them outside the door.*

FATHER HART:

> You do well, daughter, because God permits
> Great power to the good people on May Eve.

SHAWN BRUIN:

> They can work all their will with primroses;
> Change them to golden money, or little flames
> To burn up those who do them any wrong.

MAIRE BRUIN (*in a dreamy voice*):

> I had no sooner flung them by the door
> Than the wind cried and hurried them away;
> And then a child came running in the wind
> And caught them in her hands and fondled them:
> Her dress was green: her hair was of red gold;
> Her face was pale as water before dawn.

FATHER HART:

> Whose child can this be?

MAURTEEN BRUIN:

> No one's child at all.
> She often dreams that some one has gone by
> When there was nothing but a puff of wind.

MAIRE BRUIN:

> They will not bring good luck into the house,
> For they have blown the primroses away;
> Yet I am glad that I was courteous to them,
> For are not they, likewise, children of God?

FATHER HART:

> Colleen, they are the children of the fiend,
> And they have power until the end of Time,
> When God shall fight with them a great pitched battle
> And hack them into pieces.

MAURTEEN BRUIN:

> Come, sit beside me, colleen,
> And put away your dreams of discontent,
> For I would have you light up my last days
> Like a bright torch of pine, and when I die
> I will make you the wealthiest hereabout:
> For hid away where nobody can find
> I have a stocking full of silver and gold.

BRIDGET BRUIN:

> You are the fool of every pretty face,
> And I must pinch and pare that my son's wife
> May have all kinds of ribbons for her head.

MAURTEEN BRUIN:

> Do not be cross; she is a right good girl!
> The butter is by your elbow, Father Hart.
> My colleen, have not Fate and Time and Change
> Done well for me and for old Bridget there?
> We have a hundred acres of good land,
> And sit beside each other at the fire,
> The wise priest of our parish to our right,
> And you and our dear son to left of us.
> To sit beside the board and drink good wine
> And watch the turf smoke coiling from the fire
> And feel content and wisdom in your heart,
> This is the best of life; when we are young
> We long to tread a way none trod before,
> But find the excellent old way through love
> And through the care of children to the hour
> For bidding Fate and Time and Change goodbye.

A knock at the door. Maire Bruin *opens it and then takes a sod of turf out of the hearth in the tongs and passes it through the door and closes the door and remains standing by it.*

MAIRE BRUIN:

> A little queer old man in a green coat,
> Who asked a burning sod to light his pipe.

BRIDGET BRUIN:

> You have now given milk and fire, and brought,
> For all you know, evil upon the house.
> Before you married you were idle and fine,
> And went about with ribbons on your head;
> And now you are a good-for-nothing wife.

SHAWN BRUIN:

> Be quiet, mother!

MAURTEEN BRUIN:

> You are much too cross!

MAIRE BRUIN:

> What do I care if I have given this house,
> Where I must hear all day a bitter tongue,
> Into the power of faeries!

BRIDGET BRUIN:

> You know well
> How calling the good people by that name
> Or talking of them over much at all
> May bring all kinds of evil on the house.

MAIRE BRUIN:

> Come, faeries, take me out of this dull house!
> Let me have all the freedom I have lost;
> Work when I will and idle when I will!
> Faeries, come take me out of this dull world,
> For I would ride with you upon the wind,
> Run on the top of the dishevelled tide,
> And dance upon the mountains like a flame!

FATHER HART:

> You cannot know the meaning of your words.

MAIRE BRUIN:

> Then I would take and break it in my hands
> To see you smile watching it crumble away.

SHAWN BRUIN:

> Then I would mould a world of fire and dew
> With no one bitter, grave, or over wise,
> And nothing marred or old to do you wrong.
> And crowd the enraptured quiet of the sky
> With candles burning to your lonely face.

MAIRE BRUIN:

> Your looks are all the candles that I need.

SHAWN BRUIN:

> Once a fly dancing in a beam of the sun,
> Or the light wind blowing out of the dawn,
> Could fill your heart with dreams none other knew,
> But now the indissoluble sacrament
> Has mixed your heart that was most proud and cold
> With my warm heart for ever; and sun and moon
> Must fade and heaven be rolled up like a scroll;
> But your white spirit still walk by my spirit.

> (A Voice *sings in the distance.*)

MAIRE BRUIN:

> Did you hear something call? O, guard me close,
> Because I have said wicked things to-night;
> And seen a pale-faced child with red-gold hair,
> And longed to dance upon the winds with her.

A VOICE (*close to the door*):

> *The wind blows out of the gates of the day,*
> *The wind blows over the lonely of heart*
> *And the lonely of heart is withered away,*
> *While the faeries dance in a place apart,*
> *Shaking their milk-white feet in a ring,*
> *Tossing their milk-white arms in the air;*
> *For they hear the wind laugh, and murmur and sing*

Of a land where even the old are fair,
And even the wise are merry of tongue;
But I heard a reed of Coolaney say,
"When the wind has laughed and murmured and sung,
The lonely of heart is withered away!"

MAURTEEN BRUIN:

    I am right happy, and would make all else
    Be happy too. I hear a child outside,
    And will go bring her in out of the cold.

He opens the door. A Child dressed in pale green and with red-gold hair comes into the house.

THE CHILD:

    I tire of winds and waters and pale lights!

MAURTEEN BRUIN:

    You are most welcome. It is cold out there;
    Who'd think to face such cold on a May Eve?

THE CHILD:

    And when I tire of this warm little house
    There is one here who must away, away,
    To where the woods, the stars, and the white streams
    Are holding a continual festival.

MAURTEEN BRUIN:

    O listen to her dreamy and strange talk.
    Come to the fire.

THE CHILD:

    I will sit upon your knee,
    For I have run from where the winds are born,
    And long to rest my feet a little while.

                           (She sits upon his knee.)

BRIDGET BRUIN:

    How pretty you are!

MAURTEEN BRUIN:

    Your hair is wet with dew!

BRIDGET BRUIN:

    I will warm your chilly feet.

       She takes The Child's *feet in her hands.*

MAURTEEN BRUIN:

    You must have come
    A long, long way, for I have never seen

Your pretty face, and must be tired and hungry;
Here is some bread and wine.

THE CHILD:

The wine is bitter.
Old mother, have you no sweet food for me?

BRIDGET BRUIN:

I have some honey!

(*She goes into the next room.*)

MAURTEEN BRUIN:

You are a dear child;
The mother was quite cross before you came.

Bridget *returns with the honey, and goes to the dresser and fills a porringer with milk.*

BRIDGET BRUIN:

She is the child of gentle people; look
At her white hands and at her pretty dress.
I have brought you some new milk, but wait awhile,
And I will put it by the fire to warm,
For things well fitted for poor folk like us
Would never please a high-born child like you.

THE CHILD:

Old mother, my old mother, the green dawn
Brightens above while you blow up the fire;
And evening finds you spreading the white cloth.
The young may lie in bed and dream and hope,
But you work on because your heart is old.

BRIDGET BRUIN:

The young are idle.

THE CHILD:

Old father, you are wise
And all the years have gathered in your heart
To whisper of the wonders that are gone.
The young must sigh through many a dream and hope,
But you are wise because your heart is old.

MAURTEEN BRUIN:

O, who would think to find so young a child
Loving old age and wisdom?

Bridget *gives her more bread and honey.*

THE CHILD:

No more, mother.

MAURTEEN BRUIN:

    What a small bite! The milk is ready now;
    What a small sip!

THE CHILD:

    Put on my shoes, old mother,
    For I would like to dance now I have eaten.
    The reeds are dancing by Coolaney lake,
    And I would like to dance until the reeds
    And the white waves have danced themselves to sleep.

Bridget *having put on her shoes, she gets off the old man's knees and is about to dance, but suddenly sees the crucifix and shrieks and covers her eyes.*

    What is that ugly thing on the black cross?

FATHER HART:

    You cannot know how naughty your words are!
    That is our Blessed Lord!

THE CHILD:

    Here is level ground for dancing. I will dance.
    The wind is blowing on the waving reeds,
    The wind is blowing on the heart of man.

        She dances, swaying about like the reeds.

MAIRE (*to* Shawn Bruin):

    Just now when she came near I thought I heard
    Other small steps beating upon the floor,
    And a faint music blowing in the wind,
    Invisible pipes giving her feet the time.

SHAWN BRUIN:

    I heard no step but hers.

MAIRE BRUIN:

    Look to the bolt!
    Because the unholy powers are abroad.

MAURTEEN BRUIN (*to* The Child):

    Come over here, and if you promise me
    Not to talk wickedly of holy things
    I will give you something.

THE CHILD:

    Bring it me, old father!

        Maurteen Bruin *goes into the next room.*

FATHER HART:

    I will have queen cakes when you come to me!

Maurteen Bruin *returns and lays a piece of money on the table.* The Child *makes a gesture of refusal.*

MAURTEEN BRUIN:

    It will buy lots of toys; see how it glitters!

THE CHILD:

    Come, tell me, do you love me?

MAURTEEN BRUIN:

    I love you!

THE CHILD:

    Ah! but you love this fireside!

FATHER HART:

    I love you.

THE CHILD:

    But you love Him above.

BRIDGET BRUIN:

    She is blaspheming.

THE CHILD (*to* Maire):

    And do you love me?

MAIRE BRUIN:

    I—I do not know.

THE CHILD:

    You love that great tall fellow over there:
    Yet I could make you ride upon the winds,
    Run on the top of the dishevelled tide,
    And dance upon the mountains like a flame!

MAIRE BRUIN:

    Queen of the Angels and kind Saints, defend us!
    Some dreadful fate has fallen: a while ago
    The wind cried out and took the primroses,
    And she ran by me laughing in the wind,
    And I gave milk and fire, and she came in
    And made you hide the blessed crucifix.

FATHER HART:

    You fear because of her wild, pretty prattle;
    She knows no better.   (*To* The Child.)
    Child, how old are you?

THE CHILD:

    When winter sleep is abroad my hair grows thin,
    My feet unsteady. When the leaves awaken

My mother carries me in her golden arms.
I'll soon put on my womanhood and marry
The spirits of wood and water, but who can tell
When I was born for the first time? I think
I am much older than the eagle cock
That blinks and blinks on Ballygawley Hill,
And he is the oldest thing under the moon.

FATHER HART:
    She is of the faery people.

THE CHILD:
    I am Brig's daughter.
    I sent my messengers for milk and fire,
    And then I heard one call to me and came.

They all except Maire Bruin *gather about the priest for protection.* Maire
Bruin *stays on the settle in a stupor of terror.* The Child *takes primroses
from the great bowl and begins to strew them between herself and the
priest and about* Maire Bruin. *During the following dialogue* Shawn
Bruin *goes more than once to the brink of the primroses, but shrinks back
to the others timidly.*

FATHER HART:
    I will confront this mighty spirit alone.

        They cling to him and hold him back.

THE CHILD (*while she strews the primroses*):
    No one whose heart is heavy with human tears
    Can cross these little cressets of the wood.

FATHER HART:
    Be no afraid, the Father is with us,
    And all the nine angelic hierarchies,
    The Holy Martyrs and the Innocents,
    The adoring Magi in their coats of mail,
    And He who died and rose on the third day,
    And Mary with her seven times wounded heart.

The Child *ceases strewing the primroses, and kneels upon the settle beside*
Maire *and puts her arms about her neck.*

    Cry, daughter, to the Angels and the Saints.

THE CHILD:
    You shall go with me, newly married bride,
    And gaze upon a merrier multitude;

White-armed Nuala and Aengus of the birds,
And Feacra of the hurtling foam, and him
Who is the ruler of the western host.
Finvarra, and their Land of Heart's Desire,
Where beauty has no ebb, decay no flood,
But joy is wisdom, Time an endless song.
I kiss you and the world begins to fade.

FATHER HART:

Daughter, I call you unto home and love!

THE CHILD:

Stay, and come with me, newly married bride,
For, if you hear him, you grow like the rest:
Bear children, cook, be mindful of the churn,
And wrangle over butter, fowl, and eggs,
And sit at last there, old and bitter of tongue,
Watching the white stars war upon your hopes.

FATHER HART:

Daughter, I point you out the way to heaven.

THE CHILD:

But I can lead you, newly married bride,
Where nobody gets old and crafty and wise,
Where nobody gets old and godly and grave,
Where nobody gets old and bitter of tongue,
And where kind tongues bring no captivity,
For we are only true to the far lights
We follow singing, over valley and hill.

FATHER HART:

By the dear name of the one crucified,
I bid you, Maire Bruin, come to me.

THE CHILD:

I keep you in the name of your own heart!

She leaves the settle, and stooping takes up a mass of primroses and kisses them.

We have great power to-night, dear golden folk,
For he took down and hid the crucifix.
And my invisible brethren fill the house;
I hear their footsteps going up and down.
O, they shall soon rule all the hearts of men
And own all lands; last night they merrily danced
About his chapel belfry! (*To* Maire.) Come away,
I hear my brethren bidding us away!

FATHER HART:

>I will go fetch the crucifix again.

They hang about him in terror and prevent him from moving.

BRIDGET BRUIN:

>The enchanted flowers will kill us if you go.

MAURTEEN BRUIN:

>They turn the flowers to little twisted flames.

SHAWN BRUIN:

>The little twisted flames burn up the heart.

THE CHILD:

>I hear them crying, "Newly married bride,
>Come to the woods and waters and pale lights."

MAIRE BRUIN:

>I will go with you.

FATHER HART:

>She is lost, alas!

THE CHILD (*standing by the door*):

>Then, follow: but the heavy body of clay
>And clinging mortal hope must fall from you
>For we who ride the winds, run on the waves,
>And dance upon the mountains, are more light
>Than dewdrops on the banners of the dawn.

MAIRE BRUIN:

>Then take my soul.

>>(Shawn Bruin *goes over to her.*)

SHAWN BRUIN:

>Beloved, do not leave me!
>Remember when I met you by the well
>And took your hand in mine and spoke of love.

MAIRE BRUIN:

>Dear face! Dear voice!

THE CHILD:

>Come, newly married bride!

MAIRE BRUIN:

>I always loved her world—and yet—and yet—

>>(*Sinks into his arms.*)

THE CHILD (*from the door*):

>White bird, white bird, come with me, little bird.

MAIRE BRUIN:

>She calls my soul!

THE CHILD:

>Come with me, little bird!

MAIRE BRUIN:

    I can hear songs and dancing!

SHAWN BRUIN:

    Stay with me!

MAIRE BRUIN:

    I think that I would stay—and yet—and yet—

THE CHILD:

    Come, little bird with crest of gold!

MAIRE BRUIN (*very softly*):

    And yet—

THE CHILD:

    Come, little bird with silver feet!

                      (Maire *dies, and* The Child *goes.*)

SHAWN BRUIN:

    She is dead!

BRIDGET BRUIN:

    Come from that image there: she is far away.

    You have thrown your arms about a drift of leaves

    Or bole of an ash-tree changed into her image.

FATHER HART:

    Thus do the spirits of evil snatch their prey

    Almost out of the very hand of God;

    And day by day their power is more and more,

    And men and women leave old paths, for pride

    Comes knocking with thin knuckles on the heart.

A VOICE (*singing outside*):

    The wind blows out of the gates of the day,

    The wind blows over the lonely of heart,

    And the lonely of heart is withered away

    While the faeries dance in a place apart,

    Shaking their milk-white feet in a ring,

    Tossing their milk-white arms in the air;

    For they hear the wind laugh and murmur and sing

    Of a land where even the old are fair,

    And even the wise are merry of tongue;

    But I heard a reed of Coolaney say,

    "When the wind has laughed and murmured and sung,

    The lonely of heart is withered away."

The song is taken up by many voices, who sing loudly, as if in triumph.
Some of the voices seem to come from within the house.

On Baile's Strand

By W. B. Yeats

Dramatis Personae

A FOOL
A BLIND MAN
CUCHULAIN, KING OF MUIRTHEMNE
CONCHOBAR, HIGH KING OF ULSTER
A YOUNG MAN
KINGS AND WOMEN

SCENE. *A great hall at Dundealgan, not "Cuchulain's great ancient house" but an assembly house nearer to the sea. A big door at the back, and through the door misty light as of sea mist. There are many chairs and one long bench. One of these chairs, which is towards the front of the stage, is bigger than the others. Somewhere at the back there is a table with flagons of ale upon it and drinking horns. There is a small door at one side of the hall. A* Fool *and* Blind Man, *both ragged, come in through the door at the back. The* Blind Man *leans upon a staff.*

FOOL:

What a clever man you are though you are blind! There's nobody with two eyes in his head that is as clever as you are. Who but you could have thought that the hen wife sleeps every day a little at noon? I would never be able to steal anything if you didn't tell me where to look for it. And what a good cook you are! You take the fowl out of my hands after I have stolen it and plucked it, and you put it into the big pot at the fire there, and I can go out and run races with the witches at the edge of the waves and get an appetite, and when I've got it, there's the hen waiting inside for me, done to the turn.

BLIND MAN (*who is feeling about with his stick*):

Done to the turn.

FOOL (*putting his arm round* Blind Man's *neck*):

Come now, I'll have a leg and you'll have a leg, and we'll draw lots for the wishbone. I'll be praising you, I'll be praising you, while we're eating it, for your good plans and for your good cooking. There's nobody in the world like you, Blind Man. Come, come. Wait a minute. I shouldn't have closed the door. There are some that look for me, and I wouldn't like them not to find me. Don't tell it to anybody, Blind Man. There are some that follow me. Boann herself out of the river and Fand out of the deep sea. Witches they are, and they come by in the wind, and they cry, "Give a kiss, Fool, give a kiss," that's what they cry. That's wide enough. All the witches can come in now. I wouldn't have them beat at the door and say: "Where is the Fool? Why has he put a lock on the door?" Maybe they'll hear the bubbling of the pot and come in and sit on the ground. But

607

we won't give them any of the fowl. Let them go back to the sea, let them go back to the sea.

BLIND MAN (*feeling legs of big chair with his hands*):

Ha! (*Then, in a louder voice as he feels the back of it.*) Ah! ah!

FOOL:

Why do you say A-h!

BLIND MAN:

I know the big chair. It is to-day the High King is coming. They have brought out his chair. He is going to be Cuchulain's master in earnest from this day out. It is that he's coming for.

FOOL:

He must be a great man to be Cuchulain's master.

BLIND MAN:

So he is. He is a great man. He is over all the rest of the kings of Ireland.

FOOL:

Cuchulain's master! I thought Cuchulain could do anything he liked.

BLIND MAN:

So he did, so he did. But he ran too wild, and Conchobar is coming to-day to put an oath upon him that will stop his rambling and make him as biddable as a house dog and keep him always at his hand. He will sit in this chair and put the oath upon him.

FOOL:

How will he do that?

BLIND MAN:

You have no wits to understand such things. (*The* Blind Man *has got into the chair.*) He will sit up in this chair and he'll say: "Take the oath, Cuchulain. I bid you take the oath. Do as I tell you. What are your wits compared with mine, and what are your riches compared with mine? And what sons have you to pay your debts and to put a stone over you when you die? Take the oath, I tell you. Take a strong oath."

FOOL (*crumpling himself up and whining*):

I will not. I'll take no oath. I want my dinner.

BLIND MAN:

Hush, hush! It is not done yet.

FOOL:

You said it was done to a turn.

BLIND MAN:

Did I now? Well, it might be done, and not done. The wings might be white, but the legs might be red. The flesh might stick hard to the bones and not come away in the teeth. But, believe me, Fool, it will be well done before you put your teeth in it.

FOOL:

My teeth are growing long with the hunger.

BLIND MAN:

I'll tell you a story—the kings have story-tellers while they are waiting for their dinner—I will tell you a story with a fight in it, a story with a champion in it, and ship and queen, a son that has his mind set on killing somebody that you and I know.

FOOL:

Who is that? Who is he coming to kill?

BLIND MAN:

Wait now till you hear. When you were stealing the fowl, I was lying in a hole in the sand, and I heard three men coming with a shuffling sort of noise. They were wounded and groaning.

FOOL:

Go on. Tell me about the fight.

BLIND MAN:

There had been a fight, a great fight, a tremendous great fight. A young man had landed on the shore, the guardians of the shore had asked his name, and he had refused to tell it, and he had killed one, and others had run away.

FOOL:

That's enough. Come on now to the fowl. I wish it was bigger. I wish it was as big as a goose . . .

BLIND MAN:

Hush! I haven't told you all. I know who that young man is. I heard the men who were running away say he had red hair, that he had come from Aoife's country, that he was coming to kill Cuchulain.

FOOL:

Nobody can do that
>   Cuchulain has killed kings,
>   Kings and sons of kings,
>   Dragons out of the water,
>   And witches out of the air,
Banachas and Bonachas and people of the woods.

BLIND MAN:

Hush! hush!

FOOL:

>   Witches that steal the milk,
>   Fomor that steal the children,
>   Hags that have heads like hares,
>   Hares that have claws like witches,
>   All riding a cock horse
>   Out of the very bottom of the bitter black north.

BLIND MAN:

Hush, I say!

FOOL:

Does Cuchulain know that he is coming to kill him?

BLIND MAN:

How would he know that with his head in the clouds? He doesn't care for common fighting. Why would he put himself out, and nobody in it but a young man? Now if it were a white fawn that might turn into a queen before morning . . .

FOOL:

Come to the fowl . . . I wish it was as big as a pig . . . a fowl with goose grease and pig's crackling.

BLIND MAN:

No hurry, no hurry. I know whose son it is. I wouldn't tell anybody else, but I will tell you,—a secret is better to you than your dinner. You like being told secrets.

FOOL:

Tell me the secret.

BLIND MAN:

That young man is Aoife's son. I am sure it is Aoife's son, it is borne in upon me that it is Aoife's son. You have often heard me talking of Aoife, the great woman-fighter Cuchulain got the mastery over in the north.

FOOL:

I know, I know. She is one of those cross queens that lives in hungry Scotland.

BLIND MAN:

I am sure it is her son. I was in Aoife's country for a long time.

FOOL:

That was before you were blinded for putting a curse upon the wind.

BLIND MAN:

There was a boy in her house that had her own red colour on him and everybody said he was to be brought up to kill Cuchulain, that she hated Cuchulain. She used to put a helmet on a pillar-stone and call it Cuchulain and set him casting at it. There is a step outside—Cuchulain's step. (Cuchulain *passes by in the mist outside the big door.*)

FOOL:

Where is Cuchulain going?

BLIND MAN:

He is going to meet Conchobar that has bidden him to take the oath.

FOOL:

> Ah, an oath, Blind Man. How can I remember so many things at once? Who is going to take an oath?

BLIND MAN:

> Cuchulain is going to take an oath to Conchobar who is High King.

FOOL:

> What a mix-up you make of everything, Blind Man. You were telling me one story, and now you are telling me another story . . . How can I get the hang of it at the end if you mix everything at the beginning? Wait till I settle it out. There now, there's Cuchulain (*He points to one foot.*), and there is the young man (*He points to the other foot.*) that is coming to kill him, and Cuchulain doesn't know, but where's Conchobar? (*Takes bag from side.*) That's Conchobar with all his riches—Cuchulain, young man, Conchobar—And where's Aoife? (*Throws up cap.*) There is Aoife, high up on the mountains in high hungry Scotland. Maybe it is not true after all. Maybe it was your own making up. It's many a time you cheated me before with your lies. Come to the cooking pot, my stomach is pinched and rusty. Would you have it to be creaking like a gate?

BLIND MAN:

> I tell you it's true. And more than that is true. If you listen to what I say, you'll forget your stomach . . .

FOOL:

> I won't.

BLIND MAN:

> I know who the young man's father is, but I won't say. I would be afraid to say. Ah, Fool, you would forget everything if you could know who the young man's father is.

FOOL:

> Who is it? Tell me now quick, or I'll shake you. Come, out with it, or I'll shake you.

BLIND MAN:

> Wait, wait. There's somebody coming. It is Cuchulain is coming. He's coming back with the High King. Go and ask Cuchulain. He'll tell you. It's little you'll care about the cooking pot when you have asked Cuchulain that . . .

FOOL:

> I'll ask him. Cuchulain will know. He was in Aoife's country. (*Goes up stage.*) I'll ask him. (*Turns and goes down stage.*) But, no. I won't ask him, I would be afraid. (*Going up again.*) Yes, I will ask him. What harm in asking? The Blind Man said I was to ask him. (*Going down.*) No, no. I'll not ask him. He might

kill me. I have but killed hens and geese and pigs. He has killed
kings. (*Goes up again almost to big door.*) Who says I'm afraid?
I'm not afraid. I'm no coward. I'll ask him. No, no, Cuchulain,
I'm not going to ask you.

> He has killed kings,
> Kings and the sons of kings,
> Dragons out of the water,
> And witches out of the air,

Banachas and Bonachas and people of the woods.

> Fool *goes out side door, the last words being heard outside.*

Cuchulain *and* Conchobar *enter through the big door at the back.*
While they are still outside, Cuchulain's *voice is heard raised in anger.*
He is a dark man, something over forty years of age. Conchobar *is much*
older and carries a long staff, elaborately carved, or with an elaborate
gold handle.

CUCHULAIN:
> Because I have killed men without your bidding
> And have rewarded others at my own pleasure,
> Because of half a score of trifling things
> You'd lay this oath upon me, and now and now
> You add another pebble to the heap.
> And I must be your man, well-nigh your bondsman,
> Because a youngster out of Aoife's country
> Has found the shore ill guarded.

CONCHOBAR:
> He came to land
> While you were somewhere out of sight and hearing,
> Hunting or dancing with your wild companions.

CUCHULAIN:
> He can be driven out. I'll not be bound.
> I'll dance or hunt, or quarrel or make love,
> Wherever and whenever I've a mind to.
> If time had not put water in your blood,
> You never would have thought it.

CONCHOBAR:
> I would leave
> A strong and settled country to my children.

CUCHULAIN:
> And I must be obedient in all things;
> Give up my will to yours; go where you please;
> Come when you call; sit at the council-board

Among the unshapely bodies of old men.
I whose mere name has kept this country safe,
I that in early days have driven out
Maeve of Cruachan and the northern pirates,
The hundred kings of Sorcha, and the kings
Out of the garden in the east of the world.
Must I, that held you on the throne when all
Had pulled you from it, swear obedience
As if I were some cattle-raising king?
Are my shins speckled with the heat of the fire,
Or have my hands no skill but to make figures
Upon the ashes with a stick? Am I
So slack and idle that I need a whip
Before I serve you?

CONCHOBAR:
No, no whip, Cuchulain,
But every day my children come and say
This man is growing harder to endure.
How can we be at safety with this man
That nobody can buy or bid or bind?
We shall be at his mercy when you are gone;
He burns the earth as if he were a fire,
And time can never touch him.

CUCHULAIN:
And so the tale
Grows finer yet; and I am to obey
Whatever child you set upon the throne,
As if it were yourself.

CONCHOBAR:
Most certainly.
I am High King, my son shall be High King.
And you for all the wildness of your blood,
And though your father came out of the sun,
Are but a little king and weigh but light
In anything that touches government,
If put into the balance with my children.

CUCHULAIN:
It's well that we should speak our minds out plainly,
For when we die we shall be spoken of
In many countries. We in our young days
Have seen the heavens like a burning cloud
Brooding upon the world, and being more
Than men can be now that cloud's lifted up,
We should be the more truthful. Conchobar,

I do not like your children—they have no pith,
No marrow, in their bones, and will lie soft
Where you and I lie hard.

CONCHOBAR:

You rail at them
Because you have no children of your own.

CUCHULAIN:

I think myself most lucky that I leave
No pallid ghost or mockery of a man
To drift and mutter in the corridors,
Where I have laughed and sung.

CONCHOBAR:

That is not true
For all your boasting of the truth between us.
For, there is none that having house and lands,
That have been in the one family
And called by the one name for centuries,
But is made miserable if he know
They are to pass into a stranger's keeping,
As yours will pass.

CUCHULAIN:

The most of men feel that,
But you and I leave names upon the harp.

CONCHOBAR:

You play with arguments as lawyers do,
And put no heart in them. I know your thoughts,
For we have slept under the one cloak and drunk
From the one wine cup. I know you to the bone.
I have heard you cry, aye in your very sleep,
"I have no son," and with such bitterness
That I have gone upon my knees and prayed
That it might be amended.

CUCHULAIN:

For you thought
That I should be as biddable as others
Had I their reason for it, but that's not true,
For I would need a weightier argument
Than one that marred me in the copying,
As I have that clean hawk out of the air
That, as men say, begot this body of mine
Upon a mortal woman.

CONCHOBAR:

Now as ever
You mock at every reasonable hope,

And would have nothing, or impossible things.
What eye has ever looked upon the child
Would satisfy a mind like that?

CUCHULAIN:

I would leave
My house and name to none that would not face
Even myself in battle.

CONCHOBAR:

Being swift of foot
And making light of every common chance,
You should have overtaken on the hills
Some daughter of the air, or on the shore
A daughter of the country-under-wave.

CUCHULAIN:

I am not blasphemous.

CONCHOBAR:

Yet you despise
Our queens, and would not call a child your own,
If one of them had borne him.

CUCHULAIN:

I have not said it.

CONCHOBAR:

Ah! I remember I have heard you boast,
When the ale was in your blood, that there was one
In Scotland, where you had learnt the trade of war,
That had a stone-pale cheek and red-brown hair.
And that although you had loved other women,
You'd sooner that fierce woman of the camp
Bore you a son than any queen among them.

CUCHULAIN:

You call her a "fierce woman of the camp,"
For having lived among the spinning wheels,
You'd have no woman near that would not say,
"Ah! how wise!" "What will you have for supper?"
"What shall I wear that I may please you, sir?"
And keep that humming through the day and night
For ever—a fierce woman of the camp—
But I am getting angry about nothing.
You have never seen her, ah! Conchobar, had you seen her
With that high, laughing, turbulent head of hers
Thrown backward and the bow-string at her ear,
Or sitting at the fire with those grave eyes
Full of good counsel as it were with wine,
Or when love ran through all the lineaments

> Of her wild body—although she had no child,
> None other had all beauty, queen, and lover,
> Or was so fitted to give birth to kings.

CONCHOBAR:

> There's nothing I can say but drifts you farther
> From the one weighty matter—that very woman—
> For I know well that you are praising Aoife—
> Now hates you and will leave no subtilty
> Unknotted that might run into a noose
> About your throat—no army in idleness
> That might bring ruin on this land you serve.

CUCHULAIN:

> No wonder in that, no wonder at all in that.
> I never have known love but as a kiss
> In the mid battle, and a difficult truce
> Of oil and water, candles and dark night,
> Hillside and hollow, the hot-footed sun,
> And the cold, sliding, slippery-footed moon,
> A brief forgiveness between opposites
> That have been hatreds for three times the age
> Of this long 'stablished ground.

CONCHOBAR:

> Listen to me.
> Aoife makes war on us, and every day
> Our enemies grow greater and beat the walls
> More bitterly, and you within the walls
> Are every day more turbulent, and yet,
> When I would speak about these things, your mind
> Runs as it were a swallow on the wind.

Outside the door in the blue light of the sea mist are many old and young Kings, *amongst them are three* Women, *two of whom carry a bowl full of fire. The third, in what follows, puts from time to time fragrant herbs into the fire so that it flickers up into brighter flame.*

> Look at the door and what men gather there,
> Old counsellors that steer the land with me,
> And younger kings, the dancers and harp players
> That follow in your tumults, and all these
> Are held there by the one anxiety.
> Will you be bound into obedience
> And so make this land safe for them and theirs?
> You are but half a king and I but half;

I need your might of hand and burning heart,
And you my wisdom.

CUCHULAIN (*going near to door*):
Nestlings of a high nest,
Hawks that have followed me into the air
And looked upon the sun, we'll out of this
And sail upon the wind once more. This king
Would have me take an oath to do his will
And having listened to his tune from morning,
I will no more of it. Run to the stable
And set the horses to the chariot pole,
And send a messenger to the harp players.
We'll find a level place among the woods,
And dance awhile.

A YOUNG KING:
Cuchulain, take the oath.
There is none here that would not have you take it.

CUCHULAIN:
You'd have me take it? Are you of one mind?

THE KINGS:
All, all, all, all.

A YOUNG KING:
Do what the High King bids you.

CONCHOBAR:
There is not one but dreads this turbulence
Now that they're settled men.

CUCHULAIN:
Are you so changed,
Or have I grown more dangerous of late?
But that's not it. I understand it all.
It's you that have changed. You've wives and children now,
And for that reason cannot follow one
That lives like a bird's flight from tree to tree . . .
It's time the years put water in my blood
And drowned the wildness of it, for all's changed,
But that unchanged ... . I'll take what oath you will,
The moon, the sun, the water, light, or air,
I do not care how binding.

CONCHOBAR:
On this fire
That has been lighted from your hearth and mine.
The older men shall be my witnesses,
The younger, yours. The holders of the fire

Shall purify the thresholds of the house
With waving fire, and shut the outer door
According to the custom; and sing rhymes
That have come down from the old law-makers
To blow the witches out. Considering
That the wild will of man could be oath-bound,
But that a woman's could not, they bid us sing
Against the will of woman at its wildest
In the shape changers that run upon the wind.

(Conchobar *has gone on to his throne.*)

THE WOMEN (*they sing in a very low voice after the first few words so that
    the others all but drowned their words*):
May this fire have driven out
The shape changers that can put
Ruin on a great king's house
Until all be ruinous.
Names whereby a man has known
The threshold and the hearthstone,
Gather on the wind and drive
The women, none can kiss and thrive,
For they are but whirling wind,
Out of memory and mind.
They would make a prince decay
With light images of clay,
Planted in the running wave,
Or, for many shapes they have,
They would change them into hounds,
Until he had died of his wounds,
Though the change were but a whim;
Or they'd hurl a spell at him
That he follow with desire
Bodies that can never tire;
Or grow kind, for they anoint
All their bodies, joint by joint,
With a miracle-working juice
That is made out of the grease
Of the ungoverned unicorn.
But the man is twice forlorn,
Emptied, ruined, wracked, and lost,
That they follow, for at most
They will give him kiss for kiss;
While they murmur, "After this
Hatred may be sweet to the taste."

Those wild hands that have embraced
All his body can but shove
At the burning wheel of love,
Till the side of hate comes up;
Therefore in this ancient cup
May the sword blades drink their fill
Of the homebrew there, until
They will have for masters none
But the threshold and hearthstone.

CUCHULAIN (*speaking, while they are singing*):
I'll take and keep this oath, and from this day
I shall be what you please, my chicks, my nestlings.
Yet I had thought you were of those that praised
Whatever life could make the pulse run quickly,
Even though it was brief, and that you held
That a free gift was better than a forced—
But that's all over—I will keep it, too.
I never gave a gift and took it again.
If the wild horse should break the chariot-pole,
It would be punished. Should that be in the oath?

Two of the Women, *still singing, crouch in front of him holding the bowl over their heads. He spreads his hands over the flame.*

I swear to be obedient in all things
To Conchobar, and to uphold his children.

CONCHOBAR:
We are one being, as these flames are one:
I give my wisdom, and I take your strength.
Now thrust the swords into the flame, and pray
That they may serve the threshold and the hearthstone
With faithful service.

The Kings *kneel in a semicircle before the two* Women *and* Cuchulain, *who thrusts his sword into the flame. They all put the points of their swords into the flame. The third woman is at the back near the big door.*

CUCHULAIN:
O pure, glittering ones
That should be more than wife or friend or mistress,
Give us the enduring will, the unquenchable hope,
The friendliness of the sword!—

The song grows louder, and the last words ring out clearly. There is a low knocking at the door, and a cry of "Open, open."

CONCHOBAR:

    Some king that has been loitering on the way.
    Open the door, for I would have all know
    That the oath's finished and Cuchulain bound,
    And that the swords are drinking up the flame.

The door is opened by the third Woman, *and a* Young Man *with a drawn sword enters.*

YOUNG MAN:

    I am of Aoife's army.

    The Kings *rush towards him.* Cuchulain *thrusts his sword between.*

CUCHULAIN:

    Put up your swords,
    He is but one. Aoife is far away.

YOUNG MAN:

    I have come alone into the midst of you
    To weigh this sword against Cuchulain's sword.

CONCHOBAR:

    And are you noble? For if of common seed,
    You cannot weigh your sword against his sword
    But in mixed battle.

YOUNG MAN:

    I am under bonds
    To tell my name to no man; but it's noble.

CONCHOBAR:

    But I would know your name and not your bonds.
    You cannot speak in the Assembly House,
    If you are not noble.

FIRST OLD KING:

    Answer the High King!

YOUNG MAN:

    I will give no other proof than the hawk gives—
    That it's no sparrow!

    He is silent for a moment then speaks to all.

    Yet look upon me, kings.
    I, too, am of that ancient seed, and carry
    The signs about this body and in these bones.

CUCHULAIN:

> To have shown the hawk's grey feather is enough,
> And you speak highly, too. Give me that helmet.
> I'd thought they had grown weary sending champions.
> That sword and belt will do. This fighting's welcome.
> The High King there has promised me his wisdom;
> But the hawk's sleepy till its well-beloved
> Cries out amid the acorns, or it has seen
> Its enemy like a speck upon the sun.
> What's wisdom to the hawk, when that clear eye
> Is burning nearer up in the high air?

Looks hard at Young Man; *then comes down steps and grasps* Young Man *by shoulder.*

> Hither into the light.   (*To* Conchobar.)
> The very tint
> Of her that I was speaking of but now.
> Not a pin's difference.   (*To* Young Man.)
> You are from the North
> Where there are many that have that tint of hair—
> Red-brown, the light red-brown. Come nearer, boy,
> For I would have another look at you.
> There's more likeness—a pale, a stone-pale cheek.
> What brought you, boy? Have you no fear of death?

YOUNG MAN:

> Whether I live or die is in the Gods' hands.

CUCHULAIN:

> That is all words, all words, a young man's talk.
> I am their plough, their harrow, their very strength;
> For he that's in the sun begot this body
> Upon a mortal woman, and I have heard tell
> It seemed as if he had outrun the moon;
> That he must always follow through waste heaven,
> He loved so happily. He'll be but slow
> To break a tree that was so sweetly planted.
> Let's see that arm. I'll see it if I like.
> That arm had a good father and a good mother,
> But it is not like this.

YOUNG MAN:

> You are mocking me;
> You think I am not worthy to be fought.
> But I'll not wrangle but with this talkative knife.

CUCHULAIN:

Put up your sword; I am not mocking you.
I'd have you for my friend, but if it's not
Because you have a hot heart and a cold eye,
I cannot tell the reason.   (*To* Conchobar.)
He has got her fierceness.
And nobody is as fierce as those pale women.
But I will keep him with me, Conchobar,
That he may set my memory upon her
When the day's fading—you will stop with us,
And we will hunt the deer and the wild bulls;
And, when we have grown weary, light our fires
Between the wood and water or on some mountain
Where the shape changers of the morning come.
The High King there would make a mock of me
Because I did not take a wife among them.
Why do you hang your head—it's a good life:
The head grows prouder in the light of the dawn,
And friendship thickens in the murmuring dark
Where the spare hazels meet the wool-white foam.
But I can see there's no more need for words
And that you'll be my friend from this day out.

CONCHOBAR:

He has come thither not in his own name
But in Queen Aoife's, and has challenged you
Because you are the foremost man of us all—

CUCHULAIN:

Well, well, what matter?

CONCHOBAR:

You think it does not matter;
And that a fancy lighter than the air,
A whim of the moment has more matter in it.
For having none that shall reign after you,
You cannot think as I do, who would leave
A throne too high for insult.

CUCHULAIN:

Let your children
Re-mortar their inheritance, as we have,
And put more muscle on—I will give you gifts,
But I'll have something too—that arm ring, boy.
We'll have the quarrel out when you are older.

YOUNG MAN:

There is no man I'd sooner have my friend
Than you, whose name has gone about the world

As if it had been the wind, but Aoife'd say
I had turned coward.

CUCHULAIN:

I will give you gifts
That Aoife'll know, and all her people know,
To have come from me.   (*Showing cloak.*)
My father gave me this.
He came to try me, rising up at dawn
Out of the cold dark of the rich sea.
He challenged me to battle, but before
My sword had touched his sword, told me his name,
Gave me this cloak, and vanished. It was woven
By women of the Country-under-Wave
Out of the fleeces of the sea. O! tell her
I was afraid, or tell her what you will.
No; tell her that I heard a raven croak
On the north side of the house, and was afraid.

CONCHOBAR:

Some witch of the air has troubled Cuchulain's mind.

CUCHULAIN:

No witchcraft. His head is like a woman's head
I had a fancy for.

CONCHOBAR:

A witch of the air
Can make a leaf confound us with memories.
They run upon the wind and hurl the spells
That make us nothing, out of the invisible wind.
They have gone to school to learn the trick of it.

CUCHULAIN:

No, no—there's nothing out of common here.
The winds are innocent—that arm ring, boy.

A KING:

If I've your leave, I'll take this challenge up.

ANOTHER KING:

No, give it to me, High King, for this wild Aoife
Has carried off my slaves.

ANOTHER KING:

No, give it to me,
For she has harried me in house and herd.

ANOTHER KING:

I claim the fight.

OTHER KINGS (*together*):

And I! And I! And I.

CUCHULAIN:

> Back! back! Put up your swords! Put up your swords.
> There's none alive that shall accept a challenge
> I have refused. Laegaire, put up your sword.

YOUNG MAN:

> No, let them come. If they've a mind for it,
> I'll try it out with any two together.

CUCHULAIN:

> That's spoken as I'd have spoken it at your age.
> But you are in my house. Whatever man
> Would fight with you shall fight it out with me.
> They're dumb, they're dumb. How many
>   of you would meet   (*Draws sword.*)
> This mutterer, this old whistler, this sandpiper,
> This edge that's greyer than the tide, this mouse
> That's gnawing at the timbers of the world,
> This, this—Boy, I would meet them all in arms
> If I'd a son like you. He would avenge me
> When I have withstood for the last time the men
> Whose fathers, brothers, sons, and friends I have killed
> Upholding Conchobar, when the four provinces
> Have gathered with the ravens over them.
> But I'd need no avenger. You and I
> Would scatter them like water from a dish.

YOUNG MAN:

> We'll stand by one another from this out.
> Here is the ring.

CUCHULAIN:

> No, turn and turn about.
> But my turn's first because I am the older.
>
>   (*Taking up cloak.*)
>
> Nine queens out of the Country-under-Wave
> Have woven it with the fleeces of the sea
> And they were long embroidering at it—Boy,
> If I had fought my father, he'd have killed me.
> As certainly as if I had a son
> And fought with him, I should be deadly to him.
> For the old fiery fountains are far off
> And every day there is less heat o' the blood.

CONCHOBAR (*in a loud voice*):

> No more of this. I will not have this friendship.
> Cuchulain is my man, and I forbid it.
> He shall not go unfought, for I myself—

CUCHULAIN:
>I will not have it.

CONCHOBAR:
>You lay commands on me?

CUCHULAIN (*seizing* Conchobar):
>You shall not stir, High King. I'll hold you there.

CONCHOBAR:
>Witchcraft has maddened you.

THE KINGS (*shouting*):
>Yes, witchcraft, witchcraft!

FIRST OLD KING:
>Some witch has worked upon your mind, Cuchulain.
>The head of that young man seemed like a woman's
>You'd had a fancy for. Then of a sudden
>You laid your hands on the High King himself!

CUCHULAIN:
>And laid my hands on the High King himself!

CONCHOBAR:
>Some witch is floating in the air above us.

CUCHULAIN:
>Yes, witchcraft, witchcraft. Witches of the air.
>>(*To* Young Man.)
>Which of the shape changers put you to it?
>Why did you? Who was it set you to this work?
>Out, out! I say, for now it's sword on sword!

YOUNG MAN:
>But . . . but I did not.

CUCHULAIN:
>Out, I say, out, out!

Young Man *goes out, followed by* Cuchulain. *The* Kings *follow.*

KINGS:
>Hurry, hurry! We'll be too late. Go quicker through the door!
>Quicker, quicker! (*Making a confused noise. The three* Women
>*are left alone. One is standing by the door. Two remain at one side,*
>*holding bowl.*)

FIRST WOMAN:
>I have seen, I have seen!

SECOND WOMAN:
>What do you cry aloud?

FIRST WOMAN:
>The ever-living have shown me what's to come.

THIRD WOMAN:

How? Where?

FIRST WOMAN:

In the ashes of the bowl.

SECOND WOMAN:

While you were holding it between your hands?

THIRD WOMAN:

Speak quickly.

FIRST WOMAN:

I have seen Cuchulain's roof-tree
Leap into fire, and the walls split and blacken.

SECOND WOMAN:

Cuchulain has gone out to die.

THIRD WOMAN:

O! O!

SECOND WOMAN:

Who could have thought that one so great as he
Should meet his end at this unnoted sword?

FIRST WOMAN:

Life drifts between a fool and a blind man
To the end, and nobody can know his end.

SECOND WOMAN:

Come, look upon the quenching of this greatness.

The other two go to the door, but they stop for a moment upon the threshold and wail.

FIRST WOMAN:

No crying out, for there'll be need of cries
And knocking at the breast when it's all finished.

The Women *go out. There is a sound of clashing swords from time to time during what follows.*

Enter the Fool *dragging the* Blind Man.

FOOL:

You have eaten it, you have eaten it. You have left me nothing
but the bones.

He throws Blind Man *down by big chair.*

BLIND MAN:

O that I should have to endure such a plague! O I ache all over!
O I am pulled to pieces! This is the way you pay me all the
good I have done you.

FOOL:

You have eaten it. You have told me lies. You said it was done to a turn. You had eaten it all the time.

BLIND MAN:

What would have happened to you but for me, and you without your wits? If I did not take care of you, what would you do for food and warmth?

FOOL:

You take care of me! You stay safe and send me into every kind of danger. You sent me down the cliff for gulls' eggs, while you warmed your blind eyes in the sun; and then you ate all that were good for food. You left me the eggs that were neither egg nor bird. (Blind Man *tries to rise*. Fool *makes him lie down again*.) Keep quiet now till I shut the door. (*Goes up.*) There is some noise outside, a high, vexing noise, so that I can't be listening to myself. (*Shuts door.*) Why can't they be quiet, why can't they be quiet? (Blind Man *tries to get away*.) Ah! you would get away, would you? (*Follows* Blind Man *and brings him back*.) Lie there, lie there. (*Throws him down*. Blind Man *again attempts to go*.) No, you won't get away. Lie there till the kings come. I'll tell them all about you. I will tell it all. How you sit warming yourself, when you have made me light a fire of sticks, while I sit blowing it with my mouth. Do you not always make me take the windy side of the bush when it blows, and the rainy side when it rains?

BLIND MAN:

Oh, good Fool, listen to me. Think of the care I have taken of you. I have brought you to many a warm hearth, tide on the turn, he'll leave the rabbit in the snare till it is full of maggots, or let the trout slip back through his hands into the stream. (Fool *has begun singing while* Blind Man *is speaking*.)

FOOL:

> When you were an acorn on the tree-top,
> Then was I an eagle cock;
> Now that you are a withered old block,
> Still am I an eagle cock.

BLIND MAN:

Listen to him now. That's the sort of talk I have to put up with day out, day in. (*The* Fool *is putting the feathers of the hen into his hair*. Cuchulain *takes a handful of feathers and begins to wipe the blood from his sword with them*.)

FOOL:

He has taken my feathers to wipe his sword. It is blood that he is wiping from his sword. (Cuchulain *goes up to big door and throws feathers away*.)

CUCHULAIN:

> They are standing about his body. They will not awaken him, for all his witchcraft.

BLIND MAN:

> It is that young champion that he has killed. He that came out of Aoife's country.

CUCHULAIN:

> He thought to have saved himself with witchcraft.

FOOL:

> That Blind Man there said he would kill you. He came from Aoife's country to kill you. That Blind Man said they had taught him every kind of weapon that he might do it. But I always knew that you would kill him.

CUCHULAIN:

> You knew him then?

BLIND MAN:

> I saw him when I had my eyes in Aoife's country.

CUCHULAIN:

> You were in Aoife's country?

BLIND MAN:

> I knew him and his mother there.

CUCHULAIN:

> He was about to speak of her when he died.

BLIND MAN:

> He was a queen's son.

CUCHULAIN (*rushing at and seizing* Blind Man):

> What queen, what queen? Was it Scathach? There were many queens. All the rulers there were queens.

BLIND MAN:

> No, not Scathach.

CUCHULAIN:

> It was Uathach, then? Speak! speak!

BLIND MAN:

> I cannot speak. You are clutching me too tightly. (Cuchulain *lets him go.*) I cannot remember who it was. I am not certain. It was some queen.

FOOL:

> He said a little while ago that the young man was Aoife's son.

CUCHULAIN:

> She! No, no. She had no son when I was there.

FOOL:

> That blind man there said that she owned him for her son.

CUCHULAIN:

> I had rather he had been some other woman's son. What father had he? A soldier out of Alba? She was an amorous woman,— a proud, pale, amorous woman.

BLIND MAN:

> None knew whose son he was.

CUCHULAIN:

> None knew! Did you know, old listener at doors?

BLIND MAN:

> No, no. I knew nothing.

FOOL:

> He said awhile ago that he heard Aoife boast that she'd never but the one lover, and he the only man that had overcome her in battle. (*A pause.*)

BLIND MAN:

> Somebody is trembling, Fool. The bench is shaking. Why are you trembling? Is Cuchulain going to hurt us? It was not I who told you, Cuchulain.

FOOL:

> It is Cuchulain who is trembling. It is he who is shaking the bench.

BLIND MAN:

> It is his own son that he has killed.

CUCHULAIN:

> 'Twas they that did it, the pale, windy people.
> Where? where? where? My sword against the thunder,
> But no, for they have always been my friends;
> And though they love to blow a smoking coal
> Till it's all flame, the wars they blow aflame
> Are full of glory and heart-uplifting pride,
> And not like this. The wars they love awaken
> Old fingers and the sleepy strings of harps.
> Who did it, then? Are you afraid? Speak out!
> For I have put you under my protection,
> And will reward you well. Dubthach the Chafer.
> He had an old grudge. No, for he is with Maeve.
> Laegaire did it! Why do you not speak?
> What is this house? (*Pause.*) Now I remember all.

Comes before Conchobar's *chair and strikes out with his sword.*

> 'Twas you who did it—you who sat up there,
> With your old rod of kingship, like a magpie,

Nursing a stolen spoon. No, not a magpie.
A maggot that is eating up the earth!
Yes, but a magpie, for he's flown away.
Where did he fly to?

BLIND MAN:

He is outside the door.

CUCHULAIN:

Outside the door?

BLIND MAN:

Between the door and the sea.

CUCHULAIN:

Conchobar, Conchobar! the sword into your heart.

He rushes out. Pause. Fool *creeps up to big door and looks after him.*

FOOL:

He is going up to King Conchobar. They are all about the young man. No, no. He is standing still. There is a great wave going to break, and he is looking at it. Ah! now he is running down to the sea, but he is holding up his sword as if he were going into a fight. (*Pause.*) Well struck! well struck!

BLIND MAN:

What is he doing now?

FOOL:

Oh! he is fighting the waves!

BLIND MAN:

He sees King Conchobar's crown on every one of them.

FOOL:

There, he has struck at a big one! He has struck the crown off it. He has made the foam fly. There again, another big one!

BLIND MAN:

Where are the kings? What are the kings doing?

FOOL:

They are shouting and running down to the shore, and the people are running out of the houses. They are all running.

BLIND MAN:

You say they are running out of the houses. There will be nobody left in the houses. Listen, Fool.

FOOL:

There, he is down. He is up again He is going out into the deep water. There is a big wave. It has gone over him. I cannot see him now. He has killed kings and giants, but the waves have mastered him, the waves have mastered him.

BLIND MAN:

    Come here, Fool!

FOOL:

    The waves have mastered him!

BLIND MAN:

    Come here, I say.

FOOL (*coming towards him, but looking backwards towards the door*):

    What is it?

BLIND MAN:

    There will be nobody in the houses. Come this way; come quickly. The ovens will be full. We will put our hands into the ovens.   (*They go out.*)

JOHN MILLINGTON SYNGE

Edmund John Millington Synge was born in Rathfarnham, a suburb of Dublin, Ireland, on April 16, 1871, the youngest of five children. His father was a lawyer and landowner—a conservative member of the Protestant Anglo-Irish gentry. Although his mother was a devout Evangelical Protestant, Synge became disillusioned with Christianity and his English heritage at an early age, and became enamored of Ireland's history and culture. In 1889, he entered Trinity College, Dublin, where he studied Gaelic, but devoted most of his time to the study of the piano, violin, and flute, as he intended to become a professional musician. After he graduated in 1894, he traveled through Germany, Italy, and France, where he began to write poetry and dramatic pieces. In December 1896, Synge met W. B. Yeats, who suggested that he go to the Aran Islands off the Atlantic coast of Ireland. Between 1898 and 1902, Synge spent his summers among the Aran fishermen who still spoke Gaelic and led a preindustrial life. He kept notebooks of his experiences, which would later become the source material for his plays.

In 1902, he wrote *Riders to the Sea* and *In the Shadow of the Glen*. The latter caused controversy when it was produced in 1903, angering Irish nationalists who denounced its depiction of Irish life. When the Abbey Theatre opened in December 1904, Synge was appointed its literary advisor and later became one of its directors. The next year he began working on *The Playboy of the Western World*. When the play opened on January 26, 1907, it caused a full-scale riot and police had to be called in to keep order. It was decried as an insult to the nation, to Catholics, and to common decency.

That same year Synge began *Deidre of the Sorrows*, his last play, as his health started to decline. Symptoms of Hodgkin's disease, which first manifested itself in 1897, reappeared. The disease interfered with work on the play as well as postponed his marriage to the actress Molly Algood. He continued to work on the play even as he was dying. Despite several operations, Synge died on March 24,

1909. The play opened at the Abbey Theatre on January 13, 1910, with his fiancée in the title role.

Synge is today considered the most distinguished playwright of the Irish Literary Revival. *Riders to the Sea* and *The Playboy of the Western World*, both written in the last seven years of his life, are his masterpieces. His greatest work is characterized by his use of the lyrical speech he drew from the native language and dialects of Ireland, and by his accurate portrayal of Irish peasant life.

Riders of the Sea was the first play Synge wrote, and it most directly reflects his experiences in the Aran Islands. It tells the story of Maurya, who has lost her husband, father-in-law, and four sons to the sea and is expecting news of the fate of another son, Michael, who has drowned. Her last son, Bartley, is about to make a dangerous journey by horseback. This thirty-minute one-act play effectively depicts the rugged realities of life in an Irish fishing community while combining elements of Greek tragedy and the fatalistic and nihilistic character of primitive Gaelic society.

The Playboy of the Western World is Synge's finest play. It is based on a story he heard in 1898 of a man named Lynchenaun, "who killed his father with the blow of a spade when he was in a passion" and eluded the police and escaped to America. In Synge's comedy-tragedy, Lynchenaun becomes Christy Mahon, a timid boy who, through each farfetched retelling of the murder of his father, becomes a hero to the town where he has taken refuge—that is, until the "dead" father reappears.

Riders to the Sea

By John Millington Synge

Dramatis Personae

MAURYA,	*an old woman*
BARTLEY,	*her son*
CATHLEEN,	*her daughter*
NORA,	*a younger daughter*
MEN AND WOMEN	

SCENE. *An Island off the West of Ireland.*

Cottage kitchen, with nets, oil-skins, spinning wheel, some new boards standing by the wall, etc. Cathleen, a girl of about twenty, finishes kneading cake, and puts it down in the pot-oven by the fire; then wipes her hands, and begins to spin at the wheel. Nora, a young girl, puts her head in at the door.

NORA (*in a low voice*):
> Where is she?

CATHLEEN:
> She's lying down, God help her, and may be sleeping, if she's able.

Nora comes in softly, and takes a bundle from under her shawl.

CATHLEEN (*spinning the wheel rapidly*):
> What is it you have?

NORA:
> The young priest is after bringing them. It's a shirt and a plain stocking were got off a drowned man in Donegal.

Cathleen stops her wheel with a sudden movement, and leans out to listen.

NORA:
> We're to find out if it's Michael's they are, some time herself will be down looking at the sea.

CATHLEEN:
> How would they be Michael's, Nora. How would he go the length of that way to the far north?

NORA:
> The young priest says he's known the like of it. "If it's Michael's they are," says he, "you can tell herself he's got a clean burial by the grace of God, and if they're not his, let no one say a word about them, for she'll be getting her death," says he, "with crying and lamenting."

The door which Nora half closed is blown open by a gust of wind.

CATHLEEN (*looking out anxiously*):

> Did you ask him would he stop Bartley going this day with the horses to the Galway fair?

NORA:

> "I won't stop him," says he, "but let you not be afraid. Herself does be saying prayers half through the night, and the Almighty God won't leave her destitute," says he, "with no son living."

CATHLEEN:

> Is the sea bad by the white rocks, Nora?

NORA:

> Middling bad, God help us. There's a great roaring in the west, and it's worse it'll be getting when the tide's turned to the wind. (*She goes over to the table with the bundle.*) Shall I open it now?

CATHLEEN:

> Maybe she'd wake up on us, and come in before we'd done. (*Coming to the table.*) It's a long time we'll be, and the two of us crying.

NORA (*goes to the inner door and listens*):

> She's moving about on the bed. She'll be coming in a minute.

CATHLEEN:

> Give me the ladder, and I'll put them up in the turf-loft, the way she won't know of them at all, and maybe when the tide turns she'll be going down to see would he be floating from the east.

They put the ladder against the gable of the chimney; Cathleen goes up a few steps and hides the bundle in the turf-loft. Maurya comes from the inner room.

MAURYA (*looking up at Cathleen and speaking querulously*):

> Isn't it turf enough you have for this day and evening?

CATHLEEN:

> There's a cake baking at the fire for a short space (*throwing down the turf*) and Bartley will want it when the tide turns if he goes to Connemara.

> Nora *picks up the turf and puts it round the pot-oven.*

MAURYA (*sitting down on a stool at the fire*):

> He won't go this day with the wind rising from the south and west. He won't go this day, for the young priest will stop him surely.

NORA:

> He'll not stop him, mother, and I heard Eamon Simon and Stephen Pheety and Colum Shawn saying he would go.

MAURYA:

Where is he itself?

NORA:

He went down to see would there be another boat sailing in the week, and I'm thinking it won't be long till he's here now, for the tide's turning at the green head, and the hooker's tacking from the east.

CATHLEEN:

I hear some one passing the big stones.

NORA (*looking out*):

He's coming now, and he in a hurry.

BARTLEY (*comes in and looks round the room. Speaking sadly and quietly*):

Where is the bit of new rope, Cathleen, was bought in Connemara?

CATHLEEN (*coming down*):

Give it to him, Nora; it's on a nail by the white boards. I hung it up this morning, for the pig with the black feet was eating it.

NORA (*giving him a rope*):

Is that it, Bartley?

MAURYA:

You'd do right to leave that rope, Bartley, hanging by the boards.

Bartley *takes the rope.*

It will be wanting in this place, I'm telling you, if Michael is washed up to-morrow morning, or the next morning, or any morning in the week, for it's a deep grave we'll make him by the grace of God.

BARTLEY (*beginning to work with the rope*):

I've no halter the way I can ride down on the mare, and I must go now quickly. This is the one boat going for two weeks or beyond it, and the fair will be a good fair for horses I heard them saying below.

MAURYA:

It's a hard thing they'll be saying below if the body is washed up and there's no man in it to make the coffin, and I after giving a big price for the finest white boards you'd find in Connemara. (*She looks round at the boards.*)

BARTLEY:

How would it be washed up, and we after looking each day for nine days, and a strong wind blowing a while back from the west and south?

MAURYA:

> If it wasn't found itself, that wind is raising the sea, and there was a star up against the moon, and it rising in the night. If it was a hundred horses, or a thousand horses you had itself, what is the price of a thousand horses against a son where there is one son only?

BARTLEY (*working at the halter, to* Cathleen):

> Let you go down each day, and see the sheep aren't jumping in on the rye, and if the jobber comes you can sell the pig with the black feet if there is a good price going.

MAURYA:

> How would the like of her get a good price for a pig?

BARTLEY (*to* Cathleen):

> If the west wind holds with the last bit of the moon let you and Nora get up weed enough for another cock for the kelp. It's hard set we'll be from this day with no one in it but one man to work.

MAURYA:

> It's hard set we'll be surely the day you're drown'd with the rest. What way will I live and the girls with me, and I an old woman looking for the grave?

Bartley *lays down the halter, takes off his old coat, and puts on a newer one of the same flannel.*

BARTLEY (*to Nora*):

> Is she coming to the pier?

NORA (*looking out*):

> She's passing the green head and letting fall her sails.

BARTLEY (*getting his purse and tobacco*):

> I'll have half an hour to go down, and you'll see me coming again in two days, or in three days, or maybe in four days if the wind is bad.

MAURYA (*turning round to the fire, and putting her shawl over her head*):

> Isn't it a hard and cruel man won't hear a word from an old woman, and she holding him from the sea?

CATHLEEN:

> It's the life of a young man to be going on the sea, and who would listen to an old woman with one thing and she saying it over?

BARTLEY (*taking the halter*):

> I must go now quickly. I'll ride down on the red mare, and the gray pony 'll run behind me. . . . The blessing of God on you. (*He goes out.*)

MAURYA (*crying out as he is in the door*):

> He's gone now, God spare us, and we'll not see him again. He's gone now, and when the black night is falling I'll have no son left me in the world.

CATHLEEN:

> Why wouldn't you give him your blessing and he looking round in the door? Isn't it sorrow enough is on every one in this house without your sending him out with an unlucky word behind him, and a hard word in his ear?

Maurya *takes up the tongs and begins raking the fire aimlessly without looking round.*

NORA (*turning towards her*):

> You're taking away the turf from the cake.

CATHLEEN (*crying out*):

> The Son of God forgive us, Nora, we're after forgetting his bit of bread. (*She comes over to the fire.*)

NORA:

> And it's destroyed he'll be going till dark night, and he after eating nothing since the sun went up.

CATHLEEN (*turning the cake out of the oven*):

> It's destroyed he'll be, surely. There's no sense left on any person in a house where an old woman will be talking for ever.

Maurya *sways herself on her stool.*

CATHLEEN (*cutting off some of the bread and rolling it in a cloth; to Maurya*):

> Let you go down now to the spring well and give him this and he passing. You'll see him when the dark word will be broken, and you can say "God speed you," the way he'll be easy in his mind.

MAURYA (*taking the bread*):

> Will I be in it as soon as himself?

CATHLEEN:

> If you go now quickly.

MAURYA (*standing up unsteadily*):

> It's hard set I am to walk.

CATHLEEN (*looking at her anxiously*):

> Give her the stick, Nora, or maybe she'll slip on the big stones.

NORA:

> What stick?

CATHLEEN:

The stick Michael brought from Connemara.

MAURYA (*taking a stick Nora gives her*):

In the big world the old people do be leaving things after them for their sons and children, but in this place it is the young men do be leaving things behind for them that do be old. (*She goes out slowly.*)

Nora *goes over to the ladder.*

CATHLEEN:

Wait, Nora, maybe she'd turn back quickly. She's that sorry, God help her, you wouldn't know the thing she'd do.

NORA:

Is she gone round by the bush?

CATHLEEN (*looking out*):

She gone now. Throw it down quickly, for the Lord knows when she'll be out of it again.

NORA (*getting the bundle from the loft*):

The young priest said he'd be passing to-morrow, and we might go down and speak to him below if it's Michael's they are surely.

CATHLEEN (*taking the bundle*):

Did he say what way they were found?

NORA (*coming down*):

"There were two men," says he, "and they rowing round with poteen before the cocks crowed, and the oar of one of them caught the body, and they passing the black cliffs of the north."

CATHLEEN (*trying to open the bundle*):

Give me a knife, Nora, the string's perished with the salt water, and there's a black knot on it you wouldn't loosen in a week.

NORA (*giving her a knife*):

I've heard tell it was a long way to Donegal.

CATHLEEN (*cutting the string*):

It is surely. There was a man in here a while ago—the man sold us that knife—and he said if you set off walking from the rocks beyond, it would be seven days you'd be in Donegal.

NORA:

And what time would a man take, and he floating?

Cathleen *opens the bundle and takes out a bit of a stocking. They look at them eagerly.*

CATHLEEN (*in a low voice*):

    The Lord spare us, Nora! Isn't it a queer hard thing to say if it's his they are surely?

NORA:

    I'll get his shirt off the hook the way we can put the one flannel on the other. (*She looks through some clothes hanging in the corner.*) It's not with them, Cathleen, and where will it be?

CATHLEEN:

    I'm thinking Bartley put it on him in the morning, for his own shirt was heavy with the salt in it (*pointing to the corner*). There's a bit of a sleeve was of the same stuff. Give me that and it will do.

      Nora *brings it to her and they compare the flannel.*

CATHLEEN:

    It's the same stuff, Nora; but if it is itself aren't there great rolls of it in the shops of Galway, and isn't it many another man may have a shirt of it as well as Michael himself?

NORA (*who has taken up the stocking and counted the stitches, crying out*):

    It's Michael, Cathleen, it's Michael; God spare his soul, and what will herself say when she hears this story, and Bartley on the sea?

CATHLEEN (*taking the stocking*):

    It's a plain stocking.

NORA:

    It's the second one of the third pair I knitted, and I put up three score stitches, and I dropped four of them.

CATHLEEN (*counts the stitches*):

    It's that number is in it (*crying out*). Ah, Nora, isn't it a bitter thing to think of him floating that way to the far north, and no one to keen him but the black hags that do be flying on the sea?

NORA (*swinging herself round, and throwing out her arms on the clothes*):

    And isn't it a pitiful thing when there is nothing left of a man who was a great rower and fisher, but a bit of an old shirt and a plain stocking?

CATHLEEN (*after an instant*):

    Tell me is herself coming, Nora? I hear a little sound on the path.

NORA (*looking out*):

    She is, Cathleen. She's coming up to the door.

CATHLEEN:

    Put these things away before she'll come in. Maybe it's easier she'll be after giving her blessing to Bartley, and we won't let on we've heard anything the time he's on the sea.

NORA (*helping* Cathleen *to close the bundle*):

    We'll put them here in the corner.

They put them into a hole in the chimney corner. Cathleen goes back to the spinning-wheel.

NORA:

    Will she see it was crying I was?

CATHLEEN:

    Keep your back to the door the way the light'll not be on you.

Nora sits down at the chimney corner, with her back to the door. Maurya comes in very slowly, without looking at the girls, and goes over to her stool at the other side of the fire. The cloth with the bread is still in her hand. The girls look at each other, and Nora points to the bundle of bread.

CATHLEEN (*after spinning for a moment*):

    You didn't give him his bit of bread?

    Maurya *begins to keen softly, without turning round.*

CATHLEEN:

    Did you see him riding down?

    Maurya *goes on keening.*

CATHLEEN (*a little impatiently*):

    God forgive you; isn't it a better thing to raise your voice and tell what you seen, than to be making lamentation for a thing that's done? Did you see Bartley, I'm saying to you.

MAURYA (*with a weak voice*):

    My heart's broken from this day.

CATHLEEN (*as before*):

    Did you see Bartley?

MAURYA:

    I seen the fearfulest thing.

CATHLEEN (*leaves her wheel and looks out*):

    God forgive you; he's riding the mare now over the green head, and the gray pony behind him.

MAURYA (*starts, so that her shawl falls back from her head and shows her white tossed hair. With a frightened voice*):

The gray pony behind him.

CATHLEEN (*coming to the fire*):

What is it ails you, at all?

MAURYA (*speaking very slowly*):

I've seen the fearfulest thing any person has seen, since the day Bride Dara seen the dead man with the child in his arms.

CATHLEEN AND NORA:

Uah.

They crouch down in front of the old woman at the fire.

NORA:

Tell us what it is you seen.

MAURYA:

I went down to the spring well, and I stood there saying a prayer to myself. Then Bartley came along, and he riding on the red mare with the gray pony behind him. (*She puts up her hands, as if to hide something from her eyes.*) The Son of God spare us, Nora!

CATHLEEN:

What is it you seen.

MAURYA:

I seen Michael himself.

CATHLEEN (*speaking softly*):

You did not, mother; It wasn't Michael you seen, for his body is after being found in the far north, and he's got a clean burial by the grace of God.

MAURYA (*a little defiantly*):

I'm after seeing him this day, and he riding and galloping. Bartley came first on the red mare; and I tried to say "God speed you," but something choked the words in my throat. He went by quickly; and "the blessing of God on you," says he, and I could say nothing. I looked up then, and I crying, at the gray pony, and there was Michael upon it—with fine clothes on him, and new shoes on his feet.

CATHLEEN (*begins to keen*):

It's destroyed we are from this day. It's destroyed, surely.

NORA:

Didn't the young priest say the Almighty God wouldn't leave her destitute with no son living?

MAURYA (*in a low voice, but clearly*):

It's little the like of him knows of the sea. . . . Bartley will be lost now, and let you call in Eamon and make me a good coffin out of the white boards, for I won't live after them. I've had a husband, and a husband's father, and six sons in this house—six fine men, though it was a hard birth I had with every one of them and they coming to the world—and some of them were found and some of them were not found, but they're gone now the lot of them. . . . There were Stephen, and Shawn, were lost in the great wind, and found after in the Bay of Gregory of the Golden Mouth, and carried up the two of them on the one plank, and in by that door.

She pauses for a moment, the girls start as if they heard something through the door that is half open behind them.

NORA (*in a whisper*):

Did you hear that, Cathleen? Did you hear a noise in the north-east?

CATHLEEN (*in a whisper*):

There's some one after crying out by the seashore.

MAURYA (*continues without hearing anything*):

There was Sheamus and his father, and his own father again were lost in a dark night, and not a stick or sign was seen of them when the sun went up. There was Patch after was drowned out of a curagh that turned over. I was sitting here with Bartley, and he a baby, lying on my two knees, and I seen two women, and three women and four women coming in, and they crossing themselves, and not saying a word. I looked out then, and there were men coming after them, and they holding a thing in the half of a red sail, and water dripping out of it—it was a dry day, Nora—and leaving a track to the door.

She pauses again with her hand stretched out towards the door. It opens softly and old Women *begin to come in, crossing themselves on the threshold, and kneeling down in front of the stage with red petticoats over their heads.*

MAURYA (*half in a dream, to* Cathleen):

Is it Patch or Michael, or what is it at all?

CATHLEEN:

Michael is after being found in the far north, and when he is found there how could he be here in this place?

MAURYA:

There does be a power of young men floating round in the sea, and what way would they know if it was Michael they had, or another man like him, for when a man is nine days in the sea, and the wind blowing, it's hard set his own mother would be to say what man was it.

CATHLEEN:

It's Michael, God spare him, for they're after sending us a bit of his clothes from the far north.

She reaches out and hands Maurya *the clothes that belonged to* Michael. Maurya *stands up slowly and takes them in her hands.* Nora *looks out.*

NORA:

They're carrying a thing among them and there's water dripping out of it and leaving a track by the big stones.

CATHLEEN (*in a whisper to the* Women *who have come in*):

Is it Bartley it is?

ONE OF THE WOMEN:

It is surely, God rest his soul.

Two younger Women *come in and pull out the table. Then* Men *carry in the body of* Bartley, *laid on a plank, with a bit of a sail over it, and lay it on the table.*

CATHLEEN (*to the women, as they are doing so*):

What way was he drowned?

ONE OF THE WOMEN:

The gray pony knocked him into the sea, and he was washed out where there is a great surf on the white rocks.

Maurya *has gone over and knelt down at the head of the table. The* Women *are keening softly and swaying themselves with a slow movement.* Cathleen *and* Nora *kneel at the other end of the table. The* Men *kneel near the door.*

MAURYA (*raising her head and speaking as if she did not see the people around her*):

They're all gone now, and there isn't anything more the sea can do to me. . . . I'll have no call now to be up crying and praying when the wind breaks from the south, and you can hear the surf is in the east, and the surf is in the west, making a great stir with the two noises, and they hitting one on the other. I'll have no call now to be going down and getting Holy Water in the dark nights after Samhain, and I won't care what way the sea is when the other women will be keening. (*To* Nora.) Give me the Holy Water, Nora, there's a small sup still on the dresser.

Nora *gives it to her.*

MAURYA (*drops* Michael's *clothes across* Bartley's *feet, and sprinkles the Holy Water over him*):
It isn't that I haven't prayed for you, Bartley, to the Almighty God. It isn't that I haven't said prayers in the dark night till you wouldn't know what I'd be saying; but it's a great rest I'll have now, and it's time surely. It's a great rest I'll have now, and great sleeping in the long nights after Samhain, if it's only a bit of wet flour we do have to eat, and maybe a fish that would be stinking.

She kneels down again, crossing herself, and saying prayers under her breath.

CATHLEEN (*to an old* Man):
Maybe yourself and Eamon would make a coffin when the sun rises. We have fine white boards herself bought, God help her, thinking Michael would be found, and I have a new cake you can eat while you'll be working.
THE OLD MAN (*looking at the boards*):
Are there nails with them?
CATHLEEN:
There are not, Colum; we didn't think of the nails.
ANOTHER MAN:
It's a great wonder she wouldn't think of the nails, and all the coffins she's seen made already.
CATHLEEN:
It's getting old she is, and broken.

Maurya *stands up again very slowly and spreads out the pieces of Michael's clothes beside the body, sprinkling them with the last of the Holy Water.*

NORA (*in a whisper to* Cathleen):
She's quiet now and easy; but the day Michael was drowned you could hear her crying out from this to the spring well. It's fonder she was of Michael, and would any one have thought that?

CATHLEEN (*slowly and clearly*):

> An old woman will be soon tired with anything she will do, and isn't it nine days herself is after crying and keening, and making great sorrow in the house?

MAURYA (*puts the empty cup mouth downwards on the table, and lays her hands together on* Bartley's *feet*):

> They're all together this time, and the end is come. May the Almighty God have mercy on Bartley's soul, and on Michael's soul, and on the souls of Sheamus and Patch, and Stephen and Shawn (*bending her head*); and may He have mercy on my soul, Nora, and on the soul of every one is left living in the world.

She pauses, and the keen rises a little more loudly from the women, then sinks away.

MAURYA (*continuing*):

> Michael has a clean burial in the far north, by the grace of the Almighty God. Bartley will have a fine coffin out of the white boards, and a deep grave surely. What more can we want than that? No man at all can be living for ever, and we must be satisfied.

She kneels down again and the curtain falls slowly.

THE PLAYBOY OF THE WESTERN WORLD

BY JOHN MILLINGTON SYNGE

Dramatis Personae

CHRISTOPHER MAHON
OLD MAHON,   *his father, a squatter*
MICHAEL JAMES FLAHERTY, called MICHAEL JAMES,   *a publican*
MARGARET FLAHERTY, called PEGEEN MIKE,   *his daughter*
WIDOW QUIN,   *a woman of about thirty*
SHAWN KEOGH,   *her cousin, a young farmer*
PHILLY CULLEN AND JIMMY FARRELL,   *small farmers*
SARA TANSEY, SUSAN BRADY, AND HONOR BLAKE,   *village girls*
A BELLMAN
SOME PEASANTS

The action takes place near a village, on a wild coast of Mayo. The first Act passes on an evening of autumn, the other two Acts on the following day.

Act I

SCENE. *Country public-house or shebeen, very rough and untidy. There is a sort of counter on the right with shelves, holding many bottles and jugs, just seen above it. Empty barrels stand near the counter. At back, a little to left of counter, there is a door into the open air, then, more to the left, there is a settle with shelves above it, with more jugs, and a table beneath a window. At the left there is a large open fire-place, with turf fire, and a small door into inner room. Pegeen, a wild-looking but fine girl, of about twenty, is writing at table. She is dressed in the usual peasant dress.*

PEGEEN (*slowly as she writes*):
> Six yards of stuff for to make a yellow gown. A pair of lace boots with lengthy heels on them and brassy eyes. A hat is suited for a wedding-day. A fine tooth comb. To be sent with three barrels of porter in Jimmy Farrell's creel cart on the evening of the coming Fair to Mister Michael James Flaherty. With the best compliments of this season. Margaret Flaherty.

SHAWN KEOGH (*a fat and fair young man comes in as she signs, looks round awkwardly, when he sees she is alone*):
> Where's himself?

PEGEEN (*without looking at him*):
> He's coming. (*She directs the letter.*) To Mister Sheamus Mulroy, Wine and Spirit Dealer, Castlebar.

SHAWN (*uneasily*):
> I didn't see him on the road.

PEGEEN:
> How would you see him (*licks stamp and puts it on letter*) and it dark night this half hour gone by?

SHAWN (*turning towards the door again*):
> I stood a while outside wondering would I have a right to pass on or to walk in and see you, Pegeen Mike (*comes to fire*), and I could hear the cows breathing, and sighing in the stillness of the air, and not a step moving any place from this gate to the bridge.

PEGEEN (*putting letter in envelope*):
> It's above at the cross-roads he is, meeting Philly Cullen; and a couple more are going along with him to Kate Cassidy's wake.

653

SHAWN (*looking at her blankly*):

And he's going that length in the dark night?

PEGEEN (*impatiently*):

He is surely, and leaving me lonesome on the scruff of the hill. (*She gets up and puts envelope on dresser, then winds clock.*) Isn't it long the nights are now, Shawn Keogh, to be leaving a poor girl with her own self counting the hours to the dawn of day?

SHAWN (*with awkward humour*):

If it is, when we're wedded in a short while you'll have no call to complain, for I've little will to be walking off to wakes or weddings in the darkness of the night.

PEGEEN (*with rather scornful good humour*):

You're making might certain, Shaneen, that I'll wed you now.

SHAWN:

Aren't we after making a good bargain, the way we're only waiting these days on Father Reilly's dispensation from the bishops, or the Court of Rome.

PEGEEN (*looking at him teasingly, washing up at dresser*):

It's a wonder, Shaneen, the Holy Father'd be taking notice of the likes of you; for if I was him I wouldn't bother with this place where you'll meet none but Red Linahan, has a squint in his eye, and Patcheen is lame in his heel, or the mad Mulrannies were driven from California and they lost in their wits. We're a queer lot these times to go troubling the Holy Father on his sacred seat.

SHAWN (*scandalized*):

If we are, we're as good this place as another, maybe, and as good these times as we were for ever.

PEGEEN (*with scorn*):

As good, is it? Where now will you meet the like of Daneen Sullivan knocked the eye from a peeler, or Marcus Quin, God rest him, got six months for maiming ewes, and he a great warrant to tell stories of hold Ireland till he'd have the old women shedding down tears about their feet. Where will you find the like of them, I'm saying?

SHAWN (*timidly*):

If you don't, it's a good job, maybe; for (*with peculiar emphasis on the words*) Father Reilly has small conceit to have that kind walking around and talking to the girls.

PEGEEN (*impatiently, throwing water from basin out of the door*):

Stop tormenting me with Father Reilly (*imitating his voice*) when I'm asking only what way I'll pass these twelve hours of dark, and not take my death with the fear. (*Looking out of door.*)

SHAWN (*timidly*):

Would I fetch you the Widow Quin, maybe?

PEGEEN:

Is it the like of that murderer? You'll not, surely.

SHAWN (*going to her, soothingly*):

Then I'm thinking himself will stop along with you when he sees you taking on, for it'll be a long nighttime with great darkness, and I'm after feeling a kind of fellow above in the furzy ditch, groaning wicked like a maddening dog, the way it's good cause you have, maybe, to be fearing now.

PEGEEN (*turning on him sharply*):

What's that? Is it a man you seen?

SHAWN (*retreating*):

I couldn't see him at all; but I heard him groaning out, and breaking his heart. It should have been a young man from his words speaking.

PEGEEN (*going after him*):

And you never went near to see was he hurted or what ailed him at all?

SHAWN:

I did not, Pegeen Mike. It was a dark, lonesome place to be hearing the like of him.

PEGEEN:

Well, you're a daring fellow, and if they find his corpse stretched above in the dews of dawn, what'll you say then to the peelers, or the Justice of the Peace?

SHAWN (*thunderstruck*):

I wasn't thinking of that. For the love of God, Pegeen Mike, don't let on I was speaking of him, don't tell your father and the men is coming above; for if they heard that story, they'd have great blabbing this night at the wake.

PEGEEN:

I'll maybe tell them, and I'll maybe not.

SHAWN:

They are coming at the door. Will you whisht, I'm saying?

PEGEEN:

Whisht yourself.

She goes behind counter. Michael James, *fat jovial publican, comes in followed by* Philly Cullen, *who is thin and mistrusting, and* Jimmy Farrell, *who is fat and amorous, about forty-five.*

MEN (*together*):

God bless you. The blessing of God on this place.

PEGEEN:

God bless you kindly.

MICHAEL (*to men who go to the counter*):

Sit down now, and take your rest. (*Crosses to* Shawn *at the fire.*) And how is it you are, Shawn Keogh? Are you coming over the sands to Kate Cassidy's wake?

SHAWN:

I am not, Michael James. I'm going home the short cut to my bed.

PEGEEN (*speaking across the counter*):

He's right too, and have you no shame, Michael James, to be quitting off for the whole night, and leaving myself lonesome in the shop?

MICHAEL (*good-humouredly*):

Isn't it the same whether I go for the whole night or a part only? and I'm thinking it's a queer daughter you are if you'd have me crossing backward through the Stooks of the Dead Women, with a drop taken.

PEGEEN:

If I am a queer daughter, it's a queer father'd be leaving me lonesome these twelve hours of dark, and I piling the turf with the dogs barking, and the calves mooing, and my own teeth rattling with the fear.

JIMMY (*flatteringly*):

What is there to hurt you, and you a fine, hardy girl would knock the head of any two men in the place?

PEGEEN (*working herself up*):

Isn't there the harvest boys with their tongues red for drink, and the ten tinkers is camped in the east glen, and the thousand militia—bad cess to them!—walking idle through the land. There's lots surely to hurt me, and I won't stop alone in it, let himself do what he will.

MICHAEL:

If you're afeard, let Shawn Keogh stop along with you. It's the will of God, I'm thinking, himself should be seeing to you now.

They all turn on Shawn.

SHAWN (*in horrified confusion*):

I would and welcome, Michael James, but I'm afeard of Father Reilly; and what at all would the Holy Father and the Cardinals of Rome be saying if they heard I did the like of that?

MICHAEL (*with contempt*):

God help you! Can't you sit in by the hearth with the light lit and herself beyond in the room? You'll do that surely, for I've heard tell there's a queer fellow above, going mad or getting his death, maybe, in the gripe of the ditch, so she'd be safer this night with a person here.

SHAWN (*with plaintive despair*):

I'm afeard of Father Reilly, I'm saying. Let you not be tempting me, and we near married itself.

PHILLY (*with cold contempt*):

Lock him in the west room. He'll stay then and have no sin to be telling to the priest.

MICHAEL (*to* Shawn, *getting between him and the door*):

Go up now.

SHAWN (*at the top of his voice*):

Don't stop me, Michael James. Let me out of the door, I'm saying, for the love of the Almighty God. Let me out (*trying to dodge past him*). Let me out of it, and may God grant you His indulgence in the hour of need.

MICHAEL (*loudly*):

Stop your noising, and sit down by the hearth. (*Gives him a push and goes to counter laughing.*)

SHAWN (*turning back, wringing his hands*):

Oh, Father Reilly and the saints of God, where will I hide myself to-day? Oh, St. Joseph and St. Patrick and St. Brigid, and St. James, have mercy on me now! (Shawn *turns round, sees door clear, and makes a rush for it.*)

MICHAEL (*catching him by the coat-tail.*):

You'd be going, is it?

SHAWN (*screaming*):

Leave me go, Michael James, leave me go, you old Pagan, leave me go, or I'll get the curse of the priests on you, and of the scarlet-coated bishops of the courts of Rome.

With a sudden movement he pulls himself out of his coat, and disappears out of the door, leaving his coat in Michael's *hands.*

MICHAEL (*turning round, and holding up coat*):

Well, there's the coat of a Christian man. Oh, there's sainted glory this day in the lonesome west; and by the will of God I've got you a decent man, Pegeen, you'll have no call to be spying after if you've a score of young girls, maybe, weeding in your fields.

PEGEEN (*taking up the defence of her property*):

> What right have you to be making game of a poor fellow for minding the priest, when it's your own the fault is, not paying a penny pot-boy to stand along with me and give me courage in the doing of my work? (*She snaps the coat away from him, and goes behind counter with it.*)

MICHAEL (*taken aback*):

> Where would I get a pot-boy? Would you have me send the bellman screaming in the streets of Castlebar?

SHAWN (*opening the door a chink and putting in his head, in a small voice*):

> Michael James!

MICHAEL (*imitating him*):

> What ails you?

SHAWN:

> The queer dying fellow's beyond looking over the ditch. He's come up, I'm thinking, stealing your hens. (*Looks over his shoulder.*) God help me, he's following me now (*he runs into room*), and if he's heard what I said, he'll be having my life, and I going home lonesome in the darkness of the night.

For a perceptible moment they watch the door with curiosity. Some one coughs outside. Then Christy Mahon, *a slight young man, comes in very tired and frightened and dirty.*

CHRISTY (*in a small voice*):

> God save all here!

MEN:

> God save you kindly.

CHRISTY (*going to the counter*):

> I'd trouble you for a glass of porter, woman of the house. (*He puts down coin.*)

PEGEEN (*serving him*):

> You're one of the tinkers, young fellow, is beyond camped in the glen?

CHRISTY:

> I am not; but I'm destroyed walking.

MICHAEL (*patronizingly*):

> Let you come up then to the fire. You're looking famished with the cold.

CHRISTY:

> God reward you. (*He takes up his glass and goes a little way across to the left, then stops and looks about him.*) Is it often the police do be coming into this place, master of the house?

MICHAEL:

If you'd come in better hours, you'd have seen "Licensed for the sale of Beer and Spirits, to be consumed on the premises," written in white letters above the door, and what would the polis want spying on me, and not a decent house within four miles, the way every living Christian is a bona fide, saving one widow alone?

CHRISTY (*with relief*):

It's a safe house, so. (*He goes over to the fire, sighing and moaning. Then he sits down, putting his glass beside him and begins gnawing a turnip, too miserable to feel the others staring at him with curiosity.*)

MICHAEL (*going after him*):

Is it yourself is fearing the police? You're wanting, maybe?

CHRISTY:

There's many wanting.

MICHAEL:

Many surely, with the broken harvest and the ended wars. (*He picks up some stockings, etc., that are near the fire, and carries them away furtively.*) It should be larceny, I'm thinking?

CHRISTY (*dolefully*):

I had it in my mind it was a different word and a bigger.

PEGEEN:

There's a queer lad. Were you never slapped in school, young fellow, that you don't know the name of your deed?

CHRISTY (*bashfully*):

I'm slow at learning, a middling scholar only.

MICHAEL:

If you're a dunce itself, you'd have a right to know that larceny's robbing and stealing. Is it for the like of that you're wanting?

CHRISTY (*with a flash of family pride*):

And I the son of a strong farmer (*with a sudden qualm*), God rest his soul, could have bought up the whole of your old house a while since, from the butt of his tailpocket, and not have missed the weight of it gone.

MICHAEL (*impressed*):

If it's not stealing, it's maybe something big.

CHRISTY (*flattered*):

Aye; it's maybe something big.

JIMMY:

He's a wicked-looking young fellow. Maybe he followed after a young woman on a lonesome night.

CHRISTY (*shocked*):

Oh, the saints forbid, mister; I was all times a decent lad.

PHILLY (*turning on* Jimmy):

You're a silly man, Jimmy Farrell. He said his father was a farmer a while since, and there's himself now in a poor state. Maybe the land was grabbed from him, and he did what any decent man would do.

MICHAEL (*to* Christy, *mysteriously*):

Was it baliffs?

CHRISTY:

The divil a one.

MICHAEL:

Agents?

CHRISTY:

The divil a one.

MICHAEL:

Landlords?

CHRISTY (*peevishly*):

Ah, not at all, I'm saying. You'd see the like of them stories on any little paper of a Munster town. But I'm not calling to mind any person, gentle, simple, judge or jury, did the like of me.

They all draw nearer with delighted curiosity.

PHILLY:

Well, that lad's a puzzle-the-world.

JIMMY:

He'd beat Dan Davies' circus, or the holy missioners making sermons on the villainy of man. Try him again, Philly.

PHILLY:

Did you strike golden guineas out of solder, young fellow, or shilling coins itself?

CHRISTY:

I did not, mister, not sixpence nor a farthing coin.

JIMMY:

Did you marry three wives maybe? I'm told there's a sprinkling have done that among the holy Luthers of the preaching north.

CHRISTY (*shyly*):

I never married with one, let alone with a couple or three.

PHILLY:

Maybe he went fighting for the Boers, the like of the man beyond, was judged to be hanged, quartered and drawn. Were you off east, young fellow, fighting bloody wars for Kruger and the freedom of the Boers?

CHRISTY:

I never left my own parish till Tuesday was a week.

PEGEEN (*coming from counter*):

>He's done nothing, so. (*To* Christy.) If you didn't commit murder or a bad, nasty thing, or false coining, or robbery, or butchery, or the like of them, there isn't anything that would be worth your troubling for to run from now. You did nothing at all.

CHRISTY (*his feelings hurt*):

>That's an unkindly thing to be saying to a poor orphaned traveller, has a prison behind him, and hanging before, and hell's gap gaping below.

PEGEEN (*with a sign to the men to be quiet*):

>You're only saying it. You did nothing at all. A soft lad the like of you wouldn't slit the windpipe of a screeching sow.

CHRISTY (*offended*):

>You're not speaking the truth.

PEGEEN (*in mock rage*):

>Not speaking the truth, is it? Would you have me knock the head of you with the butt of the broom?

CHRISTY (*twisting round on her with a sharp cry of horror*):

>Don't strike me. I killed my poor father, Tuesday was a week, for doing the like of that.

PEGEEN (*with blank amazement*):

>Is it killed your father?

CHRISTY (*subsiding*):

>With the help of God I did surely, and that the Holy Immaculate Mother may intercede for his soul.

PHILLY (*retreating with* Jimmy):

>There's a daring fellow.

JIMMY:

>Oh, glory be to God!

MICHAEL (*with great respect*):

>That was a hanging crime, mister honey. You should have had good reason for doing the like of that.

CHRISTY (*in a very reasonable tone*):

>He was a dirty man, God forgive him, and he getting old and crusty, the way I couldn't put up with him at all.

PEGEEN:

>And you shot him dead?

CHRISTY (*shaking his head*):

>I never used weapons. I've no license, and I'm a law-fearing man.

MICHAEL:

>It was with a hilted knife maybe? I'm told, in the big world it's bloody knives they use.

CHRISTY (*loudly, scandalized*):

>Do you take me for a slaughter-boy?

PEGEEN:

> You never hanged him, the way Jimmy Farrell hanged his dog from the license, and had it screeching and wriggling three hours at the butt of a string, and himself swearing it was a dead dog, and the peelers swearing it had life?

CHRISTY:

> I did not then. I just riz the loy and left fall the edge of it on the ridge of his skull, and he went down at my feet like an empty sack, and never let a grunt or groan from him at all.

MICHAEL (*making a sign to* Pegeen *to fill* Christy's *glass*):

> And what way weren't you hanged, mister? Did you bury him then?

CHRISTY (*considering*):

> Aye. I buried him then. Wasn't I digging spuds in the field?

MICHAEL:

> And the peelers never followed after you the eleven days that you're out?

CHRISTY (*shaking his head*):

> Never a none of them, and I walking forward facing hog, dog, or divil on the highway of the road.

PHILLY (*nodding wisely*):

> It's only with a common week-day kind of a murderer them lads would be trusting their carcase, and that man should be a great terror when his temper's roused.

MICHAEL:

> He should then. (*To* Christy.) And where was it, mister honey, that you did the deed?

CHRISTY (*looking at him with suspicion*):

> Oh, a distant place, master of the house, a windy corner of high, distant hills.

PHILLY (*nodding with approval*):

> He's a close man, and he's right, surely.

PEGEEN:

> That'd be a lad with the sense of Solomon to have for a pot-boy, Michael James, if it's the truth you're seeking one at all.

PHILLY:

> The peelers is fearing him, and if you'd that lad in the house there isn't one of them would come smelling around if the dogs itself were lapping poteen from the dung-pit of the yard.

JIMMY:

> Bravery's a treasure in a lonesome place, and a lad would kill his father, I'm thinking, would face a foxy divil with a pitchpike on the flags of hell.

PEGEEN:

It's the truth they're saying, and if I'd that lad in the house, I wouldn't be fearing the looséd kharki cut-throats, or the walking dead.

CHRISTY (*swelling with surprise and triumph*):

Well, glory be to God!

MICHAEL (*with deference*):

Would you think well to stop here and be pot-boy, mister honey, if we gave you good wages, and didn't destroy you with the weight of work?

SHAWN (*coming forward uneasily*):

That'd be a queer kind to bring into a decent quiet household with the like of Pegeen Mike.

PEGEEN (*very sharply*):

Will you whisht? Who's speaking to you?

SHAWN (*retreating*):

A bloody-handed murderer the like of . . .

PEGEEN (*snapping at him*):

Whisht I am saying; we'll take no fooling from your like at all. (*To* Christy *with a honeyed voice*.) And you, young fellow, you'd have a right to stop, I'm thinking, for we'd do our all and utmost to content your needs.

CHRISTY (*overcome with wonder*):

And I'd be safe in this place from the searching law?

MICHAEL:

You would, surely. If they're not fearing you, itself, the peelers in this place is decent droughty poor fellows, wouldn't touch a cur dog and not give warning in the dead of night.

PEGEEN (*very kindly and persuasively*):

Let you stop a short while anyhow. Aren't you destroyed walking with your feet in bleeding blisters, and your whole skin needing washing like a Wicklow sheep.

CHRISTY (*looking round with satisfaction*):

It's a nice room, and if it's not humbugging me you are, I'm thinking that I'll surely stay.

JIMMY (*jumps up*):

Now, by the grace of God, herself will be safe this night, with a man killed his father holding danger from the door, and let you come on, Michael James, or they'll have the best stuff drunk at the wake.

MICHAEL (*going to the door with* Men):

And begging your pardon, mister, what name will we call you, for we'd like to know?

CHRISTY:

Christopher Mahon.

MICHAEL:

Well, God bless you, Christy, and a good rest till we meet again when the sun'll be rising to the noon of day.

CHRISTY:

God bless you all.

MEN:

God bless you.

They go out except Shawn, *who lingers at door.*

SHAWN (*to* Pegeen):

Are you wanting me to stop along with you and keep you from harm?

PEGEEN (*gruffly*):

Didn't you say you were fearing Father Reilly?

SHAWN:

There'd be no harm staying now, I'm thinking, and himself in it too.

PEGEEN:

You wouldn't stay when there was need for you, and let you step off nimble this time when there's none.

SHAWN:

Didn't I say it was Father Reilly . . .

PEGEEN:

Go on, then, to Father Reilly (*in a jeering tone*), and let him put you in the holy brotherhoods, and leave that lad to me.

SHAWN:

If I meet the Widow Quin . . .

PEGEEN:

Go on, I'm saying, and don't be waking this place with your noise. (*She hustles him out and bolts the door.*) That lad would wear the spirits from the saints of peace.

Bustles about, then takes off her apron and pins it up in the window as a blind. Christy *watching her timidly. Then she comes to him and speaks with bland good-humour.*

Let you stretch out now by the fire, young fellow. You should be destroyed travelling.

CHRISTY (*shyly again, drawing off his boots*):

I'm tired, surely, walking wild eleven days, and waking fearful in the night. (*He holds up one of his feet, feeling his blisters, and looking at them with compassion.*)

PEGEEN (*standing beside him, watching him with delight*):

You should have had great people in your family, I'm thinking, with the little, small feet you have, and you with a kind of a quality name, the like of what you'd find on the great powers and potentates of France and Spain.

CHRISTY (*with pride*):

We were great surely, with wide and windy acres of rich Munster land.

PEGEEN:

Wasn't I telling you, and you a fine, handsome young fellow with a noble brow?

CHRISTY (*with a flash of delighted surprise*):

Is it me?

PEGEEN:

Aye, Did you never hear that from the young girls where you come from in the west or south?

CHRISTY (*with venom*):

I did not then. Oh, they're bloody liars in the naked parish where I grew a man.

PEGEEN:

If they are itself, you've heard it these days, I'm thinking, and you walking the world telling out your story to young girls or old.

CHRISTY:

I've told my story no place till this night, Pegeen Mike, and it's foolish I was here, maybe, to be talking free, but you're decent people, I'm thinking, and yourself a kindly woman, the way I wasn't fearing you at all.

PEGEEN (*filling a sack with straw*):

You've said the like of that, maybe, in every cot and cabin where you've met a young girl on your way.

CHRISTY (*going over to her, gradually raising his voice*):

I've said it nowhere till this night, I'm telling you, for I've seen none the like of you the eleven long days I am walking the world, looking over a low ditch or a high ditch on my north or my south, into stony scattered fields, or scribes of bog, where you'd see young, limber girls, and fine prancing women making laughter with the men.

PEGEEN:

If you weren't destroyed travelling, you'd have as much talk and streeleen, I'm thinking, as Owen Roe O'Sullivan or the poets of the Dingle Bay, and I've heard all times it's the poets are your like, fine fiery fellows with great rages when their temper's roused.

CHRISTY (*drawing a little nearer to her*):

You've a power of rings, God bless you, and would there be any offence if I was asking are you single now?

PEGEEN:

What would I want wedding so young?

CHRISTY (*with relief*):

We're alike, so.

PEGEEN (*she puts sack on settle and beats it up*):

I never killed my father. I'd be afeard to do that, except I was the like of yourself with blind rages tearing me within, for I'm thinking you should have had great tussling when the end was come.

CHRISTY (*expanding with delight at the first confidential talk he has ever had with a woman*):

We had not then. It was a hard woman was come over the hill, and if he was always a crusty kind when he'd a hard woman setting him on, not the divil himself or his four fathers could put up with him at all.

PEGEEN (*with curiosity*):

And isn't it a great wonder that one wasn't fearing you?

CHRISTY (*very confidentially*):

Up to the day I killed my father, there wasn't a person in Ireland knew the kind I was, and I there drinking, waking, eating, sleeping, a quiet, simple poor fellow with no man giving me heed.

PEGEEN (*getting a quilt out of the cupboard and putting it on the sack*):

It was the girls were giving you heed maybe, and I'm thinking it's most conceit you'd have to be gaming with their like.

CHRISTY (*shaking his head, with simplicity*):

Not the girls itself, and I won't tell you a lie. There wasn't anyone heeding me in that place saving only the dumb beasts of the field. (*He sits down at fire.*)

PEGEEN (*with disappointment*):

And I thinking you should have been living the like of a king of Norway or the Eastern world. (*She comes and sits beside him after placing bread and mug of milk on the table.*)

CHRISTY (*laughing piteously*):

The like of a king, is it? And I after toiling, moiling, digging, dodging from the dawn till dusk with never a sight of joy or sport saving only when I'd be abroad in the dark night poaching rabbits on hills, for I was a devil to poach, God forgive me, (*very naïvely*) and I near got six months for going with a dung fork and stabbing a fish.

PEGEEN:

And it's that you'd call sport, is it, to be abroad in the darkness with yourself alone?

CHRISTY:

I did, God help me, and there I'd be as happy as the sunshine of St. Martin's Day, watching the light passing the north or the patches of fog, till I'd hear a rabbit starting to screech and I'd go running in the furze. Then when I'd my full share I'd come walking down where you'd see the ducks and geese stretched sleeping on the highway of the road, and before I'd pass the dunghill, I'd hear himself snoring out, a loud lonesome snore he'd be making all times, the while he was sleeping, and he a man 'd be raging all times, the while he was waking, like a gaudy officer you'd hear cursing and damning and swearing oaths.

PEGEEN:

Providence and Mercy, spare us all!

CHRISTY:

It's that you'd say surely if you seen him and he after drinking for weeks, rising up in the red dawn, or before it maybe, and going out into the yard as naked as an ash tree in the moon of May, and shying clods against the viságe of the stars till he'd put the fear of death into the banbhs and the screeching sows.

PEGEEN:

I'd be well-nigh afeard of that lad myself, I'm thinking. And there was no one in it but the two of you alone?

CHRISTY:

The divil a one, though he'd sons and daughters walking all great states and territories of the world, and not a one of them, to this day, but would say their seven curses on him, and the rousing up to let a cough or sneeze, maybe, in the deadness of the night.

PEGEEN (*nodding her head*):

Well, you should have been a queer lot. I never cursed my father the like of that, though I'm twenty and more years of age.

CHRISTY:

Then you'd have cursed mine, I'm telling you, and he a man never gave peace to any, saving when he'd get two months or three, or be locked in the asylums for battering peelers or assaulting men (*with depression*) the way it was a bitter life he led me till I did up a Tuesday and halve his skull.

PEGEEN (*putting her hand on his shoulder*):

Well, you'll have peace in this place, Christy Mahon, and none to trouble you, and it's near time a fine lad like you should have your good share of the earth.

CHRISTY:

It's the time surely, and I a seemly fellow with great strength in me and bravery of . . .

Someone knocks.

CHRISTY (*clinging to* Pegeen):

Oh, glory! it's late for knocking, and this last while I'm in terror of the peelers, and the walking dead.

Knocking again.

PEGEEN:

Who's there?

VOICE (*outside*):

Me.

PEGEEN:

Who's me?

VOICE:

The Widow Quin.

PEGEEN (*jumping up and giving him the bread and milk*):

Go on now with your supper, and let on to be sleepy, for if she found you were such a warrant to talk, she'd be stringing gabble till the dawn of day.

He takes bread and sits shyly with his back to the door.

PEGEEN (*opening door, with temper*):

What ails you, or what is it you're wanting at this hour of the night?

WIDOW QUIN (*coming in a step and peering at* Christy):

I'm after meeting Shawn Keogh and Father Reilly below, who told me of your curiosity man, and they fearing by this time he was maybe roaring, romping on your hands with drink.

PEGEEN (*pointing to* Christy):

Look now is he roaring, and he stretched away drowsy with his supper and his mug of milk. Walk down and tell that to Father Reilly and to Shaneen Keogh.

WIDOW QUIN (*coming forward*):

I'll not see them again, for I've their word to lead that lad forward for to lodge with me.

PEGEEN (*in blank amazement*):

This night, is it?

WIDOW QUIN (*going over*):

This night. "It isn't fitting," says the priesteen, "to have his likeness lodging with an orphaned girl." (*To* Christy.) God save you, mister!

CHRISTY (*shyly*):

God save you kindly.

WIDOW QUIN (*looking at him with half-amazed curiosity*):

Well, aren't you a little smiling fellow? It should have been great and bitter torments did rouse your spirits to a deed of blood.

CHRISTY (*doubtfully*):

It should, maybe.

WIDOW QUIN:

It's more than "maybe" I'm saying, and it'd soften my heart to see you sitting so simple with your cup and cake, and you fitter to be saying your catechism than slaying your da.

PEGEEN (*at counter, washing glasses*):

There's talking when any'd see he's fit to be holding his head high with the wonders of the world. Walk on from this, for I'll not have him tormented and he destroyed travelling since Tuesday was a week.

WIDOW QUIN (*peaceably*):

We'll be walking surely when his supper's done, and you'll find we're great company, young fellow, when it's of the like of you and me you'd hear the penny poets singing in an August Fair.

CHRISTY (*innocently*):

Did you kill your father?

PEGEEN (*contemptuously*):

She did not. She hit himself with a worn pick, and the rusted poison did corrode his blood the way he never overed it, and died after. That was a sneaky kind of murder did win small glory with the boys itself. (*She crosses to* Christy's *left.*)

WIDOW QUIN (*with good-humour*):

If it didn't, maybe all knows a widow woman has buried her children and destroyed her man is a wiser comrade for a young lad than a girl, the like of you, who'd go helter-skeltering after any man would let you a wink upon the road.

PEGEEN (*breaking out into wild rage*):

And you'll say that, Widow Quin, and you gasping with the rage you had racing the hill beyond to look on his face.

WIDOW QUIN (*laughing derisively*):

Me, is it? Well, Father Reilly has cuteness to divide you now. (*She pulls* Christy *up.*) There's great temptation in a man did slay his da, and we'd best be going, young fellow; so rise up and come with me.

PEGEEN (*seizing his arm*):

He'll not stir. He's pot-boy in this place, and I'll not have him stolen off and kidnabbed while himself's abroad.

WIDOW QUIN:

> It'd be a crazy pot-boy'd lodge him in the shebeen where he works by day, so you'd have a right to come on, young fellow, till you see my little houseen, a perch off on the rising hill.

PEGEEN:

> Wait till morning, Christy Mahon. Wait till you lay eyes on her leaky thatch is growing more pasture for her buck goat than her square of fields, and she without a tramp itself to keep in order her place at all.

WIDOW QUIN:

> When you see me contriving in my little gardens, Christy Mahon, you'll swear the Lord God formed me to be living lone, and that there isn't my match in Mayo for thatching, or mowing, or shearing a sheep.

PEGEEN (*with noisy scorn*):

> It's true the Lord God formed you to contrive indeed. Doesn't the world know you reared a black lamb at your own breast, so that the Lord Bishop of Connaught felt the elements of a Christian, and he eating it after in a kidney stew? Doesn't the world know you've been seen shaving the foxy skipper from France for a threepenny bit and a sop of grass tobacco would wring the liver from a mountain goat you'd meet leaping the hills?

WIDOW QUIN (*with amusement*):

> Do you hear her now, young fellow? Do you hear the way she'll be rating at your own self when a week is by?

PEGEEN (*to* Christy):

> Don't heed her. Tell her to go into her pigsty and not plague us here.

WIDOW QUIN:

> I'm going; but he'll come with me.

PEGEEN (*shaking him*):

> Are you dumb, young fellow?

CHRISTY (*timidly, to* Widow Quin):

> God increase you; but I'm pot-boy in his place, and it's here I'd liefer stay.

PEGEEN (*triumphantly*):

> Now you have heard him, and go on from this.

WIDOW QUIN (*looking round the room*):

> It's lonesome this hour crossing the hill, and if he won't come along with me, I'd have a right maybe to stop this night with yourselves. Let me stretch out on the settle, Pegeen Mike; and himself can lie by the hearth.

PEGEEN (*short and fiercely*):

> Faith, I won't. Quit off or I will send you now.

WIDOW QUIN (*gathering her shawl up*):

Well, it's a terror to be aged a score. (*To* Christy.) God bless you now, young fellow, and let you be wary, or there's right torment will await you here if you go romancing with her like, and she waiting only, as they bade me say, on a sheep-skin parchment to be wed with Shawn Keogh of Killakeen.

CHRISTY (*going to* Pegeen *as she bolts the door*):

What's that she's after saying?

PEGEEN:

Lies and blather, you've no call to mind. Well, isn't Shawn Keogh an impudent fellow to send up spying on me? Wait till I lay hands on him. Let him wait, I'm saying.

CHRISTY:

And you're not wedding him at all?

PEGEEN:

I wouldn't wed him if a bishop came walking for to join us here.

CHRISTY:

That God in glory may be thanked for that.

PEGEEN:

There's your bed now. I've put a quilt upon you I'm after quilting a while since with my own two hands, and you'd best stretch out now for your sleep, and may God give you a good rest till I call you in the morning when the cocks will crow.

CHRISTY (*as she goes to inner room*):

May God and Mary and St. Patrick bless you and reward you, for your kindly talk.

She shuts the door behind her. He settles his bed slowly, feeling the quilt with immense satisfaction.

Well, it's a clean bed and soft with it, and it's great luck and company I've won me in the end of time—two fine women fighting for the likes of me—till I'm thinking this night wasn't I a foolish fellow not to kill my father in the years gone by.

Act II

SCENE, *as before. Brilliant morning light.* Christy, *looking bright and cheerful, is cleaning a girl's boots.*

CHRISTY (*to himself, counting jugs on dresser*):

Half a hundred beyond. Ten there. A score that's above. Eighty jugs. Six cups and a broken one. Two plates. A power of glasses. Bottles, a school-master'd be hard set to count, and enough in them, I'm thinking, to drunken all the wealth and wisdom of the County Clare. (*He puts down the boot carefully.*) There's her boots now, nice and decent for her evening use, and isn't it grand brushes she has? (*He puts them down and goes by degrees to the looking-glass.*) Well, this'd be a fine place to be my whole life talking out with swearing Christians, in place of my old dogs and cat, and I stalking around, smoking my pipe and drinking my fill, and never a day's work but drawing a cork an odd time, or wiping a glass, or rinsing out a shiny tumbler for a decent man. (*He takes the looking-glass from the wall and puts it on the back of a chair; then sits down in front of it and begins washing his face.*) Didn't I know rightly I was handsome, though it was the divil's own mirror we had beyond, would twist a squint across an angel's brow; and I'll be growing fine from this day, the way I'll have a soft lovely skin on me and won't be the like of the clumsy young fellows do be ploughing all times in the earth and dung. (*He starts.*) Is she coming again? (*He looks out.*) Stranger girls. God help me, where'll I hide myself away and my long neck naked to the world? (*He looks out.*) I'd best go to the room maybe till I'm dressed again.

He gathers up his coat and the looking-glass, and runs into the inner room. The door is pushed open, and Susan Brady *looks in, and knocks on door.*

SUSAN:
    There's nobody in it. (*Knocks again.*)
NELLY (*pushing her in and following her, with* Honor Blake *and* Sara Tansey):
    It'd be early for them both to be out walking the hill.
SUSAN:
    I'm thinking Shawn Keogh was making game of us and there's no such man in it at all.
HONOR (*pointing to straw and quilt*):
    Look at that. He's been sleeping there in the night. Well, it'll be a hard case if he's gone off now, the way we'll never set our eyes on a man killed his father, and we after rising early and destroying ourselves running fast on the hill.
NELLY:
    Are you thinking them's his boots?
SARA (*taking them up*):
    If they are, there should be his father's track on them. Did you never read in the papers the way murdered men do bleed and drip?

SUSAN:
> Is that blood there, Sara Tansey?

SARA (*smelling it*):
> That's bog water, I'm thinking, but it's his own they are surely, for I never seen the like of them for whity mud, and red mud, and turf on them, and the fine sands of the sea. That man's been walking, I'm telling you. (*She goes down right, putting on one of his boots.*)

SUSAN (*going to window*):
> Maybe he's stolen off to Belmullet with the boots of Michael James, and you'd have a right so to follow after him, Sara Tansey, and you the one yoked the ass cart and drove ten miles to set your eyes on the man bit the yellow lady's nostril on the northern shore. (*She looks out.*)

SARA (*running to window with one boot on*):
> Don't be talking, and we fooled to-day. (*Putting on other boot.*) There's a pair do fit me well, and I'll be keeping them for walking to the priest, when you'd be ashamed this place, going up winter and summer with nothing worth while to confess at all.

HONOR (*who has been listening at the door*):
> Whisht! there's someone inside the room. (*She pushes door a chink open.*) It's a man.

Sara *kicks off boots and puts them where they were. They all stand in a line looking through chink.*

SARA:
> I'll call him. Mister! Mister!

He puts in his head.

> Is Pegeen within?

CHRISTY (*coming in as meek as a mouse, with the looking-glass held behind his back*):
> She's above on the enuceen, seeking the nanny goats, the way she'd have a sup of goat's milk for to colour my tea.

SARA:
> And asking your pardon, is it you's the man killed his father?

CHRISTY (*sidling toward the nail where the glass was hanging*):
> I am, God help me!

SARA (*taking eggs she has brought*):
> Then my thousand welcomes to you, and I've run up with a brace of duck's eggs for your food to-day. Pegeen's ducks is no use, but these are the real rich sort. Hold out your hand and you'll see it's no lie I'm telling you.

CHRISTY (*coming forward shyly, and holding out his left hand*):
> They're a great and weighty size.

SUSAN:
> And I run up with a pat of butter, for it'd be a poor thing to have you eating your spuds dry, and you after running a great way since you did destroy your da.

CHRISTY:
> Thank you kindly.

HONOR:
> And I brought you a little cut of cake, for you should have a thin stomach on you, and you that length walking the world.

NELLY:
> And I brought you a little laying pullet—boiled and all she is— was crushed at the fall of night by the curate's car. Feel the fat of that breast, mister.

CHRISTY:
> It's bursting, surely. (*He feels it with the back of his hand, in which he holds the presents.*)

SARA:
> Will you pinch it? Is your right hand too sacred for to use at all? (*She slips round behind him.*) It's a glass he has. Well, I never seen to this day a man with a looking-glass held to his back. Them that kills their fathers is a vain lot surely.

Girls giggle.

CHRISTY (*smiling innocently and piling presents on glass*):
> I'm very thankful to you all to-day . . .

WIDOW QUIN (*coming in quickly, at door*):
> Sara Tansey, Susan Brady, Honor Blake! What in glory has you here at this hour of day?

GIRLS (*giggling*):
> That's the man killed his father.

WIDOW QUIN (*coming to them*):
> I know well it's the man; and I'm after putting him down in the sports below for racing, leaping, pitching, and the Lord knows what.

SARA (*exuberantly*):
> That's right, Widow Quin. I'll bet my dowry that he'll lick the world.

WIDOW QUIN:
> If you will, you'd have a right to have him fresh and nourished in place of nursing a feast. (*Taking presents.*) Are you fasting or fed, young fellow?

CHRISTY:

Fasting, if you please.

WIDOW QUIN (*loudly*):

Well, you're the lot. Stir up now and give him his breakfast. (*To Christy.*) Come here to me

She puts him on bench beside her while the girls make tea and get his breakfast.

and let you tell us your story before Pegeen will come, in place of grinning your ears off like the moon of May.

CHRISTY (*beginning to be pleased*):

It's a long story; you'd be destroyed listening.

WIDOW QUIN:

Don't be letting on to be shy, a fine, gamey, treacherous lad the like of you. Was it in your house beyond you cracked his skull?

CHRISTY (*shy but flattered*):

It was not. We were digging spuds in his cold, sloping, stony, divil's patch of a field.

WIDOW QUIN:

And you went asking money of him, or making talk of getting a wife would drive him from his farm?

CHRISTY:

I did not, then; but there I was, digging and digging, and "You squinting idiot," says he, "let you walk down now and tell the priest you'll wed the Widow Casey in a score of days."

WIDOW QUIN:

And what kind was she?

CHRISTY (*with horror*):

A walking terror from beyond the hills, and she two score and five years, and two hundredweights and five pounds in the weighing scales, with a limping leg on her, and a blinded eye, and she a woman of noted misbehaviour with the old and young.

GIRLS (*clustering round him, serving him*):

Glory be.

WIDOW QUIN:

And what did he want driving you to wed with her? (*She takes a bit of the chicken.*)

CHRISTY (*eating with growing satisfaction*):

He was letting on I was wanting a protector from the harshness of the world, and he without a thought the whole while but how he'd have her hut to live in and her gold to drink.

WIDOW QUIN:

There's maybe worse than a dry hearth and a widow woman and your glass at night. So you hit him then?

CHRISTY (*getting almost excited*):

I did not. "I won't wed her," says I, "when all know she did suckle me for six weeks when I came into the world, and she a hag this day with a tongue on her has the crows and seabirds scattered, the way they wouldn't cast a shadow on her garden with the dread of her curse."

WIDOW QUIN (*teasingly*):

That one should be right company.

SARA (*eagerly*):

Don't mind her. Did you kill him then?

CHRISTY:

"She's too good for the like of you," says he, "and go on now or I'll flatten you out like a crawling beast has passed under a dray." "You will not if I can help it," says I. "Go on," says he, "or I'll have the divil making garters of your limbs to-night." "You will not if I can help it," says I. (*He sits up, brandishing his mug.*)

SARA:

You were right surely.

CHRISTY (*impressively*):

With that the sun came out between the cloud and the hill, and it shining green in my face. "God have mercy on your soul," says he, lifting a scythe; "or on your own," says I, raising the loy.

SUSAN:

That's a grand story.

HONOR:

He tells it lovely.

CHRISTY (*flattered and confident, waving bone*):

He gave a drive with the scythe, and I gave a lep to the east. Then I turned around with my back to the north, and I hit a blow on the ridge of his skull, laid him stretched out, and he split to the knob of his gullet. (*He raises the chicken bone to his Adam's apple.*)

GIRLS (*together*):

Well, you're a marvel! Oh, God bless you! You're the lad surely!

SUSAN:

I'm thinking the Lord God sent him this road to make a second husband to the Widow Quin, and she with a great yearning to be wedded, though all dread her here. Lift him on her knee, Sara Tansey.

WIDOW QUIN:

Don't tease him.

SARA (*going over to dresser and counter very quickly, and getting two glasses and porter*):
You're heroes surely, and let you drink a supeen with your arms linked like the outlandish lovers in the sailor's song.

She links their arms and gives them the glasses.

There now. Drink a health to the wonders of the western world, the pirates, preachers, poteen-makers, with the jobbing jockies; parching peelers, and the juries fill their stomachs selling judgments of the English law. (*Brandishing the bottle.*)
WIDOW QUIN:
That's a right toast, Sara Tansey. Now Christy.

They drink with their arms linked, he drinking with his left hand, she with her right. As they are drinking, Pegeen Mike *comes in with a milk can and stands aghast. They all spring away from* Christy. *He goes down left.* Widow Quin *remains seated.*

PEGEEN (*angrily, to* Sara):
What is it you're wanting?
SARA (*twisting her apron*):
An ounce of tobacco.
PEGEEN:
Have you tuppence?
SARA:
I've forgotten my purse.
PEGEEN:
Then you'd best be getting it and not fooling us here. (*To the* Widow Quin, *with more elaborate scorn.*) And what is it you're wanting, Widow Quin?
WIDOW QUIN (*insolently*):
A penn'orth of starch.
PEGEEN (*breaking out*):
And you without a white shift or a shirt in your whole family since the drying of the flood. I've no starch for the like of you, and let you walk on now to Killamuck.
WIDOW QUIN (*turning to* Christy, *as she goes out with the girls*):
Well, you're mighty huffy this day, Pegeen Mike, and, you young fellow, let you not forget the sports and racing when the noon is by.

They go out.

PEGEEN (*imperiously*):

Fling out that rubbish and put them cups away.

Christy *tidies away in great haste.*

Shove in the bench by the wall.

He does so.

And hang that glass on the nail. What disturbed it at all?

CHRISTY (*very meekly*):

I was making myself decent only, and this a fine country for young lovely girls.

PEGEEN (*sharply*):

Whisht your talking of girls. (*Goes to counter—right.*)

CHRISTY:

Wouldn't any wish to be decent in a place . . .

PEGEEN:

Whisht I'm saying.

CHRISTY (*looks at her face for a moment with great misgivings, then as a last effort, takes up a loy, and goes towards her, with feigned assurance*):

It was with a loy the like of that I killed my father.

PEGEEN (*still sharply*):

You've told me that story six times since the dawn of day.

CHRISTY (*reproachfully*):

It's a queer thing you wouldn't care to be hearing it and them girls after walking four miles to be listening to me now.

PEGEEN (*turning round astonished*):

Four miles.

CHRISTY (*apologetically*):

Didn't himself say there were only four bona fides living in the place?

PEGEEN:

It's bona fides by the road they are, but that lot came over the river lepping the stones. It's not three perches when you go like that, and I was down this morning looking on the papers the post-boy does have in his bag. (*With meaning and emphasis.*) For there was great news this day, Christopher Mahon. (*She goes into room left.*)

CHRISTY (*suspiciously*):

Is it news of my murder?

PEGEEN (*inside*):

Murder, indeed.

CHRISTY (*loudly*):

A murdered da?

PEGEEN (*coming in again and crossing right*):

There was not, but a story filled half a page of the hanging of a man. Ah, that should be a fearful end, young fellow, and it worst of all for a man who destroyed his da, for the like of him would get small mercies, and when it's dead he is, they'd put him in a narrow grave, with cheap sacking wrapping him round, and pour down quicklime on his head, the way you'd see a woman pouring any frish-frash from a cup.

CHRISTY (*very miserably*):

Oh, God help me. Are you thinking I'm safe? You were saying at the fall of night, I was shut of jeopardy and I here with yourselves.

PEGEEN (*severely*):

You'll be shut of jeopardy no place if you go talking with a pack of wild girls the like of them do be walking abroad with the peelers, talking whispers at the fall of night.

CHRISTY (*with terror*):

And you're thinking they'd tell?

PEGEEN (*with mock sympathy*):

Who knows, God help you.

CHRISTY (*loudly*):

What joy would they have to bring hanging to the likes of me?

PEGEEN:

It's queer joys they have, and who knows the thing they'd do, if it'd make the green stones cry itself to think of you swaying and swiggling at the butt of a rope, and you with a fine, stout neck, God bless you! the way you'd be a half an hour, in great anguish, getting your death.

CHRISTY (*getting his boots and putting them on*):

If there's that terror of them, it'd be best, maybe, I went on wandering like Esau or Cain and Abel on the sides of Neifin or the Erris plain.

PEGEEN (*beginning to play with him*):

It would, maybe, for I've heard the Circuit Judges this place is a heartless crew.

CHRISTY (*bitterly*):

It's more than Judges this place is a heartless crew. (*Looking up at her.*) And isn't it a poor thing to be starting again and I a lonesome fellow will be looking out on women and girls the way the needy fallen spirits do be looking on the Lord?

PEGEEN:

What call have you to be that lonesome when there's poor girls walking Mayo in their thousands now?

CHRISTY (*grimly*):

It's well you know what call I have. It's well you know it's a lonesome thing to be passing small towns with the lights shining sideways when the night is down, or going in strange places with a dog noising before you and a dog noising behind, or drawn to the cities where you'd hear a voice kissing and talking deep love in every shadow of the ditch, and you passing on with an empty, hungry stomach failing from your heart.

PEGEEN:

I'm thinking you're an odd man, Christy Mahon. The oddest walking fellow I ever set my eyes on to this hour to-day.

CHRISTY:

What would any be but odd men and they living lonesome in the world?

PEGEEN:

I'm not odd, and I'm my whole life with my father only.

CHRISTY (*with infinite admiration*):

How would a lovely handsome woman the like of you be lonesome when all men should be thronging around to hear the sweetness of your voice, and the little infant children should be pestering your steps I'm thinking, and you walking the roads.

PEGEEN:

I'm hard set to know what way a coaxing fellow the like of yourself should be lonesome either.

CHRISTY:

Coaxing?

PEGEEN:

Would you have me think a man never talked with the girls would have the words you've spoken today? It's only letting on you are to be lonesome, the way you'd get around me now.

CHRISTY:

I wish to God I was letting on; but I was lonesome all times, and born lonesome, I'm thinking, as the moon of dawn. (*Going to door.*)

PEGEEN (*puzzled by his talk*):

Well, it's a story I'm not understanding at all why you'd be worse than another, Christy Mahon, and you a fine lad with the great savagery to destroy your da.

CHRISTY:

It's little I'm understanding myself, saving only that my heart's scalded this day, and I going off stretching out the earth between us, the way I'll not be waking near you another dawn of the year till the two of us do arise to hope or judgment with the saints of God, and now I'd best be going with my wattle in my hand, for hanging is a poor thing (*turning to go.*), and it's little welcome only is left me in this house to-day.

PEGEEN (*sharply*):

Christy!

He turns round.

Come here to me.

He goes towards her.

Lay down that switch and throw some sods on the fire. You're pot-boy in this place, and I'll not have you mitch off from us now.

CHRISTY:

You were saying I'd be hanged if I stay.

PEGEEN (*quite kindly at last*):

I'm after going down and reading the fearful crimes of Ireland for two weeks or three, and there wasn't a word of your murder. (*Getting up and going over to the counter.*) They've likely not found the body. You're safe so with ourselves.

CHRISTY (*astonished, slowly*):

It's making game of me you were (*following her with fearful joy*), and I can stay so, working at your side, and I not lonesome from this mortal day.

PEGEEN:

What's to hinder you from staying, except the widow woman or the young girls would inveigle you off?

CHRISTY (*with rapture*):

And I'll have your words from this day filling my ears, and that look is come upon you meeting my two eyes, and I watching you loafing around in the warm sun, or rinsing your ankles when the night is come.

PEGEEN (*kindly, but a little embarrassed*):

I'm thinking you'll be a loyal young lad to have working around, and if you vexed me a while since with your leaguing with the girls, I wouldn't give a thraneen for a lad hadn't a mighty spirit in him and a gamey heart.

Shawn Keogh *runs in carrying a cleeve on his back, followed by the* Widow Quin.

SHAWN (*to* Pegeen):

I was passing below, and I seen your mountainy sheep eating cabbages in Jimmy's field. Run up or they'll be bursting surely.

PEGEEN:

    Oh, God mend them! (*She puts a shawl over her head and runs out.*)

CHRISTY (*looking from one to the other. Still in high spirits*):

    I'd best go to her aid maybe. I'm handy with ewes.

WIDOW QUIN (*closing the door*):

    She can do that much, and there is Shaneen has long speeches for to tell you now. (*She sits down with an amused smile.*)

SHAWN (*taking something from his pocket and offering it to* Christy):

    Do you see that, mister?

CHRISTY (*looking at it*):

    The half of a ticket to the Western States!

SHAWN (*trembling with anxiety*):

    I'll give it to you and my new hat (*pulling it out of hamper*); and my breeches with the double seat (*pulling it off*); and my new coat is woven from the blackest shearings for three miles around (*giving him the coat*); I'll give you the whole of them, and my blessing, and the blessing of Father Reilly itself, maybe, if you'll quit from this and leave us in the peace we had till last night at the fall of dark.

CHRISTY (*with a new arrogance*):

    And for what is it you're wanting to get shut of me?

SHAWN (*looking to the* Widow *for help*):

    I'm a poor scholar with middling faculties to coin a lie, so I'll tell you the truth, Christy Mahon. I'm wedding with Pegeen beyond, and I don't think well of having a clever fearless man the like of you dwelling in her house.

CHRISTY (*almost pugnaciously*):

    And you'd be using bribery for to banish me?

SHAWN (*in an imploring voice*):

    Let you not take it badly, mister honey, isn't beyond the best place for you where you'll have golden chains and shiny coats and you riding upon hunters with the ladies of the land. (*He makes an eager sign to the* Widow Quin *to come to help him.*)

WIDOW QUIN (*coming over*):

    It's true for him, and you'd best quit off and not have that poor girl setting her mind on you, for there's Shaneen thinks she wouldn't suit you though all is saying that she'll wed you now.

    Christy *beams with delight.*

SHAWN (*in terrified earnest*):

    She wouldn't suit you, and she with the divil's own temper the way you'd be strangling one another in a score of days. (*He makes the movement of strangling with his hands.*) It's the like of me only that she's fit for, a quiet simple fellow wouldn't raise a hand upon her if she scratched itself.

WIDOW QUIN (*putting* Shawn's *hat on* Christy):

Fit them clothes on you anyhow, young fellow, and he'd maybe loan them to you for the sports. (*Pushing him towards inner door.*) Fit them on and you can give your answer when you have them tried.

CHRISTY (*beaming, delighted with the clothes*):

I will then. I'd like herself to see me in them tweeds and hat. (*He goes into room and shuts the door.*)

SHAWN (*in great anxiety*):

He'd like herself to see them. He'll not leave us, Widow Quin. He's a score of divils in him the way it's well nigh certain he will wed Pegeen.

WIDOW QUIN (*jeering*):

It's true all girls are fond of courage and do hate the like of you.

SHAWN (*walking about in desperation*):

Oh, Widow Quin, what'll I be doing now? I'd inform again him, but he'd burst from Kilmainham and he'd be sure and certain to destroy me. If I wasn't so God-fearing, I'd near have courage to come behind him and run a pike into his side. Oh, it's a hard case to be an orphan and not to have your father that you're used to, and you'd easy kill and make yourself a hero in the sight of all. (*Coming up to her.*) Oh, Widow Quin, will you find me some contrivance when I've promised you a ewe?

WIDOW QUIN:

A ewe's a small thing, but what would you give me if I did wed him and did save you so?

SHAWN (*with astonishment*):

You?

WIDOW QUIN:

Aye. Would you give me the red cow you have and the mountainy ram, and the right of way across your rye path, and a load of dung at Michaelmas, and turbary upon the western hill?

SHAWN (*radiant with hope*):

I would surely, and I'd give you the wedding-ring I have, and the loan of a new suit, the way you'd have him decent on the wedding-day. I'd give you two kids for your dinner, and a gallon of poteen, and I'd call the piper on the long car to your wedding from Crossmolina or from Ballina. I'd give you . . .

WIDOW QUIN:

That'll do so, and let you whisht, for he's coming now again.

Christy *comes in very natty in the new clothes.* Widow Quin *goes to him admiringly.*

WIDOW QUIN:

> If you seen yourself now, I'm thinking you'd be too proud to speak to us at all, and it'd be a pity surely to have your like sailing from Mayo to the Western World.

CHRISTY (*as proud as a peacock*):

> I'm not going. If this is a poor place itself, I'll make myself contented to be lodging here.

> Widow Quin *makes a sign to* Shawn *to leave them.*

SHAWN:

> Well, I'm going measuring the race-course while the tide is low, so I'll leave you the garments and my blessing for the sports today. God bless you! (*He wriggles out.*)

WIDOW QUIN (*admiring* Christy):

> Well, you're mighty spruce, young fellow. Sit down now while you're quiet till you talk with me.

CHRISTY (*swaggering*):

> I'm going abroad on the hillside for to seek Pegeen.

WIDOW QUIN:

> You'll have time and plenty for to seek Pegeen, and you heard me saying at the fall of night the two of us should be great company.

CHRISTY:

> From this out I'll have no want of company when all sorts is bringing me their food and clothing (*he swaggers to the door, tightening his belt*), the way they'd set their eyes upon a gallant orphan cleft his father with one blow to the breeches belt. (*He opens door, then staggers back.*) Saints of glory! Holy angels from the throne of light!

WIDOW QUIN (*going over*):

> What ails you?

CHRISTY:

> It's the walking spirit of my murdered da?

WIDOW QUIN (*looking out*):

> Is it that tramper?

CHRISTY (*wildly*):

> Where'll I hide my poor body from that ghost of hell?

The door is pushed open, and old Mahon *appears on threshold.* Christy *darts in behind door.*

WIDOW QUIN (*in great amusement*):

> God save you, my poor man.

MAHON (*gruffly*):

> Did you see a young lad passing this way in the early morning or the fall of night?

WIDOW QUIN:

> You're a queer kind to walk in not saluting at all.

MAHON:

> Did you see the young lad?

WIDOW QUIN (*stiffly*):

> What kind was he?

MAHON:

> An ugly young streeler with a murderous gob on him, and a little switch in his hand. I met a tramper seen him coming this way at the fall of night.

WIDOW QUIN:

> There's harvest hundreds do be passing these days for the Sligo boat. For what is it you're wanting him, my poor man?

MAHON:

> I want to destroy him for breaking the head on me with the clout of a loy. (*He takes off a big hat, and shows his head in a mass of bandages and plaster, with some pride.*) It was he did that, and amn't I a great wonder to think I've traced him ten days with that rent in my crown?

WIDOW QUIN (*taking his head in both hands and examining it with extreme delight*):

> That was a great blow. And who hit you? A robber maybe?

MAHON:

> It was my own son hit me, and he the divil a robber, or anything else, but a dirty, stuttering lout.

WIDOW QUIN (*letting go his skull and wiping her hands in her apron*):

> You'd best be wary of a mortified scalp, I think they call it, lepping around with that wound in the splendour of the sun. It was a bad blow surely, and you should have vexed him fearful to make him strike that gash in his da.

MAHON:

> Is it me?

WIDOW QUIN (*amusing herself*):

> Aye. And isn't it a great shame when the old and hardened do torment the young?

MAHON (*raging*):

> Torment him is it? And I after holding out with the patience of a martyred saint till there's nothing but destruction on, and I'm driven out in my old age with none to aid me.

WIDOW QUIN (*greatly amused*):

It's a sacred wonder the way that wickedness will spoil a man.

MAHON:

My wickedness, is it? Amn't I after saying it is himself has me destroyed, and he a liar on walls, a talker of folly, a man you'd see stretched the half of the day in the brown ferns with his belly to the sun.

WIDOW QUIN:

Not working at all?

MAHON:

The divil a work, or if he did itself, you'd see him raising up a haystack like the stalk of a rush, or driving our last cow till he broke her leg at the hip, and when he wasn't at that he'd be fooling over little birds he had—finches and felts—or making mugs at his own self in the bit of a glass we had hung on the wall.

WIDOW QUIN (*looking at* Christy):

What way was he so foolish? It was running wild after the girls may be?

MAHON (*with a shout of derision*):

Running wild, is it? If he seen a red petticoat coming swinging over the hill, he'd be off to hide in the sticks, and you'd see him shooting out his sheep's eyes between the little twigs and the leaves, and his two ears rising like a hare looking out through a gap. Girls, indeed!

WIDOW QUIN:

It was drink maybe?

MAHON:

And he a poor fellow would get drunk on the smell of a pint. He'd a queer rotten stomach, I'm telling you, and when I gave him three pulls from my pipe a while since, he was taken with contortions till I had to send him in the ass cart to the females' nurse.

WIDOW QUIN (*clasping her hands*):

Well, I never till this day heard tell of a man the like of that!

MAHON:

I'd take a mighty oath you didn't surely, and wasn't he the laughing joke of every female woman where four baronies meet, the way the girls would stop their weeding if they seen him coming the road to let a roar at him, and call him the looney of Mahon's.

WIDOW QUIN:

I'd give the world and all to see the like of him. What kind was he?

MAHON:

A small low fellow.

WIDOW QUIN:

And dark?

MAHON:

Dark and dirty.

WIDOW QUIN (*considering*):

I'm thinking I seen him.

MAHON (*eagerly*):

An ugly young blackguard.

WIDOW QUIN:

A hideous, fearful villain, and the spit of you.

MAHON:

What way is he fled?

WIDOW QUIN:

Gone over the hills to catch a coasting steamer to the north or south.

MAHON:

Could I pull up on him now?

WIDOW QUIN:

If you'll cross the sands below where the tide is out, you'll be in it as soon as himself, for he had to go round ten miles by the top of the bay. (*She points to the door.*) Strike down by the head beyond and then follow on the roadway to the north and east.

Mahon *goes abruptly.*

WIDOW QUIN (*shouting after him*):

Let you give him a good vengeance when you come up with him, but don't put yourself in the power of the law, for it'd be a poor thing to see a judge in his black cap reading out his sentence on a civil warrior the like of you. (*She swings the door to and looks at* Christy, *who is cowering in terror, for a moment, then she bursts into a laugh.*)

WIDOW QUIN:

Well, you're the walking Playboy of the Western World, and that's the poor man you had divided to his breeches belt.

CHRISTY (*looking out: then, to her*):

What'll Pegeen say when she hears that story? What'll she be saying to me now?

WIDOW QUIN:

She'll knock the head of you. I'm thinking, and drive you from the door. God help her to be taking you for a wonder, and you a little schemer making up the story you destroyed your da.

CHRISTY (*turning to the door, nearly speechless with rage, half to him-self*):

To be letting on he was dead, and coming back to his life, and following after me like an old weazel tracing a rat, and coming in here laying desolation between my own self and the fine women of Ireland, and he a kind of carcass that you'd fling upon the sea . . .

WIDOW QUIN (*more soberly*):

There's talking for a man's one only son.

CHRISTY (*breaking out*):

His one son, is it? May I meet him with one tooth and it aching, and one eye to be seeing seven and seventy divils in the twists of the road, and one old timber leg on him to limp into the scalding grave. (*Looking out.*) There he is now crossing the strands, and that the Lord God would send a high wave to wash him from the world.

WIDOW QUIN (*scandalized*):

Have you no shame? (*Putting her hand on his shoulder and turning him round.*) What ails you? Near crying, is it?

CHRISTY (*in despair and grief*):

Amn't I after seeing the love-light of the star of knowledge shining from her brow, and hearing words would put you thinking on the holy Brigid speaking to the infant saints, and now she'll be turning again, and speaking hard words to me, like an old woman with a spavindy ass she'd have, urging on a hill.

WIDOW QUIN:

There's poetry talk for a girl you'd see itching and scratching, and she with a stale stink of poteen on her from selling in the shop.

CHRISTY (*impatiently*):

It's her like is fitted to be handling merchandise in the heavens above, and what'll I be doing now, I ask you, and I a kind of wonder was jilted by the heavens when a day was by.

There is a distant noise of girls' voices. Widow Quin *looks from window and comes to him, hurriedly.*

WIDOW QUIN:

You'll be doing like myself, I'm thinking, when I did destroy my man, for I'm above many's the day, odd times in great spirits, abroad in the sunshine, darning a stocking or stitching a shift; and odd times again looking out on the schooners, hookers, trawlers is sailing the sea, and I thinking on the gallant hairy fellows are drifting beyond, and myself long years living alone.

CHRISTY (*interested*):

You're like me, so.

WIDOW QUIN:

I am your like, and it's for that I'm taking a fancy to you, and I with my little houseen above where there'd be myself to tend you, and none to ask were you a murderer or what at all.

CHRISTY:

And what would I be doing if I left Pegeen?

WIDOW QUIN:

I've nice jobs you could be doing, gathering shells to make a whitewash for our hut within, building up a little goose-house, or stretching a new skin on an old curragh I have, and if my hut is far from all sides, it's there you'll meet the wisest old men, I tell you, at the corner of my wheel, and it's there yourself and me will have great times whispering and hugging. . . .

VOICES (*outside, calling far away*):

Christy! Christy Mahon! Christy!

CHRISTY:

Is it Pegeen Mike?

WIDOW QUIN:

It's the young girls, I'm thinking, coming to bring you to the sports below, and what is it you'll have me to tell them now?

CHRISTY:

Aid me for to win Pegeen. It's herself only that I'm seeking now.

Widow Quin *gets up and goes to window.*

Aid me for to win her, and I'll be asking God to stretch a hand to you in the hour of death, and lead you short cuts through the Meadows of Ease, and up the floor of Heaven to the Footstool of the Virgin's Son.

WIDOW QUIN:

There's praying.

VOICES (*nearer*):

Christy! Christy Mahon!

CHRISTY (*with agitation*):

They're coming. Will you swear to aid and save me for the love of Christ?

WIDOW QUIN (*looks at him for a moment*):

If I aid you, will you swear to give me a right of way I want, and a mountainy ram, and a load of dung at Michaelmas, the time that you'll be master here?

CHRISTY:

I will, by the elements and stars of night.

WIDOW QUIN:

Then we'll not say a word of the old fellow, the way Pegeen won't know your story till the end of time.

CHRISTY:

And if he chances to return again?

WIDOW QUIN:

We'll swear he's a maniac and not your da. I could take an oath I seen him raving on the sands to-day.

Girls run in.

SUSAN:

Come on to the sports below. Pegeen says you're to come.

SARA TANSEY:

The lepping's beginning, and we've a jockey's suit to fit upon you for the mule race on the sands below.

HONOR:

Come on, will you?

CHRISTY:

I will then if Pegeen's beyond.

SARA TANSEY:

She's in the boreen making game of Shaneen Keogh.

CHRISTY:

Then I'll be going to her now.

He runs out followed by the girls.

WIDOW QUIN:

Well, if the worst comes in the end of all, it'll be great game to see there's none to pity him but a widow woman, the like of me, has buried her children and destroyed her man. (*She goes out.*)

Act III

SCENE, *as before. Later in the day.* Jimmy *comes in, slightly drunk.*

JIMMY (*calls*):

Pegeen! (*Crosses to inner door.*) Pegeen Mike! (*Comes back again into the room.*) Pegeen!

Philly *comes in in the same state. To* Philly.

Did you see herself?

PHILLY:

I did not; but I sent Shawn Keogh with the ass cart for to bear him home. (*Trying cupboards which are locked.*) Well, isn't he a nasty man to get into such staggers at a morning wake? and isn't herself the divil's daughter for locking, and she so fussy after that young gaffer, you might take your death with drought and none to heed you?

JIMMY:

It's little wonder she'd be fussy, and he after bringing bankrupt ruin on the roulette man, and the trick-o'-the-loop man, and breaking the nose of the cockshot-man, and winning all in the sports below, racing, lepping, dancing, and the Lord knows what! He's right luck, I'm telling you.

PHILLY:

If he has, he'll be rightly hobbled yet, and he not able to say ten words without making a brag of the way he killed his father, and the great blow he hit with the loy.

JIMMY:

A man can't hang by his own informing, and his father should be rotten by now.

Old Mahon *passes window slowly.*

PHILLY:

Supposing a man's digging spuds in that field with a long spade, and supposing he flings up the two halves of that skull, what'll be said then in the papers and the courts of law?

JIMMY:

They'd say it was an old Dane, maybe, was drowned in the flood.

Old Mahon *comes in and sits down near door listening.*

Did you never hear tell of the skulls they have in the city of Dublin, ranged out like blue jugs in a cabin of Connaught?

PHILLY:

And you believe that?

JIMMY (*pugnaciously*):

Didn't a lad see them and he after coming from harvesting in the Liverpool boat? "They have them there," says he, "making a show of the great people there was one time walking the world. White skulls and black skulls and yellow skulls, and some with full teeth, and some haven't only but one."

PHILLY:

It was no lie, maybe, for when I was a young lad there was a graveyard beyond the house with the remnants of a man who had thighs as long as your arm. He was a horrid man, I'm telling you, and there was many a fine Sunday I'd put him together for fun, and he with shiny bones, you wouldn't meet the like of these days in the cities of the world.

MAHON (*getting up*):

You wouldn't, is it? Lay your eyes on that skull, and tell me where and when there was another the like of it, is splintered only from the blow of a loy.

PHILLY:

Glory be to God! And who hit you at all?

MAHON (*triumphantly*):

It was my own son hit me. Would you believe that?

JIMMY:

Well, there's wonders hidden in the heart of man!

PHILLY (*suspiciously*):

And what way was it done?

MAHON (*wandering about the room*):

I'm after walking hundreds and long scores of miles, winning clean beds and the fill of my belly four times in the day, and I doing nothing but telling stories of that naked truth. (*He comes to them a little aggressively.*) Give me a supeen and I'll tell you now.

Widow Quin *comes in and stands aghast behind him. He is facing* Jimmy *and* Philly, *who are on the left.*

JIMMY:

Ask herself beyond. She's the stuff hidden in her shawl.

WIDOW QUIN (*coming to* Mahon *quickly*):

You here, is it? You didn't go far at all?

MAHON:

I seen the coasting steamer passing, and I got a drought upon me and a cramping leg, so I said, "The divil go along with him," and turned again. (*Looking under her shawl.*) And let you give me a supeen, for I'm destroyed travelling since Tuesday was a week.

WIDOW QUIN (*getting a glass, in a cajoling tone*):

Sit down then by the fire and take your ease for a space. You've a right to be destroyed indeed, with your walking, and fighting, and facing the sun (*giving him poteen from a stone jar she has brought in*). There now is a drink for you, and may it be to your happiness and length of life.

MAHON (*taking glass greedily and sitting down by fire*):

God increase you!

WIDOW QUIN (*taking men to the right stealthily*):

Do you know what? That man's raving from his wound to-day, for I met him a while since telling a rambling tale of a tinker had him destroyed. Then he heard of Christy's deed, and he up and says it was his son had cracked his skull. O isn't madness a fright, for he'll go killing someone yet, and he thinking it's the man has struck him so?

JIMMY (*entirely convinced*):

It's a fright, surely. I knew a party was kicked in the head by a red mare, and he went killing horses a great while, till he eat the insides of a clock and died after.

PHILLY (*with suspicion*):

Did he see Christy?

WIDOW QUIN:

He didn't. (*With a warning gesture.*) Let you not be putting him in mind of him, or you'll be likely summoned if there's murder done. (*Looking round at* Mahon.) Whisht! He's listening. Wait now till you hear me taking him easy and unravelling all. (*She goes to* Mahon.) And what way are you feeling, mister? Are you in contentment now?

MAHON (*slightly emotional from his drink*):

I'm poorly only, for it's a hard story the way I'm left to-day, when it was I did tend him from his hour of birth, and he a dunce never reached his second book, the way he'd come from school, many's the day, with his legs lamed under him, and he blackened with his beatings like a tinker's ass. It's a hard story, I'm saying, the way some do have their next and nighest raising up a hand of murder on them, and some is lonesome getting their death with lamentation in the dead of night.

WIDOW QUIN (*not knowing what to say*):

To hear you talking so quiet, who'd know you were the same fellow we seen pass to-day?

MAHON:

I'm the same surely. The wrack and ruin of three score years; and it's a terror to live that length, I tell you, and to have your sons going to the dogs against you, and you wore out scolding them, and skelping them, and God knows what.

PHILLY (*to* Jimmy):

>He's not raving. (*To* Widow Quin.) Will you ask him what kind was his son?

WIDOW QUIN (*to* Mahon, *with a peculiar look*):

>Was your son that hit you a lad of one year and a score maybe, a great hand at racing and lepping and licking the world?

MAHON (*turning on her with a roar of rage*):

>Didn't you hear me say he was the fool of men, the way from this out he'll know the orphan's lot with old and young making game of him and they swearing, raging, kicking at him like a mangy cur.

A great burst of cheering outside, some way off.

MAHON (*putting his hands to his ears*):

>What in the name of God do they want roaring below?

WIDOW QUIN (*with the shade of a smile*):

>They're cheering a young lad, the champion Playboy of the Western World.

More cheering.

MAHON (*going to window*):

>It'd split my heart to hear them, and I with pulses in my brainpan for a week gone by. Is it racing they are?

JIMMY (*looking from door*):

>It is then. They are mounting him for the mule race will be run upon the sands. That's the playboy on the winkered mule.

MAHON (*puzzled*):

>That lad, is it? If you said it was a fool he was, I'd have laid a mighty oath he was the likeness of my wandering son (*uneasily, putting his hand to his head*). Faith, I'm thinking I'll go walking for to view the race.

WIDOW QUIN (*stopping him, sharply*):

>You will not. You'd best take the road to Belmullet, and not be dilly-dallying in this place where there isn't a spot you could sleep.

PHILLY (*coming forward*):

>Don't mind her. Mount there on the bench and you'll have a view of the whole. They're hurrying before the tide will rise, and it'd be near over if you went down the pathway through the crags below.

MAHON (*mounts on bench,* Widow Quin *beside him*):

>That's a right view again the edge of the sea. They're coming now from the point. He's leading. Who is he at all?

WIDOW QUIN:

> He's the champion of the world, I tell you, and there isn't a hop'orth isn't falling lucky to his hands to-day.

PHILLY (*looking out, interested in the race*):

> Look at that. They're pressing him now.

JIMMY:

> He'll win it yet.

PHILLY:

> Take your time, Jimmy Farrell. It's too soon to say.

WIDOW QUIN (*shouting*):

> Watch him taking the gate. There's riding.

JIMMY (*cheering*):

> More power to the young lad!

MAHON:

> He's passing the third.

JIMMY:

> He'll lick them yet!

WIDOW QUIN:

> He'd lick them if he was running races with a score itself.

MAHON:

> Look at the mule he has, kicking the stars.

WIDOW QUIN:

> There was a lep! (*Catching hold of Mahon in her excitement.*) He's fallen! He's mounted again! Faith, he's passing them all!

JIMMY:

> Look at him skelping her!

PHILLY:

> And the mountain girls hooshing him on!

JIMMY:

> It's the last turn! The post's cleared for them now!

MAHON:

> Look at the narrow place. He'll be into the bogs! (*With a yell.*) Good rider! He's through it again!

JIMMY:

> He neck and neck!

MAHON:

> Good boy to him! Flames, but he's in!

Great cheering, in which all join.

MAHON (*with hesitation*):

> What's that? They're raising him up. They're coming this way. (*With a roar of rage and astonishment.*) It's Christy! by the stars of God! I'd know his way of spitting and he astride the moon.

He jumps down and makes for the door, but Widow Quin *catches him and pulls him back.*

WIDOW QUIN:

Stay quiet, will you. That's not your son. (*To* Jimmy.) Stop him, or you'll get a month for the abetting of manslaughter and be fined as well.

JIMMY:

I'll hold him.

MAHON (*struggling*):

Let me out! Let me out, the lot of you! till I have my vengeance on his head to-day.

WIDOW QUIN (*shaking him, vehemently*):

That's not your son. That's a man is going to make a marriage with the daughter of this house, a place with fine trade, with a license, and with poteen too.

MAHON (*amazed*):

That man marrying a decent and a moneyed girl! Is it mad yous are? Is it in a crazy-house for females that I'm landed now?

WIDOW QUIN:

It's mad yourself is with the blow upon your head. That lad is the wonder of the Western World.

MAHON:

I seen it's my son.

WIDOW QUIN:

You seen that you're mad.

Cheering outside.

Do you hear them cheering him in the zig-zags of the road? Aren't you after saying that your son's a fool, and how would they be cheering a true idiot born?

MAHON (*getting distressed*):

It's maybe out of reason that that man's himself.

Cheering again.

There's none surely will go cheering him. Oh, I'm raving with a madness that would fright the world! (*He sits down with his hand to his head.*) There was one time I seen ten scarlet divils letting on they'd cork my spirit in a gallon can; and one time I seen rats as big as badgers sucking the life blood from the butt of my lug; but I never till this day confused that dribbling idiot with a likely man. I'm destroyed surely.

WIDOW QUIN:

And who'd wonder when it's your brain-pan that is gaping now?

MAHON:

Then the blight of the sacred drought upon myself and him, for I never went mad to this day, and I not three weeks with the Limerick girls drinking myself silly, and parlatic from the dusk to dawn. (*To* Widow Quin, *suddenly.*) Is my visage astray?

WIDOW QUIN:

It is then. You're a sniggering maniac, a child could see.

MAHON (*getting up more cheerfully*):

Then I'd best be going to the union beyond, and there'll be a welcome before me, I tell you (*with great pride*), and I a terrible and fearful case, the way that there I was one time, screeching in a straitened waistcoat, with seven doctors writing out my sayings in a printed book. Would you believe that?

WIDOW QUIN:

If you're a wonder itself, you'd best be hasty, for them lads caught a maniac one time and pelted the poor creature till he ran out, raving and foaming, and was drowned in the sea.

MAHON (*with philosophy*):

It's true mankind is the divil when your head's astray. Let me out now and I'll slip down the boreen, and not see them so.

WIDOW QUIN (*showing him out*):

That's it. Run to the right, and not a one will see.

He runs off.

PHILLY (*wisely*):

You're at some gaming, Widow Quin; but I'll walk after him and give him his dinner and a time to rest, and I'll see then if he's raving or as sane as you.

WIDOW QUIN (*annoyed*):

If you go near that lad, let you be wary of your head, I'm saying. Didn't you hear him telling he was crazed at times?

PHILLY:

I heard him telling a power; and I'm thinking we'll have right sport, before night will fall. (*He goes out.*)

JIMMY:

Well, Philly's a conceited and foolish man. How could that madman have his senses and his brain-pan slit? I'll go after them and see him turn on Philly now.

He goes; Widow Quin *hides poteen behind counter. Then hubbub outside.*

VOICES:

>There you are! Good jumper! Grand lepper! Darlint boy! He's the racer! Bear him on, will you!

Christy *comes in, in Jockey's dress, with* Pegeen Mike, Sara, *and other* Girls, *and* Men.

PEGEEN (*to crowd*):

>Go on now and don't destroy him and he drenching with sweat. Go along, I'm saying, and have your tug-of-warring till he's dried his skin.

CROWD:

>Here's his prizes! A bagpipes! A fiddle was played by a poet in the years gone by! A flat and three-thorned blackthorn would lick the scholars out of Dublin town!

CHRISTY (*taking prizes from the* Men):

>Thank you kindly, the lot of you. But you'd say it was little only I did this day if you'd seen me a while since striking my one single blow.

TOWN CRIER (*outside, ringing a bell*):

>Take notice, last event of this day! Tug-of-warring on the green below! Come on, the lot of you! Great achievements for all Mayo men!

PEGEEN:

>Go on, and leave him for to rest and dry. Go on, I tell you, for he'll do no more.

>   *She hustles crowd out;* Widow Quin *following them.*

MEN (*going*):

>Come on then. Good luck for the while!

PEGEEN (*radiantly, wiping his face with her shawl*):

>Well, you're the lad, and you'll have great times from this out when you could win that wealth of prizes, and you sweating in the heat of noon!

CHRISTY (*looking at her with delight*):

>I'll have great times if I win the crowning prize I'm seeking now, and that's your promise that you'll wed me in a fortnight, when our banns is called.

PEGEEN (*backing away from him*):

> You've right daring to go ask me that, when all knows you'll be starting to some girl in your own townland, when your father's rotten in four months, or five.

CHRISTY (*indignantly*):

> Starting from you, is it? (*He follows her*). I will not, then, and when the airs is warming in four months, or five, it's then yourself and me should be pacing Neifin in the dews of night, the times sweet smells do be rising, and you'd see a little shiny new moon, maybe, sinking on the hills.

PEGEEN (*looking at him playfully*):

> And it's that kind of a poacher's love you'd make, Christy Mahon, on the sides of Neifin, when the night is down?

CHRISTY:

> It's little you'll think if my love's a poacher's, or an earl's itself, when you'll feel my two hands stretched around you, and I squeezing kisses on your puckered lips, till I'd feel a kind of pity for the Lord God is all ages sitting lonesome in his golden chair.

PEGEEN:

> That'll be right fun, Christy Mahon, and any girl would walk her heart out before she'd meet a young man was your like for eloquence, or talk, at all.

CHRISTY (*encouraged*):

> Let you wait, to hear me talking, till we're astray in Erris, when Good Friday's by, drinking a sup from a well, and making mighty kisses with our wetted mouths, or gaming in a gap or sunshine, with yourself stretched back unto your necklace, in the flowers of the earth.

PEGEEN (*in a lower voice, moved by his tone*):

> I'd be nice so, is it?

CHRISTY (*with rapture*):

> If the mitred bishops seen you that time, they'd be the like of the holy prophets, I'm thinking, do be straining the bars of Paradise to lay eyes on the Lady Helen of Troy, and she abroad, pacing back and forward, with a nosegay in her golden shawl.

PEGEEN (*with real tenderness*):

> And what is it I have, Christy Mahon, to make me fitting entertainment for the like of you, that has such poet's talking, and such bravery of heart?

CHRISTY (*in a low voice*):

> Isn't there the light of seven heavens in your heart alone, the way you'll be an angel's lamp to me from this out, and I abroad in the darkness, spearing salmons in the Owen, or the Carrowmore?

PEGEEN:

If I was your wife, I'd be along with you those nights, Christy Mahon, the way you'd see I was a great hand at coaxing bailiffs, or coining funny nicknames for the stars of night.

CHRISTY:

You, is it? Taking your death in the hailstones, or in the fogs of dawn.

PEGEEN:

Yourself and me would shelter easy in a narrow bush, (*with a qualm of dread*) but we're only talking, maybe, for this would be a poor, thatched place to hold a fine lad is the like of you.

CHRISTY (*putting his arm round her*):

If I wasn't a good Christian, it's on my naked knees I'd be saying my prayers and paters to every jackstraw you have roofing your head, and every stony pebble is paving the laneway to your door.

PEGEEN (*radiantly*):

If that's the truth, I'll be burning candles from this out to the miracles of God that have brought you from the south to-day, and I, with my gowns bought ready, the way that I can wed you, and not wait at all.

CHRISTY:

It's miracles, and that's the truth. Me there toiling a long while, and walking a long while, not knowing at all I was drawing all times nearer to this holy day.

PEGEEN:

And myself, a girl, was tempted often to go sailing the seas till I'd marry a Jew-man, with ten kegs of gold, and I not knowing at all there was the like of you drawing nearer, like the stars of God.

CHRISTY:

And to think I'm long years hearing women talking that talk, to all bloody fools, and this the first time I've heard the like of your voice talking sweetly for my own delight.

PEGEEN:

And to think it's me is talking sweetly, Christy Mahon, and I the fright of seven townlands for my biting tongue. Well, the heart's a wonder; and, I'm thinking, there won't be our like in Mayo, for gallant lovers, from this hour, to-day.

Drunken singing is heard outside.

There's my father coming from the wake, and when he's had his sleep we'll tell him, for he's peaceful then.

They separate.

MICHAEL (*singing outside*):

> The jailor and the turnkey
> They quickly ran us down,
> And brought us back as prisoners
> Once more to Cavan town.

He comes in supported by Shawn.

> There we lay bewailing
> All in a prison bound. . . .

He sees Christy. *Goes and shakes him drunkenly by the hand, while* Pegeen *and* Shawn *talk on the left.*

MICHAEL (*to* Christy):
The blessing of God and the holy angels on your head, young fellow. I hear tell you're after winning all in the sports below; and wasn't it a shame I didn't bear you along with me to Kate Cassidy's wake, a fine, stout lad, the like of you, for you'd never see the match of it for flows of drink, the way when we sunk her bones at noonday in her narrow grave, there were five men, aye, and six men, stretched out retching speechless on the holy stones.

CHRISTY (*uneasily, watching* Pegeen):
Is that the truth?

MICHAEL:
It is then, and aren't you a louty schemer to go burying your poor father unbeknownst when you'd a right to throw him on the crupper of a Kerry mule and drive him westwards, like holy Joseph in the days gone by, the way we could have given him a decent burial, and not have him rotting beyond, and not a Christian drinking a smart drop to the glory of his soul?

CHRISTY (*gruffly*):
It's well enough he's lying, for the likes of him.

MICHAEL (*slapping him on the back*):
Well, aren't you a hardened slayer? It'll be a poor thing for the household man where you go sniffing for a female wife; and (*pointing to* Shawn) look beyond at that shy and decent Christian I have chosen for my daughter's hand, and I after getting the gilded dispensation this day for to wed them now.

CHRISTY:
> And you'll be wedding them this day, is it?

MICHAEL (*drawing himself up.*):
> Aye. Are you thinking, if I'm drunk itself, I'd leave my daughter living single with a little frisky rascal is the like of you?

PEGEEN (*breaking away from* Shawn):
> Is it the truth the dispensation's come?

MICHAEL (*triumphantly*):
> Father Reilly's after reading it in gallous Latin, and "It's come in the nick of time," says he; "so I'll wed them in a hurry, dreading that young gaffer who'd capsize the stars."

PEGEEN (*fiercely*):
> He's missed his nick of time, for it's that lad, Christy Mahon, that I'm wedding now.

MICHAEL (*loudly with horror*):
> You'd be making him a son to me, and he wet and crusted with his father's blood?

PEGEEN:
> Aye. Wouldn't it be a bitter thing for a girl to go marrying the like of Shaneen, and he a middling kind of a scarecrow, with no savagery or fine words in him at all?

MICHAEL (*gasping and sinking on a chair*):
> Oh, aren't you a heathen daughter to go shaking the fat of my heart, and I swamped and drownded with the weight of drink? Would you have them turning on me the way that I'd be roaring to the dawn of day with the wind upon my heart? Have you not a word to aid me, Shaneen? Are you not jealous at all?

SHANEEN (*in great misery*):
> I'd be afeard to be jealous of a man did slay his da.

PEGEEN:
> Well, it'd be a poor thing to go marrying your like. I'm seeing there's a world of peril for an orphan girl, and isn't it a great blessing I didn't wed you, before himself came walking from the west or south?

SHAWN:
> It's a queer story you'd go picking a dirty tramp up from the highways of the world.

PEGEEN (*playfully*):
> And you think you're a likely beau to go straying along with, the shiny Sundays of the opening year, when it's sooner on a bullock's liver you'd put a poor girl thinking than on the lily or the rose?

SHAWN:

> And have you no mind of my weight of passion, and the holy dispensation, and the drift of heifers I am giving, and the golden ring?

PEGEEN:

> I'm thinking you're too fine for the like of me, Shawn Keogh of Killakeen, and let you go off till you'd find a radiant lady with droves of bullocks on the plains of Meath, and herself bedizened in the diamond jewelleries of Paraoh's ma. That'd be your match, Shaneen. So God save you now! (*She retreats behind* Christy.)

SHAWN:

> Won't you hear me telling you . . . ?

CHRISTY (*with ferocity*):

> Take yourself from this, young fellow, or I'll maybe add a murder to my deeds to-day.

MICHAEL (*springing up with a shriek*):

> Murder is it? Is it mad yous are? Would you go making murder in this place, and it piled with poteen for our drink tonight? Go on to the foreshore if it's fighting you want, where the rising tide will wash all traces from the memory of man.

Pushing Shawn *towards* Christy.

SHAWN (*shaking himself free, and getting behind* Michael):

> I'll not fight him, Michael James. I'd liefer live a bachelor, simmering in passions to the end of time, than face a leaping savage the like of him has descended from the Lord knows where. Strike him yourself, Michael James, or you'll lose my drift of heifers and my blue bull from Sneem.

MICHAEL:

> Is it me fight him, when it's father-slaying he's bred to now? (*Pushing* Shawn.) Go on you fool and fight him now.

SHAWN (*coming forward a little*):

> Will I strike him with my hand?

MICHAEL:

> Take the loy is on your western side.

SHAWN:

> I'd be afeard of the gallows if I struck him with that.

CHRISTY (*taking up the loy*):

> Then I'll make you face the gallows or quit off from this.

Shawn flies out of the door.

CHRISTY:

    Well, fine weather be after him, (*going to* Michael, *coaxingly*) and I'm thinking you wouldn't wish to have that quaking blackguard in your house at all. Let you give us your blessing and hear her swear her faith to me, for I'm mounted on the springtide of the stars of luck, the way it'll be good for any to have me in the house.

PEGEEN (*at the other side of* Michael):

    Bless us now, for I swear to God I'll wed him, and I'll not renege.

MICHAEL (*standing up in the centre, holding on to both of them*):

    It's the will of God, I'm thinking, that all should win an easy or a cruel end, and it's the will of God that all should rear up lengthy families for the nurture of the earth. What's a single man, I ask you, eating a bit in one house and drinking a sup in another, and he with no place of his own, like an old braying jackass strayed upon the rocks? (*To* Christy). It's many would be in dread to bring your like into their house for to end them, maybe, with a sudden end; but I'm a decent man of Ireland, and I liefer face the grave untimely and I seeing a score of grandsons growing up little gallant swearers by the name of God, than go peopling my bedside with puny weeds the like of what you'd breed, I'm thinking, out of Shaneen Keogh. (*He joins their hands.*) A daring fellow is the jewel of the world, and a man did split his father's middle with a single clout, should have the bravery of ten, so may God and Mary and St. Patrick bless you, and increase you from this mortal day.

CHRISTY AND PEGEEN:

    Amen, O Lord!

Hubbub outside.

Old Mahon *rushes in, followed by all the crowd, and* Widow Quin. *He makes a rush at* Christy, *knocks him down, and begins to beat him.*

PEGEEN (*dragging back his arm*):

    Stop that, will you. Who are you at all?

MAHON:

    His father, God forgive me!

PEGEEN (*drawing back*):

    Is it rose from the dead?

MAHON:

    Do you think I look so easy quenched with the tap of a loy? (*Beats* Christy *again.*)

PEGEEN (*glaring at* Christy):

> And it's lies you told, letting on you had him slitted, and you nothing at all.

CHRISTY (*catching* Mahon*'s stick*):

> He's not my father. He's a raving maniac would scare the world. (*Pointing to* Widow Quin.) Herself knows it is true.

CROWD:

> You're fooling Pegeen! The Widow Quin seen him this day, and you likely knew! You're a liar!

CHRISTY (*dumbfounded*):

> It's himself was a liar, lying stretched out with an open head on him, letting on he was dead.

MAHON:

> Weren't you off racing the hills before I got my breath with the start I had seeing you turn on me at all?

PEGEEN:

> And to think of the coaxing glory we had given him, and he after doing nothing but hitting a soft blow and chasing northward in a sweat of fear. Quit off from this.

CHRISTY (*piteously*):

> You've seen my doings this day, and let you save me from the old man; for why would you be in such a scorch of haste to spur me to destruction now?

PEGEEN:

> It's there your treachery is spurring me, till I'm hard set to think you're the one I'm after lacing in my heart-strings half-an-hour gone by. (*To* Mahon.) Take him on from this, for I think bad the world should see me raging for a Munster liar, and the fool of men.

MAHON:

> Rise up now to retribution, and come on with me.

CROWD (*jeeringly*):

> There's the playboy! There's the lad thought he'd rule the roost in Mayo. Slate him now, mister.

CHRISTY (*getting up in shy terror*):

> What is it drives you to torment me here, when I'd asked the thunders of the might of God to blast me if I ever did hurt to any saving only that one single blow.

MAHON (*loudly*):

> If you didn't, you're a poor good-for-nothing, and isn't it by the like of you the sins of the whole world are committed.

CHRISTY (*raising his hands*):

> In the name of the Almighty God. . . .

MAHON:

> Leave troubling the Lord God. Would you have him sending down droughts, and fevers, and the old hen and the cholera morbus?

CHRISTY (*to* Widow Quin):

> Will you come between us and protect me now?

WIDOW QUIN:

> I've tried a lot, God help me, and my share is done.

CHRISTY (*looking round in desperation*):

> And I must go back into my torment is it, or run off like a vagabond straying through the Unions with the dusts of August making mudstains in the gullet of my throat, or the winds of March blowing on me till I'd take an oath I felt them making whistles of my ribs within?

SARA:

> Ask Pegeen to aid you. Her like does often change.

CHRISTY:

> I will not then, for there's torment in the splendour of her like, and she a girl any moon of midnight would take pride to meet, facing southwards on the heaths of Keel. But what did I want crawling forward to scorch my understanding at her flaming brow?

PEGEEN (*to* Mahon, *vehemently, fearing she will break into tears*):

> Take him on from this or I'll set the young lads to destroy him here.

MAHON (*going to him, shaking his stick*):

> Come on now if you wouldn't have the company to see you skelped.

PEGEEN (*half laughing, through her tears*):

> That's it, now the world will see him pandied, and he an ugly liar was playing off the hero, and the fright of men.

CHRISTY (*to* Mahon, *very sharply*):

> Leave me go!

CROWD:

> That's it. Now Christy. If them two set fighting, it will lick the world.

MAHON (*making a grab at* Christy):

> Come here to me.

CHRISTY (*more threateningly*):

> Leave me go, I'm saying.

MAHON:

> I will maybe, when your legs is limping, and your back is blue.

CROWD:

> Keep it up, the two of you. I'll back the old one. Now the playboy.

CHRISTY (*in low and intense voice*):

Shut your yelling, for if you're after making a mighty man of me this day by the power of a lie, you're setting me now to think if it's a poor thing to be lonesome, it's worse maybe to go mixing with the fools of earth.

Mahon *makes a movement towards him.*

CHRISTY (*almost shouting*):

Keep off . . . lest I do show a blow unto the lot of you would set the guardian angels winking in the clouds above. (*He swings round with a sudden rapid movement and picks up a loy.*)

CROWD (*half frightened, half amused*):

He's going mad! Mind yourselves! Run from the idiot!

CHRISTY:

If I am an idiot, I'm after hearing my voice this day saying words would raise the topknot on a poet in a merchant's town. I've won your racing, and your lepping, and . . .

MAHON:

Shut your gullet and come on with me.

CHRISTY:

I'm going, but I'll stretch you first.

He runs at Old Mahon *with the loy, chases him out of the door, followed by crowd and* Widow Quin. *There is a great noise outside, then a yell, and dead silence for a moment.* Christy *comes in, half dazed, and goes to fire.*

WIDOW QUIN (*coming in, hurriedly, and going to him*):

They're turning again you. Come on, or you'll be hanged, indeed.

CHRISTY:

I'm thinking, from this out, Pegeen'll be giving me praises the same as in the hours gone by.

WIDOW QUIN (*impatiently*):

Come by the back-door. I'd think bad to have you stifled on the gallows tree.

CHRISTY (*indignantly*):

I will not, then. What good'd be my life-time, if I left Pegeen?

WIDOW QUIN:

Come on, and you'll be no worse than you were last night; and you with a double murder this time to be telling to the girls.

CHRISTY:

I'll not leave Pegeen Mike.

WIDOW QUIN (*impatiently*):

Isn't there the match of her in every parish public, from Bing-hamstown unto the plain of Meath? Come on, I tell you, and I'll find you finer sweethearts at each waning moon.

CHRISTY:

It's Pegeen I'm seeking only, and what'd I care if you brought me a drift of chosen females, standing in their shifts itself, maybe, from this place to the Eastern World?

SARA (*runs in, pulling off one of her petticoats*):

They're going to hang him. (*Holding out petticoat and shawl.*) Fit these upon him, and let him run off to the east.

WIDOW QUIN:

He's raving now; but we'll fit them on him, and I'll take him, in the ferry, to the Achill boat.

CHRISTY (*struggling feebly*):

Leave me go, will you? when I'm thinking of my luck to-day, for she will wed me surely, and I a proven hero in the end of all.

They try to fasten petticoat around him.

WIDOW QUIN:

Take his left hand, and we'll pull him now. Come on, young fellow.

CHRISTY (*suddenly starting up*):

You'll be taking me from her? You're jealous, is it, of her wed-ding me? Go on from this. (*He snatches up a stool, and threatens them with it.*)

WIDOW QUIN (*going*):

It's in the mad-house they should put him, not in jail, at all. We'll go by the back-door, to call the doctor, and we'll save him so.

She goes out, with Sara, *through inner room. Men crowd in the doorway.* Christy *sits down again by the fire.*

MICHAEL (*in a terrified whisper*):

Is the old lad killed surely?

PHILLY:

I'm after feeling the last gasps quitting his heart.

They peer in at Christy.

MICHAEL (*with a rope*):

Look at the way he is. Twist a hangman's knot on it, and slip it over his head, while he's not minding at all.

PHILLY:

Let you take it, Shaneen. You're the soberest of all that's here.

SHAWN:

Is it me to go near him, and he the wickedest and worst with me? Let you take it, Pegeen Mike.

PEGEEN:

Come on, so.

She goes forward with the others, and they drop the double hitch over his head.

CHRISTY:

What ails you?

SHAWN (*triumphantly, as they pull the rope tight on his arms*):

Come on to the peelers, till they stretch you now.

CHRISTY:

Me!

MICHAEL:

If we took pity on you, the Lord God would, maybe, bring us ruin from the law to-day, so you'd best come easy, for hanging is an easy and a speedy end.

CHRISTY:

I'll not stir. (*To* Pegeen.) And what is it you'll say to me, and I after doing it this time in the face of all?

PEGEEN:

I'll say, a strange man is a marvel, with his mighty talk; but what's a squabble in your back-yard, and the blow of a loy, have taught me that there's a great gap between a gallous story and a dirty deed. (*To* Men.) Take him on from this, or the lot of us will be likely put on trial for his deed to-day.

CHRISTY (*with horror in his voice*):

And it's yourself will send me off, to have a horny-fingered hangman hitching his bloody slip-knots at the butt of my ear.

MEN (*pulling rope*):

Come on, will you?

He is pulled down on the floor.

CHRISTY (*twisting his legs round the table*):

Cut the rope, Pegeen, and I'll quit the lot of you, and live from this out, like the madmen of Keel, eating muck and green weeds, on the faces of the cliffs.

PEGEEN:

And leave us to hang, is it, for a saucy liar, the like of you? (*To* Men.) Take him on, out from this.

SHAWN:

    Pull a twist on his neck, and squeeze him so.

PHILLY:

    Twist yourself. Sure he cannot hurt you if you keep your distance from his teeth alone.

SHAWN:

    I'm afeard of him. (*To* Pegeen.) Lift a lighted sod, will you, and scorch his leg.

PEGEEN (*blowing the fire, with a bellows*):

    Leave go now, young fellow, or I'll scorch your shins.

CHRISTY:

    You're blowing for to torture me. (*His voice rising and growing stronger.*) That's your kind, is it? Then let the lot of you be wary, for, if I've to face the gallows, I'll have a gay march down, I tell you, and shed the blood of some of you before I die.

SHAWN (*in terror*):

    Keep a good hold, Philly. Be wary, for the love of God. For I'm thinking he would liefest wreak his pains on me.

CHRISTY (*almost gaily*):

    If I do lay my hands on you, it's the way you'll be at the fall of night, hanging as a scarecrow for the fowls of hell. Ah, you'll have a gallous jaunt I'm saying, coaching out through Limbo with my father's ghost.

SHAWN (*to* Pegeen):

    Make haste, will you? Oh, isn't he a holy terror, and isn't it true for Father Reilly, that all drink's a curse that has the lot of you so shaky and uncertain now?

CHRISTY:

    If I can wring a neck among you, I'll have a royal judgment looking on the trembling jury in the courts of law. And won't there be crying out in Mayo the day I'm stretched upon the rope with ladies in their silks and satins snivelling in their lacy kerchiefs, and they rhyming songs and ballads on the terror of my fate? (*He squirms round on the floor and bites* Shawn's *leg.*)

SHAWN (*shrieking*):

    My leg's bit on me. He's the like of a mad dog, I'm thinking, the way that I will surely die.

CHRISTY (*delighted with himself*):

    You will then, the way you can shake out hell's flags of welcome for my coming in two weeks or three, for I'm thinking Satan hasn't many have killed their da in Kerry, and in Mayo too.

Old Mahon *comes in behind on all fours and looks on unnoticed.*

MEN (*to* Pegeen):
> Bring the sod, will you?

PEGEEN (*coming over*):
> God help him so. (*Burns his leg.*)

CHRISTY (*kicking and screaming*):
> O, glory be to God!

He kicks loose from the table, and they all drag him towards the door.

JIMMY (*seeing* Old Mahon):
> Will you look what's come in?

They all drop Christy *and run left.*

CHRISTY (*scrambling on his knees face to face with* Old Mahon):
> Are you coming to be killed a third time, or what ails you now?

MAHON:
> For what is it they have you tied?

CHRISTY:
> They're taking me to the peelers to have me hanged for slaying you.

MICHAEL (*apologetically*):
> It is the will of God that all should guard their little cabins from the treachery of law, and what would my daughter be doing if I was ruined or was hanged itself?

MAHON (*grimly, loosening* Christy):
> It's little I care if you put a bag on her back, and went picking cockles till the hour of death; but my son and myself will be going our own way, and we'll have great times from this out telling stories of the villainy of Mayo, and the fools is here. (*To* Christy, *who is freed.*) Come on now.

CHRISTY:
> Go with you, is it? I will then, like a gallant captain with his heathen slave. Go on now and I'll see you from this day stewing my oatmeal and washing my spuds, for I'm master of all fights from now. (*Pushing* Mahon.) Go on, I'm saying.

MAHON:
> Is it me?

CHRISTY:
> Not a word out of you. Go on from this.

MAHON (*walking out and looking back at* Christy *over his shoulder*):
> Glory be to God! (*With a broad smile.*) I am crazy again! (*Goes.*)

CHRISTY:

Ten thousand blessings upon all that's here, for you've turned me a likely gaffer in the end of all, the way I'll go romancing through a romping lifetime from this hour to the dawning of the judgment day. (*He goes out.*)

MICHAEL:

By the will of God, we'll have peace now for our drinks. Will you draw the porter, Pegeen?